D0312057

JO GRIMOND

Michael McManus

JO GRIMOND

Towards the Sound of Gunfire

Foreword by
Jim Wallace

Birlinn

First published in 2001 by
Birlinn Limited
West Newington House
10 Newington Road
Edinburgh EH9 1QS

www.birlinn.co.uk

The publisher acknowledges subsidy from the Scottish Arts
Council towards the publication of this volume.

ISBN 1 84341 006 0

British Library Cataloguing in Publication Data
A Catalogue record for this book is available from the British Library

Typeset in Adobe Garamond by Brinnoven, Livingston
Printed and bound by Creative Print and Design, Ebbw Vale, Wales

To my parents, who have always helped with everything –
but especially with this!

Foreword

As a child growing up in the '50s and '60s, I had an unusual hobby. I was fascinated by politics and followed the progress of elections via the BBC, so my first memory of Jo Grimond is of a tall man with a lock of unruly hair, who could command the instant attention of the viewer in a party political broadcast or in a panel discussion.

When I became a member of the Liberal Party in his post-leadership years in the '70s, Jo was an elder statesman of the party, although for several weeks in 1976 he stood in again as leader. As a new prospective candidate, I was the recipient of spirited weekly commentaries on the political scene. I was present at the rally in Llandudno in 1981 when Jo followed David Steel, Shirley Williams and Roy Jenkins to the rostrum and delivered a speech celebrating our new Alliance and bringing a spellbound audience to our feet. A vision looked as if it might be becoming a reality.

It was not until 18 months later, when I was adopted as the candidate for Orkney and Shetland, that I first met the man I hoped to succeed as MP. He was nearly 70, growing deaf and his hair was even more unruly, but he was still a witty and charismatic man who could readily command an audience, be it on a political platform or around his own dinner table at the Old Manse in Orkney. He proved to be an amusing and wise adviser after I was elected; but that advice had to be sought, it was never unsolicited.

The present day Liberal Democrats owe a great deal to Jo – but for him the Liberal party of the 1950s might well have sunk without trace – and much of what Jo fought for politically has come to pass, not least devolved government for Scotland and Wales. Although I suspect he would still be a doughty critic today of red tape and unnecessary regulation.

He is still greatly revered within Liberal Democrat circles and by his former constituents in Orkney and Shetland, but there was much more to Jo than the public persona. As well as a politician, he was a son, a husband, a father and a friend, and in those roles, which made up the private man, others knew him far better than I.

Had he been Labour or a Tory, there is no doubt that his political stature and ability would have gained him Cabinet rank and possibly even the top job itself. It is perhaps surprising therefore, that this book is the first biography of Jo Grimond to be published. Michael McManus has researched all aspects of Jo's life, from childhood to old age, to provide a rounded picture of this complex man who made an impression on all who met him. It acknowledges too the role played by Laura, not only behind the scenes but as a notable politician in her own right.

It will, I am sure, prove to be a valuable source of information and insight for all those with an interest in politics, particularly Liberal and Scottish politics. But most of all, for those of us privileged to have known him, it will find an honoured position on our bookshelves as a reminder of a very special man . . . there will never be another Jo.

Jim Wallace

Acknowledgements

I am immensely in the debt of the Grimond and Bonham Carter families, notably Grizelda, Johnny and Magnus Grimond and Raymond Bonham Carter, for their unobtrusive and admirably non-interventionist support and encouragement from the earliest days of my work on this book. They bear no responsibility for any shortcomings in this book, but I do sincerely hope that they enjoy it.

I should also like to record particular gratitude to Jim and Rosie Wallace, for the hospitality and support that they have provided, way beyond the call of duty.

If anyone else deserves to be singled out, it must be Russell Reid, not only for years of friendship and support, but also for introducing me to Dundee and St Andrews many years before this book was even a twinkle in Hugh Andrew's eye. Without those foundations, this book would have been far more difficult to write.

I have been diligently helped and supported throughout by Hugh, Liz Short, Neville Moir and all the team at Birlinn and would like to add my own voice to the chorus of praises for Morag Lyall, an efficient and sensitive editor. My literary agent, Andrew Lownie, played an essential part both in initiating this project, and in bringing it to fruition. Fiona Morrison did sterling work to ensure that news of the book was suitably promulgated.

Jo Grimond was not a man to keep a diary, nor was he prone to hoarding the type of documents that might have come in handy for a future biographer. In the course of researching this book, therefore, I called upon the services of a number of archives, from New York and Hamburg to Edinburgh and Berlin. I am immensely grateful to the following for their invaluable help in piecing together the jigsaw of a long and varied life:

Mrs Penny Hatfield at the Eton College Archive; Catherine Mason, Liz Turner and their colleagues at the Bodleian Library, Oxford; Stuart Adams at the Middle Temple Library;

Susanne Semmroth at the Kempinski Hotel Atlantic, Hamburg; Marilla Guptil and Aurora Tangkeko in the United Nations Archive, New York; Carolynn Bain, Archivist of the National Trust for Scotland; The Special Collections Team at Birmingham University; The British Library of Political

and Economic Science; Ray Smith and his colleagues at News International;
Charles Moore and *The Daily Telegraph*; IPC Magazines; Boris Johnson and
The Spectator; Elke Berger at the Deutsch-Englische Gesellschaft, Berlin; Iain
Brown and his colleagues at the National Library of Scotland; The staff of
the Dundee University Archive; David Stockdale at the McManus Galleries,
Dundee; Gill Poulter at Dundee Industrial Heritage; Eileen Moran and her
colleagues at Dundee City Library; Phil Astley and his colleagues at the
Orkney Archive.

I must also record my heartfelt thanks to a long list of friends, colleagues,
interviewees and those who have given me permission to reproduce text
or images:

Ken Amer, Robert Armstrong, David Astor, Eric Avebury, Tim Beaumont,
Professor and Mrs Samuel Beer, Tony Benn, Honor Blackman, Jane Bonham
Carter, Raymond Bonham Carter, Duncan Brack, Luke Borwick, Virginia
Brand, Dr David Butler, Pratap Chitnis, Alyce-Faye Cleese, John Cole, Clive
Collins, Harry Cowie, Dr Ron Cox, Iain Dale, Tam Dalyell, J H Darton,
Carol Djukanovic, Mrs Srdja Djukanovic, Tim Dumas, Frances Edmonds,
Lionel Esher, Ginny Felton, Geordie Fergusson, Nick Fernyhough, Paul
Fiander, Catherine Fisher, Iain Flett, Ron Forbes, Karen Geary, Alec Gilchrist,
Sir John Gilmour, The Duke of Grafton KG, Hamish Gray, Tony Greaves,
Josh Gutbaum, Sir Nicholas Henderson, Richard Holderness, Richard Holme,
Chris Holt, Emlyn Hooson, Geraint Howells, Margaret Howl, Ian Hunter,
Roy Jenkins, John Jensen, Russell Johnston, Michael Jones, Russell Jones,
Charles Kennedy, Sir Ludovic and Lady Kennedy, Archy Kirkwood, James
Landale, Chris Layton, Grant Lindsay, Magnus Linklater and Baroness
Linklater, Lizz Loxam, Ruth McInry, George Mackie, David McKie, Sue
McLeod, Michael Meadowcroft, Alasdair Milne, Bobbie Mitchell, Richard
Moore, Jim Naughtie, Robin Needham, Beatrice Nesbit, Sian Norris-Copson,
Leslie Norton, Steve O'Brien, David Partner, Edward Pearce, Tony Petit, Dr
Mark Pottle, Steve Pound, Jo Preece, Francis Pym, William Rees-Mogg, Sir
Adam Ridley, Professor Richard Rose, Conrad Russell, George Russell, Eoin
Scott, Dr Geoffrey Sell, Dougie Shearer, Barry and Ester Slater, Sir Cyril Smith,
Trevor Smith, Iain Sproat, Michael Steed, Sir David Steel, Anthony Steen,
Lady Stormonth Darling, Major David Summers, Robert and Fiona Syms,
Charles Tait, Dick Taverne, Jeremy Thorpe, John Thurso, Hilary Wainwright,
Richard Wainwright, William Wallace, Alan Watkins, Alan Watson, George
Watson, Susanne Weber, Keith Wedmore, Ruth Williams, Harold Wilson, Sir
Richard Wilson, Margaret Wingfield, the Hon Mrs Catherine Zelenkiewicz.

1

IN THE SUMMER of 1913, the Liberal government led by H H Asquith
was beset with difficulties. Serious divisions, both personal and political,
were threatening to open up between its senior figures. Its Bill to introduce
Home Rule for Ireland was bogged down in Parliament, and there was talk
of a snap general election to clear the air, as the government considered
seeking a mandate for this controversial proposal. One prominent peer, Lord
Lansdowne, argued that the government would do better to consult the
people on the Bill, directly and specifically, by means of a referendum. The
conservative *Spectator* echoed this call on 26th July. Although this organ much
disliked the Asquith administration, borrowing Disraeli's famous phrase in
describing it as an 'organized hypocrisy', it did believe that this issue was so
difficult, so intractable, that only the full force of the people themselves –
one way or another – could cut the Gordian knot. It doubted, however, that
Liberals would allow the people to express their view directly, since they
would be reluctant to set a dangerous precedent, which might put an end
to all 'progressive legislation'. This caution, argued the *Spectator* forcefully,
would haunt the Liberals for years to come. It was right.

On Tuesday, 29th July 1913 in the House of Commons it was very much
business as usual, with three notable Liberals of the day heavily occupied
with their governmental duties. Asquith himself was answering questions
about land tenure in Ireland; the Chancellor of the Exchequer, David Lloyd
George, was delivering a lengthy and detailed speech in a debate on the
government's Revenue Bill; and the Postmaster-General, Herbert Samuel, was
attempting to defend the terms and conditions enjoyed by shorthand typists
in the Post Office. Samuel personally was still enduring the aftershocks of a
scandal springing from the government's dealings with the Marconi Company,
a scandal that would gravely damage the long-term image of the Liberal
Party. On that mild summer's day, in a town circumscribed by Asquith's own
constituency of East Fife, comparatively unheralded and unnoticed, an event
took place that would in due course have a great, and positive, influence on the
fate of the Liberals. At 8 Abbotsford Crescent, St Andrews, Fife, Joseph ('Jo')
Grimond was born, the youngest child and only son of Joseph ('Joe') Bowman
Grimond and his wife Lydia, *née* Richardson.

Joseph Grimond was born into a stable and contented family, whose considerable prosperity derived from the spinning and manufacturing of jute in Dundee. Jo's father wanted his family to enjoy the quality of life that existed in the more favoured atmosphere of St Andrews, and commuted daily by train to the family firm. The Bowbridge Works of J & A D Grimond, in Thistle Street, their gates adorned with the Grimond family symbol of a man (alleged, presumably spuriously, to have been modelled on T E Lawrence) resting against a camel, could for many years be numbered amongst Dundee's most famous landmarks. The Grimonds were well known in Dundee, having for many years lived in its pleasant suburb of Broughty Ferry, which the jute industry at its nineteenth-century height reputedly turned into the wealthiest community in Great Britain. The Grimond family could trace its roots in the textile business back to the beginning of the nineteenth century, and the family jute firm had been founded by Joseph B. Grimond's grandfather, Joseph Grimond (the 'J' of the company title), in partnership with his brother Alexander ('AD'). The brothers were born at Lornty, Blairgowrie, where their father David and uncle James played a major part in founding the jute-spinning industry. Joseph, the fourth son of David Grimond, was born in 1821. He served his apprenticeship in Dundee at David Martin & Co. flax and green cloth merchants, and then went to Manchester in 1844, where he became a merchant and manufacturer of oil-cloths and tarpaulins, rapidly raising sufficient capital to invest in a sizeable factory there. While Joseph Grimond was in Manchester, his younger brother Alexander (born in 1823) remained in Dundee, where he bought cloth for forwarding to Manchester. In 1848 A D Grimond decided to set up looms in Dundee for the manufacture of hessians, acquiring small premises in Commercial Street, where half a dozen workers would work hand-looms. Within less than a decade, the company had expanded dramatically, first into the nearby Maxwelltown works, then into the Bowbridge works, which had to be specially built. By the time Joseph Grimond died, on 2nd November 1894, while he was visiting his daughter in Liverpool, the company was employing between 2,500 and 3,000 people. The Bowbridge works had recently been valued at over £200,000 and Grimonds had subsidiaries in India, Canada and the United States (where the incorporation was based upon that of the Brennan Self-feeding Nose Bag Attachment Company). By 1910 the assets/liabilities of J & A D Grimond had risen to a then extremely substantial figure of over £450,000.

Dundee in the late nineteenth century, known as 'Juteopolis', was dominated by the jute industry, whose chimneys and stalks jutted above the town's skyline. The jute barons became immensely wealthy, very quickly, rewarding themselves with a series of grand houses. In 1861 Joseph Grimond bought Kerbat House in Broughty Ferry and turned it into Carbet Castle, with a series of richly decorated extensions and accretions. Its east and west wings were designed by Thomas Saunders Robertson, and the ceilings of the west wing, some of which survived the demolition of the house, were extravagantly decorated by the French artist Charles Frechou. The castle was populated with objects of beauty or interest brought home by Joseph Grimond from his extensive trips to Europe and America. When Jo Grimond was born in 1913, Carbet Castle was still occupied by an unmarried aunt. In 1919 it was valued at £7,500 and sold off. Although Joseph Grimond was notoriously impatient with stupidity and laziness, both Carbet Castle and his country home at Kinnettles (acquired from the Bank of Scotland in 1884) were renowned for their very convivial atmospheres, and Grimond was a loyal and highly sociable friend, with a genuine love for Scotland, and for the poetry of Robert Burns. He was a devout member of the Church of Scotland, an animal lover and a quiet philanthropist. 'His benefactions were secret, liberal and unceasing, and to-day many a poor home will miss him,' declared his obituary in the *Dundee Record*, which also noted his 'sympathy for the Irish people': he was a friend and ardent supporter of John Bright, who broke with Gladstone after helping to defeat his government's Home Rule Bill in 1886 and became a Liberal Unionist. Despite his strong Liberal sympathies, therefore, Joseph Grimond was towards the end of his life very much out of tune with the Liberal Party itself.

His brother AD was a member of the non-conformist Free Church of Scotland, and an 'out-and-out Liberal' who, in 1868, helped to break the long Tory reign in Perthshire. As vice-president of the Dundee and District Liberal Association, he helped to fund their new headquarters and even provided carriages for the conveyance of voters during an ill-fated local election campaign. He was a Justice of the Peace, a patron of art and a discerning lover and collector of good books. When he died in 1903, without ever having married, his possessions were sold off in two tremendous auctions. On 16th and 17th June 1903 his massive personal library came up for sale at the Dundee Auction Rooms, and the catalogue of the sale reveals him to have been a highly cultured and discerning man. Many of his books related to poetry and language, with some political tracts leavening the mixture – notably a collection of speeches in Scotland by Gladstone.[1] He had also assembled a fine collection of beautiful historical etchings. In that catalogue, some 580 items are listed in detail. In November another auction followed, of the domestic and agricultural possessions from his estate at Glenericht, Perthshire. The auctioneer's notes provide a full record and dissection of a rural life in that era. Items listed in painstaking detail include chairs, knives, forks and spoons, hoes, weddocks, branks, stits, stirks, a 'hand turnip machine', a number of turnip cutters, and livestock including many horses, sheep and hens. The auction raised over £4,260 in total, of which over £350 was paid exclusively for turnips and dung.

Jo Grimond had no illusions about management practices in the jute industry, and was the first to admit that his great-grandfather in all probability 'treated his work people no better and no worse than did his contemporaries'.[2] In fact, contemporary records suggest that the Grimonds were comparatively enlightened, by the standards of the time, taking care that their properties were safely laid out and well ventilated. Bowbridge had a big hall for amusements or lectures, a comfortable dining room and modern sanitation. The family also invested money in a trust fund to provide pensions for former employees who were in desperate need of support. At the time of Jo's birth the jute industry was already in decline. Both 1911 and 1912 were grim years for jute: mills were closing and prices were depressed. Then in January 1912 the problems were particularly compounded for Grimonds, which found itself in the front line of the battle for union recognition. Attempts were even made to 'black' Grimonds' goods at the docks. Dundee's Lord Provost had to intervene and, in effect, the firm began a process of capitulation. The following year, however, brought a remarkable, and quite unexpected, revival: indeed 1913 is described in one authoritative account as perhaps the most remarkable year that the industry had ever enjoyed – and almost certainly the best since the American Civil War (when the Dundee mills had managed to sell vast quantities of cloth to both sides). That proved in time to be a last, false dawn, as jute went back into decline. In 1920 Joseph B Grimond was obliged to sell out to a consortium organised by a hated rival, Hatry. He himself did not want to sell, but his fellow managing director and cousin, Louis Macintyre, wanted to get out of the industry and built up enough of a coalition amongst other shareholders in the extended family to outvote him. As an independent company, J & A D Grimond was wound up at an Extraordinary General Meeting on 8th October 1920, and the minutes of the next directors' meeting, held a fortnight later, record that Joseph B Grimond had tendered his resignation from the board. The other directors 'accepted this resignation with regret and . . . resolved to ask Mr Grimond to remain on as General Manager at his present salary for such time as might in the opinion of the Board be necessary'. Mr Grimond was not interested in that, which was probably for the best; he was now at least able to spend the few years remaining to him in relative comfort and peace.

Jo was always delighted in later life to cross paths with anyone who had been connected with J & A D Grimond. A porter once came up to him on Dundee station, several decades after Grimond's father sold out, and asked whether he was related to the jute barons of the same name. He confessed that he was, and the man lamented how his life in the world of jute had deteriorated after the Grimonds had sold out: 'It was all fun then, now it's all productivity and no chat.'[3] He told Grimond how in the old days the workers used to roll jute bales down the hill and tilt at each other on trolleys. After the firm had been consolidated into Jute Industries, such practices had been replaced by modern business methods and time-and-motion studies.

In contrast with his capitalistic forebears, Jo Grimond's father (known to friends and close colleagues as 'Joe', with an 'e') was a gentle man, and not obviously suited to the management of a large family firm, into which he had been pitchforked by fate. Studious and meticulous, but not academic, his only son later reflected that he might have made an admirable lawyer. Although his health had never properly recovered from a serious childhood illness, he combined working hard with being a doting and assiduous father. He was also practical, neat and well organised, and the young Jo would clamber over him, forever trying to gain access to the four pockets of his waistcoat, in which he would keep a small range of essential tools: his watch, his keys, a penknife and his railway season ticket. The young Jo was particularly close to him. He loved going for a putt with him on the Bruce embankment (latterly a car park) after he returned from work, light permitting, and playing games with him in the smoking room, before he went off to his club for some light recreation. Jo Grimond's father was anything but a hard-nosed businessman. He hardly drank, evinced no interest in card games and took little pleasure in the traditionally boisterous activities enjoyed by his colleagues and rivals. His love of travelling, of nature and of the semi-rural way of life he certainly passed on to his son.

Jo Grimond had two sisters, Gwyn and Nancie, respectively fourteen and eleven years older than he was. Because of the age difference, the girls were effectively partly siblings, partly aunts for young Jo. They both flowered into flamboyant 'good-time girls'. Grimond always joked that he would recommend having older sisters to any boy: they pampered him, and their suitors generally recognised the diplomatic benefits of making a fuss of him. Gwyn married in 1919, when Jo was only six years old. Her husband, 'Billy' Corbett, had been awarded the Military Cross in the war, and was still recovering from his wounds. He was the nephew of the Grimonds' next door neighbour Mrs Curran and, in later life, as Lord Rowallan, became Chief Scout. As a child Jo thought the world of him, not least because he possessed the extended family's only car and took him on countless jaunts in it – on one occasion to see a captured German submarine on the Tay. Jo was a pageboy at the wedding, looking rather diminutive alongside Mrs Curran's older and larger son, Geoffrey. 'The camel yoked to the ass,' she reputedly remarked.

Amongst the great pleasures for the young Jo Grimond were regular visits to Rowallan, Billy Corbett's family seat near Kilmarnock. The old castle of Rowallan had been built in the sixteenth century and was for much of its existence uninhabited and in a ruinous state. When Billy's parents, the Liberal MP Archie Corbett and his ambitious wife, acquired the property, Mrs Corbett decided not to restore the old castle, but to have a new Rowallan built about half a mile away. Sir Robert Lorimer was retained to design the new house, and did so with his customary flourishes. As a child, Grimond loved the place. It could have been designed specifically with children in mind: its rambling interior was full of nooks and crannies, mysterious passages and spiral staircases. Nancie, in contrast with Gwyn, remained at home until the 1930s. She then followed her sister in marrying a holder of the Military Cross: Willie Black of Fife. Before settling down with him, however, she 'always had wide-ranging tastes in young men with perhaps a passing bias for the undesirable'[4] and, like her sister, was evidently a constant source of stimulation, amusement and joy for her young brother.

Although trips to Rowallan were regular features of Jo's youth, as his father no longer possessed a car (though he had owned one when they first became available), weekend jaunts were generally out of the question. Nor did the Grimonds believe that anything of great interest was to be found in the Fife hinterland:[5] 'a pretty savage place, inhabited by lunatic lairds and other peculiarities'. Unless Billy Corbett happened to be in the vicinity, everything had to be done by train, with the family ordering a bus to carry them and their possessions in stately fashion to and from the station, where a one-armed guard called Lees reigned supreme. This gave Jo a lifelong love of the railways which, later in life, he likened to a well-loved dog: 'endearing, friendly, with some notable exceptions rather useless, messy, apt to be smelly and require a great deal of cosseting'.[6] Some of these longer family holidays must certainly have broadened his horizons. After he learned to fish, Jo enjoyed trips to Devon or Aberdeenshire in pursuit of piscine quarry and, later, after his father had retired and long vacations had become a possibility, sojourns of between four and eight weeks in the South of France. Father and son also engaged in some gentle bird-watching, possibly the beginning of Jo's lifelong fascination with animals. These trips certainly nurtured not only Grimond's ravenous constitution (in France he discovered, and devoured, a plenitude of patisseries and *oeufs en cocotte*) but also his sense of the absurd or, perhaps more appositely, his appreciation of the *recherché*. One trip to a Devon boarding-house came to an abrupt end after only one night when Jo's mother discovered incontrovertible evidence of damp in the beds. She thrust a hand mirror between the sheets as a precaution, it misted up slightly, and the family decamped at once. Damp meant croup, and she was not risking that.

Although Grimond's mother, Lydia Grimond, came from Birkenhead, she was a considerable St Andrews character, becoming in Jo's words one of the 'powerful contingent of formidable women' who dominated society in the town. She always kept a close eye on her young son, lest he fall into bad habits. It caused her great perturbation, for instance, when in his teens Jo attended a pantomime and went backstage afterwards to see the actresses. Her brother, Foster Richardson, and her sister had also migrated from Merseyside to St

Andrews, living close by the Grimonds. Foster worked for J & A D Grimond in Dundee and he partnered Jo's father at golf. In St Andrews in 1924 they won the Calcutta Cup Foursomes, an annual handicap tournament restricted to members of the Royal and Ancient. After A D Grimond died in 1903, along with Joseph B Grimond and one of his cousins, Louis Grimond Macintyre, Foster Richardson took turns as chairman of the company board. He also remained with the successor company, Jute Industries, for many years after Joseph B severed all connections. Lydia Grimond too was athletic, and all three children inherited from her a strong sense of the importance of what Grimond even in old age would call 'games' – competitive sport in all its forms. She was a notable golfer and encouraged her offspring in all their sporting pursuits. Close to the local station stands Kinburn House, a gloomy, baronial place built originally by a Dr Buddo who, according to Grimond, died insane after shooting dead a boy who he thought was stealing apples from his garden. Kinburn's main plus, in the eyes of the Grimond clan, was its tennis courts. The Kinburn tournament each August hosted Scotland's hard-court championship, and Grimond's sisters were keen and effective participants.

Gwyn was a wonderfully elemental character, full of energy and vigour and a great favourite of her brother, who described her admiringly and affectionately as 'a child of nature . . . spontaneous . . . she dragged less certain spirits in her wake . . . Gwyn liked happiness and wanted everyone to be happy too . . . Though a moderately observing Christian, her behaviour was pagan.'[7] She and a family friend, Ian Collins, were for a time the mixed doubles champions of Scotland. Jo Grimond inherited the sporting enthusiasms of his family. He played tennis with his sisters and their friends, indeed played it well into middle age. His family still recall how effectively he could serve, even when well out of practice. He also graduated from the putting green to golf on the main course at St Andrews. He was brought up to play the game seriously although, by his own admission, he never played especially well. By tradition golf on the Old Course was free to ratepayers and Grimond in later life would hark back to the marvellous, unique character of that course, which 'catered for duffer as well as pro'.[8]

The family home, 8 Abbotsford Crescent, was rented from the white-bearded Professor McIntosh, an academic at the university, neighbour and formidable property speculator. It had five floors including a basement, with three bathrooms and two indoor lavatories. The Grimonds had baths rather often by middle-class standards – many respectable households apparently considered a weekly immersion perfectly adequate. As was customary in Fife at that time, the dining room was on the ground floor, and the drawing room on the first floor. Jo Grimond's family generally observed the contemporary formalities and rituals. In common with most of the St Andrews bourgeoisie, they would change for dinner on every night except Sunday. They would consume alcohol only when their visitors, all of whom were expected to arrive at a quarter past eight on the dot as per their invitation, were offered 'sherry and only sherry' before dinner and were never, ever kissed. Christian names were used only sparingly and, even to most of his intimates, Grimond's father would sign himself formally, 'J B Grimond'. Only to a few of his closest business associates (usually in the United States) would he sign off as 'Joe'. Nobody would be asked inside the Grimond house unless Mrs Grimond had first 'called'. When Jo Grimond was a child, there were never fewer than four servants at any one time.

Nothing was ever routine or dull in Jo Grimond's life, and even the house of his birth had an interesting history. The development of which it was part dated back to the mid 1840s, and the major investor had been none other than John Gladstone, aged patrician of the great Liberal family, and father of W E Gladstone. As he came to the end of his life, he had reduced his shareholdings in the railways and joined with James Hope (changed to Hope-Scott after he married Sir Walter Scott's grand-daughter) to build three linked streets of what were then described as 'gentlemen's houses' to the west of the old town in St Andrews. The burgeoning popularity of golf was bringing new life to the town, and Gladstone always had a good eye for an investment. The scheme was in deliberate imitation of the New Town of Edinburgh. Any pretensions were not confined to the houses: at the end of the crescent was a raised 'crossing', and over the gutter outside the Grimonds' home was a mounting block. The completion of the houses coincided with the final decline of sedan chairs in the town. A previous tenant of the house was one Mr Boothby, who had stayed there with his son, Bob, later a Conservative MP and a significant figure in the downfall of the Chamberlain government.

Jo Grimond had the early experiences typical of someone of his class. His elderly nurse, Jessie Anderson, had also nurtured his sisters and father. He was, by his own admission, an unrepentantly tiresome charge. In particular, if Jessie fell asleep when reading to him, he would prod her awake without mercy. She seems to have endured all this in good humour, taking the young Jo on portentously slow walks along the Ladebraes – a mile-long burn at the edge of town. He had already developed a prodigious appetite, and she would indulge him most evenings with a taste of her supper. When Jo was deemed old enough, Jessie was supplemented by a governess, Miss Mathieson, whose enthusiasm for history rapidly infected Jo. Then, for a time, he attended a school in the town. Those early lessons also consolidated Jo's sense of Scottishness, which was later to survive more than a decade of English education: 'I remember very well as a child being a passionate partisan of the Scots in history. I remember my first sense of something wrong when as a boy I went to Edinburgh and found an empty palace.'[9]

St Andrews was a prosperous and varied town, and the young Jo found plenty there to fascinate him. There were countless points of interest for a bright youngster and, as the child of a well-to-do family, Jo was regularly indulged by many of the tradesmen whose activities so intrigued him. He loved to watch the blacksmith's roaring forge and Miss Robertson, the local grocer, would give him bars of chocolate. Amongst Grimond's familiars were the Patons and the Boases, scions of two notable, and inter-related, St Andrews families. Dr Paton was the doctor at St Leonard's School in the town, and his son John was Grimond's closest childhood friend, and later a contemporary at Oxford. He and his only brother, Neil, were both destined to perish in the Second World War. Grimond later wrote poignantly: 'of all my St Andrews friends John is the one I miss most.'[10] From an early age, Jo used to enjoy taking ineffective pot shots at the local wildlife, particularly on the Eden, admitting rather proudly in adulthood that he hadn't reduced the stock very much. The highlight of his 'shooting season' came at Christmas each year, when Philip Boase would round up the St Andrews boys, including Jo and the Patons, and some of their parents, taking them off to Leuchars, whose wide fields of oats and potatoes provided a nutritious environment for partridges. Beaters would attack the field from a right angle to a single file of armed hunters. Few partridges died and, even more amazingly, no people ever did. St Andrews was not, however, an exclusive playground for the rich. It had its share of poverty too, although even the poorer children of the town, whose lives were certainly spartan, were for the most part spared the squalor and violence that routinely prevailed in the cities. All in all, this childhood must have provided Jo Grimond with splendidly robust and secure foundations for life, making him, in his own phrase, 'rather self-contained and rather satisfied'.

Once Jo had outgrown the ministrations of his home tutor and the local primary, it was a different matter. He was soon sent away to London, where he had a horrible time. Although he would later write of having enjoyed a childhood home life that was sheltered or even pampered, Grimond appears to have endured a thoroughly unpleasant existence whenever he was away from home. At the age of eight he had one term at a preparatory school, Gibbs, on London's Sloane Street, the only school that he actually enjoyed attending, largely because he was able to play football there. Like most of his family, Jo Grimond was blessed with a naturally powerful physique and a good eye for a ball, and throughout his time at preparatory school he was an enthusiastic sportsman. He boxed, and at cricket he became a useful bowler. Tennis was confined to his vacations, but ensured that he kept his eye in even when he was home with the family. He later wrote of the 'ecstasy' playing football at Gibbs and reckoned that it was on the football pitches at Putney at the age of eight that he reached his 'zenith as an athlete'.[11] He remained convinced throughout his life that as many people as possible should participate in sport, since the playing of sport could play a useful role, and not only in team building and improving the fitness of individuals. It could also play an important role in channelling the violent instincts of the male of the species. But he never much enjoyed the sedentary activity of watching games. He was one of the first politicians to point out that the watching of sport, far from channelling or neutralising aggressive and anti-social behaviour, was all too often a stimulus and focus for it. There isn't, he felt, too much of the Corinthian spirit abroad on the average football terrace.

After that single term at Gibbs, Jo was sent to Evelyn's, a 'private' boarding-school in West Drayton, Middlesex, which he thoroughly hated. Just as many old soldiers will not discuss their experiences of war's horrors, Grimond preferred to draw a veil over his time in Mr Worsley's school. He merely referred anyone evincing interest to Evelyn Waugh's *Decline and Fall*. In Waugh's novel, one of the characters explains how such schools are divided into four categories: 'Leading School, First-rate school, Good School and School . . . Frankly, School is pretty bad.' There is no doubt whatsoever that Jo Grimond was very much at a 'School'. It did nothing to slake his thirst for reading, however, and between the ages of eight and ten he 'would have read anything on which I could lay my hands . . . While suffering from measles I became expert on the complications of civil war in China by absorbing every article I could find on this abstruse subject.'[12] This independence of mind, combined with an ability to absorb ideas at speed, would stand Grimond in good stead as he continued his education and throughout his political life.

Although he had a miserable time boarding at his preparatory schools, Grimond never thought to hold this against his parents. He came to accept, as a child and later as an adult, that his parents 'no doubt thought it would be good for me to leave home . . . they perhaps rightly or wrongly felt that some of the English schools gave a better education than their Scottish equivalents.'[13] In the first (unpublished) manuscript draft for his *Memoirs*, he reflected on this matter: 'I loathed school but though I have resentment about many things I did not bear any resentment against my parents for having sent me there. The contrast between the foreign, cold atmosphere of school, the compulsion, the curious people who were to be found teaching, and the warmth and enjoyment of home life remain vivid to this day. I sympathise with those who want security.' The beginning of his final term, at least, was greatly enlivened when the train on which he was travelling to London was affected by the General Strike, which had seemed so remote to people in St Andrews. Losing time all the way, the train limped into York and the twelve-year-old Jo spent the night in York's station hotel instead of back at school, having seen trains with their windows all smashed in Edinburgh, troops guarding the level crossings in Northumberland and an overturned train in North Yorkshire. It was, perhaps, an appropriate end to what had been a disagreeable preparatory schooling. For the final stage of his schooling, he was sent on to Eton College from his hated preparatory school in the Autumn Half (term) of 1926, at the age of thirteen, 'largely for snobbish reasons'.[14]

The privacy that he now enjoyed was a welcome revelation to him, as were the far greater degree of freedom and the 'huge teas' that he could now devour to his heart's content. As Grimond's near-contemporary Bernard Fergusson put it in his marvellous account of the school at this time: 'never will the new boy feel so grand again as when he looks on his Eton room for the first time . . . He has said goodbye for ever to the bleak cubicle or dormitory which has hitherto been thought good enough to house him . . . Here he will eat, sleep, work, rag, read, sing, and play the fool with his friends for many months to come.'[15] At the beginning of his Etonian career, Jo Grimond discovered new freedoms and bloomed as he had never been able to before. He was about to enjoy traditional English education at its very highest level, yet he would emerge from it with his sense of Scottishness not only intact, but also refined and redefined. Much has been written about the nature of this unique institution, and it would be otiose to repeat it in detail. Suffice it to say that Eton, then as now, was one of the cradles – arguably by far the most significant one – of the British ruling class, that it gave boys an unusual degree of power over their own affairs, that it had more than its fair share of brilliant teachers and characters, and that no boy could fail to emerge unaffected by its values, sense of history and academic excellence. Fergusson describes the Eton of this time as 'one of the most tolerant places in the world . . . There are few cliques; everybody's tastes are respected; the lion lies down with the lamb; the athlete messes with the sap; the pugilist with the poet.'[16] If there were gaps in the education provided, the place seems at least to have been founded upon a system that was respectful towards the individual, and highly liberal in spirit. Grimond himself was always full of praise for the way in which values and traditions were passed on at Eton – but felt that he had never received the slightest scrap of practical instruction.

Jo Grimond's housemaster was Mr Howson, in the Etonian firmament perhaps no more than a safe pair of hands but by any more generally applied yardstick evidently an admirable individual, who had recently resigned as the Eton Scouts' Quartermaster in order to take over the house. Etonian houses are curious corporate entities, with short lives. They are named not after the building that they inhabit, but after the housemaster. When a housemaster steps down, the common identity can change totally. In the early part of this century this sense of transience was intensified by the almost federal nature of the school. Each pupil's parents in effect contracted with the housemaster to provide board and lodging to their son – with teaching subcontracted to the college. The physical state of the school, and of Mr Howson's boarding-house in particular, would hardly be acceptable today. For the younger boys, classes routinely numbered thirty or more – the best teaching came later, in seminars and tutorials – and Mr Howson's house boasted little in the way of facilities, offering only two baths, a multitude of woodworm and no fire escape.

Jo admired the way in which the school inculcated a really deep and abiding loyalty towards itself even in the most wayward staff, whose criticisms of the place always seemed to spring from a sense of belonging; it was 'all within the family' as it were. Above all he enjoyed the fact that pupils were encouraged to develop self-reliance more or less from day one. The academic approach impressed him less and, with a degree of hyperbole, he would write that 'at the end of a lengthy and expensive education no boy of my time could speak a foreign language, read a balance sheet, mend a motor car, cook, type, darn or knit'.[17] In his early period at the school, Grimond established himself as a gifted schoolboy, without ever quite storming the heights. Towards the end of his first year, he won a Holiday Task Prize and the Brinckman Divinity Prize. Academically he seems to have cruised somewhat thereafter. In his *Memoirs,* Grimond claimed that at Eton he soon learned the value of a crib and how, as he put it, 'to cheat acceptably'. He also admitted that, by the time he made it into the 'middle reaches' of his time at Eton, he was 'virtually unteachable and should have been put out to grass'.[18] Caught between the initial excitement of his arrival, and his subsequent emergence as one of the school's leading 'swells', he found Etonian life distinctly underwhelming and 'at no time would I not have leaped at the chance of going home'.[19] On 26th February 1929 came a bitter personal blow, with the death at fifty-four of Grimond's father, Joseph B Grimond, who had been in delicate health for some time. The young man had been particularly close to his father, and this must have set him back badly. It can hardly be a coincidence that this event marked the beginning of Grimond's least productive time at Eton: in 1929 his name is notably absent from Eton's copious and comprehensive lists of academic and sporting achievements.

In due course, however, Grimond's emergence from the chrysalis of adolescence did bring with it the esteem of his fellows. Few individuals come through the intense experience of Eton life without forging at least some close friendships that will sustain them in later life. Jo Grimond, always a clubbable sort, was no exception. Either because he was ambitious, or because he liked them better, he seems to have spent a lot of time with boys who had joined the school a year or more before him. One older pupil who particularly influenced him was Bernard Fergusson (later Baron Ballantrae), who was three years ahead of him and became a lifelong friend. In later life Grimond was fond of recounting how, when he and a group of friends went walking in the Highlands in the late 1930s, Fergusson, a future hero of the Burma campaign, got blistered feet and had to take a bus. When Grimond committed this to paper in his *Memoirs*, he received a jocular letter from Fergusson, who wrote how much he had enjoyed the book 'despite the gross libel . . . For which I would thrash you with a horse-whip on the steps of your Club if only you belonged to a decent club.' Another older boy with whom Grimond fell in was Con O'Neill, later to resign three times from the Foreign Service in a series of notable protests, but who ultimately distinguished himself by leading the UK official delegation in the successful accession negotiations with the EEC in 1970–72. Jo Grimond subsequently became godfather to O'Neill's daughter Onuora, herself now a distinguished academic. Grimond and O'Neill were in some ways the unlikeliest of chums, proving that opposites can attract. O'Neill had none of the consensual qualities that Grimond had even by then developed. He was throughout his life a dry, acerbic character. When, in the wake of British accession to the European Community, O'Neill found among his new responsibilities that of assessing corn crops throughout the Community, Grimond commented wryly that it was 'typical of Con' to earn his corn by assessing how corny corn was. Through Con O'Neill, Jo also became a close friend of Jasper Ridley, regarded by most who knew him as one of the most remarkable talents of his generation. Jasper was the grandson of the last Czarist ambassador in London, and a constantly stimulating companion with a penchant for Socratic conversations of intellectual discovery. The foundations of friendship between this trio were put in place at Eton, but it was later in the decade that their travels together, and their continued proximity at Oxford, created a deep bond that only Ridley's tragically early death during the war brought to a cruel close.

Amongst his other near-contemporaries, Grimond had several other intimates who went on to great things. As well as visiting Ulster with Con O'Neill, with Dick (later Sir Richard) Levinge, his house captain, he visited Knockdrin, the Levinge family seat at Mullingar in Ireland. It was Levinge who drove Grimond to sit for his scholarship examination at Oxford. Towards the end of his time at Eton, Jo Grimond added to his already impressive roster of talented friends Lionel Brett, a King's Scholar and Captain of the School, who ended up as principal of the Royal College of Art, and Guy Branch, whom Grimond particularly admired. It seemed to Grimond that the particular personal qualities of Guy Branch foreshadowed a less arrogant and complacent Etonian style that had started to emerge in the 1930s, shorn of the old sense that the school conferred almost mystical qualities, including a 'right to rule'. Out of all of his friends, it was probably for Branch that Grimond had the highest hopes. These hopes were dashed by Guy Branch's death in the Second World War. Grimond gave his friend a touching tribute in his *Memoirs*: 'Guy was clever but not rich and certainly not arrogant, nor did he attach much importance to games although he kept wicket for Eton . . . He was rather more sophisticated than his contemporaries, amusing, detached, a discoverer of odd corners in life, whether in personalities or literature, sanguine about the future, engrossed in the present.'[20]

Through his friendship with William Douglas Home, who was a year ahead of him in Mr Howson's house, Grimond became acquainted with William's father Lord Home, and the Homes' family seat, Douglas, attending summer parties there. He admired the eccentricities of the family and their home, where the irregular supplies of electricity, food and drink kept guests guessing – and even trips to the lavatory promised new adventures in a building that could be plunged into complete and unyielding darkness at any moment. Lord Home and his extended family evidently took to the young Grimond, and derived much amusement from the fact that some or all of the household's five sons would attempt to entice him into snipe-shooting every day. 'Going shooting again?' asked Lord Home on one such occasion. 'How do you know that poor old Grimond doesn't want to stay at home and think today?' A number of staff at Eton left their mark on Grimond, notable amongst them his history teachers Henry Marten and Robert Birley. Birley, later knighted, was by any token a remarkable figure, whom Grimond described as a 'master of genius',[21] ensuring that Grimond's nascent interest in history was kindled into genuine academic enthusiasm and even expertise. He it was who provided, in David Astor's words, the 'chief intellectual stimulus'[22] to the teenaged Grimond and also, by Grimond's own testimony, convinced him of the virtues of liberalism. He remained a major influence on Grimond for half a century. Yet undoubtedly the most notable figure of Grimond's time at Eton was not a mere master, but the provost, M R James, perhaps best known today for his peerless ghost stories. In his first manuscript draft for his *Memoirs*, Grimond wrote of James that:

> He was the most uncontradictable man I ever met. Not Churchill or de Gaulle, though perhaps in the same class, ever struck me as being as formidable as James . . . From him I learnt that position, recognition, place in the lists of worldly esteem are inessential. I also learnt the virtues of benevolent selfishness . . . He was by ordinary standards a selfish man. But that meant that he did not impose on others. He wanted people to enjoy themselves. He had no mission to make them better. No mission either to put himself to any great truth on their behalf. A bad thing, perhaps, if universally applied. But how excellent, how restful, how agreeable in him . . . As he never taught me, I cannot claim to have learnt anything from him (though one of the greatest scholars of his time) except a passing acquaintance with Shakespeare. But I think that he was both a salutary antidote to ambition and subservience and an example of the importance of people as people and not as office-holders.

Grimond first met James socially at an unusually early juncture in his school career, after Bernard Fergusson suggested his name as a suitable dinner guest. This dinner not only gave Grimond his first opportunity to observe the great man at close quarters. It also ended with him getting drunk for the first time, having been plied with claret and port. Grimond would often question some aspects of the education provided at Eton, but always commended the system of streaming by ability: 'the school,' he wrote in his *Memoirs,* 'as far as ability was concerned, was comprehensive, ranging from boys of incurable stupidity up to brilliant scholars.' Grimond was never quite as physically inactive at Eton as he would later claim to have been. Although England's most celebrated boarding-school never stripped him of his Scottish sensibilities, it did afford him the opportunity to hone his skills at the very English game of cricket. During his first three years at the school, Jo Grimond became something of a star cricketer for his house. In his first summer at the school, he was making his mark as a bowler in junior competitions – taking 24 wickets at an average of just under 15 runs. The following year his bowling average fell into single figures across the season, and the *Eton College Chronicle* singled him out for praise when, in June 1928, he took 4 wickets for only 10 runs in one match. In his final year as a junior cricketer, the young Grimond took 44 wickets in the season, costing a very acceptable average of only 6.7 runs. In his last two years, although he never quite made it into the first team, he was a mainstay of the school's second team – interestingly a Second XII, where even the Twelfth Man got a game. The most surreal and satisfying entry on a surviving scorecard from this period is from a match on 4th June 1931 – Eton's most significant day each year, on which it celebrates the birthday of its benefactor King George III – when Grimond played against the Eton Ramblers. The school side batted first, and Grimond lost his wicket cheaply: out caught by one W G L F Lowndes for six runs. He exacted cruel and worthy revenge, as the Ramblers' scorecard testifies:

W G L F Lowndes (c Scaramanga b Grimond) 99

One or two of his future political rivals might have done well to take note. Also on 4th June 1931, Grimond made it into the crew of *Monarch,* joining his friends Con O'Neill and William Douglas Home in the celebrated ten-oar boat that still takes pride of place (albeit a rather ceremonial and sedate one), captained by the school's Captain of Boats, in the annual Procession of Boats. All in all he was quite a 'swell'. In his late teens, Jo Grimond was also a highly accomplished Fives player, usually playing in partnership with his close friend Robert McNeile, and on at least one notable occasion representing the school, deputising for the 'Keepers' (the first pair) by playing against a highly competitive army team in March 1932 and winning by 62 points to 58. As a consequence, Grimond was able to add a 'Fives Choice' (the Etonian equivalent of an Oxford or Cambridge Blue) to the house colours he had already gained. The *Eton College Chronicle* reported that, in the army match, 'the play was consistent and steady throughout, and the rallies were extraordinarily long, but the game was remarkable more for its nerve-shattering closeness than for any particular display of brilliance on the part of the players'.

As he made his way through Eton, Grimond not only proved himself to be a fine scholar and historian. He was also an enthusiastic supporter of the school's various societies, which he praised for doing 'much indirect good . . . they make people feel pleasanter to themselves and their fellows'.[23] The societies would generally meet between nine and ten in the evening and afforded boys an opportunity to exchange ideas and, no doubt, to show off after hours. Each society's fortunes waxed and waned according to the enthusiasm – or lack of it – within each generation of Etonians. A detailed explanation of these societies, and their significance, can be left to Jo Grimond himself, for in his last year at the school he wrote a lengthy essay about them. This was published in an impressive independent magazine, or ephemeral, entitled *Change*, which he co-edited with a quartet of contemporaries including Lionel Brett. Grimond had obviously reflected deeply before putting pen to paper. It is an impressively mature piece, tautly argued and providing a fascinating insight into the school and its relationship with the outside world. There are interesting parallels too between Grimond's paean to the societies and much of his later thinking: for instance his enthusiasm for volunteering and the importance he would attach to 'intermediate institutions' and shared values. There is also no mistaking the air of pre-emptive nostalgia with which the piece is imbued, or the early signs of an instinctive liberal distrust of committee structures:

> Learning is now made attractive by books written for the popular taste, by instructive cinemas, and generally by not only thrusting knowledge down the throat of the public, but also by wrapping the pill in a liberal coating of sugar. At Public Schools it is becoming distinguished instead of disreputable to be highbrow . . . Eton is the stronghold of the classics, and of an education which prides itself not on its attraction but on its repulsion . . . here the athlete is the god . . . but even here . . . the new ideas are beginning to be felt . . . Masters support [the Societies] as a means of rousing the interest of boys. The boys come to them because they are interested, and because to go out at 9pm flatters their self-importance. Both enjoy them because the Englishman loves to meet and join in a committee.

In Grimond's view, the best of the mainstream societies, and the most prestigious, was the invitation-only Shakespeare Society, which gathered around the fire in the provost's dining room. James himself was, according to Grimond, a 'marvellous, even-toned reader' and an indulgent overseer:

> The room, whether lit by sunlight or a log fire, makes a stage which can have few equals in England . . . But it is not the room, nor the boys, who now sit under the portraits of the predecessors *progeniem vitiosorem* [the children of the corrupted ones – quoting Horace] no doubt, which lend this Society its glory: it is the Provost. No matter how trying the day has been, no matter how bad the reading (and it must be sometimes painful to him), every member under his benign influence is soon sunk in the beauty and peace of his surroundings.[24]

Grimond was also a fairly assiduous contributor to the rather high-minded Essay Society, at which one pupil would deliver a paper to a dozen or so others, and then be subjected to their scrutiny. He read papers, *inter alia*, on the author 'Saki' and on Eton itself. But the most obvious groupings to receive his attentions were the Debating Society and the Political Society. The latter had been founded by Lord Curzon when he was at Eton, and became Grimond's pride and joy, blossoming under his ambitious leadership. A series of MPs and eminent public figures came to make their case to the assembled company, including HRH the Prince of Wales (the future King Edward VIII), who addressed them in June 1931, and Hilaire Belloc, who addressed the society on the subject of 'Historical Evidence' in July 1932. Party political speakers included Sir Archibald Sinclair, soon to become leader of the independent Liberal Party, Austen Chamberlain and, only two days after him, John Buchan. Each received an attentive hearing and, in all probability, with the exception of HRH, some good-natured and allegedly well-informed heckling.

Perhaps the most unexpected and interesting acceptance to an invitation from the society during this period came from Mahatma Gandhi, who addressed them on Friday, 23rd October 1931. Grimond did not warn the school authorities that he had invited such a controversial character and, when word leaked out, there was the most almighty furore. Luckily for him, the headmaster defended him against the attacks of splenetic Old Etonians. There was still no question of providing a guard of honour for Gandhi, however, although he was offered overnight accommodation. Grimond and one of his friends went to meet him very informally at the station. He was not much taken with this particular guest: 'He bristled with curious habits and demands, some to the British bordering on the unsavoury',[25] and he was very struck by the fact that the policemen charged with looking after Gandhi had all taken a dislike to the man. Gandhi's performance in front of the society did little to redeem him in anyone's eyes and Grimond in particular found him rather a disappointment. He did not answer questions directly or frankly, and the boys thought him evasive and slippery. The best that Grimond could contrive in exculpation was that Gandhi was both exhausted and nonplussed by questions asked in an English context, in contrast with his own thoughts, which were focused on India. Gandhi also demonstrated beliefs that the young Etonians found eccentric and distinctly unappealing: an almost superstitious belief in handicrafts, and a strong attachment to the Hindu religion, which Grimond as an adult purported to admire, but never to understand. In fairness to Gandhi, he was at that time negotiating with the British government and, as Grimond himself later reflected, he was a famously shrewd, Machiavellian negotiator and never knew who might be listening. Grimond compared Gandhi's performance particularly unfavourably with that of the hard-line Muslim leader Maulama Shaukut Ali, whose manner and appearance seem to have been as demotic as they were demonic. Grimond again:

> He was a flamboyant personality and in every way a contrast to Gandhi: a magnificent looking man, dressed in flowing robes with a great stick with an ivory head . . . He said the British were hell. He flourished his stick and said: 'I've killed twenty people with this myself,' and with the young this went down very well. 'Do you believe in violence?' 'Oh yes, I believe in violence.' He was a leader of the Muslims but he didn't have to play his hand like Gandhi.[26]

Although the Debating Society was in a fairly shaky state throughout Grimond's time at the school, he seems to have done his bit on those rare occasions when a meeting did take place. A solitary report exists of one thinly attended meeting during this period, when the society discussed a motion demanding that legislation should be brought in at once to curb the powers of the press. The *Eton College Chronicle* reported that Jo Grimond, not for the last time in his long life, opposed this talk of censorship: 'Grimond, with ruthless logic, attempted to prove that the proposed censorship would be a party censorship, and would not apply to the biased Conservative newspapers.' Despite his hostility, however, the motion was carried by 12 votes to 11. Jo Grimond would later deplore the apathy that undermined the Debating Society, but recognised too that those debates that did take place were not always a convincing advertisement for the genre. He clearly felt that more could be learned from the shortcomings of his colleagues than could ever be gleaned from their better features. He also reminisced with pleasure upon a debate in which two masters, Mr Routh and his respected history teacher Robert Birley, locked horns on the subject of free trade. Once again a single-vote margin separated the two camps, the free-trading Birley losing to an opponent who, in Grimond's view, 'had the weakest case but the bias of the audience'. He also confessed that he himself 'got lost several times'.[27]

The poor condition of the Debating Society, and the infrequency of its meetings, must have put Grimond at something of a disadvantage, since any aspirant politician needs opportunities to develop his ability to master both argument and the elusive art of public speaking. However at least one part of the politician's armoury – oratory pure and simple – could get a regular outing through the Etonian tradition of 'Speeches', for which leading lights in the school memorise and deliver lengthy prose passages. Grimond's friend Con O'Neill had been a particular star at this activity and, in his own last year, Grimond sought to follow in his footsteps. He performed three times and, although it is essential to make allowance for the fact that his friends on the *Chronicle* were no doubt enjoying a laugh at his expense, their reports still give us the best extant accounts of the mannerisms and speaking style of Jo Grimond at the age of eighteen. As a rule he seems to have been a little nervous but, once he had settled into his stride, he evidently succeeded in becoming quite a crowd-pleaser. This may explain the rather grudging praise that he elicited from the reviewers – comments that rather foreshadow the kind of notices he would receive later in life for his parliamentary performances. He made his debut in October 1931, choosing a political theme:

> Grimond began with a passage from Lord Rosebery's *Life of Pitt*. He set an excellent example of audibility. His speech was far from easy. Two difficulties at least stood in the way of complete success. The style of the passage is in itself so emphatic that the greatest skill is needed to avoid over-emphasis in declamation. And Grimond did over-emphasise too many words. Secondly the author's device of piling short sentence upon short sentence to produce the deadweight of the calamities which surrounded Pitt makes the speaker apprehensive of being monotonous. Here he tries to invest each new sentence with fresh life and interest, instead of dwelling on the monotonous sequence of disasters. Therefore we lost a little of the meaning of the piece and the rhythm of the writing. But the speech was far from a failure, as the applause at the end testified.

In February 1932 his choice of text was 'The Broadcast Hoax', an essay by Father Ronald Knox, an Old Etonian clergyman, editor, literary critic, humorist and writer of detective stories, who in the 1920s laid out his 'ten rules' for detective fiction in its so-called Golden Age. The surviving account of Grimond's performance describes how difficult he found it to walk the line between declamation and a 'greater realism', and it seems that he once again took a little time to conquer his nervousness. 'He began in the grand manner, but whether because he realised that that would not do, or because in the face of much hilarity throughout the audience, he could not keep it up, he soon abandoned this, and the speech gained at once in effect from his more natural but no less satirical tone of voice.' On 4th June 1932, the last occasion on which Grimond took part in the school's annual festivities, he again participated in Speeches. It seems that he had by now grown in confidence, though his precise choice of text – helpfully described only as *A Ballad* by 'Anon' – is impossible to identify now. The *Eton College Chronicle* reported that, of the twenty presentations that day, his was 'the most courageous':

> Grimond's *Ballad* was very difficult indeed, and he came within only a little of brilliant success. He has a fine powerful voice, and showed considerable skill in his variations of strength and tone. He made many intelligent and telling pauses, but was always in danger of spoiling them by a nervous fidget or a disturbing habit of swaying backwards and forwards. It is possible that this criticism is ungenerous, for there is no doubt that he made a deep effect upon his audience. But in the writer's view these little blemishes just prevented him from doing himself full justice.

More prestigious even than Speeches was the Eton Society – better known by its pet name of 'Pop'. Con O'Neill proposed Grimond for Pop in March

1931, and he was elected at the first time of asking – a rare honour, and a clear sign of his remarkable popularity – with only two dissentients (five or more would have been fatal to his cause). For his last four terms, therefore, Grimond was a member of Pop and, for his very last term, he was its president. He appears to have enjoyed himself thoroughly, and used all his influence to win admittance to the society for his younger friends, most notably Guy Branch who finally won admission at the fourth time of asking. The presidency of Pop was the most sought-after prize in the school, and one of which Grimond, at least at the time, was shamelessly proud:

> [The Eton Society] has a history which might be made into a whole article, and the article would be as boring as most school records; in which we enjoy only the sight of our own name in print . . . It is self-elective, and its members are chosen for athletic skill, for distinction, but most of all for popularity . . . its very excellence lies in the fact that it is open to every danger and could never have originated in the brain of a schoolmaster.[28]

In that final phrase we clearly apprehend the authentic, politically non-conformist voice of Jo Grimond.

The economic tribulations of 1931–2 were felt even within the Etonian stockade and, in a note to his successor as president of Pop, Grimond warned that even the Eton Society itself would have to introduce certain economies. Under pressure from the school authorities to show some kind of lead in a country hit by austerity, a Pop sub-committee led by Grimond had at first proposed the outright abolition of the customary and distinctive waistcoats worn by members, marking them out from the rank and file. It is easy to imagine the outcry that forced them into a rethink:

> On reconsideration of the matter it was seen that this was little or no economy, most of the waistcoats worn being secondhand. It was therefore decided that no change should take place in the rules or customs of the society. The society has been left untouched by the authorities on the understanding that it curbs its own expenditure. It is to be hoped that it can do so without rules being laid down.

Grimond's last year at Eton seems to have had a profound effect on him. When his friend William Douglas Home, the House Captain, left in summer 1931, in his own words he 'handed on to a large, cheerful and untidy boy, Jo Grimond'.[29] As well as succeeding to the house captaincy, Grimond set the seal in his final year upon an academic career that, although it did not mark him out as one of the greatest minds of his generation, certainly showed much distinction. He had an essay 'sent up', eight distinctions in Trials and proved his credentials as a historian in March 1932 by winning the prestigious Rosebery Scholarship. He also voluntarily traversed the traditional adolescent 'poetry period', devouring the works of Donne, Burns, Keats and Shelley 'in the back benches of history classes'.[30] Despite his precocious advocacy of liberal values for the nation, the school had evidently inculcated in Jo Grimond a strong streak of old-school paternalism, combined with a willingness to dole out judicious applications of traditional punishments when required. He was not beyond beating the younger boys. Consequently, while some of the juniors, by all accounts, virtually hero-worshipped Grimond (including the future Duke of Grafton, his fag in that year, who much admired Jo and found him to be 'considerate and very intelligent'), others never forgave him for the indignities that they suffered at his hands. On one occasion, Grimond was charged with meting out punishment to everyone in the house below 'Debate' (roughly below the age of sixteen), after an unknown hand had bashed in all the new top hats that had been delivered to 'M'Tutors' for 4th June 1932. The entire house was summoned to the house library and Grimond delivered an ultimatum. Either the guilty party or parties must own up, or everyone would have to be beaten. He held up a stopwatch and waited. Nobody said a word in response, so Grimond meted out six strokes to each and every potential suspect – a 'general tanning'.

In addition to his thoughts on Pop and the school's societies, Jo Grimond left behind at the end of his final term one of the most notable documents of his life. The lengthy testament that he composed at the end of his last term, in July 1932, runs to a couple of thousand words, inscribed in his own inimitable and virtually indecipherable longhand in a huge tome intended to be handed on through his line of successors as House Captain. It contains both his personal philosophy and the kind of introspection that is not uncommon in young men of his age. The composition was obviously written over a period of time – variations in the handwriting make that clear to the reader – and it is an unusually personal and heartfelt document, largely setting out those aspects of Etonian life that least appealed to the eighteen-year-old Grimond, and his suggestions for their abolition or amelioration. In places here, Grimond is self-critical to a degree that even he would surely have considered excessive only a few years later. The senior members of one of the old public schools enjoy a great deal of independence and autonomy. They are expected to grow up fast, both regulating and helping their younger colleagues. In this essay, Grimond displays all the earnestness, and lack of perspective, that can be expected of a talented, sensitive and serious young man in his position. Although Grimond's own thesis is fairly unsteady and unstructured in places, there are elements within it that tantalisingly and engagingly adumbrate his adult thinking. Most interesting of all is the favourable comparison he makes between the relative anarchy of his own house and the more disciplined regimes that evidently predominated more or less everywhere else in the school. There is no mistaking his pride in the role he had played in maintaining a reasonably laid-back regime, the regrettable incident of the 'general tanning' apart:

The spirit of individualism, enquiry and some might say insubordination, agrees ill with military discipline and the blind obedience to do or die has never been one of our characteristics. Why should we march ten miles for no reason; why should the lunch be given round in half an hour military fashion when it could be done in a quarter civilian fashion? Then on our notice-board you will see no expanse of white sheets neatly pinned at each corner.

There is never a row of regulations showing fines for offences, laying down the law as to the exercise to be taken and giving the duties of all and sundry. We live on the minimum of house-rules and none of them are to be found on our notice-board . . . The members of the house are treated as members and are left to fend largely for themselves. I hold that this is the ideal system.

It is all too easy to be content with a nicely working house in which everyone and everybody hangs on a peg. The result may be a stereotyped set of boys and no great enthusiasm that will last. Secondly though possibly admirable for some boys who need to be dragged about it does not suit those who do not. So that though the average may be better, there may be no-one outstanding . . . the best Etonians do not seem to come out of the best run houses.

Yet Grimond worried too that he had not done nearly enough to ensure that the more indolent boys made good use of their time. Although he was concerned about the effects of a house carrying too many inactive bodies, even as a teenager he saw far greater virtue in activities undertaken voluntarily and enthusiastically than he did in any form of compulsion. He recognised that true team spirit is elusive: if it is to be sustained with enthusiasm, it must come from within. 'It is best,' he reflects here, 'that all the house should go to watch a lower boy tie of their own accord.' That is all very well, however, and raises another question: 'Is it better that only three-quarters should go of their own accord or that the whole should go under compulsion?' He had struck upon a classic liberal's dilemma: the balance between the individual and the community. On balance, in the time-honoured spirit of *mens sana in corpore sano*, he reluctantly accepted and propounded the view that general morale would improve if more compulsory sporting activities could be laid on: 'It does not seem to follow that boys keen on Athletics are moral, though it seems likely that boys who do nothing of an afternoon will be dingy and though they may not do anything their talk may be rather gloomy.' On matters of discipline, Jo Grimond now professed to have become a good liberal. He was opposed to doling out punishments gratuitously:

If boys make a noise in a quarter of the house where it can disturb no one there is no need to prowl round continuously to catch them. If you come across it stop it. Otherwise be content with dealing with noises which disturb you or other people . . . Two boys play cricket regularly in their room. It may be good for them to be stopped if it is annoying the boys below. If not, what good does stopping them do?

Grimond may have erred on the side of *laisser-faire*, but he also learned that a pragmatic streak came in handy. In his Utopian House there would be no 'general tickings off . . . they may be sometimes necessary but they are a sign that you have let one part of the house go astray'. If punishment had to be meted out, however, it had to be effective, which, in his view, meant that offenders should be punished individually. The Utopian House, conjured up by Grimond in his testament to his successors, would be a dictatorship, but a benign one. The senior boys should get on well together and, although the system of fagging would persist, 'as in the feudal system, the master must be in some degree responsible for his fag . . . He should enquire after his games, work, and general well-being and see he sometimes has a clean collar . . . We must risk familiarity breeding contempt.' The closing section of the testament verges on self-pity:

> Isn't all the stuff I have written in this book revolting. Only very late at night or very early in the morning will it be tolerable and then no one will take the trouble to read . . . I have captained the house by whim and laziness. I could have done more if I had been energetic enough, but I never would be. I can't say it has been a success (shame shame fishing for compliments) . . . we have been beaten in the first round of everything. Everyone is much the same or rather worse than they were except one or two who have grown nicer with age.
>
> Well, boring, pompous (*very* pompous), presumptuous, sad. There is much more I should like to say and much more I have said which in a year I shall wish unsaid . . . Perhaps my successors more gifted and more vigorous than I, will supply these. Anyway they should not leave everything to the last minute like this. They must get down to it.

The young Jo Grimond was no doubt a matter of taste. He was gifted at sport, but by no means a sporting hero. He was charming and mature, to be sure, but was also capable of making his own contribution to the streak of callousness running through the institution to which he belonged. He was certainly bright and good at examinations, but he was fairly lazy, so he was also far from being an academic paragon. In almost every aspect of his Etonian existence, with greater application Jo Grimond could have achieved so much more than he did. A similar quality would arguably be only too apparent in the adult politician. Reaching the eminence that Jo Grimond did within his school community, particularly without provoking a serious degree of resentment and jealousy amongst his peers, must have taken some doing. He seems to have managed that but, like many in his position, found the end of his last term a great wrench. For a young man with ten years' experience of enjoying considerable personal autonomy far from home, even the prospect of going up to one of the great universities can be comparatively unalluring, representing in many respects more of the same, rather then an exciting departure. After eighteen months at Oxford, Grimond would reflect: 'As [the Public Schools] become more and more like a University, the University grows more and more like an anti-climax. The freedom from routine and the stimulation of wider opportunities are wasted because the Public School boy is free at sixteen and has long grown contemptuous of opportunities.'[31] At the age of eighteen, Jo Grimond must have been conscious that many people had already marked him out for stardom. But he was intelligent enough and imaginative enough to realise in darker moments that, if things didn't go his way, he already had a long way to fall.

2

WHEN THE EIGHTEEN-YEAR-OLD Jo Grimond first arrived in Oxford, to sit his scholarship examination, it had a remarkable, almost mystical, effect on him. In his own phrase, he 'experienced some emotions faintly like those which it is said Luther experienced when first seeing Rome'.[1] He was deeply impressed not only with the architecture and the academic atmosphere, but with the dons he met during his brief stay in Balliol, the college to which he had applied. The austere nature of the rooms was never going to dismay an Etonian, nor was he likely to be easily intimidated by the bookish qualities of the first Fellow whom he encountered: 'Sligger' Urquhart, the first Roman Catholic to have been made a Fellow of Balliol since the Reformation. Grimond went on to win his entrance award, the prestigious Brackenbury history scholarship. The biggest change noticed by Grimond when he went up to Oxford in 1932 was that he was suddenly made to feel as though his views mattered. No longer was he being prepared merely for examinations. Now he was really treated as an adult, with thought processes and views of his own, who was expected not simply to absorb received wisdom from textbooks old and new, but to think deeply and seriously about historical matters. Bluffing could be attempted, but bluffs were always prone to be called, according to the whims of individual dons. Grimond also found that he now had to organise his own schedule to a far greater degree. More familiar to him were certain spartan features of life at Balliol: baths and lavatories that were some hundred yards or so away from his rooms, as he put it 'across country'. This was typical of Oxford as an institution, he reflected: 'It is strange how little it uses modern science considering how conscious it is of its effects . . . It talks glibly of distance annihilated and man supreme over nature, but it trudges a hundred yards through snow to a bath . . . Rivetting machines may have ousted nightingales from poetry, but many undergraduates have a strong antipathy to a gas-fire'.[2]

Grimond's first-year history course was taught by men whose names belong to Oxford's roll of honour, including the great medievalist Vivian Galbraith and Humphrey Sumner, whose love of the abstruse probably amused more than it edified. Of Galbraith, Grimond later wrote that 'he thought that the world had gone downhill since the end of the Middle Ages . . . it was a revelation for a boy coming from school to be taught by someone who did not take the orthodox view.'[3] But Grimond in due course followed his instincts, and his growing interest in politics, by switching in 1934 from History to 'Modern Greats' – Politics, Philosophy and Economics. Grimond's change of school brought him into contact with more of the great men of Oxford in the 1930s: the philosopher A J Ayer, then at the beginning of a long and distinguished career, and his economics tutor, W M Allen. It was Allen who gave Grimond his biggest boost, for 'he had a genius . . . for attaching the most erudite meanings to any stumbling proposition which one put forward'.[4] In History he won the Jenkyns Prize; in his later school of study he was awarded the James Hall Prize. But it is hard not to conclude that, despite some of the marvellous teaching that he must have had at Oxford, the more significant influences on Grimond's intellectual development had come at Eton, not at Oxford, and that it is his wider accomplishments at university that are of greater interest. On reflection Grimond came to feel that too little was expected of undergraduates. 'It is from Reasonableness if not from Reason that Oxford is suffering,' he once wrote. 'It does a reasonable amount of work, plays a reasonable amount of cricket and makes reasonable mistakes . . . nothing in excess has become excel at nothing.'[5]

Like many students, Grimond took pleasure not only in the formal teaching at Oxford, but also in the general ambience of the place. He loved the University Dramatic Society (OUDS), studiously avoided the Oxford Union (though he played a role in the Liberal Society) and, above all, enjoyed a varied social life, which extended through all his vacations. On his staircase in his first term were his brilliant, unpredictable old schoolmate, Jasper Ridley; and Norman O Brown, later an academic and author. Other familiar Etonian faces at Balliol were those of Con O'Neill and Guy Branch, both of whom Grimond deeply respected. There was something shamelessly and wonderfully self-indulgent about the reaction of Grimond and his friends to Oxford. They really loved being there, and took every possible advantage of it. After his second year, Grimond joined a group of friends, including fellow Etonians Jasper Ridley and Mark Pilkington, in digs at 21 Beaumont Street. Their group, in combination with others at 9 Beaumont Street, soon became one of the best known in the university – for its intellectual and political cut and thrust as well as for its aloofness and good-natured disdain towards the mainstream of university life. Grimond and his friends, though not Conservatives, took a mildly positive view of Baldwin. This penchant for unfashionable Tory leaders never deserted him; in later life he would always leap to the defence of both Eden and Heath. Not for Grimond and his clique of friends the committees and other bureaucratic diversions that he was to denounce in a later generation of students. This group lived life to the full, and Jo Grimond himself was no exception. In due course he became treasurer of the Gridiron Club, which largely shared the values of the Beaumont Street gang. The final stanza of a poem written about the club by Jasper Ridley for *Isis* magazine gives a flavour of its attitudes:

> Secure from the people who bore us
> We sing in our smug little chorus
> How charming a fate
> That the people we hate
> Should all of them choose to ignore us

A later resident of the Beaumont Street digs, Philip Toynbee, wrote of the early members, including Grimond, that 'they were intellectuals, but . . . their first principle was an almost harsh demand for emotional integrity . . . Friendship, for example, was never to be taken for granted.'[6] Towards the end of his first year at Oxford, the traditional time for undertaking such extra-curricular diversions, Grimond involved himself with *Isis*, the main student weekly in Oxford. In announcing his appointment, the paper described him as being 'already distinguished as a brilliant litterateur'. In the Michaelmas (autumn) Term of 1933, he became sports editor, which involved much collating and editing but not much writing. His hand can, however, be detected elsewhere in the magazine. There is a very up-beat review of a Liberal rally in the Town Hall at which Isaac Foot had spoken, in which the anonymous author boldly proclaims that, 'in Oxford liberalism is undoubtedly on the up-grade'.[7] The Oxford University Liberal Club evidently wasn't so sanguine, and within a week had sought out as a guest speaker one who presumably had experience of breathing new life into the dead – one Baron Franckenstein! There is also a pretty self-indulgent review of the annual *Isis* party, which was evidently something of a reunion for Grimond and his friends. He is featured in a photograph with Lionel Brett, Dick Levinge and John Paton; and other Etonian contemporaries such as Con O'Neill, Brian Johnston ('Johnners' of cricket broadcasting fame) and Jasper Ridley all feature in the text, 'talking of times at the old school'. The only substantial article with Grimond's by-line in those early days was a surreal paean to the merits of taking snuff in the run-up to Christmas 1933:

> Every Englishman feels it his duty to celebrate with inanity the season of good cheer. The National Government having relieved him of his traditional Christmas, national pride still imposes the penance of a paper cap . . . let us recommend to you snuff this Christmas, for it will clear your head, it will fit you to play the role of your roistering forefathers, and since you are a race of pigeon-chested micro-pneums, you will sneeze. By sneezing you will exercise and strengthen the muscles of the soul.[8]

For a time at least, Grimond preferred pipe smoking.

The following term, Grimond was literary editor and effectively deputy editor. His hand may surely be detected in a piece headed 'Political Roundabout' in one of that term's earliest editions, which denounces left and right with equal contempt while, in contrast, 'Liberalism alone of all creeds places internationalism before nationalism.'[9] Grimond was quoted too in the rather mild *Isis* gossip column 'Heard in the High', having proffered this piece of Liberal compromise: 'If one cannot realise one's ideal, one may as well idealise the real.'[10] In one sense, Grimond was as good as his word. He and some of his fellow students made a serious effort to help unemployed people on Tayside during one vacation by carting cheap fish back from the harbours for them. For the summer term of 1934, Grimond took full charge of *Isis* as its editor. He subsequently claimed to have done this very badly. In fact, as he did throughout his life, he wrote very well, and the collection of his editorial essays, scribbled down no doubt between engagements in his delphic hand, constitutes an impressively precocious corpus of work. The style, especially when contrasted with Grimond's much gentler late journalism, is perhaps slightly self-conscious: the younger Grimond rarely uses a simple word where a polysyllable will do, or a sentence where a paragraph will suffice, or indeed a concrete example where an allusion can be employed. Nonetheless, he ruminated very competently, on a weekly basis, upon a series of questions that he believed should be of interest to his contemporaries.

When he became editor, Grimond resolved both to maintain the dissident tone of his predecessors and to indulge himself in some pretty purple prose. He retained the affectation of writing editorials in the first person plural and rarely ran scared of metaphors or pomposity. 'Since [Oxford's] sentiments remain conservative in a love of destruction, if in nothing else,' he wrote, 'we shall continue to put into English, good English, the futile gropings of the illiterate masses of the University.'[11] But he had no intention of following the national press in its desire to sensationalise every story in the hope of increasing circulation: 'We deplore the results of this debauchery and the overlay of convictions by motives of mercenary gain which by now should be satisfied.'[12] Halfway through his term, Grimond penned what was perhaps his first endorsement of the 'social market'. In May 1934, for neither the first nor the last time, the Oxford Playhouse closed down. The Oxford Playhouse has more lives than a family of cats and few students can have spent their three years in Oxford without it closing and opening, or opening and closing, at least once. In an editorial in *Isis*, Grimond argued that, however marvellous and talismanic the Playhouse might be, it would be foolish to make an argument for keeping it open without at least some reference to the obvious economic problems afflicting it. It was not enough to argue that the place would be missed, nor that 'Oxford ought to have a repertory company', nor even that 'Oxford ought to have opportunities for seeing famous plays'. What heartened Grimond was that a spontaneous community campaign had sprung up in a matter of days, which showed every sign of raising the necessary capital to keep the old place open: 'Oxford might subscribe to the Playhouse for its own enjoyment even if it does not pay dividends, but we believe that under new management it will not have to subsist on charity'.[13] Grimond was full of praise for this enterprise, which could 'preserve the Playhouse for future generations'. In time, it was precisely this kind of community initiative that he would come to regard as the means by which liberal democracy could revive the nation.

By both associating himself with the Beaumont Street crowd and running *Isis*, Grimond consciously risked appearing rather aloof and elitist. As he himself conceded: 'it is a just complaint against Oxford periodicals that they are written for and by small cliques.'[14] None of this worried him, however, and he did at least shun membership of another institution whose popularity amongst the main body of student opinion has never been certain. Although most of his politically active contemporaries made a beeline for the Oxford Union Debating Society and polished their rhetorical skills there, Grimond never regretted his own decision to avoid it almost totally. He had a wonderful time doing other things instead. He also had some pretty trenchant criticisms of the place's ethos. One of the earliest *Isis* pieces to carry a Grimond by-line was a review of the bleak volume *Memoirs of the Unemployed* published by Victor Gollancz, containing an explicit dig at the pomposity of the Union:

> Every means is legitimate which will vivify the squalor and degradation of the unemployed labourer. Here, where the air hums with theories and dogmas, it is essential that we should have the horror of life on the dole thrust upon us as they are [sic] for those who live thus and not in the figures of economic text books . . . no one will deny that Oxford should do its utmost for the unemployed and that in its adulation of orators and theorists it should not forget those men who work unknown in the slums, be they curates or agitators.[15]

In short, Jo Grimond thought that the denizens of the Union were a bit of a pain, no more than a bunch of name-dropping nonentities who generally brought political discourse into disrepute: 'It could – I put it no higher – encourage that view of politics which expresses itself in clichés suitable for speeches or articles . . . It has been a little responsible for the superficiality of much political comment, the sneering, the desire to appear to be on the inside and claim a spurious intimacy with political figures even if you have never exchanged a word with them'.[16] Many Oxford alumni before and since would no doubt echo much of that, yet it is hard not to wonder how differently Grimond might have performed as a parliamentarian had he chosen the obverse path, for he never quite became one of the great parliamentary orators. Thanks perhaps to his lawyer's training, he became one of the better questioners in the House of Commons, but the House rarely held its breath for him when he delivered a set-piece speech.

In their Beaumont Street digs, the group were well looked after by a long since departed breed of housekeeper. Grimond travelled little outside Oxford during term-time, except when he began to take his dinners at the Middle Temple, but in their vacations members of the group often holidayed together, usually in decrepit cars that they either bought for a pittance or borrowed from relatives. Grimond travelled to Zarauz in the Basque country and Madrid, marvelling at the 'terrifying, empty, scorched plains of Spain' and visited 'Sligger' Urquhart's chalet above Saint-Gervais and below Mont Blanc. Less idyllically, he and Con O'Neill happened to be driving through southern Germany together in June 1934 when Hitler's agents carried out their first large-scale murders, during the 'Night of the Long Knives'. As they made their way through thronged roads, a young man stopped them and begged them to take him with them to France. Without realising the implications of what they were doing, and more amused than scared, they let him hide himself under some rugs in the back of their car and smuggled him as far as the French border, where he leaped out just before they left Germany. Not until French police virtually stripped their car hours later did it strike them that serious matters were afoot.

There was also a summer 'tour' with David Astor and Adam von Trott, during which the three young men hoped to discover for themselves how industrial England really operated. Though their intentions were undoubtedly noble, they never quite 'slummed it'. They began their tour from the Astors' Cliveden home and after that von Trott suggested that they should spend the next night in a plain boarding-house. In the event, baulking at the cold reality of a 'pretty awful' cheap boarding-house, they spent the first night in the Queen's Hotel, Birmingham, and took things from there in the same, rather less than Spartan, spirit. Astor and von Trott carried on to an Astor property on Jura, for some shooting; Grimond made his apologies and went home to St Andrews. The extent of their industrial exploration seems to have been a visit, arranged through their schoolfriend, Mark Pilkington, to the famous glass-blowing firm of that ilk at St Helens, followed by a tour of a tyre factory and an audience with Mr Vinogradoff, foreign editor of the *Manchester Guardian*. Grimond's most vivid recollection of it all was the scene in the crowded lift in the newspaper's office in Manchester. Adam von Trott had acquired a painful boil 'on a vulnerable spot' and half of Manchester's population seemed intent upon banging into it as violently as possible. Adam von Trott went on to find his place in history as an epitome of the 'good German'. He was a Rhodes Scholar and a man of impeccably liberal views, horrified at the madness that was gripping his homeland. Though his friends enjoined him not to risk his life by returning, he ignored their entreaties because he felt that it fell to him, as a German, to return home and attempt to put an end to the Nazi regime. When he was executed as an associate of von Stauffenberg after the unsuccessful attempt to kill Hitler in July 1944, he was mourned by many friends in many lands.

Grimond was also a regular visitor to East Anglia, usually staying with Jasper Ridley and his family, and in this period became a friend and protégé of Sir Archibald Sinclair, leader of the independent Liberals and MP for Caithness. He had first met Sinclair, and caught his eye, when he had come to speak at Eton, and renewed the acquaintance when staying at a hunting lodge, Glut, on the Caithness moors with Mark Pilkington, a friend from Eton days. Sinclair's own shooting lodge, Dalnawillan, was next door, and the two young men were invited to join Sinclair in a hare shoot. Subsequently Grimond and several of his friends were invited to stay at Dalnawillan. Though guests were allowed to rise late, they were then expected to ride vigorously for most of the day in search of grouse and, after bathing upon their return, to provide lively and entertaining company during and after a splendid dinner. Guests could expect to be kept on their toes. Grimond once wrote how 'whenever I put forward – even as a withdrawable kite or balloon – some doctrine which I imagine knit tightly into Sir Archibald's heart, it is sprung upon by the Sinclair family as a sign of some fearful and subconscious heresy.'[17] They were also expected to compete in Highland sports alongside the four Sinclair children against keepers and ghillies led by a formidable individual named McNicol, in the 'Dalnawillan Games'. Participants had their mettle tested as they ran, tossed the caber and were knocked off slippery poles with stuffed sacks. On one visit Grimond was even prevailed upon to perform as an actor before the same audience, this time in the Dalnawillan nursery, as the Good Witch to Jasper Ridley's Bad Witch, in a one-act play written by Sinclair's ten-year-old son Angus.

As his Finals drew near in the summer of 1935, Grimond knew that he had a serious chance of getting a first-class degree and accordingly withdrew at least partially from the social whirlwinds of Beaumont Street to spend more time in the university's libraries. He got his First. He took this very much in his stride, rather modestly perhaps taking the view that this did no more than confirm what everybody already knew: that he was highly competent academically, with a particular talent for sitting examinations. Like many before and since, with typical modesty he found the First rather an embarrassment. On April Fool's Day 1975, Grimond was interviewed by the then doyen of the *Today* programme, Brian Redhead, along with two of his friends from Eton and Oxford, William Douglas Home and Brian Johnston. Redhead asked the trio what degrees they had got. Douglas Home, by then a highly accomplished playwright, owned up to a Third. Grimond then admitted with reluctance that he had got a First, and it was Brian Johnston who somehow came out on top by proclaiming that he had got a Fourth.[18] Half a lifetime later, Grimond would suggest 'the idea of a degree as setting a permanent stamp on a man which he carries through life may have to be revised.'[19] Balliol is an unusual college, its power to repel just as notable as its power to attract. Although, after leaving Oxford, Grimond claimed that 'the approbation far outweighs the fury',[20] his relationship with the place never seems to have been all that close. Nonetheless, when Balliol was looking for a new Master in the 1990s, Grimond was on the lookout in case the position went to someone whose commitment might be open to question. He had his doubts about the claims of Chris Patten, former Tory minister and by then the 'last governor', charged with preparing Hong Kong for its handover to Peking. Grimond commented that, 'If Chris Patten would be prepared to live in Balliol, and give most of his time to Oxford affairs, he would be an excellent choice in keeping with the traditions of the college . . . But, if he were to use it as a platform for a return to Westminster, or to divide his time between Oxford and lucrative jobs in the City, he would not be acceptable'.[21]

By the time he sat his Finals, Grimond had a fair idea of how his future might be mapped out. He had decided early on in his time at Oxford that the law would provide him with the ideal foundations for a political career. It would guarantee both a substantial income and, if necessary, a handy safety net in case his political fortunes waned. He wrote later that 'the law interested me – up to a point – and seemed a suitable career for an aspiring politician to attempt.'[22] He had sent off his admission form to the Middle Temple in early October 1933, at the beginning of his second year at university, paying the requisite fee of 100 guineas, and was admitted on 21st October 1933. Just one other aspirant lawyer was admitted to Middle Temple on that particular day: his friend Jasper Ridley. Neither man wasted any time in satisfying the arcane tradition of 'eating dinners', turning up at the Inns of Court to consume an (allegedly less than delicious) evening meal there for the minimum three times a year. By the time he left Oxford, Jo Grimond had set his sights on becoming a Liberal Member of Parliament. Even though Grimond came from a Liberal family background, this was an extraordinary decision. During the early 1930s the Liberals had fallen into a dramatic political and financial decline, until by late 1933 they were little more than a pathetic remnant of a once-great party. They seemed to have no real prospects of their own, and squabbled continuously amongst themselves about which of the other parties they disliked more, or less, in a series of debilitating skirmishes between the Liberal Nationals, the Samuelites and Lloyd George and his clan. In Grimond's own backyard of East Fife in 1931 a Liberal National had even stood against the official Liberal candidate. In 1935 Jo Grimond attended his first political meeting, which was addressed by the Scottish Nationalist candidate at the East Fife by-election, Eric Linklater, who subsequently became a useful and stimulating friend. Grimond was at first taken aback by the unimpressive physical appearance of one who could write so trenchantly and even romantically about his beloved Scotland: 'I expected a romantic hero; I found a stocky figure in plus-fours over whose owl-like face rose an impressive but bald head.'[23] Although he would later compare Linklater, in looks and behaviour, with Captain Mainwaring of *Dad's Army,* Grimond soon came to terms with how Linklater looked, and simply breathed in the atmosphere of the meeting: 'I can recall the *feel* of it very vividly . . . It was in a temperance hall which obviously had taken a great deal of trouble to live up to its name, for it was as dark and cheerless as cold tea . . . Eric Linklater . . . battled valiantly against that chilly hall . . . But I fear that the hall won.'[24] It was not a great meeting, but the politics bug had bitten Grimond.

Then, during the general election campaign of 1935, Grimond enjoyed what he would term his 'first foray' into electioneering, spending a few days helping Arthur Irvine, the Liberal candidate for Kincardine and West Aberdeenshire. Grimond had met Irvine at the end of his time at Oxford and had been greatly impressed by this 'extremely active, attractive figure'. What Grimond does not mention in his *Memoirs* is that Irvine was, by any standard, a very young candidate (at twenty-six years of age) and not much older than Grimond himself. Indeed, though he would later become Solicitor-General in a Labour government, Irvine was still thought of at that time as one of Lloyd George's praetorian guard of 'young men'. Another unusual feature of this contest was that there were only two candidates: the sitting Unionist member, Charles Barclay-Harvey, and Irvine. Barclay-Harvey was a local laird and, throughout a rancorous contest, the local press openly favoured him. Grimond made his first political speech during that campaign – on Friday, 25th October 1935, as Irvine's warm-up man under the cliffs of the coast at Johnshaven. He did not much enjoy this initiation into political public speaking, feeling conscious from the start that he was being listened to with a mixture of indifference and incomprehension. But speak he did, and survive he did – as a speaker, and as a Liberal. The National government won the general election handsomely and this constituency followed the national trend, returning Charles Barclay-Harvey to Parliament with 12,477 votes against Irvine's total of 9,841.

The *Mearns Leader and Kincardineshire Mail* noted that there was 'little sign of downheartedness'[25] amongst local Liberals after the result had been declared at Stonehaven Town Hall. They gave Irvine a great send-off, throwing a great party with music, dancing and even a recitation by Irvine's agent, Mrs Ronald, whose abilities, Grimond observes in his *Memoirs,* deserve commemoration 'on some shelf of history'. Grimond's experiences on the campaign trail confirmed him in his view that it was in the Liberal Party that he must make his way. The old Tory–Radical division was everywhere apparent, and Grimond knew from the outset on which side of that line he belonged. Along with Robert Birley, Irvine was one of the most important influences on Jo Grimond. When, as leader of the Liberal Party, Grimond developed the strategy of a 'realignment of the left', he might have volunteered an attribution to his old mentor Arthur Irvine. Witness this report of a speech in Oxford by Irvine, taken from the Liberal weekly the *Oxford Guardian*: 'The speaker tried to envisage the Progressive Party of the future, composed of what is now the Liberal Party, the Trades Unionists, and the right wing of the Labour Party. Such a combination would, when the country came to recognise its aims and abilities, be irresistible.'[27] Across the country, the general election of 1935 marked a new low point in the fortunes of the Liberal Party. Of its 161 candidates, only 21 were returned, and the party leader Herbert Samuel was narrowly defeated. This had a direct effect on Grimond, as his friend and mentor Archibald Sinclair, who had held on at Caithness, took charge of the denuded party. The rift with Lloyd George was patched up and, in due course, Sinclair would become a greatly respected national figure.

Although it is quite clear that the law was never likely to be an end in itself for Grimond, he still brought all his formidable talents to bear on it. In particular, he set about improving his financial position as a young lawyer by applying for a Harmsworth Scholarship. These awards were made possible by a series of bequests made in the 1920s by the Viscount Rothermere, in memory of his late father Alfred Harmsworth. Between 1924 and 1928 some £170,000-worth of capital was handed over on condition that it would remain intact, and interest accruing from it should be made available to aspirant barristers attached to the Middle Temple. The original terms of reference were refreshingly lacking in any semblance of political correctness. Scholarships of £200 per year, to last over a period of three years, would be awarded each year to a number of students – all male – to be nominated exclusively by the vice-chancellors of Oxford and Cambridge. A committee of senior barristers would interview and assess the candidates. There was no right of appeal, but unsuccessful candidates were welcome to try again. Not yet wholly reconciled to tearing up his Oxford roots, Grimond also applied for a fellowship at All Souls' and, for once in his academic career, he was unsuccessful.

In the summer of 1935 Grimond's was one of twenty-seven names put forward in total by Oxford and Cambridge for that year's batch of Harmsworth scholarships. He was one of the youngest applicants, which made him an obvious candidate for deferment. He also chose August 1935 as a suitable month for one of his lengthy European sojourns, suggesting perhaps that he didn't rate his chances too highly. As a consequence, when the secretary of the Memorial Fund, T F Hewlett, wrote to all the candidates on 26th July inviting them for interview on Monday, 14th October, he heard nothing in response from Grimond for over a month. The suitably apologetic letter despatched by the young man on 28th August, in which he explained that 'I have been wandering about the continent and no letters have been forwarded', seems to have done all the necessary placating. When he came to be interviewed, however, not only did Jo Grimond's considerable personal charm count in his favour. The application form that lay before the committee had two obvious virtues. Naturally enough it gave due prominence to the candidate's undoubtedly impressive academic attainments, but it also included a tribute from Oxford's vice-chancellor that might have made even a nascent politician blush:

> Mr Grimond is recommended to me by his Tutor, Mr B H Sumner, MA, who says that he has first-class intellectual gifts which he uses to excellent effect, a great capacity for hard work, and interest in and ability for both philosophy and politics and economics . . . Mr Grimond is expected to obtain a First Class in the Final School of 'Modern Greats' this year. He is a man of quite exceptional promise, of excellent character, good sense, good taste, and remarkable personality. Mr Sumner adds that he is a prominent and well-liked member of his College and the University, with a wide variety of interests and of all-round distinction.

The committee's terms of reference required it to base its judgements upon 'the character and scholarship of each candidate, his intention to practise at the English Bar and the likelihood of his so doing, and loyally following its traditions'. The trustees of the fund considered this final criterion important, and the two vice-chancellors were repeatedly reminded of the requirement that candidates should be serious about their commitment to a legal career. The young Jo Grimond evidently convinced the assessors that he was serious about it (he was, in his own words, 'a very serious boy') and won the scholarship at the first time of asking. A year later, Jasper Ridley would follow Grimond in being elected to a scholarship – although the fact that he was already on the verge of being called to the Bar would prevent him from taking full advantage of it.

As he set about mastering the English law with the benefit of his latest scholarship, Grimond went into a firm of solicitors close to Ludgate Circus, White & Leonard & Nicholls & Co. at 4 St Bride Street. He found the clerks there highly congenial, always recalling them affectionately as the first 'loveable cockneys' of his acquaintance, and his happiest memories seem to have been of the occasions when they took their young protégé on picaresque pub-crawls. He started with them in February 1936 and finished a year or so later, when he was called to a different kind of Bar. Grimond applied for his Bar exams in the Hilary (winter) term of 1937. As usual he progressed without undue difficulty, and was called to the Bar on 26th January 1937. He continued his studies by going into the chambers of Gordon Alchin, twenty years Grimond's senior and one of the great legal characters of his age. Known as the 'Flying Judge', Alchin had been awarded the Air Force Cross for his exploits in the Royal Flying Corps, which he joined in 1915. Grimond now bought his first car, a blue Morris of which he was inordinately proud. When he first took it to Teasses on a visit to his sister Nancie, it vanished from outside the house. It was found at the bottom of a steep bank: he had left the brakes off, and the car (fortunately undamaged) had to be dragged out of a ditch with a large tractor. Grimond particularly enjoyed his forays into East Anglia, often made in the company of his flamboyant friend and colleague Hugh Boileau, whose motto was 'Hunt on Saturdays, court on Sundays' and who gladly allowed Grimond to drive his impressive Daimler. Jo Grimond took immense pleasure in acquainting himself even more closely with the small towns and landscapes of Norfolk and Suffolk, which he already knew thanks to his regular visits in recent years to Jasper Ridley and his family.

For a time, Grimond did work full-time as a lawyer and, in the Law List of 1938, was listed as practising on the South-East circuit. He joined chambers at 4 Paper Buildings EC4, a business address that was listed against his name throughout the conflict of 1939–45 and up until the Law List of 1953, by which time he had presumably come to the view that politics would now provide him with the necessary security of tenure. Nonetheless, his name at least still appeared annually in the List until 1964 – the year in which he enjoyed his greatest political success – albeit shorn in later years of any chambers address.

Although his opposition to the death penalty predated his brief legal career, Grimond's support for abolition was hardened by one especially poignant case that he encountered in his work as a counsel for the defence in a case of murder. The defendant was the misanthropic captain of a barge that sailed to and fro between London and Ipswich. The only crewman was also the captain's only known friend or close associate, and the two of them regularly went ashore together on drinking bouts. After one of these sessions, the skipper had shot his mate dead. He himself did not deny what he had done, but could offer no reason whatever for his action. As Grimond wrote later, his client cut a figure both tragic and absurd amidst the arcane and archaic rituals of a criminal court: 'all this was as remote from our client as a visit to the moon or an exegesis of Virgil'.[28] The bemused fatalism of the killer, to Grimond, made his preordained destiny the more gruesome, with the caveat that 'the only scintilla of justification for hanging him was that I could not think what otherwise within the possibilities of the time could have been done with him . . . To shut him up in prison would have been as cruel as to keep a wild animal in a small cage.'[29] When, at the close of proceedings, the condemned man smiled courteously and shook the hands of all involved, Grimond felt the mixture of deference and ingenuous bewilderment that he displayed would have moved the coldest of hearts.

While he made good use of his legal training throughout the rest of his life, Grimond's experiences as a barrister did nothing to convince him that the prevailing legal system served the people as well as it might. He quickly became critical of the 'closed-shop' aspects of the legal profession, comparing the KCs' juniors to the notorious 'Plumber's Mates' of old – synonymous with restrictive practices – and asking 'how men so able, so humane, so uncorrupt as lawyers could stride on, turning a blind eye to the enormities of their profession'.[30] This was a theme that he would develop further in 1963:

> If any trade union conducted itself like the Inns of Court, the outcry would rise to high heaven. Barristers' fees and the general expenses of going to law are far too high . . . Restriction of entry to the profession by making it so expensive, extra fees charged for the offence of, for instance, taking a barrister off his circuit, medieval jargon and Dickensian language and procedure should have been reformed long ago.[31]

He also felt that young lawyers were taught to be quite literally a law unto themselves, cut dangerously adrift from any social or political moorings. When he was put in charge of a review body to look at the internal workings of Birmingham University, one of Grimond's major crusades was to see that the structure of faculties should be adjusted to bring law students into closer contact with the social sciences: He had long believed that lawyers should have some knowledge of sociology and politics.

During his time in London, the handsome, Oxford-educated young lawyer was inevitably much in demand for dinners and parties, and he took full advantage. At one such social occasion, probably some time in 1936, he met Cressida Bonham Carter, almost four years his junior, and quickly fell for her. She was the eldest child of Sir Maurice 'Bongie' Bonham Carter, who had been Asquith's private secretary at No. 10, and his remarkable wife Lady Violet, Asquith's only daughter from his first marriage. Cressida and her younger sister Laura belonged to the last generation of the 'Liberal girls', among them Asquiths, Sinclairs and Bonham Carters, who had more or less enjoyed a 'season' of their own in the pre-war era. In defiance of the party's declining electoral fortunes, the Liberal establishment still enjoyed considerable prestige and the Liberal girls were much sought after by the ambitious, upwardly mobile young men and poodlefakers of the era. Later in life Laura was keen to dispel what she believed to be the myth that the 'Liberal girls' were terribly glamorous. In fact, she once explained, 'the aristocratic deb world thought us rather dingy, too blue-stocking, and they suspected us of being serious-minded – they either thought us too critical, or not smart enough, parvenues almost, not glittery'.[32]

Grimond was soon invited to stay at the Bonham Carters' country retreat Tilshead, on the edge of Salisbury Plain. They did not stand on ceremony. During his first visit there, Grimond was astonished to find himself being cross-questioned by Bongie Bonham Carter about Calvinism, and tried unsuccessfully to bluff his way through the conversation. He quickly learned to avoid such entanglements, lest he be cornered again. Cressida and Laura were an extraordinary duo who, had they belonged to a later generation, would certainly have expected to go on to a good university. As it was, both girls missed out because mainstream education, especially to degree level, was not in those days seen as 'suitable for a lady'. They had both followed their mother in being tutored and going, for a time, to continental Europe for their 'finishing', though neither of them developed Lady Violet's taste for Wagner. Despite their excellent political pedigree, however, at this stage the girls evinced little interest in politics. They preferred reading, riding and playing cricket. They were nonetheless Liberals, which fact Laura attributed not to their parents but to their nanny, who was evidently quite a force to be reckoned with: 'She was a strong Liberal, though her parents hadn't been, and she brainwashed us – it was an assertion of independence and the right to stand up for yourself.'[33] Many of the young men to cross the paths of the Bonham Carter girls quickly fell in love with either, or both, of them.

For a time, Jo and Cressida's friends were convinced that he would successfully woo her. In the spring of 1937, however, she made it clear to him that, much as she valued him as a friend, she did not envisage a long-term relationship or marriage. By all accounts, this was a considerable setback to Grimond. Fortunately he soon carved out an opportunity to get away from it all and reflect on the matter, as his legal credentials combined with a useful family connection to provide him with a first taste of America. He travelled there in the early summer of 1937 with Hugh Sharp, the only son of his father's friend Fred and some fifteen years older than Jo. When his father had died five years earlier, Hugh Sharp had inherited his financial interests, primarily the Alliance Trust Company in Dundee, which owned acres of land and herds of cattle in and around San Antonio. The Trust was engaged in litigation there and, in return for the trip, Grimond was to provide legal advice. The parties chose, and paid, a judge who would sit only after midday because he hunted in the morning. Grimond was charmed by the Drought family, which had represented the Trust in Texas for generations. Old Mrs Drought told Jo that she had not been able to marry until a director of the Trust had come over and given his approval. She was a Southern *grande dame* of the old school, who would reminisce: 'I was a married woman before I knew "damned Yankee" was two words!'[34] Once matters had been sorted out in Texas, the two men travelled extensively across the States, which left Grimond with a lifelong affection for America and the American way of life.

But the trip also marked another, far more personal, turning point in his life. Although they certainly had plenty in common, Jo Grimond and Cressida Bonham Carter were probably not that well suited. Cressida was a rather serious young woman who lacked the frothy and mischievous sense of fun that Jo Grimond never wholly managed to subdue in himself. Her sister Laura was quite different, sharing not only Grimond's political outlook, but also his natural exuberance and his relaxed love of sport. Although, in her own way, Laura shared her sister's tremendous integrity, she was in character far closer to Grimond. She mirrored his curious combination of an iron will and an equally distinctive love of frivolity. Their surviving friends from that time recall, above all, how the two of them would laugh together. By the time he set foot back on British soil, Grimond had apparently concluded, as his friend Lionel Brett later put it, that it was Laura who best epitomised 'Keats's coupling of Beauty and Truth . . . inseparable, in one person'[35] and, in June 1939, it was Jasper Ridley who would lead Cressida up the aisle. The courtship of Laura got off to a less than propitious start. Almost as soon as he started to woo her, Grimond managed to give her chicken pox. Lady Violet was concerned lest her youngest, Raymond (aged eight), should contract it too, and packed poor Laura off to an isolation hospital.

Despite this inauspicious start, however, Jo and Laura were soon engaged to be married. Their destinies became inextricably linked in September 1937, as he drove her south from Dalnawillan, where they had both been staying with the Sinclairs. They spent most of their time at Dalnawillan together, and then left together. By the time Grimond dropped Laura home in London, they were engaged. Coincidentally, it was also from Dalnawillan that they both first glimpsed Orkney, which would play such a role in their lives. From this time on it is quite impossible to disentangle the relationship between Laura and Jo from the background of association with the Liberal Party that they always shared. Jo was at first worried that his bid for Laura's hand might have caused perturbation in the Bonham Carter household, and wrote to Lady Violet at once:

> I love Laura, only I know how much and I can't describe it with adjectives. But that you know and it is, or will be, obvious. What I most want to say is that even in the days when I did not love her; when the future did not depend on her; when my actions were not related to her and my imaginings did not take shape around her, I looked on her as unique . . . If she were to be killed now, the world, apart from the feelings of anyone in love with her, would feel a loss not of someone with promise only, not of someone destined for success and virtue, but of someone complete, not to be repeated, for whom substitutes could not be found, someone not earthly if earthly things can only be explained in prose.[36]

A few days later, Jo Grimond was back at Tilshead, explaining himself to the Bonham Carters. When he woke up the following morning, he found on his pillow a letter from Lady Violet, in which she assured him that she had no objections to the match, and would be proud to have him as a son-in-law. Grimond's own mother presented more of a problem. Jo brought Laura to meet her at St Andrews, and she took to the young woman at once ('Jo is so happy and proud of her that already I feel grateful to her'[37]). The only disappointment came when Mrs Grimond asked Jo whether Laura was a good tennis player. 'No,' he admitted, adding as an afterthought, 'but she is a good jumper!'[38] Although she would subsequently describe Laura to Jo as 'a girl for whom anybody would do anything',[39] his mother believed that the couple were too young to get married for at least two years, and wrote to Lady Violet in that vein: 'I am thinking of Laura, more than Jo, she is just a gay, happy child, as she should be at eighteen.'[40] Jo recruited Lady Violet in support of his desire to marry the following spring or summer, and the campaign was a success. Shortly after the arrangements had been agreed, Lady Violet wrote a lengthy letter from Petworth House on 27th November to her brother Herbert ('Beb') in London, informing him of the news. This letter gives an early indication of the intensity that would develop in the relationship between Jo Grimond and his mother-in-law. Lady Violet did not attempt to disguise her excitement:

> Laura is engaged to be married – to Jo Grimond – the young man you met at Tilshead – & liked – (I am glad to say!) Of all the young men who have loved her in the last 18 months (& they have been many and various) I like him far the best – so I am overjoyed – My only regret is her youth (just 19) – I hoped she would go on 'shaking a loose leg' (as father called it) for many years more – & I shall hate losing her so soon – But I couldn't like Jo better – He has very good brains – really delightful looks (I think), & a character of gold – I can well imagine being in love with him – which is such a help for a prospective Mother-in-Law![41]

It was not only Grimond's personal charm that appealed to Lady Violet. She had also needed convincing that Laura would be able to live in the manner to which she was accustomed: 'I am glad to say that he has enough money to marry on apart from the precarious "Bar" – which is also a comfort. They won't be married until the summer – & I don't quite know when we shall announce it so please don't tell anyone except Cynthia [Herbert Asquith's wife] yet – & seal her lips.'[42]

Lady Violet Bonham Carter was a truly extraordinary figure. She was the fourth child, and the only daughter, of Asquith's marriage to his first wife, Helen. She was from her teenage years onwards a relentless political campaigner and socialite, counting amongst her more notable friends the war poet Rupert Brooke and the errant politician Winston Churchill. When Violet's father set out to revive his political career at the Paisley by-election in 1920, she threw herself into it with gusto, becoming a talismanic figure in his robust and energetic campaign there and playing a major part in getting him elected. That was in many ways a false dawn, for him personally and for the Liberals, whose schisms took a while longer to heal. It did, however, help to establish Violet in the public mind as a formidable figure in her own right. Her daughter Laura became equally celebrated as a businesslike and tireless by-election campaigner. Lady Violet was a lifelong devotee of the Asquith brand of liberalism and, equally, a violent opponent of socialism in all its forms. Although she never succeeded in a parliamentary election, she did make it, very belatedly, into the House of Lords.

Once the engagement had been announced, Jo Grimond became an even more regular fixture in the Bonham Carter circle. From his stint as Asquith's private secretary, Bongie Bonham Carter had learned the art of dividing his life between bursts of rapid and intense hard work, alternating with periods of relaxation that were no less intense. At Tilshead he kept everyone on his or her toes with bursts of activity, then caused hilarity by falling asleep quite unexpectedly. Although Grimond hugely admired Bongie's character – which he described as 'saintly' – he recognised too the flashes of spleen and impatience that he possessed. By the time Grimond knew him, Bongie had developed a slightly narcoleptic quality, sometimes collapsing snoring when he went upstairs to wish the younger children goodnight. He was also something of a Mrs Malaprop, substituting surreal replacements for misplaced vocabulary, on one occasion reputedly addressing a meeting of shareholders as the 'charwomen of the company'. Bongie was the youngest son amongst a dozen siblings, and the Bonham Carter diaspora spread far and wide. When relatives came to dinner, the conversation also grew picaresque. On one occasion Grimond delighted in one of Bongie's brothers improbably commencing some great exposition with the words, 'When I was running a small brewery in the Azores'.[43] At weekends, Laura and Cressida would invite their friends to Tilshead, and the group would ride on the plain then, in Oxonian fashion, debate and discuss every topic under the moon into the small hours. Life at Tilshead sounds like an Edwardian dream. There were horses in the stables, servants, endless and generous meals – and stimulating conversation and excellent company were in infinite supply. Grimond and several of his friends and contemporaries from Eton and Oxford found a temporary nirvana there.

Even in those early days, Grimond did at times find Lady Violet's ambition, and her desire to control, rather overbearing. In later years, when he was leader of the Liberal Party, he was even known to go upstairs into self-imposed exile when she came to visit Laura at the Grimonds' London home. Violet Bonham Carter wanted her family to be brilliant and successful, rich not only in spirit but in material ways too. He loved her for her loyalty and her energy, but would sometimes find it difficult to plough his own political furrow without a sense of her slightly disapproving presence at his elbow. He nonetheless played up to her, sending her between Christmas 1937 and New Year 1938 a series of jocular postcards, likening himself to 'a child who, having a wild, incredulous longing for Wendy, is taken as a special treat to see *Peter Pan*. On leaving Drury Lane he is told not only that Wendy is real but that he may live with her for ever in the never never land . . . My only fear is that by thrusting my head into the sky I may cloddishly rub some of the gold dust off the clouds.'[44] A few weeks later, after going to the theatre in London with his brother-in-law Billy Corbett, Jo Grimond had a 'vision' of Laura (who was at Tilshead) and wrote her a touching letter: 'last night I was taken with a great surge of love for you . . . you were unbearably beautiful so that I forgot I was engaged to you and only knew that I was in love with you but could never love you enough . . . I experienced the pain of ecstasy which I supposed only unreturned or thwarted love could give . . . pray heaven that you do not cease to love me or die.'[45]

Jo and Laura's wedding, on 31st May 1938, was by any standards a grand event. Thanks to the Bonham Carters' parliamentary connections, they were married in St Margaret's Church at Westminster, the spiritual home of MPs. Jasper Ridley was best man, and an entire chorus of 'Liberal girls' acted as bridesmaids. Laura's brother Raymond and Gwyn Corbett's son Joseph were the pages. The Asquiths and the Bonham Carters turned out in force, as did most of the contemporary Liberal establishment. Viscount Samuel, former leader of the Liberals, was there with his wife, as was Sir Archibald Sinclair with his. Also present was Clementine Churchill, wife of Lady Violet's dear friend Winston. So too were many of Jo's friends, among them Guy Branch and Lionel Brett from Eton and Oxford, and Gordon Alchin and Hugh Boileau, colourful colleagues from his professional life as a barrister. Harcourt 'Crinks' Johnstone, formerly a Liberal whip and the man who at one stage had to pay the salaries of Liberal staff out of his own pocket, contributed what Grimond described as the 'largest bottle of brandy ever known'.[46] Lady Violet hosted the reception at 1 Hyde Park Gardens, borrowed for the day from her friend Sir Ian Hamilton. The couple went to France for their honeymoon, starting in Paris, where they enjoyed the hospitality of the Morhanges for a week or so, before moving on to Provence for a few days.

Grimond had been living in digs at 35 South Eaton Place, where William Douglas Home also had a room, all under the care of Mr and Mrs Crisp, former domestic servants. He was a retired butler (affectionately known to the residents as 'Crippen') and a 'gentleman's gentleman' of the old school; she was tolerant, good-natured and a very good cook. When Grimond left after getting married, moving briefly into a flat and then lodging with Lady Violet, his room was taken over by Brian Johnston, another contemporary from Eton days. Within only a few weeks, Laura was pregnant. It was a difficult pregnancy, and Laura endured a lot of sickness in the early weeks. After suffering an attack of giddiness in the street, she was effectively confined to barracks for a time and, in early August, Mrs Grimond senior came down to London to help care for Laura, and look for rented accommodation suitable for the couple in the longer term. According to her son, this was not always plain sailing: 'I continually disown her as she button-holes postmen, Austrian maids and any other passers-by with demands as to whether there are any houses to let. Her manner with maids is most successful, we penetrate to the innermost dungeons without passes or keys. She emerges triumphant from commodious cupboards under the backstairs crying 'A sepulchre, Jo, a black sepulchre'. The owners are not so pleased.'[47] On 26th March 1939, almost exactly ten months after Jo and Laura Grimond were married, their first child, Joseph Andrew ('Jag'), was born.

Grimond always insisted that he went into chambers intending to stick at it, at least for a decent time. It just transpired that he was 'not temperamentally suited' to legal life and, in the event, it was not politics that tore Grimond away from the Bar but the dark forces that were gaining strength across the English Channel. Grimond had seen for himself the threat that Nazism represented and, after the invasion of Poland, in common with most of his generation, he was both quick to volunteer his services to the war effort, and very modest subsequently about his contribution to it. When Britain declared war on Germany on 3rd September 1939, Grimond had already been granted an emergency commission, as a 2nd lieutenant, the day before. On the advice of his brother-in-law Willie Black, now a brigadier, he had enlisted at Dunfermline in 'A' Squadron of the 2nd Fife and Forfar Yeomanry. The history of the Fife and Forfar Yeomanry could be traced back to the end of the eighteenth century. It had, however, undergone many changes of name and function. The most recent had been in 1919, when it had been designated the Twentieth Armoured Car Company. Towards the end of 1938, with war looming, the regiment expanded from company strength (about 200 officers and other ranks) to an establishment of 32 officers and 403 other ranks. In April 1939 all Territorial units had been instructed to double their strength. Only the London Scottish achieved this more quickly than did the Fife and Forfars. The 2nd Fife and Forfars, thus established, were called up on a full-time basis as war was declared. Although Grimond was, nominally at least, to remain on the strength of the 2nd Fife and Forfars for the duration of the war, his service with them was interrupted by postings elsewhere and, finally, by his permanent move to the staff of the 53rd (Welsh) Division. Although Fate had decreed that it was to be in peacetime that Grimond would earn renown for serving his country with distinction, during the war and its confused aftermath the seal was destined to be set on Jo Grimond's character as well as his political outlook.

3

GRIMOND WAS NOT called up until the end of September 1939, and he made good use of the intervening weeks by helping with the harvest at Teasses, home of his sister Nancie. When the summons did come, he and his unit were at first stationed in his hometown of St Andrews, where they occupied the Drill Hall that he knew well, in its normal role as a centre for badminton. Their first commanding officer was Major Andrew Brown, the formidable proprietor of the Argyle mineral water factory and a veteran of the First World War. They were soon moved away, initially to Cupar and then to Markinch. Grimond was amongst those who had to take the bus to Cupar; since he had no uniform, he was not allowed to march. It was at Markinch that Grimond was appointed to teach the men about the dangers of gas warfare. After two weeks there, he was deemed sufficiently knowledgeable to pass on his newly acquired expertise, in the form of lectures to small groups of the men. One of them, Alec Gilchrist, still recalls the rhyme that Grimond taught the men to remind them how to recognise one particular gas:

> If you have a funny feeling and a smell of musty hay,
> You can bet your bottom dollar that there's Phosgene on the way –
> You may for garlic and for onions have a cultivated taste
> But if you smell them both in wartime, leave the area in haste

Grimond subsequently bemoaned how soldiers were battered into submission by all the lectures they had to endure; they became so inured to it all, indeed, that they thought little of it when one of Grimond's fellow officers 'went slightly off his head and took to lecturing on his family tree . . . He gave universal satisfaction until removed in the army equivalent of a strait-jacket.'[1] Grimond was the first to concede that it was his wife Laura who, in many respects, had the more difficult time of it during the war, particularly in the early days. As well as caring for Andrew, she had to make all the necessary wartime arrangements, such as getting the family's furniture moved out of London. It was perhaps inevitable, however, that Andrew, less than six months old when the war broke out, would bear much of the brunt of the family's wartime dislocation. Grimond's first thought was to send his infant son away from danger ('I was rather keen on Canada, or even New Zealand') but, in the event, Laura spent most of her time in Scotland, based with Jo's mother in the family home in Abbotsford Crescent, St Andrews. Although Lydia Grimond now lived alone, she still managed to retain at least one maid and lived in some comfort. She formed a particularly close bond with Andrew, talking with him at length and teaching him a range of card games. Meanwhile Jo was on the move. In January 1940 the 2nds moved south, to take over Beaumont Barracks at Aldershot from the 1st Fife and Forfars who had crossed the Channel to join the British Expeditionary Force (and who, within the space of a few months, would win distinction during the retreat to Dunkirk). They remained in Surrey until June 1940. In the early days of the war, Laura and Jo would be together when he came home on leave to St Andrews, or during those periods when wives were permitted to join their husbands where a unit happened to be stationed. In May 1940 Jo and Laura were able to leave Aldershot for Wiltshire to visit Laura's mother, Lady Violet Bonham Carter, for what turned out to be a remarkable family reunion. Both Laura's brother Mark and Jasper Ridley, who were also serving in the forces, managed to get back for that precious weekend. In due course, despite the hardships and enforced separations of war, both Laura and Cressida would bear a child during 1942: Jo and Laura's only daughter Grizelda, born in Edinburgh in February of that year, and Jasper and Cressida's only child, Adam, who was born three months later. The Bonham Carters had for a time taken a house in Westmorland but continued to travel around a great deal. Lady Violet disliked being away from London for any length of time and commuted regularly between her London home and the comparative safety of the family's home in Wiltshire. When she was in the capital, she was in occasional contact with Churchill and, via her friend Toto Morhange, with events in France.

In June 1940 the 2nd Fife and Forfars were despatched to Dungannon in Northern Ireland. As they approached the town, their train turned out to be too heavy to climb the gradient to the station, and ground to an ignominious halt. A Fawltyesque scene ensued, with the fireman seen to hit the side of the engine repeatedly with a hammer. They made it to their destination in the end, their task to protect the border with Eire against any incursion from the south by German forces, or the possible depredations of the IRA. They had to take particular care to protect their considerable stocks of ammunition, and to avoid accidentally crossing the border with the Republic. Any trespasser would have been interned for the duration of the war. Once they were safely ensconced in Dungannon, the soldiers and the locals got on famously. When they were told that their visitors would have to transfer less than a week before Christmas 1940, the townspeople, who had prepared special Christmas festivities for their adopted sons, sent a telegram to the Prime Minister, asking for their departure to be deferred. Their pleas were in vain: the regiment spent Christmas thirty miles away, at Bessbrook. Throughout its time in Ulster, the regiment was, inevitably, in need of training to attain the standards required in combat and, equally of concern, they were painfully short of equipment.

Grimond was anything but an inadequate officer, always able to impress. One of his colleagues from that time, Tony Petit, remembers him as 'delightful, unassuming and amusing . . . He was immensely popular among all ranks . . . I remember especially his sense of humour and the quiet way in which he got things done.'[2] Just as he always became bashful on the subject of his academic attainments, however, Grimond evidently enjoyed concealing his rather high degree of competence behind a naturally humorous and sardonic persona. As in later life, he simply refused to take himself, his position, or events around him too seriously. Witness this account, from the regimental journal, of a training exercise in the Lough Neagh area on 14th August 1940, evidently after Grimond had transferred to 'B' Squadron:

> The battle starts about 0500 hrs on the 14th – 3 enemy Bren carriers being destroyed. Later on, a tank troop under the intrepid command of 2nd Lt. Grimond (minus one of its members whose turret was last seen projecting from a bog) severely shoots up the 3rd Mons Regt and wipes out its Brigade Headquarters, including the CO who cannot see the B Squadron point of view and is none too pleased . . .

Jo Grimond must have taken particular pleasure in putting one over on a group of Bren carriers. Alec Gilchrist recalls trying to teach Jo how to master the controls of an early Bren carrier, in the winter of 1939–40. It was beyond him. The carriers were not the most manageable of vehicles, possessing rather clumsy steering wheels instead of the joysticks common in tanks of the period. Grimond himself was the first to admit that his hands were not the most dextrous in the business, once comparing the teaching methods of the British army favourably with those at Eton in his time because, whereas Eton taught him nothing practical whatsoever, the army remarkably trained him, 'whose fingers are all thumbs, to strip, reassemble and fire a Vickers machine-gun in a fortnight'.[3] When it came to mastering the controls of what he described as 'this bloody car', however, not even the army's most skilled instructors could help Grimond overcome his lack of dexterity. Many years later, his parliamentary colleague David Penhaligon watched with total incomprehension as Jo struggled to open a plastic marmalade container.[4]

Having already given lectures to his own men about the dangers of gas warfare, Grimond thought for a time that he might be sent to the 'Gas School', where soldiers were taught *en masse* about that subject, but this plan was frustrated by a senior officer. Grimond was not best pleased, writing that 'I have no special job & no mechanical knowledge & I am not particularly brilliant as a troop leader.'[5] Nonetheless, he did rather enjoy himself in Dungannon. The locals were generally amiable and, although he discouraged Laura from joining him there, he liked his billet at the Northland Arms Hotel, whose proprietor had acted at the Old Vic. He also took pleasure in the company of his men, whom he observed with a politician's eye and thought 'delightful': 'I am not sure that Winchester, Eton or Oxford would have done them any good, on the other hand unless you tap these sort of people it is no good broadening the basis of education.'[6] Grimond continued his own education, writing to Lady Violet that he was reading books about political economy, including Trotsky's account of the Russian Revolution ('alas my brain which was never incisive is as blunt as a bayonet now'[7]). Following with interest the political situation at home, he was appalled that David Margesson, who had been government chief whip under Chamberlain, had been appointed to the Ministry of War:

> It may be that he is not as incapable as he is vicious but I can't help feeling he is a disastrous appointment. If you want an organizer why have a politician at all? If you have a politician he ought to have some decent episodes in his political history. To promote a tarnished, discredited Fouché or Chiappe on the grounds that they successfully stifled the very feeble rays of decent Conservative feeling seems to me to smack of Vichy . . . the worst of it is that it saps my faith in Churchill, Sir A, Bevin (if one ever had any) etc.[8]

In January 1941 Grimond was called to higher things, when he was appointed General Staff Officer Grade 3 (GSO 3) at the headquarters of the 53rd (Welsh) Division, to which the 2nd Fife and Forfars were at that time attached. Ten days later he was appointed acting captain. The official history of the regiment records 'the loss of several excellent officers who had gone to staff jobs . . . One of these was 2nd Lieutenant Jo Grimond . . . Grimond was a remarkable man who never seemed to be daunted by any circumstances. That, perhaps, is why at the time of writing this chronicle, he is the leader of the Parliamentary Liberal Party'.[9] Even before Grimond became a staff officer, he was encouraged to put his legal experience to good use, regularly representing soldiers in the military courts. Two instances demonstrate how Grimond's decent, and slightly subversive, instincts survived the military experience intact. A sergeant from Grimond's regiment had been arrested by two military policemen in a bar in Brighton, accused of being drunk. Grimond was asked to represent him at his court martial. The sun had not shone for days, but Grimond put it to the court that the man was suffering not from over-consumption of alcohol, but from sunstroke. His cross-examination tied up the military policemen 'in knots', and a very effective and valuable sergeant was acquitted. In another case, Trooper Ron Forbes, out on a tank exercise, had been ordered by his accompanying sergeant instructor to take the turret of the tank. It was getting dark and the vehicle's lights were poor, and the instructor drove straight into a disabled tank. The authorities were not best pleased: the instructor was charged with negligence and severely reprimanded, and Forbes himself, initially called as a witness, was charged too. He was summarily informed that his leave had been cancelled and he had been docked fourteen days'-worth of pay, without any appeal. When he sat grumbling about his situation in the NAAFI, Grimond's batman told him to put his case to Grimond, who listened attentively and set about putting right the injustice that had been meted out. He succeeded: Forbes had his leave reinstated and lost not a single day's pay. Almost sixty years later, Ron Forbes wrote that: 'Jo was like myself not a good tidy soldier and it was so nice to be able to sit and relax and unburden one's troubles to him . . . His batman declared he was the nicest officer anybody could wish to look after but he always had to be tidying up after him. On parade he always wore his beret like a bowler hat!'[10]

Grimond's first period on the staff lasted from January 1941 until April 1942. The move to divisional headquarters, one senses, brought with it wider horizons and a new circle of friends including, for a time, one Lieutenant A D Powell, already a successful novelist and man of letters, and destined to be even better known in post-war years as the author of *A Dance to the Music of Time*. The character of Widmerpool, who links the twelve books of that series, though he signally lacks Grimond's charisma, shares with him his rank, his Etonian background and a measure of his natural existentialism. Although Grimond fully recognised the grim dangers that the country faced, he was ill suited to the disciplines of army life and never took them too seriously. In the spring and summer of 1941, Grimond was back in Fife, which made it easier for Laura to come and visit him. 'I am very selfish about pressing her to come over,' he wrote in early May. 'It isn't a very cheerful life for her living alone in an hotel: or worse still in the company of other wives. But I miss her so much when she is away and enjoy her so much when she is here that I am quite unscrupulous.'[11]

On the basis of records supplied by the Ministry of Defence, it seems that by the summer of 1942 Grimond had once again been called back to the staff after a brief break. In February 1943, as a staff captain, he was posted to headquarters, Fife Sub Area. He did then spend a brief period lecturing on gas at the Army Staff College at Camberley and, after three short postings to staff jobs, was promoted to acting major, with the appointment of Deputy Assistant Adjutant General (DAAG) at the headquarters of the 53rd (Welsh) Division, where his staff career had commenced. The title of major, he once joked, was 'dreary . . . if you cannot become a colonel, better remain a dashing captain!'.[12] The 53rd Division was a 'first-line' Territorial unit, whose framework had been kept in being throughout the inter-war period. It spent much of the war training, and did not see action until shortly after D-Day, in June 1944. Thereafter, however, it was engaged in fighting until the end of the European war, in May 1945. It took heavy casualties in Normandy, and then fought its way through the Low Countries, the 'Battle of the Bulge', the Reichswald Forest, the crossing of the Rhine and the final clearing of resistance in northern Germany. In the process some 9,800 casualties were suffered (almost half of the divisional strength). As a staff officer and amongst new colleagues, Grimond again established himself as something of a character, not least in alliance with Graeme Hutchison, with whom he would later dabble in publishing – 'Graeme and I were incurable . . . we looked as though we had slept in our uniforms.'[13] He was reputedly the life and soul of the 'A' Mess, which was often almost deserted, as most of the senior officers preferred to spend time in their temporary homes nearby. By all accounts, those of Grimond's colleagues who did not have that option had good cause to be grateful for his amusing banter.

In the summer of 1943 Jo Grimond was the only one of his family's men-folk to be actively involved in the war. Jasper Ridley had been captured in northern Africa in June 1942 and was being held in Italy. He had shown grim determination from the outset to play his full part in a successful prosecution of the war against Germany, and his imprisonment must have been purgatory to him. Laura's brother Mark too had been captured after the dreadful battle of 16–17 March 1943 at the Mareth Line in Tunisia, the only officer from his company to survive. He was subsequently held at Arezzo and Modena. Grimond's reaction to the news of Mark's capture was one of relief rather than distress. Writing to Lady Violet during a home leave at the Grimond family home in Abbotsford Crescent, St Andrews, in April 1943, he expressed relief: 'I am so glad Mark is safe . . . It is the best that could be hoped for. I am sure the Italians are the best people to be a prisoner among and the climate of Italy will be reasonable even in a prison camp . . . I selfishly & possibly ignobly heave a sigh of gladness when any of my friends are out of harm's way.'[14] Within less than nine months, however, Mark had valiantly escaped from his prisoner-of-war camp and made it back to England. After the announcement of the Italian armistice on 8th September 1943, an estimated 50,000 allied prisoners-of-war made a break for home, trying to get clear before the Germans arrived to occupy their camps and move them northwards. Mark and another officer who had been captured on the same night, Major Tom Butler, hid in a hole at their camp and waited for it to be evacuated. It then took them thirty days to cover over 400 miles, as they avoided all roads and bridges on their way to the allied lines about 100 miles east of Rome. Fewer than 5,000 of the 50,000 made it to safety by the end of the year. When Mark made it home in time to celebrate New Year 1944 in Wiltshire with Jo and Laura, Lady Violet and his young brother Raymond, a new optimism seemed at last to be justified. Mark and Butler were both mentioned in despatches, but a bitter blow was still to strike the family.

Cressida's husband, Jasper Ridley, had also escaped, leaping from a train with two colleagues when they were being moved northwards after the allies attacked Salerno in the autumn of 1943. As Mark Bonham Carter had been, Ridley was at first sheltered by a well-disposed Italian, in this instance a schoolmaster. Then he heard, on the wireless, of his brother-in-law's successful bid for freedom. This galvanised him into following Mark's example by pressing on homewards, and he resolved at once to move on from his shelter. For several months after he left the safe house, nothing was heard of him. But he had left with the schoolmaster a letter to Cressida, to be delivered to her after the village had been liberated. By a cruel twist of fate she would receive it six months later, only a day after the War Office had at last announced that he was missing, presumed killed. He had never seen his infant son, Adam, and the family were devastated. One of the bright lights of a generation had been extinguished, and war had deprived Grimond of a close friend and much-loved brother-in-law. It transpired that Jasper had perished when attempting to cross a minefield in December 1943, about eighty miles south-east of Rome.

Grimond's view of his own life in the army was characteristically detached. He records the fact that, removed from regimental obligations, life at divisional headquarters was relatively peaceful. Indeed, even after D-Day he never had to fire a shot in anger. His adventures were decidedly removed from the horrors of the battlefield and, as recounted by him, generally had a comic quality. Shortly after he arrived in Normandy, for example, his memories of earlier visits to mainland Europe failed to stand him in good stead. He forgot that people drove on the right and, consequently, he was knocked over almost at once by a motorcycle. Once he had settled into life in Normandy, Grimond managed to obtain some splendid samples of brie cheese. He proudly sent one back to the Bonham Carters and another to his mother in St Andrews. The Bonham Carters gratefully devoured theirs and wrote to thank him. He heard nothing from his mother, subsequently discovering that she had decided that the cheese, no doubt distinctly and potently ripe on arrival, was in fact off and had thrown it away without a second thought. He had plenty of time to reflect upon 'the gulf', as he put it, between the risks constantly faced by those in the front line, and the comparatively docile life enjoyed by those in the army's 'tail'. Since the German forces were generally in retreat, he felt that 'once you were behind the infantry you were as safe as in London during an air-raid . . . Even the gunners suffered very few casualties and our long tail practically none.'[15] This question of the administrative 'tail' would intrigue Grimond throughout his life, and came to symbolise for him the bureaucratic mind-set out of which the British were unable to shake themselves after the war. During his time in northern Europe, he was never convinced that the 'top-hamper of staffs and hangers-on' borne by British and Canadian troops could be justified, likening them to the bureaucrats that followed in peacetime: 'the forerunners of the modern quangos and advisory bodies, civil government, ABCA, liaison officers . . . It was in the army too that I first noticed the absorption of public officials, at this time regular army officers, with their allowances, perks and badges of offices.'[16]

For Jo Grimond at least, 1945 did not begin propitiously. He was struck down with acute appendicitis and his appendix was removed at a field hospital. He was then transferred to a hospital in Glasgow, where it was left to the ward matron to 'first-foot' him for New Year 1945. Thereafter, once he was fit enough, he recuperated for a time at Lady Violet's home in London ('I couldn't have had a more pleasant illness – if illness it can be called'[17]), evicting Toto Morhange from his room and exiling him for a time to Brooks's Club. By the end of February 1945, Grimond was back in close touch with developments on the front line, sometimes sleeping within only a few hundred yards of the enemy. In a letter to Laura in mid March 1945 he foresaw that the war would be over within six weeks and, in a letter to Lady Violet, he suggested a premonition of the work that would be occupying him full-time before the end of the year: 'Goodness knows how long it will take to re-house the French, Belgians, Greeks, Yugo-Slavs, Dutch, Poles, Germans etc. I can't help feeling slight pleasure that Germany is being destroyed not because one wants the wretched civilians killed or terrified but because I really think it may bring home to them what they have done to other people. They have never suffered the humiliation of being refugees.'[18] Of Grimond's personal achievements during his time with the 53rd Division there is little to be found in his own writings. The fact that he reached the rank of major, and was appointed DAAG in time for the invasion of Normandy, is evidence enough that he was an effective staff officer. The CO of the division, Major-General 'Bobby' Ross, was a formidable and respected figure and would never have tolerated serious inefficiency among his staff. Not only did Jo Grimond become an (acting) major, but also he achieved the 'substantive' (that is, permanent) rank of captain, as he would recount later in life with genuine pride and a touch of *amour-propre*, and was once mentioned in despatches – purely to make up the numbers, he modestly claimed years later. Grimond's only failure, so far as it is possible to ascertain, came when he was rather improbably put in charge of the officers' mess, and the then divisional commander, General Wilson, was so appalled by a meal there on one visit that Grimond was summarily relieved of his post. Grimond's time in charge of the mess was not wholly wasted, however. For the first time in his life, he had to master the rudiments of a balance sheet – something that he had never been taught about at Eton.

In the winter of 1944–5, Lionel Brett, who was serving as a gunner in the European campaign, visited Grimond at his headquarters on a social call. Many of their mutual friends had already perished during the conflict and, as Brett later recalled, the two men, torn from their natural environments by circumstances, could recapture a little bit of the spirit of Beaumont Street: 'There he was . . . surrounded by people completely unlike himself so that he seemed a different animal, a noble beast in a farmyard. He was the same, elusive, shrewd, as difficult to grasp as quicksilver, kind, vague, humorous.'[19] Another acquaintance serving in the same campaign was Graeme Hutchison. He would tell the story of driving along with his column one filthy night and coming across a solitary figure in a heavily shelled farming area. 'Who the hell are you?' he demanded. 'I'm Grimond,' came the firm reply. 'I am the officer in charge of the burial of dead cattle.' The two became firm friends.

When the Germans surrendered, on 3rd May 1945, Grimond was just outside Hamburg, which Hitler had originally planned to turn into a fortress, to be defended 'to the last man'. As soon as the surrender was confirmed, he and a colleague, Jim Cooper, were despatched to the bomb-wrecked city to find a suitable headquarters for the division. They were astonished to discover that the city's renowned Atlantic Hotel had survived the war almost intact. Despite intensive allied bombing of the city, the hotel had never taken a direct hit and, even more amazingly, was still more or less functioning as in peacetime. Jim Cooper takes up the tale: 'General "Bobby" Ross sent Jo Grimond and me into Hamburg the day *before* the troops went in, to take over the surrender. Jo went to reserve "A" Mess and offices at the Hotel Atlantic. I took the Schauspielhaus Opera (2,000 seats) for show business. Again a sincere confirmation of Bobby's concern for the welfare of the Division – I was instructed to arrange a cabaret for the Divisional dinner.'[21] The Hotel Atlantic served as divisional headquarters and was, in essence, taken over as a going concern with its manager for the previous thirteen years, Oscar Geyer, still in day-to-day charge. The British turned out to be, in the words of the official history of the Atlantic Hotel, 'fair and cultivated victors'.[22] A photograph taken on the allies' first night in the hotel shows Grimond seated at the divisional victory dinner held at the Hotel Atlantic, the left sleeve of his battledress tunic still bearing the regimental tartan of the Fife and Forfars. His senior colleagues had cause to be grateful to him that evening for his lifelong devotion to food. Finding the hotel's kitchens fully operational, Grimond organised the kind of menu that even for senior officers must have long since vanished into the mists of time. They dined on iced melon and 'Clear Turtle Soup' followed by crayfish 'English style', roast spring chicken, raspberries and praline ice – all washed down with champagne, brandy and liqueurs. Oscar Geyer's shrewd political instincts were every bit as impressive as his organisational ability: he remained in charge of the hotel for a further twenty years.

During what was to be a relatively short stay at the hotel, Grimond still had time to be involved in one item of political drama, when members of the division stopped a car at a checkpoint, and discovered that one of the occupants was Artur Seyss-Inquart, for five years the brutal and feared Reichskommissar of the Netherlands. Since all senior officers were absent, as apparently they were wont to be, Grimond and several colleagues of equivalent rank had to decide what to do. Contact having been made with their superiors, they were told to put their captive into a staff car and send him to army

HQ. Since they were chronically short of such vehicles and Seyss-Inquart was famously evil even by Nazi standards, they thought this was a bit rich and asked for written confirmation. This having failed to appear, they treated him as an ordinary prisoner, searching him, removing a concealed knife from him, and then tossing him into a military police cell for the night. He was subsequently found guilty at Nuremberg of crimes against humanity and executed there along with nine of his most notorious colleagues by an American sergeant-hangman on 16th October 1946.

On a lighter note, it was not only supplies of food that had miraculously maintained their pre-war quality in Germany's second city. General Ross's penchant for having his men entertained enabled Grimond to see what he described thirty-five years later as 'the best cabaret I have ever encountered',[23] including a man who balanced on one finger. The author's father recalls seeing the same performer on BBC Television in the mid 1950s, and has ever since been trying to work out how the feat was achieved. But Hamburg proved to be but a short intermission. Within a few weeks, Grimond was to return to home shores. Grimond later improbably claimed that, amidst the turmoil of war, he had more or less forgotten the fact that he was a prospective parliamentary candidate. In 1940 the Liberals' prospective candidate for Orkney and Shetland, the Lady Glen-Coats, had felt obliged to stand aside, having found the strains of travelling to and from the islands, and around them, too much to endure. She knew Grimond through the Sinclairs, and recommended him as her successor. Although he had never been to either archipelago, the seat had been Liberal until a conservative, Basil Neven Spence, had gained it at the general election of 1935 and Grimond accepted what looked like a reasonably good opportunity. He did once try to get to Orkney during the war, but it was no easy proposition. There were no civilian air services and, by the time he made it as far as Perth, everything was deep in snow and he gave up.

Grimond concluded that he would rather fight a less remote constituency. Around Easter 1945, Laura wrote to him and informed him that the Liberals in Banff were looking for a candidate. He was at once interested, and wrote to Lady Violet asking for her advice about how he might extricate himself from his commitment to Orkney and Shetland, ideally without incurring the wrath of his predecessor as candidate: 'Lady Glen-Coats I know wants me to go on where I am and she is, more or less, the Scot Lib Fed that rather blocks that line of approach. On top of it all we are of course very busy and moving all the time. If you can get me put forward for Banff I should be most grateful.'[24] With the war in Europe won, the Labour party conference effectively forced Churchill to call a general election for 5th July 1945, and Jo Grimond was on his way home. A few months earlier he had written a letter to Sir William Beveridge, praising his plan for the social services, which would come to transform the relationship between state and citizen throughout the United Kingdom: 'You have said that you want from the Liberals a policy far more radical than Socialism . . . I agree entirely and it wants to be an immediate programme.'[25] It was in that spirit of radicalism that Grimond came home to fight his first election campaign as a parliamentary candidate.

As a major, Grimond was chauffeur-driven in a Mercedes to meet his ferry back to England. One of its wheels flew off en route, but after an otherwise uneventful journey, Grimond was on his way to London and, thence, to St Andrews. The 1945 general election might more accurately have been termed a 'general muddle', an unexpectedly early poll that left many voters irritated and confused. The Liberals were in a particularly confused and confusing state, with some candidates not sure in their own minds whether they wished to run as National Liberals, or as independent Liberals under the banner of Sir Archibald Sinclair. Although the independent Liberals stood to fight only a minority of the 640 seats, they were hopeful of making some progress. Sinclair himself had been close to Churchill ever since serving with him in the Royal Scots Fusiliers in 1916 and, as Minister for Air, he had certainly had a 'good war'. In Orkney and Shetland, Grimond soon discovered that none of the party organisations was up to much, ten years after they had last contested an election. His first port of call in Shetland was Peter Goodlad, a Lerwick lawyer who had been pencilled in to act as Lady Glen-Coats's agent. Goodlad consulted some files and discovered that the Liberals had indeed retained the services of his firm in the past, so he would of course be happy to help. But out of curiosity, for which party did Grimond propose to stand? Despite this unpromising start, Grimond soon gathered up around him the remnants of the islands' once-considerable radical tradition. Perhaps most helpfully of all, Grimond discovered that two of the local newspapers stood firmly in that tradition, and would endorse him. Both the *Orkney Herald* and the *Shetland Times* would be invaluable allies in the years ahead. In Orkney he enlisted the help of another lawyer, Cecil Walls, who had no experience of campaigning and drove around the islands in a huge Daimler.

Within only a few days, Grimond was genuinely unsure about whether to contest the election. The local Liberals appeared to have done little or nothing since losing the seat in 1935, and he was understandably daunted at the thought of having to build up an efficient campaigning organisation from scratch. Given a few months in which to get himself better known, and to build up some kind of network of supporters, he was confident that he might have a fighting chance. Faced with a general election in only five weeks, however, he did not believe that he could make enough impact upon such a scattered electorate. Grimond was dismayed to discover that Labour was determined to put up its candidate, a well-established (though not, according to him, especially well liked) secretary of the local Seamen's Union. He was also struck by how many people in the islands were now dependent upon subsidies from the government. This, he believed, explained their lack of enthusiasm for political change or controversy. On the other hand, he did sense a radical spirit in the islands, and was loath, as he put it, 'to sell the rights' to the Labour Party by leaving the field clear for them. From Lerwick, Grimond wrote a lengthy letter to Lady Violet, which resonates with profound pessimism:

> I myself am not very happy. I think that in a straight fight in October, Orkney & Shetland would be a good chance. At the moment I am grappling with several formidable difficulties . . . I am in some doubt about the whole matter. My supporters say quite cordially that with Labour standing my chances are nil . . . I am beginning to doubt whether it is worth standing. It is a blow to give up but in the face of local advice and a July election it seems extremely doubtful whether I shall do Liberalism or myself much good if I go on. It will mean of course that Labour get in here as the official opposition and may at some future election win the seat . . . Lady Glen Coats will be dreadfully upset if I don't stand and I sympathize with her because I do feel that in more favourable circumstances Orkney & Shetland are a good Liberal chance in a straight fight. But there are still 5 weeks to go to the election and they may get someone else . . . I haven't definitely decided not to go on – indeed I am starting a tour, speaking in several places – but I have told the local people that we will discuss it again in about a week and I have warned Edinburgh.[26]

Grimond did go on and, though his campaign was by his own admission pretty sporadic, in fairness he was a first-time candidate in what turned out to be an exceptionally difficult election for his party. He also rapidly discovered, as he and Laura came to terms with the peculiar geographical challenges that Orkney and Shetland present, that he did not much like the process of fighting an election. Comparatively few candidates have to spend a sizeable proportion of their campaign being tossed around on rough seas in tiny boats, but Grimond was very game and got to as many of the smaller islands as he could. After all, even though his constituency had one of the smallest electorates in the country, as he was fond of reminding people, it stretched from tip to toe as far as the distance between London and York. In both Orkney and Shetland many people have strong Nordic antecedents, widely reflected in family names and place-names. The Viking raids of earlier centuries truly left an enduring legacy: a recent (2001) scientific study confirmed that present-day islanders in Orkney have a distinctly Norwegian element in their DNA, and the magnificent twelfth-century cathedral that dominates Kirkwall is dedicated to St Magnus (and contains his bones). There are places on Orkney with more standing stones and ancient burial chambers per square mile than anywhere else in Europe. For a base on the Orkney mainland in the 1945 campaign, the Grimonds used the Royal Hotel in Kirkwall, the only hotel in Orkney available for civilian use at that time. With a war still raging, the hotel was not even in a position to serve a proper dinner, so Jo and Laura had to take their choice between a 'high tea',

taken before the evening's round of public meetings, or fish and chips by the
sea. They usually opted for the latter, or dined at the homes of supporters. They
also ended up having to spend much of the election campaigning separately, to
cover as much ground as possible. This only worried Jo when he was in Orkney,
and Laura was up in Shetland: although Cecil Walls was a highly decorous
and well-behaved person, his opposite number in Shetland was quite a character.
When Laura and Goodlad were campaigning together, Grimond once joked,
'they might well land me in jail between them!'[27]

Laura tried very hard to get Jo to address the electors informally, in
particular from a soapbox outside the old picture-house in Kirkwall, but he
retorted that this was 'just not my line', preferring to stick to public meetings –
many of which were extremely well attended, and at which by all accounts he
made a very favourable impression. Before one such meeting, Grimond was
warned that he should expect a lot of technical questions. Perceiving the faces
of his thirty or forty interlocutors only by dim candlelight, he returned fire
pretty effectively. These questioners were made of stern stuff, however, and as
Grimond set off for the next meeting on his itinerary (he sometimes took in
several meetings in one evening), most of his audience clambered aboard their
various forms of transport and followed him there. In his election literature,
Grimond tried to deal with the National Liberal question by stating that
he and, he expected, fellow Liberals, would willingly continue to work with
Churchill at least until the war against Japan had been successfully prosecuted.
His first campaigning slogan was a play on the name of Basil Neven Spence,
his Tory opponent: 'A Liberal vote is double-barrelled – best for Orkney, best
for Britain'. He campaigned for the centralisation of the state to be reversed,
and for greater devolution, not just to new tiers of government, but to put
'power in the hands of the people'. It was a theme to which he would return.

Westminster and London seemed half a world away. When Churchill made
his notorious remark to the effect that electing a Labour government would
mean seeing the 'Gestapo' on British streets, it seemed like a controversy
from a different planet. In the islands, people shrugged – and laughed –
off the hyperbole that supposedly scandalised more cosmopolitan opinion.
Throughout the campaign, Grimond had only the vaguest sense of what might
be happening locally: he and his team never asked people how they intended to
vote; in the small communities of the islands, Grimond had been warned, this
would be considered impudent. On one occasion, Laura made very delicate
enquiries about how well, or otherwise, the Liberals might be doing in one
locality. She was met with a dusty response: 'The people of this parish will
vote as they see fit. They will vote Liberal if they be of that mind.' Outside
the public meetings, therefore, electioneering took the comparatively gentle
form of visiting people, chatting with them and taking tea with them. The
cause was not always helped by Cecil Walls, who did little more than take

Grimond to meet his own friends, most of whom turned out to be committed Conservatives. He spent a day with Eric Linklater and his wife. Although he failed to convince them to vote for him on this occasion, he came away convinced that the meeting had been 'very useful' and, only a few years later, he was proven right. When he was despatched to visit a minister of the Church of Scotland in Shetland who was believed to be a Liberal of long standing, Grimond was surprised when he was received no more than politely. It transpired that his intelligence was out of date: this man was a locum, who had come to Shetland on a temporary basis as a favour to his good friend Basil Neven Spence. By the end of the campaign he was learning the tricks of campaigning in such tight communities. One of his supporters took him to the settlement of St Margaret's Hope, where a local shopkeeper, Herbert Mackenzie, was believed to be sympathetic. Mackenzie immediately downed tools, asked a friend to mind his shop and took Grimond around personally, introducing him to all the locals. It was a masterstroke, and marked the beginning of a campaigning style that would stand Grimond in good stead thereafter. Grimond certainly made an impression in 1945: one of his helpers from that election still recalls asking a ninety-year-old relative how she intended to vote. 'I think I'll vote for the bonny man,' she concluded firmly.[28]

Because of the need to include the votes of active service personnel, the results of the 1945 election were not announced until three weeks after polling day. Grimond was not even present at the count in Orkney and Shetland. He was astonished when he was telephoned by one of his election team and informed that he had lost by only 329 votes. He knew at once that, with some extra effort, he might have won. This was the story of the election for a painfully large number of Liberals. His had been far from a well-known face in the constituency, and he had wasted too much time early in the campaign learning his way around and 'taking tea with Tories'. Yet he had made an excellent impression on those he did meet, and local Liberals assumed that they would be seeing a lot more of him in future. Nationally the Liberals met with another disaster. Although their total poll, at around 2¼ million votes, was the highest since 1929, this only came about because they were running 306 candidates, as against 161 in 1935 and 118 in 1931. The bitterest blow came at Caithness, where, in a painfully tight three-way contest, Sir Archibald Sinclair had come third. Only twelve independent Liberals made it into the House of Commons – five from England, seven from Wales – and even that small group was seriously divided. The leadership of the party fell to a talented but little known and rather conservative Welsh lawyer called Clement Davies, whose sole claim to fame was the important background role that he had played in the downfall of the Chamberlain government in 1940 (when, on his advice, the motion designed to bring down the Chamberlain administration was made technical, rather than substantive, effectively guaranteeing its success).

Churchill still had a number of National Liberals operating under the aegis of the Conservative Party, and he resolved at once to take over what remained of his old party if he could.

Grimond personally had to take stock. He was the father of two young children, and needed to be mindful of his family's needs. Money was never a desperately pressing issue for him, but he had concluded from his own childhood experiences in St Andrews, and commuting to and from school, that children above all prize some sense of stability and continuity. An itinerant life, either through a protracted continuation of his army service, or because he was a prospective parliamentary candidate for such a remote constituency, had little appeal. Grimond was therefore dismayed to be ordered back to Catterick Camp in Yorkshire to complete his military training. When he was on leave in London during the summer of 1945, Grimond took the opportunity to ask his friends and contacts if they could help him find a job that could reunite him with his young family. In search of advice, he went to see Toto Morhange, who was now playing a major role in the rebuilding effort, having taken on in March 1944 the post of finance director in the European Regional Office (ERO) of the United Nations Relief and Rehabilitation Administration (UNRRA). He referred Grimond immediately on to the ERO director of personnel, Colonel Whiteley, with his personal recommendation. Hearing that Grimond had been a DAAG in the army, Whiteley wasted no time in settling the young major's career plans, asking, 'I don't suppose you'd like my job?' What followed was arguably the most testing and rigorous period of Jo Grimond's career outside politics, as he abruptly found himself in charge of 130 people, who had to help organise a major part of the international effort to bring relief to countries liberated from the enemy. At the beginning of September, Grimond joined UNRRA, which he described in a letter to some supporters in Orkney as 'a rather dubious organisation'. This effectively marked the end of Grimond's military service, and he later discovered how contentious his own appointment had been. When he was brought in, his predecessor told his UNRRA superiors virtually nothing about him. All they knew was that he was a serving officer, and that he had unsuccessfully contested a parliamentary seat. They assumed for a time that he was a spy reporting to the British War Office – and never did receive any biographical information about him.

By autumn 1943 the allied forces had been confident that the tide of the war had turned, and victory over the remaining Axis powers was only a matter of time. In November of that year the United Nations – at that time heavily US-dominated – passed a forward-looking resolution setting out ways in which international efforts might best be organised to give the citizens of liberated nations 'aid and relief from their sufferings, food, clothing and shelter, and in the prevention of pestilence and in the recovery of health of the people'. The UN also resolved to play an early and active role in arranging the speedy return of refugees to their homelands, and to offer 'assistance with the resumption of urgently needed agriculture and industrial production and the restoration of essential services'. This meant setting up, entirely from scratch and inevitably on a very short-term basis, an organisation that would be able to deliver relief on a huge scale. When UNRRA was set up in 1944, with its HQ in Washington, one of its first actions was to set up a European Regional Office, in London, to be headed by a Personal Representative of the Director-General (PRDG). Shortly after Grimond joined UNRRA, a new PRDG arrived, in the shape of Sir Humfrey Gale KBE, formerly deputy chief of staff to General Eisenhower. For much of Grimond's time at UNRRA, the Director-General was Fiorello La Guardia, former Mayor of New York. Europe would account for an estimated 80 per cent of UNRRA's activities, and the ERO was responsible not only for recruiting its own staff, but also for 'the recruitment of most of the British and other European staff of the Administration'.[29] Although a management system of sorts was in place from the beginning, it is hard now to capture the chaotic fashion in which UNRRA operated.

The personnel functions were a particular source of friction between Washington and the ERO. In the early days of UNRRA, the ERO had attempted to arrogate to itself not only the day-to-day running of personnel in Europe, but also matters of policy. UNRRA HQ had different ideas, regarding the ERO as no more than a directly-controlled executive body, which should take its instructions entirely from senior staff in Washington. By the time Grimond joined UNRRA, a gradual process of more clearly defined delegation had begun to take place and his responsibilities took in virtually every aspect of personnel and training for the European region. Although Grimond himself had evidently been recruited in an unorthodox manner, an advisory committee did exist with the job of vetting possible senior UNRRA employees. Amongst those deemed to be unsuitable 'for reasons such as age, health, political affiliation, personality or lack of ability' were several men whose paths crossed Grimond's at some point, such as Philip Noel-Baker, Arnold Toynbee and Harold Laski. Grimond arrived in the wake of three short-lived predecessors and joined an organisation whose usual and inevitable state of flux was now bordering on chaos.

One of Grimond's first tasks at UNRRA was to placate the outgoing head of finance and administration, Sir Frederick Leith Ross, who was in a fury about a personnel matter that had been unsatisfactorily dealt with by Grimond's predecessor. Although Sir Frederick was in a distinctly disagreeable mood when Grimond arrived, he was perfectly courteous and ordered tea for two. The tea arrived. Sir Frederick Leith Ross promptly upset it, over himself and his desk. Tea spread over his papers, dripping from drawer to drawer. By the time the two men had finished crawling around and mopping up, try as he might, Sir Frederick could not remain plausibly angry. Grimond did not need to inspect the spilled tea leaves to detect in this a portent of chaos to come. On one occasion, twenty Peruvian doctors arrived, unannounced, at Southampton expecting to play their part in UNRRA's activities. Some huge ploughs, designed to be dragged by caterpillar tractors, were sent to Ethiopia at the behest of a bustling lady Democrat from the USA who had been seconded to UNRRA. The women of Ethiopia went into open revolt: they were used to carrying ploughs on their heads, it transpired, and were not impressed at the unintended implication that they should do so in the case of these huge contraptions. Another instance of bureaucracy at its worst came when the Royal Aircraft Establishment at Farnborough offered to lend teams of its students to UNRRA during the summer. It seemed mad to Grimond that the administration could not find a way of taking up this offer, but to his intense irritation the response amongst ERO staff and field officers alike was to find the pitfalls and the problems, instead of being imaginative or radical.

Within days of joining UNRRA, Grimond was pouring his heart out to Lady Violet about how dreadful the situation was: refugees from Russia in particular had been reduced by the war to a pitifully primitive state, and UNRRA simply did not have the means to relocate them, still less to make good the gaps in their education and training. Not only were some of the young men a danger to the women of central Europe, they were a danger to themselves. In August, just as Grimond arrived, a senior US official, Posner by name, was sent to the ERO to find out what was going on. He cabled back to his superiors that the place was in a state of 'confusion, inertia, low morale and lack of coordination'.[30] Grimond himself had come to a rather similar view when he arrived and, in the absence of any clear policy from on high, had at once set about drawing up his own salary schedules and personnel policies in cooperation with a like-minded colleague – quite independently not only of headquarters, but also of most of his senior colleagues at the ERO. One of Grimond's first tasks was to help with the production of a manual, already into the final stages of drafting, which would codify the terms and conditions of UNRRA employees. Earlier in the year, staff at the ERO had become so frustrated with a lack of leadership on the part of the US headquarters that they had begun to draft their own manual for personnel in the field stations. The new manual codified and superseded some 80 administrative orders, 200 general bulletins and at least 200 cables that had accreted in only a few months. Through his persistence, Grimond had not only played a major part in its final drafting, but he had also won a victory over the bureaucrats by rendering it into simpler English and decentralising at least some of UNRRA's personnel functions. After the manual was published, however, differences of opinion and interpretation continued to arise between London and Washington.

In particular, the ERO seemed determined to go its own way on the contentious question of what headquarters termed 'meritorious pay increases'. This had always been a bone of contention between London and Washington. The ERO view had originally been that officers whose services had been satisfactory should receive an automatic annual increment. This became the general rule, accepted and applied by Washington, and hardened into a *de facto* policy of either granting employees an annual increment, if their work was up to the required standard, or simply getting rid of them if it wasn't. Grimond unilaterally attempted to change all that, because he wanted to use merit pay more flexibly, as a means of rewarding outstanding employees for whom there were no imminent opportunities for promotion. He felt that 'meritorious awards' should be just that: that they should create some genuine spur to better performance, rather than coming round regularly and automatically, which was now Washington's policy. He had grown especially weary of the approach to this question adopted by UNRRA's British staff, who came in and 'asked for a small rise for the whole grade, not on the grounds that they were any good, but because they had not had one for six months . . . On being refused they shuffled out again, wrapped in grumbles, to wait for another six months.'[31]

From mid 1946, UNRRA was due to start contracting. When Grimond joined the organisation, he realised at once that not enough thought had been given to the immense personnel difficulties inherent in running down such an organisation within a short space of time. Junior staff whose positions had been terminated by UNRRA missions had taken to wandering around Europe and turning up at other missions in search of employment, which was causing consternation and embarrassment. Grimond's main concern was that it would be virtually impossible to keep UNRRA running at all once it had begun to contract, because the pattern of staff departures was impossible to predict – and recruitment was likely to be nigh impossible. In January 1946 he sent a confidential minute to his immediate superior, warning that the recruitment of junior staff in particular was likely to present serious problems: 'suitable recruits in general must be young and energetic . . . UNRRA offers no future to such men . . . The general demand for their services in civilian life is likely to increase for the next six months to a year.'[32] Grimond hoped that the strategic policy decisions of the administration might take account of the personnel bottlenecks that he foresaw, and he suggested that UNRRA should offer new recruits some kind of safety net – in the shape of guaranteed twelve-month fixed-term contracts and the suggestion that other UN bodies might take over at least some of those made redundant by UNRRA as it wound down. Within his own division, Grimond now proposed to turn over one of his recruitment sections to terminations and reassignments.

Washington then came forward with a proposal that chilled Grimond's blood, to establish a general policy that promotions should be frozen, at least above a certain level, with exceptions to be allowed in individual cases, each of which would have to be negotiated bilaterally with Grimond's team at the ERO. He at once recognised in this a recipe for administrative chaos, arguing that, since people were becoming redundant or 'semi-redundant' so quickly across the organisation, and anything even resembling a normal career structure was therefore going to become impossible to maintain, UNRRA needed to undergo a far more radical restructuring in the final phase of its existence.

As part of that process, Grimond again wanted to improve incentives to staff: 'meritorious increments should be more liberally used to reward employees whom [sic] it is considered are deserving of a higher salary'. In the event an only very slightly amended version of the American proposal was put into effect, and a bureaucratic nightmare beckoned. Grimond's UNRRA work enabled him to observe at first hand the increasing influence of American thinking on how international organisations operated. The private, internal history of UNRRA held by the UN suggests that it was in the field of personnel policy that the culture clash between the Americans and the British was most extreme. Even though America was supposedly the home of individualistic freedom and enterprise, Grimond noted that the Americans in fact brought some very bureaucratic habits with them to UNRRA. It was they, not the British, who generated mountains of paper, with everything copied to everyone.

The culture clash was greatly exacerbated by an almost total lack of any exchange of personnel across the Atlantic. Most of the senior figures at headquarters never once visited an UNRRA field mission. Grimond was, however, always willing to accept any net additions to his empire and welcomed to the ERO two senior officials from the States. One of them, Carol Laise (who subsequently became an ambassador), joined the ERO as an extra deputy to Grimond. 'Welcome to the chaos of UNRRA,' he proclaimed when she arrived. When he first saw a printed copy of his *Memoirs*, Grimond saw her described in his text as 'a charming, cute and tactful girl'.[33] He was furious – he had originally written 'astute' not 'cute'! At UNRRA Grimond learned all about the futility of lengthy discussions and conferences that neither came to clear conclusion nor led to any significant activity, and saw for himself the dangers of over-centralisation. He was also confirmed in his view that, even if the people working within them are talented, motivated and well intentioned, bureaucracies are by their very nature unresponsive and inefficient.

By early 1947 it was clearly time to look for any credible opportunity to move on. The winding up of field operations was almost complete, and the remainder were due to end by 30th June: by far the busiest part of Grimond's empire was its 'Reduction and Closure Coordination Committee'.

Some time around New Year 1947, Commander Jackson, a senior UNRRA official, went to see Hector McNeil, recently promoted to Minister of State at the Foreign Office, to explain to him how difficult it was becoming for UNRRA to hang on to talented senior personnel. McNeil wrote to Sir Humfrey Gale, Grimond's UK boss, in the smooth vernacular of a later Sir Humphrey, explaining that 'His Majesty's Government will do their best to find suitable employment for any of the highly qualified members of your staff whom you feel obliged to persuade to stay on until the end of your operations . . . this is not, of course, an absolute guarantee, but it does express our definite intention.'[34] The minister also requested details of any such individuals. Sir Humfrey Gale therefore asked Grimond to compile a list of seven or eight of his most notable and 'highly qualified' officers, to which Gale himself added Grimond to spare his blushes. This he sent on to Sir Edward Bridges, Permanent Secretary at His Majesty's Treasury, on 25th February 1947. Gale asked that the individuals named should be helped if possible, and gave Grimond a short and effective reference: 'A very intelligent type. An attractive personality & has learned much in UNRRA of the complexities & difficulties of personnel work. Is legal trained & approaches all his problems with an unbiased mind.'[35]

Jo Grimond's critics often accused him of being a dilettante. Whilst at UNRRA he proved himself to be highly competent and conscientious. He flagged up many of the problems associated with winding down UNRRA well before anyone else had thought seriously about them. He also put into effect some of the principles that he would later advocate in his political life, notably a greater emphasis on participation and incentives. On the other hand, he had already developed a capacity for being at times an intensely irritating colleague. His penchant for tossing ideas into the air without due care and attention would never desert him, nor would his habit of impatiently or playfully redrafting text without due authority. But his charm and style generally saw him through, and he was never less than considerate and humane towards UNRRA field personnel. In the event Jo Grimond was not to need help from either Hector McNeil or Sir Edward Bridges, but there can be no doubt that his experiences with UNRRA would be an enormous help to him throughout his career. Although work at the ERO certainly had its frustrations, it was never dull. The immense toll taken by the Second World War saw to that. Furthermore, despite its internal problems, UNRRA did succeed in returning some 7 million displaced persons to their countries of origin and provided camps for around a million refugees who were unwilling to be repatriated.

4

I^T WAS PERHAPS the ERO's London location that in time became the greatest burden for Grimond, since he still wished to keep open the option of fighting another election somewhere in Scotland. On 18th February 1947 the Orkney Liberals met in Kirkwall to discuss 'the question of resuscitating the local Liberal Association'. They constituted a committee, whose first tasks were to affiliate the Orkney Liberals with the Scottish Liberal Party – and to write to Jo Grimond, 'inviting him . . . to come forward again as prospective Liberal Candidate for the constituency'.[1] Although he had come far closer to winning in Orkney and Shetland than anyone had imagined he would, and he certainly wanted to keep open the option of fighting there again, Grimond was not willing to commit himself at this stage, presumably in case a better opportunity presented itself – or the Liberal Party completely collapsed. Although there is no evidence to suggest that Jo Grimond ever considered fighting under any colours other than Liberal, he may have had half an eye on Archibald Sinclair's old seat at Caithness, which had a strong Liberal tradition and was easier to reach than the islands. Either way, Grimond must have known that, their natural Liberal leanings notwithstanding, the people of the Highlands and Islands would only vote for a man whom they knew, liked and trusted. He therefore needed a job somewhere in Scotland, and ideally a job that would allow him the necessary flexibility to travel, and to spend the occasional week in the north, as and when the need arose.

Grimond knew socially the Scottish architect Robert Hurd, who was at that time working on a commission from the National Trust for Scotland (NTS) to lead a radical renovation programme at Culzean Castle in Western Scotland. Hurd was also a founder member of the new Propaganda Committee that the NTS had established to proliferate word of its work. The NTS came into the field later than its English counterpart, having been established in 1921. Although it was by no means immune from post-war austerity, thanks to ambitious leadership from the young Earl of Wemyss and March, it was by 1947 determinedly looking to expand its empire and influence. Culzean was a huge undertaking, indeed one whose financial implications would in time come to threaten the very existence of the Trust. But, happily for Grimond, the policy of gentle expansion meant that new blood was required at the

NTS headquarters in Edinburgh. The secretary of the National Trust for Scotland is responsible not only for minuting meetings and overseeing the maintenance of properties in the Trust's care. In effect the secretary is also the guardian of the Trust's constitution, a crucial link between the membership and the bureaucracy. Since the pre-war era, this position had been held by the redoubtable Colonel Edward (later Sir Edward) Stevenson CVO MC, operating from his spare bedroom and with only a single secretary for support. Stevenson and Wemyss were, as Grimond later wrote, 'the unpaid pioneers of conservation, which is now big business'.[2] As he steadily moved towards full retirement, Stevenson had initially agreed to do the job on an 'expenses-only' basis, later acting as secretary for no remuneration whatsoever. By late 1946 he was finding the demands of a full-time position rather excessive, and made up his mind to vacate the front line in favour of a paid professional, with a managed hand-over to take place in the summer of 1947. Stevenson was himself against advertising the post and undertook in November 1946 'to communicate with the labour exchange about a suitable type of man'.[3]

The job was never advertised. Robert Hurd recommended Jo Grimond as an ideal candidate and, on 26th March 1947, the NTS executive remitted the matter to Lord Wemyss and Sir Ernest Wedderburn, who represented the Royal Society of Edinburgh on the executive, with powers to interview and appoint Grimond to the post. His salary was to be £1,000 per annum, rather more than the £700 that had originally been planned, but far less than the very substantial £2,155 that he was earning by the time he finished with UNRRA. If the interview proved successful, he would be invited to start with the NTS in mid July 1947. During the weeks that followed Grimond was interviewed both by Lord Wemyss and by the Trust's Business Committee. The path to appointment was unusually smooth and, on 22nd April, Colonel Stevenson wrote to Grimond at his home in Holland Park offering him the post of assistant secretary at a remuneration of £1,000 per annum, with a view to becoming secretary upon his own retirement in September. At that point Stevenson would take up the position of 'Honorary Secretary General'. This was manna from heaven to Grimond. It would pay his bills, get him away from London – and give him an invaluable foothold in Scotland's public life. In all conscience, however, he knew that the appointment was never likely to be more than a stopgap. He made no attempt to disguise this fact, and negotiated terms to his contract that would allow him the greatest possible flexibility. Difficulties therefore quickly arose when the precise terms were discussed, because the Trust ideally wanted rather more commitment than Grimond was in a position to offer.

Grimond took a little while to reply to Stevenson's letter of 22nd April. Although he explained this away on the basis that his UNRRA superior Sir Humfrey Gale had been away and could not therefore be consulted, it is absolutely clear that the ten-day interval afforded Grimond an important period of reflection. Never a man prone to dissembling, Grimond no doubt recognised that, should he prevaricate about his likely intentions at this juncture, his reputation amongst the 'great and good' north of the border might suffer incalculable harm in the longer term. When he replied on 2nd May, his letter crossing with a mildly irritated chaser from the NTS, Grimond therefore set out civilly but firmly and clearly his feeling that the six-months' notice period proposed by the NTS was rather too severe. He was also absolutely open about the fact that he was unwilling to be tied down to an open-ended commitment:

> I would . . . prefer, though I do not suppose that the point will be vital, to make the appointment subject to three rather than six months notice on either side . . . As to the length of the appointment, it has been spoken of as indefinite and I have the impression that while the appointment would be terminable on notice by either side the Trust hope to secure a permanent secretary . . . I feel it only fair to state that, although this suggestion is not embodied in the conditions of service, I attached in my own mind considerable importance to it. I am a young man still and many things may happen. I do not therefore want to bind myself morally (I am clearly not bound legally) to stay as secretary of the Trust for the rest of my career.

At the very least, this letter demonstrated a sublime combination of the lawyer, the Oxford PPE scholar and the Liberal politician. The Trust decided to ignore the hint and appointed him anyway. Not everyone was satisfied, even at the outset. Edward Stevenson's reaction, for example, foreshadowed tensions to come. He had made up his mind to move on from the post and, if Grimond didn't want the job, then there was an urgent need to advertise and recruit somebody else. He therefore made no attempt to disguise his irritation at what he evidently regarded as pettifogging and selfish behaviour on the part of someone to whom a substantial improvement in terms and conditions had already been granted. He minuted Lord Wemyss at once about Grimond's letter, warning that he was 'feeling a little unhappy about it'. The Grimond charm had worked, however, and David Wemyss's mind was made up. When the exchange of letters between Stevenson and Grimond was discussed by the NTS executive on 28th May 1947, it approved his appointment. The minutes record that the NTS Business Committee had indeed told Grimond that his position would be reviewed after three years; and that, any future differences of emphasis notwithstanding, the executive wanted Colonel Stevenson to secure Grimond's services without further ado – presumably on whatever terms Jo Grimond found acceptable. On Tuesday, 22nd July 1947, a week and a day later than originally planned, Grimond arrived at the National Trust for Scotland as its secretary-designate. A week later, he cheekily used his UNRRA contacts to obtain some surplus office equipment for use in the National Trust's new offices at a favourable price. In February 1948, the chairman shared with the

NTS Council his view that the new secretary 'had taken a very firm grip on the whole thing and he (the chairman) had been very much impressed with the way he had tackled difficult problems and dug out into the past and was carrying on the business of the Trust in a most capable manner'.[4] Wisely, perhaps, the new secretary did not allow false, or genuine, modesty to dilute that part of the record! Some of the problems faced during this time were indeed difficult, and it soon became apparent that the independent existence of a National Trust for Scotland might not be sustainable.

As part of the deal with Grimond, the Trust undertook to help him find accommodation for himself and his family, which now consisted of Laura and three highly energetic children: Andrew and Grizelda, who were both at school, and Johnny, who was 'beginning to run about'. With the Trust as landlord it was never going to be an ordinary house and in the end the Grimonds were offered a most unusual property, the Hamilton Dower House in Prestonpans, an old mining village east of Edinburgh. This house had been built in 1628 by Sir John Hamilton as a dower house for his widowed mother; and it had seen some action since then. It was reputed to have been used by troops loyal to Bonnie Prince Charlie before the Battle of Prestonpans in September 1745, held to be the explanation for marks on the stone window frames which had supposedly been cut by soldiers sharpening knives or bayonets. Some local sages even claimed that the prince himself had been in the house. It was used as barracks again by troops preparing for the French invasion predicted in 1814 and then became an inn towards the end of the 1800s. In the early twentieth century the house fell into disrepair and, in 1934, the county council of East Lothian declared the building to be unfit for human habitation, scheduling it for demolition as part of a road scheme. The council report for that year, adduced as justification for that decision, stated that 'the northern portion is empty – and the remainder occupied as working class houses'.[5] The newly established National Trust for Scotland was having none of it, however, and won a reprieve. In 1938–9 the house was renovated under the leadership of none other than Robert Hurd. The Grimonds rented it for £110 per annum (the market rent was estimated at around £150 per annum).

In addition to his routine tasks as secretary to the Trust – visiting properties, taking minutes and so forth – Grimond immediately found himself supporting his chairman in his ongoing struggles to keep the Trust financially viable. Throughout the late 1940s, the finances of the Trust came under the most terrible strain. The ongoing renovation of Culzean (still, to this day, a jewel in the crown of the NTS) was proving ruinously expensive, and income was far from covering liabilities. By the summer of 1948, there was no disguising the seriousness of the position and, in July of that year, Lord Wemyss wrote to those members of the Trust Council who were not members of the executive, setting out the scale of the problem and four possible ways of ameliorating the situation. First of all, commitments had to be curtailed, which cast a shadow over further property acquisitions in the foreseeable future. A big public appeal was required, both to stimulate short-term income and to generate good PR. Other grant-giving trusts would be approached. And then there was the taxpayer. In 1946 the English National Trust had received a substantial government grant in the form of a 'Jubilee Grant' and a year later its Scottish counterpart had registered a bid for something similar. The good news was a long time in coming, but in the autumn of 1948, a Mr Cunningham of the Scottish Home Department finally answered the *cri de coeur*. The government was now proposing a fundamental reassessment of how the National Trust should deal with historic buildings, he wrote, but *pro tem* there was some good news: 'I am glad to be able to tell you . . . that the Chancellor of the Exchequer agrees that in the meantime the National Trust for Scotland cannot be allowed to collapse and he is accordingly ready to agree to a grant.'[6]

The grant came to £12,500 towards capital expenditure, and £7,500 towards the recurrent costs of administration. This afforded no more than a breathing space of a couple of years, but the prospect of immediate liquidation had been averted. An indication of Grimond's liberal politics came in his measured response to these tidings at an executive meeting on 19th January 1949. He feared that this contribution from the Exchequer might presage a far more serious intervention by the government: that, with the Trust at its most vulnerable, a socialist government might wish to move towards taking it over entirely: 'This [contribution] would almost certainly mean a large measurement of government control of the Trust . . . [He] was not necessarily averse to this, but he thought the implications of government support on these lines should be carefully considered.'

Despite these financial dire straits, Grimond still managed to drive through the acquisition of two major properties. The first comprised the house and gardens at Threave, south-west of Dumfries. The Threave Garden and Estate take their name from the original title of the castle built on the site in the fourteenth century for Sir James Douglas, a leading supporter of Robert the Bruce. The present Threave House was built by a Liverpool businessman, William Gordon, for himself and his family. The estate includes several farms and totals approximately 1,400 acres. The last generation of Gordons to inhabit the house were two bachelor brothers, the elder of whom, Colin, had died in 1942. His younger brother, Major Alan Gordon DSO MC, who had served in the Irish Guards between 1914 and 1934, approached the National Trust for Scotland in 1947 to see if it might be willing to take over the property. Grimond met Major Gordon in December 1947 and they discussed possible terms on which such a transfer might be viable. Gordon was beginning to find the costs of maintaining the property excessive and wished to make long-term arrangements for its upkeep. As part of the arrangement he wished to carry on living at Threave until his death, pursuing – albeit in a less vigorous fashion than before – his enthusiasms for estate management, gardening and wildlife.

Grimond was only too aware that the options before him were limited. With its finances in an increasingly precarious state, the Trust should ideally be cutting back on its commitments and liabilities, not adding to them. But equally it must not completely abjure its very *raison d'être* by turning down an unrepeatable offer such as this, which would undoubtedly have resulted in the estate being broken up forever. He therefore secured an offer from Major Gordon that not only the property, but also an endowment of around £60,000 would be given over to the Trust. This proposal, in Grimond's words, 'appeared to be very generous and adequate'. The Trust's Business Committee came down in favour of the acquisition, but only with certain caveats. The executive first considered Threave at its meeting on 21st January 1948 and, at its meeting two months later, was ready to take on Threave. By that time Major Gordon had added to his original offer a three-sevenths share in the Neish Estate in Dundee, to fund continuing provision for employees on the estate and their widows. With the consent of the Trust, he lived on in the house 'with the full enjoyment of the gardens and policies' and, as he had wanted, retained the right to help himself to the produce of the gardens, even to the point of giving some of it away to friends 'within reason'. After his adroit handling of such a negotiation, it is certainly easier to understand how Jo Grimond came to navigate the waters of Liberal assemblies with such sangfroid. This really was a job well done. Later that spring his brother-in-law Billy Corbett tried to induce the Trust to take on Rowallan. Nothing came of that, but another property with great significance to the Grimond family was also in the frame: the Hill of Tarvit near St Andrews.

The Hill of Tarvit is the site a few miles south of Cupar where, between 1773 and 1904, the former Wemyss Hall had stood. The old Scotstarvit Tower still stands today. It was bought in 1904 by Fred Sharp, a friend and associate of Grimond's father, who in turn brought in Sir Robert Lorimer to build a new property on the site in the years 1907–8. The new mansionhouse, as it was called, would serve not only as a family home but also as a showcase for his impressive collection of memorabilia from all over the world – notably Flemish tapestries, Chinese porcelain and bronzes and furniture from France and England. As fate decreed it, however, the new house would serve as a home to only two generations of the family. Fred Sharp had two children, his son Hugh and Elizabeth, twelve years his junior. After Hugh's tragically early death in 1937 in the Castlecary train disaster, Fred's widow Beatrice and daughter Elizabeth lived retiring lives in the property. Beatrice died in June 1946 and, when Elizabeth succumbed to cancer just over two years later at the age of thirty-eight, she left the Hill of Tarvit to the National Trust, together with its contents (bar a few personal items which were to go to friends) and an allowance for its upkeep. Grimond was eager for the Trust to take it over, and to make a success of it. It was sheer bad luck that the offer of this property, which meant so much to Grimond personally, should come so soon after Threave and at the very nadir of the Trust's financial fortunes. He rapidly came to the conclusion that Hill of Tarvit would only be made financially viable if the Trust could find someone to live there. His first thought was that it would make an appropriate official residence for the Secretary of State, but there was no interest from that quarter. He therefore embarked on a search for a tenant, which, though not particularly systematic, was certainly eclectic. In a few short months he corresponded with such diverse institutions as the Society of Authors, the Scottish Council of Social Service, the English Speaking Union and even the Holiday Fellowship in Hendon. Taking full advantage of his range of contacts in the vicinity of the property, Grimond also wrote to the Principal of St Andrews, receiving instead a response from Ronald Cant, an academic he knew and admired, not least for his definitive history of the University of St Andrews.

Grimond and other representatives of the Trust visited Hill of Tarvit several times during the months that followed. There were many significant opponents of its acquisition, generally on grounds of economy. Jo Grimond was determined, however, and at a meeting of the NTS executive on 19th January 1949 he had to fight his corner vigorously on this question, warning that: 'There might be a contradiction in saying that the Trust believed that country houses should be preserved and that they [the National Trust] were the body to do it and, at the same time, refusing Hill of Tarvit . . . if the Trust felt any doubt about taking Hill of Tarvit on financial grounds, they might have to reconsider their whole attitude to country houses.' The deliberations on Hill of Tarvit continued for several months, to the intense irritation of Jo Grimond and the executors of Elizabeth Sharp's will. At a series of executive meetings throughout the early part of 1949, the question was kept open repeatedly. Finally, in March 1949, a decision in principle was arrived at and Grimond recorded tartly that 'it was finally decided that the Trust should accept with gratitude the bequest of Hill of Tarvit', albeit on a basis the details of which were still to be ironed out. What other officers and officials of the Trust made of that 'finally' wearily interpolated by the secretary may safely be left to the imagination. Meanwhile the search for a viable tenant went on. The offer of Rowallan was refused with regret at the same meeting. The Trust couldn't afford the estimated £10,000–£12,000 needed for repairs to the fabric of the building.

Added to problems with the Hill of Tarvit was the new distraction of having to prepare draft evidence for the National Trust for Scotland to present to the Committee on Houses of Outstanding Historic or Architectural Interest which had been appointed in December 1948 by the Chancellor of the Exchequer, Stafford Cripps. Grimond circulated members of the NTS executive with a first draft of the evidence, in which he set out the Trust's recent experiences of running country houses and argued the case for an expansion of their activities. However, even as he wrote it Grimond was clearly aware of a lacuna in his own argument: that he could hardly adduce any overwhelmingly convincing evidence of notably beneficial interventions by the Trust. On the contrary, its record was decidedly mixed. Grimond was fearful too that members of the executive were failing to take seriously the possibility that the Labour government might 'nationalise' the Trust, warning in his notes accompanying the draft that:

> If [the Trust] wants to hold country houses then I can see no logical, or indeed possible, half-way house: it must have funds and staff to acquire, endow and develop whatever class of houses it is decided should be preserved . . . if it is to continue taking on large properties – houses or open country – it will inevitably meet development problems . . . In my view that means an overhaul and expansion of its organization, government grants on a large scale and with them some degree of government control.

The draft was discussed at an executive meeting on 3rd February 1949 and was generally well received. Perversely perhaps, this served to irritate Grimond, who himself recorded in the minutes that:

> He [Grimond] felt that the members had on the whole been over-complimentary about the draft. On reading it through he did not feel entirely satisfied with it. It struck him as diffuse and not very well written or arranged . . . Rather incongruously perhaps the Trust concluded [in the draft evidence] by saying that in the face of this unsatisfactory experience they were confident that they could deal with most houses of historical or architectural importance provided they were given a very large sum of money.

This outburst appears to have had the intended effect, stimulating the Executive into adopting a rather more aggressive and explicit defence of the Trust's unique qualities in the next draft of its evidence: 'They have a very wide discretion which enables them to make the best use of these houses in the public interest . . . and they feel that where any portion of the house is to remain in private occupation they can establish better relations with the owner than would be possible if they were handed over to any government department.'

The committee report, published in 1950, was immensely satisfactory from the NTS point of view, recommending that a new governmental Historic Buildings Council be set up, for England and Wales, with a sister council for Scotland. The Trust was described as 'a non-governmental organisation of the highest standing',[7] and the option of taking it over wholesale as the foundation for the new state body was considered – and decisively rejected. The committee wanted the Trust to work with its new governmental colleagues, but not to jeopardise 'its freedom and elasticity and informal relations which subsist between it and those with whom it deals'.[8] This was a knock-out victory, and a crucial turning point, for the National Trust both north and south of the border. Grimond's experiences at the NTS convinced him that keeping the original occupants, their descendants or at least their personal possessions on site was by far the best way not only of maintaining the fabric of historic buildings, but also of maintaining public interest in the buildings, a point he revisited a few years later:

> What the visitors enjoy is not only seeing beautiful pictures or architecture. They enjoy seeing the imprint of the owner's last letter, and that sort of thing. I have been taken around his house by the noble Lord the Member for Dorset, South (Viscount Hinchingbrooke). I should hate to liken him in any way to an ancient monument, but there is no doubt that what pleases the people who visit his house is not only its beauty but the fact that he occasionally takes them round the house.[9]

In fact Grimond did not always have the easiest time with former owners occupying properties in the care of the Trust. The present Father of the House of Commons, Tam Dalyell MP, still believes that: 'Jo Grimond regarded the National Trust as a stepping stone to be used, and cared little or nothing about the Trust for its own sake.'[10] The Dalyells had handed over their ancestral home, the Binns, to the Trust in 1944 and, like most former owners who had stayed on as occupiers, they were always highly sensitive to even the slightest indication that their concerns were not being listened to, and rapidly acted upon, by the new owners. Dalyell senior found attempting to get in touch with Jo Grimond a trying business: 'the blighter is spending all his time in Orkney and Shetland wanting to be an MP rather than dealing with the problems of the Trust,' he complained.[11] This wasn't quite fair; in fact, Grimond could more justly be accused of doing too little, rather than too much, in the constituency that he had fought in 1945: when the Liberals of Orkney and Shetland wrote to Grimond in 1947 asking him to stand again, his response was non-committal, and the minute book of the Orkney Liberal Association records that, a little over a year later, by which time he was firmly ensconced at the Trust, he was still playing 'hard to get': when the Liberals of the islands resolved to press the issue with Grimond in March 1948, this time to a firm conclusion, they still had to wait patiently for a year before eliciting a definite response.

All the evidence suggests that, for a time at least, Jo Grimond really had lost interest in fighting Orkney and Shetland again. This is hardly surprising: after their disastrous result in 1945, the Liberals had found it virtually impossible to make any impact under the low-key leadership of Clement Davies. Their parliamentary strength had been further curtailed with the defections of two MPs, Gwilym Lloyd George and Tom Horabin, to the Tories and Labour respectively. In 1946 there had been an abortive attempt at forging a pact with progressive Conservatives, something that Davies himself had torpedoed at the eleventh hour. Sensing an historic opportunity, the Tories had responded by making a sustained pitch for the residual Liberal vote, which could still determine the outcome of an election. In May 1947 the Liberal Nationals and the Conservatives had effectively merged at last, with the Liberal Nationals in many areas retaining their Liberal label and, by the autumn of 1947, independent Liberals were regularly losing their deposits in by-elections. Clement Davies and his dwindling party can hardly have made an impressive pitch for a talented and charismatic young hopeful. The Scottish Liberal Party too put Grimond under considerable pressure, as George Mackie recalls: 'Jo was very doubtful about standing again at Orkney and Shetland and the boys in the Scottish Liberal Party at that time had a hell of a job in persuading him to stand again in 1950. He had a certain amount of fear about what would happen to the Liberal Party. He was reluctant. He needed pushing to stand again.'[12]

Although the national picture for the Liberal Party looked fairly dire, local Liberals in both Orkney and Shetland had assured Grimond that they were getting their respective acts together and, in November 1948, he returned to the islands to assess how things had progressed. The minutes of a meeting of the Orkney Young Liberals record the presence of 'Major J Grimond, Liberal candidate at the last election, and, we hope, the prospective candidate for the next election'.[13] Electrified by Grimond's presence, the Young Liberals deferred discussion of their forthcoming Christmas fair, and turned their attentions instead to an 'open discussion on wide and varying political topics'. Six days later they reconvened to discuss naming the doll, cake-weight guessing and numbered jam pots. Grimond left Orkney feeling greatly heartened. He felt that Liberal support was holding up better than expected, particularly in Shetland, and believed that the departure of many wartime labourers would now hit Labour badly. He did, however, doubt that he would get in, writing to Lady Violet that 'I have to make up my mind whether to be adopted or not. If I do intend to stand I ought to spend some time there next summer which probably means that I must give the Trust notice as I don't think I could take say 6 weeks off and in any case I doubt if I could remain Secretary and at the same time be an active politician.'[14]

On his way home, Grimond stopped off at Dalnawillan to see his old mentor and friend Sir Archibald Sinclair. He was anxious about two aspects of Liberal policy, and he took them up with Sinclair. First of all, he feared that the Liberals had not properly thought through their policy for profit-sharing. Parts of the economy were in something of a trough, and Grimond feared that, in some industries, profit-sharing might turn into ruinous loss-sharing. His second point was a more general one. He was troubled by the party's 'advocacy of large expenditure on every sort of thing from social services to Highland

Development while at the same time saying that we were living beyond our means'.[15] He found Sinclair 'far saner than I expected', as he answered the younger man's points 'in foxiest highland vein about taking any resolutions passed by a party conference with a large pinch of salt'.[16]

In late 1948 Grimond was still hesitating about whether or not to let his name go forward in the islands. Lady Violet's tales of woe about the state of the party centrally did little to encourage him, but he had enjoyed his trip to Orkney and still felt a certain moral obligation towards the Liberals there. It is clear that he was beginning to be swayed:

> After being a little encouraged by my visit to O&S I, quite irrationally – and perhaps because of talking to Archie – began to feel that the party could not be quite so foolish and ineffective as I feared it had become . . . I really feel that it is maddeness [sic] to stand but yet I would like to do so. The trouble is that one can't insulate even Orkney or Shetland . . . This façade of looking neither to right nor left, when one knows that all the well-known figures are in fact looking over each shoulder in turn is very dangerous . . . I rather think that in the end, against my better judgment and loathing the prospect of an election, I shall stand.[17]

Grimond spent Christmas 1948 with his mother, who was now bedridden, and then joined the rest of the family at Rowallan for New Year. He was still uncertain about how to proceed. He found his job at the National Trust very congenial, and enjoyed living in Prestonpans and working in Edinburgh. As he wrote to Lady Violet, though he was feeling less than enamoured of the Liberal Party, the other options still seemed even worse: 'Laura and I become more and more Blimpish . . . the only antidote to becoming a Tory is to spend a day or two in the company of Tories: that, luckily, is frequently our lot.'[18]

Problems between the Liberal Party and the Bonham Carter clan soon became personal. In mid February the Liberal *News Chronicle* welcomed the inauguration of Chaim Weizmann as the first President of Israel, and Lady Violet responded by sending a letter to the paper drawing attention to the plight of Palestinian refugees. She had not intended that it should be published, but the chairman of the *News Chronicle*, Walter Layton, had talked her into letting it appear 'in the public interest', publishing it in a special box. Her letter was immediately attacked by the Liberal chief whip, Frank Byers, in what looked like an official rebuke from the party: 'I deplore the substance and tone of Lady Violet Bonham Carter's letter, and so must every genuine Liberal in the country.'[19] She responded by writing to Clement Davies asking whether this was indeed a line authorised by the party. In the midst of this furore, while she was considering leaving the party once and for all, Grimond sent his mother-in-law a supportive letter:

> As you know I am passionately anti-Zionist. I always thought that they had the weaker case and their behaviour passes all bounds . . . [Byers] must be mad, as

your previous correspondence with him indeed indicates . . . if you do [quit the party] I wonder what Archie & Samuel will do? Even if Archie stays I don't think it will be worth going on unless he will come out and lead. We can't go on with Clem and Byers . . . The Orks and Shets look bleaker than ever!'.[20]

Matters came to a head at a rancorous meeting of the party executive on 8th March, during which Lady Violet discovered that the Byers letter had indeed been discussed by members of the committee before it was sent. In turned out too that the original draft had accused her of both anti-semitism and racial discrimination, charges that had been taken out, respectively, by Viscount Samuel and the editor of the *News Chronicle*. She demanded a 'public repudiation' of the Byers letter, reminding her colleagues of her long service for the Jewish cause and asking both Byers and Clement Davies how many Jewish refugees each of them had personally guaranteed. She was strongly supported by most members of the committee and, rather sheepishly, Viscount Samuel conceded that an apology should be made and a formal statement prepared – 'Byers looking hot red & speechless & Clem [Davies] inexpressibly foolish'.[21]

Early in 1949 a vice-president of the Scottish Liberal Party, Tony Stoddart, visited the islands, urging local Liberals at a meeting in Lerwick to set about forming an association. In conversation with some of his audience afterwards, he also mentioned in passing that, should Grimond decide not to fight the seat again, he might be persuaded to stand in his stead. One of those present was Basil Wishart, the redoubtable editor of the *Shetland Times*, who at once made it his business to go to Edinburgh for a summit with Grimond. Wishart later recounted the fateful meeting: 'I went to Edinburgh, was coldly received by Jo Grimond, but told him bluntly that he would have to show his face in the place if he intended to stand again.'[22] Grimond was also visited by Edwin Eunson, chairman of the Orkney Young Liberals, with a very similar message. When Eunson attended the special conference in 1988 that dealt with the merger of the Liberals and the SDP, he listened as speaker after speaker proclaimed that it was Grimond who had brought them into the Liberal Party and justifiably itched to stand up and tell the world that it was he who had brought Jo Grimond into the Liberal Party. The joint pleas of Wishart and Eunson had the desired effect, stirring Grimond into belated action. At the beginning of March 1949, he informed senior members of the National Trust executive that he now intended to move on, in order to pursue a political career, and the minutes of the Orkney Liberals for April 1949 record that 'Mr Joseph Grimond had accepted the invitations of the Orkney and Shetland Liberal Associations to become prospective candidate for the constituency and that he intended to come north in the summer months; this announcement being received with great enthusiasm.'[23]

Although he continued in office until the early summer, Grimond quickly became something of a lame duck. When his decision to relinquish the secretaryship was recorded for the first time, at the executive on 31st March 1949, surprisingly there is no mention in the minutes of any expression of regret at his departure. All that is recorded is Colonel Stevenson's robust sentiment that there was 'no question of despondency' and that the whole question of the secretaryship should be approached in a 'spirit of optimism'. Stevenson had devoted much of his life to the well-being of the Trust, and had mixed feelings about Grimond's sudden departure. Once again the post was not advertised. This time around, the Trust Council formally registered its unhappiness with such a procedure although, once reassurances had been given, it did grudgingly leave the matter in the hands of the executive. A successor was found quickly through the good offices of the Ministry of Labour: Jamie (later Sir Jamie) Stormonth Darling, a man who would subsequently devote his life to the Trust. He was installed so quickly and with so little ceremony that his formal acceptance of the position was actually written on Trust paper. He arrived in May 1949 and took over as secretary after Grimond left on 13th June. As Stormonth Darling settled in at his new desk on his first day, Jo Grimond came in and tossed on to his successor's desk a bundle of folders tied up in pinkish string. These, he informed the bemused newcomer, were the legal papers that he would soon need when the National Trust for Scotland had to be wound up. Fortunately those fears were misplaced.

The minutes of the first meeting of the council after Grimond had announced his intention to move on – recorded by Grimond himself – are also terse to the point of chilly on the question of the secretaryship. They merely record that 'the Secretary had tendered his resignation . . . This had been accepted by the Executive.'[24] It was only at Jamie Stormonth Darling's first executive meeting as secretary, after Grimond's departure, that an appreciation of sorts was at last recorded with regard to the outgoing secretary of the Trust:

> The Chairman proposed that an expression of their deep gratitude and an appreciation of all the invaluable and most thorough work which Mr J. Grimond had done during his time as Secretary should be recorded in these Minutes . . . It was the wish of the Executive that Mr J. Grimond should be formally thanked by the Chairman and informed of their very sincere feelings expressed at this Meeting.[25]

The stilted English tends to intensify, rather than dilute, the sense that Grimond's rapid departure was not totally appreciated at the time. However, the retrospective encomium to Grimond in the Trust's annual report for 1948–9 suggests that his former colleagues had now come to terms with losing him: 'In his all too brief tenure of office Mr Grimond's work has covered a wide field, and his attention has penetrated so deeply into many matters of importance, that he has left a mark on the Trust quite out of proportion to the time spent as its Secretary . . . The Trust must deeply regret that Mr Grimond has felt it necessary to take his talents elsewhere.'

Although he left when the Trust was still in a gravely weakened state and, by most accounts, could have been rather more emotionally engaged in its affairs, Jo Grimond had clearly left at least some powerful friends behind at the National Trust for Scotland. After all, despite Grimond's own pessimism about its prospects, the Trust had not actually gone under. A powerful defence of his tenure as secretary subsequently came from his acquaintance from St Andrews, Ronald Cant, who wrote to him in July 1979 as he was putting the final touches to *Memoirs*: 'I hope that you will give due justice to your period as Secretary of the National Trust for Scotland which, for all that has happened since, still seems to many people the point at which the Trust broke through to a true measure of national significance.'[26] In his *Memoirs*, Grimond disregards this advice by dismissing his time at the Trust in approximately four lines. The house at Prestonpans gets a little more, as does the ghost seen there by Johnny. Although his stint at the National Trust for Scotland was certainly not the most fulfilling time of Grimond's life, he did enjoy himself there and remained on excellent terms with most of his former colleagues. Grimond remained for a time on the Council of the Trust and occasionally raised matters on its behalf in the House of Commons, giving the Scottish Trust an independent voice at Westminster during its chrysalis days in the early 1950s, when all too few people in government knew of its separate existence. Yet it is still more or less impossible to regard this period of Grimond's life, in retrospect at least, as anything other than a convenient and necessary interlude, a staging post en route to Westminster, via the Highlands and Islands of Scotland.

Once he had resolved to leave the National Trust for Scotland, Grimond was in a position to inform the Orkney Liberals that he would, after all, allow his name to go forward once again. He now staked everything on a really serious attempt at winning Orkney and Shetland. He took a career break, retained occupancy of the house at Prestonpans, and followed Basil Wishart's advice by engaging in some serious campaigning up in the islands, which he had almost totally neglected since the 1945 poll. He undertook a 'summer tour' of both Orkney and Shetland, making a series of speeches, which his loyal supporting newspapers were delighted to report. He generally adopted an orthodox, liberal-radical line, claiming that he and the Liberals understood, and could help to reverse, the 'lack of enthusiasm in the country, and pessimism about the future . . . I believe that is partly because people no longer feel responsible for their own destinies . . . Their lives are subject to controls which seem arbitrary and exasperating.'[27] He called for lower taxation, more competition and an end to doctrinaire nationalisation, and demanded that more be spent on improving transport links to, from and between the islands. He was also not above making the occasional populist appeal to the islanders' self-interest and sense of isolation, demanding that government should at least 'spend a comparatively small sum on cheapening transport to Orkney and Shetland rather than a far bigger sum on problematical groundnuts in Africa'.[28] He acknowledged too that aspirations in Orkney and Shetland for greater autonomy were unlikely to be satisfied merely by the setting up of a new body based in Edinburgh:

> The Liberal party is in favour of greater control in Scotland of Scottish affairs . . . down to county and town councils, so that people will again feel that they are taking a more direct part in their government . . . We do not want severance from England; we want more power in Scotland . . . we have many problems which exist only in Scotland which are vital to us, but which must seem very small and remote in London where they will never get attention.[29]

In the autumn, Grimond was back in the islands. This time he had company, in the shape of his mentor and friend Sir Archibald Sinclair. Sinclair had decided to contest his old seat at Caithness again, and he had strongly encouraged Grimond to do the same in Orkney and Shetland. Grimond and Sinclair spent two days together on the islands, jointly addressing meetings in Orkney one day and Shetland the next. According to the *Orkney Herald*, Sinclair was accorded 'tumultuous receptions by packed halls'.[30] The effect on Liberal morale of having the party's charismatic, even heroic, former leader visit was electrifying. He treated his audiences to lengthy and detailed expositions not only of Liberal policy, but also of the shortcomings of the Labour government. Most of the achievements that it claimed for itself, he pointed out, were the results of policies initiated by the wartime administration, often stimulated by Liberals. He also reiterated the party's commitment to a Scottish Parliament. After Sinclair had left the islands, Grimond continued on a two-week tour of his own, hopping from community to community and island to island, speaking to farmers' groups, in town halls and in village halls. He followed Archibald Sinclair in repeatedly pointing out how much influence Liberals – in an unbroken line through Asquith, Lloyd George, Keynes, Beveridge and Sinclair himself – had enjoyed over the major policy reforms of the first half of the century. The warm response to this message buoyed him and appeared to confirm that the radical tradition was alive and well in Orkney and Shetland. Orkney in particular struck him as fertile Liberal territory:

> Orkney seemed to him to be the sort of community Liberals wanted to see . . . No one was very rich but few were very poor . . . Orcadians had made their county by their own efforts – largely because many of them owned their own land or houses, and most of them felt that by their own efforts and their own hard work they could lead a decent life and improve the lot of themselves and their families . . . That was a Liberal attitude.[31]

As he concluded his speaking tour, Grimond began to concentrate his fire on the Conservatives, warning that they offered no forward-looking policies of their own: 'they always relied on an appeal to men to vote against something.'[32] Although Grimond, no doubt mindful of the ever vigilant Lady Violet scrutinising his utterances, never attacked her old friend Winston Churchill personally, he was coruscating about the party he led, observing that 'the same men who would have nothing to do with Mr Churchill in the days when his leadership might have saved us from war, now attempt to hide behind him from the spectre of their own past'.[33] One of the local Conservatives still did him a good turn, however, albeit unwittingly. Grimond was in a Kirkwall hotel during this tour and needed someone to witness a legal document that he had drawn up. He asked the only other person in the room, who duly signed the document. The signature was that of Mr D Kneale, the recently appointed Unionist organiser for the islands. 'I hope I haven't signed away the constituency,' he joked wryly. Although Grimond had come close to not fighting the 1950 election at all, this period of intensive campaigning must have convinced him that there was a real chance of victory in Orkney and Shetland. He must also have been greatly cheered by Archibald Sinclair's very evident determination to stage a serious comeback.

During the course of his campaigning, Grimond would pledge to become a full-time MP, and to buy a family home in the islands if elected. For the time being, he stayed either in hotels or in the homes of friends and supporters. Laura and the three children continued to be based at Prestonpans, joining him for some of his stints in the islands. Andrew was now boarding at a school that he detested, while his younger brother Johnny ('Toad') had developed what his father described as 'the most alarming psychic powers',[34] regularly seeing the ghost of a woman in the Dower House and, on occasions, even scaring his parents with the intensity of his accounts. Grimond always felt most at home north of the border, and the thought of using his expertise at the English law to provide a fall-back career had faded almost entirely with the passing of the years. By the end of 1949, his interest in publishing and the close friendship between the Grimond and the Collins families had produced an offer of employment with the Glasgow publisher. In preparation for this, Grimond spent a few weeks at a printing works in the town. He found that so stultifyingly dull that it hardened his resolve to campaign all-out at the general election – and win. As the election approached the Grimonds borrowed a cottage close to the Loch of Harray, about twelve miles from Kirkwall on the mainland of Orkney, from Elspeth Cormack, sister of Eric Linklater. It served until they found a property of their own. The cottage was snug and convenient, and Grimond even took the opportunity to catch some fish in the loch. In the campaign itself, Grimond generally relied upon his own resources, oratory and charm; the Liberal Party had precious few national figures, and the islands were a long way from home for almost all of them. Grimond therefore had to make a substantial political impact for himself. He put out publications such as *Liberal Orkney,* an unusually cogent and challenging personal manifesto, in which he set out a range of Liberal policies, alongside messages of support from Archibald Sinclair and Clement Davies. There is a clear exposition of the policy on home rule for Scotland: 'to form a separate Scottish Parliament to sit in Edinburgh . . . [while] Scotland will continue to be represented at Westminster with a full say in matters affecting the whole country'.[35] At his large meeting in Kirkwall at the beginning of the campaign, according to a report: 'it was interesting to note that the heartiest rounds of applause came for his backing of the policy of home rule for Scotland and his outlining of the Liberal plan for the development of the Highlands and Islands.'[36]

Even the best friends of Cecil Walls, Grimond's Orkney agent in 1945, could not have claimed that he was a brilliant campaigner and, for the 1950 campaign, Grimond's supporters secured for him the services of a new election agent, a solicitor from Stromness by the name of Jackie Robertson, who had never met him. Basil Wishart took over as the Shetland sub-agent. Robertson later reminisced: 'I accepted the job as a challenge . . . a few days later a tall, handsome figure called at my office, stooping slightly as he entered my room door, and modestly announced, "I'm Grimond."'[37] This happy association lasted for over forty years, the only problem being Robertson's seasickness, which emerged during the 1950 campaign. As Grimond once told Michael Meadowcroft, no doubt with a measure of hyperbole: 'mine is not an appropriate constituency for anyone suffering from such a malady – I spent an entire election campaign holding his head over the side of boats and arranging hotels for him on the islands.'[38] A meeting at St Margaret's Hope on South Ronaldsay presented a different challenge. South Ronaldsay is linked to the Orkney mainland by the Churchill Barriers, built (largely by Italian POWs) during the Second World War to protect the British fleet from incursions by U-boats, in the wake of the sinking of the *Royal Oak* in Scapa Flow. The meeting ended late, and Grimond and Robertson headed for home at around midnight. The roads atop the Barriers are narrow and, in those days, there were no fences or other protection on either side of them. That night a terrific gale was blowing up, sending heavy spray across the Barriers and enveloping any vehicle whose driver was bold enough to risk the journey. Grimond thought this was tremendous fun, but Robertson (who was driving) was terrified that the engine would flood and the car would stop, to be swept away by the elements. He kept the engine running fast in low gear and, fortunately, they made it across. One of Grimond's earliest supporters, who had recommended that he should find a new agent, asked him after a time how he was getting on with Robertson. 'He's no more efficient than Cecil [Walls],' he responded, 'but he's less apologetic!'[39] Grimond was ony joking: he was as devoted to Robertson as Robertson was to him.

The one big name to venture north in his support was the formidable figure of his mother-in-law, Violet Bonham Carter, who stayed with the Sinclairs en route, also speaking in support of Sir Archie. Lady Violet spent ten days in the islands and, when she took the stage alongside Laura in Kirkwall on Saturday, 18th February, less than a week before polling day, despite suffering from a cold she was in punchy form. She denounced socialists for having the wrong answers to the nation's problems and dismissed the Conservatives because they had none at all. She made a personal appeal to the voters to vote not only for Liberalism, but also for Grimond the man, whom she described with almost embarrassing warmth:

> I am the mother-in-law of the Liberal candidate, and it is universally recognised that mothers-in-law are the worst kind of relation, interfering, cantankerous and altogether unnecessary – and so I feel rather proud that my son-in-law has asked me to come here and lend a hand. I notice that since my arrival he has always been on a different island from myself – but as he is not here, I would like to say a word or two about him. You can take it from me that it will be very unbiased, because mothers-in-law are apt to be critical . . . He is a nice young man, and rather a nice looking young man, but that of course is a matter of taste . . . he is a very able young man, and if you send him back he will leave no stone unturned, and no effort unmade, to serve your best interests in Parliament . . . He is a man of principle and integrity . . . If he had been out to get a seat by hook or by crook, he might easily have scrambled on the Labour or Conservative bandwagon, but Liberalism is with him in faith, a faith of fairness and freedom, a faith that puts human needs, human rights, first before all else.'[40]

At the end of one of Lady Violet's eve-of-poll speeches in Orkney, at the old Dounby School close to the Grimonds' borrowed cottage, the chairman of the meeting, a well-known farmer, became the latest person to be swept away by her outspokenness. He stood up at the end to give the vote of thanks and proclaimed, 'Surely this must be a good man when even his mother-in-law is speaking for him.'[41]

The weather during the late-winter campaign was dreadful, so both Grimond and his rivals for the seat spent a lot of time enduring rough seas as they travelled from island to island. Basil Neven Spence once lost an entire day to the weather, when the boat he was on had to heave-to behind an island for shelter. On one of Grimond's trips he and his crew had a hungry killer whale for company. In total, Grimond addressed over a hundred meetings, some attended by only a handful of people, and some held impromptu at the end of a pier during the short stopover of a boat. After a few milder days, the weather in the islands on polling day itself was bitterly cold. In Shetland it snowed, which filled the Liberals with foreboding, as the polling stations were so far between, especially amongst the outer islands. They need not have worried. The people of the islands had decided to 'Go for Jo'. One illiterate voter who had heard Grimond at a public meeting even turned up to vote with a picture of him, demanding, 'That's the man I want to vote for!' Grimond owed an immense debt to his band of devoted supporters. First and foremost was Laura, throughout her life an indefatigable campaigner and, in that first campaign, an absolute mainstay. In Orkney the foundations of success were built over the years by the likes of his new agent Jackie Robertson and Edwin Eunson, by 1950 very much Grimond's right-hand man and in later years convenor of the Orkney Islands Council. The Eunson family home had already become one of Grimond's main election bases, filled with election addresses, envelopes, letters and posters. Edwin's mother Mrs Eunson, the matriarch of the family, provided hospitality in the form of infinite quantities of excellent tea, the brew that has sustained so many campaigners across the generations. Further support came from Grimond's supporters in the local press, which was blatantly, indeed shockingly, partisan even by today's standards. There were four local papers: two were unashamedly Tory, two were Liberal. Basil Wishart of the *Shetland Times* would in time co-author with Grimond much of the Liberal campaigning literature. Grimond had cause also to be grateful to the Twatt family, owner-editors of the *Orkney Herald*. As an endnote, Grimond mentioned in his *Memoirs* that he once met one of the sons of that ilk, working in England for Marconi, but with his surname changed to Watt. Grimond asked why. The answer was self-protection: 'He said that people in the south couldn't believe his name was Twatt so he had obliged them by dropping the "T".'[42]

When the poll was declared on Monday, 27th February 1950, Grimond was in by almost 3,000 votes. In Grimond's own words, his predecessor, Sir Basil Neven Spence, had been 'rejected for no better reason than the electors thought he had been in Parliament long enough'.[43] It was not quite that simple. Grimond and his team had learned the lessons of their near miss in 1945, and fought an aggressive and effective campaign. They had convinced the voters that a Liberal vote was anything but a 'wasted' vote, and they had vigorously reasserted a radical tradition that is never far below the surface in the islands. Jo Grimond's success provided a late, and precious, shaft of light for the Liberals – one of only three gains they made at the election. By the time news of Grimond's win came through, his party had lost three of the nine remaining seats from 1945 that it defended. Archibald Sinclair had lost again in Caithness, so Clement Davies was reaffirmed as leader of the parliamentary party and, when he arrived at the House of Commons, Jo Grimond had never before met any of his colleagues. The party's chief whip, Frank Byers, had been narrowly defeated in his Dorset constituency and, within only a few days, Davies asked Grimond to take over as whip. Even though Grimond's flock consisted of only eight other colleagues, it was to prove quite a challenge.

5

B ETWEEN 1950 AND 1955 Jo Grimond began to demonstrate that he intended
to realise the potential that others had perceived in him from his earliest
years, taking full advantage of the opportunities available to a member of
a small, loosely organised parliamentary grouping. He also developed his
liberalism in various important ways. In the early 1950s the very existence of a
Liberal Party was open to question. It could be argued that it no longer served
any useful purpose, and the party was steadily losing members, including
some of its highly limited supply of public figures. Grimond was amongst the
first to recognise that, if the party was to earn any kind of political revival,
it must first generate its own intellectual renaissance. He was helped by the
ideological lethargy within the Conservative Party and, no doubt, by the
pretty illiberal and unattractive methods used by the Gaitskellites against
Nye Bevan and his followers. Genuine liberalism was indeed in short supply
in those years, but Grimond reasoned that this was a vacuum that nature
must abhor. In speeches and articles, and within the inner counsels of his
weakened party, Grimond made the case for a reformulation of liberalism
based upon the time-honoured tenets of individual freedom and responsibility,
community action and shared values. In all of this, the people of Orkney
and Shetland were indispensable not only because they rewarded Grimond
with a parliamentary base: they also provided, with their down-to-earth,
communitarian outlook, a genuine inspiration to their young Member of
Parliament. Grimond assiduously cultivated his constituents and quickly
fulfilled his promise to live among them. They responded not only with
support at the ballot box, but also with the beginnings of a reciprocal affection
that would go on to sustain one of the more remarkable political marriages of
the century.

Small as it was, the Liberals' parliamentary party represented more or
less the full spectrum of liberalism. Some of the MPs appeared to have
virtually nothing in common politically with their colleagues, notably Megan
Lloyd George and Rhys Hopkin Morris. Hopkin Morris was a staunch and
courageous advocate of the most classical, traditional form of liberalism, a man
who had voted against Lloyd George becoming party leader. He was sceptical

about the benefits of virtually every aspect of state activity and, even within his own constituency of Carmarthen, would refuse to play to the gallery, telling miners that uneconomic pits must close, and farmers that 'guaranteed prices' were just stuff and nonsense. In contrast, Megan Lloyd George was 'already so much in love with Labour' and its post-war settlement, to which she was increasingly prone to offer the posthumous advocacy of her father.[1] She was almost totally out of place. Most of the left-wing Liberals had already left the party, and her reasons for not following suit were largely sentimental. She was in favour of virtually everything that the Attlee government had done, and deeply opposed to cooperation in opposition with the Tories.

Of the two, it was Hopkin Morris whom Grimond found more congenial, and who had by far the greater influence on him. He invariably presented his case in a clear and rational manner, argued from first principles and painstakingly presented. Grimond admired him for the way in which he epitomised the traditional Liberal 'admiration for integrity and a dislike of ostentation, material ambition and blowsiness'.[2] In his endeavours to become an effective party whip, Grimond had not only to contend with his own naturally lazy inclinations and the constant disagreements that broke out amongst his colleagues. He also found Clement Davies, though amiable and decent to the core, to be lacking in essential leadership skills. In his determination to hold his mixed bag of parliamentary colleagues together, Davies tried to hard to achieve the impossible: to please each and every one of them on as many issues as possible. On one symbolic occasion he left a meeting of Liberal MPs apparently convinced that conscription should be abolished, after a fine libertarian exposition from Hopkin Morris. He then bumped into Violet Bonham Carter (who took the opposite view) on his way to the Liberal Party Committee. By the time he addressed the committee, he had performed a complete U-turn under pressure from Lady Violet.

Grimond made his maiden speech on the morning of 10th March 1950, in the wake of a speech by Bob Boothby, who had used his own oration to attack the Liberal Party's proposals for Scottish self-government. Grimond gave the conventional *tour d'horizon* of his constituency, confessing that since the war the islands had 'on the whole enjoyed a fair measure of prosperity' but warning 'lately, there have been very serious clouds over the future of Shetland'.[3] He went on to launch a counter-attack on Boothby, setting out in general and impressionistic terms his own vision for devolution. The consistency between this speech and Liberal Democrat policy up to the present day is most striking:

> We do not in the least want to break away from England . . . Of course, if the question is approached in a spirit of enmity it will be a failure . . . I do feel that we should have more control over our own affairs so that we shall not again have our problems pushed aside . . . and I see no reason why this proposed

solution should not lead to greater friendship in Europe . . . It may be that some form of federal government is the ultimate solution for all Europe . . . One of the most important things today is that government should be in close touch with the people.[4]

As an early advocate of British participation in European integration, Grimond most unusually acted as a 'teller' (counter of votes) alongside a Tory whip in crucial votes on Europe in June 1950, after a debate in which Churchill had declared that, in contrast with the socialists, 'the Conservative and Liberal parties declare that national sovereignty is not inviolable'.[5] The Attlee government, which wanted no part of the Schuman process, defeated the Conservative motion by a majority of twenty. Four of Grimond's eight colleagues supported the motion, and none opposed it.

Winston Churchill's close friendship with Grimond's mother-in-law Violet Bonham Carter brought him into regular contact with the new Liberal whip. Ever conscious that Churchill felt himself bound by sentiment to his old party, Lady Violet was constantly nagging Churchill to do something about the electoral system, to give the Liberals a fairer deal. Just as the Liberals' deputy leader, Megan Lloyd George, increasingly believed that the Liberals should be part of a radical coalition with Labour, Lady Violet wanted to help Churchill find a way of building an anti-socialist alliance, including Conservatives, Liberals and National Liberals, to keep Labour out of power. One can only feel sympathy for the young Emlyn Hooson, who used to occupy the single seat between these two formidable ladies at meetings of the Liberal Party Committee. In 1947 the Woolton-Teviot Agreement had consolidated the assimilation of the National Liberals into the Conservative Party, and many of the merged Conservative Associations took the opportunity to describe themselves as 'Conservative and Liberal' and, in many instances, particularly in 1951, there was no Liberal to challenge their claim to the label. In the run-up to the 1950 general election, Churchill had written to Clement Davies urging him to enter into some kind of anti-socialist electoral pact. Over lunch on 18th April 1950, Churchill informed Grimond and Lady Violet in confidence that he had charged Rab Butler with preparing plans for collaboration with the Liberals precisely along these lines. The Conservative Party, he informed them, would not at this stage swallow electoral reform, but most of its more thoughtful members would understand the advantages of sustaining a non-socialist third party as an extra bulwark against Labour. Butler was himself present at another lunch later that month, held at Chartwell, at which these thoughts were developed further. Churchill ordered that the party's enquiry into electoral reform should be made public as soon as possible. Rab Butler concurred, but warned both Grimond and Lady Violet on their way home that they should not overestimate Churchill's influence within the party he led. Churchill had recently put the case for looking at the electoral system to a meeting of the Conservative 1922 Committee, and the committee's members had given him a hard time. Although Butler didn't believe that Churchill would ever be in a position to deliver, Lady Violet and her allies never gave up.

Less than three months into the new Parliament, one newspaper reported that the fragile, contradiction-ridden coalition that was the parliamentary Liberal Party had voted in unison only four times in the twelve main divisions since the election.[6] One of the biggest controversies dividing the Liberals at this time had begun in 1950 with the election of Donald Wade as Liberal MP for Huddersfield West. In the run-up to the election, Wade had promised that he would not support a Labour government in a confidence vote. In return, the Conservatives had agreed not to put up a candidate against him, whilst in Huddersfield East, the Liberals would give the Tories a free run. Although several other Liberal MPs, including Clement Davies himself, were not opposed by Conservative candidates, they made no formal undertakings. Many Liberals feared, with some justification, that the Tories planned not to sustain the Liberal Party, but to turn it into a political stooge. Three of Grimond's parliamentary colleagues were particularly troublesome for their inexperienced chief whip. As well as Lady Megan Lloyd George, nominally the Liberals' deputy leader, two other colleagues, Emrys Roberts and Edgar Granville, were increasingly inclined towards the Labour Party.

On 19th September 1950 Grimond surprised even himself by successfully cajoling all three of his wandering sheep into the opposition lobbies in support of a motion moved by Churchill himself, criticising Labour's policies towards the steel industry. Grimond must have been helped in his task by the behaviour of the principal Conservative and Labour speakers in the debate: Herbert Morrison attacked the Liberals vitriolically, prompting a robust and instant response from Clement Davies, while Churchill went out of his way to woo his old party. The government won the division by 306 votes to 300. Matters did come to a nasty head only a couple of months later, however, when Lady Megan and her two allies finally broke ranks, voting against a Conservative housing amendment on the King's Speech while their colleagues supported it. The official story given to the media was that the party had originally intended to abstain. Then, supposedly, Grimond had heard that this trio had voted with the government. He had therefore felt obliged to cancel them out, he claimed, which he did by rounding up the rest of his flock and marching them into the opposition lobby. In any case, argued Grimond, such disagreement as there was related not to important matters of principle, but to mere parliamentary tactics. This attempted explanation never rang true and, the following day, although Megan Lloyd George had signed the Liberal amendment on the cost of living, she and the same two colleagues failed to support it in the relevant division. Later that day, they abstained again, this time on a further Conservative amendment.

The three rebel MPs effectively became a left-wing pressure group within the party, proudly styling themselves as 'Radical Liberals'. When they attempted to explain away their behaviour in a joint statement the following week, the implicit criticism of Davies and Grimond was unmistakable. The problem, they claimed, was that the Conservative Party was manipulating the parliamentary situation, 'forcing a series of divisions purely for the sake of opposition, thereby artificially keeping in being a state of political crisis'.[7] Although they agreed in principle with the Liberal amendment on the cost of living, they felt that it was inappropriate to vote against the government on it 'in the atmosphere of a vote of confidence'.[8] They indicated that they had no intention of coming back into line at anyone's behest, and Grimond baulked at bringing undue pressure to bear on his insubordinate colleagues. It is interesting to compare their arguments about the 1950–51 Parliament with Grimond's own tactics in the 1964–6 Parliament, in which the parliamentary arithmetic was similar: he had evidently come to share their distaste for the 'harrying' so beloved of the Tories.

Throughout the autumn of 1950 tentative negotiations between the Liberals and the Tories on a range of topics continued, after Davies and Churchill resumed contact and Churchill put Davies directly into contact with the Conservative Party chairman, Lord Woolton. Grimond was keen that his own presence at the meetings between Churchill and Lady Violet should be kept secret, lest Davies think that he was plotting behind his back. He was worried too that Davies might lack the necessary resolve in any formal negotiations that might emerge: 'There are the usual unknowns which centre round Clem,' he informed Lady Violet. 'Attlee has shown a slight tendency to pat him in the head. This of course is nectar to him.'[9] He feared that, while Churchill might attempt to establish a formal pact with the Liberal leaders, Attlee might appeal directly to party members and supporters, over their heads. Grimond informed Lady Violet that Davies was now planning to use his forthcoming speech to the Liberal assembly to call upon Labour to drop socialism, so that a broad-front radical Lib-Lab set-up could be established: 'he expects to draw a derisive reply from the Socialists. Winston can then weigh in with a conciliatory anti-Socialist speech & local arrangements can follow . . . Winston says apparently that he is getting his way with the Tories, and hopes for 30 Liberal members & some sort of electoral reform in the Tory programme.'[10]

Jo Grimond himself was very unsure about which way the party should jump. On the one hand, the party was short of money, workers and support: 'therefore if we want a Parliamentary party we have got to swallow some unpalatable medicine'.[11] On the other hand, Churchill was now proposing to visit certain seats to persuade their local Conservative Associations to stand down in favour of a Liberal, all of which could give the impression that the Liberals had given up their independence. Grimond was worried too that Davies had committed a potentially fatal error in the negotiations with Churchill, having admitted that, in most circumstances, the presence of a Liberal candidate took more votes from Labour than it did from the Conservatives. Meanwhile, in conditions of the utmost secrecy, just as Lady Violet Bonham Carter was meeting with Churchill to discuss an anti-socialist alliance, Lady Megan was discussing with Herbert Morrison how the Liberals could prevent the Conservatives from regaining power. In the face of what seemed to be incipient collapse, Clement Davies understandably considered resigning as leader. He didn't quit and, in name at least, Lady Megan stayed on as his deputy. Whenever the party intended to do something in a parliamentary division that seemed to her unconscionable, she just went quietly home before the division bell rang. The Liberals also had problems in the House of Lords. A number of Liberal peers, sensing that the total disintegration of their party might be on the cards, began to drift towards the Tory Party. At Grimond's insistence, the former party leader Lord Samuel took charge of stemming this trickle before it became a tide; this he did with considerable success.

Westminster was by no means Jo Grimond's only concern in those early years. He had first of all to find the home for himself and his family that he had undertaken to buy if elected. Knowing that another election could not be far off, local Liberals were delighted to learn that the Grimonds had acquired the Old Manse of Firth, in Orkney, for a little over £3,000. Orkney Tories were rather less impressed than their Liberal counterparts. 'What's he doing?' one of them asked. 'He must think he's got a permanent job here!' The Grimonds brought with them from Prestonpans their devoted housekeeper Miss Ray Russell, whose good-natured support proved invaluable during an inevitably unsettling period. She was also a fierce and effective gardener. The garden would in due course become Grimond's pride and joy, and his sanctuary. Today it stands still, a living memorial to him. Even when he was in his suit, ready to 'go south', as the Orcadians put it, he would snatch a last few moments in the garden, either in the main, decorative area closest to the house, or in the secluded 'secret garden', where he grew fruit and vegetables. He planted trees himself, rarities in Orkney, and they too survive. Grimond was always loath to prune or cut back any of his beloved plants; but as soon as he was away, Laura, ever practical, would set about them with pruning shears.

The house itself has tremendous character, overlooking Orkney's dramatic Wide Firth and quietly commanding the local landscape. Since it is perched on a spur of high ground, the wind blows through it without mercy. It has a marvellous maze of rooms, and must be one of the few double-glazed homes in the United Kingdom where the curtains still flap violently when the wind is up. The Liberal Democrat MP Archy Kirkwood, by any measure a well-travelled man, recalls that, 'I was there overnight once, and I've never spent a colder night in my life.'[12] Yet it suited the Grimond family perfectly, and became virtually an open house for friends and neighbours. The Bonham Carters' doll's house was installed in the attic, and the birthday parties of the Grimond children were legendary, with even Jo obligingly concealing his huge frame in games of hide-and-seek. Adults were welcome too, with guests over the years including such illustrious figures as Lord Reith of the BBC and the Poet Laureate, Sir John Betjeman. Until they became too old for wholly sleepless nights, Jo and Laura Grimond would host Hogmanay parties at the Old Manse, which were supplanted in due course by drinks at 11 a.m. on New Year's Day itself. Guests from those parties recall how they would hear Jo's voice gradually, but unmistakably, rising in volume and cutting through the general hubbub until everyone shut up to listen to what he had to say.

The considerable publicity about the purchase of the Old Manse dovetailed with a period of intense hard work. At no stage of his career did Jo Grimond take for granted the votes of his constituents. When he was away at Westminster, Laura carried much of the responsibility, acquiring a number of honorary positions and busily going about opening events, dedicating lifeboats and generally convincing the locals that the Grimonds deserved to become a real local fixture. As was her nature, she was always embarking on some worthwhile project, usually of a charitable or an archaeological nature. As the couple laboured away at winning over the islanders, Jo in particular had to learn not to flinch when they were at their most outspoken. At one early election meeting, at Finstown School just across from the Old Manse, Ned Sinclair, a friend of the Grimonds, let slip casually in conversation that, in his view, 'a vote for the Tories is a vote against Jesus Christ'. Grimond just smiled beatifically in response, knowing that such sentiments could be neither endorsed nor dismissed, at least without causing offence. Once the family had settled in Orkney, Jo Grimond established his practice of travelling up from London every second week or so, and on to Shetland every four or five weeks. He usually travelled by the overnight sleeper to Aberdeen, and flew on from there. When he went to the parliamentary Fees Office to make the necessary arrangements for these regular trips to be paid for, he was handed the requisite sheet of paper to fill in. When it came to naming the nearest railway station, he put down Bergen. In the case of Shetland at least, this was quite true. In later years, Grimond tried to talk the Fees Office into letting him make his journeys between London and his constituency by plane via Copenhagen, mainly as his way of making a protest against the poor direct services from the UK mainland. They didn't take too kindly to that either.

As chief whip, Grimond carved out a niche for himself independently of his role as one of the 'usual channels' of communication between parties. He was elected as one of three members on a tri-partisan committee established to urge on the government the claims for compensation of those who had been prisoners-of-war of the Japanese. Like many of Grimond's campaigns, this one too came to fruition only after his death. In June 1950 Grimond co-signed a letter to *The Times,* with Richard Crossman and Woodrow Wyatt, requesting the government to clarify its intentions with regard to Formosa (Taiwan), where the former Nationalist government of China was defiantly parading its political independence from the mainland. The co-signatories feared that the US might get dragged into conflict with both Communist China and the USSR if it maintained its hawkish stance on Formosa, and that Britain might find itself reluctantly dragged in behind. At the time of writing, this tension has still not totally evaporated. In January 1951 Grimond also joined the Liberal Party Committee as an ex-officio member.

Even when Grimond was at Westminster, however, his efforts were targeted largely towards helping his chances of getting re-elected in Orkney and Shetland. The speeches he made in the House of Commons in 1950–51 were predominantly on subjects of particular interest to the people of the islands. He also played an active role in the Scottish Committee of the Commons. It was only in later years that he developed his habit of wandering in to the committee's meetings, speaking, then apologising for the fact that he had to leave and going out again. While he was learning the ropes, Grimond was rather more assiduous. In early 1951, well before the general election of that year, he also served on the parliamentary standing committee examining the Labour government's Sea Fish Industry Bill. He provided something of a lone voice in support of inshore fishermen, and those of Shetland in particular. The Bill was rather biased towards the trawlermen, and even to whaling. It also, in Grimond's view, failed to acknowledge the inevitable international dimension of fishing and the need to prevent over-fishing of Britain's territorial waters by foreign vessels. With support from backbenchers of both other parties, Grimond successfully moved an amendment, requiring the government's new White Fish Authority to take at least some responsibility for either equalising or reducing freight charges. This question, he warned, 'is a matter of the utmost importance, not only to the fishing industry in my constituency, but to the whole question of whether life and work shall go on there'.[13] Orkney and Shetland were well served.

When Grimond did come to defend his seat for the first time, at the general election of October 1951, the Liberal Party was in a far more parlous state, financially and organisationally, even than it had been at the previous election only twenty months earlier. It managed to put up only 109 candidates, against 475 in 1950. One of those candidates was Lady Violet Bonham Carter, standing in Colne Valley with Conservative support. Churchill even spoke there in her support. The general decline in Liberal ambitions was reflected in the party manifesto, which could not even make any pretence that a Liberal government might be elected. It concentrated instead on making the case for the party's very existence. This general decline was in many ways the making of Jo Grimond. He had always recognised that, even in Orkney and Shetland, the Liberals' poor standing nationally might jeopardise his chances of re-election and drafted his election literature accordingly. A new edition of *Liberal Orkney* was distributed, whose anonymous author vouchsafed that: 'the Liberal Party by its very existence, and irrespective of its success or failure at the polls, exercises a salutary influence on the action of other parties.'[14] Given the need to be so defensive about the party, it is hardly surprising that Grimond's pitch for re-election concentrated upon local issues, and upon his own personality and achievements. To judge by this material, Jo Grimond might almost have been an independent candidate. He was a 'free representative', the voters were assured, 'who hates wrangling and all the meaner forms of debate . . . his interest lies in making a wider, happier, nobler life for all through the instrument of democratic action.'[15]

Meanwhile, less than two years into his parliamentary career, Grimond's party was already promoting him as a national figure. Despite their obvious decline, the Liberals were allowed to retain the same broadcasting entitlements during the course of the campaign as in 1950: two ten-minute radio slots and one of twenty minutes at the end of the campaign. Almost one in four of the adult population heard Jo Grimond make the second of those broadcasts, at 6.15 p.m. on 12th October 1951. He was no doubt buoyed by a tribute to him featured in that morning's edition of the *Daily Despatch*, which described him as a 'man of great personal charm and good humour', who 'should get back' in the election. In the first of the Liberal broadcasts, three days earlier, Dingle Foot had portrayed the Liberals as a moderate party, seeking to further the interests of the ordinary consumer. In contrast, Grimond's broadcast included a shameless pitch for the Celtic fringe, with a great emphasis on how difficult it was for further-flung constituencies to get any sense out of the man in Whitehall. He also used this opportunity for a flash of free-marketry, advocating lower taxes and improved incentives for industry to invest and produce, together with a radical extension of employee share ownership. He sought to emphasise the priority that Liberals gave to foreign policy questions. Although such matters might seem remote to many voters, he said, they were of the utmost importance to the well-being of the nation, which had to ensure that it was 'too strong to be worth attacking'. Britain also had to exploit to the full its unique position in the world, building up peace and friendship, initially among the western nations, and subsequently spreading that gospel of coexistence more widely. Every policy, every sentiment would be repeated by Grimond countless times throughout his long life, forming the basis of Liberal policy for decades. In those difficult days a national broadcast was a precious and rare opportunity for a Liberal. By all accounts, Grimond used it to good effect – even allowing for the fact that he felt obliged to devote a significant proportion of his talk to justifying the very existence of his party.

He did the same in an article published five days later in the Liberal-supporting *News Chronicle*. He was at pains to emphasise the great and benign influence that Liberals, Keynes and Beveridge in particular, still had on the way people lived, and argued that their party must therefore not be allowed to wither away: 'The seeds it sows blow far and wide. We welcome it when they take root in the Conservative or Labour parties, but we must tend and water the plant from which they come'. This piece also gives one of the clearest expositions we have of Grimond's strategic and philosophical thinking at this early stage of his parliamentary career: 'Why am I a Liberal? Not merely for negative reasons. It is because I want to see Britain's – and the world's – future unfold in liberal pattern . . . I believe that the only valuable things in this world are people. The State has no value except indirectly in making people better and happier. And what it is worthwhile being and doing each individual must find out for himself.'

In common with most of his colleagues, Grimond went off to spend most of the campaign in his own constituency. Lord Rea, chairman of the Liberal Campaign Committee, was generally left in charge at Liberal HQ in Victoria Street. The election was nearly fatal for the Liberals, who won only six seats. In those seats they fought both in 1950 and in 1951, the average fall in their share of the vote in less than two years was 4 per cent. Of the six winners, only Grimond had faced a Conservative opponent. The four other Liberal MPs from the 1950–51 parliament to face a three-cornered fight were all defeated – albeit narrowly. Frank Byers was again defeated in his old Dorset seat, so Grimond would carry on as chief whip. Only forty-three Liberals retained their deposits by winning the required 12½ per cent. Jo Grimond was an eye-catching exception in this depressing picture. He had quickly discovered that he had far less of a fight on his hands than he had feared. The islanders had taken to their outspoken, charismatic new MP and his young family. Grimond took nothing for granted, in this or any subsequent election, but as he went from island to island addressing audiences ranging from a handful to several hundred, he must have realised quickly that there was not the slightest threat to his position. No other Liberal came within 5,000 votes of victory in a three-way fight, but Grimond saw his share of the vote rise from 47 per cent to 58 per cent, and his majority increase from 3,000 to over 6,000. He would never again need to worry about losing his seat, but he was now the only Liberal MP in Scotland, the unexpected 1950 gain of Roxburgh having been reversed. He also knew that he would have to carry an increasing share of the Liberal burden in Parliament, if the party was to survive at all. If 1945 and 1950 had been setbacks for the Liberals, 1951 was truly a disaster. They would have to pull together as never before. The result did have one interesting knock-on effect for Jo Grimond. Along with her two left-leaning allies, Messrs Granville and Roberts, Megan Lloyd George, the increasingly semi-detached deputy leader of the party, had been defeated. She was not replaced in that post and, as parliamentary chief whip, Grimond would rapidly become her *de facto* successor.

Shortly after resuming the premiership in 1951, Churchill made renewed overtures to Clement Davies, offering him a cabinet post in charge of education, together with junior ministerial positions for two of his colleagues, if the six Liberals cared to follow the National Liberals, and Churchill himself, into the Tory fold. Davies had refused to help abolish his party on at least two previous occasions and, after consulting with senior colleagues including Grimond, he rejected the overture of 1951 as well. His refusal to countenance the proposition that the Liberals should be subsumed in this way was without doubt a remarkable act of political courage and statesmanship. In 1951 Violet Bonham Carter thought that Davies had made a mistake. When she said so to colleagues on the party council, she was generally excoriated. If Davies had been seduced by Churchill's gambit, it is unlikely that he could have carried more than a few of his party colleagues with him into a long-term arrangement with the Conservatives.

Within weeks of the election, Grimond was off on his travels, going to Australia and New Zealand as part of a four-man parliamentary delegation. On behalf of the House of Commons, the group presented a silver mace to the Australian House of Representatives in celebration of the golden jubilee of the Australian Commonwealth, becoming the first parliamentary delegation to cross the bar of the Australian House. When Grimond sought refreshment in one of the local MPs' favoured watering holes during the stopover, he was surprised to encounter Henry Gullett, chief whip of the Australian Liberal Party, who had been attached to the Fife and Forfars during the war. Gullet was missing a series of important debates because he had been suspended for the rest of the sitting, and Grimond was shocked to learn that in Australia this was regarded as a perfectly normal occurrence. In New Zealand the quartet presented a new Speaker's chair to the Lower House, in acknowledgement of twenty years of full parliamentary government in the former British dominion. It was an extraordinary honour for the Liberals, with their six MPs, to be thus treated as equals to the two larger parties, but then this was still the age of Churchill.

The 1951 result meant that Grimond had to speak even more in the Commons. Not only did he have to catch the Speaker's eye on behalf of the entire Scottish Liberal Party, but he had also to set out Liberal views on a rather wider range of issues than he had in the short-lived Parliament of 1950–51. Although he took the opportunity to float some interesting ideas about the economy and about foreign affairs, *Hansard* reveals that Scottish affairs remained the mainstay of his parliamentary activity. In the chamber of the Commons and in its committees, Grimond continued to demonstrate a remarkable mastery of the complexities of life in the islands, speaking with authority about everything from the catching and freezing of fish and the various types of boat that were in use, to the requirements of crofters and the structure of freight tariffs in the north of Scotland. He also campaigned with particular vigour against the increasing abuse of the title 'Shetland wool' to describe wool from anywhere in the world. He bemoaned the lack of capital afflicting would-be entrepreneurs in Orkney and Shetland, though at this stage he could suggest no more radical solution than the introduction of cheap loans or grants, which would presumably have to be provided by central government. There seemed to him to be no other way of breaking the vicious circle of economic decline. Although Grimond was himself appointed in February 1952 to the Highlands Panel that the Attlee government had established in 1947, he regarded the panel as an inadequate response to the needs of the region. It was made up almost entirely of politicians and civil servants and, since most of the problems in the Highlands and Islands were essentially economic, he quickly became convinced that more private sector input was required. By the time he fleshed out his proposal for a Highlands and Islands Development Board, his doubts about the effectiveness of government action had grown substantially, and he foresaw a far more significant, even dominant, role for the private and cooperative sectors on the board.

In the 1952–3 parliamentary session, Grimond introduced a Bill for the first time, relating to harbours, piers and ferries in Scotland. With help and encouragement from the Conservative government, and the unanimous support of his parliamentary colleagues from the Highlands, Grimond introduced a modest but worthy piece of devolutionary legislation. Many of the islands were threatened with depopulation if they could not improve sea access and the intention in this Bill was to grant local authorities greater discretionary powers over harbour and pier work. They had long been hamstrung by the need to apply for provisional orders from central government whenever they proposed to spend more than £5,000 on such work, and there was general agreement that this must be changed, if only to take account of inflation. Grimond knew that, even though there was general support for the principle of what he was proposing, anything that smacked of extravagant increases in spending would be squashed by the Treasury. The parliamentary time necessary to secure the passage of a Bill like this was entirely in the gift of the government. He therefore recognised that, if he was too ambitious and proposed too high a limit for discretionary spending, then a single Treasury-led objection from the government could kill his Bill entirely. He therefore proposed raising the cut-off figure to £25,000 – a comparatively modest, but still significant, sum that ministers had indicated privately to him would be acceptable.

In February 1953 Grimond joined other senior Liberals on a further visit to Winston Churchill to discuss the voting system. Lady Violet, who led the Liberal delegation, warned Churchill that, although local pacts along the lines of those in Huddersfield and Bolton might well be effective in keeping Labour out, they had a dispiriting effect on the party organisation. They were also not to the taste of many party workers. What was needed was a more representative voting system, under which such pacts would be unnecessary. Churchill knew only too well that electoral reform was a long-time totem for Liberals and, under pressure from this barrage, he agreed to look again at the findings of the factual enquiry that he had set up into the likely effects of proportional representation, but held out no real hope for progress. The measure just would not have the necessary support in the House of Commons. Churchill had in the past himself advocated electoral reform, at least within larger towns, and he could not disguise his frustration and sadness at being unable to deliver the results that he wanted. Lady Violet perfectly understood that her old friend's hands were tied, writing in her diary that evening: 'what alarms me is that the Tory Party should still run so true to form'.[16]

Back in the chamber of the House of Commons, Grimond was beginning to follow the example of Hopkin Morris by treating the Commons to some unashamedly intellectual expositions on how the Western system of liberal democracy should be developed and improved. When the Commons discussed abolishing the colour bar – arguably the most significant piece of anti-discrimination legislation to date – Grimond made one of his most memorable early interventions. Having said that he would not in the least mind his own daughter marrying a black man – so long as he was kind to his father-in-law – he went into an expansive and philosophical mode:

> There may be only a short time for the white people, with their Western civilisation and their Christian ideals, to convince the neutrals of the world whether they are sincere and whether they really have something better than what is offered by Communism . . . I believe that it is one of the aims of civilisation to get past the primitive reactions of mankind against people who are different to them . . . we must get rid of this primitive, barbaric and, to me, rather horrible, instinct that people of a different colour are therefore inferior to us.[17]

Two main strands are apparent in Grimond's parliamentary activities during the remainder of the 1951–5 Parliament: a tremendous emphasis upon issues of particular concern to his constituents (notably the crofters) and a series of telling contributions in a wide range of debates about foreign and Commonwealth affairs.

The Grimond family now clearly needed a long-term base of its own in London, as well as in Orkney. After their stint in London as house guests of Lady Violet in Paddington for a couple of years, Jo and Laura had in

January 1953 acquired a large property, Beaufort House in The Butts, Brentford, situated between the Thames and the Great West Road. The house was in a state of almost total dilapidation and, on reflection, they had concluded that the months of renovation it needed did not really appeal. They therefore had almost immediate second thoughts, and relocated across the river only a matter of months later to a house conveniently close to the District Line, in the vicinity of Kew Gardens. The Brentford house was sold to the Labour MP Elwyn Jones and his wife, the writer Pearl Binder, while its successor in Kew would serve the Grimond family well for several decades. There was still the problem of dividing lives between Orkney and London, since parliamentary recesses and school holidays were never quite coterminous, but the Grimonds could always count upon the understanding of teachers and friends at both ends of their long lines of communication. Grimond also dabbled again in publishing in the early 1950s, along with Martin Secker and Graeme Hutchison helping to found a small and short-lived publishing house called the Richards Press. Their most notable publication was probably a collection of gripping reminiscences (published in 1953) from Count Constantine Benckendorff, Jasper Ridley's uncle and the son of the last Tsarist ambassador in London. He was also, for a time, a director of an electronics firm called Sykes Robertson.

In 1953 Grimond also acquired the services of a new private secretary, Catherine Fisher, who had been working at Liberal headquarters. Originally taken on for six months as cover for Grimond's own secretary, who had gone on her travels, after ten years working for Grimond, Cate Fisher would ask him whether she should now consider that the position was a permanent one. She evidently thought the world of Grimond, positively looking forward to Monday mornings, when she could again be exposed to his particular brand of *joie de vivre*. One of Cate Fisher's great skills was her ability to decipher Grimond's 'hieroglyphic' handwriting, an ability that she laughingly attributes to her wartime training as a code-breaker with the WRNS. Even she had sometimes to improvise, however, Grimond asking her on one occasion as he read over something that she had typed, 'am I now using words that aren't even in the dictionary?' Many constituency problems came to Miss Fisher not in the form of letters posted from Orkney and Shetland, but as scrawled notes, made by Grimond on whatever was to hand – an old envelope, a flattened cigarette box – when he was buttonholed in the street. Amiably vague as he was, Grimond would rely on Cate Fisher to run virtually every aspect of his professional life. He would even ask her from time to time where Laura was – 'I thought she was in Orkney, but I can't find her' – and depended utterly on her ability to organise his travel itineraries. Although Grimond did have his own, famously elderly, dinner jacket, Cate Fisher's black WRNS tie came in handy, too; she kept it in a drawer in the office, and it adorned Grimond at countless funerals and state occasions.

Grimond liked to be extremely punctual and, even if he was only a few minutes late for an appointment, he would get Miss Fisher to call ahead and warn whomever he was meeting. He regarded this as good manners, as, indeed, he regarded being cheerful as good manners. If anyone – particularly Young Liberals – turned up late for a meeting with him, Grimond loathed waiting, and might refuse to do so for more than few minutes. So far as Cate Fisher recalls, although he often cut things fine and always relied upon public transport to get him to stations on time he never once missed a train. With the terrific pace that he set himself, Grimond's travelling must have taken a heavy toll on him. If he urgently needed to take a script with him on a journey, he would stand over the typewriter as she typed it out, taking out the sheets one by one as they were completed. He rarely dictated, scrawling most things down on scraps of paper as and when his schedule allowed him to. On many occasions, for example, he would get as far as Aberdeen on his way to the islands and then have to come back to London if the weather prevented him from flying on. On his way south, he could sometimes spend an entire day stranded at Kirkwall airport, waiting for the all-clear to fly.

Immediately after Christmas 1953 Grimond went on his first ever trip to the Middle East, as part of a three man parliamentary delegation to a number of important states, emirates and protectorates. The month-long visit was funded by a rich and noted Lebanese Christian businessman and politician, Sayed Emil Bustani, who happily disbursed vast sums of his oil-derived wealth on attempts to improve relations between the United Kingdom and the Middle East. No doubt MPs would think twice about accepting such an invitation today, but those were less strangulated days. The group started its tour in Bahrain and moved on to Qatar, where their interview with the sheikh was interrupted by a band of his praetorian guard, who had come to protect him from possible attack, since his uncle was in the vicinity. Grimond and his colleagues were then impressed (rather than scandalised) to hear that there were British army officers in the British protectorate at the time of their visit, subduing some revolutionary elements in a quietly businesslike way. They moved on to Kuwait on 31st December, seeing in the New Year at a 'ghastly' New Year's Eve party at an American house there. After a couple of days of shooting at bustards from speeding Cadillacs in Kuwait, the trio moved on to Basra. From there they went on to Israel, where they attended the Coptic Christmas mass in the Church of the Holy Nativity in Bethlehem. The headman of a refugee camp nearby then browbeat them about the iniquities of the Americans and the British. In Jordan they were granted an audience with the twenty-year-old king, Hussein ibn Talal, who impressed upon them his powerful attachment to England. Thence to Syria, where they met the military ruler General Shishakly, who struck them as an important pillar of stability in the region – that is, until he fled his country only a few days later.

Their next port of call was the Lebanon, whose political establishment, like their host Emil Bustani, was predominantly Maronite Christian. Everywhere they met members of the ruling elite, and everywhere they were conscious that British influence was on the wane. This was the era in which 'Pan-Arabism' was taking wing, and Grimond and his travelling companions were left with the impression that there now existed in the region a strong will to see Jordan and Iraq form a federation in due course, possibly also including Syria.

The regime in Egypt, their final port of call, was essentially secular and military in nature. Egypt was in the middle of negotiations with the British about the future of the British Suez Canal Zone Base, and was certainly their most important destination. Grimond and his colleagues met Egypt's powerful Minister of the Interior, Gamal Abd al-Nasser, for what was described as an 'amicable' talk, lasting over three hours. They found him persuasive, but never for a moment doubted that inside the velvet glove was a brutal iron fist. Their visit to the base itself did little to convince them that Egyptian intentions were friendly. Although the base was effectively under siege, and the object of constant small-scale irritations and attacks, morale was good and the quality of military leadership was impressive. Their meeting with the country's nominal ruler, General Neguib, was the most formal interview of the entire tour. There was no unpleasantness as such, but the general wanted to discuss serious matters and he was not in a mood to compromise. He left them in no doubt that the negotiations on the canal zone were going to run into trouble. They failed to make progress towards breaking the deadlock between the British and Egyptians regarding the future of the base, and came home fearing the worst. Grimond wrote subsequently that, although he had always regarded himself as being sympathetic to the Arab cause, this trip had convinced him that 'the Arabs are the worst possible advocates for their own cause . . . after hours of strident harangues, the goodwill of the most fervid pro-Arab must wilt.'[18]

Less than a year earlier, Grimond had co-signed a letter to *The Times* with Charles Waterhouse, a renowned hardliner on policy towards the Middle East, chastising the newspaper for publishing a report in which the British government was described as a 'suppliant' for facilities on Egyptian territory. Not so, claimed the correspondents. The British were no 'humble petitioners': their case was 'incontrovertible on legal grounds'.[19] After his return from his trip, Grimond evinced none of his earlier stridency. His approach now was quietly pragmatic and offered no easy solutions to the difficulties surrounding the proposed withdrawal – indeed he acknowledged that there were none – but he did have a few observations to make: 'I am sure that our prestige depends not upon force or violence but upon the wisdom and consistency of our policy. If we had to use force on a big scale in Egypt, it would be a confession of failure.'[20] He had been struck by the poor conditions that British servicemen were forced to endure there, and took up their case with the government. He also dealt with the state of the continuing Anglo-Egyptian negotiations over the 80,000 British army personnel who were due to leave Egypt by 1956. Many British politicians now felt that Britain's strategic interests and prestige would be fatally undermined by this withdrawal and the Arab world was beginning to suspect that Churchill and his ministers were deliberately dragging their feet.

Grimond foresaw the consequences of the government's attitude, which seemed to him dilatory and arrogant in equal measure. He saw no reason to assume that the Egyptians' assessment of where their best interests lay would coincide with the British view, and feared that the government mistakenly believed that it could bluff Egypt, whose President Neguib was by now engaged in a bitter power struggle with his even more hardline former ally, Nasser:

> I do not believe that time is on our side. If we get too near to 1956 the Egyptians will be only too happy to let the time run out . . . At that stage we shall be taken to the United Nations, world opinion will be against us and we shall have to leave Egypt in a most ignominious fashion . . . If we cannot come to an agreement with Egypt, I feel that it would be better if we left the base and abandoned £300 million of stores rather than prevaricate about our policy all through this part of the world'.[21]

He developed this point four months later: 'What is to happen if there is [local aggression] in the Middle or Far East and the Egyptians for reasons which may seem to us very short-sighted – and the Egyptians are not always moved by the most logical calculations – should decide to interfere with our shipping in the Canal?'[22]

As well as developing a reputation for thoughtful speeches on international affairs, Grimond made good use of the intellectual foundations provided by his study of economics. The British economy in the post-war years suffered from chronic stagnation, and the Conservative Party of that time, although no friend to nationalisation, had not developed the strain of economic liberalism that has come to characterise it in more recent times. Its leadership seemed bereft of new ideas and, perhaps worst of all, failed to foresee the effects of the creeping plague of inflation that was beginning to afflict the country. Grimond was amongst the first parliamentarians to warn of the threat of ruinous inflation. Many leading politicians of the time were still in the mind-set of austerity and price controls, or even of the Great Depression, and greatly underestimated the dangers of an inflationary culture. Anything, even ingrained inflation, seemed to them preferable to a return to the mass unemployment of the 1930s. One of Grimond's very best parliamentary speeches came in a debate about the cost of living when he was chief whip. Of course, this speech has to be taken very much in context; so much of what Grimond was saying is now the common currency of economic debates, but in 1955 it must have sounded very heretical. The war had naturally seen considerable curtailments of liberties, in the economic field as well as the social. What annoyed Grimond was the fact that post-war governments, both Labour and Conservative, had failed to move back the frontiers of the state. If anything, they had further curtailed individual initiative.

Grimond already foresaw dire economic and social consequences unless the tide of corporatism could be reversed, and the liberal spirit of free enterprise revived. He argued in particular that unemployment was becoming increasingly localised, the consequence of structural change, not of inadequate demand in the economy as a whole. Transitional unemployment, as old industries died and had to be replaced, was going to be a feature of life from now on, and there was no point in pretending that it could be totally avoided. The only pertinent question was how it could be dealt with. The 'Keynesian' solutions – increased demand, subsidies, lower interest rates and so forth – were no longer relevant. Indeed adding 'froth' to an economy that in many places was bubbling along nicely would create inflation and add to the long-term malaise. The other main inflationary problem was that wage settlements were getting out of hand. Generally negotiated and agreed at a national level, they took little heed of productivity or profitability; these were the days of the 'going rate' and fixed differentials that gave not the slightest regard to changes in economic circumstances, however obvious they were. Grimond's suggested remedy characteristically did not take the form of an all-embracing philosophy of economics. He suggested that only a judicious mixture of policies, some familiar and some radical, could provide a way forward: tighter monetary policy; a more aggressively interventionist regional policy to mitigate the effects of industrial change in declining areas; a new determination on the part of government to take up the consumer's case, promoting competition and attacking monopoly and oligopoly; and progress towards decentralised wage bargaining. Unless these policies were embraced, he warned, the scourge of inflation would go on setting the weak against the strong, the organised mass against the individual, the employed against the unemployed – and Britain would just go on chasing its own inflationary tail. Grimond was not, however, deceived by the serious nature of the problem into advocating the kind of deflationary policies that would do more harm than good. When he warned that the suggested cures for inflation were in many instances worse than the problem itself, he was asked to 'give an example of where that could be so'. 'Having one's head cut off to stop a common cold,' he replied sardonically.[23]

In a debate on the compulsory acquisition of land and property, Grimond set out the basics of an approach to politics that would sustain him for the rest of his life, in one of his clearest rhetorical expositions of 'Grimond liberalism', in which he particularly denounced the centralising and unaccountable tendencies of socialism:

> The history of this country has shown many examples of the struggle of ordinary people against tyranny, and tyranny has taken many forms . . . The State, the King, the Executive, have many times formidably threatened the lives and liberties of the ordinary people, and if there is a threat today it does not, in my view, come from powerful individuals, but again from the Executive and also from certain powerful corporations, public and private, which have grown up within the body politic.[24]

All this high-faluting talk was never, however, intended for the consumption of Grimond's constituents. Grimond used to joke – even when he was leader – that he didn't want Liberal Party literature upsetting the people of Orkney and Shetland, so he arranged for it 'all to be stopped at the ports'.[25] Although Grimond consistently espoused most of the tenets of economic liberalism, he was always conscious of the particular difficulties faced by his own constituents. If left entirely at the mercy of the unfettered free market, he reasoned, many of the smaller islands would soon be totally depopulated. In an early speech to the House of Commons Scottish Committee about agriculture, he departed by some way from the principles of liberal economics: 'I support a guaranteed price . . . I think that we ought to keep the subsidies going, if we are going to have them, for as long as possible and chop and change as little as possible . . . With these long-term improvements in land we need better houses and I am glad to hear that the grant is going to be raised.'[26] This kind of talk could easily be attacked as inconsistent or even hypocritical. The case for the defence is surely that Grimond regarded the needs and problems of Orkney and Shetland as so far from the norm that general principles had to be suspended. Unless those in power were forced to take careful and specific note of the needs of such islands and their inhabitants, then government policies were likely to be wholly inappropriate for them. Nonetheless, as Grimond listened to his colleague Rhys Hopkin Morris, member for Carmarthen with all its post-industrial hardship, showing the courage to damn the dangerous practice of economic intervention without any apology or qualification, Grimond must have at least felt a pang of embarrassment.

Jo Grimond also took care of the interests of his constituents in more straightforward ways. He often found himself stuck with attending certain time-consuming standing committees that were examining legislation relating to Scotland, even when he had little or nothing to contribute. For instance, between February and April 1954, he attended seventeen sessions of the Scottish Committee as it examined that year's housing bill – without saying a word. When planning matters came up he always defended the peculiar 'udal' law (a system of freehold rights based upon uninterrupted possession and prevalent across northern Europe before the feudal system) that prevailed in matters of tenure across most of Orkney and Shetland. Whenever agriculture was discussed, he could also be relied upon to be present, making the case for the humble crofters of Orkney and Shetland. Grimond much admired crofters. He reckoned that one of the only two truly contented people he had ever met was a crofter in his constituency (the other being the Duke of Devonshire). Nonetheless, Harry Cowie recalls Grimond once telling him that he was rather embarrassed at having inherited a totally intact croft in Perthshire from a relative, and not knowing what to do with it. Despite Cowie's protestations about its likely historical significance, Grimond apparently had it destroyed.

Crofting is still a significant tradition in the Highlands and Islands of Scotland. It involves the cultivation of patches of hard terrain, usually for the grazing of animals, and it is an activity for hardy souls. Sometimes it is carried on as a means of self-support; for others it can be a seasonal undertaking, or a part-time relief from the stresses of urban life. Crofting land is generally of a poor quality and private-sector landlords have consequently had few illusions about its value. Out of a combination of tradition and decency, they would almost without exception take a reasonably enlightened attitude towards their tenants. Increasingly hardship was being caused by the fact that so much crofting land, especially in Orkney and Shetland, was held in trust – and the trustees were often constrained to look after the narrow interests of the beneficiary. If a crofter defaulted or fell ill, they were often unable to take a generous view. Although Grimond hugely admired the crofters of Orkney and Shetland, and wanted to see the tradition maintained, he had no illusions. Unless the practice could become more remunerative, it would inevitably vanish from the landscape, leaving it even bleaker. Too many aged crofters were forced to endure a miserable old age, and too few of them were handing on their crofts for continued cultivation. What was needed, Grimond argued, was more capital going into the crofts. 'No more than anyone else,' he later explained, 'do I want the crofter to live for ever on charity or to be in a specially privileged position against the cottar [a tenant cottage-dweller] or the dweller in the small town.'[27] What was required, above all, was new ways of generating more capital locally, of using the savings potential of the local community to greater effect.

In 1954–5, the government's Crofting Commission failed to produce a unanimous report about a way forward, and Grimond feared that the existence of both a majority and a minority report would be used as an excuse for inaction. The differences between the two were often highly technical, relating to possible changes in the rating system and reflecting divergent views amongst commission members about the role of private landlords. Grimond said from the outset that, since either set of proposals would be better than none, he would like the government to choose between them, and then get on with improving the position of the crofters. He also warned repeatedly that the governmental approach to the Highlands and Islands should not be limited to helping the crofters. Other long-term needs must be addressed too. The specific problems of crofters were to some extent legal, relating to land holdings, but they suffered too from the general economic problems of the area: the need for alternative employment opportunities and improved amenities. Roads were a particular problem. Without dramatic improvements to the roads in Orkney and Shetland, and particularly to the by-roads, not only would tourism be unlikely to take off in the islands: agriculture, forestry and fishing would also continue to decline. Grimond also stressed that government action must be sensitively organised: 'the crofter is a man of independent outlook who is very much attached to his home and his way of life, and he must be handled with care and tact.'[28]

When the government did introduce a Crofters (Scotland) Bill in 1954–5, Grimond was an assiduous contributor to debates. He pressed the government to populate its reconstituted Crofting Commission with at least a number of successful figures from the private sector. This chimed perfectly with his view that the Highlands and Islands Development Board, whose creation he had always advocated, should be dominated not by civil servants, but by entrepreneurs with a real feeling for the region. It was necessary to break the vicious economic circle by demonstrating that the north of Scotland could produce real success stories, and that they could be replicated. To help achieve that, Grimond advocated tax inducements rather than subsidies or the establishment of further government bodies. Indeed, he argued that the proliferation of different, indeed sometimes competing, governmental and quasi-governmental bodies was beginning to bring more confusion than relief to the lives of the humble crofter. Here surely were the beginnings of the 'bureaucratic blight' that he would later vehemently denounce. Given Grimond's hard work in highlighting the problems of the Highlands and Islands, it must have been gratifying to him when the only really impressive Liberal result of the 1951–5 Parliament came at a by-election held in a snowstorm at Inverness on 21st December 1954. John Bannerman gained 36 per cent of the vote in a seat that the Liberals had not contested in 1951, running the Tories a close second in what had been a safe seat. Sceptics pointed out, however, that this was an obvious one-off. The seat was naturally fertile territory for the Liberals – being far-flung and 'Celtic' – and turnout had fallen from almost 70 per cent at the general election to below 50 per cent at the by-election. The result nevertheless provided a rare shaft of light for the Liberals. The *News Chronicle* declared: 'Let us have more Invernesses!'

As the Liberals gathered in Llandudno in April 1955 for their spring assembly, shortly after taking over the premiership from Winston Churchill and with an unusual six weeks' notice, Anthony Eden announced that a general election would be held on Thursday, 26th May. Grimond was charged with winding up the assembly in place of Clement Davies, who was already suffering from the illness that would keep him out of the election campaign. Hitherto, Grimond had never particularly pushed himself forward at assemblies. This time he came out with guns blazing. A new age needed new political leadership, he told his audience, and 'I am not interested in causes which are perpetually lost . . . I am not attracted by the wistful glamour of defeat.'[29] Winston Churchill had gone and Clement Attlee, another great wartime figure capable of appealing beyond the bounds of his own party, was now on his way out too. Indeed, Mr Attlee was in danger of losing not only his position but also his dignity. He had emerged from his last tilt with Mr Bevan 'with his hat knocked over one eye',[30] making it little wonder that Britain's place in the world was now open to question. 'Democracy,' said Grimond, 'is not only a matter of counting votes but of influencing minds.'[31] Many people still speculated about whether the Liberal Party would live or die, yet the audience that day was transfixed by Grimond's sturdy rhetoric, and Frank Byers's appeal for funds after the speech reaped twice as much as it had the previous year. Grimond was ready to move into the limelight, and into the political premier division.

6

For the general public the 1955 general election was almost a non-event, especially so far as the Liberal Party was concerned. For a start, the party leader, Clement Davies, was unwell for most of the campaign and was not able even to launch it. But this very fact confirmed that, for Grimond personally, this election was not going to be an irrelevancy. Although Grimond was still nominally only the party's chief whip, his starring role at Llandudno had underlined his clear position as Davies's heir-apparent. Critics might say that it was just a question of there being no one else, but that would be to underestimate the very real respect and affection that Grimond now commanded in the party. The experience of conducting an election campaign with a sick leader convinced most of the leading Liberals that it was now time for a change at the top. The election result would reinforce them in their conviction. The party's manifesto was widely criticised, for lack of invention and for its turgid style. In fact, belying its curiously diffident tone, it was both radical and far-sighted, advocating closer British involvement in Western European integration; parliamentary assemblies for Scotland and Wales; measures to counter monopolies; and protection of the civil liberties of individuals against the effects of racial prejudice, union harassment and even against the state itself. The number of candidates, at 110, was precisely one higher than in 1951.

As the likelihood of a comfortable, outright Conservative victory hardened in people's minds to certainty, the third party became something of a bystander, cited only when spokesmen of the other parties proudly set themselves up as the 'true heirs' of the Liberal tradition. The only intervention by a Liberal to receive significant press attention was a speech by Lord Samuel in which he poured scorn on the pretensions of both socialists and Conservatives. Grimond threw himself into the campaign in Orkney and Shetland with his customary vim. The result was never in doubt, but he was determined to drive down the residual Tory vote to something suitably derisory. Although he was predictably criticised by his opponents for neglecting his parliamentary duties, Grimond began campaigning as soon as it was clear that an election was imminent, and undertook another punishing schedule of public meetings across the length and breadth of the constituency. According to contemporary accounts, he was at times in brilliant form. As in 1951, Grimond in his election address emphasised not only his liberalism, but also his independence from the 'relentless political machines . . . and "bloc" votes' of the Labour and Conservative parties. Although the result was never in much doubt, towards the end of the campaign Grimond received a welcome fillip when his campaign team was able to release a letter to him from Eric Linklater. Although Linklater was a long-standing friend of Grimond's, he was known to have been a nationalist-minded Tory supporter in the past, and had never before offered him explicit political support. This time he did endorse him, expressing the hope that he would 'be returned with an overwhelming majority . . . not because I am in the process of becoming a Liberal . . . simply because I am permanently interested in the welfare of Orkney and Shetland, and I am sure there is no one more capable than you, and more zealous than you, in promoting their welfare'.[1]

Although, unlike in 1951, Grimond was not pushed into one of his party's precious broadcasting slots, he did get the opportunity to pen a few articles in the national press. They are as fluent and radical as might be expected. These writings by Grimond are brilliant statements of social liberalism and, really for the first time, he begins to foreshadow elements of the intellectual revolution that gripped Britain in the 1980s. It is hard to imagine such thoughtful articles appearing in print during the heat of election battle in this age of disposable rhetoric. In the *Daily Mail*, for instance, he wrote that: 'No person, no nation can 'go it alone' – irrevocably our lives are bound up with another . . . Particularly are our lives entwined with the lives of the peoples of the Western World . . . It is man's duty to emulate the harmony of Nature in his conduct and affairs, for it is the absence of the discordant which leads to individual enjoyment, a happy community, and a peaceful world.'[2] There are also strong elements in the same piece of pure economic libertarianism, as when Grimond writes that: 'without economic freedom the Western World is no more than a defence mechanism . . . A civilisation upholding the essentials of liberty in the economic sphere must, as its members grow rich in knowledge and happiness, spread naturally to those parts of the world where tyranny is now the order.'[3] He was making a connection – which we now recognise as a fundamental and irrevocable connection but was then too rarely articulated – between economic liberty and political liberty. Elsewhere in this thoughtful essay, Grimond went further than his party in advocating devolution at all levels, widespread co-ownership in industry and vastly increased home ownership.

In two further articles, published in the national press during the week before the election, Grimond launched scathing attacks on those who argued that a Liberal vote was a wasted vote. In fact it was any other vote that would be the wasted vote, he maintained, because neither Labour nor the Conservatives had the faintest idea about how to modernise Britain and protect its freedoms. He was admirably even-handed in his twin critique of the two larger parties, and certainly did not regard Labour as radical or progressive in any meaningful sense. Its leaders had no taste for the kind of changes that might enhance freedom and enrich people's lives. People were fed up with paying for socialism, he wrote and, furthermore: 'Mr Bevan does not appear to them as a large-minded, humane champion of good causes, but as an unbalanced politician with a rag-bag of unfortunate phrases and ill-assorted ideas which raise doubts about the good management of any Labour government.'[4] His explicit advocacy of a large-scale political realignment was still some years in the future, but there is a clear foretaste of it in his *Observer* piece, as he denounces in turn the failure of the Conservative Party to recast itself as 'a progressive alternative to socialism' and predicts rather hopefully that 'the mass vote of the Conservatives or Socialists . . . is showing signs of disintegration'.

When election day came, the party reforms of the previous two years bore fruit. Not only Grimond, but his parliamentary colleagues too, benefited significantly from improved organisation. All six were re-elected, three in Wales, two in England and Grimond in Orkney and Shetland, once again the only Liberal MP to have been opposed by a Conservative. At this election he received almost 64 per cent of the vote, 6 per cent higher even than his impressive 1951 result. Nationally the Liberal share of the vote rose slightly, from 2.5 per cent to 2.7 per cent, and only sixty deposits were forfeited. The party hadn't reached the 5 per cent suggested by the first poll of the campaign, but at least the years of decline seemed to have been arrested, and the nascent practice of seat targeting seemed to have been moderately successful. There were no Liberal gains, but the party enjoyed some impressive, though frustrating, 'near misses'. Inverness, a few months earlier the scene of the Liberals' best by-election result in a generation, came even closer to turning, the Conservative majority dropping to below 1,000 votes as the Labour vote was squeezed further. Tremendously hard work in North Devon (where Jeremy Thorpe virtually doubled the Liberal share of the vote) and North Cornwall transformed safe Conservative seats into serious future prospects for the Liberals. In time all three seats would come the Liberals' way. For the first time since the 1930s, Liberals could feel some mild satisfaction at an election result. They had consolidated rather than advanced, but here were foundations upon which any new leader could build.

Grimond continued to blossom as a parliamentarian. In July 1955 Grimond deputised for Clement Davies at a NATO parliamentary conference, and his speeches in the House of Commons began to cover virtually the whole gamut of policy. He hardened his position on dealing with inflation, which he now perceived as potentially the most serious problem facing the nation, advocating a robustly monetarist approach to controlling it: 'better a few bruises now than a smash in a year or two.'[5] This became his theme for the summer. He believed that the Tories' surprisingly easy victory at the election had convinced them that all was well, and that they would ultimately pay a heavy political price for not taking advantage of the strength of their position. They should have introduced some painful, but necessary, measures while things were running their way. Why hadn't the Chancellor, Rab Butler, come down hard on inflation while he had the chance? 'There would have been a fearful squeal if he had put up the Bank rate and made some real cuts in public expenditure,' Grimond conceded, 'but if prices had steadied up and he could have come back in six months or so with inflation really under control, what praise he would have got!'[6] Nor had Butler taken any of the long-term measures that would have driven inflation out of the system for good: nothing had been done about the wage-bargaining system, the structure of public expenditure or about the organisation of the nationalised industries. 'We must make up our minds,' proclaimed Grimond, 'whether wages and salaries are to be earned by successful work or are to become a sort of welfare payment with rises every year . . . We cannot for ever live beyond our means and try to conceal our extravagance by inflation.'[7] In the same radical vein, Grimond argued that the blanket subsidising of council houses should end, and be replaced with a system of targeted income support – a measure that was eventually taken forward by the Heath and Thatcher governments. Grimond can, of course, be accused of advocating from the luxury of the opposition benches policies of whose consequences anyone in government would have to take more serious account. That would be unfair.

In 1956, government cuts were visited upon Grimond on his own doorstep with the announcement that that the famous naval base at Scapa Flow would be closed down because of defence cuts. He recognised that, having advocated a policy of spending cuts in general, it would be hypocritical to make political capital out of attacking them in this specific instance. Grimond was on top form for a debate about the Trinidad Oil Company, which had been controversially sold to American interests. During the exchanges in the Commons, a number of MPs expressed their concern about the Western world's growing dependency on oil. For Grimond, wider questions were raised, largely about the ability of the British economy to generate the necessary funds for industrial investment. He pointed out that, although private industry generated 40 per cent of UK output, it was getting its hands on only around 25 per cent of savings. The state was hoovering up the rest, not for investment purposes but for sinking into such things as housing and welfare services. This 'crowding out' of private-sector investment was making British and Commonwealth interests vulnerable to take-over from overseas. The most interesting section in his remarks dealt with the welfare state, which was already under strain as it attempted to reconcile the infinite expectations of citizens, as users, and the palpably finite resources of those same citizens, in their separate roles as taxpayers:

> We have created a gigantic organisation for consumption . . . We should say that we cannot further extend the Welfare State until we have built up production and built up the investment savings which are necessary for higher production . . . A great deal of the Welfare State has been built up on the thinking of the thirties, when mass unemployment and the need to pump extra purchasing power into the economy were what was wanted . . . I believe that a reduction in taxation would give some incentive to production and would result in extra savings.[8]

Just as interesting as these early signs of Grimond's economic radicalism are the first indications of the strategy that would sustain his leadership, that of a 'realignment of the left'. Since Aneurin Bevan and his supporters had broken ranks with Attlee to denounce the H-bomb, Grimond had become convinced that Labour was on its way out. Whoever replaced Attlee in the leadership change that now seemed imminent, the fundamental divide between Bevanites and Gaitskellites seemed impossible to bridge. More importantly, neither wing of the party seemed to Grimond to have anything close to the policies that the country needed. He admired some radical elements of the platform put forward by the left, but regarded many on the left as pro-Communist 'fellow travellers'. Equally, whilst he fully recognised that some of the Gaitskellites, notably Roy Jenkins, shared many of the Liberals' aspirations, most of the right-wing machine politicians who lurked behind Gaitskell, buttressed as they were by trade union block votes, were also anathema to Grimond. What was necessary was to sift out the liberals and the radicals from all parties, and to bring them together as a potent force, united in support of individual freedom and responsibility, progress towards equality of opportunity, a participative society and a new internationalism. Grimond was convinced that there were forces at work in society that would in time provide a massive impetus behind this strategy, and it was in 1955 that he first made a pitch on behalf of the Liberals for the new class of voter that he thought was coming into being, those younger, educated professionals who 'will live in a land between the old working and the old middle classes'.[9] The block-vote approach could have no appeal to this new, classless generation, he was convinced, in which case, 'who is heir to the spirit of the Left, the spirit which grasps at new ideas, the spirit of human, expansive happiness, reason and goodwill?'[10]

Grimond was also trying to re-energise the party's presentational and campaigning techniques, which were rather conventional and old-fashioned. At the Executive Committee in May 1954 he 'urged that the Committee should get away from the old fashioned idea of an Assembly and arrange, instead, an impressive Party Rally without our having the embarrassment of resolutions, the adoption of which created little if any advantage but usually led to trouble'.[11] He was far-sighted in fearing that, if the party did revive and began to enjoy more media coverage, its assembly might prove more than capable of causing genuine and lasting embarrassment. By mid 1955 Grimond was responsible for leading high-level discussions about the future organisation of the Liberal Party and in November of that year he suggested that the Executive Committee should ask federations and certain constituency associations to arrange rallies on particular themes, as a means of generating increased interest and publicity at a regional or even national level. The stresses of travelling and fretting about the future of the Liberals did not engender weight loss in Jo Grimond. Just before Christmas 1955, Sandeman's cellars in London revived an ancient tradition, that of weighing in guests at dinner against bottles of port. One by one they sat in a flimsy chair, balanced on an antiquated platform, and a count was taken. When Grimond took part, extra bottles had to be sent for to match his fourteen-stone frame. It was all too much for the decrepit contraption: when he stood up again, all the bottles crashed unceremoniously to the floor.

After the general election of 1955, the senior Liberals who were really serious about restoring their party's fortunes came round to the view that their most pressing need was for a change of leader. During the 1955–6 parliamentary session Clement Davies was never openly challenged and he survived more or less unscathed. Yet, although the party rank and file remained devoted to Davies, he was now over seventy years old and, having played virtually no part in the 1955 election, could hardly be presented as a credible leader four or five years down the line. Paradoxically another factor that probably damaged Davies's position was the early emergence of some fragile signs of Liberal recovery. The party enjoyed a number of unexpected gains in the local elections of May 1956 and, in the manner of Inverness, parliamentary by-elections began to bring more heartening news. At Torquay on 15th December 1955 Peter Bessell increased the Liberal vote by almost 10 per cent. Two months later, at Gainsborough and at Hereford on 14th February 1956, the Liberals did rather well again, increasing their share from 25 per cent to over 36 per cent. The Liberal candidate in Hereford, former newspaper editor Frank Owen, had enlisted the campaigning help of Dominic Le Foe, a Liberal activist, theatrical agent and former professional magician who was also a long-standing associate of Jeremy Thorpe. These signs of revivification only added weight to the argument that, with new blood at the top, the Liberals might actually be able to achieve something. Then came the first act of a drama that would, without exaggeration, transform the political landscape. Following the refusal of the Americans and British to finance the Aswan Dam in southern Egypt, in July 1956 the Egyptian President Nasser summarily nationalised the Suez Canal. A crisis ensued that would bring the British political establishment to breaking point, and which would fundamentally change many people's perceptions of the Conservative Party. A huge opportunity was about to be created for a re-energised Liberal Party.

It is impossible now, some forty-five years on, to discern how exactly Clement Davies was induced to renounce his position as Liberal leader. Grimond always claimed that Davies's resignation came as a shock to him. He had spoken with Davies in July 1956, at the beginning of the summer recess, and there had not been the slightest indication that he was considering calling it a day. By the time the Liberals assembled for their autumn assembly in Folkestone towards the end of September 1956, however, everyone seemed to know that something was afoot with regard to the party leadership. Even Davies's many admirers within the Liberal Party must now have realised that, with Suez threatening to engulf Britain in a national crisis, more energetic leadership was desperately needed. There was only one credible candidate. Jo Grimond was not only the most impressive performer in the parliamentary party; he was also a *de facto* deputy leader, and had an electoral independence that none of his colleagues enjoyed as the sole Liberal MP to have defeated opponents from both other parties. The problem was that, though Grimond was now ready to pick up the mantle, Davies had grave problems coming to terms with standing down, and still needed a little pushing. Grimond himself did not wish to be implicated in any kind of enforced departure. He was also nervous because he was committed to flying off to the United States just before the end of assembly week, for a six-week visit as a guest of the English Speaking Union. He could see no way of even significantly curtailing the commitment, still less of cancelling it altogether. Never discouraging his supporters from doing what they had to do, Grimond resolved to let events take their course. He need not have worried. The political journalist John Cole, who was attending his first Liberal assembly that week in Folkestone, recalls attending an informal press reception on the first evening of the assembly. He and his colleagues were left in no doubt whatsoever as to what was going to happen: Davies was going to stand aside.

The weekend before the assembly, 'Crossbencher' in the *Sunday Express* had hailed the 'wealth of purpose and punch' that Grimond could bring to the job of leader[12] and, during the week, both the *Guardian* and the *News Chronicle* had been induced to inform their readerships that Davies was intending to call it a day in his closing address. There was no formal procedure in place for a change of leader, so it had fallen to party *éminences grises* such as Frank Byers and Philip Fothergill, in Grimond's phrase, 'to take soundings and if necessary bell the cat'.[13] Once the assembly had begun, Grimond helped matters along by making one of his better speeches the day before Davies was due to address the assembly. He always took immense care over his major assembly speeches, which he wrote himself. They would generally go through a number of drafts, with Grimond sending out for advice, facts or figures as he worked.

At Folkestone he spoke on the potentially deadly dull subject of industrial development and the potential benefits of automation, but his speech was masterful, containing some robust and thoughtful arguments, all nicely spiced with humour and ably delivered. The choice of subject, slightly mystifyingly, was his own. Grimond's choice of such a non-controversial subject suggests that he scrupulously wished to avoid looking too much like a man indecently eager for the limelight, particularly after his triumph at Llandudno the previous year. From the beginning of the assembly, there was no mistaking the significance of the response provoked even by the mention of Grimond's name.

Despite Grimond's own unwillingness to play Brutus, the campaign to crown him leader had acquired its own, unstoppable momentum. Even he could not ignore the atmosphere, commenting as the delegates stood cheering him that, 'I thought for a moment I was expected to lead the singing in a verse of the National Anthem.'[14] As one rapturous delegate cried out in the heat of the moment, he was 'the hope of the Liberal Party', and the stage was set for his succession. As one report on the assembly put it, the Liberals could be more confident about their future than they had been for a long time, since 'in Mr Grimond they have a Prince Charming'.[15] It is hard not to feel a good measure of sympathy for Clement Davies. He had stepped willingly into the breach for his party at an appalling juncture in its fortunes. Without him, it would surely have died. He had subsequently turned down office for himself in order to protect the independent existence of his party, and he had never been other than competent, decent and utterly true to his Liberal instincts. But the fact remained that he was hardly a national figure and, in the elections between 1945 and 1955, the Liberals had looked increasingly like the largest of the minor parties, rather than the smallest of the major parties. He simply had to go, and Grimond was about to be, as he put it himself years later, 'improperly and undemocratically elected'[16] as party leader.

When Davies entered the hall to deliver his leader's speech, he received a lengthy standing ovation and the words with which he acknowledged it confirmed that his renunciation was indeed imminent. 'Thank you for that wonderful reception,' he said as the tumult subsided. 'Especially do I thank you this morning.'[17] His speech was masterful. He spoke for over an hour, ranging across virtually every area of policy. But at no stage did he try to disguise how painful the day was for him. Liberalism, he told his audience, was for them all a faith, almost a religion, and one for which they were prepared to make almost any sacrifice. Then he went into his heartfelt coda. 'It is time that the tiller were placed in the hands of a younger man,' he told the assembled company, 'and a new voice should be calling upon the ship's company, rallying them to the great cause which we all have so much at heart . . . Fortunately I can step down knowing that there is a worthy successor waiting, one who has fully earned his master's certificate.' His voice genuinely cracking with the emotion of the moment and his eyes filling with tears, Davies then dispensed with any ambiguity. To one or two cries of 'Oh no' and 'No, Clem, don't do it',[18] he confirmed that the end had come: 'I step down from the bridge, and go below.'[19] These scenes were painful to behold, and nobody could credit the Liberals with handling the transition particularly well. 'How maladroitly the king-making Liberals plucked the leader's mantle from a loved veteran,' wrote the special correspondent of *The Times,* 'whose one fault is that he has grown old.'[20] Grimond himself was not present for Davies's valedictory address, nor was his name mentioned at any point in it. It did not need to be: there was no other possible candidate. Once it became clear that Davies was willing to go, after a meeting with Byers and Fothergill, Grimond had panicked about whether he should cancel his American trip. Davies was having none of it. 'Off you go, my boy,' he told his putative successor, 'and have a good time.'[21] Only a few hours after all this drama, therefore, Jo Grimond flew off from London Airport to the USA. In theory the choice of a new leader would be a matter for the six Liberal MPs as soon as they reassembled at the beginning of the new parliamentary session. But nobody doubted what they would do. When Clement Davies was interviewed later that day, he said that, although 'the question of leadership is always a matter for the Members of the House . . . I am almost sure that my colleagues will choose unanimously Joseph Grimond.'[22]

Grimond had always wanted the leadership of the Liberal Party, and now it was his for the taking. Even the *New Statesman and Nation* had to admit that, 'not even the jaundiced staff of this journal has anything but praise for him'.[23] At an eve-of-session dinner on 5th November 1956, shortly after arriving home from the USA, Jo Grimond was unanimously elected as leader of the Liberal Party. Even Grimond's trip to the USA had taken an unexpected turn. Encouraged by some American friends, he rapidly abandoned his itinerary and inveigled himself into the entourage of Adlai Stevenson, the Democrats' candidate for the presidency. His magic touch had not deserted him, but he now faced one of the biggest challenges in contemporary politics. There was no question in Grimond's mind about what his political priorities must be. He had to find policy areas on which the Liberals could outflank their opponents, and there was the pressing question of party organisation. This was hardly his forte, but some of the by-elections towards the end of Clement Davies's tenure as leader had demonstrated that mid-term elections could be fertile ground for a third party. To exploit that potential to the full, the party had not only to buff up its policies: it had to develop new methods of targeting its very limited resources and convince people that a Liberal vote was not, in the time-honoured phrase, 'a wasted vote'. Most urgent of all, however, was the situation at the Suez Canal, which was turning into a national and international crisis. Though they were few in number, his parliamentary colleagues were seriously divided on this question, and he had to show decisive leadership. Grimond therefore resolved to try and stake out a distinctively Liberal position around which his colleagues could unite. His initial instincts towards Nasser's summary occupation of the Canal Zone had been to return to the fairly aggressive stance towards the Egyptian regime that he had first evinced. At a Liberal Party Committee meeting on 31st July 1956 he had laughingly described himself as 'the Captain Waterhouse of the Liberal Party' and drew parallels between Nasser's actions and Hitler's invasion of the Rhineland that might subsequently have scandalised a Liberal audience. As the months went by, however, the cold reality of Eden's unilateral Suez expedition appealed less and less to him.

In a statement on 18th August 1956 Grimond had already denounced the government's pompous behaviour at the Suez conference. He was certain that, as soon as Nasser had nationalised the canal, 'the best that could be hoped for from the conference was a compromise by which the Egyptian act of nationalisation would be virtually accepted, while the canal administration was placed under some sort of international control'.[24] To his credit, he also foresaw longer-term problems arising from oil and the Middle East. On Thursday, 13th September 1956, along with Arthur Holt and Donald Wade, he gave the Eden government the benefit of the doubt by supporting it in two critical divisions on Suez. Rhys Hopkin Morris had in private evinced robust support for Anthony Eden's stance at Suez, but as a deputy Speaker he kept these views off the public record and did not take part in these controversial divisions. Grimond himself was absent (in the USA) for the next crucial votes, on Thursday, 1st November 1956, when Arthur Holt abstained but Davies, Wade and Roderic Bowen switched to supporting the Labour opposition. By the time Grimond returned from the USA to take up the reins as the party's parliamentary leader, he had become far more suspicious of Eden's motives, and had arrived at the view that the Liberals could not afford to sit on the fence. He was supported in this by the officers of the Liberal Party Organisation, who agreed on 2nd November that, 'the policy of the Government, because it has dealt a serious blow at the establishment of the rule of law, would stand condemned even if it were successful.'[25] He had discovered for himself that American opinion was just as divided as that in Britain. But he had a problem. Both Rhys Hopkin Morris and Arthur Holt still sympathised with Eden's actions, and Donald Wade too had to be mindful of his vulnerable situation in Huddersfield should he become too outspoken in his criticisms.

As the crisis developed Grimond remained in close and regular touch with his old friend David Astor, whose *Observer* had been against the whole adventure from the start, minting the word 'fraudulent' as a description of the government's behaviour. Suez convinced Astor that the Conservative Party was infected with a strain of 'nationalist-imperialist' thinking, and he set up an informal anti-Suez group including several Tories (among them Edward Boyle), which continued to meet well into 1957. Although his public stance was slightly equivocal in the early days, Astor recalls that Grimond was privately at one with the sceptics from the start, regularly attending meetings of this group from its inception. He arrived at this position by an impeccably rational process. The Liberals had always been in favour of a stronger United Nations, and had long argued that it should ideally have set up some kind of international 'police force' to deal with just this type of situation. As it was, the British and the Israelis were dealing with the problem in their own way, which could not be tolerated. As the Korean War so nearly did, it could have dragged the superpowers into a conflict that was being waged by their allies and surrogates. Even the UN as it was, short on respect, might and firepower, would be a better arbiter at Suez than Eden and his post-imperial 'might is right' coalition. Up in Bolton Arthur Holt continued to argue that, until the UN was up to the job, the British and their allies were perfectly entitled to get on with it by themselves. On that basis, Grimond could argue, the disagreement was about tactics rather than principles.

Grimond and his party colleagues stood genuinely shoulder to shoulder on another contemporary question. While the government was arguing that Nasser must not be appeased, it was ignoring another human tragedy far closer to home, and another one that was symptomatic of the weakness of the UN and other international organisations. On 25th October 1956 police in Hungary had fired upon anti-government demonstrators, killing 300 of them. In retaliation, a furious crowd had stormed and ransacked the Communist headquarters in Budapest, and violence had continued sporadically thereafter. On 4th November 1956, after a brief ceasefire, Soviet tanks invaded Hungary and imposed martial law. Many Hungarians felt that the West, particularly the 'Voice of America', had encouraged them to make a stand against hardline socialism. They had then been left to their fates. Grimond and his colleagues were disgusted by the way in which the Eden government and other Western powers had exploited the Suez situation to avoid taking a stand on events in Hungary. Some cynics had even compared Britain's actions at Suez with the Russian oppression of Hungary. The British government had initially done little to help those who had fled the persecution in Hungary and, in early November, Grimond and Arthur Holt led a delegation to the Home Secretary, Gwilym Lloyd George, in the hope of convincing him that the government had a responsibility to induce local authorities to set up refugee reception committees, which they duly did. Grimond also volunteered subsequently to go to Hungary in person, to act as an international observer at the trials of some of the participants in the uprising.

On 12th November Grimond set out the Liberal position in a robust article in the *News Chronicle*. He acknowledged that many people in Britain had shown admirable concern about events in central Europe, but warned that there were important general principles at stake: 'the lesson of Hungary is in danger of being overlooked in our agony at the sufferings of the Hungarian people and our anxieties about Egypt'. He rejected any comparison between Suez and Hungary and warned that, unless the West established a firm policy towards the USSR, such an atrocity could easily happen again: 'we have never made up our minds as to how far we are prepared to go in the defence of justice and freedom against the threat of the hydrogen bomb . . . If we are not clear, the Russians can check-mate any move by simply threatening total war.' He was echoing an article he had penned a year earlier, in which he had attacked what he considered to be Bevan's irresponsibility in pressuring Attlee to sign up to a 'no first use' policy for nuclear weapons: 'No one in his senses could have expected a Leader of the Opposition, pledged to a policy of deterrents [sic], to give a public pledge that under no circumstances would he use the new weapons against any attack whatsoever by conventional weapons.'[26] Grimond's solution to the Hungarian situation was astonishingly bellicose. In effect, he argued that, despite the fact that their governments were nominal signatories to the Warsaw Pact, the oppressed peoples of Europe could still be brought under the protection of the West: 'the Governments of the free world should urgently consult and make it clear in what circumstances they will feel bound to intervene through the United Nations or other treaties, regardless of the consequences . . . If only we had done that already we could now be in a position to go to the help of the Hungarians, not with words but with arms.'.[27]

In his first speech in the House of Commons as Liberal leader, Grimond was cheered to the echo from the opposition benches when he mocked the Eden government's claim to have inspired the creation of a United Nations force to sort out the mess at Suez. This, he said, 'was rather like a burglar's claiming that his skill and violence compelled the police to improve their methods'.[28] Grimond felt that the Suez crisis had been the inevitable consequence of years of weak policy towards the region, and pressed the government to adopt a sustainable and coherent attitude towards the Middle East. He now proposed what he described as a policy of the 'extreme centre', under which clear guidelines would be drawn up for the final stages of decolonisation – and for NATO to prepare a firm policy with regard to any further Soviet military incursions into central Europe. Britain would also have to play a leading role, working through the Commonwealth and Europe, in setting up really effective international mechanisms for dealing with future flare-ups in the Middle East and elsewhere. In his New Year message for 1957, Grimond warned against Britain becoming a new Middle West: 'midway between Europe and America, understanding neither, vaguely resentful of both, trying to wrap jingoism around us and vent our troubles on foreigners; yet expecting the same foreigners, particularly the Americans, to lend us money and give us oil.'[29] Suez had in many ways provided Grimond with a wonderful political opportunity. By the time of the last critical vote on the crisis, on Thursday, 6th December, he was able to lead all his colleagues into the opposition lobby. Furthermore, along with the question of colonial policy, Suez had the effect of dramatically radicalising a section of public opinion. By playing up the Liberals' opposition to Eden's policy, Grimond greatly enhanced their image as an 'anti-system' party. For the thousands of people who were stimulated into political activity by their opposition to Suez, the Liberals now looked like a serious and attractive proposition. The crisis also gave Grimond the opportunity of making a mark in Parliament. As Ian Trethowan, a future Director-General of the BBC, wrote in the *News Chronicle*: 'day by day, he was able to wait until some luckless Minister had backed himself into a corner . . . Then, gracefully but mockingly, Grimond rose to deliver the knock-out.'[30]

A week after becoming leader in November 1956, Grimond had had to put in an early appearance at a highly unpromising by-election, speaking at a rally in the city of Chester two days before polling day. This was not the kind of seat that he would have chosen for his first target as leader. The Liberals had won only 11 per cent of the vote there in 1955, and the best that the party could hope for was to retain its deposit. On 15th November its candidate failed to achieve even that modest target. The Liberal share of the vote rose by an infinitesimal amount, and the Conservatives held the seat comfortably. Compared with other by-elections in the previous twelve months or so, this was a dreadful result. Shortly afterwards, an even more dangerous by-election loomed for the Liberals after Sir Rhys Hopkin Morris died suddenly and unexpectedly at his home in Sidcup on the night of 21–2 November 1956. Hopkin Morris had won his seat by fewer than 500 votes in both 1950 and 1951 and, although his majority had risen to over 3,000 in 1955, he had a sizeable personal vote and Carmarthen was by any token a highly marginal seat. Then came a double bombshell: news that the Labour candidate was to be none other than Megan Lloyd George, formerly deputy leader of the Liberals, and that the local Liberals were minded to select a candidate who shared Hopkin Morris's pro-government views on Suez. The minutes of the party's Executive Committee meeting on Friday, 14th December 1956 indicate that Donald Wade and Roderic Bowen had tried to take charge of the situation in Carmarthen and steer the members there towards selecting a less outspoken candidate, but had been thwarted by an unhelpful intervention from Herbert Harris, the party's Director-General. A meeting of the Executive Committee in Carmarthen two days before, consisting of some sixty–eighty people, had indeed chosen as candidate John Morgan Davies, a staunch supporter of the government's

Middle East policy. Grimond had to decide quickly whether he should disown a candidate with whom he disagreed on a matter of such national significance, or swallow his pride and his principles by campaigning alongside Morgan Davies to retain the seat. In a decision that he later rather regretted, Grimond decided to campaign for Morgan Davies and to paper over the disagreements between them. He could at least count upon the support of his colleagues. Even Clement Davies agreed to do his bit, addressing a meeting during the campaign. The whole business left a bad taste in the mouth, however, greatly affirming Grimond's view that the party needed to become more coherent and more professional.

At the beginning of 1957 Anthony Eden resigned as Prime Minister. Although Grimond had tormented him over his bungling of the Suez crisis, he felt some sympathy with a man who had, at least, also been opposed to appeasement when that had made sense. At the Liberal Executive Committee on Saturday, 12th January 1957, Grimond talked to his colleagues about 'the recent political crisis arising from the resignation of the Prime Minister . . . He stressed the utter confusion there had been in the Conservative Party during the last two months, and the vital need to show to the country that the new Liberalism stands for a new age.'[31] Although Grimond followed convention in welcoming Harold Macmillan's appointment as Prime Minister in suitably generous terms – 'In my view he has "guts" and has shown great courage in his political career and is now reaping the reward'[32] – he would come to regard Macmillan as a singularly unsuccessful premier. Suez had created a national climate of self-doubt, and Grimond hoped that the new Prime Minister might capitalise on this by pressing forward with some radical policies. Macmillan, however, did nothing to curb the growth of the state; he did nothing to bring the trades unions within the ambit of the law; and he made no positive move towards the European Economic Community (EEC), which had just been established by the Treaty of Rome. Thus were historic opportunities missed.

Even with the shadow of the forthcoming by-election at Carmarthen hanging over him (the by-election didn't take place until the last day of February 1957), Grimond was able to take forward the process of regenerating the Liberal Party and reshaping it into an effective campaigning organisation. Grimond knew that he was no organiser, and left such matters to Frank Byers, who had been such a mainstay of the party since 1945. Grimond himself got on with doing what he did best – filling the role of the charismatic front man – and Donald Wade was put in charge of arranging a series of lunches at which Grimond cultivated a range of businessmen. For the first few months of 1957 Grimond undertook a regional tour or a major rally virtually every week, in addition to his duties in the House of Commons and his regular trips back to Orkney and Shetland. He was in demand everywhere and soon found that he had set himself an initial pace that he just could not maintain. By the

Grimond's great-grandfather, and co-founder of the family firm, A D Grimond

Grimond's father, Joseph Bowman Grimond

Grimond's mother, Lydia (*née* Richardson) (1896)

Jo Grimond's sisters, Nancie (left) and Gwyn (1907)

The camel trade-mark symbol of J & A D Grimond – 'alleged by ribald Dundonians to be an early Grimond' (Photograph: D.C. Thomson)

The Grimonds' Bow Bridge works in Dundee (D.C. Thomson)

Grimond and his father playing golf at St Andrews (c. 1921)

Grimond as a member of the Eton Society ('Pop')

Co-editor of *Change* – Grimond, attending an editorial meeting, is on the right, with beard and monocle

A young Laura Bonham Carter with her brother, Mark (c. 1928)

Voyage of Discovery – Jo photographed by his friend Hugh Sharp on his first journey to America, 1937 (The National Library of Scotland)

Laura on holiday in the Highlands of Scotland

Grimond on holiday in the Highlands

Grimond with Sir Archibald Sinclair (standing, left) and a Sinclair family group

Laura Bonham Carter and her
father, Sir Maurice, on her
wedding day, May 1938

Jo and Laura Grimond on their wedding day, May 1938

Outside the family home in St Andrews

summer he had told colleagues that his stamina was being sorely tested and minutes of the Executive Committee meeting on Saturday, 7th September 1957 record that the party's general director was now advising that: 'Mr Grimond could accept no further engagements until Christmas, none during January or February, and had only two dates free in March and April, on one of which he had accepted an invitation to speak at the London Rally of the NLYL [the National League of Young Liberals]. Mr Grimond wishes to do many other things and particularly to spend much more time in Parliament. It [is] time we were building up other speakers as attractions.'[33]

In addition to his local, regional and parliamentary duties, Grimond also had to act as the main national media focus for the Liberals. In a party political broadcast on 1st February 1957 he dealt with both domestic and foreign policy. He warned that Britain was in danger of becoming addicted to inflation. The cure, like that for alcoholism, might well be unpleasant in the short term, but it could be found if the government had the will to seek it out and implement it. He also set out some of the Liberals' views on devolution and a wider distribution of property. On foreign affairs, he argued that it was only by being realistic about its limitations in the post-war world that Britain could find new ways of leading the search for peace. Better machinery for cooperation was needed, and it was time for Britain to stop paying lip service to European integration and the need to bind the Commonwealth together: the government had to commit itself wholeheartedly to the machinery of internationalism. But his main message, no doubt with Carmarthen in mind, was that he was sick of people telling him that they were Liberal at heart, but didn't want to waste their votes. 'What is the use of that,' he asked, 'if we all wait for each other to vote Liberal . . . we shall never get anywhere – and we shall certainly never get Liberalism.'

In domestic affairs, Grimond's predominant theme was the need to curb the activities of the state, and to reduce personal taxation. He was concerned that a 'nanny state' was reducing the population into what he termed a classic 'proletariat', lulled into the belief that they must pay more and more in taxes, in return for which the state would then allow them to slough off their civic responsibilities. Meanwhile far too little was done to stimulate enterprise and create wealth. He would in due course attack the Conservatives' 1957 Budget for reducing allowances on capital investment. The Chancellor, he warned, was stifling investment through his refusal to introduce incentives to 'risk investment' when he should 'go all out for enterprise and hard work to give us the goods to justify high consumption'.[34] In a vivid speech at a rally in Huddersfield on 15th February 1957 he set out a very robust view of what he saw as the madness gripping the country:

> The music goes round and round. An anguished cry from the shopkeepers about
> rates increases, so the thumbscrews are tightened on householders. Shrieks from

them, so industry is put on the rack. And all the time the taxpayers – that is all of us – are being bled white. There is no magic way out. Neither the Government nor the local authorities make any wealth or have any money of their own. If we want them to spend more and more we have to pay. The remedy is in our hands. Stop running to them asking them to do this, that and everything under the sun – and demand instead that they stop doing and spending so much. In fact we need a national do-it-yourself campaign in national and local affairs.[35]

Then came the by-election at Carmarthen. Not only had the process of candidate selection got out of hand: the campaign itself was fraught from the outset. Hopkin Morris had held the seat through little more than the force of personality and tradition. The local Liberals were short of manpower, and the agent who had been drafted in, Mr Hardy, was not Welsh-speaking, which caused all sorts of difficulties in rural Wales. His health then broke down, and he had to be replaced. Less than three months into his tenure as party leader, Grimond now had to share a platform with someone who profoundly and openly disagreed with the lead that he had given on what remained the defining issue of politics. Whilst Mr Morgan Davies's statement that the Eden government had 'acted with speed, resolution and great courage' was not so very different from what Arthur Holt had been saying in Bolton, Grimond's embarrassing situation was not lost on Labour. When asked about her views on Suez, Megan Lloyd George would respond with a smile that, 'I agree with Mr Grimond.' Most of Grimond's colleagues told him that he had both to accept the local decision, and to fight hard to retain what was, after all, one of only a tiny handful of Liberal seats. Grimond was grateful to Jeremy Thorpe for acting as a lightning conductor in this embarrassing situation: the two of them even addressed meetings jointly during the campaign. 'It was an unhappy affair,'[36] he wrote later with characteristic understatement. The campaign culminated in the loss of the seat to Lady Megan by 3,000 votes.

Recognising that the loss at Carmarthen would be a severe blow to morale in the party, Grimond gave a major speech two days later, on Saturday, 2nd March 1957, to a meeting of the Home Counties Liberal Federation in an attempt to regain at least some of the initiative. He had already been attacked in the wake of the defeat by what he described as 'those two great organs of liberalism' – the *Manchester Guardian* and the *News Chronicle* – for failing to impose internal discipline on his party and allowing serious divisions on policy to blight its electoral prospects. He now set out the strongest case he could for supporting the Liberal at Carmarthen. 'I think they are wrong,' he said of the pro-Suez faction in the constituency, 'but that is not the point . . . Should we take action to impose our views . . . Should we become more dictatorial than Abbey House [Conservative Central Office] or Transport House?'[37] The result had another effect on Grimond, which was already apparent in his speech that afternoon. He reconciled himself to the fact that the Liberals were faced with a long march. 'We are not likely to form a government ourselves for some years,' he conceded. 'Our influence on affairs must be exerted on governments of other parties . . . we ought therefore to support and encourage governments which do Liberal things.'[38]

With Suez and Carmarthen out of the way, Grimond really began in earnest to lead his party on its long march. He made 1957 the year in which he made his personal imprint on the Liberal Party. In a series of speeches throughout the year he set out a distinctive platform for the party. The first of these was delivered on Saturday, 9th March, on a visit to Bolton in support of Arthur Holt. At the party assembly the previous year, the Liberals had toyed with a policy of not only banning H-Bomb tests, but also ending British manufacture of such weapons. The party leadership had not felt ready to embrace such a radical policy, however, and the proposal had been omitted from the official party platform. Grimond now wanted to press the point. 'Does this country need to build up a nuclear striking force itself?' asked Grimond rhetorically in his Bolton speech. 'I doubt it . . . If we were to decide not to continue to manufacture nuclear weapons nor to compete with America and Russia in arms, then we gain elbow room not only for diplomatic negotiations, but for strengthening our economic situation.'[39] Later the same month, the parliamentary party issued a joint statement to the same effect. This effectively marked the birth of a new Liberal policy, later refined and formally adopted at the party's 1958 assembly, of shedding the independent British nuclear deterrent whilst continuing to make a full contribution to the US nuclear shield.

The controversy over Suez reared its head again at the end of March, when the French press first leaked word of what became known as the Sèvres Protocol, the secret document in which collusion between Britain, France and Israel had been formalised during the struggle against Nasser. The government had explicitly denied in the House of Commons that Britain had any foreknowledge of the Israeli attack on Egypt: so, said Grimond, if these French disclosures were true, they would demonstrate that the Eden government was 'made up of rogues and their dupes – not to mention incompetents'.[40] Outside the furnace of Westminster twenty years later, Grimond was able to take a more relaxed view: 'while I personally rather welcome the veil which has been drawn over this incident – there may well be occasions when ministers must lie in the national interest – yet the contrast between the treatment of the dissemblers on this occasion and the way that others have been expelled from public life for lesser offences, is strange to say the least of it.'[41]

Grimond was determined that the Liberals must have their own radical persona. In April 1957 he attacked 'Clause Four' socialism, and the way in which nationalisation had been implemented. Why had the opportunity not been taken, he asked, to turn the nationalised industries into genuinely cooperative ventures? Why had the government not pioneered new methods of partnership? 'We reject the Socialist arguments about "basic" industries,' he explained. 'The railways are no more basic than the woollen industry, or the coal mines than agriculture.'[42] Later in the year Labour floated the idea that the state might acquire shares in major industrial concerns. This 'semi-nationalisation' earned particular scorn from Grimond. By socialist standards, he argued, this seemed pathetically timid; by any sane standards it would smack of unwarranted interference in the workings of the market. Although Labour's leaders appeared to recognise that traditional socialism was defunct, he said later in the year, 'yet they prefer to rummage among the bones of bygone controversies rather then turn to the future'.[43] At that same meeting, Grimond again provided a voice in the wilderness on the need to crack down on inflation before it was too late. 'Inflation has killed more democracies than any other disease,' he observed. 'It is their cancer. Like cancer, it can be brought on by apparently agreeable habits. It leads to disaster and dictatorship.'[44] Nobody but the government could do anything about the problem, yet neither of the major parties had the necessary resolve to take the unpopular decisions that could douse the flames of inflation: 'let anyone suggest a remedy to inflation which might actually bite home, and they are up in arms.'[45] Grimond also sought out other distinctively Liberal issues to promote. He was not frightened of controversy, joining the Young Liberals in discussing a liberalisation of the law in some controversial areas such as licensing, homosexuality and prostitution. Speaking in support of the Liberal candidate at the North Dorset by-election in June, he highlighted other civil liberty questions, in the light of a recent phone-tapping scandal. This was Frank Byers's old seat and the party had high hopes of a good result. Although, as in Carmarthen, the local party was weaker than might have been expected, there was a strong candidate *in situ*, Alun Emlyn Jones, who had fought the seat at the previous general election. The association was also a member of the party's By-election Guarantee Fund, so most of its by-election expenses would be underwritten. The party had set itself the ambitious target of a 100 per cent canvass, and party agents from across England were drafted in to help. The candidate had an encouraging result on 27th June, substantially denting the Conservative majority but still failing to win by a fair margin.

Grimond was also at his coruscating best in a short debate called at Hugh Gaitskell's insistence to discuss the conduct of Major Niall Macpherson (later Lord Drumalbyn), an under-secretary at the Scottish Office. Macpherson was the Tory MP for Dumfries and had been implicated in the sacking of the editor of the *Dumfries and Galloway Standard*, who had been replaced six months after a meeting between Macpherson and the directors of the paper, at which Macpherson had bemoaned the paper's hostile editorial line towards the government. The editor had been sticking to the traditionally Liberal line of the paper, and felt that he was now being victimised because of unfair pressure from the minister. Harold Macmillan, in defending Macpherson, could not deny the sequence of events, nor did he attempt to deny that pressure had been brought upon the directors. Instead he attempted to draw a distinction between Macpherson the minister and Macpherson the MP, making this a constituency matter and not one for the government. Grimond was having none of it, and forced the Prime Minister on to the back foot in a battle that was rejoined only a week later:

> There does not seem to be any dispute that pressure was brought upon this paper by a member of the Government . . . But I imagine that the Prime Minister will not want to go on the record as saying that it does not matter because it is a small paper, or even because it is a Liberal paper . . . I am sure that the Prime Minister will agree that it is improper that a member of the Government should seek to influence a paper in this way.[46]

Macpherson survived, but Grimond had further enhanced his reputation as an effective parliamentary cross-questioner.

Grimond spent much of the summer of 1957 in Orkney, reflecting on the future and talking to his constituents, punctuating his stay there with occasional speeches and a steady stream of journalism. There was a good piece on reforming Parliament, in which Grimond was highly critical of the suggestion that life peerages might be introduced. The House of Lords, he argued, should be completely rethought, not just mildly ameliorated in this way. It should represent legitimate interests that, for whatever reason, were not properly represented in the House of Commons. Both ministers and MPs were overstretched, he argued: the former because they had accumulated the debris of expanding government activities and were poor at delegating; the latter because they had no means of obtaining the specialised information they needed if they were to do their jobs properly. Members of Parliament had also lost sight of their original function: instead of helping to control public expenditure, under the pressure of increasingly well-organised lobbying from constituency and other interests, they were now constantly pleading for increases in spending. This is where the upper house could have a particular role: free from pressures of this kind, it could be better placed than the Commons to assert the general over the particular: 'This to me is going to be the test of democracy's survival. If it can find no way of putting the general interest above that of particular groups, no restraint upon its own demand for more bread and circuses, then a dictatorship of some sort may be inevitable.'[47]

Grimond's first assembly as party leader was buoyed by a more encouraging by-election result. On 12th September 1957 the Liberal candidate at Gloucester, Patrick Lort-Phillips, won over 20 per cent of the vote, in a seat that the party had not contested in 1955. These votes came almost entirely from the Conservatives, turning a Labour ultra-marginal into a safe seat. Some Tories reacted bitterly by suggesting that the Bolton and Huddersfield pacts could be jeopardised by similar Liberal interventions in future. Grimond's response to such talk was robust. He proclaimed that the Liberals were not 'going to ride on the Tory tiger'. Before the party assembled, Grimond said on television that the country might have a Liberal government within ten years. As the Liberals gathered, the government was forced to put up the bank rate from 5 per cent to 7 per cent to defend the pound, and Grimond was positively triumphant. He even intervened two days before he was due to deliver his leader's speech with an 'I told you so' interjection. The government had cut interest rates only three months earlier, and Grimond claimed that nobody could now have any confidence in its ability to run the economy. 'What they have done vindicates what Liberals have been saying for five years,' Grimond went on to tell the assembly, to cheers. 'The prime duty of the Government is to protect the pound and stop the rise in the cost of living.'[48] This was good fighting talk, but Grimond knew that a stream of effective knocking copy would not suffice. He needed to say something positive about liberalism.

This conference demonstrated the growing influence of the party's Radical Reform Group, which Jeremy Thorpe had helped to establish some years before, and the presidency of which Grimond would take on in January 1958. Lort-Phillips, though by no means a young man himself, joined in, warning that the party must bring its policies and principles up to date if it wished to take full advantage of disillusionment with the other parties. So long as it didn't get out of hand, this revolution suited Grimond's purposes very well. The party still contained a solid phalanx of economic Liberals, many of them inclined to be anti-European, and he desperately wanted the more radical, often younger, social Liberals to rise through the ranks. Several of them did so, attempting to refer back to the party executive motions that were regarded as excessively vague. On the final day of the assembly, Grimond spoke with great style. He still slightly underplayed his witticisms, highlighting them too little and moving on from them too quickly, before delegates had spotted them, but many of his arrows went home. He rejected any notion that the Liberals could content themselves with becoming some kind of pressure group, operating outside the mainstream of political activity and satisfying themselves purely with the effectiveness of their attacks on others. 'I am not prepared to lead a party of eunuchs,' Grimond declared, 'I am not prepared to lead a party which has forsworn direct political action.'[49] They must be a serious campaigning party, interested in power and influence, not a brains trust: 'To say that we may fail is to say nothing new at all . . . What is interesting is that Gloucester has shown that we may succeed.'[50] As it stood, the party was poorly equipped to take full advantage of its new opportunities. It did not lack for enthusiasm, but desperately needed to increase its membership and restore its financial position. Its organisation was inadequate. It was necessary for Liberals to evangelise, he said, to convince people to become Liberals through the force of argument and an appeal to their idealism. He deprecated those who shared the party's aspirations and values, but would not put their shoulders to the wheel. In one of his most famous phrases, he summed up the Liberal position as he saw it: 'The old lifebuoys which have kept this party afloat so long are now dropping astern and in the next ten years it is a question of "Get on" or "Get out" – let's make it "Get on".' The speech was so effective that the text was immediately printed and distributed.

The party now faced another by-election, at Ipswich, where the Liberal candidate was a young woman by the name of Manuela Sykes, who brought glamour and even a degree of slickness to campaigning. The Liberals had not contested the seat in 1955, but Grimond was determined to make a decent showing. The seat was a Labour marginal, and it was Labour who came in for a scathing, indeed hyperbolic, attack when Grimond addressed a meeting in the constituency. 'Socialist fingers are itching to get hold of the steering wheel of Government . . . If they succeed . . . we are going to get the old dose of high taxation, restrictions, controls and, possibly, eventually rationing.'[51] The Liberal polled just over 21 per cent, apparently taken in a ratio of one-third from Labour and two-thirds from the Conservatives.

The next development for Jo Grimond was an invitation to appear on the BBC television version of the *Brains Trust*. He was among the first senior politicians to recognise the importance of television as a campaigning medium. Mindful of the need to look his best, he even went on to a diet towards the end of 1957. ('Why Jo is putting on weight when he's always rushing about so much, I don't know,' commented Laura Grimond. 'But all the same he's got to get rid of it!') During the general election campaign of 1955, any programme (other than party election broadcasts) that might have influenced viewers had been scrupulously dropped from the schedules. As television proliferated, both the BBC and the ITA wanted to institute a more relaxed regime. In January 1958 Jo Grimond attended a seminal conference organised by David Butler at Nuffield College, Oxford to discuss how political broadcasting might be developed. Other delegates included Hugh Gaitskell, Rab Butler, Tony Benn and Edward Heath. In a journey that could itself have provided the basis for a fine television show, Grimond gave Benn and Heath a lift back to London. Of all those present, it was Grimond who would master television most convincingly – and his interest in its potential was to be reaffirmed very soon, for there were two far more significant by-elections just around the corner, one of which would be remembered as the first 'television by-election'. Both were in seats that the Liberals had failed to contest in 1955, but also in areas with a strong radical and nonconformist tradition. Interestingly, both would be fought in the Liberal interest by first-rate candidates whose Liberalism had been affirmed by a combination of Suez and Grimond.

The first was at Rochdale, where the late Conservative MP had defeated Labour with a wafer-thin majority of just over 1,500 votes in a two-horse race. One of the more glamorous figures whom Grimond had enticed into the party, the writer and broadcaster Ludovic Kennedy, put his name forward for the candidacy. Labour really had to win this by-election, but the Conservatives were desperate to make a fight of it. Ludovic Kennedy was no politician, but after hearing a speech by Grimond shortly after he became leader, he had felt moved to join the party. The Kennedys and the Grimonds later became firm friends, dining together and going to the theatre *à quatre*. Kennedy and his glamorous wife, the celebrated ballerina and writer Moira Shearer, waged a highly effective and charismatic campaign. Mrs Kennedy brought in her wake huge media interest, including an unexpected visitor from Finland, one local paper reflecting that, 'never in the history of politics can so much press publicity have been devoted to one constituency'.[52] Most significantly of all, inspired at least in part by the presence of a well-known ITN newscaster among the candidates, Granada Television made an unprecedented intervention in the by-election. Before the Suez crisis blew it away, there had until recently been a ban (incidentally opposed by Grimond and the Liberals) on television broadcasting anything about any political subject that was due to be debated in Parliament in the next fourteen days. The television companies still took the view that by-election campaigns were totally off-limits. Not this time. Granada had taken legal advice and come to the view that, so long as balance between the opposing camps was maintained, they could broadcast whatever they liked. All three candidates were twice featured on regional television, once making statements and once answering questions. A lasting blow had been struck for media freedom. Even though Kennedy felt that he had the most to lose from this innovation, he welcomed it and played his full part. He was nervous that, although he was a newscaster not a politician and was used to delivering a prepared script, he would be judged by harsher standards than his competitors. In fact, he acquitted himself perfectly well.

Grimond spent a day alongside the Kennedys a week before polling day, ending with a meeting in the Town Hall, whose initially euphoric atmosphere the chairman of the local Liberals almost killed stone dead by asking for a minute's silence in honour of the victims of the Munich air disaster. Grimond attacked the Conservatives vigorously for their failure to offer a positive alternative to socialism – 'on the contrary, they are engaged in conserving its worst features'[53] – and came away convinced that a remarkable result might be on the cards. When he first met Moira Shearer that day, he is alleged to have asked her what she was doing there. She replied that she was 'helping Ludo'. Naturally he sympathised. 'How embarrassing,' was his response. The campaign was highly energetic and widely publicised, and the final weekend saw all three parties holding protracted mass rallies in the town hall square of the town. The Conservatives plummeted from first to third place, their share of the vote slumping from over 50 per cent to below 20 per cent. Their candidate received fewer then 10,000 votes, compared with over 26,000 votes in 1955. Labour won, but with a decreased vote. Ludovic Kennedy received a remarkable 17,603 votes. The Tory result was so bad that the party chairman, Quintin Hailsham, privately offered his resignation to Harold Macmillan, who turned it down. The Tories had some hard thinking to do.

Liberal confidence was immensely boosted by the Rochdale result. Ludovic Kennedy was convinced that he had laid to rest the old 'wasted vote' argument once and for all and, the minutes of a meeting of the party's council just three days after the Rochdale poll record, he told his fellow Liberals that: 'this had been the real turning point in the Liberal Party's affairs . . . He was certain that our re-birth would spread throughout the United Kingdom.'[54] In the wake of Rochdale, Grimond promptly went off to the USA for a three-week lecture tour organised by the English-Speaking Union, explaining before he left that it was 'very important' that people there should 'know what the Liberal policy is'. 'Perhaps,' responded one sarcastic observer, 'but what about the people here?'[55] He made eight radio and television appearances in five days while he was in the US and was greatly impressed by the informality of the broadcasters, as compared with all the ceremony to which he was used: 'someone just bears down on you with a microphone and you are on the air!'[56] In fact, Grimond and his loyal lieutenants were working away behind the scenes trying to strengthen the party's image. One of the concerns was that, although Grimond's leadership had given the party an immense fillip, it was generally perceived as a 'one-man band'. Although he certainly had his vain streak, and in some ways enjoyed all the attention, nothing would have pleased Grimond more than the emergence of other figures who could easily and effectively deputise for him. It was all very well getting himself across as a plausible personality, but where was his shadow cabinet, his administration in waiting? The Executive Committee resolved on 15th March 1958 that the party 'must build up twenty, thirty or forty personalities to try and convince the electors that we had some good men and women for Mr Grimond's team as well as a good policy'.[57] Although they never succeeded in realising this ambition, at least some help was now on the way.

7

IN THE WEST COUNTRY, with its strong Liberal traditions, another promising by-election was already looming. The Conservative member for Torrington in North Devon had succeeded to his father's peerage, creating a vacancy. The Liberals already had a well-established prospective candidate in place, a local man by the name of Ambrose Fulford. The by-election was not totally unexpected, and Fulford had already warned Grimond and Jeremy Thorpe the previous year that he did not feel that he would be up to the demands of a by-election. He therefore stepped aside and Mark Bonham Carter, who had once fought part of the constituency in 1945 on old boundaries, was invited to fight the seat. The departure of a well-known local face caused some controversy early in the campaign, but it soon died down. Just as the Suez crisis began, Bonham Carter had been going through the necessary procedures for signing up to the Tories. The potent combination of Suez and Grimond's accession had put paid to that, and Mark was now a loyal and highly active Liberal, and one of the party's most experienced and effective campaigners. His mother, Lady Violet, wrote in her diary that: 'I can see that Mark's mouth waters for the fray.'[1]

Bonham Carter signed up to a gruelling timetable, involving a daily press conference at 9.30 a.m., followed by a full day's campaigning and a series of meetings every evening. His Conservative opponent, Anthony Royle, was also an accomplished operator and had the benefit of far more impressive political machinery behind him. Lady Violet and Jeremy Thorpe, whose relentless and charismatic campaigning in the neighbouring seat of North Devon had elevated him into something of a regional celebrity, threw their full weights behind the campaign, she memorably likening the Conservative candidate to the 'hind legs of a Tory pantomime horse'. Grimond spent a day in the constituency, addressing three meetings and, despite himself, being surprised by the welcome that he received. At the last meeting, in Torrington itself, he had an audience of around 1,200 people, the biggest attendance of the campaign. Ludovic and Moira Kennedy also attended. Towards the end of the campaign, local polls indicated that Mark Bonham Carter could win. In a message to his brother-in-law, Grimond emphasised the party's commitment to a 'comprehensive policy for the countryside as a whole'.[2] According to Bonham Carter's own analysis, this was the most attractive element of the Liberal platform. Despite a warning to the electors from the *Daily Telegraph* that 'a vote for Liberalism turns out in the end to be a vote for Socialism',[3] Mark Bonham Carter did win the seat, after a recount, by a slender but historic margin of just over 200 votes. This was the first Liberal gain at a by-election since March 1929. Lady Violet was predictably ecstatic, as was Jo Grimond himself. She likened the revived Liberals of Torrington to a liberating army and sent out a message to Liberals elsewhere: 'Hold on, hold on, we are coming!' Bonham Carter, to whom Jo Grimond had long been close, would subsequently become his closest confidant and, for a time, his most important parliamentary lieutenant. Many people feel that, with a reliable parliamentary seat, he might even in due course have become Grimond's successor as leader.

After Torrington, Grimond penned an important article, which appeared in the *News Chronicle* on 29th March 1958. He was sensitive to the charge that many of Mark Bonham Carter's voters in Torrington had been voting against the shortcomings of other parties rather than giving a positive endorsement to Liberalism, so some difficult questions had to be answered. 'Where do Liberals go from here,' he asked rhetorically. 'We carve out a niche for ourselves Left of Centre . . . in the sense that we stand for personal freedom against authority . . . in the sense that we believe there is still too much poverty, too many slums and too much cruelty . . . in the sense that we want and mean to have a wide dispersal of property and power.' Yes, he conceded, it could be argued that a Liberal vote was a protest vote, but then 'all votes are' in some sense and, at least, a Liberal vote 'isn't a protest vote against one particular thing . . . It is a protest against the whole of politics since the war . . . It is a protest against broken promises and bumbledom [bureaucracy].' Grimond also set out clearly for the first time his formula for how the Liberals might behave if they ever held the parliamentary balance of power: 'We would throw our weight behind Liberal measures whoever proposed them and try to get them on the statute book . . . We would create a Liberal atmosphere in this country and in the Western world.' But what was so important was the fact that people were seriously asking such a question: 'Our opponents used to say that a Liberal vote was a wasted vote. Torrington has killed that dead.' When Mark Bonham Carter took his seat in the House of Commons, the faint cheers of his new colleagues were drowned out by laughter and jeers from the other parties.

Four by-elections in a row – Gloucester, Ipswich, Rochdale and now Torrington – had served Liberal purposes very well. Then the Liberals had disappointing results in the county council elections in April, and Labour too performed only moderately well, gaining a handful of seats. It was Labour that began to panic; Gaitskell and his team were aware of widespread disaffection with the Tories, but they seemed unable to harness it. In contrast, by choosing carefully where to intervene, the Liberal Party was at least managing to capture between 20 and 40 per cent of the vote at parliamentary by-elections. For the remainder of the Parliament, the Liberals devoted a considerable amount of effort and of their limited resources to contesting residential and agricultural seats at by-elections. But Harold Macmillan was beginning to make his mark as Prime Minister and, as 1958 progressed, the initiative was slipping away from the opposition parties. In the House of Commons Bevan tried to put one over Macmillan by dubbing him 'Mr MacWonder'. 'What a bloody silly thing to say,' Grimond whispered to Mark Bonham Carter.[4] Grimond was amongst the first to realise that, for all his old-world mannerisms, this new Conservative Prime Minister was going to prove far more formidable than most people had expected.

In the wake of Torrington, Grimond both embarked upon a process of policy renewal, and continued to grapple with the party's organisational shortcomings. As the party gained in confidence and it became more assertive, the question arose of whether it should now look to go all out, contesting every seat in the land and abjuring all pacts with other parties, at least until the 'New Alignment' had come into being. Grimond had to speak with forked tongue. On the one hand, he wanted to sound bullish and confident, commenting after the Rochdale result: 'at one time many constituencies were fought by three parties . . . I think it would be a good thing if we got back to that situation.'[5] He knew full well, however, that Arthur Holt, in Bolton, and Donald Wade, in Huddersfield, were most unlikely at that stage to remain in Parliament if the Conservatives decided to end the pacts in those towns. So Grimond always carefully limited his remarks to a condemnation of any *national* arrangement, something that the party's executive too ruled out in a statement issued shortly after Torrington. On local arrangements Grimond's view was more equivocal. 'In my view,' he told one political correspondent in response to the executive's trenchancy, 'this does not touch the question of local pacts.'[6] This line became harder to hold once the Liberal assembly in 1958 asserted that, 'the Liberal Party can, in no foreseeable circumstances, enter into pacts with either the Conservative Party or the Labour Party on the national or local level', but Grimond always loyally defended both Wade and Holt.

Grimond's mind was now turning to the next general election. By-elections had demonstrated the importance of effective campaigning techniques, so he wrote a formal letter to Donald Wade, the party's parliamentary whip, setting out what he regarded as the party's organisational requirements. On Friday, 9th May 1958, the party's Executive Committee discussed his proposals. At their core was Grimond's conviction that it was now essential to establish a new, powerful Pre-Election Strategy Committee, whose chairman should be either the chief whip or the chairman of the executive, and whose vice-chairman should be someone who was not participating in the general election as a candidate. In the period before the campaign proper, the committee should ideally consist of ten or eleven people, half of whom could be candidates. Then when the election beckoned, the others could remain at HQ during the campaign itself. Of those candidates, at least two should be MPs. Scotland and Wales should both be represented; and the new committee shouldn't duplicate the work of other committees. Its main emphasis should be on collecting material for election leaflets and other aspects of the national campaign. It should work closely with the party's Candidates' Committee in mapping out the broad outlines of the campaign, and should take responsibility for ensuring that the manifesto was ready in good time. It should also coordinate plans for major rallies, and prepare lists of 'personalities' for broadcasts. The minutes record that 'Mr Grimond qualified these points by indicating that most of the better known personalities of the Party would have to spend time in their own constituencies. Three of the Members of Parliament had very large agricultural constituencies, which would occupy them full time. Broadcasts need very careful consideration. He himself could not leave Orkney and Shetland.'[7] That last sentence has a chilling finality about it.

Grimond wanted Frank Byers (as effective chairman) and Arthur Holt to run this new committee for him. At the crucial meeting, the minutes record,

> Mr Donald Wade MP said that Mr Grimond was certainly very anxious not to do anything unconstitutional and did not wish to override the Executive in any way. He would like to feel that the Parliamentary Party and the other representatives of the Party were making such preliminary plans as were possible so that we were ready when the time came. Mr Grimond himself would be Chairman but when the election came he would have to go up to the Orkneys. It was mainly for this reason that he had put forward suggestions.[8]

The Executive Committee signed up to his initiative which, in time, became the basis for a thoroughgoing (and controversial) reform of the entire structure of the Liberal Party.

Another electoral test soon beckoned. On 12th June 1958 by-elections were held in five constituencies in what the national press labelled a 'Little General Election'. This was hyperbole since, in all honesty, none of the seats promised much of an upset. Three were safe Tory seats; two were Labour strongholds. The Liberals had only contested one of them in 1955, the strongly Conservative constituency of Ealing South, where their candidate had won just under 10 per cent of the vote. They would much rather have not contested such an unpromising seat again, but felt obliged to do so for fear of looking defeatist. The other two Tory-held seats, Argyll and Weston-Super-Mare, looked like better prospects. The party fared poorly in Ealing but did better than respectably in those other constituencies by winning around a quarter of the vote, but falling well short of the high-water marks of Rochdale and Torrington. Ludovic Kennedy and Mark Bonham Carter had so raised expectations that to increase the vote from a standing start to 25 per cent now seemed positively lacklustre. As he became better known, Grimond travelled more and more, confiding in one candidate that what got him down most was neither the travelling itself, nor the people he met: 'It's awful, you know – you go into this house, you are briefly introduced to the children, who then scurry off into the kitchen where you then hear them having a gorgeous fry-up. You've had nothing to eat all day, and you're offered a few crisps and nuts – and then you're expected to go off and make a speech!'[9]

During this busy time, Grimond even went out to sea with the Shetlanders, one of whom told journalists that Grimond was 'one of the hardiest seafarers you could meet and enjoys a night out with the fishing fleet . . . one skipper has not yet recovered from the novelty of having a Member of Parliament sitting on deck gutting fish in the early hours.'[10] The islands came as close as any part of the United Kingdom to the kind of Liberal ideal that Grimond espoused. The people were hardy and self-reliant, their communities were democratic and cohesive, and they were unimpressed by the considerations of status that so obsessed the political class down in London. This, of course, meant that the 'man in Whitehall' could more or less ignore them, a fact that Grimond bemoaned in a speech to some of his constituents:

> The outer isles of Orkney are guilty of nothing but working for their living: result, no transport subsidy and electricity. The best way to get help would be to stage a sit-down strike or ensure that the population is reduced to vanishing point. Then, when it is too late, help will be showered upon you. Your gradual decline into a nature reserve will be made comfortable by lavish public expenditure on service which only officials will be left to use. The Highlands are overrun by authorities which have too little money, too little business ability and insufficient powers.[11]

Grimond was also concerned that the Parliamentary Boundary Commission might decide to merge some of the constituencies in the Highlands and Islands. The average electorates were (and still are) extremely low in Scotland's most northerly seats, but they have endured because of the huge geographical areas that they cover. When talk of political merger with the mainland began, Grimond was having none of it. The Highlanders were splendid people, but the people of the islands had different needs, traditions and interests: 'Patriotic as I am, I cannot suggest that every Shetlander or Orcadian is worth two and a half Londoners in an election . . . [But] in considering the size of constituencies, we must remember not only the Member's difficulties, but the constituent's. He wants to see his Member occasionally – and we might, incidentally, make it easier for him to vote.'[12]

After the summer break, Grimond had to endure one of the most difficult

Liberal assemblies of his career. No single element of the Liberals' Torquay assembly in 1958 made it into a shambles, but a shambles it most certainly was. Since gathering in Southport a year earlier, the Liberals had enjoyed one of their better years, but their assembly degenerated into a farce, with delegates squabbling about procedural problems and hair-splitting amendments while totally ignoring the important questions of substance that lay before them. The president of the assembly, the eminent Liberal lawyer Sir Arthur Comyns Carr, regularly held a sheaf of papers in the way of the microphone, so his remarks were all too often lost on all but his immediate neighbours. Many of the speeches from the platform were inaudible, delegates often didn't know what they were voting on, and the defeated candidate from the Gloucester by-election, Colonel Lort-Phillips, was inexplicably accorded a bigger welcome by the assembly than Mark Bonham Carter received. There was also a series of unedifying squabbles between Oliver Smedley, unofficial leader of the party's remaining hardline free traders, and some of the party's younger members who felt that his calls for 'unilateral free trade' were archaic and impractical. Jo Grimond delivered rather a good speech, but to little avail. His attacks on the shortcomings of the other parties seemed almost laughable. He claimed that he did not regret 'by one tittle' the disagreements and chaotic episodes of the week. This was not a matter for shame. At least the Liberals were open about their debates, rather than settling everything behind closed doors. This all sounded a little desperate. More significant, perhaps, was Grimond's firm call upon Liberals 'to give some cohesion not only to long-term Liberalism but also to the Liberal impact on immediate current events'.[13] Not surprisingly, even Jeremy Thorpe could not make a success of the financial appeal at the end of the week – the total was half that of a year earlier. This was a hammer blow: even though membership had approximately doubled since Grimond had become leader, the party's finances were ill prepared for another general election. The publicity accorded to the assembly was almost uniformly dreadful and Grimond, who had never been a great admirer of assemblies, resolved that this must never happen again. The most outspoken and newsworthy section of Grimond's speech was a vigorous attack on privilege, as epitomised by the Conservative and Labour machines:

> We make ourselves a laughing stock . . . Time was when we used to laugh at Balkan princelings and South American generals with strings of titles and breasts full of medals. But we are getting worse. We give the impression that Britain is a sort of elderly fossil, a preserve for tourists. Peerages, life peerages, knighthoods, directorships, perquisites of every sort, are showered on those the Prime Minister and the ruling party choose to honour. I see no more reason for bowing to TUC knights than to Tory knights . . . There is real danger that the leadership of the TUC is becoming a frozen hierarchy of office, which is out of touch with its members and failing to perform useful service for the community.[14]

If Grimond was looking for controversy, he certainly found it. The Labour-supporting *Daily Mirror* carried this section of his speech in full on its front page the following Monday, with a banner proclaiming that 'This is <u>TALKING! THIS</u> should be the policy of Britain's Labour Party!' Not everyone in the Labour movement was so impressed. There ensued a rancorous exchange of correspondence with Clement Attlee, who felt that Grimond was making an implicit personal attack on his conduct as Prime Minister. Attlee claimed that he had known the political affiliations of only three of the peers whom he had nominated – two Conservatives and one Liberal. Grimond was polite but unrepentant, defending his right to make public criticisms of the system for disbursing honours. He was raising a point of principle, not making any personal attacks. Attlee's curt rejoinder to this challenged Grimond either to give specific examples of abuses, or to withdraw his allegations about the system. Rather appropriately, Grimond was then fogbound in Shetland and the next act of this drama was delayed. The two men ultimately agreed to disagree, Grimond sticking to his line that it was perfectly in order to criticise such a manifestly arcane method of handing out honours.

The next time the party gathered was on 6th November 1958, at a massive rally in the Royal Albert Hall. An anonymous donor contributed the use of the hall, and all 5,000 reserved seats were sold. This time nothing was left to chance. Grimond took the opportunity to give one of his first expositions of the 'realignment of the Left' (a phrase borrowed from Mark Bonham Carter), stating that 'the long-term objective is clear: to replace the Labour Party as the progressive wing of politics in this country.'[15] Into this new progressive movement, based around the Liberals, he would sweep 'not only Liberals, but liberal Socialists and liberal Tories, and make it a great movement for the shaping of a Liberal society'.[16] He also launched a new fund-raising plan, under which members would give a commitment to contribute annually to the party. Although Grimond gave one of his better speeches, the real star of the evening was the party's former leader Viscount Samuel, contributing to the 'revivalist' atmosphere on his eighty-eighth birthday. By all accounts he received the biggest cheer of the night.

Grimond had to work harder than ever throughout to maintain a significant profile in Parliament. He did not confine himself to the big set-piece occasions in the chamber itself. It may seem incredible to think now, but he had to continue serving on parliamentary standing committees, dealing with the details of legislation, for much of his time as leader. As the sole Liberal representative from Scotland, for example, he served on the committee considering the 1956–7 Housing and Development Bill. Although he didn't make a single intervention, between March and May he attended ten out of the committee's nineteen half-day sessions. During the following session he sat on the Scottish Standing Committee as it ground its way through

Bills on Land Drainage and Local Government. His only interjection during the former was to record his sadness at the death of his old friend Walter Eliot; on the latter he was more outspoken, deploring the government's failure to introduce Home Rule and, interestingly, advocated that local authorities should be obliged to take greater account of the prevailing economic situation as they took decisions on expenditure. His most interesting interventions, however, came at meetings of the Scottish Grand Committee, which consists of all Scottish MPs plus other ad hoc members, and exists not to play a part in legislation but to fulfil the time-honoured role of scrutinising and discussing the work of government. Grimond was concerned about the proliferation of semi-autonomous bodies that the government was funding, and the limited methods available to MPs for examining their performance. What was needed was 'development and not mere administration'. The Highlands and Islands came under the aegis of an unusually high number of such bodies, and Grimond wanted to see them simplified. Some of his parliamentary colleagues had been involved in public clashes with such bodies, and Grimond warned that this would be unavoidable unless ministers could establish a new culture of accountability: 'The dangerous situation now is that there are many of these boards which are groping about in a sort of limbo. Parliament does not control them adequately and our constituents do not know how to tackle them. Nor are these boards open to the strains and stresses of commercial life . . . It is the Minister who must take responsibility.'[17]

Grimond also called regularly for improved transport for the islands, not just for the purposes of encouraging tourism, but also for the local people themselves. Although he did not use the phrase 'Integrated Transport Strategy' (but how many politicians since have done so, without ever finding one), as a regular long-distance commuter he was well qualified to moan about the absence of 'close cohesion between the nationalised industries of airways and railways, let alone between these industries, steamers, road services and the Government'.[18] He felt that the people of Orkney and Shetland were being victimised and denied the kind of financial support that others routinely received because of their independence of spirit and their reluctance to complain. Some crofters were benefiting from government policy, it was true, but did the government realise how much it was discriminating against the owner-occupier since 'crofters' were, for the purposes of the Crofters Commission and its system of grants, by definition tenants and only tenants? Although the Highlands and Islands were crying out for capital and 'have to put up with the disadvantage of high taxation by the State',[19] they were getting nothing like as much industrial assistance as certain other regions, notably Northern Ireland. With so much else on his plate – national campaigns, major policy reforms, endless party committee meetings, not to mention a young family – Grimond never allowed his advocacy of constituency concerns to flag.

There were two more promising by-elections in early 1959. At the end of January, Southend West offered some encouragement when the Conservative majority fell by more than 10,000 and the Liberal share of the vote increased by over 9 per cent. Then, in April, the Liberals came second in a by-election at Galloway, another seat that they had not contested in 1955, taking a third of Labour's vote and reducing the Conservative share from 67 per cent to 50 per cent. Buoyed by this limited progress, Grimond rather tempted fate by predicting that the Liberals might take twelve to eighteen seats at the forthcoming general election. As 1959 progressed, Grimond sensed an ebbing of the Liberal tide. The protest votes that had so enlivened by-elections seemed now to be returning to their atavistic homes. He launched a minor 'spring offensive' against Labour, mainly on defence policy, which helped restore the Liberals' poll rating into double figures. In particular he mocked Hugh Gaitskell, whose real problems with the nuclear disarmers were now beginning, denouncing the 'utter cynicism' of Labour's home policy and attacked the trade unions for their advocacy of Britain joining the 'non-nuclear club'. Frank Cousins of the Transport and General Workers' Union had been the prime mover in this new anti-nuclear initiative. Grimond's response was that he 'seems more dangerous to his own wicket keeper than to the Tory batsmen'[20] – the unions would be better occupied advising their members on demarcation disputes. He did also argue, however, that the Conservative government retained its attachment to an independent nuclear deterrent not on strategic grounds, but purely to nurture and indulge its imperial pretensions. 'Do not delude yourself that the British bomb is designed to frighten the Russians,' he told an audience at Kirriemuir. 'It is designed to frighten the Americans.'[21] On defence at least, Grimond did walk a fine line between the Tory position and that of the Labour Party.

The Liberals' progress as a freshly reminted progressive party was proving to be a mixed blessing for Arthur Holt. Holt had campaigned with great vigour for Ludovic Kennedy as he tried to win the Conservative seat of Rochdale, and many Tories in Bolton felt that, in doing so, he was guilty of breaching the spirit of his non-aggression pact with them. The position was not helped by Liberal encroachment into traditionally Conservative areas at local government level in the town. At a poorly attended meeting in early 1959, the Executive Council of the Bolton West Conservative Association voted to end the arrangement with the Liberals by putting up a candidate against Arthur Holt. The chairman of the association resigned in protest, blaming the influence of the association's women members – Bolton Wanderers had been playing Preston on the evening of the vote and, consequently, only 75 of the council's 200 members had been present. The pact made sense, he said, because it had resulted in the election of 'two first-class MPs and . . . two anti-socialist votes in Parliament'.[22] Arthur Holt suspected from the outset that the decision might well be reversed and wisely kept his own counsel. Both the Conservative agent for the north-west and the party chairman, Lord Hailsham, advised the Bolton association to think again and Holt must have breathed a sigh of relief as Bolton West Conservatives decided by an overwhelming majority at their 1959 AGM to reverse the earlier decision to contest his seat. Holt did recognise, however, that an arrangement born in the early 1950s in very different political circumstances was beginning to come under impossible pressure. A deal of this sort, even without any written foundation, was now a serious embarrassment to the Liberal Party nationally. 'The question of a pact on previous lines does not arise,' he conceded as soon as he heard the good news.[23] Nonetheless the *pro tem* about-turn was welcomed not only in Bolton, but also in the *Daily Telegraph*, which urged Conservatives and Liberals elsewhere, 'where local conditions permit . . . to follow Minerva rather than Mars'.[24]

At Grimond's insistence, the Liberals also ran a summer campaign in 1959, founded upon a series of articles on policy in *Liberal News*, which had now been sharpened up considerably by Arthur Holt. Grimond was determined that everyone must remain on a war footing, and the summer of 1959 afforded him the opportunity for one more major speech before the flag went up for the autumn election that most people now expected. As the main keynote speaker at the Liberal summer school in Oxford, he set out a broad Liberal vision for both domestic and foreign policy. He foresaw that, as the influence of mainland European habits spread, the traditional British division between politicians and civil servants could be blown away. If a new breed of highly paid and influential *énarques* was to take charge of our affairs, he warned, they should be accountable: men and women 'open to criticism and over whom the ultimate sanction is the sack'.[25] Meantime, the House of Commons should get back to its original and fundamental job of scrutinising the executive, and stop trying to take direct control over more and more aspects of national life. He argued that inflation was not only a monetary phenomenon: it had also afflicted the honours system, reducing modern-day Britain to a parody of a banana republic, 'living in a stuffy, egotistical world of her own creation, worshipping the maces, wigs and general paraphernalia of a political system to the suitability of which, for modern life, neither the Conservative nor Labour parties have given any thought whatsoever'.[26] In foreign affairs, Grimond argued that Britain really must shed its old definition of sovereignty, urging the creation of a 'Western Foreign Office' with its own cabinet of heads of state, to pull together the strands of foreign policy across the Western powers.

Grimond always took great interest in the difficulties in Cyprus, the Mediterranean island that had played such an important part as a British outpost for a good many years. In light of their determination to retain a major role in the Middle East, successive post-war British governments resolved to keep Cyprus as a colony. During the early 1950s a movement for Cypriot union with Greece (Enosis) grew up and, from 1955, a more violent campaign against the British colonial presence was waged by the EOKA organisation. The British occupying forces met violence with violence, and Grimond was amongst the first to denounce the swift recourse to force. Under pressure, the British government belatedly suggested that Cyprus, rather than uniting with Greece, might become a member of the Commonwealth. There was little goodwill towards Britain on the island at that point, however, and this gambit was coolly received. Grimond from the outset believed that the people of Cyprus should be allowed to determine their own future, pointing out vigorously that 'it is particularly unfortunate that we should be behaving in a totalitarian manner on an island that is celebrated throughout history for its courage as an outpost of Western civilisation.'[27] The main focus for most pro-independence activities was Archbishop Makarios III, head of the Cypriot Orthodox Church. In 1956 some diaries by the Secretary of State for the Colonies, Alan Lennox Boyd, were deliberately released, implicating Makarios in the violence in an apparent attempt to discredit him. Grimond called the government's bluff, asking why, if he was so wicked, Makarios had not been brought to trial; the British authorities baulked at that, however, and had him deported to the Seychelles.

Although the British government was always reluctant to let Cyprus go, its policy towards the island was inevitably tempered in the wake of Suez. After becoming Liberal leader, Grimond restated his belief that Britain should, as a first step, declare that it had no selfish or national interest in Cyprus, ultimately allowing the islanders to decide their own fate. With David Astor, he was a leading member of a group of public figures who met covertly with Greek and Greek-Cypriot representatives to discuss possible ways of breaking the deadlock. By 1958, although the British still maintained that they would not give up their bases on the island, they had begun to concede that full British sovereignty over the island must now be negotiable. There was already another unpredictable and dangerous factor at play, in the shape of a sizeable Turkish minority on the island. Grimond and the Liberals warned all along that any stable settlement would have to safeguard the rights of ethnic Turks, foreseeing a role for international law and the United Nations in guaranteeing that.

Towards the end of 1958, Laura discovered that, at the age of forty, she was pregnant with the couple's fourth child. Magnus Grimond was born on 13th June 1959 and, although his parents hoped that this late fecundity might be repeated, he proved to be their last child. Johnny, meanwhile, was about to start Eton and Grizelda was at St Pauls, where, a fellow parent from the time remembers, Jo Grimond's own appearances were eagerly awaited, as he was 'by far the handsomest father'. It was an extraordinary reflection on Laura Grimond that, with so many other responsibilities, she was willing even to consider another child at this stage of her life. Throughout her husband's development from judicial neophyte through unambitious soldier to parliamentarian and public figure, Laura provided crucial support, both moral and practical. The energetic fashion in which she threw herself into campaigns, particularly in Orkney and Shetland and in by-elections, was legendary, and her own career in public life should never be underestimated. She was, at various stages and *inter alia*, on the Liberal Party Executive Committee, a parliamentary candidate, a magistrate, a local councillor, President of the Women's Liberal Federation and a laudably robust member of the Alliance Defence Commission. It is no secret that the Grimonds' was not the easiest of marriages, particularly during the long periods when Laura was in Orkney and her husband was in London, but its ultimate endurance marks it out as one of the great political partnerships.

While Laura was nursing her infant son Magnus, the troubled life of her eldest, Andrew, took a turn for the worse. He had ended his career at Eton under something of a cloud after contracting tuberculosis, a disease to which some vestigial stigma was still attached, and spent some time in a sanatorium in Sussex. Even as a young child, Andrew had preferred the company of adults and this experience, which both broke his bond with Eton and brought him into extended contact with older TB patients, seems to have affected him profoundly. Despite this setback, however, Andrew was able to take up his place at Magdalen College, Oxford. Although he was by inclination a historian, he opted to study the subject at which his father had excelled – Politics, Philosophy and Economics (PPE) – almost certainly an unhappy misjudgement. Both Andrew and his parents soon had high hopes that he was putting his earlier unhappiness behind him. At Oxford he seemed to blossom, making many new friends and enjoying life generally. Then disaster struck. The university had recently introduced a policy of 'two strikes and you're out' for first-year PPE students. When Andrew failed his preliminary examinations in summer 1959, at the end of his first year, he faced an immediate ultimatum: he had to retake them at the beginning of the autumn term and, if he failed again, he would be sent down. Tragically for him, he did fail. He was severely traumatised. It is impossible to say whether he already harboured the seeds of mental instability before his Oxford career was so abruptly cut short – he had certainly been an unusually absent-minded teenager, prone to introspection and rather serious – but he now suffered a period of severe withdrawal, at times bordering on catalepsy. He seemed to feel that he had not only let himself down. He had failed to match up to the impressive yardstick set by his father, who later reflected: 'high aspirations are prolific causes of family trouble.'[28] All the Grimonds were greatly relieved when, in the autumn of 1960, he was able to return to his studies at London University, having regained some internal equilibrium and transferred to a more congenial history course.

When a press conference was convened at the National Liberal Club on Thursday, 3rd September 1959 to discuss the proposed agenda for that month's Liberal assembly, Mark Bonham Carter was in acerbic mood. Harold Macmillan had just given a televised broadcast from No. 10 featuring himself in conversation with President Eisenhower. This, said Bonham Carter, meant that an election was unquestionably in the offing, in which case they were all probably wasting their time talking about the assembly. It would either be happening in the first week of an election campaign, or not at all. Losing their assembly in this way, conceded Arthur Holt at the same press conference, 'would make it very tricky'[29] for the Liberals, who needed all the publicity they could get. Mark Bonham Carter was right. Harold Macmillan, buoyed up by improved opinion poll ratings and in search of his own mandate, called a general election for 8th October 1959. The Liberal assembly at Scarborough was indeed cancelled, supplanted by a one-day campaign launch meeting on Tuesday, 15th September. Grimond had done most of the gruelling spadework in fashioning a party in his own radical image. Now the time really had arrived for him to 'get on' or 'get out'. A day later, a series of photo-calls with London candidates was cancelled at short notice because Grimond had to drive Johnny off to Eton for the beginning of his first term there.

Grimond cannot have felt terribly confident going into the 1959 general election. He had made considerable strides in regenerating the party intellectually, but as a campaigning outfit it was still worryingly ineffective and most of its six seats were vulnerable. The burst of support that had buoyed the party through the earlier part of the 1955 Parliament had more or less evaporated, and the triumph of Torrington was a distant memory. There had also been the terrible blow of Philip Fothergill's death, at the cruelly early age of fifty-two, on 31st January 1959. This deprived Grimond of a stalwart supporter and friend with an apparently infinite capacity for uniting the party. Fothergill was an extraordinary and indispensable figure for the Liberal Party in the post-war era, chairman of the party for 1946–9 and arguably an even more crucial figure than Clement Davies in holding the party together during an almost impossibly difficult time. Grimond always referred to Fothergill, with a mixture of irreverence and respect, as 'Foth', and never underestimated his political skills. He was an ever-present source of inspiration and support for almost two decades whom Grimond described as 'father confessor and favourite uncle, old family nurse, friend for a pleasant evening and purveyor of good ideas'.[30] He also played a crucial role in ensuring that Clement Davies went quietly.

Although Grimond had by now firmly stamped himself upon his party, he was still finding it difficult to make a more general impact and the state of the party's finances still curtailed its advertising and organisation. Only Grimond himself and, to a far lesser extent, Frank Byers were in any sense national figures and a Gallup poll in March 1959 had shown that almost 60 per cent of voters said that they didn't know what the party stood for. Nonetheless, Grimond could take some encouragement from the widespread disenchantment that he detected towards politics in general, and the two major parties in particular. Although Grimond was naturally averse to making too strong a pitch for 'negative' votes, he had at least in part to swallow his pride. This was apparent when he launched the party's campaign at a thinly attended rally in London on 15th September. Since they looked like fielding just over 200 candidates, Grimond could not pretend that the Liberals had a chance of winning the election, and he skirted around any question of how they might behave if they held the balance of power in the new Parliament. He argued instead that, if many more of the millions of people with liberal instincts had the courage of their convictions and voted Liberal, they could rein in 'the real blimp Tories and stop the Socialists who want more nationalisation . . . You may not determine whether you get a Tory or a Socialist government – but what is more important, perhaps, is to influence how a Tory or Socialist Government will behave.'[31]

The following day, at a press conference, Grimond conceded the election to the Conservatives, admitting that, 'we are not at this election, though we shall be in subsequent ones, passionately interested in contending for office.'[32] There would have been no point in pretending that the Liberals were in a position to win outright, but it did still surely smack of defeatism to concede so early in the campaign that, even as part of a coalition, power was just not on the menu. The same 'negative' message was to some degree reflected in the Liberals' manifesto, which came out rather late, on 21st September. Although this document, entitled *People Count,* certainly contained plenty of policies, its main emphasis was on a personal appeal from Grimond himself, who advised people to break away from the politics of the big party machines. 'A Liberal vote is a protest against the British political system being divided up between two powerful Party machines,' he claimed, 'one largely financed by the employers and the other by the Trade Unions.'[33] Grimond was widely criticised in 1959 for whittling down his draft tour itinerary to just one day of campaigning outside his Orkney and Shetland redoubt, and remaining in the islands for over two weeks solidly, between 17th September and 2nd October. His fear of defeat appeared to verge on the neurotic, which for a time alienated even those closest to him. He was still fearful that the islanders would take it amiss if he appeared to be taking them for granted now that he was leader, and even asked Violet Bonham Carter to come and campaign with him in Orkney and Shetland, something that she hadn't done since 1950. She was not amused, recording in her diary that 'I know he is as safe as a church whereas Mark is fighting for his life at Torrington & Malindine [North Cornwall] & Jeremy [North Devon] might win seats.'[34]

   Grimond's absence from the national front line was a significant personal
misjudgement that did little to help the party. Frank Byers, as campaign
chairman, and the party's general director Herbert Harris took charge of press
conferences and did their best to gain publicity. With their best asset tucked
away in the far north, however, the Liberals found it just as difficult as in 1955
to win a place at the political top table. In Grimond's absence, the party's
first television election broadcast was not a notable success. It was clumsily
put together and far from coherent, presenting an obviously contrived and
not especially stimulating discussion between five of the party's more notable
candidates, including Mark Bonham Carter and the broadcasters John Arlott
and Robin Day. Grimond did at least pen the odd article, including one
for the *Daily Mirror*, in which he issued a vigorous call for a more exciting
and honest brand of politics. Somewhat bizarrely he also sounded off against
some of the 'evils' afflicting Scotland: 'violence, drink . . . sexual promiscuity
and feckless weakness'.[35] When Grimond did at last return to the national
battlefield, he made an immediate impact. On Friday, 2nd October he gave
a speech in Inverness, still a target seat for the Liberals. He then travelled
immediately south to London by sleeper that same night. Herbert Harris
summoned all the party's agents in London to attend upon Grimond as he
arrived. They trooped to King's Cross at crack of dawn, the sleeper duly
arrived and crowds of people poured forth on to the concourse. Of Grimond
there was no sign. The group went hunting, and found their leader in the
luggage van at the back of the train, struggling to retrieve his baggage – in the
shape of the famously heavy Gladstone bag that he took everywhere which, as
Basil Wishart once joked, 'from its condition, may well have belonged to the
GOM himself'.[36] They then took him to party HQ in a motorcade.
   Grimond's first task in London was to give a press conference; the second
was to deliver the party's second and final television broadcast live that evening.
At the press conference he reiterated his view that the Liberals stood to win
between twelve and eighteen seats at the election. He dictated his script for the
broadcast himself to a pair of secretaries at Liberal headquarters and then, on
arrival at the studio in Wembley, decided to rework its peroration substantially
at the last minute, with help from Basil Wishart, who had accompanied
him down from Shetland to act as his PA for the brief English sojourn.
'Come on, Wishart,' he demanded, 'why d'you think I brought you here!?!'[37]
Carefully playing the patrician, Grimond spoke directly to the viewer without
contrivances or gimmicks of any kind, bidding for the 18 per cent of voters
shown by the most recent polls still to be undecided. Distancing himself
from the crude partisanship of the other parties, he emphasised the value of
the Liberals' independence in an age of party machines. Although he again
failed to address the knotty question of exactly what he and his party might
do if they did get a large vote and ended up holding the balance of power

in Parliament, he signed off by claiming that a Liberal vote could make a difference. It was not, to use the phrase that for so long haunted his party, a 'wasted vote'. His improvisation made him overrun, and ITV viewers were deprived of his peroration because he was jeopardising the commercial break. The broadcast made it into the week's 'Top Ten' programmes: almost 5 million homes tuned in to it, in a mere 311,000 of which sets were turned off before the end. The doyen of American political commentary, Ed Murrow, subsequently revealed in a lecture that he had found this broadcast 'as effective as anything presented during the campaign . . . He did not appear to be speaking down to us from Cloud Seven.'[38]

On Monday, 5th October, Grimond had his only full day of campaigning outside Orkney and Shetland, taking the night train to Bodmin and joining Basil Wishart, whom he had sent on ahead the day before, for breakfast at a hotel in Newquay. Grimond had apologised to Wishart for the fact that he felt unable to put him up at the family home at Kew – it was not in an immaculate state, and a mouse had just been sighted running across the dining table. Wishart stayed at the National Liberal Club. One of the porters had gone out to fetch the morning papers for them and, leaving the hotel, Grimond suggested to Wishart that they should tip him half a crown. 'I've already given him a pound,' responded Wishart, 'and put it on your expense account.'[39] They then undertook a one-day helicopter tour of target seats, taking in the West Country and Hereford and ending up at Manchester and Rochdale, where Ludovic Kennedy was standing again. Grimond's exchanges with voters and party workers in the West Country did wonders for his confidence and he began to talk of a 'sweeping tide of Liberalism' and of a coming 'landslide to liberalism in certain places'. At the day's close, Grimond and Wishart were driven through the night from Rochdale to Glasgow, whence they flew back to the islands on the 7.15 flight the following morning.

When Grimond and Wishart arrived in Orkney, Laura appeared in a flurry, clutching a batch of carpet samples and demanding that Jo should select one suitable for the dining room at the Old Manse before he was allowed to carry on to Sumburgh. As usual, she too had been campaigning hard, despite the fact that she was nursing an infant child. Carrying four-month-old Magnus swaddled in a Moses basket and 'tied with a luggage label in case he was mislaid during a meeting',[40] Laura sailed indomitably around the islands addressing a series of public meetings. The more remote the island, the better: 'If Jo had gone,' she joked of one of them, 'he might have been stranded and missed the whole election.'[41] Grimond's three-day burst of higher-profile campaigning may have come rather late in the day, but it was by no means ineffective. At last the Liberals got some decent publicity for their efforts, and a post-election Gallup poll found that 42 per cent of those who voted Liberal in 1959 had decided to do so only during the election campaign itself.

Yet not everyone was filled with admiration for the Liberal approach. Robin Day, standing for the Liberals at Hereford, found it 'depressing that so few of the local Liberals seemed to be interested in contemporary Liberalism as preached by Jo Grimond and myself'.[42] Day increasingly resorted to anti-Tory populism as the campaign wore on. Despite the hard work of his admirable agent, Ted Wheeler, and a visit from the skies by Grimond, Day lost by over 7,500 votes. He severed all connections with the party thereafter, and would write scathingly about the tensions and contradictions that, in his view, would always undermine the credibility of Grimond's Liberals: 'as an organisation, the Liberal Party was a shambles . . . it was likely to be hopelessly divided between the old traditionalists and young radicals . . . To many of its supporters it was a party of the reasonable centre. To many of its activists it was a party of the militant left. A political party could be either of these, but not both.'[43]

In the wake of the election Grimond's agonies and dilemmas about how to behave in a hung Parliament could be set to one side. Macmillan was back in with an increased majority – and the Liberals still had only six seats. Worst of all, Mark Bonham Carter had lost at Torrington, even though his share of the vote had risen slightly. Grimond described this as 'a heavy and by me unexpected blow'.[44] Despite his defeat, Bonham Carter remained Jo Grimond's main lieutenant throughout his leadership. The defeat at Torrington was to some extent countervailed by an impressive gain in a neighbouring constituency: on a swing of almost 8 per cent, Jeremy Thorpe had taken Devon North by 362 votes. Although 56 of the 216 Liberal candidates at the 1959 election lost their deposits, 27 others came second, compared with only 11 in 1955. In five of these instances – Bodmin, North Cornwall, Torrington, Merioneth and Rochdale – the party won over a third of the vote. Although the Liberals did not receive the 2 million votes for which Grimond had hoped, they did better than their rivals had expected, more than doubling their total from 722,000 votes in 1955 (2.7 per cent of the total) to 1,641,000 (5.9 per cent). In the seats that they fought both times, the Liberals saw their share of the vote go up too: from 15.1 per cent to 16.9 per cent. The real blow to Grimond was the Liberals' failure to win a significant parliamentary bridgehead. Indeed, eight of the ten seats where the Liberal vote actually fell in this election were seats in which the party had won over 30 per cent of the vote in 1955. Since the party had achieved that in only thirteen seats, the 1959 result shows just how poorly the party did in targeting its efforts and getting out what remained of its 'core' vote.

The West Country had traditionally been home to a strong Liberal tradition and, as Grimond had hoped, there were now clear signs that this might be reviving. Many Liberal votes in the east of the region had come from a squeeze on Labour; to the west, the Tories' own vote had proved vulnerable to a Liberal advance, Peter Bessell coming within 3,000 votes of capturing Bodmin, and Edwin Malindine missing out in North Cornwall by the painfully slender margin of 989 votes. In Cornwall as a whole, the Liberals came a good second, with almost 30 per cent of the vote. This regional revival would form the basis of intensive campaigning in the years ahead and Thorpe's tireless efforts in North Devon would become the inspiration for an entire generation of candidates. Between 1951 and 1959 he had increased the Liberal share of the vote from 19.4 per cent to 42.9 per cent. In the 1959 campaign Thorpe, Bonham Carter and several of the other more active Liberal candidates in the region, particularly in Cornwall, had emphasised the party's commitment to a regional plan, capitalising upon localised pockets of high unemployment. Interestingly, in the wake of the 1959 election, not only did the Liberals nationally target the West Country, but also within the region itself the party began painstakingly to rebuild its presence at the municipal level. The practices of 'community politics' and ruthless seat targeting took another step forward.

Grimond's majority in Orkney and Shetland increased very slightly, from 7,993 to 8,612. The 64.2 per cent of the vote that he received compared with only 18.5 per cent for the Conservative, still his nearest rival, making rather a nonsense of his professed pre-election fears. Donald Wade's majority in Huddersfield West increased to almost 10,000. In Bolton West, however, Arthur Holt had been made to look distinctly vulnerable in the face of a concerted campaign by an energetic young Labour candidate, who reduced his margin of victory to fewer than 4,000 votes (less than 10 per cent of the total). Roderic Bowen looked safe in Cardigan, but in Montgomeryshire a Conservative intervention had reduced Clement Davies to a majority of fewer than 3,000 – as fragile-looking as the man himself after years of declining health. All in all, this was a highly equivocal result. The significance of the 1959 result was appreciated only in the years that followed, as the Liberals assimilated the lessons of an election that had promised so much but delivered so little. Grimond was bitterly disappointed, but knew that he had to put a brave public face upon it. The day after the election he claimed that he was not downcast about the long-term implications of the Tories' massive win, but 'hopeful that the result will be the creation of a new progressive movement'.[45] Grimond's one consolation was the widely held view that Labour could not survive another general election defeat, and he seized the initiative by inviting a journalist called Mark Arnold Forster to Orkney to interview him for the *Observer*.

In this interview Grimond not only reaffirmed his belief in a realignment of the left, but also appeared to imply that he wanted some kind of union between Labour and the Liberals, stating that, unless the progressive and radical elements in politics got together, 'the Left may be in opposition for years and years'.[46] Almost as soon as he had given the interview, Grimond began to regret it. Not only had he been more candid than he had intended, but he was also not sure that he had explained his thinking with sufficient clarity. He telephoned the editor of the *Guardian,* Alastair Hetherington, in a panic on the Sunday morning. The day's newspapers had not yet reached Orkney, and he feared that he might have made a dreadful hash of the *Observer* interview. Hetherington told him that the paper had made great play of his comment that, on certain vital issues, the opposition parties 'can and must combine' and had splashed the story across its front page with an eye-catching headline. Grimond confided in Hetherington his fear that the party council would give him a hard time over his comments, and grumbled that he was already weary of the 'continuous performing seal act' that he had to maintain, just to keep the Liberal Party going. On the same Sunday evening, Grimond told *The Times* that 'I really mean nothing more than I have been saying on the subject for some time . . . I am not talking about any immediate coalition, and I am merely speaking for myself.'[47] Many people were not convinced.

Grimond may be faulted for giving such an ambiguous interview on such a sensitive topic, but he certainly kept the Liberals in the headlines. Within the week he had several opportunities to clarify what exactly he had meant. The point missed by many was that Grimond was proposing not collusion with Labour as currently constituted: he was suggesting the creation of a completely new and progressive non-socialist party in opposition to the Conservatives. But still what everyone wanted to know was whether he now foresaw a coalition of any kind with Labour. Many party members, after all the splits and secessions of the past fifty years, cherished above all else the party's independence. This talk of coalitions and alliances made them restless. Furthermore, given the Liberals' paltry parliamentary representation, as Grimond later admitted, 'the idea that the Liberal Party should be the mainstream of realignment was regarded as a Grimond eccentricity'.[48] Through a series of media, including a BBC broadcast of the popular *Any Questions* show, he explained that, although he wanted to see radicals from all parties coming together, he did not think that a formal pact or agreement between Labour and the Liberals was on the cards. What he did foresee, however, was a 'growing together of radical opinion on some issues that may come up in the next few years' as part of a longer-term process of realignment.[49]

The weekend after the election, Hugh Gaitskell had hosted a gathering of some of his most important supporters, ostensibly as a farewell for Hugh Dalton, which turned into more of a wake for the party itself. Gaitskell privately shared Grimond's belief that Labour would be lucky to sustain another defeat without fragmenting. At that party, Douglas Jay advocated some kind of arrangement with the Liberals, 'even up to merger'. Gaitskell said angrily that he was having none of it. Then that same evening, over dinner with Gaitskell, Woodrow Wyatt, Labour MP for Bosworth, suggested an electoral pact with the Liberals. Gaitskell again demurred. His view was that the Liberals would gain disproportionately from any such arrangement – Labour voters would certainly prefer them to the Tories – but he never believed that the Liberals could possibly deliver their votes for Labour. It was extraordinary that Labour had been so quickly reduced to talking in these terms. They really did see Grimond's Liberal Party as a threat, primarily because an unusually high proportion of new Liberal voters at the 1959 election had come from the Labour Party, in complete contrast to other elections since the war, when Liberal interventions had generally damaged the Tories more than Labour. Morgan Phillips, Labour's general secretary, estimated that Labour lost as many as three votes to the Liberals for every one that switched from the Tories. Shortly afterwards, Hugh Gaitskell confided to Alastair Hetherington that he not only liked Jo Grimond personally, he was also rather sympathetic to some of his ideas: it was just impossible to do anything about them at present. What Gaitskell would have liked, presumably, was not an alliance or pact with the Liberals – it was more like a complete annexation by Labour.

An up-and-coming Labour candidate, Merlyn Rees, echoed Gaitskell's darkest fears shortly afterwards in an article in the *Political Quarterly*. His view was that the effects of social and economic change on political allegiances had been overestimated. Labour had an image problem because it adhered to certain principles and dogmas that looked out of date. Unless it sorted itself out, therefore, another electoral defeat 'might throw the opposition ball into Mr Grimond's court'.[50] The authors of the celebrated treatise *Must Labour Lose?* sifted through the evidence in greater detail. Their conclusion was similar, but not identical, to that of Merlyn Rees. The tide of history, they argued, was now against socialism, but Labour could still survive by adapting itself to new values and needs. Even though 'the ethos of class solidarity [was] beginning to crumble in the face of the new fluidity',[51] there was no reason to believe that society itself would break up. The case for public provision of certain goods and services could still be made, and 'the generous impulses of man'[52] that created and sustained so much of socialist thinking were still in existence. Indeed, as society became more prosperous, people would be better able to afford to act on these impulses. When Labour assembled at Blackpool in late November for a conference, Gaitskell had to fight for his political life. The party was fundamentally divided on the question of public ownership, and there was no disguising the rancorous atmosphere as attempts were made to draw up a compromise between fundamentally opposed philosophical outlooks: pluralistic social democracy and hardline state socialism. In a speech in Cambridge, Grimond rubbed salt into the wounds, praising Gaitskell as 'by far the ablest' of Labour's senior figures but pouring scorn on the idea that deeply held convictions could be sensibly compromised. Either people believed in state socialism or they did not: 'You can't have a doctrine which is ostensibly founded on the belief of the rightness of Socialism and the wrongness of capitalism . . . submitted to the sort of examination which is going on now at Blackpool. It is as if the Roman Catholic Church were to begin to vote as to whether God existed.'[53]

This situation was encouraging for Grimond, but so far he had only succeeded in introducing the first stage of the revolution that he had planned for the Liberal Party. Although the Liberals had done reasonably well in the 1959 election, Grimond was uncomfortably aware that even the tiniest swing in public opinion – not to mention future Conservative interventions against his parliamentary colleagues – could still have left him looking very lonely on the Liberal benches. If the party wanted not only to survive and to consolidate, but also to take full advantage of new opportunities, then its organisation needed further radical reform. The Liberals had to be ready for any by-elections that might come along, and several of his colleagues impressed upon him the importance of taking local government elections more seriously. For the past few years, the Liberals had begun to make gains in this area without really trying. In 1950 fewer than 100 Liberal councillors were elected out of a total of over 3,300. By 1955 the figure was closer to fifty. Then, in 1956, the party had gently turned a corner by beginning to gain seats without particularly trying or expecting to, albeit at a modest rate. Now, with the right kind of targeting, they could start to make serious inroads. Grimond also wanted to take the process of policy renewal far further. In the run-up to 1959 he had driven through a new defence policy, and he had sharpened up the party's lines in various other areas, notably Europe and economic policy. But he wanted more fresh and new ideas, with a more radical tinge. He also had in his sights the general director of the party, Herbert Harris, a survivor from the Clement Davies era whose political judgement he distrusted. Nobody would ever attest to a single incident through which Harris particularly alienated Grimond and his cadre of supporters, though one oft-quoted remark of his, made during a party assembly, cannot have strengthened his position: 'If, in the process of getting to Liberalism, we put a Socialist Government in, we cannot help that . . . That is something you must suffer on the road.'[54] The Conservatives cited that remark for years as evidence that a vote for the Liberals was effectively a vote for Labour, and for socialism. Each time they did so, they helped to push Mr Harris closer to the political precipice.

8

ALTHOUGH GRIMOND AND his chief lieutenants – Frank Byers, Arthur Holt and Mark Bonham Carter – had good reason to be proud of the 1959 general election result, they knew that greater momentum was now needed. They therefore displayed a resolve, ruthlessness even, in the following months that re-energised the party. Holt in particular proved to be an indispensible intermediary between Grimond and the hardworking party staff and members. The first action was to sustain the life of the special committee that had been set up to prepare the party for the 1959 poll, which had taken a grip on policy and organisation for the election run-up as well as during the campaign itself. Grimond had concluded that the party's main decision-making bodies, its council and the Executive Committee, had grown unwieldy and ineffective. They were ill suited to the guerrilla war that the party leadership now planned to wage in Parliament, at by-elections and at local council elections. When Grimond addressed the Party Council on 14th November 1959, he made it plain that Liberals must now waste no time in picking themselves up, dusting themselves down and preparing themselves for new battles. He indicated that he wanted the general election committee to turn into 'a small steering committee . . . to give continual thrust and direction to our efforts'.[1] The party could be proud of its achievements at the recent election, he warned, but it could not afford to underestimate how much hard work remained to be done. When he went on to talk about policy, for the first time he gave top priority to environmental matters, as well as dealing with more familiar territory such as industrial and economic policy, foreign affairs and the need for political reform. His speech was followed by a private question and answer session for parliamentary candidates.

The party's officers duly accepted that the committee should be given new life, and recommended to members of the executive that they give the new arrangement their blessing, but by all accounts this was done with a marked lack of enthusiasm. To many Liberals, the pre-election committee had been an unpleasant necessity, its concentration of powers offensive to their sensibilities but acceptable in the short term, before such a crucial poll. Many now felt that they were being 'bounced' by the leadership, which had insensitively announced details of the reconfigured committee's membership and functions in advance of the executive's deliberations. This was, at the very least, discourteous. Nonetheless the party executive did rubber-stamp the rebranded Standing Committee, although a dissenting minority made its views very plain. Grimond and Byers had won an important victory. The executive had signed up to the broad terms of reference necessary to ensure that the committee could expand its brief in just about any direction without overstepping the mark: in theory the Standing Committee was charged with upgrading party organisation, but the executive had now explicitly given it delegated authority to do whatever was necessary to 'strengthen the impact of Liberalism upon the electorate'.[2] The small membership, with Frank Byers in the chair and Mark Bonham Carter as his deputy, was made up of a cadre of Grimond supporters consisting of Richard Wainwright, Jeremy Thorpe and Arthur Holt. To calm nerves in the Liberal Party Organisation (LPO), Heather Harvey from the press office was also invited to attend some of the meetings.

Now began the real Grimond revolution – bloodless but deceptively ambitious, with almost all the nitty-gritty carried out by surrogates. Within two days of the Standing Committee coming formally into existence, its chairman Frank Byers had produced draft proposals for a radical reorganisation of the party. These pointedly excluded a general director, and Byers suggested to the person who had occupied that position since it had been established in March 1953, Herbert Harris, that he might wish to go quietly. Harris was understandably taken aback by this turn of events and took the view that, as the executive had appointed him, it was for them, and only them, to dismiss him. This they duly did, on 8th January 1960, and at the end of that month he departed without ceremony, a profoundly unhappy man. Grimond's revolution in the wake of the 1959 general election had claimed its first, and most significant, sacrifice. Harris would be swiftly followed by an ally, Reginald Smith, the editor of *Liberal News*. At the end of February, Herbert Harris held a press conference to clear away 'the cloud of mystery' that hung over his departure, at which he gave a remarkable insight into some fairly robust and illiberal behaviour by Frank Byers. Harris described his last day in the office as 'quite fantastical, if not comical': only one person had come to say goodbye to him, and he had received no message of any kind from Grimond himself. 'Had I been a leper,' he mused, 'had I been guilty of some great offence, I could not have been more ostracized.'[3] In response to Harris's public outburst, Mark Bonham Carter co-signed a terse letter claiming that Harris had merely been the unfortunate victim of redundancy arising from 'the changed position of the Liberal Party in the country today'.[4] No aspersions had been cast on his integrity and no false conclusions should be drawn.

In the midst of such controversy, it is hardly surprising that the main topic of discussion at the very first meeting of the new committee, on 19th January

1960, was the need to allay the 'immediate suspicions' towards it. By the time of the committee's second meeting, on 7th February 1960, any residual sense of embarrassment had been dismissed, as Mark Bonham Carter took charge of Research, Press, Publications and *Liberal News*, Richard Wainwright agreed to sort out Local Government Affairs and Training Schools, and Jeremy Thorpe took on a special brief to ensure that the party would take full advantage of future by-elections. During the remainder of 1960 the Standing Committee systematically arrogated more and more powers to itself. At its meeting on 29th February 1960 it resolved to begin taking a grip on the leader's forward diary, noting that 'The Wigston Rally [near Market Harborough], addressed by Mr Grimond, was not altogether successful and the hall was not full. Response to the appeal was small . . . in future Mr Grimond's rallies should be Headquarters' responsibility.' A week later, the committee was already sorting out how the now-departed Mr Harris should be replaced, agreeing on 7th March that a 'Co-ordinating Secretary' should be appointed: 'It must be made plain that the Co-ordinating Secretary would be the Chief Executive of the Party, that Policy would be decided by the Committee . . . he would be undisputed head of the office.'[5] This is what Grimond had wanted from the start: an explicit division between policy-making and organisation, with his own closest allies in overall charge of both. It was the former that would in due course receive the leader's attention. As Jeremy Thorpe once put it, Grimond 'had no idea what was going on in the organisation . . . on policy, yes – he liked writing articles, and the more difficult they were to understand, the more brilliant people thought they were.'[6]

In his New Year message to the party for 1960, Grimond had told members that they must make this the year in which they would 'make their principles bite'. Mark Bonham Carter's success at Torrington in 1958 had provided a huge boost to Liberal morale and, as and when promising seats came up at by-elections in the new Parliament, the party had to be ready to campaign hard. One of the innovations of the Standing Committee was the way in which its members kept a close eye on constituencies where by-elections were pending, and did not mince their words if any association prized its independence too highly. After a poor result at Harrow West in March 1960, the committee began to intervene directly in the process of candidate selection for by-elections. It also did its bit to help Grimond assert the Liberal view more strongly in the House of Commons, recognising that other demands on his time and energies would have to be curtailed. The committee accordingly 'Resolved that in future Mr Grimond should never substitute for anyone else.'[7] Not everyone was impressed by the party reforms that Grimond had inspired. One of the party's treasurers, Colonel Lort-Phillips, resigned, complaining that he had in effect been made redundant by the introduction of the Standing Committee, which excluded him from its decisions. 'I wanted a job of work,' he opined, 'and not the prestige of an empty title . . . Now that I have no job I do not intend to keep the empty title.'[8] Lort-Phillips expressed a fairly widely held view that, through Mark Bonham Carter's leading role in the Standing Committee, Grimond was turning the party into little more than a family business. Bonham Carter himself protested, assuring everyone that, as soon as the new co-ordinating secretary was appointed, his own 'day-to-day appearances will become fewer'.[9] These tensions between the voluntary party and Grimond's own coterie would not be dissipated until they had been justified by substantial evidence of political progress. There were also certain tensions within Grimond's immediate circle. His relationship with Byers was always slightly ambivalent. Perhaps Grimond never forgot that, until an accident of fate saw him win in Orkney and Shetland while Byers lost narrowly in Dorset, it was Frank Byers who hade been Clem Davies's chief whip and heir apparent. There had also been Byers's ill-advised attack on Lady Violet. Nonetheless some people did think Grimond peculiarly graceless when he developed the habit of putting Frank Byers in his place from time to time. When Byers was a director of Rio Tinto Zinc, he would sometimes host meetings in his office and Grimond would make fun of him 'lounging on his chaise longue'. Despite the banter, a hint of genuine rivalry between Grimond and Byers was never far from the surface.

Another growth area was local government. From the beginning of 1960, Richard Wainwright helped finance the establishment of a local government department at party headquarters under Pratap Chitnis, a formidable organiser recruited from the Coal Board. Chitnis epitomised the Grimond era. He had been inspired to join the Liberals after attending the Liberal rally in the Royal Albert Hall in November 1958 and had acted as a party agent in 1959. His activities now were fundamental to the long-term revival of the Liberal Party. The decline of municipal Liberalism had already begun to turn around in 1955 and 1956, with the Liberals recording modest net gains in both years. In 1957 their net gain was 27; in 1958 it was 76; and in 1959 it was 33. In the early months of 1960 the Liberals prosecuted a more sustained attack on local council seats. In the run-up to the local elections in May, their candidates were polling around 25 per cent of the vote. Progress continued in May, with the party taking 130 seats. Despite these advances, Chitnis harboured no illusions that Grimond had any abiding personal interest in local government. From the early days of his leadership, this had been one of the many areas of which he knew little and which he was only too happy to ignore, or at best to delegate to others. He did, however, give Chitnis all the authority he needed to instigate a revolution and, in due course, gradually became persuaded of the importance to the party of successes in local government. He would become a close friend of Chitnis, dubbing him 'Podsnap', after the lumbering but reliable Dickensian gent in *Our Mutual Friend*.

Alongside the development of the Standing Committee came another burst of Grimondian 'ad-hoccery'. Although Grimond was an enthusiast for ideas, he was suspicious of detailed policy commitments, loathing the very idea of a manifesto. Mark Bonham Carter provided a counterweight to this view, convincing Grimond that the party could be taken seriously only if it began to formulate a credible platform to compete on equal – or comparable – terms with those of the Tories and Labour. He gradually convinced Grimond that the Liberals must put before the electorate a thoroughly considered and radical set of policy ideas. The party had plenty of policies – and a number of committees for developing and propagating them – but many of the policies were growing stale and hoary. They had become mantras, words without thoughts.

Between 1958 and 1960 Grimond gradually supplanted the established committees with a series of 'ad hoc' groups comprised of specialist counsellors, many of whom were not even party members. These were largely drawn from the impressive roster of academics he had attracted into the party, and their brief was to breathe new life into the party's policies, and they had the advantage of being able to publish their conclusions without tying the party to anything specific, though their suggestions could, of course, be put to the assembly for approval as policy. The exceptional quality of the individuals who agreed to serve was entirely down to Grimond, who himself chaired some of these so-called 'New Directions' groups personally. He even played a part in drafting one or two of their papers – notably that on Europe – but none of them was ever, strictly speaking, a formal statement of party policy. It would be easy to suppose that the Standing Committee and these groups might have had a slightly uneasy relationship. Not a bit of it. They operated hand-in-glove with each other, which fact served to confirm that the ad hoc groups were a means of using the Liberal Party machine to propagate Grimond's preferred ideas, whilst avoiding the tiresome bother of getting policies past an often truculent party assembly. During the same period, Grimond continued to devote time and attention to groups from outside the mainstream of party activity. These included three early think tanks: the Oxford Liberal Group and the New Orbits Group in addition to George Watson's Unservile State Group. He also encouraged the development of the Young Liberals.

All this varied activity would in due course be supported by the creation of a research department, largely funded by money from the Rowntree Trust and headed by Harry Cowie, a talented young investment analyst who joined the party organisation in September 1960. In due course Cowie built up a core team of half a dozen or so researchers, under the sponsorship of Arthur Holt and, later, Mark Bonham Carter, as head of the Research Committee. This was part of the Liberal Central Association, separate both from the LPO and from the parliamentary party, which gave Cowie a free hand. Harry Cowie shared Grimond's view that the Liberals had for too long lived off tired old policies – a mixture of free trade, once radical proposals for constitutional reform that now looked rather dusty, plus some elements of Asquithian social liberalism with a bit of Lloyd George populism thrown in for good measure. When the research department did produce, in its slightly erratic way, a range of policies, according to Cowie, Grimond was usually reluctant to see them published. Grimond did not undertake a vow of silence as he waited for his committees to report. He continued in more or less the same vein as before, acting as a kind of freewheeling political commentator and doing his best to give the Liberals' image a harder edge. It was really hard for a Liberal leader to gain publicity in those days, and Grimond scarcely missed a trick, even presenting a forty-five-minute ITV programme about venereal disease: *The Shadow of Ignorance.*

Throughout this time, Grimond's main rival on the centre-left, Hugh Gaitskell, had seen much of his authority evaporate. When Labour produced an unconvincing compromise on nationalisation in the spring of 1960, Grimond was by turns scathing and mocking:

> The real New Testament was not written because a Gallup poll showed that the Old Testament was unpopular. It was written because there was a fiery new prophet who said what he meant. I wonder what would happen if the Labour Party restated the Ten Commandments? 'Thou shalt love thy neighbour as thyself' would have a gloss attached to it showing that this was only to be carried out so long as he joined the right union and refrained from making any goods cheaper than they could be made in Britain.[10]

Grimond also pressed on with the development of a distinctive Liberal position on foreign affairs. His was amongst the first voices to denounce the Sharpeville massacre of March 1960, and he recognised at once that few people would ever be able to think of South Africa the same way again:

> I believe that something happened at Sharpeville which has made a dividing line in history such as we sometimes see. I do not think that things will ever be quite the same again . . . the prime cause of all this is the attempt to impose a wholly unworkable and repugnant system – a system of race superiority . . . I do not think we should drive South Africa out of the Commonwealth. On the other hand, I do not think we should compromise about the underlying nature of the Commonwealth so as to keep South Africa in'[11]

As in the previous Parliament, in addition to his more global responsibilities, Grimond had also to serve on the standing committee dealing with Scottish Bills. He was a notable participant in the passage of the Highlands and Islands Shipping Bill in 1959–60 which had been introduced at least in part because of pressure from him, and he was an assiduous contributor to the process of honing it. Sea services in the islands were both expensive and painfully slow: as Grimond pointed out, it took longer to travel from Westray to Kirkwall (twenty miles as the crow flies) than it took to fly to New York and back. Services between the islands were provided on an entirely commercial basis. As a consequence, Grimond argued, the islanders were being penalised for their willingness to pay up and endure a rickety service. In contrast, London Transport was given special permission to run up an accumulated deficit.

Jo Grimond always based his argument for subsidy on first principles, and on 'the wider argument for encouraging and sustaining communities in the more remote parts of Britain'.[12] On that basis, the islands deserved not a patchwork of temporary subsidies, but a long-term commitment from government. He fought a running battle with ministers during the passage of the Bill, since its effect initially appeared to be confined to journeys made on the open sea. In other words, Grimond feared that the Bill would not make it any easier for subsidies to be granted either to ferries or to routes any part of which involved travelling over land. There was also an apparent error in the drafting of the Bill, which could have tied the Secretary of State's hands by excluding local authorities and their subsidiaries from applying for grants or subsidies, since only organisations that were 'wholly or mainly engaged in providing sea transport services' would be considered as valid candidates.

As the Bill came into its final straight, Grimond was evidently finding it somewhat harder to retain his good humour. In alliance with Sir David Robertson, a former Conservative MP who had been re-elected the previous year as an Independent, he attacked what seemed to be an edge of mean-spiritedness towards the islands. Grimond believed that, although the transport situation in the islands did stand to improve as a consequence of the Bill, the Highlands and Islands ultimately failed to appeal to a government that set too great store by prestige projects. It had recently been reported that the government was considering a subsidy to Cunard, for the building of luxury liners – as Grimond put it, 'a subsidy not to the poor but to rich, expense-account travellers . . . Are they considered of first priority?'[13] Almost eighteen months later, the House of Commons came to vote on the North Atlantic Shipping Bill of which the Cunard grant was part. Grimond demonstrated admirable consistency by chalking up the unusual achievement of being the sole MP to vote against it, assisted by two rebel Labour MPs who acted as 'tellers' in the division and had the arduous task of counting him through.

Grimond also continued to advocate a Highlands and Islands Development Board, a single unit with the power to act promptly and advance economic diversification in the islands. There were plenty of smaller enterprises springing up, but no organisation existed to help nurse them through their early years. 'I do not believe,' Grimond once warned the Scottish Grand Committee, 'that we can run the Highlands on a shoestring, at the end of a highly industrialised society and a few years behind the times, and then set up a Commission and, while suffering depopulation, await reports demanding extra powers, and then settle down for three or four more years before deciding what is needed to be done.'[14] On a standing committee considering the 1960–61 Crofters (Scotland) Bill, Grimond would describe this complacency in government even more vividly: 'There is no other part of this country – and this is saying a great deal – in which more stable doors have been locked after the horses have gone than in the Highlands and Islands. I do not say that these horses have bolted: nothing as dramatic as that. They have ambled out of the stable while successive Secretaries of State have leaned against the doorpost chewing straws.'[15]

When Grimond had become leader, his secretary Cate Fisher was 'petrified' by the thought that the pleasant *modus operandi* of his office would come to an abrupt halt. In the event, the new demands of leadership had not even necessitated an extra member of staff, and Cate Fisher had continued to enjoy working for him just as much as before. In the new climate of activity post-1959, however, many of those close to Grimond began to press him to take on a personal assistant, in addition to Miss Fisher. Grimond fought stubbornly against this proposition: the last thing he wanted was a stooge from the party organisation dogging his every move. For several years Grimond succeeded in hitting the proposal into 'long grass', Cate Fisher breathed a sigh of relief and life carried on much as usual. Although it was not beyond him to sit in glowering silence if he was upset with someone, Grimond never lost his temper, and always radiated his love of life. He would sometimes have a party for the Liberal MPs and their staff, not on any special pretext, but purely and simply because he liked parties. Yet, although Grimond certainly presented an informal and approachable persona outwardly, and would always leaven the day with humour, still he maintained an unmistakable and indestructible carapace when dealing with colleagues. Jeremy Thorpe, for instance, commented to the author, 'Jo I worked with closely, but I never really got to know him.' Grimond was also not very good at recognising people whom he had only met once or twice, a failing to which many supporters and colleagues over the years did not take especially kindly.

In the summer of 1960, events outside Grimond's control brought one internal party controversy to a head, when the Bolton East seat fell vacant after the sitting Conservative MP, Philip Bell, was appointed a judge. As Grimond led his party in an ever more radical direction, the Bolton and Huddersfield deals with the Tories, those relics of the Davies-Churchill era, looked increasingly archaic if not absurd. The Liberals now had to decide whether they could afford to challenge the Tories in the eastern half of Bolton; or, to put it another way, whether they could afford not to. The opinions that mattered most were those of Grimond himself and Arthur Holt. Although Holt never claimed that the Liberals were likely to win Bolton East (he believed that they would probably come second, after the Tories), he did tell a Standing Committee meeting on 27th June 1960 that 'all the local officers, with the possible exception of the Secretary, wished to fight.'[16] He claimed that his own division of Bolton West could now be held in a three-party fight, while conceding that the figures in 1959 appeared to tell a different story, and asserted that 'a successful fight in Bolton East would assist Bolton West.'

Grimond would almost certainly have supported Holt either way, and appears to have put no pressure on him. But everyone knew that this was not just a tactical decision for Bolton Liberals. This was a question of strategy for the entire party. If they did fight at Bolton, at least two of the party's six seats could be put at serious risk; if they opted out, however, their enemies could accuse them of running scared and their pretensions as an independent force would be in tatters. At the Standing Committee meeting on 11th July, Holt effectively took the plunge: 'the issue of whether to fight or not could not be seen solely in the local context and that from the national point of view the seat should be fought – and, indeed, had to be fought, since the consequences of not fighting would subsequently be harmful, not only in Bolton West but also at by-elections in constituencies elsewhere in the country.'[17] Former party leader Clement Davies, still in the House of Commons as member for Montgomery, would have been less than delighted to know that the likelihood of a by-election in his seat before the end of the Parliament was also considered at this meeting as an important factor.

The decision taken by the Bolton Liberals to contest this by-election was one of the most significant of the Grimond years. Although it was taken at a local level, there was never any doubt about the support that the decision would have from Jo Grimond and his close supporters. On hearing the news, Grimond commented bullishly that 'I am confident that Liberals can win both Bolton seats on their own merit whether Conservatives stand against them or not.'[18] The entire party was electrified. Nobody doubted the massive contribution that Arthur Holt and Donald Wade were making to Liberalism, but the basis on which they had been elected was increasingly embarrassing. In due course Frank Byers was unanimously selected to fight Bolton East. He threw himself wholeheartedly into this highly symbolic contest – unlike several candidates for other forthcoming by-elections due in the autumn, one of whom had vanished unexpectedly on a long summer vacation to Sicily.

Meanwhile Grimond was also developing his policies in new and interesting directions. In economic matters, he came ever closer to the German notion of a social market economy. He thought that Labour's advocacy of a so-called 'mixed economy' was not to be trusted, at least until socialists openly and unashamedly embraced free enterprise. As he wrote in a seminal article in the *Observer,* this meant accepting 'a competitive economy, mobility of labour and the removal of many windbreaks which shelter inefficiency and failing industries.'[19] A corollary of that, according to Grimond, was rejecting the option of retreating back into nationalisation or subsidies, which should be supplanted by 'a high level of public expenditure . . . not only for the present Welfare Services but for new roads, town-planning etc . . . The taxation system and the techniques of economic and financial control would have to be improved.'[20] In the same article, Grimond suggested that a really enterprising economy should have a place for 'certain undertakings developed on a modern form of syndicalism, control being largely kept to their management and workers'.[21]

It is possible to detect a further toughening of Grimond's public rhetoric during this period. As he and his close colleagues were earnestly debating the pros and cons of taking on the Tories in Bolton, he made a powerful and impatient speech to the Women's Liberal Federation. He reverted to his theme of 'get on, or get out', imploring all Liberals to show renewed vigour and sense of purpose in the months ahead, and telling his listeners to urge 'all members who are in any sort of responsible position in the party' to 'make up their minds between now and the autumn on . . . how much time and energy they can devote to Liberal causes or organisations . . . If they cannot for one reason or another make their contribution to the present party line they should consider very seriously what the party should do – or how long they can rely on others to carry on the fight'.[22] Liberals, he warned, should stop harking back to the trappings of office. A small party like theirs was only likely to succeed as and when it 'really goes to town on some issues'.[23]

This was inevitably a turbulent and busy time for the entire Grimond family. Grizelda was now studying History at Oxford, while Johnny was coming towards the end of his time at Eton. Andrew was preparing to go on to London University. In spring 1960 Laura resigned as a magistrate in Richmond after four years. The busier Jo got, travelling all over the country, the more of a burden she found herself carrying up in Orkney and Shetland as well as within the family. She had taken a twelve-month sabbatical from the bench when she was pregnant with Magnus, but now found that the combined pressures of bringing up a family alongside her various political and social activities were too much. At the beginning of June, after a long and debilitating illness, her father died. Although this was by no means unexpected, the loss of Sir Maurice Bonham Carter was felt far and wide. Lady Violet's own tender account of her husband's final illness is unbearably poignant. Jo Grimond too would greatly miss the amiable patriarch who had welcomed him so warmly into what was perhaps the greatest Liberal family of the age.

The 1960 assembly at Eastbourne was crucial to Grimond's plans. The planned assembly of 1959 had been knocked out by the autumn election, making this the first full assembly since the debacle of 1958. Delegates were given the opportunity to register their views on the next wave of proposed changes to the party structure, and they would be able to vote on a proposal to reduce the size of the party executive from around fifty members to something more like thirty. The fear was that many in the voluntary party might now be feeling that the powers of the leader and the parliamentary party were beginning to get out of hand. When Edwin Malindine, chairman of the Agenda Committee and a close supporter of Grimond, launched the assembly agenda with a press conference, he was asked about the relationship between the assembly and the MPs and he carefully put the assembly firmly in its place, replying that the MPs were 'answerable for their own views in the House of Commons, and are certainly not to be dictated to by the party conference . . . That is a cardinal principle of our Liberal activities.'[24]

To clarify matters further, the party issued a document with an alarming orange cover entitled *This is YOUR PARTY.* In theory its purpose was to clarify the 'complex and widespread' structure of the Liberal Party. In practice, this document was intended to show everyone who was in charge, and to stimulate a major fund-raising effort. 'The Annual Assembly and the Party Council,' it explains, 'define the general objectives of the Party and stimulate, guide and organise its work in all parts of the country.'[25] There is a *cri de coeur* on behalf of the parliamentary party, whose many tasks are listed in detail and which 'is provided only with minimum secretarial assistance . . . It needs far more.'[26] Grimond's policy committees also make an appearance here – and a plea is made for them to receive the support of 'additional qualified staff'.[27] The requirements of the party HQ are set out in detail and it is quite extraordinary, from the vantage point of a new century, to read just how few of the usual appurtenances of a national political party the Liberals possessed at that time. The 1960 budget of Liberal HQ, at around £30,000, was estimated to be less even than that of the Communist Party. Its press and publicity operation, amazingly, was effectively a one-woman show. It couldn't afford to run a library service, and didn't even have a typing pool. It was estimated that the party needed to raise an additional annual sum in the order of £100,000 (the equivalent of some £1.5 million today) to enable its HQ to do its job effectively. If the publication of this pamphlet was intended to pre-empt or defuse any controversy at the assembly about Grimond's party reforms, however, it was at best partially successful.

Grimond's prefatory remarks at the assembly's opening session were unusually potent. He reminded delegates that they had for years been demanding leadership. Now, he said, they had got it; and he wasn't joking. The message was unambiguous. There must be no foolish self-indulgence before the television cameras. The streamlined assembly agenda and party reforms were necessary, and they were here to stay: the ghosts of the 1958 assembly had to be exorcised once and for all. The attendance was the biggest since the war, and delegates overwhelmingly endorsed the leadership's policy of negotiating terms for joining the Common Market. This marked the final victory for Grimond and his allies over the remnants of the free-trade Liberals, led by Oliver Smedley, and marked a significant landmark in his take-over of the party at grassroots level. Of the record turnout of almost 1,100 delegates, an estimated 800 were under forty years old (the rest, one person in attendance commented, seemed to be over sixty), and Grimond deservedly got most of the credit for establishing the party's remarkable new appeal to younger people. His own main speech was not one of his most memorable, but it was perfectly effective and received a warm welcome. As was now traditional, Jeremy Thorpe took charge of the appeal for party funds on the final day, and raised over £15,000 – an impressive and unprecedented sum. In his closing address, Grimond made a point of referring to the transformation of party organisation, and the fact that the party now had a credible plan for its future development. Most of it was given over to sheer exhortation. It was now up to all the party's members to go out and win the votes that would really put them into the running: the party needed 'two million more votes, 60,000 more workers – only about 100 more a constituency – and 100 new dedicated publicists and policy-formers . . . Liberals are made today, not born . . . We have to go out and make them.'[28] The second half of November alone would bring eight by-elections, including that at Bolton East. What was needed, said Grimond in his one truly memorable phrase of that day, was 'another heave'.[29] He also made a point of singling out Frank Byers for praise.

Although Grimond could be well pleased with the Eastbourne assembly, he had real reason to celebrate the following week, watching in astonishment as Labour met at Scarborough and proceeded to blow itself apart, the trade union block votes delivering a policy of unilateral nuclear disarmament in defiance of Hugh Gaitskell's famous pledge to 'fight, fight and fight again' to save the party he loved. Grimond wasted no time in picking over Labour's bones. As its leadership attempted to reach a compromise over defence, on which the two wings of the party were fundamentally divided, Grimond proclaimed that Labour was now becoming the Conservatives' best friend because it was attempting to bridge over a fundamental political fault-line. What was needed was a full-scale realignment. 'The task of the Left is not to wrangle,' he warned, 'but to get the Tories out and get on to another great era of progress . . . can be done honestly and effectively if we rally together and cease to look for compromises where no compromise is possible'.[30] Labour's problem, Grimond suggested, was its conservative approach to most contemporary problems: 'It may be true that the Labour Party cannot be led from the Right: but what is the Right in that party? A change in our attitude towards Europe, for instance, which some "Left" Labour would dislike, must have far more radical results than nationalising another industry or two.'[31]

In November and December 1960 Grimond began to find the physical demands of his job rather too much and, from looking at his schedule, it is easy to understand why. He was carrying an immense burden on behalf of his party. He was undertaking an unnervingly high proportion of the speaking engagements that were offered to him, but still found all too often that events were poorly organised and suffered from disappointing attendances. He also adhered to his well-established constituency routine, going up to the islands a couple of times per month. He even had to go straight from Eastbourne to a dinner in Lerwick given by Shetland Liberals in belated celebration of his tenth anniversary as their MP in February 1950. They presented him with a hand-woven dressing gown and silver cufflinks, to add to the rather splendid chair that their counterparts in Orkney had already given him. Laura was given a silver brooch. Grimond had a summit meeting with Douglas Robinson, the Liberals' new organising secretary, at which he made it clear that he was no longer willing to make himself available for a rally a month over a period of a year as he had originally agreed. The Standing Committee in due course agreed that Grimond should be asked to undertake only six rallies during 1961. If he was satisfied with these, he could then be asked to undertake a further three, making nine in all. Both the committee and Robinson agreed that Grimond should be asked to undertake only those rallies which measured up to the standards set by headquarters, in areas where the constituency associations were fully active.[32] The committee also agreed, at the urging of Donald Wade, that Grimond need not speak at every single by-election that the party was contesting. They decided that his involvement in by-elections should be decided by the general principle of whether the constituency was one 'where Liberals might win a seat or come a very good second',[33] the responsibility for that decision resting with the Standing Committee and not with Grimond himself.

Grimond was already feeling quite frustrated enough by the difficulties of getting a fair press for the Liberals, when the depressing (but not wholly unexpected) news came that the only national newspaper to support the party, the *News Chronicle*, was closing down. He could not conceal his dismay, mourning the loss of 'a staunch friend not only of the Liberal Party but of all who value freedom, reporting and lively comment'.[34] Fortunately a more pleasant distraction now presented itself, when a young student by the name of David Steel talked Grimond into standing for election as rector of Edinburgh University, a post whose responsibilities include chairing the university's governing body and representing the interests of the students. Steel was president of the Student Representative Council and, for him at least, the stakes were very high indeed. At the previous rectorial installation, for the actor James Robertson Justice, a barrage of flour bombs and tomatoes had been hurled at the platform, and a toilet roll had landed at the feet of Prince Philip, the chancellor of the university. There was now a serious threat that the university authorities might totally abolish the tradition of electing the rector if that outrage was ever repeated. Steel therefore urged everyone to calm down this time around. When Grimond agreed to stand, Steel quickly secured the signatures of 186 fellow students in support of his nomination. The other candidates in the election, to be held on 11th November 1960, were the Labour MP Philip Noel-Baker (with 76 declared supporters) and press magnate Roy Thomson (with 79 supporters). Thanks to overwhelming support from students of the Arts Faculty, including a number of young Orcadians, Grimond won a handsome victory, receiving almost 58 per cent of the total votes and becoming the first politician to be elected as rector at Edinburgh since Churchill in 1929. During the traditional pitched battle in the Old Quad of the university between supporters of the opposing candidates, which Steel had been unable to tone down, 'bags of soot and flour were thrown and clothing torn'. Police and ambulancemen who tried to intervene were booed and hissed and, when a group of Grimond supporters (most of whom were alleged to be Orcadians) went on the rampage in the city after his victory was announced, the army garrison at the castle had to lock the gates against them.

Almost as unpleasant was some of the mud-throwing at the by-election campaigns going on at the same time. Six of the contests were due on Wednesday, 16th November, all in Conservative-held seats; a seventh, in solidly Labour Ebbw Vale, would be held a day later. The Liberals did not win any of the by-elections. At Tiverton they came close, with 36.7 per cent of the votes on a swing of almost 14 per cent, but elsewhere they peaked in the high 20s. Most disappointing of all was Frank Byers's third place in Bolton East. The electoral system had cheated the party again, but Grimond put a brave face on it. 'I have never believed,' he told a reporter from the *Guardian*, 'that we should expect dramatic results at this stage.'[35] In the London *Evening News*, Grimond went on to set out a realistic assessment of how the Liberals might carry on strengthening their position: 'We aim to come second or within striking distance of being second in more and more constituencies . . . We shall go for the rewarding places first . . . Only lunatic commanders assault the strongest part of the enemy lines . . . The Little Election marked another milestone passed . . . It has rallied a few thousand more recruits to our ranks.'[36]

Christmas 1960 began badly for Grimond and his daughter Grizelda (surreally redubbed 'Gresondor' in the *Yorkshire Post*). On Christmas Eve their car collided with a lorry on the new Stamford by-pass in Lincolnshire as they travelled up to Scotland for Christmas. The front of the car was smashed, its windows were shattered and its roof was buckled. Fortunately, after treatment for cuts, bruises and shock, they were able to continue their journey by train. Presumably this brush with death was not responsible for the hint of asperity in Grimond's New Year message for 1961, which maintained his questioning and challenging tone of recent months. 'The question for

1961,' he argued, was 'what the politically attached are going to do . . . Will they come in and help build this radical alternative, or are they determined to remain on the touchline? If they choose the latter course, they have no one to blame but themselves if the life goes out of politics.' One of the early controversies of 1961 was the battle between the Mirror Group and Thomson Newspapers for control of Odhams, the publishers of the *Daily Herald*. The government was under pressure to intervene in the public interest, to prevent further concentration of power and influence, but Harold Macmillan felt that he was powerless to make any such dramatic move. When Macmillan made a statement to the House of Commons on 31st January, in his response Grimond was in sparkling form. So effective were his rejoinders to the Prime Minister that, to the astonishment of politicians and journalists alike, Macmillan crossed the floor of the House for a private, explanatory tête-à-tête with him.

There was more trouble too over African affairs. In Congo (Zaire), sudden independence from Belgium the previous year had created a climate of appalling instability. The Soviet Union wasted little time in stirring up trouble, and Grimond could not conceal his frustration with the unwillingness of the West to acknowledge that the 'really shocking and disgusting feature' of the growing crisis was the 'behaviour of Russia', which was blatantly destabilising attempts to establish a durable constitution for Congo. This was a favourite theme for Grimond in this period: he thought that liberal opinion in the West was, quite literally, letting the Soviet Union get away with murder.

> There are a great many people in this country who seriously say that the blame for the international situation is shared as much by the Americans as by the Russians . . . a most extraordinary reaction to the Russians' behaviour of the last two or three months. No one in the West has undertaken the massacres that have gone on in Russia over the years and, on their side, the Russians have not offered anything like the Marshall Plan that the Americans have undertaken.[37]

As for South Africa, liberal opinion had generally come to the view that it was time for the Commonwealth to look at the option of expulsion. Yet the British armed forces were constantly implicated in the apartheid regime. Grimond must have been dismayed to find himself forced to ask why 'the Marine band from HMS *Victorious* gave a performance from which all non-whites were turned away' on a visit to Cape Town.[38] Laura echoed him in a speech that she made two weeks later to the annual conference of the Women's Liberal Federation, in which she criticised the Macmillan government for using South Africa's membership of the Commonwealth as a 'pretext for Britain to act as counsel for the defence every time apartheid was an issue at the United Nations'.[39] Later that month her husband returned to the attack, leading anti-apartheid demonstrators in a march from Marble Arch to Trafalgar Square, carrying a 'Remember Sharpeville' banner with the assistance of a leading

member of the South African United Front in London. He also delivered one
of several speeches to the gathering in the square and, in June 1962, became
one of the first British politicians to meet Nelson Mandela when he came
incognito to London with the assistance of David Astor. The following week in
the House of Commons he made another of his better speeches, in which he
too accused the Macmillan government of hypocrisy towards South Africa:

> Let us suppose that there was a Commonwealth country in which a very large
> white population was oppressed by a small black population. Would he say that
> it was no concern of other white people in other parts of the Commonwealth?
> Would he say that it was an internal matter of the country concerned? I doubt
> whether he would take that view . . . I believe that the relationship of the black
> and white races is one of the two or three most important questions of our
> time . . . I believe Britain and her Commonwealth could make an immense
> contribution simply on this subject.[40]

Amidst all this serious political activity came Grimond's installation as
rector at Edinburgh. In view of the students' refusal to dispense with their
antics during the election itself, the University Court had initially decided
that Grimond should be installed not at the traditional open ceremony in
the McEwan Hall, but at a much smaller private ceremony in the university's
Upper Library. David Steel was alarmed. He called a mass meeting of
his fellow students and warned them that, unless they did now agree to
comport themselves with a little dignity, not only would they be excluded
from the installation, but the rectorship itself might indeed be abolished.
'There is nothing particularly amusing,' Steel admonished his fellow students,
'in inviting a distinguished man to be Rector and then giving him dog's
abuse when he comes.'[41] The students' promise of good behaviour was
accepted, Steel's appeal to the authorities was successful, and Grimond would
subsequently write that 'I have yet to find any students unbearably rude, even
the hecklers at my rectorial address to the University of Edinburgh . . . In my
experience, student hosts and student audiences are the most courteous and
the most receptive you can have.'[42] Grimond quickly, if unwittingly, repaid
Steel by seating him next to a young woman called Judy MacGregor at his first
rectorial dinner. She, in due course, became Mrs David Steel.

At his installation, Grimond delivered a marvellous speech. His mood had
lifted after the exhausting days of late 1960, and he felt confident enough
to appeal directly to the idealistic instincts of his audience. It is not hard
to understand why the students were by all accounts far more attentive and
far less boisterous for him than they had been for most of his predecessors.
He urged them not to disparage the political process, which in his eyes was
an integral part of human existence and, as ever, he used humour to good
effect when making his point. 'Put five professors of science into a room
and what do they talk about?' he speculated. 'Nuclear fission? Not a bit

of it. They talk about the politics of the faculty. They gang up. They plot against the humanities.' Politics should not be artificially divorced from life, said Grimond: without the ebbs and flows of politics the open society would wither away. He also struck a communitarian tone, with a plea on behalf of the 'intermediate institutions' – charities, clubs and societies – through which people voluntarily improve the human condition. Decentralisation and participation were his watchwords, and he ended with a very clear plea to the students not to forsake the political parties: 'I urge you all to become politicians, Liberals preferably, but if you can't manage that even Labour or Conservative politics are better than none. I urge you because politics are important, because politics are rewarding, but, most of all, because politics are one of the greatest, most natural and most enjoyable of human activities.'[43]

Appropriately, Grimond was cheered to the rafters after his speech and then borne from the hall on a red chair by a group of students, to be paraded through the streets of the city in a horse-drawn landau. He was a great success as rector, handing the rectorial reins back over to his own predecessor, James Robertson Justice, who had been elected for a second term. At the handover ceremony, Robertson bowed theatrically to Grimond and then began, 'As I was saying before I was interrupted . . .' In her diary on the evening of Grimond's own installation, Violet Bonham Carter wrote an unrestrained flood of praise for her son-in-law. She was more than ever impressed by his originality and informality, as well as his sense of humour which, 'as Mark says . . . is almost <u>too</u> good for his job!'.[44] Her only sadness was that he had to carry so great a burden: 'Would that he could be given by Fate a better armoury of material weapons, in the way of money & organization & above all a group of abler followers & henchmen approaching his own stature.'[45] In an interview with the Edinburgh student newspaper, Grimond again made a favourable impression, telling his interviewer that, in his view, 'students should have some say in the determination of academic curricula, especially where the more antiquated courses need to be brought up to date.'[46] He gave the impression of being a rector who would 'fill his role in a quiet and diplomatic, but effective, way . . . He lays great stress on corporate life and does not want mass production in education . . . most important of all, he has taken on a job and is keen to do it.'[47] Edinburgh must have been a pleasant diversion for Grimond. It reaffirmed his position as one of the most charismatic and popular politicians of his generation, but he had still not demonstrated that the party he led could be turned into a really formidable political machine.

9

IF 1960 WAS a year of internal reform and political consolidation for Grimond and the Liberals, the story of 1961 was the story of what might have been. The shine went off Harold Macmillan and his government almost as soon as they were re-elected in 1959 – and Labour was still tearing itself apart. On 16th March 1961 the Tories held four parliamentary seats with reduced majorities. At both Worcester and Derbyshire, High Peak the Liberal candidate was within 10 per cent of the winner. Nonetheless, despite averaging over a quarter of the vote across these by-elections, the Liberals still came third in every constituency. A month later, John Bannerman, the chairman of the Scottish Liberal Party who had so nearly snatched Inverness in both 1954 and 1955, stood for the Labour seat of Paisley. Although the seat had strong Liberal connections (Asquith had relaunched his political career there in February 1920), the party failed to contest it in 1959. Bannerman, with active support from Grimond, lost out by only 1,658 votes, as the Conservative share of the vote fell from 42.7 per cent to a humiliating 13.3 per cent. 'Everyone is rather depressed,' wrote Macmillan in his diary four days later.[1] This was one of the great near misses: had the Liberals won Paisley, both Labour and the Tories would surely have been more than 'rather depressed'.

The next by-election was one of history's curiosities, with Grimond again actively involved – but not on behalf of a Liberal. Tony Benn had been a Labour MP in Bristol for ten years when his father, Viscount Stansgate, died in November 1960 and he automatically inherited his peerage. He fought a protracted battle in the courts to establish his right to remain a commoner and, from the outset, Grimond and Lady Violet Bonham Carter were both hugely supportive – far more so, indeed, than Hugh Gaitskell ever was. When Benn was physically barred from entering the chamber of the House of Commons and his seat was declared vacant, triggering a by-election, Grimond described the Tories' unwillingness to help him as 'mean and niggardly'. He gave Benn informal legal advice and, encouraged by Lady Violet, resolved to help him win the by-election, helping to prevent the local Liberals from running against him. The Liberal Organising Committee was content for him to address a meeting in support of Benn, so long as the meeting 'should confine itself to the single issue of Mr Wedgwood Benn's right to remain in the House of Commons'. In the event, when Grimond delivered his speech, he did not run shy of the implication that he and Benn might share a certain strain of radicalism. He was there, he said, because he wished to be counted 'among those who dislike not only what is being done to Benn and Bristol, but dislike all the implications of the Government's reaction to the Benn case'. This was not personal, it was an issue of principle: the 'mere accident of peerage' should not be allowed to prevent the people of a constituency from choosing someone to represent them. There was a real risk that Parliament would become ridiculous if it was associated with such 'obvious absurdity and injustice'.[2]

In the May local elections, Labour seemed to hit bottom, and almost 200 Liberal gains left the party with the largest groups on several councils, including Huddersfield and Darwen, and control of three: Bacup, Saddleworth and Fletton. The foundations for a lasting recovery were being built and yet Grimond was at low ebb. Since the demise of the *News Chronicle* national publicity for the Liberals was virtually non-existent, and he felt that his parliamentary colleagues were failing to pull their weight. Only Arthur Holt could be relied upon to deliver speeches of any significance. There was also worrying evidence of a Labour revival; or, more specifically, of a substantial improvement in the personal popularity of Gaitskell. Although Tory voters were certainly continuing to defect to the Liberals, the risk now was that Labour would be the main beneficiary in terms of seats gained. The Liberals badly needed to win a by-election, both in order to grab the headlines and to increase the parliamentary party, but the right seat never came up. As was his custom, Grimond spent most of the 1961 summer recess at home in Orkney with the family. His friend and supporter Ernest Marwick, of the *Orkney Herald,* wrote a piece for the *Liberal News* about Grimond the constituency member, contrasting the pacific calm of the islands with the frenetic activity at Westminster and, for that matter, within the Old Manse. Even after becoming leader of the party, Grimond made a point of visiting all the agricultural shows in Orkney and Shetland every August, and of making a trip to every significantly populated island within the constituency at least every second year.

By the time of the 1961 autumn assembly in Edinburgh, the party had increased its national total of aldermen and councillors from 621 to 993 in only twelve months, and morale was high, with another record-breaking attendance. The party felt itself to be on the crest of a wave. The Berlin Wall had been constructed without warning the month before, and this panicked the assembly into its sole dalliance with danger, when it passed a motion calling for the *de facto* recognition of East Germany, as the precursor to serious East–West dialogue about the future of Berlin in particular and Europe in general. Representatives of the Liberals' West German sister party, the Free Democrats, walked out in protest. Many delegates too felt that the new policy represented an unforgivable concession to totalitarianism. Bridges with the Free Democrats were soon mended, but the Liberals learned to be slightly more circumspect about the 'German question' at future assemblies. In his speech, Grimond made it plain that there would be no softening in his own opposition to Communism. He attacked pacifists and unilateralists, and likened the position of the West to that of 'people condemned to live in a small house with a man of violent habits and objectionable opinions . . . We can't hope to frighten him or lock him up . . . All we can do is try to agree to keep apart, find out what makes him angry and try to iron out possible causes of trouble.'

One of Grimond's great achievements as leader was re-establishing the Liberals' intellectual credibility and, by this time, he was attracting into the party an unparalleled influx of young people with both talent and real political ambition. Each successive autumn term saw Grimond intensifying his previous campaigns to recruit in the universities, and an entire generation of undergraduates was transfixed. At Oxford and Cambridge in particular, the Conservative and Labour clubs suddenly found that the Liberals were out-recruiting them. Leading party figures of the future came on board under the personal influence of Grimond, who seemed to them to offer a way out of the stark dichotomy between state socialism and increasingly technocratic conservatism. Alan Watson, later a president of the Liberals, was a Conservative before he arrived at Cambridge as part of the first generation of students to have been spared national service. After hearing Jo Grimond speak one Sunday afternoon, he was among a number to be converted and, within a couple of years, the membership of the Cambridge University Liberal Club unexpectedly came to rival that of the Conservative Club. William Wallace, Richard Holme and many others tell a similar story. Grimond carried with him at this time an irresistible aura of confidence, a sense of being the 'man of the moment'. For all his charm and his undoubted ability to rouse a hall with his speeches, however, Grimond still drew up short of any kind of intimacy with all but the tiniest group of confidants. Although he was on first-name terms with colleagues, he rarely socialised with them, retaining a mixture of aristocratic aloofness and professional detachment, and few of them ever got to feel that they really knew him well personally. When he went to East London to hand over the leadership to David Steel in 1976, he gave the party president, Margaret Wingfield, a welcoming kiss. 'This is a great thing, you know,' Laura confided in her, 'because he never kisses anyone.' Mrs Wingfield commented to the author that, 'I think he had an inner resistance to being well known.'

On 31st October 1961, on the eve of the new parliamentary session, it was announced that Jo Grimond was to become a Privy Counsellor. Membership of the Privy Council would entitle him to be called by the Speaker of the

House of Commons ahead of other 'backbenchers', and to be entrusted with certain state secrets on a privileged basis. He had been leader of the Liberals for five years. Clem Davies had had to wait only two years before this particular privilege had been conferred upon him, but then Clement Davies had never represented quite the threat to the political fortunes of Her Majesty's Government that Grimond now did. For five years, Grimond's formal standing in the House of Commons had been no greater than that of any other MP who had never achieved office. This had enabled anti-Liberal journalists to criticise him for failing to make sufficient impact in the chamber, as the larger parties squeezed him out of debates by bringing in their own big guns. Not that everyone in the other parties was totally antipathetic to Grimond and his Liberals. In mid November Woodrow Wyatt stirred things up by going public with his suggestion that Labour should 'come to terms with the Liberals'. His gambit provoked a dusty response from senior figures in his own party. Grimond's initial reaction too was to reject this idea out of hand. Why, he asked, would the Liberals wish to tie themselves up with 'a Labour Party machine which is bureaucratic and out of date, quite apart from being riddled with dissension'.[3] He then called a meeting of his own senior colleagues. Although they could not decide unanimously on what strategy should be adopted, they did at least agree with Grimond that to be tied up with Labour in its present state would be suicidal. Labour was having a pretty bad time of it, and the Liberals knew that every Labour failure would help to bring about the realignment whose virtues their leader proclaimed. There would be no sense in propping up the socialists whom they wanted to supplant. On the other hand, a poll in late November showed substantial support amongst Liberal voters for what Wyatt was proposing – and, astonishingly, majority support amongst Labour supporters for some kind of arrangement with the Liberals.

Shortly afterwards Richard Crossman interviewed Grimond for the *Guardian* on this subject. Grimond identified a number of areas on which disagreement between the two parties was at that time unbridgeable. For a start, socialists still argued vehemently against joining the EEC because that would make it impossible to carry out 'a Socialist programme of economic reconstruction at home'. In contrast, Liberals wanted to deal with the shared problems of Europe on a common basis. With such a fundamental disagreement over policy, the chances of an arrangement between Labour and the Liberals didn't look too promising, yet Grimond would not rule it out indefinitely. 'In the immediate future it's obviously out,' he explained, 'but politics is unpredictable – nearer, or after, the election, or particularly in the event of a national emergency caused by the bankruptcy of Tory policy, people may be thinking very differently.'[4] Crossman was left with the clear impression that Grimond was by no means inimical to the thought of a pact;

he just wanted the Liberal Party to be in a substantially stronger position before negotiating. There was, of course, some common ground, for example with regard to the government's Immigration Bill which, in Grimond's view, missed the point entirely:

> It is common knowledge that about 95 per cent of the West Indians who come to this country find jobs, it is common knowledge that we would have difficulty in manning the hospitals and the London Transport services if that flow did not come . . . What the Government have made no proposals about is housing. It is the consequent overcrowding which is the problem. Therefore, their proposals are totally irrelevant to the only problem raised by immigration.[5]

As Labour and the Liberals marched through the parliamentary lobbies together opposing the Bill, Grimond sent Gaitskell a note, no doubt at least slightly tongue-in-cheek, saying, 'the Lib-Lab pact seems even closer than Woodrow envisaged'.[6] Gaitskell would not be drawn. Like Roy Jenkins, he thought well of Jo Grimond and Mark Bonham Carter, but he recognised that many of the Liberals' supporters were now well to the right of them – 'Poujadistes' as Jenkins once put it – so it probably once again did Labour more good to have them intervening in seats than to have them stand down. He also thought that many Tory defectors to the Liberals were too 'snobbish' ever to vote Labour. He was polite enough to send a reply, but it was decidedly non-committal.

In the Liberal Party, policy development had largely gone into abeyance. Grimond had already won significant victories in the areas that mattered to him – notably defence, Europe and economic affairs – and recognised the good sense of allowing the party's new platform to bed down. Then, on the subject of the monarchy, Grimond arguably allowed his radical instincts to get the better of him. Writing in the magazine *Encounter,* Grimond claimed that the monarchy was growing dangerously out of touch with the real world. By insulating itself from criticism and change, he warned, it was in danger of withering away. He argued that the Crown and court should be drawn into new fields and into natural contact with a far wider range of people. The Crown could also have shown a more entrepreneurial aspect: 'it could by its example have made it respectable for every local authority and big company to mind about the quality of its buildings and furnishings . . . It could have founded a Glyndebourne or continued with more enterprise the tradition of the Royal Picture Collections.'[7] He also argued that the monarch should be more closely associated with other Commonwealth territories, and with development issues. This may have sounded heretical at the time, but it is hard to imagine the present Prince of Wales disagreeing with much of it.

Although 1962 began badly for Grimond – his car was stolen in Kew – he knew that he had to maintain the considerable momentum that he had built up. He allowed *Liberal News* to run a feature in which a Liberal 'shadow cabinet' was chosen by the paper's readership. This was an obvious part of a very necessary campaign to kill off the 'one-man band' allegations and although, for obvious reasons, the people on the list generally lacked ministerial (and, in most cases, parliamentary) experience, they were by no means an unimpressive group. Mark Bonham Carter would surely have given the Foreign Office a much-needed shake-up, and Ludovic Kennedy might have made a notably liberal Home Secretary. Shortly afterwards, in the columns of the *New Statesman,* Woodrow Wyatt returned to his unauthorised proposals for a Lib-Lab pact, this time accompanied with tables of his own devising, which purported to show how the pact might work in practice. This time Grimond struck a more emollient tone. Although he could not see any likelihood of a share-out of candidacies between the parties, he did accept that 'it would be intolerable for the country and suicide for the parties concerned if Liberal and Labour cut each other's throats.'[8] Any arrangement would have to be part of a general realignment of the progressive side of British politics: 'there are clearly within the Liberal and Labour parties many personalities and large groups which could work together and which, indeed, would attract many people at present calling themselves Conservatives . . . agreement on attitude and on the main issues must come before any talk of an arrangement about seats.'[9] In other words, it would be cynical and self-defeating to set up any deal with a party that was still weighed down by left-wing enthusiasts for both nationalism and nationalisation. Grimond's latest statement was no marriage proposal – it was another cheeky take-over bid for the pro-European right wing of the Labour Party. The pact question then went quiet for a very good reason: the general secretary of the Labour Party, Morgan Phillips, told Wyatt to shut up or face expulsion from the party.

By the beginning of 1962 there had been almost thirty by-elections since 1959, yet none had occurred in a seat where the Liberals had more than the remotest chance of victory. They had not contested over half of these seats in 1959 and, in those they had contested, their highest share of the vote had been exactly 20 per cent, at High Peak. With the party buoyed by opinion poll ratings that had risen steadily from the low teens to the low twenties during the second half of 1961, the by-elections pending in 1962 looked far more promising. Grimond never expected to win at Lincoln, where the party had no organisation worth speaking of, but the vacancies at Blackpool North and Orpington looked far more intriguing. Blackpool North was historically a safe Conservative seat, but the Liberal candidate in 1959 had gained over 20 per cent of the vote, coming only a handful of votes behind Labour. Orpington looked better still. The position there in 1959 had been virtually identical to that in Blackpool, but Orpington had since become one of the places where the Liberals' new emphasis on local government campaigning had most dramatically borne fruit. Prior to 1955, the Liberal Association had about

200 members – compared with the 10,000 or so in the local Conservative Association – then in 1956 its members decided to form ward committees and contest local elections. In that first year Liberal candidates won under 10 per cent of the votes cast in elections to Orpington Urban District Council, and no seats. They built up patiently from there. By 1959 they had overtaken Labour, with over 30 per cent of the vote, and won two seats. By 1961 they had overtaken the Conservatives in votes cast, and had twelve members on the thirty-three-member council.

When the Conservative MP for Orpington, Donald Sumner, resigned from Parliament towards the end of the 1961 summer recess, local Tories were understandably worried about their ability to hold the seat. Accordingly, the Conservative whips in the House of Commons delayed moving a by-election writ for several months. Although the seat fell vacant on 1st October 1961, the Conservatives opted to wait until the new electoral register was in place, the following February, before moving the writ. They nonetheless wasted no time in selecting a candidate, Peter Goldman, an uncharismatic individual with no obvious local connections who was a close associate of Iain Macleod. The new ruthlessness of the Liberal Party organisation was soon called into play when the local party agent had contacted Donald Wade to advise him of news about the prospective Liberal candidate, Jack Galloway, which could have proved politically ruinous. It turned out that he had not understood the technical terms *nisi* and absolute, and had innocently remarried before his first marriage had been properly dissolved. He was put under pressure to step aside, which in due course he did. Wade advised the local Liberals to replace him with another local man. They selected Eric Lubbock, a local councillor and professional engineer with deep family roots in Orpington. Lubbock was an archetypal 'Grimond Liberal', having only joined the party in 1960, soon after which he had found himself on the local executive committee. In May 1961 he had gained a Tory council seat, Downe, with 75 per cent of the vote. Before the end of the year, the *Daily Mail* speculated that the word Orpington might come to be 'engraved on the coffin of the Macmillan government'.[10]

Pratap Chitnis, who had masterminded so many of the Liberals' advances in local government, was drafted in as agent. By mid February, with Chitnis firmly ensconced at Orpington, the Liberals were so eager to get the by-election under way that Grimond and Donald Wade presented a petition in the House of Commons urging that the writ be moved without further delay. This had the desired effect almost immediately, and the by-election was called for Wednesday, 14th March 1962. Lubbock had already visited every street in the constituency. Now he planned to revisit them all.

Jo Grimond himself only went to Orpington once during the by-election campaign. He and Eric Lubbock were driven around in a white Cadillac loaned by a local supporter, and addressed an evening meeting that was almost revivalist in its fervour. He went back to Westminster, a week before polling day, believing firmly that Eric Lubbock had a real chance of victory, proudly informing Cate Fisher on his return that 'I think we're going to do rather well!' The by-election held at Blackpool North the day before Orpington no doubt enhanced his optimism as, to general astonishment, the Conservative majority fell from almost 16,000 to under 1,000. When Grimond appeared on the ITV late-night by-election special the following night, however, he was still not fully prepared for the drama of the result. Eric Lubbock was in all right. He was in by almost 8,000 votes, having earned the biggest swing ever recorded. The Liberal share of the vote, on a turnout of over 80 per cent, had increased by a shade under 32 per cent. We are now inured to the voters inflicting such punishment on our leaders. In 1962, however, such a result seemed seismic. Grimond seemed almost embarrassed. When Michael Meadowcroft had spoken to Grimond earlier in the evening from Orpington, he proclaimed, 'We've won!' 'Yes, I can see we have,' responded Grimond, 'disgustingly well!' On television he could still not disguise his astonishment at the scale of the triumph. 'My God, an incredible result!' he exclaimed, before adding some deeper reflections: 'It is a wonderful victory . . . Orpington was won as a result of seven years' hard work in the constituency . . . We have shown that only the Liberals can make real inroads into the present Tory vote.'[11] Even the vice-chairman of the Conservative Party, Lord Aldington (whose resignation as an MP precipitated the by-election in Blackpool), conceded live on the air that this was a 'sensational result'.[12] At the celebration at party HQ, Chitnis was assailed with congratulations and good wishes. One colleague after another told him that he must now surely take a good holiday, to recuperate after all his hard work. Grimond, however, had different ideas. With a twinkle in his eye, he took Chitnis on one side and said, 'The sooner we can get you off to another by-election the better!'[13] Intellectually Grimond must have known that he could not afford to read too much into the result at Orpington, but such was the emotion at the time that, for a while at least, he evidently really did begin to believe that the citadel of the party system had been breached. Despite the assurances of Eric Lubbock's team, he had never dared to hope for anything better than a close-run result.

The authors of *Must Labour Lose?*, writing in 1960, were primarily concerned with the fortunes of the Labour Party, but they also included a small section identifying a potential Liberal coalition that could, in time, have a critical influence on British politics. Their analysis of the voters who might vote Liberal still provides a useful guide to anyone trying to unpick what happened at Orpington. The first paradigm identified by Abrams and Rose is the *anti-political* voter, repelled by the squabbling and division that characterise party politics and regarding the Liberals as a sanctuary away from mainstream politics. The second type is the *anti-class-conflict* voter, described as 'a social equivalent of the anti-political voter' and disenchanted with the class basis of the two main parties. The third is the *socially responsive* voter, who is subject to conflicting political pressures, perhaps at work as against at home, and resolves them by 'opting out' in some degree – either by voting Liberal or by abstaining. The fourth and final type is the *halfway-house* Liberal, a defector from one of the two class-based parties who draws up short of giving direct succour to his atavistic enemy. In the by-elections of 1956–8, it had been this last type of voter who had swelled the Liberal ranks – only to return to his or her traditional allegiance in 1959, or else complete a switch across the spectrum. In the circumstances that prevailed between 1960 and 1962, it is easy to see how every part of this curious coalition increased in size. The Conservatives were tired and desperate, while Labour was divided and obstreperous: only the Liberals looked fresh, and united. Grimond's talk of political revolution, in combination with his Etonian cadences, could excite the radical and soothe the moderately inclined in almost equal measure.

In the immediate wake of Orpington, Grimond penned two significant pieces for the broadsheet newspapers. In the first, for the *Guardian* on 16th March, he explained that he wanted to help create a new party, based upon the Liberals and rooted 'in the warm tradition of British radicalism', which would 'harness the type of talent which in America is available to the Kennedy administration'. He accepted that many people were still unsure about what exactly the Liberals stood for, but laughed off the suggestion that they lacked policies: 'I think we have almost come to the state of having too much policy'. What people needed to understand was not every detail of every policy, but the general thrust of the Liberal response to the challenges of the 1960s. He was also careful to play down short-term expectations: 'we know that we have a long way to go and we fully expect that there may be setbacks along the road'. A day later, in a rather weightier article in *The Times,* Grimond did in fact deal with specific policies in far more detail, and explained more clearly what he meant by a 'realignment' of politics. He claimed to see the writing on the wall for the Tories – 'the picture of the Conservative Party as the party of managers competent to run the country's business is shattered' – but argued that the left's response to changing circumstances had been fragmented and ineffective, largely because 'the divisions in politics fall in the wrong places'. The sort of radical, progressive policies for which the country was crying out could never emerge from Labour, or from the Liberals alone. Because Labour was so fundamentally split, its leadership was utterly incapable of taking the decisions needed, and the Liberal Party's role now was to provide the foundations of a 'broadly based progressive party' in opposition to the Tories.

By a happy coincidence, exactly a week after Orpington came the Liberals' one television allocation of the year for a party political broadcast. Rather than speaking to camera or wheeling out a number of familiar and semi-familiar faces, Grimond threw himself at the mercy of a group of students from Imperial College, none of whom he knew. Only one of them professed himself a Liberal, but Grimond dealt easily enough with their questions. For one used to campaigning in Orkney and Shetland, this was hardly a trial, and Grimond looked very impressive. He took the opportunity to explain, in clear and concise terms, the Liberal view of politics. He also began the process of calming everyone's expectations of the Liberals down to a more realistic level, conceding that the Liberal Party was still far from able to compete with its larger rivals on anything approaching an equal footing: 'It is quite true that it is short of money and is building up from very low levels . . . We have been built up a lot by the press, but we know full well that we have got to do a lot of hard work . . . We don't regard Orpington, or any of these by-elections, as the end – we regard them as the beginning.'[14] The broadcast equalled *Coronation Street* and *Sunday Night at the Palladium* as the second most popular television programme of the week. Luck had been a lady for Grimond for most of March 1962. Then, two days after Grimond's broadcast, his predecessor as party leader, Clement Davies, died in a London clinic. He had already announced his intention to stand down as MP for the Liberal stronghold of Montgomery at the next general election, but his death still came as a blow to Grimond. It also meant that the Liberals would soon be on the defensive at a by-election. Would they prove to be effective gamekeepers as well as poachers?

Grimond may have done his level best, at least after the first few days, to dampen down the post-Orpington euphoria, but it was an impossible task. Even Harold Macmillan was convinced that some great historical shift was taking place. In his view the Conservative government he led was becoming the victim of its own success. He was scornful of the Liberals, whom he regarded as 'purely opportunist', but still feared the damage they might be able to wreak against his own party. He wrote in his diary on 25th March that 'perhaps . . . we have killed the class war and the fear of socialism . . . so, by removing their fear, we have made it possible for people to gratify their exasperation at minor difficulties by voting against the Government . . . In a word, we have made England safe for Liberalism!'[15] Macmillan may have been inclined to take the spate of by-elections in spring 1962 rather too personally: Orpington bordered his own constituency of Bromley and now another by-election was due at his former seat of Stockton. Under pressure from panic-stricken colleagues and party activists, Macmillan decided to break with convention by taking part in the campaign at Stockton.

The sense of panic in the Conservative camp intensified when two opinion polls towards the end of March put the Liberals in first place and demonstrated that nearly 40 per cent of the population now thought that Grimond would make a good Prime Minister. Speaking to the annual conference of the Women's Liberal Federation on 29th March, Grimond was upbeat, telling delegates that 'We can have a Liberal Government – and not in the too far distant future either.'[16] He also took the opportunity to kick into touch any talk of a coalition or alliance with the Labour Party as it was then constituted, which he deemed an 'out-of-date tie-up'.[17] Orpington turned out to be a high point, not the inauguration of a golden age. In the wake of their debacle, the Conservatives launched an extensive and expensive period of self-examination. They identified faults in the party's image, its campaigning methods and its process of candidate selection. Patrick Kemmis, a former civil servant who had taken over as head of the Liberal Party Organisation the previous summer, had already warned privately that even the most optimistic Liberal should have serious doubts about the staying power of the new Liberal voters. He felt that the Blackpool result was more representative than that at Orpington: it had provided some favourable headlines, but came about largely because of the high number of voters who had opted to stay at home. Compared with the previous general election, the Tories had seen their vote fall by 12,000 but the Liberals had seen their total rise by only 2,500. The Liberals soon followed the Tories in investigating in detail what lessons they could draw from Orpington.

The Liberals' own private study echoed the fears of Kemmis, warning that Orpington looked dangerously like a one-off: Eric Lubbock had won by a landslide because, in that particular constituency, everything was just right for the Liberals. True, certain factors would apply elsewhere as they had in Orpington. The Macmillan government was becoming generally unpopular, which helped, but local factors had both damaged the Tories and positively helped the Liberal. Above all, from the outset there had been no 'wasted vote' argument in Orpington, because the Liberal always looked credible, with Labour looking down and out. Such a conjunction was a dream come true for the Liberals. It was also extremely unlikely to recur in more than a handful of seats at a general election. In parallel with this report, Timothy Joyce, one of the bright young Liberals attracted to the party by Grimond, was charged with suggesting how further 'Orpingtons' could be achieved. He put his intermediate conclusions to the Organising Committee in April 1962. His view was that the Liberals would achieve similar breakthroughs in future only if they established a clear image for the party, which should look efficient and up-to-date, with a particular appeal to younger people. He also concluded that far greater emphasis should be given to local and regional issues and campaigns. Everything possible should be done to kill off the 'wasted vote' argument in as many seats as possible, and the Liberals must be shameless in exploiting the growing sense in the country that the Tories believed that they had a 'right to rule'.

Grimond was soon back to the steady grind of opposition politics, albeit secure in the knowledge that he would henceforth get rather more press attention than in the past. He memorably deemed the April 1962 Budget a 'mouse of a Budget'[18] and warned that, until the government really committed itself to wholehearted participation in the EEC, it could never get to grips with the country's underlying economic problems. He found his visit to the by-election at Stockton dispiriting after the high tide of Orpington. Again he was driven into the town in an open car, but this time he found few admirers en route and, when he claimed that he detected a change of allegiance in the air in Stockton, he was forced to admit that he had never visited the place before. Still he put a brave face on things, claiming that the Liberals could win, and must have been heartened when his evening meeting in the town's Holy Trinity Hall was packed to overflowing. He then, inexplicably, made not even a fleeting appearance at Derby North, which was due to poll a week later. 'Don't say I am disappointed,' commented the Liberal candidate there through gritted teeth, 'just say it would have been nice if Mr Grimond had looked in'.[19] In both seats Labour held on with a reduced majority and the Liberals came a good second. The obvious next priority was for the Liberals to capitalise on Orpington by throwing everything into the forthcoming local elections. On Saturday, 28th April 1962, Richard Wainwright was able to report to the Executive Committee that there would be 2,199 Liberal candidates in the local elections – compared with 1,365 in 1961. Even taking into account the fact that 320 of those were contesting metropolitan boroughs, which had not been up for grabs in 1961, that was impressive. The Liberals threw everything into these local elections and consequently enjoyed another advance, recording net gains of over 500 seats.

Approximately a third of the party's candidates at those elections were elected. In many places this came about because the party succeeded in winning an entirely new vote. Writing in the *Political Quarterly* later in 1962, R H Pear propounded the theory that local elections and by-elections were intimately related. As the Liberals exploited dissatisfactions with both Labour and the Tories, they gave the 'British non-socialist voter' the chance to register 'his disapproval of a Tory government's progress'.[20] This was in essence an imported variant of the 'ticket-splitting' so common in the USA, where voters regularly vote for different parties in presidential and congressional elections, sometimes on the same day, but provided little useful information about what might happen at a general election. In contrast with this pessimistic view, Grimond himself, influenced by Pratap Chitnis, argued that successes in local elections were fundamental to the job of building up the long-term strength of the party organisation: 'If we have more Liberals in local government, beginning with such parochial matters as moving bus stops, they are becoming valuably trained in public administration . . . And in their local papers the public can read about Liberal councillors and learn that the Liberal Party is not made up of remote intellectuals or fireworks in the House of Commons'.[21]

It was essential to keep the Liberal bandwagon on track at the forthcoming by-election in Montgomery, where Emlyn Hooson had been selected to defend Clem Davies's majority of below 3,000 votes. Even though Hooson seemed to be the ideal candidate (he had effectively been nursing the constituency for years and was married to the daughter of the Lord Lieutenant of the county), Grimond still sensed troubling potential parallels with the disaster at Carmarthen that had marred his early months as leader. He need not have worried. On a turnout of over 85 per cent, Hooson more than doubled the previous Liberal majority and, in the wake of such an advance, Grimond could go back on to the offensive. On television, he opened up slightly on the fraught question of how the Liberals might behave in a hung Parliament, telling Malcolm Muggeridge that he stood 'nearer the aims of the Labour Party'[22] than those of the Conservatives. He did not, however, foresee a coalition across the board with the Labour Party, as it was then constituted. He would consider offering conditional support to a Labour administration on certain issues, to 'make a Government possible for a limited time until the country can pronounce again'.[23]

In a speech to a gathering of the newly elected Liberal councillors the following day, Saturday, 19th May 1962, Grimond warned that the Liberals must waste no time in capitalising upon their new-found success: 'We failed to follow up Torrington as vigorously as we might have done. We must get those who have joined us tied tightly into the work of the party so that they feel it is their party and they have a stake in it. Now, while the iron is hot, our imprint can be cast on it.'[24] He also claimed that the time had now come for the Liberals to be taken seriously: 'From now on the Liberal Party is neither playing solitaire on its own, nor is it a mere guerrilla on the fringe of other people's battles.'[25] He went on to clarify how he foresaw any future relationship with Labour: 'The Labour Party may rest on its oars hoping to be swept into office on a Liberal current . . . We are not interested in pacts merely for power . . . Nor shall we do other than work for the creation of the Liberal Britain which is our goal.'[26] Oddly, in a rival newspaper the same day, Grimond appeared rather more enthusiastic about a coalition with Labour, saying that he would consider joining one so long as 'Labour were in the political lead' and 'there was genuine agreement on major heads of immediate policy'.[27]

Arguably the party in fact missed an excellent chance for 'another Orpington' very soon afterwards. A by-election was held in West Derbyshire on 6th June 1962. This was not self-evidently promising territory for the Liberals, and there were some voices raised against fighting the seat at all. In the event Colonel Ronald Gardner-Thorpe, a competent but fairly unassuming and not especially charismatic member of the party's executive committee, agreed to contest the by-election if nobody else would. They wouldn't, so he did. Once the campaign got under way, Peregrine Worsthorne, writing in the *Sunday Telegraph*, was astonished by how much support Gardner-Thorpe was attracting, describing him as 'abysmally poor, with a platform manner which is all ham and no tongue'.[28] Some local wags had nicknamed him 'Colonel Limp'. Yet he was clearly the man to watch in this contest. How, asked Worsthorne, might a really high-calibre Liberal candidate be doing? Gardner-Thorpe lost by only 1,500 votes. It is not necessarily the case that another candidate could have closed the gap, but a more vigorous campaign by the party nationally and locally might well have done. Both Grimond and Mark Bonham Carter would in later years rue West Derbyshire as another great missed opportunity to build on Orpington, by claiming another seat well removed from the Celtic fringe.

The growing credibility of the party continued to manifest itself in all sorts of ways. In spring 1962 Grimond's effigy was introduced at Tussaud's. He was the only living Liberal to be thus honoured, and the management had to decide where to put him. He obviously didn't belong in the Conservative cabinet or amongst their Labour shadows, nor did it seem appropriate to place him alongside Gladstone and Lloyd George, amidst the statesmen of the past. His effigy ended up, rather enterprisingly, sharing a platform with those of Drake, Nelson and Wellington. A more serious problem came in the shape of Iain Macleod, who in June 1962 launched a counter-offensive against Grimond and his troops with the theme 'If you really want Socialism then vote Liberal'. Macleod, himself very much a Tory radical, had always recognised the potential danger of maintaining Churchill's policy of reprieving most of the Liberal MPs from the Conservative interventions that might have cost them their seats. He was now charged with enacting a political death sentence on Grimond and his colleagues. From now on, everything that Grimond or his party did would go into a dossier at Conservative Central Office. As Grimond had hoped, it was now open season on the Liberals again. 'We can make many friends and recruits among Tories,' was Grimond's response to this news when he addressed the Scottish Liberal Congress, 'but the Tory machine, when frightened, lashes out in all directions.'[29]

Grimond feared that some Liberal faint-hearts might start to enjoy their politics rather less if they came under serious fire from the other parties for the first time: 'The adventure on which we are embarked is not one for those who have an aversion to the in-fighting of politics . . . It is not for those whose confidence may falter when they are met with the chorus of threats and dreadful warnings that any attempt to put reforms into practice always brings.'[30] The main Tory leaflet attacking the Liberals claimed that their proposals would leave a 'spending gap' of more than £4,000 million, an immense sum in those days. Arthur Holt furiously attacked this propaganda as 'grossly irresponsible' and a 'complete distortion',[31] and Grimond described the figure of £4,000 million as 'forlorn and unsupported'.[32] When Iain Macleod produced his detailed figures, it turned out that the Tories had a reasonable case. Approximately half of the total took the form of tax cuts that Liberals had advocated; the balance was made up of spending pledges that they had made. Too many loosely phrased proposals had been floated over the years and, when they were subjected to proper scrutiny for the first time, they simply didn't add up. This was a timely warning for Grimond and his advisers. Macleod became his party's main mouthpiece for attacks on the Liberals for some time, claiming that he didn't know what Grimond's views were and once describing Liberalism as a 'cave and a refuge'[33] in which people would find no lasting succour.

A more serious and knotty issue arose at the same point about the system for allocating political broadcasts. For many years discussions on this question had been held between the two major parties, with a Liberal as neutral chairman. While this arrangement had been acceptable so long as the Liberals were effectively moribund, the other parties no longer felt that it was acceptable. Furthermore, it was the Liberals who were now pressing for a change in the allocations. Recent by-election results had convinced Grimond that the Liberals deserved more coverage all round, that the media should treat them not as the largest minor party but as the smallest major party. When Grimond had addressed a major Liberal rally at Central Hall in Westminster the previous March, it had gone virtually unreported, with only the *Guardian* carrying even a small mention. The Liberals had also been engaged in a running battle with the BBC to get a party spokesman included on its pre-budget show. At this stage the Liberals were granted a single television broadcast annually, with a duration of fifteen minutes. Labour and the Tories both had four broadcasts, each enjoying a total of eighty minutes on the air. Things began to come to a head in May 1962, after both Grimond and a group of senior Labourites had taken to the airwaves putting their case against the Budget. The Conservatives claimed that these programmes amounted to off-ration political broadcasts. For months there was controversy about this entire question. Then, in August, a new formula was agreed, which would take account not only of the previous general election but also, towards the end of a Parliament, of by-election results since the election. This gave the Liberals around 15 per cent of the broadcasting time available.

For the remainder of 1962 Grimond concentrated less upon policy development, and more upon image. Although he genuinely believed that the Liberals should style themselves as a party of the progressive left, Grimond knew that he had to be careful to avoid giving the impression that the Liberals were irredeemably pro-Labour and anti-Conservative. Many Liberals were at least as hostile towards socialism as they were towards anything espoused by Harold Macmillan, so Grimond occasionally had to slap down talk of a Lib-

Lab pact. He explained on radio that: 'if you have a cold-blooded agreement to keep the Tories out at elections I don't think this would be effective . . . I don't think I would go in for a pact for the sole intention of keeping the Tories out.'[34]

A major reform initiated under Grimond's leadership during this period was a radical development of seat targeting through the establishment of a Special Seats Committee under Jeremy Thorpe, which formally came into existence in July 1962 and enjoyed tremendous freedom of action. It had only three members: Thorpe himself, Dominic le Foe and Ted Wheeler. Dominic le Foe was a friend of Thorpe and Peter Bessell, a PR man and former professional magician who had played a major part in stage-managing the Liberal revival in the south-west, and who was formally appointed as the party's publicity consultant in November 1962. Ted Wheeler, in contrast, was an archetypal party agent of the old school. Their brief was simple. They had to assess where the Liberals had a serious chance of winning under the first-past-the-post voting system; then they had to get the local organisation into shape and ensure that adequate funds were being raised. Wheeler would visit individual seats, seeing for himself what state the party was in locally and then submit a detailed survey and report to his two colleagues. The committee in turn discussed each report, worked out schemes tailored to each constituency and visited the constituencies to discuss these plans with the local officers. The constituencies would be set targets for membership, branches and fund-raising and, if they met their targets, they would get assistance. By the autumn of 1963, Thorpe could report that the committee had given advice and financial assistance to eighteen constituencies in England and Wales, and to nine in Scotland. Fifteen new agents or sub-agents had already been appointed as a consequence of the committee's activities. The only problem was the usual one: finance. In its first year, the committee had been given only £1,000 to disburse, of which £400 had gone to Orpington alone.

The Liberal by-election challenge was maintained into the summer of 1962, again without quite delivering another gain. Although the Liberals were now back in third place (albeit a strong third place) in the opinion polls, on 12th July their man came within a whisker of taking the hitherto unpromising seat of Leicester North-East. The Conservative candidate's tumble from a close second place to a distant third precipitated Harold Macmillan's 'Night of the Long Knives', the second that Grimond had experienced at first hand, in which a third of his senior ministers were sacked. Violet Bonham Carter recorded in her diary that Grimond seemed 'far less exhilarated by the rumpus over the massacre'[35] then she had expected him to be. She was surprised to find him unsure about whether he should speak in favour of the censure motion that Labour had put before the House of Commons as a response to the sackings, commenting that 'the <u>only</u> ingredient he lacks as a political leader is passion'.[36] Grimond never displayed any uncertainty in public. 'The logic of the situation,' he commented tersely, 'is that the whole Government should resign.'[37] He also came close to drowning himself not on gore, but in a veritable flood of metaphor and cliché, when he claimed that: 'The people have sold too many Tory pigs in a poke to fall for any promises of cats in the bag . . . Mr Macmillan in the last five years has swept so many questions under the carpet that the floors on which we tread are heaving with unfaced decisions.'[38] He was even more trenchant in the censure debate:

> No motion of censure which the House can pass can be nearly as devastating as the vote of censure passed by the Prime Minister on his own Government . . . it is the conduct of the Borgias, on one of their more unsavoury evenings . . . The most regrettable casualty of the past three weeks has been public confidence in the processes of the government . . . in the decency of politicians . . . and any belief that any party has any principle except . . . sticking to office through thick and thin.[39]

Early in 1962, Grimond had to rebut suggestions that he should forsake Orkney and Shetland for a more conveniently located constituency. He explained that he had no intention of upping stakes and moving south. 'I like the place and I like the people,' he retorted. 'It gives me a firm foundation.'[40] It also, of course, gave him a firm majority at elections. To prove the point, he had to go on making his presence felt on the Scottish Committees of the House of Commons. The Grand Committee was little more than a sop to those who advocated devolution. It had no executive powers, no sustained influence and no real parliamentary powers, beyond a very notional one of scrutiny. In Grimond's view it did nothing to address the need to bring government in Scotland closer to the people. It was a wearisome 'talking shop' that he had to attend for the sake of appearance, but which in his view needed to 'suppress its love of rhetoric and get down to expert examination of Ministers, and, indeed, senior officials'.[41] Despite his impressive attendance record, Grimond spoke only rarely at these gatherings and, when he did speak, he trod familiar ground, pressing the case for a Highlands Development Authority and impressing upon ministers the need for more capital in agriculture, providing piers and more reliable electricity supplies. He also made regular fun of the dilatory way in which the Scottish Office went about its business, once remarking that he sometimes thought that 'when Doomsday comes there will be an excellent band of people in the Scottish Office busy drafting legislation following a report by a working party – and it would not be surprising if there were a Crofters' Bill shortly after we had all been buried by a hydrogen bomb.'[42]

The extra demands on the Liberal Party machine in the aftermath of Orpington soon necessitated another reorganisation. Once again Grimond was reshuffling a very limited pack. At the beginning of September 1962 it was announced that Donald Wade, who had served as whip for the six years since Grimond became leader, would become deputy party leader, with special responsibility for policy matters. His place as whip was taken by Arthur Holt, who accordingly took charge not only of the party's parliamentary affairs, but also of a great deal of its general organisation and administration, including the party's Candidates Committee and liaison between the party's Executive and Organising Committees. Wade would take on a number of tasks from Grimond himself, as well as serving as a link between the MPs and Harry Cowie's research department. Tim Beaumont, the wealthy Anglican priest who was already helping to finance the party's activities and would soon become the party's treasurer, had been nagging Grimond for some time to appoint a researcher or personal assistant, as much as a status symbol as anything else. Grimond's response had always been that the House of Commons had a perfectly good library, with admirable specialists at the beck and call of MPs, so he didn't need anyone else. When Grimond quite unexpectedly caved in, Beaumont had to find a suitable person for the job. He struck upon Christopher Layton, who was the son of a Liberal peer and very active as the prospective parliamentary candidate for the forthcoming by-election at Chippenham. With the one proviso that he was hoping to win Chippenham, Layton was an obvious person, and Beaumont recommended him to Grimond on the basis that 'he will have lots of stimulating, bright ideas for your speeches'. Grimond's response was that 'I don't want anyone to provide stimulating ideas for my speeches – I have six bright, stimulating ideas before breakfast. What I want is someone to get me from A to B on time.'[43] George Scott, the journalist who had done so well as the party's candidate at the two recent Middlesbrough by-elections, was brought in as head of a new political division at headquarters. His job was to coordinate press and publicity, publications, research and information. At last, the three main headquarters functions – administrative, organisational and political – had been separated into streamlined divisions.

The 1,500 delegates who gathered for the 1962 Liberal assembly, held at Llandudno in September, were in high spirits and had plenty to talk about: in a matter of little over a week just before the assembly, the Liberals rushed out seven policy documents for delegates to discuss. Grimond himself looked notably relaxed and fit, and spent a great deal of time on the platform, listening intently to the debates. His very presence was now enough to ensure that the party would not throw away its new prominence by falling into the trap of faction fights. To help enhance his profile, Christopher Layton was afforded considerable prominence at the assembly, and he played a major role in inducing the party to accept that its accumulated proposals for public expenditure were now such that the party could not credibly promise a reduction in taxation. He also warned that the party would suffer unless it destroyed the old perception that it was 'full of cranky ideas and . . . all things to all men'. Other policy discussions were as earnest as ever, culminating in a significant hardening of the party's pro-EEC policy. No longer were the Commonwealth or fellow EFTA members to have any kind of implied veto. It was now a hard-and-fast policy to get into the EEC as soon as possible. Nor were the Liberals now minded to let the terms of entry weigh too heavily on their minds. To do so, said Grimond, would be 'as if at the Reformation someone had said they were unable to make up their minds until they knew what price the monasteries were likely to fetch'.[44] This was thrown into sharp relief when Hugh Gaitskell, whose personal popularity had been surging in recent months, made a sublimely timed intervention.

In a television and radio address the evening before Grimond was due to address the assembly, Gaitskell issued a warning to the nation against joining the EEC. Grimond rewrote much of his speech for the next day. Where he had intended to concentrate his fire on the Conservatives, Grimond now opened up on two fronts, saying that Gaitskell's broadcast 'would have been a credit . . . to any Conservative Prime Minister . . . It was well-spoken, cautious, pessimistic . . . It showed a proper suspicion of all foreigners and a considerable distrust of all change . . . It was imbued with the honourable sentiment in favour of things as they are.'[45] Grimond was disappointed in Gaitskell. Although so many of his supporters shared the Liberals' radical zeal for joining the EEC, on this question Gaitskell himself had, in Grimond's words, 'fallen off the fence, rather limply, on the wrong side'.[46] Grimond believed too that Gaitskell was failing to rise to the challenge of what should have been a debate about the future of a great continent, reducing it instead to a disagreement about machine tools and the price of tinned peaches.

During the autumn of 1962 Grimond was back on the political treadmill, delivering speeches, producing articles and explaining Liberal policies to the voters. He clarified the Liberal position on industrial democracy, telling one journalist that 'although we think that workers should have an influence on their company, we do not – at least, I do not – envisage them running it'[47] and, although the scale of the Cuban missile crisis left little room for a third-party profile, Grimond still did his best to plead for calm and balance. Although 'the murderers of Hungary should not be in a strong position to condemn interference by America in neighbouring countries,'[48] he argued, there was a whiff of hypocrisy in the violent reaction of the Americans to what the Soviets planned in Cuba: they themselves had long since set up nuclear arsenals of their own close to the border of the USSR.

The one opportunity that Grimond identified for arresting the slide of Liberal fortunes was the forthcoming Chippenham by-election. Christopher Layton was just the sort of person whom Grimond wanted in the House of Commons – a cogent speaker as well as an original thinker – and a local opinion poll confirmed that he had a real chance of winning, even though the

Liberal candidate had come third in 1959. Unfortunately for him, the Labour vote held up at the by-election and he was narrowly denied, by the absence of tactical voting, what would have been a fine victory. On the same day, at Dorset South and Glasgow Woodside, a collapse of Tory votes to the Liberals delivered the seats to Labour – even though at both seats the Labour share of the vote actually fell. In advance of the Conservative conference, Iain Macleod had already used a party political broadcast to warn that the problem with the Liberals was no longer that they had no policies: 'To judge from some of their debates at Llandudno their policies are even more to the Left than those the Socialists, anyway officially, would wish to put forward.'[49] The Dorset and Glasgow by-election results provided Macleod with even better ammunition, since they clearly demonstrated that the consequence of Tories switching to the Liberals had been victory for the socialists. Meanwhile the polls suggested that the Liberals had peaked. Between March and December 1962 their support fell from the high 20s to the low teens. Around the time of Orpington, Labour's own private tracking polls had shown that Grimond was more popular than Gaitskell, but that too had now been reversed. The country no longer needed politicians to tell it that the Orpington 'bubble' had well and truly burst. Now it was up to Grimond to prevent this turning into a complete collapse.

10

B Y THE END of 1962, the Liberals once again looked to be a declining force. Orpington seemed more and more like a one-off and even the diehards were beginning to wonder whether the break in the clouds might not have passed. It must have become clear to Jo Grimond very quickly that he and his party were losing the political initiative. The cause was simple enough: after years of self-inflicted wounds, Labour was beginning to pull itself together. This confronted Grimond with a tremendous test of nerve and character. In his early days as a Liberal MP, he could never have envisaged that so much could be achieved, so quickly. Now, however, he was a potential victim of the expectations that Orpington had so dramatically raised. He had to stabilise his party before retrenchment turned into a rout. The dark cloud of the Chippenham by-election result did at least have a silver lining for Grimond – although he hadn't wanted a PA, he was now forced to have one for a time, and he would certainly draw extensively upon Layton's expertise in European affairs, as the government's application to join the EEC hit turbulent waters. Grimond attacked Macmillan for 'blowing hot and cold' on Europe, and suspected the Conservatives of deliberately playing up problems in the negotiations in order to extricate themselves from a politically embarrassing corner. He also attacked Macmillan's handling of the Nassau meeting with President Kennedy, which in due course gave Charles de Gaulle the perfect justification for vetoing the UK application. In a speech to the party executive on Saturday, 15th December 1962, Grimond lamented the fact that Britain's many friends overseas were devastated to see Britain 'sunk in touchy Conservative complacency', constantly opting out of new international developments and trying unconvincingly to play the role of a supposed superpower.

Grimond spent the run-up to Christmas 1962 working extremely hard in the House of Commons, delivering a particularly impressive and impassioned speech about the need to reduce unemployment in the regions. The country needed economic expansion, he warned, but must take measures to ensure that it was not lost through 'gross inflation'. This required ministers not only to talk about an incomes policy, but also to apply one – to themselves as well as to others. He was particularly scornful of the decision by Lord Kilmuir (formerly

David Maxwell Fyfe) to quit politics and take up a highly paid position in industry. Either salary and wage increases must be a free-for-all, for all, or else public figures must start to set a better example: 'It is perfectly reasonable to say that one does not accept restraint . . . But how can it be reconciled with appeals for wage restraint, with talk of an incomes policy, with telling people like nurses . . . that they, of course, must not have any more? One must either make it a genuine policy or drop the cant.'[1]

In January 1963 Grimond went on a trip to North America, taking in Yale and Harvard and meeting President Kennedy for a private discussion. While he was there, the party released details of its biggest campaign since 1959. Despite Grimond's own misgivings about such exercises, individual letters bearing his facsimile signature were to be sent to all of the party's 250,000 or so members, appealing to them to work flat out for the party in the months ahead. There was also to be a new policy leaflet and a poster campaign focusing on Grimond personally. During Grimond's time abroad, British politics were shaken to their foundations by two events that many had feared but few had predicted. Britain's negotiations with the EEC broke down when the French President vetoed British entry and, on 18th January, Hugh Gaitskell died after a sustained period of ill health. Grimond's reaction to both of these seismic events was arguably less than inspired, although he did manage to despatch a short message of sympathy about Gaitskell before returning home. On arriving at London Airport, perhaps unwisely, Grimond allowed himself to be drawn on whether Gaitskell's death might present a political opportunity to the Liberals, when he might have done better to emphasise his sympathy for his late rival's family. Harry Cowie recalls that, although Grimond's return was the focus of considerable media attention, he was reluctant to take full advantage and ducked out of several possible interviews. In response to criticism at the time, Grimond pointed out that, on his return from the USA, he had 'given a press conference and then done five radio and TV appearances on that same evening',[2] but the sense remained that he might have managed rather more.

After Gaitskell's death, Grimond was for a time the leading figure of the left, but he never really succeeded in pressing home this advantage, though he did make the most memorable of the speeches given in honour of Hugh Gaitskell the following day in the House of Commons, praising his late rival for demonstrating 'the best political manners of anyone I have known – and they flowed from deep conviction and a thoroughly generous nature'.[3] Although Grimond had regarded Gaitskell as being insufficiently radical, a figure trapped by the confines of the Labour movement, he had never had cause to doubt either his integrity or his innate decency. Another political death close to Grimond followed soon after. On the evening of 5th February 1963 Lord Samuel, who had led the party between 1931 and 1935, died at the age of ninety-two. Samuel, said Grimond, 'stood for something very dear to Liberals and was not only deeply respected but loved by all who knew him'.[4] For many years Grimond had been one of the senior Liberals who had regularly visited Samuel on his birthday to pay homage and present a gift. 'I feel just like Rabbit or Christopher Robin going off to Eeyore's party with a present,'[5] he once joked. At Samuel's memorial service a fortnight later, Samuel was praised as the 'greatest Postmaster General of our epoch' (between 1910 and 1916). As he departed from the synagogue after the service, Grimond told Jeremy Thorpe, 'My boy, let that be an example to you – if you work hard, you may be thought of at 92 as the second greatest Postmaster-General of our epoch!'[6]

Since joining Grimond's staff, Christopher Layton had worked hard to prepare a new Liberal line on Europe. His view was now that Grimond should now attempt to outflank de Gaulle, in the wake of his veto, by proposing both a new impetus for political union in Europe, and the creation of a new defence community. In Layton's phrase, Grimond did 'mutter about' these ideas, but he was not willing to make a serious attempt at seizing the initiative. Layton believes that Grimond's reluctance to grasp this nettle was a consequence of his meeting with President Kennedy, who had assured him that de Gaulle did not deserve to be taken seriously and could just be 'pushed over'. The French President had had his opportunity to participate at Nassau but had refused, said Kennedy, and had therefore opted out of serious international power politics. Instead of offering a new and dramatic lead, therefore, Grimond poured scorn on de Gaulle's 'posturing without power': 'France has about one and a half divisions of troops in the line. Her nuclear deterrent does not exist. She is wholly dependent on her allies. Let President Kennedy withdraw his protection and Gaullism could collapse like a pack of cards.'[7] Two weeks later, speaking to European Liberals, Grimond did finally heed Layton by making a half-hearted and poorly executed attempt to add impetus to the debate, calling for a new European political community 'to match the economic, atomic and coal and steel communities'.[8] This would supposedly not be a rival to the Common Market; it should, he said, grow from within it, in combination with the EFTA countries. The problem was, it was not at all clear how Grimond's suggestion differed from initiatives that were already being taken by the 'Six' – or even from the Treaty of Rome itself. His speech barely earned a mention in the broadsheets.

At the beginning of March 1963, the Liberals produced their most comprehensive economic policy for decades, drafted by Arthur Holt and Christopher Layton. Some political historians argue that the Conservatives shot the Liberals' economic fox in 1962 by creating the National Economic Development Council (NEDC or 'Neddy'), a shamelessly corporatist body, to study economic growth and propose ways of improving it. Surely this would provide precisely the kind of 'planning' envisaged by Grimond and his allies?

Grimond had extricated himself from that problem, if indeed it was a problem, with great skill. He argued that the NEDC was merely a means by which the Conservative government could wash its hands of economic problems. What was needed was a 'political decision to make growth the first object in the economy'.[9] Industrial production in the UK had risen by only 14 per cent between 1955 and 1960; in the EEC it had risen by 40 per cent. The figures for export growth over the same period were a derisory 13 per cent in the UK, as against 63 per cent for the 'Six'. It was for the government to lead the way out of this mess, for 'it will be a most serious setback if once again manufacturers find that, having increased their capacity, through Government policies they are unable to use it . . . In those circumstances, I wonder whether they will ever do it again.'[10] He was particularly scathing about the government's failure to take the necessary long-term measures to eliminate some of the structural weaknesses that were dogging the UK economy, even when things did go better for a time.

Much of the new Liberal policy was microeconomic rather than macroeconomic in character, building upon the arguments about incentives repeatedly set out by Grimond a year before. Presenting the new package, he denounced the 'utterly barren' debate about privatisation and nationalisation and called for an end to 'stop-start' economic policies. The centrepiece was a revised version of the Liberals' five-year plan. This plan seems to be not a *dirigiste* plan as such, under which resource allocation would be centrally directed. The intention seems to have been to introduce greater stability, thereby enabling industries to plan for the future with confidence. There are several positive 'supply-side' elements to the proposals here, largely designed to improve the incentives for business and relating to capital write-offs and simplification of corporation tax. There is also a proposal (no doubt at least partially with the EEC in mind) to replace purchase tax with sales tax or value-added tax, though for economic liberals there is still rather too much emphasis on the role of government – in the shape of the national planning body and the subsidiary Regional Planning Authorities that are proposed. What was perhaps most interesting was the emphasis given to cutting taxation, in clear contrast with a policy adopted only months before by the party assembly, largely at the instigation of Christopher Layton himself. The party leadership tried to square this circle by claiming that the shift in policy was a consequence of the economic downturn. This was half-credible at best and, despite the best endeavours of some very clever people, the party's economic policies remained confusing not only to the voters, but even to specialists.

A hugely important by-election was now looming, at Colne Valley, a Labour-held seat in which the Liberals had driven the Conservatives into third place at the 1959 general election. The candidate was Grimond's great friend and supporter Richard Wainwright. Here was a seat in which the Liberals had an opportunity to prove their credentials as a progressive party, by wounding Labour in its heartland. More prosaically, if they picked up further Tory votes in such a seat, for once it would hurt Labour rather than enabling it to steal victory, as had happened in Dorset and Glasgow a few months earlier. At Colne Valley, Grimond revisited his celebrated quip when asked what he would do for the working class. To cheers he responded that he would abolish it, along with the entire class system. On 21st March 1963, as they waited for the result from Colne Valley, the Liberals held a rally at the Royal Albert Hall in London, at which the tension was palpable. The Executive Committee had wanted this occasion to be 'a militant one', but it fell well short of that, and Grimond talked about reforming the rating system. Colne Valley provided another frustrating near miss: Wainwright halved the Conservative share of the vote, but he couldn't manage the extra yard, losing to Labour by 2,000 votes. His subsequent analysis caused great concern. Although he believed that he had won a fair number of votes from manual workers, he felt that Labour had won over a significant number of converts directly from the Conservatives. In short, really disillusioned Conservatives had largely voted Labour, not Liberal. The Liberals had also made the mistake of claiming early in the campaign that they were confident of winning the seat. Consequently a perfectly respectable result looked rather disappointing. In retrospect, it can be seen that the row of near misses during 1962–3 – West Derbyshire, Leicester North-East, Chippenham and Colne Valley – marked the end of the high tide of Grimond Liberalism. If the party had won two or three of these seats, it might have been possible to maintain momentum. As it was, a few extra second places – added to so many others – hardly caused a ripple in the political pond. Colne Valley, like Paisley and Leicester North-East, was particularly important because it was a Labour seat.

The local elections of May 1963 partially obscured the extent to which Liberal momentum had been lost. The party fielded over 2,000 candidates, rather more than in 1962, and a record number of associations contested every seat, with twenty-seven borough associations fighting for the first time. The seats being fought had last been contested in 1960 – a flat year for the Liberals and a good one for the Tories. Liberal gains outweighed losses to the tune of approximately 250 councillors, but this was still a poor result compared with a year earlier. Although the party could now claim the allegiance of over 1,800 councillors – compared with 475 in 1959 – the real story of this particular night was a huge haemorrhaging of votes and seats from Conservative to Labour. The Tories lost over 1,000 seats net and Labour gained almost as many. It was clear that the Liberals now had to work rather harder for their gains and, as Colne Valley had adumbrated, the Labour vote was beginning to harden considerably as the voters' thoughts turned to a general election. There was also evidence that the Tory fight-back against the Liberals was having some effect. Grimond himself conceded that he was 'not elated . . . we are not doing so well as we were at the time of Orpington.'[11] Part of the problem, he would admit in private, was that there were not enough first-rate brains among the party's new recruits: whereas 100 good men were needed, only about twenty had come in. The one lasting bonus was that Orpington had led, more or less directly, to a more generous allocation of broadcasting time to the Liberals. It had also helped Grimond to convince his party that it must concentrate on a particular, 'Orpington type', of voter, along with some older, radical working men with an interest in politics.

On 15th May 1963 Grimond delivered a television broadcast in which he called for a more equitable share-out of Britain's wealth. It took first place in the week's Top Twenty programmes. President de Gaulle wanted a French bomb, and the Liberals had been struggling to find a response. Grimond therefore authorised Christopher Layton to publish a pamphlet, *Europe after the Wreck*, in which he floated the idea of a common European deterrent. Then the Profumo case exploded. Grimond's view from the outset was that Macmillan himself should resign: 'Either he knew the dangers of the company which his Secretary of State was keeping and took no action,' he said in London, 'or he did not know and he failed to make effective inquiries, for there were plenty of warning rumours.'[12] Grimond had to postpone a trip to Sweden in order to make his contribution to the crucial debate on Profumo in the House of Commons. When Macmillan and his government claimed that they would respond to the crisis of confidence by launching their own 'clean-up' campaign, Grimond was scornful: 'to suggest that the present Tory administration is in a position to lead from the top in some Puritan campaign is again the best evidence of where the rot lies.'[13] Grimond feared that there were 'unhappily certain trends in the moral life of the nation at this time which should cause concern to all thoughtful people'.[14] He didn't blame the Tories entirely for this situation, but denounced them for evading responsibility for their own shortcomings: 'nothing is ever their fault . . . almost anything is justified as long as they remain in office.'[15] In the House of Commons he echoed that view.

Although he personally had never questioned the integrity of the Prime Minister, he said, the nation had to resolve, 'whether his Government can now command respect and prestige sufficient to rule the country'.[16] At the end of June, Grimond was back in the West Country, making a surprisingly relaxed tour of target seats. Macmillan should go, he reiterated in Plympton, because 'sometimes to swap horses in mid-stream is the sensible thing to do if the horse you are on is drowning'.[17]

The Profumo affair provided Grimond with a distraction – possibly a welcome one – from the tedious grind of preparing for the next general election. In particular, he still had to resolve the problem of deciding whom to put in charge of the forthcoming campaign. At a meeting of the Executive Committee on 22nd June an interesting discussion took place, during which members reflected that the Liberals needed more publicity, particularly if they were to make inroads into Labour areas, which task was always tough and especially so when the Conservatives were in government. Interestingly, the minutes also record 'a widespread feeling the Party criticised the Government too much and the Labour Party too little'.[18] There is no doubt that this view increasingly influenced Grimond in the closing stages of the 1959–64 parliament. At the same meeting Desmond Banks, a founder member of the Radical Reform Group, returned to the thorny old question of whether the balance of power might not be set as the party's election target – or, failing that, at least 'decisive influence' as a realistic and credible fallback position. In July, Grimond was forced to reshuffle his parliamentary team. Arthur Holt, who never fully recovered from the privations he was forced to endure as a prisoner-of-war at the hands of the Japanese, was finding the strains of being party whip unendurable. Looking after over 350 parliamentary candidates added a huge burden to the comparatively modest demands of organising the votes of six colleagues. Eric Lubbock took over from him.

Another scandal soon rocked the political establishment, when Kim Philby was exposed as a Soviet spy. When Grimond tried to probe into the matter in the House of Commons, Macmillan put him down, remarking, 'if he had any experience . . . of the operation which we are forced to undertake in the present condition of the world, he would not have put his question.'[19] Macmillan also refused to share with him any of the secrets that he divulged to the Labour leadership about the Philby affair on a Privy Counsellor basis. Despite the attempts of Grimond's opponents to belittle him, however, the voters continued to regard him as a man whose independence and goodwill could be trusted and relied upon. When he made a scheduled trip to Aberdeenshire, for example, he was asked to lend his support to a campaign to keep open a hospital at Fyvie. He willingly met campaigners, but had to confess, 'at the moment I don't know if I can do anything'.[20] Unusually, the Tories called a by-election that year in the middle of August, at Stratford-upon-Avon. Grimond's heart must have sunk at the result: despite a Liberal intervention, the Labour share of the vote actually rose, the first time this had happened since 1959. Nonetheless, the Liberal did receive over 20 per cent of the vote from a standing start. After the by-elections of the next twelve months, the Liberals would look back on that as a minor triumph. For Harold Wilson, a more emollient figure than the brittle Gaitskell, was succeeding in bringing the conflicting wings of his party into agreeing some kind of truce. As a consequence, Labour was beginning to look electable and the gap in the market that Grimond and the Liberals had identified and exploited in recent years was being closed.

Grimond's attitude and strategy towards Labour at this time seem to have been genuinely confused. He regarded the Tories as a spent force and he had no reason whatsoever for wishing to be identified with them in any way, yet his entire strategy for forcing a realignment of the left necessarily depended upon competing in the first instance not with the Conservatives but with Labour. Unless he could demonstrate that the Liberals were an essential part of any acceptable, sustainable and electable coalition on the centre-left, then that strategy was doomed, yet all the short-term logic, and the relentless probing of journalists, gradually induced him to admit again that he saw himself in long-term opposition to the Conservatives and could easily foresee circumstances in which he would lead his troops into the lobbies in support of a Labour government. He told Hugh Massingham, for instance, 'if the Liberals held the balance, they would then have to decide what to do . . . In some ways we would be sympathetic to Labour . . . I wouldn't mind Wilson throwing a sprat or two to the Left.'[21] He also conceded that the Liberals might be willing to offer such support even to a Government that didn't particularly need it, without demanding any concessions in return: 'we shall support those policies of social justice in which we believe, but we are determined to use our influence and power to prevent any further doctrinaire nationalisation'.[22] Yet still Grimond would attack both Labour and socialism as out of date and ineffective. It is little wonder that many people were unsure about what, if anything, the Liberals stood for.

Hugely helpful to Grimond, during this difficult time for the party, was the surprisingly bullish mood amongst party members, in defiance of the odds and the polls. Membership continued to rise into 1963 (to a remarkable peak of around 350,000 as against around 75,000 in 1953) and a general consensus persisted that the party should still, despite its plummeting ratings in the opinion polls, be marketing itself as a potential government. This came through clearly in a survey of candidates initiated by Arthur Holt before he stepped down as party whip, which returned the unambiguous message that the Liberals should now be trying to look every bit as serious as the other parties. Some candidates felt that the party should not 'plug' Grimond too much, lest people conclude that it had nobody else. There was also some criticism of Grimond's frequent admissions that a Liberal government would be long delayed, and also of Grimond's persona, which was too academic for some people's taste. One candidate even criticised him for being 'too slovenly in dress', which was 'trivial but important'. The general thrust was that candidates feared that the party would be perceived as a 'one-man band' without any serious pretensions to government. Years later, acknowledging the dangers of hindsight, Grimond commented: 'I think I should have been more unreasonable than I was. I think that I should have made claims that were clearly unsupportable. I should have made outrageous suggestions that the

Liberals were really going to sweep the country. I have learned that outrageous suggestions are nearly always picked up by the media and retold as if they were sensible.'[23]

During that summer, a new election committee was finally appointed. Its membership was slanted away from those contesting seats at the forthcoming election, in order that it should be able to supersede the Organising Committee as election day approached. This was very much Grimond's committee. Its terms of reference had his imprimatur; it would determine the line on campaign issues in constant consultation with him; and it would keep him fully up to date with budget preparations for the campaign. It would also prepare for, and direct, the campaign itself and take a leading role in sorting out Grimond's tours, with a view to ensuring that he would not be overtired, in order that he would appear fresh when appearing on TV and at major rallies. Those rallies would be in big population centres – ideally where the party was reasonably strong – while smaller centres could be added to the main itinerary on a whistle-stop basis. The committee also set up three sub-committees, to deal separately with organisation, political propaganda and finance. This was the new businesslike approach that Grimond had always wanted, and made a remarkable contrast with the party's limited state of readiness for 1959.

The party's assembly in 1963, held in Brighton, was arguably the most important during Grimond's tenure as leader. Since Llandudno, the party had failed to make the breakthrough that had then still seemed so close at hand, and the Liberals' poll rating had fallen by half. Even worse, as the Liberals convened, a Gallup Poll taken in their fifty best seats suggested that since 1959 they had actually lost ground where it most counted. The approach this time was not to invent new policies every day, but to establish three clear themes that could be promoted as being distinctively Liberal: modernisation, classlessness and internationalism. There was a rancorous debate on a motion to lower the voting age to eighteen, at the end of which Grimond himself abstained, although he personally favoured this innovation. The motion was narrowly lost. In the debate on industrial and economic policy, Christopher Layton again tried to clarify what the Liberals meant by 'planning'. To some Liberal ears it sounded like a form of state socialism; to others, it didn't sound like planning at all. Grimond himself had long been an advocate of 'planning', and Layton now tried to explain how this could not only be consistent with a free market economy, but could in fact energise it. He was not altogether successful. It was all a question of whether or not government was effective or not. The new party president, the former Labour minister Lord Ogmore, also fell short of greatness at this assembly. In one of the more obvious hostages to fortune, he asked in his speech whether the Liberal Party could form a government. Instead of the roar of approbation he expected, only a few voices raised a half-hearted 'Yes' for him. It was more obvious than ever before at this assembly that the party was increasingly polarised on age lines. As a special correspondent put it in the *Daily Telegraph*: 'there seemed to be masses of 17-year-olds, masses of 70-year-olds . . . The long, sad decades in between seemed to be more sparsely represented.'[24]

The stage was set for Grimond. He had to make the speech of his life, to help his party find a new balance and perspective now that their former over-confidence had been superseded by an unmistakable sense of anticlimax. He did not disappoint. In what remains his most celebrated speech, he swept away the technical questions about how the Liberals might behave in a hung Parliament. The important thing was to get Liberals elected, so that they could influence things in a Liberal direction. He deplored the decline of standards in public life, and the abrogation of responsibility by the government, inherent in its decision to bring in a judge to investigate the Profumo affair. 'Since when,' he asked, 'have the people of this country had to call in a High Court judge, however eminent, to carry out a roving commission into the private lives of various individuals so that we may be informed whether we are behaving ourselves or not?'[25] Alone amongst the political parties, the Liberals had been able to recognise and acknowledge the true enemy: the self-indulgence, shiftiness and downright laziness that now marred public life. All the other parties offered was 'complacency and inertia in the face of incompetence and injustice'. Grimond, as the party's leader, knew what was expected of him in the face of an enemy of such magnitude. In his most famous phrase, he declared, 'in bygone days the commanders were taught that, when in doubt, they should march their troops towards the sound of gunfire – I intend to march my troops towards the sound of gunfire!'[26]

Those who worked closely with Grimond at this time all attest to how seriously he took his responsibilities as a speaker. He would write his own speeches, often working his way through many drafts, and rehearse them meticulously. He would pace backwards and forwards in a world of his own backstage before performing – and he would often rather revel in transmitting his own nervousness to others by turning up at the last minute for major events. The pre-delivery manuscript of this remarkable speech from September 1963 gives an insight into just how thorough he was. He left nothing to chance, which helps to explain his almost faultless timing and delivery. Even pauses for applause and laughter are included with sensible foresight and an admirable lack of false (or genuine) modesty. As a platform speaker, this was perhaps Grimond's finest hour – and he knew it. One journalist even caught him watching a videotape of himself in a television van afterwards with evident, and rather vain, pleasure. Grimond remained firmly in the public eye during the other parties' conferences. When Harold Wilson addressed his first Labour conference as Labour leader, Grimond denounced Labour's plans for extending nationalisation and other aspects of the role of the state. When

the Tories met at Blackpool, however, it was they who went on the attack.
Iain Macleod deliberately poured scorn on the Liberals' pretensions: 'We need
not waste time on Mr Grimond's Fred Karno [a music-hall comedian known
for his 'comic confusion' act] effort about marching his troops towards the
sound of gunfire. It's a long, long way to Tipperary. And if and when Mr
Grimond ever gets to the battlefield, he will find we have been there for a very
long time.'[27]

When it was announced at that conference that Harold Macmillan was
resigning from the premiership on grounds of ill health, Grimond was
generous towards the man but less so towards the Tories as a party. They chose
as their new leader Alec Home, who immediately exercised the new right of
resigning from the House of Lords. A parliamentary seat had to be found for
him and young hopeful George Younger (latterly Lord Younger) was bumped
out of a promising by-election at Perth to make way for him. Although he had
known Alec Home for most of his life, Grimond was sceptical about the Tories'
choice. 'He has many admirable qualities,' he jibed, 'but they do not seem to
have counted as much as the fact that he did not want the job – that surely
is an insufficient reason for giving it to him.'[28] As for parachuting the new
Prime Minister into a parliamentary seat, that merely reduced parliamentary
democracy to farce. The end of the 1962–3 parliamentary session was severely
affected by this situation, as was the opening of the new session. With no
Prime Minister in the House of Commons to question, the government
curtailed questions, arguing that MPs could still question ministers privately
if they had anything to get off their chests. Grimond was furious. 'It is
quite possible to run a system by which controversy is carried on in private,'
he pointed out, 'it is the way in which it is carried on in all dictatorial
states.'[29] The situation seemed to him not merely a short-term expedient, but a
symptom of the contemptuous way in which the Conservatives now routinely
treated Parliament as little more than a vehicle for the promotion of their own
party advantage. If the new Prime Minister wanted matters to improve, said
Grimond, let him 'strike a blow against this continuing denigration of the
House of Commons – this tendency to deal with important matters either
through Royal Commissions or over the air'.[30]

On 22nd November 1963, less than a year after Grimond had been so
impressed by meeting him in person, President Kennedy was shot. Grimond
took part in the live tribute broadcast by the BBC and it is hard to imagine
that he ever had a more difficult political task. Everything that could be said
about this 'numbing tragedy' had already been said by Alec Home and Harold
Wilson. Nonetheless a sombre Grimond did not conceal his admiration for
Kennedy's style: 'firm but not offensive in defence of our rights and freedoms'.
Tragedy rapidly turned to farce when Grimond was invited to join Alec
Home and Harold Wilson on a special flight for VIPs attending Kennedy's

funeral. He forgot his passport and had to follow on separately on a PanAm plane with an emergency travel document. The pantomime extended to an entire planeload of people on the way back: the return flight was diverted to Manchester by fog, and Grimond was amongst a group that enjoyed emergency hospitality at Chatsworth House thanks to the quick thinking of the Duchess of Devonshire. As Grimond tested his vast four-poster bed, another of the party popped his head into the room: 'you could get the whole of the parliamentary Liberal Party into that one,' he ventured. Grimond's response was not recorded for posterity.

Grimond was feeling less jocular within a couple of weeks, when December brought some truly dreadful Liberal by-election performances. At St Marylebone, the Liberal share of the vote rose by a minuscule amount, to a feeble 13.3 per cent. At Sudbury in Suffolk, it actually fell to an equally miserable percentage. With a general election due in the next twelve months, the two-party squeeze did indeed seem to have set in with a vengeance. Not everything was going badly for the Grimonds, however. In November Laura was elected to the party's executive at her first attempt, adding that position to several others that she had effortlessly accumulated.

In the more down-to-earth political battles, in the House of Commons and out in the country, Grimond and the Liberals continued to plough their own furrow. Although they were generally critical of the government, they did offer qualified support to one of its most radical and controversial measures, the abolition of Resale Price Maintenance. This system had long forbidden shops to offer goods at discount prices to consumers. One way around the legislation was for some shops to offer 'trading stamps', which people would collect and then redeem for goods. As Grimond put it, he 'would rather see people getting things cheaper in the shops, paying cash and having what they like, than being given free green trading stamps so that they can have a decorated duck'.[31] When the government had a close call on an amendment about medical supplies, the abstentions of Grimond and three of his colleagues were decisive – helping to deliver a majority of one. December saw a hardening of the Liberals' policy towards inflation when, in a speech in Aberdeen, Grimond returned to the idea of an 'inflation tax', which he had floated before in speeches and in a pamphlet. This question had not been resolved at the assembly, and Grimond now argued that, although collective bargaining should be free and decentralised, the case for minimum wages had long been accepted. Was it not therefore reasonable to conclude, 'we are bound to reach the stage when maxima are also set'?[32] He did not believe that these could be enforced rigidly by law, but employers could be penalised through the tax system if they 'grossly exceeded what was justified'. This was a classic instance of Grimond going AWOL, and a party spokesman quickly made the extraordinary claim that 'this is not necessarily Liberal policy . . . Mr

Grimond was just throwing out new suggestions.'[33] Grimond pressed on with his point, however, by clarifying a week later what he meant. His point, he told the party council, was that the share-out of the economic cake just wasn't fair: there was too much friction between management and the 'ordinary weekly wage earners', who created most of the wealth. Unless everyone started to pull in the same direction, Britain faced the 'father and mother of all inflations'.[34] In private, although Grimond personally believed that inflation would become the most dangerous issue facing the country, he was dismayed by the widespread complacency about inflation that he encountered in the country. He took many of his soundings amongst the railway porters that he met as he travelled to and fro, and the cost of living never seemed to loom large in their day-to-day concerns.

The party failed to organise any kind of autumn campaign in the closing months of 1963. Grimond tried to make up for that in January and February 1964 by campaigning especially hard, touring Yorkshire, East Anglia and Manchester and, on 27th February, addressed a major pre-campaign rally at the Royal Albert Hall. There was nothing much new in the speeches that Grimond delivered on his travels: his priority was to raise morale amongst activists. In a party political broadcast on 5th February, Grimond tried to turn the question of 'negative votes' on to its head. He admitted that there was a mood in the country for a change after over twelve years of Tory government, but insisted that nobody much wanted socialism. In that situation, even the two main parties would be relying on a lot of 'anti' voting. Grimond wanted these voters to stop being negative and go for something really different: 'collectively they could exercise a tremendous positive influence in politics'.[35] It required a major effort on Grimond's part to look and sound reasonably fresh, and he cannot have been pleased by an attack on him by Christopher Booker in *New Outlook* magazine, in which it was suggested that 'his day as the Liberal Party's chief asset is over . . . the boyish charm has worn thin.'[36]

The Liberals' expenditure proposals now came under renewed attack from both Labour and the Conservatives. Iain Macleod's attack two years earlier had drawn blood, and a more concerted barrage now began. Although nobody thought it much mattered whether or not the Liberals' proposals for government added up – they were down to single figures in some polls by this stage – both major parties needed to mop up defecting Liberal votes and felt that effective attacks on this perceived Achilles' heel might deliver them. Grimond tried to square the circle with a mini-campaign entitled Waste Week at the end of February 1964, drawing attention to ways in which public expenditure could be more efficiently organised. At the end of Waste Week he strained his back digging and had to cancel a tour of Essex and Kent and ended up wasting a week himself – in bed. At least his itinerary wasn't wasted, as Emlyn Hooson substituted for him at short notice. On ITV's programme *This Week* on 12th March, Grimond effectively drew a line under the 'Orpington era', conceding that the Liberals had no chance of winning the election, even though they would be contesting a majority of seats. He added that, though the Liberals were not seeking the balance of power in Parliament, he personally 'would not be frightened of it'. Grimond was also working hard in support of Liberal candidates for the Greater London Council (GLC) elections on 9th April. London had not been good territory for the Liberals for many a long year, but they had hopes of snatching a seat or two: in the London boroughs they had increased their representation from fifteen councillors to over 200 in only five years. For the first time since he moved into the borough ten years earlier, Grimond also spoke for the Liberals in Richmond. His efforts in the capital were to no avail: though they won half a million votes, the Liberals were swept away in the Labour tide, winning not a single seat. In the county council elections, the Liberals had another mediocre result.

Grimond fully shared the general irritation at the game of cat-and-mouse that Alec Douglas Home was playing with regard to the date of the forthcoming general election. He felt that the Conservatives had long since betrayed, and lost, the confidence placed in them by the voters in 1959, and believed that they should therefore go to the country without delay. Not to do so was, he said, just another aspect of the way in which they were 'debasing government in this country'.[37] Grimond claimed not to believe that a Labour win was in any sense inevitable, though he did concede: 'there is a feeling abroad that the top tycoons in the City are already clambering aboard the socialist ship, which seems so much more navigable than Sir Alec's lugger, where the mutineers pop up through every hatch.'[38] Two days later, Grimond gave a broadcast on the BBC. At a preview he noticed that the prop map of the UK that served as background included Orkney, but not Shetland. His whole empire must appear, or he would not, he informed the producer. Just in time, a full version was pasted up. One visitor to that empire during this period was the young comedy writer and actor John Wells, whom Grimond had seen performing with some of his fellow students from Oxford. He invited Wells to Orkney to discuss whether he might be able to leaven his speeches with some jokes, something that Wells later likened to 'God ringing you up and asking you to write the first chapter of Leviticus'.[39] The arrangement came to nothing: according to Wells, Grimond tried his jokes out on the sheep, and they all fell asleep.

At the 1964 local elections a remarkable total of 3,075 Liberal candidates stood, in 412 constituencies. The results were poor. Only 236 of them were elected, representing a net loss of 84. In the same month, the Liberals performed badly in by-elections at three seats – Devizes, Winchester and Bury St Edmunds – where a year earlier they might have had high hopes. Grimond and his team decided to avoid further by-elections until after the general election. They also recognised the need to cut back on the party's general election plans. There had for some time been significant voices raised against the 'broad front' policy of fighting over 400 seats, an approach originally advocated by Frank Byers. Word of Jeremy Thorpe's target seats campaign had inevitably leaked out, and many Liberals now felt that this must be the main focus of the party's efforts. As early as December 1963, Grimond had told the party council that, although party morale was good, some constituencies were still very weak and, accordingly, although the party wanted to fight every constituency, it should not fight where it was not ready. Even at the end of May 1964 the party executive could not quite bring itself to admit that the Liberals were on the ropes, hedging its bets in a statement claiming that the party intended to contest every seat 'where it is possible to fight with a reasonable organisation, a good candidate and adequate finance . . . Liberals further believe that each election fought by a constituency is a stage towards eventual victory.'[40] The executive also recognised that even candidates who lost badly did at least add to the party's aggregate vote. The loss of confidence within the space of two years was quite extraordinary. Grimond was even forced to confirm on television that he would 'soldier on' as leader as speculation grew that he had grown weary of the demands of his job. The *Sunday Express*, admittedly never an admirer of Grimond, took great pleasure in describing him somewhat fantastically as 'the saddest, most desolate figure in Parliament today'.[41]

On Saturday, 20th June 1964, Grimond made a bold attempt to regain the initiative, launching a 'charter for new men' at Carlisle. He evoked the spirit of Orpington, targeting his appeal at the 'enterprising professional, managerial, technical and skilled workers' who felt that the Tories were out of touch, but rejected socialism. Unless these men of the future were given their heads, British industry would remain outmoded and inefficient and the standard of living would continue to lag. He followed this up with a fierce attack on the right wing of the Conservative Party. The hardline conservative Senator Barry Goldwater was coming to prominence in the USA as a possible presidential contender (promising, *inter alia,* to liberate central Europe from the Soviet yoke, if necessary by force) and, at Blaenau Ffestiniog, Grimond claimed to detect a similar tendency in the British Conservative Party. He said that he was far more frightened by the 'Goldwaters of the Tory Party, the men of Munich and Suez, than by any Goldwaters-in-reverse said to lurk in the Labour Party'.[42] Two days later he fired off a salvo at the left, deploring new trade union proposals that the heavy engineering industry should be brought under state control, which he described as 'rather like treating a case of frost-bite with an ice-pack'.[43] From now until the general election, Grimond adopted a robust policy of keeping both main parties at arm's length. He got no sympathy from the Conservative Party. Even though Grimond's old nemesis Iain Macleod had refused to serve on Alec Douglas Home's front bench, the Tories maintained their fire on Grimond, releasing a record entitled 'Songs for Swinging Voters', including an oddly touching song recorded by Ian Wallace entitled 'Poor Old Jo', based upon the old Paul Robeson favourite, in which they poked gentle fun at him for supposedly helping the Labour cause: 'I hope to hear anguished Tory cries of woe – another seat for Labour won by Poor Old Jo.'

For what remained of the parliamentary term before the summer, Grimond worked incredibly hard. In the spirit of the new targeting strategy, he went back to the West Country and made a visit to Cheadle, a seat in the north-west with a similar profile to Orpington, where the local Liberals had high hopes. Grimond's anger at the arrogant behaviour of the Labour-Conservative duopoly was intensified when the new list of life peers in July 1964 once again included not a single Liberal name. Lord Rea, the Liberals' leader in the House of Lords, had twice submitted names to the Leader of the House, Lord Carrington, but nothing had been done. Grimond had originally opposed the introduction of life peerages because he thought that the system would be abused. He must have felt vindicated as well as angered. In early 1964 Grimond had held crucial meetings with the Liberals' main general election team, the Scottish Liberal Party and his own supporters from Orkney and Shetland, at which he had agreed that it would be disastrous to repeat his 1959 mistake of vanishing to the islands for long periods. This time he signed up to a full election itinerary for himself and his small entourage: his indomitable secretary Cate Fisher, the party's press officer *par excellence,* Phyllis Preston, and another official from HQ, by the name of Grierson. So heavy was it, indeed, that upon seeing it in its first draft Grimond protested that 'you haven't even given Cate [Fisher] time to wash her hands!' Arbitrage between the main Liberal Party and the Scottish Liberals was complicated and protracted. Although George Mackie, who ran the Scottish party as a separate outfit, was convinced that the Liberals could make a clean sweep of the Highlands and Islands, the party's central staff were reluctant to tire out their leader in the vast constituencies of the north, when there was so much work to be done elsewhere. During the summer it was announced that Grimond was expected to make something like 100 speeches during the course of the forthcoming election campaign, in seventy-four different constituencies. This would entail travelling some 8,400 miles, mostly in a chartered aircraft, and Grimond's life had to be insured for £250,000.

At the end of August, Grimond did Mackie's bidding and made a tour of the Highlands of Scotland. In Caithness and Sutherland, the candidate (Mackie himself) and his family seemed to be the only people at Grimond's meetings who were under fifty years old and, in the little Sutherland town of Golspie, he was introduced as the leader of the Labour Party. Yet even the hardened journalists who observed Grimond on his gruelling five-day tour had to concede that he brought it all off with great style. His statesmanlike manner belied the fact that he was the leader of a parliamentary party of only seven, his meetings were all well attended and everywhere he was received with respect. Nonetheless, with his party down to 7 per cent in the latest Gallup poll, Grimond faced an uphill struggle. He was not particularly helped when the prospective candidate for Inverness, Russell Johnston, went off on an unauthorised flight of fancy by proposing that the Royal Mint should be relocated in his constituency, minting future coinage from aluminium. Sitting next to him, Grimond was observed commendably not to flinch. Back in Orkney and Shetland, Grimond could not conceal his fear that the Liberals were going to be squeezed out of the picture when he warned that the major parties would use the election 'purely as an auction, using the public purse to bribe the voters'.[44]

David Steel, at that time still an employee at the headquarters of the Scottish Liberal party, acted as Grimond's bag-carrier during this tour (for his stopover in the Highlands during the general election campaign itself, Grimond would not be so lucky – he had to carry his own bags or rely on the assistance of journalists). Steel still recalls two particular incidents. When Grimond arrived at Dingwall Town Hall in the constituency of Ross and Cromarty and met the candidate there, Alasdair Mackenzie, for the first time, there was not a great meeting of minds. A sixty-one-year-old crofter, Mackenzie was no orator and did not want to make a supporting speech, although he was willing to make a brief financial appeal at the end. In the event, however, he was manoeuvred into taking questions. When he was asked about the Liberals' defence policy, both Steel and Grimond held their breath. Mackenzie rose to his feet and, with great deliberation, proclaimed that 'the Liberal Party will defend Britain, the Commonwealth and the free world'.[45] With that, he sat down to general acclamation. Less impressive was a photo call in the Western Isles, when Grimond was snapped with an aspirant candidate at Stornoway Airport – who turned out to be the local Labour MP, rather than the Liberal who hoped to supplant him. Steel himself had been the beneficiary of considerable sponsorship from Grimond. Some months earlier, the Liberal candidate for the formerly Liberal seat of Roxburgh had been forced to resign after falling out with the local party. A desperate search for a new candidate had ensued. Although he had been actively engaged as prospective parliamentary candidate for Edinburgh Pentlands, Steel had quickly come into the frame. Grimond had come into Steel's office at Atholl Place in Edinburgh to discuss possible successors. None had appealed to him, so he told Steel with a grin, 'I suppose you'll have to do it then!'[46]

By the time the 1959 Parliament went into its last summer recess, the Labour Party's post-Orpington recovery in the polls had stabilised for almost two years and the Liberals had fallen far from the dizzy heights of 1962. Privately,

Grimond now admitted that he might have been wrong all along, that the party system could be more or less as strong as ever after all. He had come to rue the prominence given to Orpington and its aftermath, and the attendant implication that anything less than a major parliamentary breakthrough would represent failure on a grand scale for the Liberals. Furthermore he would have gleefully traded a chunk of Eric Lubbock's extravagant majority at Orpington for a win at West Derbyshire only three months later. Although he now feared the worst, however, he could at least console himself with the thought that the abject failure of the Conservative Party to pull itself together left the Liberals with a continuing opportunity. At the very least, the Liberals should be able to gain a handful of seats at a general election for the first time in a generation. It was a matter of complete bafflement to Grimond that the Tories were proving so utterly incapable of capitalising on, or even mentioning, their strengths and achievements in office. The mood for radical change that he had sensed back in the heady days of 1961–2 had evaporated, which potentially hurt Labour almost as much as it hurt the Liberals. Yet the Conservative Party seemed to be too weary to take advantage. The younger, more attractive and radical senior figures whom Grimond admired – such as Keith Joseph, Ted Heath and Edward Boyle – were afforded far less prominence than seemed sensible. Alec Home himself – by no means a man without charm – was being underplayed and, most mystifying of all, even a solid economic recovery had brought virtually no political dividend. Grimond was convinced that the Tories, if they could only show sufficient signs of life, had every opportunity of doling out a hugely damaging fourth consecutive defeat to the Labour Party. In Grimond's view, unless Alec Douglas Home gambled and put someone like Duncan Sandys in charge of the forthcoming campaign, the electorate would more or less sleepwalk into electing a Labour government – through *ennui* alone.

By and large Liberals were as weary as anyone of the Tory grip on power and, in the balanced Parliament that appeared now to be a distinct possibility in view of recent polls, their overwhelming instinct was to side with the Labour Party. Although Grimond doubted that Harold Wilson would make many, if any, of the radical changes that Britain in his view desperately needed, he could not deny that the Labour leader had demonstrated himself to be a party manager *par excellence*. While the thought of propping up Alec Home in power was anathema, however, there was already a serious shadow over any putative Lib-Lab arrangement: Labour's determination to renationalise the steel industry. In August 1964 Christopher Layton and Eric Lubbock held a press conference on this question, reinforcing the Liberals' hostility to nationalisation. Something that Grimond deplored in both major parties was their unwillingness even to mention the unions, and certainly they had no intention of taming them. In contrast, in a pre-campaign speech in the Midlands, Grimond warned that 'unless the trades unions are prepared to streamline their structure and undertake the new opportunities which open out to them for the next 50 years, they will inevitably sink back into unimportance.'[47] This would necessitate getting back to their industrial role and gradually disengaging from the organic link with politics and the Labour Party.

By the beginning of the campaign proper, Ladbroke's would be offering 25–1 against a hung Parliament, as compared with previously reported odds of 50,000–1. Very sensibly Grimond always sidestepped the issue of which party he would prefer to support in government. For a start he knew full well that cold arithmetic might well dictate that the Liberals had no choice in the matter, if their numbers were few. Furthermore, he needed to hold together a disparate collection of supporters through what promised to be a very partisan election campaign. He therefore began to set out his message to the voters, a message that finds echoes even today in appeals from leaders of the Liberal Democrats: that a Liberal vote could now be effective again for the first time in a generation, if only for its effect on the other parties. To some of his more hotheaded colleagues, this all seemed a bit defeatist, but Grimond was determined to be realistic. Nonetheless his difficulties as leader were intensified by those who insisted that the Liberals should conduct themselves as though they were, in every respect, a major party worthy of the same treatment and credibility as their larger rivals. This pretence occupied much of Grimond's time, as he toured a range of hopeless constituencies making speeches at thinly attended meetings. As Grimond himself would observe privately, this cost money and energy that the party could ill afford. The party's aspiration to re-establish itself as a major force right across the country was hugely ambitious. Even a couple of months before the general election, a substantial number of adopted candidates were still regarded as 'doubtful' – likely to withdraw for want of a deposit, a campaign team or the chimerical motivation necessary to sustain an individual in pursuing a perceptibly lost cause. In August 1964 Pratap Chitnis told the media that he would be in position to announce the party's full roster of candidates by the beginning of September. He wasn't, and the press had to wait until the party conference, which was itself truncated and transformed into a platform for the election campaign. In the summer of 1964 the party's General Election Committee had the final version of the manifesto printed. They also reversed an earlier decision to print a 'popular' version, only loosely based on the full version, and resolved instead to issue a full miniature version.

At first, the delay of the election into 1964 had caused frayed nerves amongst Liberals, who feared further losses of support as a more partisan and rancorous political atmosphere developed. As 1964 progressed they began to feel more robust, as it became apparent that their strength in their better areas, and the morale of their activists, was proving to be surprisingly resilient. The sense of anti climax after Orpington steadily receded. Nobody believed that there was going to be a Liberal government, but Jeremy Thorpe was confident that the targeting strategy was beginning to work in the twenty-five seats that the party had identified as being really 'winnable', in all of which the party was fighting as if a by-election was taking place. By the autumn, Thorpe confidently predicted that the party would win in at least fourteen of those constituencies. This made a positive contrast with Grimond's private view of the early summer that the best the party could hope for was to scrape into double figures. Throughout his career, Grimond liked to write for himself everything that went out in his name. As the 1964 general election campaign approached, however, he was forced to concede that the demands upon him might be too great for this general rule to be applied in the heat of battle. Tim Beaumont was deputed to take over this 'ghosting' operation and, from the beginning of September 1964, he set about imitating the great man. Patrick Kemmis also charged him with checking through the many supportive messages from Grimond to constituencies and candidates. At the same time the party's election theme, 'If you think like a Liberal, Vote like a Liberal', was given its first run out, in a party political broadcast delivered straight to camera by a Welsh QC, Alun Talfan Davies. The intention in this broadcast was clear: as well as covering familiar ground such as old age pensions and devolution, it set out radical and (at that time) distinctively Liberal positions on electoral reform and the trade unions. Almost two decades before anyone did anything about it, the Liberals advocated abolition of the closed shop and the enforcement of secret ballots on industrial action. Somewhat against Jo Grimond's personal instincts, they also attempted to push electoral reform up the agenda (or, more realistically, on to it).

The two-day Liberal assembly between 4th and 5th September was inevitably disorganised and uninspiring, but it did just about serve its purpose. Grimond himself was very tired and accordingly rather tiresome behind the scenes, though he did speak well, telling Liberals that they were 'aiming at power' – although precisely what that meant was never explained – and firing off broadsides at both of the main parties. 'Ask for the moon,' he warned, 'and the Government, which found it impossible to pay nurses decently in 1962, will gladly arrange free trips there in 1964.'[48] As for Labour, 'it is nationalistic . . . it has no belief in socialism, but no desire to make the free enterprise system work better . . . It approaches the prospect of office with all the caution of a cat approaching a bowl of cream.'[49] There was also an unexpectedly outspoken passage in which Grimond execrated those who sat on the sidelines complaining about the state of politics without ever making the slightest effort to improve matters:

> Politics is not a job for people who think they are superior – these are the people
> who have been the bell-ringers of tyranny all through history . . . If you want

to take part in politics you have to get into the kitchen with the heat and nasty
smells . . . I would rather have Senator Goldwater, with all his faults, than some
of these sissy Pharisees who claim that politics is too dirty for them to soil their
hands in it.[50]

The financial appeal by Jeremy Thorpe raised £21,000 and Frank Byers's
closing speech, short, effective and to the point, sent activists away in good
heart. There was a reasonable amount of coverage in the broadsheet press,
but the more popular titles still took the view that the Liberals might as
well not exist. Large-scale live coverage was another luxury not afforded to
the party, although the evening news carried helpful items. One method
employed to improve this situation in the election run-in was to produce a
special conference issue of *Liberal News*, to which individual constituency
Liberal parties could add their own front page. This had the added advantage
of dramatically boosting the paper's shaky cash flow. The party was as ready
as it could be for the election, and certainly in better heart than it had
been months earlier. As a campaigning unit, however, it still lacked the
resources and discipline that would have enabled it to rub shoulders with its
mightier opponents. In the run-up to the election, the Conservative Party
produced the most comprehensive dossier yet of contradictory statements from
senior Liberal spokesmen – on policies ranging from taxation to trade unions,
nationalisation to defence. This was, indeed, the 'sound of gunfire'.

11

THE GENERAL ELECTION was called for Thursday, 15th October 1964, virtually the last possible date. Grimond was soon cheered to discover almost no enthusiasm out in the country for a Wilson-led government, and everywhere he took the opportunity to ram home his message that, 'If you think like a Liberal, vote like a Liberal.' As Grimond put it in East Anglia during his pre-election tour: 'it would be as foolish for those people who believe in liberalism to vote for any other parties, as it would be for those who believe in one church to worship in another simply because at present it has a bigger congregation.'[1] On the morning of Monday, 21st September, the day that formally marked the beginning of the election campaign, Grimond was back in London after a few days in Orkney, plaguing Tim Beaumont with changes to his tour itinerary. At least Grimond's fear of losing his own seat had now receded, and he conceded that he would not, after all, require the full-time services of Kim Malcolm, an LPO staff member, when he was up in Orkney, providing the LPO press office with a very welcome extra pair of hands. In his assembly speech at Brighton a year earlier, Grimond had boldly and optimistically proclaimed: 'we shall have over 400 candidates into the field at the election.' In the event, the Liberals did well to field 365 candidates, but Grimond's style during the campaign itself was anything but apologetic or defensive. Although he never totally overcame his fear of 'putting his foot in it' in front of the media, the impression he gave was one of almost relentless dynamism, sometimes delivering a series of ten-minute speeches in a number of constituencies on a single morning or afternoon. At Shrewsbury, startled onlookers watched as he leaped on to a four-foot-high rostrum without any steps and then departed as quickly as he had come. Wherever he went, he attracted sizeable crowds. His speaking style out in the constituencies had an evangelical quality that he generally lacked at Westminster, and he used humour to good effect, beginning one of his earlier speeches with a reference to this 'unexpected election, which must come as a shock to all'.[2] Grimond's splendid campaign was sustained no doubt by two cases of white wine half-bottles bought from Green's champagne bar for his packed lunches.

His press conferences were well attended and unexpectedly widely reported. He also made a fine early impression on the BBC's *Election Forum*, answering questions fluently in a vigorous head-to-head with Kenneth Harris, Robin Day and Ian Trethowan. Once he even chided Kenneth Harris for butting in with a new question before he had finished answering the previous one. Despite being subjected to considerable pressure from these highly experienced interlocutors, Grimond doggedly refused to be browbeaten into giving any commitments about how he might behave in a hung Parliament. 'I should be defeating democracy and the election,' he proclaimed with beautifully understated pomposity, 'if I stated in advance of the decision of the public what I was going to do.'[3] He also set out one particular scenario in such detail that he must have had an uncanny hunch about the parliamentary situation that the forthcoming election would precipitate: 'There would be some subjects, I hope, on which we could agree for a limited programme. When we had reached the end of agreement, that would no doubt be the time to put the matter back to the people, who have the ultimate say in politics, and there would be another election.'[4] Frank Byers was drawn more successfully on this question a few days later, when he admitted that the Liberal Party had far more to gain from a Conservative victory than from a hung Parliament: 'this would create a real possibility for a realignment on the left with the progressive Conservatives, the Liberals and non-socialist Labour acting together.'[5] This intervention was not helpful in an election campaign, though it did neatly encapsulate the Liberals' dilemma.

When Harold Wilson challenged Alec Douglas Home to a televised debate mid campaign, Grimond tried to get in on the act and made his bid for a share of the limelight. It was, he thought, surprising that the Conservatives didn't accept the suggestion with alacrity: 'I am not at all convinced,' he commented, 'that Mr Wilson could hunt the Prime Minister around the ring.'[6] The very thought of giving the Liberals such a platform was dismissed by Labour: 'we are interested in people involved in political power,'[7] commented a spokesman, rather bitchily. Labour was well advised to be wary, as Harold Wilson would have been reduced in political stature by conceding that the Liberal leader had an entitlement to appear alongside him with equal billing. It soon became clear that the political oxygen of all this regular television exposure was dramatically breathing new life into the Liberals. Despite his punishing itinerary, Grimond himself was flourishing, as Laura told a reporter during the campaign: 'He is phlegmatic and not easily ruffled. He sleeps like a log. There are no pills or tranquillisers in the house. He enjoys every moment of it. But it is obviously a great responsibility. He relaxes by reading detective stories.'[8]

Going into the second half of the election campaign, Tim Beaumont was busily finalising the details of the second and third party election broadcasts. In the first of these, the celebrated *Avengers* star Honor Blackman, who never met Grimond but admired him enormously, had added some glamour to the campaign. Ludovic Kennedy closed the broadcast live, with a direct appeal straight to camera. In the second, Grimond himself would be the star, first introducing a selection of other candidates from around the country and then closing the broadcast with a 'talking-head' appeal to camera. This direct appeal to the voters, on 10th October, was arguably the best broadcast of all. As Labour and the Tories had converged in the polls and slugged it out with renewed vigour, the Liberals' poll ratings had begun to rise, and Grimond therefore made a play for the 'non-political' or even 'anti-political' vote, emphasising how he sympathised with everyone who was fed up with the election campaign, and the 'endless bickering between the Tory and Labour parties'. What was needed, he said, was 'some touch of idealism in politics'. His final appeal was for 'Liberal members with a massive Liberal vote behind them'.[9]

Jo Grimond was effective on television – and he knew it. He was among the first advocates of televising Parliament and thoroughly enjoyed appearing in every kind of show, formal or informal. 'If television had determined this election,' wrote Philip Purser in the *Sunday Telegraph* four days before polling day, 'Mr Grimond would be forming a Government on Friday . . . there is little real disagreement that of all the official party broadcasts only the Liberals' have appeared to have been addressed by human beings to their fellows.'[10] The day before the election, Grimond confidently proclaimed: 'the wasted vote argument is dead – millions of people have seen us on television, and they've liked what they've seen.'[11] The definitive study of the effects of television on the 1964 general election supports his claim with a detailed analysis of the effects of the Liberal campaign on voters' perceptions of the parties and their leaders. In the words of the authors: 'the party which stood no chance of winning the 1964 *election* had won the preceding *campaign*.'[12] Fewer than half of the Liberal votes in their sample came from people who had intended to vote Liberal at the beginning of the campaign. The contingent that switched to Grimond and his party was characterised, above all, by its unusually high exposure to political broadcasts during the campaign. They demonstrate too how, through the campaign, Grimond's own position had strengthened ahead of his party's. On a wide spectrum of questions ranging from his integrity and sincerity to his straightforwardness and likeability, every single shift in perception of Grimond personally was positive. Above all, during the campaign Grimond was increasingly perceived as inspiring, strong and confident. The more people saw of Grimond – and of the other two leaders, Home and Wilson – the more likely they were to favour the Liberals. If his carefully contrived, errant forelock was already familiar to television audiences by the time this campaign began, by polling day it had secured a place in their hearts. Grimond succeeded in shifting the agenda towards what the authors describe as a 'modernising' agenda. The 'new Liberals', and especially those who switched during the campaign, were anything but apathetic. They were knowledgeable and keenly interested in the issues, and their imagination was caught by Grimond's appearance as a courageous and disinterested radical standing up to the party machines of Labour and the Tories. His was a tremendous personal achievement. In the equivalent book about the effects of television on the 1959 general election, the first of its kind, the Liberals receive only the slightest mention in passing.

On the campaign trail, Grimond worked hard until the bitter end. James Pickles, latterly a celebrated legal personality, was standing for Brighouse and Spenborough. This was not a target seat but, since Grimond was due to pass through the constituency, Pickles talked him and his entourage into making the briefest of flying visits en route – for long enough to inscribe a tablecloth for the local Liberal ladies, and to have his picture taken with the candidate. Pickles later recalled: 'he looked so tired that I don't think he really realised who I was or where he was'.[13] Nor were Orkney and Shetland totally neglected. The gradual advent of television in the more far-flung islands had more or less killed off the old-style public meetings of Orkney and Shetland. Grimond was always convinced that it was a bad sign if large numbers of people turned up at election meetings organised by an incumbent MP, and when only a lone supporter turned up for the scheduled meeting at Mid Yell he was immensely heartened. He invited the stalwart soul to have a lengthy heart-to-heart with him in his car. At a meeting on Burra, the chairman pressed those present to ask questions of their candidate: 'Next time you see Mr Grimond on the little square box, he won't be able to answer you!' 'It sounds like my funeral,' responded Grimond.[14] At another meeting, a well-known local Tory started to make a speech, beginning with the words 'the point I want to make...' Grimond interrupted him before he got into flow, saying, 'the point is that you want to make a speech, while I pay for the hire of this hall!'[15]

A new optimism was in the air, as both opinion polls and reports from the constituencies confirmed a significant shift towards the Liberals. Grimond was immensely heartened when he visited the West Country, before heading back to the Highlands and Islands for the last few days of the campaign. Before flying north, Grimond recorded a final radio broadcast, in which he predicted that his party would create a modern record by polling in excess of 3 million votes. He particularly counselled his listeners to be prepared for any 'last-minute scare' from the Tories. He developed this theme in his whistle-stop tour of the Liberals' target seats in the Highlands and, by the eve of the poll, he was confident enough to predict that the House of Commons would be 'revived by an influx of new Liberal members backed by a large Liberal vote'.[16] He was also unable to conceal his amusement at an attack on the Liberals from Quintin Hogg, who said that people would have to be 'bonkers' to vote for them. He was less amused by an intimation from Conservative Central Office that people would do better to vote Labour than

Liberal, indignantly criticising the two major parties for 'rolling along arm-in-arm, trying to take up the whole of the political highway'.[17]

Although the Liberals did get their 3 million votes on 15th October 1964 (11.2 per cent of the total), a tremendous achievement after the frustrations and disappointments of 1963, election night itself was hardly a joyous occasion for Grimond, who came back to London for the result. Donald Wade and Arthur Holt were both defeated, Holt falling from first to third in Bolton West. Both defeats represented a terrible blow for Grimond. The West Country brought further disappointment: Mark Bonham Carter again lost at Torrington, and North Cornwall remained Conservative by another slender majority. Eric Lubbock held Orpington with a reduced majority while, building on his by-election result, Richard Wainwright drove the Labour majority in Colne Valley down to only 187 votes. What really mattered to most voters, however, was the fact that Alec Douglas Home was out and Harold Wilson seemed to be in – albeit by a wafer-thin majority. It never crossed Wilson's mind to go to the Liberals seeking succour. So far as Labour was concerned, Jo Grimond and his Liberals could like it or lump it. In public, Grimond did his best to hide his disappointment. He failed.

The day after the election, Jo Grimond flew back home to Kirkwall. While he was en route, two bastions of the north fell to Liberals – George Mackie winning Caithness and Sutherland, and Alasdair Mackenzie gaining Ross and Cromarty – adding to Russell Johnston's fine win at Inverness. The Liberals won nine seats in total, the first time they had increased their parliamentary representation at a general election since 1929. Their regional campaigns enjoyed mixed success, delivering three new MPs in the Highlands and a solitary English gain, at Bodmin. This net increase of two seats was a poor return for 3 million votes, but did at least enable Grimond to proclaim a 'great triumph for Liberalism in the crofting counties'.[18] That was not the only good news awaiting him as he stepped off his plane at Kirkwall on the evening of Friday, 16th October. Those present were struck by how relieved he looked when it was confirmed to him that Labour had, in fact, scraped together its narrow majority (of five seats). Although Grimond had long advocated the politics of coalition, in the circumstances of 1964 he felt little enthusiasm for a delicately balanced Parliament. He had been at pains during the campaign to emphasise that, though they did not seek the balance of power in Parliament, the Liberals would be willing to accept the responsibility. In fact, he had dreaded that outcome. For all his sermons about realignment and the politics of coalition, Grimond was under no illusions: his party was just not ready to play a part in government.

The Liberal result in 1964 was less patchy than at previous landmarks in the party's long recovery. In 54 seats the party received over 25 per cent of the vote, compared with 23 seats in 1959. They also came second in 54 seats as against 27 in 1959. They broke into the home counties, gaining substantial and impressive footholds in a number of areas where they had been moribund for years. That was the good news. The problem, as Grimond knew at once, was that, with the Tories now out of office again after thirteen years, the 'protest' votes that had flowed so readily from them to the Liberals would almost certainly begin to dry up. If the Liberals were seen to be getting too close to Labour, many of the defectors from the Tories picked up in 1964 could vanish as quickly as they had appeared. It seemed likely too that Alec Home would soon be replaced by a more potent figure, which made a squeeze on the Liberal vote in any snap election even more likely. Labour had received its lowest total poll since the war, and its share of the vote had increased by only 0.3 per cent. The increase in the Liberal vote – and the Labour win – had come almost entirely as a consequence of Conservative votes switching to the Liberals, providing the basis for a familiar counter-attack from the Conservatives: that a vote for the Liberals only let in the socialists. Grimond gave as good as he got on this point, retorting: 'they themselves have let Labour in, in Colne Valley and Huddersfield and in Bolton East and West.'[19] This was a fine, robust rhetorical flourish, but Grimond knew that he had to proceed with caution. Although the parliamentary arithmetic did, theoretically, give the Liberals an unusual degree of potential influence, this was an accidental situation that any second election would almost certainly bring to a rapid end. Grimond did not approach Wilson about a parliamentary arrangement, nor did Labour approach him. Although there were informal contacts throughout the Parliament, this situation never really changed. Grimond knew that an alliance with Labour would have upset many Liberals. He knew also that rejection by the Labour Party was certain. Yet he could not give up on the possibility, while this Parliament lasted, of imposing at least some Liberal influence on the direction of government policy.

With its constantly shifting balance of seats and advantage, the 1964–6 Parliament always seemed to be on the verge of collapse. Yet, despite a majority that started at four or five (depending upon the method of calculation) and ultimately fell to zero, Harold Wilson never really lost control of the situation. Although Labour stayed ahead in the polls for the first six months of the new Parliament, Wilson did not want the voters to think that he had capriciously sprung another general election upon them. He resolved to keep going for as long as possible. In the wake of defeat, the Conservative Party turned in upon itself and was for some time in no fit state to fight an election. With the possible exception of the determined and ambitious Ted Heath, newly appointed as shadow Chancellor, the last thing on Tory minds was forcing an election. All this greatly strengthened Wilson's hand and weakened Grimond's, leaving him in the most appalling quandary. The parliamentary arithmetic certainly gave the Liberals the opportunity, on some issues at least, to influence government decision-making, an accidental situation that Grimond was keen to sustain. On the other hand, the Liberals could not afford to be seen as mere stooges of the Labour Party. It was a delicate balancing act.

The weekend after the election, Grimond immediately set out his stall. Although he warned that, in his view, 'there will have to be a new election fairly soon',[20] he emphasised that the Liberals would not take part in any parliamentary campaign to 'harry' the new government. This was a reference to the Conservatives' tactics in the Parliament of 1950–51, when Labour was forced to marshal sick and dying MPs for crucial division after crucial division in the face of a merciless parliamentary onslaught. In fact, both Grimond and Wilson had already come to the view that Alec Home and his colleagues, recently defeated rather than resurgent, were pretty unlikely to try such a tactic in any case. Grimond also emphasised that the Liberals would not allow their desire for electoral reform to get in the way of the immediate measures that were needed to sort out the nation's economic problems. In due course, he would edge away from that position, eventually coming to the view that electoral reform was the only prize that could justify going into a coalition. Although a year seemed to him a reasonable term for a government with such a slender majority, Grimond was determined while the Parliament lasted to prove that the 3 million Liberal votes 'have been really effective and will have a major influence on what happens in the House of Commons'.[21] The Liberals had no intention of giving Labour a *carte blanche* and would 'oppose anything which we think will be against the national interest'.[22] In particular, they would resolutely oppose any attempt to nationalise the steel industry, and maintain a critical view of Labour's proposals for land reform. On nationalisation, the Liberals' position had been too clear, for too long, for them even to consider an about-turn. 'I do not believe that the Government of this country should get into the business of being bankers,' Grimond had once proclaimed in the House of Commons. 'Nor do I think that they should get into the general business of managing companies.'[23]

For as long as this parliamentary situation endured, Grimond had no intention of lining up with the Conservatives unless he absolutely had to; the Liberals wanted to see stable government 'for a reasonable period of time' and would give Wilson a fair wind in the hope that he might introduce some of the radical, liberalising measures that the Liberals advocated. He also emphasised all along that, if Labour chose to make an approach to the Liberals with the objective of securing an understanding between the two parties, they would be given a fair hearing; but any arrangement would have to be reached on the basis of a mutually agreed programme. That, in turn, would mean that the Liberals would wish to have access to confidential Treasury information about the state of the economy before signing up to any economic programme. In the absence of an all-embracing agreement, the Liberals would not support legislation that they held to be against the national interest purely for the purpose of deferring an election. By the time Grimond discussed parliamentary tactics with a meeting of the Liberal Party Council, on Saturday, 31st October, two Labour rebels – Desmond Donnelly and Woodrow Wyatt – had already broken ranks with Wilson by announcing publicly that, like the Liberals, they could not countenance supporting steel nationalisation. Suddenly the Liberal position really did take on an unquestioned importance. Wyatt in particular also returned to Grimond's theme of realignment, suggesting in a newspaper piece that a full-blown pact be established to provide a stable, centre-left majority in the House of Commons, with Grimond in the cabinet.

This was not, however, what Grimond meant by realignment. He wanted to see a new progressive party established, shorn of the die-hard socialists and nationalisers but united around a progressive and radical vision. He did not want to lend Liberal respectability to a government that wanted to nationalise steel. Grimond therefore reiterated what had always been his view: the Labour government deserved qualified support on a range of issues where its policies might have a radical hue that appealed to Liberals – on legal reform, for example, the social services and restrictive practices – but with regard to steel, the Liberals had to remain true to their fundamental beliefs. Although the 'Lib-Lab' idea being floated by Wyatt and Donnelly certainly had its attractions, and Grimond was delighted to 'welcome their agreement with a number of things that we have been saying for a number of years',[24] he did also point out that the two men 'at present speak only for themselves . . . No one, so far as I am aware, with any official standing, has ever suggested a pact . . . It seems to me that most of the talk about this pact comes from the too-vivid imagination of Liberals.'[25] The minutes of the council meeting record that 'Mr Grimond, in his reply to the debate, made the point that he did not see why he should repudiate suggestions made by backbench Labour MPs, although he doubted if anyone was more opposed to pacts than he was.'[26] However, as he joked to the party council: 'we should not take up this rather spinster-like attitude that, if two individuals say the Liberal Party is splendid, we should instantly hitch up our skirts and lock the door.'[27] Wyatt had made a similar overture when Hugh Gaitskell's battles against CND were at their fiercest, but had received no support from the leadership, and Grimond must have known that Harold Wilson was likely to be at least as cool towards realignment as his more social democratic predecessor had been. Grimond always found Wilson difficult to talk to, and instead sent his personal assistant Christopher Layton to see Roy Jenkins to explore possibilities for inter-party cooperation. Jenkins told Layton that he would 'put a line out' within Labour to see if there was any possibility. For a time, no more was heard. Nonetheless, Liberal whip Eric Lubbock did meet the junior government whip John Silkin regularly

A MESSAGE FROM

THE LIBERAL CANDIDATE

MAJOR JOSEPH GRIMOND.

✦ ✦ ✦ ✦

Ladies and Gentlemen,

Let me begin by paying tribute to Mr Churchill and to the great coalition of all Parties which he has led.

Liberals often worked with Mr Churchill before the war, and gladly served under him during the war. I would willingly join with him again if it is the wish of the people that a truly national Government of all Parties be formed to finish the war against Japan—which is the first essential.

Major Joseph Grimond's 1945 general election address

With Lady Violet Bonham Carter and her elder son, Mark (? 1945/6)

The Old Manse at Firth (Dougie Shearer)

Jo Grimond in conversation with Mrs Frank Byers

The Grimond family outside the Old Manse, c.1951 (*left to right*) Andrew ('Jag'), Johnny ('Toad'), Jo, Laura and (kneeling) Grizelda

Another election, another celebration. Jackie Robertson, Grimond's Orkney agent (Charles Tait)

Sent packing? Campaigning at an Orcadian egg-packing plant

Grimond with Richard Dimbleby in 1958 (BBC)

Mark Bonham Carter, Frank Byers and Donald Wade; to the right a glimpse of a splendid hat, to the left the unmistakable Grimond forelock (Srdja Djukanovic)

JG looking distinctly unperturbed as he is interviewed on television by Robin Day (BBC)

Eric Lubbock (left) leads the applause at Orpington (Srdja Djukanovic)

'Orpington Man' is born – the count at the Orpington by-election, March 1962; the defeated Conservative candidate can be seen to the left of the photograph, putting a brave face on things (Srdja Djukanovic)

Jealous of the attention? Grimond looks all made up, but the same cannot be said of Harold Wilson (BBC)

for lunch – every month or so –and discussed forthcoming parliamentary business each week.

Meanwhile the Liberals, flushed with their successes at the election and mildly intoxicated with an unfamiliar whiff of power and influence, endorsed Grimond's plan to give the government a fair wind. A whip-round from amongst the party's grateful candidates generated £275 for their leader, who bought himself a painting. Grimond's contribution to the debate on the Queen's Speech four days later was arguably the most important parliamentary speech by a Liberal leader since the 1930s. The party council had given him the free rein he needed, and Grimond went on to set out his position with clarity, offering a qualified welcome to the incoming administration: 'We welcome the proposals to modernise and develop the health and welfare services and to abolish prescription charges, again, always subject to the overriding need to provide the wealth with which this can be done.'[28] On steel, however, Grimond cast doubt upon Wilson's mandate for pressing on with nationalisation in the face of the reservations expressed about it on all sides of the House of Commons: 'I have never been a great upholder of the doctrine of the mandate, for I do not think that it has played any part in British constitutional history – but I understood that the Prime Minister yesterday claimed a mandate for the nationalisation of steel – and that, of course, is something which he cannot claim.'[29] What was needed, as elsewhere in the economy, was a war against restrictive and monopolistic practices.

The Liberals quickly put forward a compromise plan of their own on the future of the steel industry. When no one else was willing to lead the line, Emlyn Hooson put this case in the House of Commons on 9th November. So turbulent and rowdy was the atmosphere that Hooson felt almost as though he was talking to himself. Hooson set out clearly on the record the Liberals' intention to oppose, 'with all the power and influence at our disposal', any doctrinaire nationalisation of steel. He did not attempt to set out a detailed proposal, preferring to 'indicate the lines on which sensible negotiations can take place'.[30] The Liberal 'lines' would have involved the government taking a 51 per cent stake in a limited number of steel companies and establishing competition between state-owned and privately owned industry. This was a rather vague attempt to split the difference between the other parties, and one that proved difficult to maintain. At the end of the debate, all nine Liberals voted for the Conservative amendment, which was defeated by 307 votes to 300, Wyatt and Donnelly both voting with the government. When the government introduced a *de facto* autumn Budget shortly afterwards, the Liberals found it impossible to support the Conservatives on two more crucial votes, one on petrol tax and another on income tax. On the latter they actually supported the government.

In due course Wilson was canny enough to throw a few encouraging straws into the wind for the Liberals. Just a fortnight after the election, he told the House of Commons that the government was 'considering various proposals for electoral reform, and hope to arrange for discussion between the parties shortly'.[31] Wilson and his senior colleagues kept Grimond and the Liberals wiggling nervously on the end of that particular line for the duration of the Parliament. Grimond welcomed this statement with 'applause' on behalf of the Liberal Party and its supporters. Wilson and his allies followed this up with a number of private conversations with the Liberals, always implying that, could they but resolve some of their internal party problems, they would like nothing more than real progress towards electoral reform. Wilson did in due course set up a Speaker's Conference on electoral reform, but nothing of lasting significance came of it. By 1966, Grimond would grow very sceptical of the ministers who spoke to him sympathetically about electoral reform, believing that it would only come about as part of a 'full-scale Lib-Lab arrangement to be negotiated after an election'.

Grimond was conscious of the need to keep members of his own party, as well as the wider audience, fully briefed on how the Liberals voted in the House of Commons, and why. A regular *Campaign Bulletin* was instituted, setting out the main arguments, often in the form of lengthy quotations from Grimond's speeches and statements. The *Bulletin* also regularly featured a detailed breakdown of the voting record of the Liberal Parliamentary Party, usually accompanied by pithy justifications of their actions. When the Liberals decided to vote both against the Wilson government's first Queen's Speech, and also against a self-congratulatory Conservative amendment to it, the robust argument in *Bulletin* explained that the Queen's Speech 'contains all Labour proposals including renationalisation of Iron and Steel, Land Commission etc. If we voted for this we should join the Labour Party.'[32] As for Alec Douglas Home's amendment, since it stated that Labour would damage the Conservatives' 'programmes of modernisation already in train', it could hardly be supported since 'Liberals know of no evidence that Conservatives had any real modernisation programmes.'[33] A running tally of partisan votes was kept up throughout the lifetime of the 1964–6 Parliament, demonstrating that the Liberals opposed the Wilson government more often than they supported it. This was only partially effective, and Grimond was always angered by the fact that even members of his own party fell for the canard that he and his colleagues were bailing out Harold Wilson at every available opportunity. For instance, a tetchy message was conveyed to the Organising Committee on 10th December 1964 from the party executive, requesting that the party's MPs should start making more effort to come to its meetings. The MPs were criticised for being out of touch with party opinion and, according to the executive, 'appeared to be too readily supporting the Labour Party in Parliament'.

One of the few concrete gestures of goodwill made by the first Wilson administration towards the Liberals was the creation of three Liberal life peers, something that no Conservative government had been willing to grant since the introduction of life peerages. All three were notable and formidable in their way. Although the Huddersfield Liberals had announced within days of the general election that they wanted him to stand again in his former division, Donald Wade was easily persuaded to go instead to the upper house. In contrast, Frank Byers had long since given up any thoughts of re-election and made a more obvious candidate for elevation. The Liberals were initially offered two peerages, but Grimond managed to negotiate with Wilson that they could have three, so long as the third was Lady Violet Bonham Carter. Lady Violet had long been regarded as a natural candidate for the upper house by her many admirers, but she had by now suffered a minor stroke and her general health was increasingly fragile. Wilson therefore agreed that the Liberals could have two 'working' peerages – for Wade and Byers – and a third, 'honorary', one for Lady Violet, on Wilson's own nomination.

Wilson meanwhile had added to his own problems by precipitating a by-election in one of Labour's own seats. The shadow Foreign Secretary, Patrick Gordon Walker, had been defeated at Smethwick in the West Midlands after the local Conservatives exploited the issue of race in an area of high immigration, a result that Grimond had denounced in fierce terms: 'a damned disgrace . . . the most disgraceful thing that has happened in the election . . . I only hope the rest of the country at any rate will repudiate this.'[34] Harold Wilson echoed these sentiments with equal vigour. His displeasure was greatly enhanced by the fact that the Smethwick result had left his first choice as Foreign Secretary without a parliamentary seat. Wilson appointed Gordon Walker to the post regardless and told his whips to find someone in a reasonably safe Labour seat who would be willing to stand down. Despite his initial reluctance, they eventually prevailed upon the veteran Labour MP for Leyton, Reg Sorensen, to accept a peerage, precipitating a by-election at which Gordon Walker would be the candidate. Sorensen's majority at the general election had been just under 8,000 votes. Wilson also prompted a similar situation in Nuneaton, a rather safer seat, in order to make way for the trade unionist Frank Cousins, whom he wished to appoint as Minister for Technology.

The parliamentary situation inevitably meant that Grimond had to spend more time at, or close to, the House of Commons, and the opportunities for developing new policies were inevitably curtailed. He had already produced two significant books, and Hodder and Stoughton sensed that the new political situation might provide a perfect opening for a third. Grimond was realistic enough to realise that whatever market there was had probably by now been saturated. 'I have already written two books on Liberalism,' he wrote in response to the publisher's opening gambit, 'and I do not think I can do a third on this subject.'[35] He did not close the door entirely, however, sensing that there might be value in publishing some kind of definitive work on the experience of holding the ring in a Parliament where the government's majority was wafer-thin: 'something about specific Liberal reactions to certain major events . . . This, however, would require some research and in the present state of Parliament I doubt if I am able to undertake it.'[36] This was a pity: if Grimond had been more able or willing to delegate, he might have produced a third major work, and one of lasting value to political historians. Half-hearted negotiations would continue into early 1965, but never really looked like setting the stage for a *magnum opus*.

Grimond's 'New Year Message' to Liberals for 1965 conceded that this would be a 'year of some risk . . . we are now playing for higher stakes in national politics.'[37] He also sought to reassure his supporters that, under his leadership, the Liberal MPs would 'emphasise their decisive and distinctive role'.[38] There was also strong encouragement to Liberal councillors and local associations, who should be as active as possible in the months ahead. In this important document Grimond also set out how Liberal influence might be maximised in whatever time was left for the House of Commons elected in 1964:

> We must play our important role by getting the Government to implement measures of social and economic reform about which all radicals can be united . . . The most fundamental trouble with the Government's policies so far has been their failure to make clear what they expect to be the driving force in the economy. Liberals believe that this must be the free enterprise system with its benefits more widely spread.

In the first fortnight of 1965 the Liberals bolstered their numbers again in the House of Lords, picking up two converts from the crossbenches. Both were former ambassadors. Lord Franks (formerly Sir Oliver Franks) had been British ambassador in Washington from 1948 to 1962 and had been close to the Liberals for some time. Lord Gladwyn (formerly Sir Gladwyn Jebb) joined because he strongly agreed with the Liberals' positive policy towards the EEC. When Gladwyn went to see Grimond to enquire about joining the party, he asked him what the main ethos of the party was. 'Wool, wool and wool-gathering,' responded Grimond with a grin.[39]

Later that month the results at Nuneaton and Leyton landed a serious blow on both Labour and the Liberals. The voters' collective judgement on Labour's '100 Days' in government was far from encouraging. Although Frank Cousins held Nuneaton with a reduced majority, the Tories gained Leyton with a majority of 205 votes. This clearly looked bad for Harold Wilson, but the lesson for Grimond was, if anything, even more serious. In both seats the Liberal vote had slumped as voters defected to the Tories. Grimond put a brave face on things and tried to reassert his independence. 'If Mr Wilson wants to stay in office,' he counselled, 'he really must start doing things which appeal to a wider public than the hard-core of Left-wing Socialist voters . . .

the Government's measures have been negative and harmful.' Leyton was soon forgotten: three days later, Winston Churchill died at the age of ninety and no other story mattered. Churchill was the symbol not only of Britain's victory in the Second World War. He was also a symbol of the old Liberal Party and its long battle against its rival, socialism. Grimond had paid a marvellous tribute to Churchill less than a year before, when the former premier attended his last session in the Commons before retiring at the 1964 general election:

> He has on occasions been very angry with the House of Commons. He has been ignored by the House of Commons. He has been howled at by the House of Commons. He has received almost unparalleled adulation from the House of Commons and, in over 50 years, he has held the highest offices . . . He has also had a book thrown at him in the House of Commons, and a point of order has been taken against him for attempting to vote in his pyjamas. But he has never attempted to patronise or belittle the House of Commons . . . Few people can fail to be moved by the meticulous care which he takes to pay his respects to this assembly, in which his whole life, almost, has been spent.[40]

When he heard of Churchill's death, Grimond described him as 'the largest human being of our time, the greatest man of action that this nation has ever produced'.[41] Grimond had been in his early twenties when he first met Churchill, under the sponsorship of Lady Violet. In his newspaper column he remembered that first meeting: 'As a person, Sir Winston liked everyone to have the best champagne, figuratively and literally. He wasn't one of those who graded his hospitality according to the standing of the guest.'[42] As leader of the Liberals, Grimond now took part in a special ceremony to honour Churchill as he lay in state in Westminster Hall, the oldest surviving part of the Palace of Westminster. Harold Wilson, Alec Home, Grimond and the Speaker of the House of Commons, Sir Harry Hylton-Foster, stood on guard together for five minutes. Grimond borrowed suitable attire from the Serjeant-at-Arms, Sir Alexander Gordon-Lennox. He combined a black waistcoat loaned by Gordon-Lennox with a tailcoat that his mother-in-law recognised as being the one in which he had been married almost thirty years earlier. Laura then told her mother that Grimond had recently sought assistance from the same source when he had to attend a dinner party 'with decorations'. When he arrived, Grimond had discovered that he was wearing the Burma Star, never having been to Burma in his life. The BBC added a macabre touch to the Churchill Memorial Day by sending Grimond an urgent message in which they asked him to record an obituary of Harold Wilson. Presuming that the BBC had been stimulated by Churchill's death into checking that its political obituaries were all up to date, Grimond speculated that Wilson and Home had probably received similar messages about him.

Once the period of mourning was over, Grimond returned to the campaigning fray at a moderately promising by-election, due to be held at East

Grinstead on 4th February. The Liberal candidate was Richard Holme, one of Grimond's most talented protégés, who had run a reasonably strong second in the seat at the general election. The Liberals were so keen to capitalise upon tactical voting by Labour supporters that they incurred the self-righteous wrath of the Labour candidate after they claimed in a leaflet that 'in East Grinstead you have a choice between a Conservative and a Liberal', rather giving the impression that there wasn't a Labour candidate at all. The result was solid rather than spectacular, a collapse in the Labour vote resulting in a modest swing to the Liberals that fell far short of threatening the Conservative majority, as the Conservative share of the vote rose slightly. Taken together with Leyton and Nuneaton, this appeared to demonstrate that, although Conservative support had at the very least stopped falling, anti-Conservative tactical voting was continuing. It therefore offered some sustenance to Grimond's continuing campaign for political realignment.

On 2nd February 1965, no doubt with East Grinstead in mind, Grimond began an offensive against the Conservatives, who that day in the House of Commons moved a motion of censure against the Labour government. Although the Liberals were perfectly willing to vote against the government on a substantive motion, in a decision reminiscent of the attitude of the 'Radical Liberals' in 1950–1, as a matter of principle they had agreed amongst themselves that they would not support Tory gestures of this kind. In the party's *Campaign Bulletin* the following week, the explanation was that the Motion 'condemned all Government actions, some of which Liberals can support, and ignored Conservative failings over 13 years . . . The Motion was "political shadow-boxing".' This uncannily echoed the line taken by Megan Lloyd George in 1950–1. Grimond, always sensitive to charges that the Liberals were being squeezed in the bi-partisan atmosphere, recognised that this action would be adduced by the Tories as further evidence that the Liberals were no more than Labour stooges. This angered Grimond; after all, the Tories themselves had recently abstained on an important substantive motion relating to the Burmah Oil Company, a matter far more likely to bring down a government than a censure motion. In the House of Commons, Peter Bessell, the flamboyant and idiosyncratic MP for Bodmin, fought his own, one-man guerrilla war against the government, merrily disrupting parliamentary conventions and putting down batteries of questions to ministers.

Conscious that Wilson was likely to call another election as and when it best suited him, Grimond and Frank Byers knew that they had to keep their weary troops on an election footing. At the first meeting of the party's Executive Committee after the general election, on 30th October 1964, Frank Byers had taken the opportunity not only to set down the party's gratitude to Grimond 'for his personal contribution', but also expressed his hope that non-essential demands on Grimond's time 'should be kept down to the absolute minimum'.[44] With another election in the not-too-distant future looking like a racing certainty, the executive agreed to a proposal from Frank Byers that something akin to the General Election Committee should be kept in being *pro tem*. On 26th February 1965 the committee embarked upon another shake-up of the party organisation in advance of the next general election, and the reassembling of a suitable team. Mark Bonham Carter warned that there was a lot of work to do, not least in retaliating against some highly effective disinformation: 'the Liberal role in Parliament had been the subject of a deliberate and unscrupulous campaign by Conservative MPs.' In fact Labour always had a majority in the House of Commons, not least because of the steady flow of vacancies in Tory-held constituencies, so the Liberals' role was fairly peripheral.

Timothy Joyce was put in charge of a spring campaign to rid the party of inertia. During February alone, the committee was proudly informed, the press department had put out 36 written handouts – 22 speeches, 7 statements and 7 general handouts – and, on average, over two verbal statements a day were being phoned over to agencies. During the month, Grimond himself had been on *Tonight*, *Gallery*, *Division* and *Ten o'clock*. On 27th March 1965 the spring cleaning continued: 'In the view of the Organising Committee and Mr Grimond,' it was resolved, it was now necessary to 'make the Party Committee a larger body than the Constitution laid down . . . the Executive agreed that this appeared to be unavoidable.'[45] One victim of the changes was Patrick Kemmis, who had been head of the party organisation since 1961. Kemmis was a former civil servant, who repeatedly made the mistake of taking both himself, and Jo Grimond, too seriously. Once he had arranged for a Liberal rally in London and had made the mistake of not formally clearing the date with Grimond in advance. When he told Grimond that a hall had been booked at great expense, and all the necessary arrangements set in train, Grimond deliberately wound him up by saying that he couldn't be there, as he had a dinner arranged – which was not true. Kemmis blew his top, asking Grimond whether he was serious about politics and whether he realised how important the event was. By the end, Kemmis was hardly on speaking terms with Grimond. He was replaced by Tim Beaumont.

In the House of Commons Grimond took the battle to the Conservatives, in one caustic performance ironically claiming to be rather flattered by the very notion that he and his small band alone could be held responsible for keeping a government in office, and reminding the House, to ministerial cheers and laughter, that 'however many of the opposition vote this evening, we cannot defeat the Government . . . This does not even need matchsticks . . . There is nothing that terrifies the Opposition Chief Whip more than if he thinks there is going to be a near division . . . He rushes out and people are locked in lavatories.'[46] He reiterated this point on Independent Television that evening, warning that what the Conservatives 'really want is a Labour Government and to blame the Liberals for it',[47] an argument that he developed further two days later:

> Does anyone believe that the Tories themselves want an election before they have settled their leadership, and at least have some semblance of policy? Of course they don't . . . They are as brave as lions when the Government have a comfortable majority – as they have at the moment, with five by-elections impending in Tory-held constituencies. But whenever there has been a real danger of embarrassing the Government, the full Tory strength is not put into the voting lobby.[48]

At two other by-elections in early 1965, at Salisbury and Altrincham and Sale, the Liberal vote again fell. These were signs of things to come throughout that Parliament. The journalist Ian Waller, admittedly no friend of Grimond or the Liberals, claimed that their 'timid behaviour in the Commons is obviously now working against them'.[49] Although Grimond privately feared that his critic might have a point, there was plenty of evidence that tactical voting was at work, rather than a real collapse in support for the Liberals. For the remainder of spring 1965 Grimond plugged away, making a series of short trips and tours on which he spoke with vigour and was generally received with enthusiasm. Constantly he reiterated the essence of the Liberals' approach to the parliamentary situation. It was not the business of an opposition party to assume the responsibilities or attitudes of government, he asserted, and the Liberals would continue to vote according to the merits of individual cases. What Grimond wanted for the remainder of the Parliament was for the Wilson government to concentrate on the introduction of policies that enjoyed support beyond the confines of the Labour Party – for example on regional policy and certain economic measures. The government must also be pressed into giving some indication of how it would reform and modernise the economy: 'Britain is saddling her producers with a vast weight of unproductive expenditure . . . We are like a family with a house full of elderly relatives who take up a lot of room, expect three square meals a day, television and attendance, but don't bring in anything.'[50] Talk of a coalition or general arrangement between the parties was pointless unless and until the Labour Party made some kind of formal approach to the Liberals. Even though the Conservatives were now in opposition, it was from their weakness that the Liberals drew most of their strength, and Grimond's hopes must have been buoyed when a Gallup poll in March 1965 suggested that 51 per cent of people thought that he would be a better leader of the opposition than Alec Home.

Grimond was also kept busy in his own political backyard. Although, much to his relief, he now had Liberal colleagues from Scottish constituencies to share the burdens of the Grand Committee, he still had to attend to the specific demands of his own constituents. He scarcely reduced his constituency commitments and campaigned tirelessly on behalf of the sixty residents of Fair Isle, the lonely island between Orkney and Shetland, when they petitioned to have their own resident doctor. Then there was a running battle over the methods employed by Labour in the introduction of a Highland Development Board, something for which Grimond had long called. First of all, Grimond wanted to be sure about how the new board would be financed and operated. Furthermore he wanted it to be staffed with professionals 'in the prime of life'. He was also determined to fight for a democratic element in any programme of regional development – the only guarantee that it would represent a genuine shift of power away from the centre. In return for this, Grimond was more than happy to witness the demise of some existing bodies: 'in the Northern area of Scotland there are a great many organisations, some of which are not very effective, and I think that some of these could be thinned out.'[51]

Any pleasure that Grimond might have experienced at Labour's apparent willingness to press on with regional development was more or less blown away when the two major parties attempted to squeeze the Liberals out of the parliamentary picture as the Highland Development Bill progressed. The Liberals now represented four of the six constituencies affected by the Bill, yet the thirty-five-member committee nominated to scrutinise its passage included only one Liberal name, that of Russell Johnston. The Liberals took the unusual and extreme step of tabling motions in the House of Commons criticising both the Committee of Selection and the Speaker himself. Frustrated in the face of such arcane procedures and problems, Grimond commented bitterly that 'Russian astronauts are not the only people floating about in space attached to their fellow men by only the thinnest cord . . . the same is true of MPs trussed up by the party system and out-of-date protocol.'[52] The problem was exacerbated when only two Liberals were called in the second reading debate on the Bill, Grimond complaining bitterly that 'the House owes its first obligation to the people and not to any of its own procedures or party arrangements.'[53]

Despite his irritation with Labour over the Scottish question, in March 1965 Grimond did give new impetus to the 'Lib-Lab' debate by setting out in public some thoughts on how the Liberals might behave if Labour's slim majority did erode further, or vanish entirely, and the Conservatives decided to start giving the government a run for its money in the voting lobbies of the House of Commons. After a spate of by-elections, the opposition was now back up to full strength. In an interview with *The Times*, Grimond explained that, if that combination of circumstances did arise, then the *ad hoc* approach that Liberals had adopted towards votes in the House of Commons thus far might have to be seriously reconsidered in the interests of stable government. If the Labour Party actually went into a minority, then 'either we must have some reasonably long-range agreement with the Government or a general election – we must have an agreement for a few months on some purpose we both want . . . I should be very much opposed to going back to the 1929 system, in which the Labour Government and the Liberal Party made practically daily *ad hoc* decisions on the business of government.'[54] He foresaw Labour and the Liberals reaching some kind of agreement on 'certain things both parties want to get through', under which the Liberals would support Labour 'on all issues, however minor, until that is done'.[55] This far-reaching gambit was regarded by some Liberals as premature and by others as extreme apostasy. It certainly stirred up the political establishment.

When Roy Jenkins approached him in early 1965 for help, Grimond was immediately inclined to be positive. Jenkins was already a great friend of his brother-in-law Mark Bonham Carter, and epitomised the kind of liberal-minded social democrat who would certainly belong in the new progressive party that Grimond envisaged. On this occasion, Jenkins wanted to establish whether the Liberals might be willing to provide him with support, tacit or explicit, in the House of Commons during some difficult times that he foresaw arising out of his decision to cancel the TSR-II aircraft. Grimond asked his parliamentary team for their views. Eric Lubbock, the party's aviation expert, liked the TSR-II and wanted to defend it, and Russell Johnston in particular wanted to heed him. Meanwhile Bessell and Thorpe, according to one of the parliamentary party at that time, were 'absolutely terrified of what the Tories would say down in the West Country' if the Liberals supported the Labour government on such a controversial policy. George Mackie, who had since the general election inclined to favour a link with Labour, was particularly loath to lose this opportunity to influence events. 'For God's sake, put it to them that you'll resign unless they back this chance,' he told Grimond, who demurred.[56] The cancellation of the TSR-II was announced a few weeks later, not by Jenkins but by the Chancellor of the Exchequer, James Callaghan. The Conservative Party put down a motion criticising the government and, although the Liberals agreed to vote against it, Lubbock was highly critical of the government in his contribution to the debate. The opposition motion was comfortably defeated, by 316 votes to 290 votes.

Although promising by-elections were few and far between for the Liberals between 1964 and 1966, a contest now loomed at Roxburgh, Selkirk and Peebles. At the 1964 general election David Steel had turned this Tory seat, which had been briefly held by a Liberal between 1950 and 1951, into a marginal. The re-elected Tory MP had now died and Steel was confident of a by-election victory. Although he and his team detected a slight loss of Liberal voters to the Conservatives, they were certain that enough Labour supporters would switch for them to close the gap of fewer than 2,000 votes. George Mackie continued jealously to guard the independence of the Scottish

Liberal Party, and when Jeremy Thorpe tried to take charge in Roxburgh he was politely invited to join the team – no more, no less. Grimond made two lengthy sojourns in the constituency during the short campaign. Steel won by 4,607 votes and Grimond observed that 'wherever Liberals have a chance of winning, people express their disgust with the shadow-boxing of the other parties . . . After five months of Labour Government, people can see no real difference from 13 years of the Conservatives.'[57] At Saffron Walden, where Rab Butler had stood down, the other side of the same coin was in evidence, as the Liberals in third place were badly squeezed in a seat where they stood no chance of winning. Yet speaking in the constituency during the campaign, Grimond had been warmly received, a collection at the end of his speech yielding over £64 and one egg! Buoyed by Steel's win, Grimond became more sanguine about an early election. 'Let Parliament either do a job,' he told the Women's Liberal Federations in a strong speech, 'or get out.'[58] With the Conservatives in such disarray, and now openly looking for a new leader, Harold Wilson must have felt tempted to follow that lead. But, for reasons of his own, he did not.

In the wake of Roxburgh, Grimond continued to pummel the Tories: 'Far be it from me to defend the Labour Party, but I think that we should be told what wicked things it has done . . . what are the Conservatives going to conserve? I do not ask the Tories to tell us what positive measures they would take, but they should tell us what parts of the Labour Government's programme they would change'.[59] In the same speech, the Wilson government came in for some criticism too: 'I still believe that there is a widespread feeling that, although the Labour Party does not really believe in Socialism, it is not wholeheartedly committed to private enterprise.'[60] The Liberals and their Labour soul mates Wyatt and Donnelly maintained their unyielding opposition to steel privatisation throughout all of this, but still Wilson would not risk provoking outrage on the Labour left by totally shelving the policy. He did, however, delay it substantially by issuing a White Paper on the industry in the spring of 1965, rather than pressing straight on with a Bill. Although much credit belonged to the Labour rebels, this was arguably the first concrete evidence of Liberal achievement after 1964. Grimond was not satisfied with this partial victory and, when the White Paper came out, he at once denounced it on television, describing his reaction as 'wholly unfavourable – I would feel bound to oppose it', and reiterating his view that old-fashioned nationalisation of the industry would do nothing to reduce its monopolistic characteristics, nor to deal with the nation's immediate problems.[61]

In May 1965, for the first time since the election, Labour's opinion poll ratings began to sag – and both Labour and the Liberals suffered major setbacks in the local elections. A bitter blow came at Maidenhead, where the Conservatives regained control of one of only two Liberal-held borough councils in England and Wales. The party had a net loss of almost 250 seats. Harold Wilson must have consoled himself with the thought that the Liberals probably didn't want an election any more than he did. Nonetheless, they must have added to his worries by voting against the government on 6th May, when the steel industry was debated. The government's majority was down to only four in that division, despite George Brown's success in negotiating quite literally last-minute support from Messrs Wyatt and Donnelly. On the evening of 10th May 1965 the Liberals flexed their muscles again by voting with the Conservatives on the Finance Bill, this time bringing Wilson down to his notional majority of three votes, on the most fundamental legislation of all for any government. Grimond made a fine speech, in which he explained why the Liberals could not endorse Labour's economic philosophy: 'The doubts about the country's economy are largely centred upon the high level of Government expenditure and the fact that much of the expenditure is not productive . . . The Government sometimes seem to be afraid of individual enterprise and to have little faith in the capacity of individuals to order their own affairs.'[62] He later explained that, 'unless amended, the Bill will create a closed economy, with a high level of taxation, isolated from the rest of the world and it will do great damage.'[63] Apart from the slow-tracking of steel, there were few signs of Labour moderating its plans and, in a major speech to the Scottish Liberals, Grimond repeated his warning that Britain could soon find itself 'the most highly taxed country in the world'.[64] Meanwhile two other long-cherished Liberal policies were hanging in the balance. A Speaker's Conference on electoral reform was beginning its work, its terms of reference including consideration of a preferential voting system. Grimond knew only too well that this would be blown out of the water at once by any incoming Tory administration. Then there was the question of Europe. He pressed home well-rehearsed Liberal arguments for British accession to the EEC, warning against putting too much trust in President de Gaulle and his 'antediluvian and futile ideas of national grandeur'.[65]

Up to the end of May 1965 the Liberals had voted with the government forty times, and against it eighty-five times. This still left open the question of what might happen if Labour lost its majority altogether. Although the Liberals preferred a period of peace, they were busily preparing for war. Encouraged by the party's Organising Committee, Grimond set up a new party panel of seventeen Liberal spokesmen, all of them outside the House of Commons, to complement the parliamentary team. Amongst the better-known names were those of Mark Bonham Carter (foreign affairs) and Christopher Layton (economic affairs), alongside several of Grimond's academic allies. Mr ADC Peterson, head of the department of education at Oxford, and industrial relations expert Michael Fogarty, both of whom had helped to frame policy in advance of 1964, were also included. For a small party, it was undeniably a strong team. In the newspaper column that he had penned for the old *Sun* newspaper virtually every week since the general election, Grimond regularly tested the waters, but usually in terms of realignment rather than a pact. A few weeks earlier, for instance, he had written that: 'Whatever the party machines may say, there is a radical coming together of the two non-Conservative parties . . . The new radicals . . . want a fresh look at old problems . . . The Liberal Party have to be the kernel of this new coalition.'[66] This had prompted no comment or response. Perhaps everyone thought that it was an April Fool's joke.

Grimond's seminal piece published two months later was certainly no joke. In a section that was often quoted (and misquoted) in the months that followed, he wrote that:

> If I were Mr Wilson I would consider it common sense to approach the Liberals . . . Having missed his chance of holding an Election this spring, Mr Wilson must surely want to survive a bit longer. Yet at any moment he may lose control of the Commons. To avoid that he must concentrate on measures which Liberals and liberal opinion in the country can support. If you are living on a small majority it is common sense to approach the Liberals – and here I include the whole of liberal opinion, three or four million people – with proposals for active co-operation. Or at least to concentrate your proposals within a range where their support is likely. Otherwise, by the logic of Parliamentary procedure, you force them more and more into opposition.[67]

Within ten days, Liberal headquarters had effectively retracted the article, explaining that Grimond had never meant it to be 'a formal invitation to a pact-making exercise'.[68] Then, just as his troops were making their weary way back to the bottom of the hill, Grimond appeared to march them back up again. In a sound broadcast on the evening of 23rd June 1965, he pressed the point again. Although the main thrust of the broadcast was about his favourite theme of realignment – in other words, the proposition that Labour should fragment, with the more agreeable sections amalgamating with the Liberals – Grimond did in this broadcast make a point of setting out what kinds of arrangement with the Wilson government might or might not be acceptable to the Liberals. Although the broadcast did not, strictly speaking, mark any shift in Grimond's position, or that of his party, such was the febrile atmosphere of the time that the professional Kremlinologists of the broadsheet newspapers were dissecting every word of his every utterance on this subject. They chose to underplay the substantive criticisms that he had made of the Labour government as it stood, which he described as 'in some ways . . . too pessimistic and conservative to call out the full effort of modern Britain',[69] whilst making great play of his observation that a spontaneous Lib-Lab movement seemed to have sprung up at recent by-elections, as anti-Tory voters had coalesced behind the candidate of the left most likely to win in each seat. Most also failed to quote Grimond's clear declaration that Liberals would 'continue the work which they have urged for the last 10 years – to give this country a real and radical alternative to Tory rule . . . having built up the party . . . on the hard slogging of voluntary workers up and down the country, we are not selling our beliefs for any temporary advantage.'[70] The response from Labour was cool: the government had been having a hard time of it in the voting lobbies during the passage of its Finance Bill, and Wilson assumed that Grimond had chosen his moment accordingly. Senior Labour figures professed themselves far from impressed.

Ignoring Labour's refusal to play, as well as tensions within his own party, Grimond would not let the matter drop. In an 'exclusive' interview with Mark Arnold Forster, published the day after that broadcast in the *Guardian* under the deliberately provocative headline 'Coalition Offer to Labour by Mr Grimond', he explained that he thought that it might now be sensible for Labour and the Liberals to have a talk about 'a serious agreement on long-term policies'. He didn't much like the way in which Labour had conducted itself thus far, he conceded, but 'it would be a setback to the general political condition if the country decided to go back to Toryism because it thought Labour had failed.'[71] Any such agreement would have to be more or less on the Liberals' terms, according to Grimond, because 'we could not make an agreement to keep a Labour government in office simply to see it go on in the way it has gone these last nine months . . . we have shown quite clearly the sort of policies we want.'[72] None of this meant that the long-term aim of realignment was dead. Although he was still not willing to force the issue when the country was in severe economic difficulties, electoral reform did remain a fundamental plank of the Liberal platform, and not simply as 'a method of . . . ensuring the election of more Liberals – electoral reform . . . could lead to the reform and liberalisation of the administrative machine as a whole'.[73]

After what had happened when the same journalist interviewed him in October 1959, Grimond can hardly have been surprised either by the sensational headline or by the response that it provoked in the country. Fortunately, on this occasion he had discussed in advance with his parliamentary colleagues the line he intended to take. He received positive support only from Jeremy Thorpe and new recruit David Steel: the remainder no more than acquiesced, Emlyn Hooson arguing that a pact with Labour was impossible, and Peter Bessell thinking it pretty undesirable. Grimond followed the article up with two major broadcast interviews that day. In one of these, for a show called *Scene,* Grimond clarified one important point in particular. He was not looking for an electoral arrangement with Labour: 'I don't think, you see, there's any chance of a pure deal for electoral advantage – if there's going to be any growing together of the parties, this has got to come about, first of all, from the people themselves in the grassroots [sic] and, secondly, because we really believe in the same things.'[74] In the other interview, for *Gallery,* Grimond clarified why he would not condemn Wilson and the Labour government out of hand: 'we would, as I say, like to see them put back on the rails because we don't want the country just to be forced back onto a Tory Government'.[75]

This gambit provoked furious activity amongst the media, as well as within the counsels of the Liberal Party. Grimond received a mountain of mail, which was evenly divided on the merits of his actions. He was not unduly perturbed by the volume of opposition since, as he would put it privately, his task was to 'educate his own party and the public – and this would take time'. Furthermore, in his view, many of his critics had 'no idea how Parliament worked'. Political features writers across the length and breadth of the land owed Grimond a great debt, as they churned out column yards about his initiatives. Whether their readers were equally grateful is a matter of conjecture. After all, most of the arguments had been well rehearsed by now. The one significant change was that Labour's opinion poll ratings were in a trough, so it seemed probable that Wilson would now wish to hang on for a time. Set against that was the fact that the Liberals too had begun to suffer from the mild Conservative resurgence. The talk was still of a new Tory leader and, with the name of Ted Heath very much in the frame, Grimond personally feared that the Liberals could lose out further. Heath was a grammar-school boy made good, a firm pro-European with an image as a moderniser. He could have been invented, feared Grimond, to appeal to precisely those 'New Men' whose votes the Liberals badly needed. What Grimond also knew, however, was that Wilson was perfectly capable of hanging on for a time. As the shrewd political editor of the *Financial Times,* Ronald Butt, pointed out: 'in no single Commons division in this first Session of Parliament has the Government owed its survival to the Liberals.'[76] Although their support had bottomed out, the Conservatives were by no means ready as an organisation to fight another election. Alec Home had put Heath in charge of a complete policy overhaul and, until that was complete, they would find it hard to draft a manifesto. Grimond too had another say on the matter, this time in the letters page of the *Guardian,* where he challenged the headline that had appeared over the interview with him the day before. The initiative for the interview had come from the newspaper, he pointed out, and not from him or the Liberal party. All he had done, rather than taking any great initiative, was 'to reiterate the views which I had expressed before about the general background to any possible approach by Labour'.[77]

Grimond's manoeuvrings prompted the establishment of a Liberal 'Independence Committee', set up by four former parliamentary candidates. In an open letter, the four warned Grimond against 'saving the Labour Government from the ruin it so richly deserves', which would leave Liberal principles 'submerged in socialism'.[78] Such a direct attack could not easily be shrugged off, particularly as the four men were all advocates, not opponents, of Grimond's strategy of realignment. How, they asked, could a party that wished to supplant Labour rush to its rescue when it found itself in difficulties? Emlyn Hooson, the Liberal MP for Montgomery, was also openly critical. The Liberals had only one option, he asserted: 'to soldier on in complete independence of any arrangement with Conservative or Labour and to press the policies in which we believe'.[79] In reality, there was no great distance between Grimond and his critics. He shared their antipathy towards any long-term arrangement with Labour and recognised that Labour's success was the Liberals' failure. He just wanted to make the most he could of the Liberals' limited, and short-term, parliamentary influence.

As the parliamentary session limped uninspiringly into the summer of 1965, Grimond carried on seizing every opportunity to publicise his views. In a newspaper interview he explained that the Liberals had to face facts: the day might come when they either had to support the government, or bring it down. It made sense to work out tactics before that day actually arrived. He was less than complimentary about those in his party who cared only for its 'independence': 'It's no good saying that although everyone else is playing football, we want to play hockey . . . In fact, we are engaged to play football.'[80] The Liberals had to get out of the mind-set of eternal opposition. Then, moving on to what he meant by realignment, Grimond said something very interesting: 'I've always fought against the view that the Liberal Party was in the centre, except in the sense that everyone is in the centre . . . Anyone who can squeeze between Roy Jenkins and Ted Heath is a very slim figure indeed.'[81] It was very rare indeed for Grimond to name possible allies from the other parties in this way, and it provides an early pointer for how his thinking would develop in the late 1960s and 1970s.

As Parliament went into recess in the summer of 1965, a by-election was held in the safe Conservative seat of Hove. Fighting for his deposit in what was then solidly Tory territory, the Liberal candidate described Grimond's behaviour in hinting at a Lib-Lab pact as 'one of the great political absurdities of our time'.[82] In seats such as Hove, the very suggestion was death on the doorstep. Grimond was not to be put off by this kind of broadside and, in the event, the Hove result was perfectly respectable. Although Grimond was still highly active as a political figure, however, all the stresses and strains of leadership were beginning to take a great toll. For all his fighting talk in public, Grimond was in fact beginning to intimate to family members and certain close colleagues that he had grown weary of his position and wanted to resign as leader. As he struggled to hold the ring in Parliament and came under increasing fire from within Liberal ranks, he was no longer enjoying himself and, as he had once told Herbert Kretzmer (later to become the successful translator into English of the musical Les Misérables): 'if politicians feel their life is something of a grind, or that they are misunderstood, all they have to do is give it up – there is no lack of aspirants, heaven knows!'[83]

Alastair Hetherington, the editor of the *Guardian,* was both a friend of Grimond and a staunch advocate of 'Lib-Labbery'. In the summer of 1965 he made it his business to get Grimond and Wilson talking. Shortly before the summer recess, he received a message from Harold Wilson informing him that he would indeed be having a private talk with Jo Grimond. Afterwards, Grimond informed Hetherington that his meeting with Wilson had been cordial and interesting, but that he did not expect anything to come of it. They had talked about the economic situation and, showing either professional optimism or a marked lack of frankness, Wilson had told Grimond that he thought the country was now over the worst of the crisis. Any discussion about the government's forthcoming legislative programme had been brief and very general in nature, although Wilson had sought to leave Grimond with the clear impression that it would be acceptable to the Liberals. Wilson had emphasised to Grimond that, in the light of the conversation that they were now having, the Liberal MPs would, of course, be welcome to talk to ministers at any time. As Grimond commented to Hetherington: 'we can do that anyway.'[84] All in all, Grimond was not impressed. This was not consultation in any meaningful sense, and he had seen no real evidence that Labour intended to provide a genuinely radical, reforming government. He concluded that Wilson's only thought in inviting him in for a chat was to assess the Liberals' intentions for his own purposes. Wilson, in turn, became more convinced than ever that Grimond could not deliver his party into any long-term arrangement. When Wilson told his cabinet colleagues about this meeting a few weeks later at Chequers, he claimed that he and Grimond had not met to discuss a pact, although the question had been briefly mentioned – and Grimond had, according to Richard Crossman's account, 'observed that there could be no question of a Lib-Lab pact'.[85] The Liberals would therefore continue to vote according to their consciences, division by division and issue by issue.

12

Had it not been for the prospect of an early general election, Jo Grimond would almost certainly have vacated the leadership of his party during the summer of 1965. As it was, he just had to soldier on. In August 1965 the Conservatives resolved their leadership problems. Edward Heath had impressed his colleagues enormously earlier in the year with his relentless and effective campaign against Labour's Finance Bill and, in August 1965, they rewarded him with the leadership after Alec Douglas Home's resignation and, for a brief time, the Tories took the lead in the opinion polls. When Heath's first act as Tory leader was to put down a censure motion in the House of Commons against the government, the Liberals put down a 'reasoned' amendment of their own, somewhat short of an outright denunciation of the government. It was not called. Both Grimond and Eric Lubbock would have liked to vote with Labour against the Conservatives' censure motion, but Peter Bessell demanded a special meeting of the parliamentary party, which took the opportunity to make its position clear. There had been enough Lib-Lab for now, and they agreed to abstain *en bloc*. Tony Benn would record in his diary at the end of that week his belief that 'there is a reasonable chance that the Liberals will abstain in crucial censure debates, giving us another year at our job.'[1] Although Grimond certainly used the opening and closing sections of his long and impressive speech to criticise the shortcomings of the Wilson government, he also explained why he could not bring himself to support a censure motion from the Conservatives. Grimond readily conceded that Heath must 'awaken some appreciation in Liberals', he was far from convinced that he could achieve the 'Herculean task' of changing the Conservative Party into a positive and radical force. One radical policy that Grimond now embraced, but which was too strong for the Tories, was his suggestion that 'there was a case last year . . . for making the £ float'.[2]

In the days that followed, the press became convinced that the Liberals were drifting away from Labour. Grimond was still waiting for any positive Labour response to his various initiatives, though his covert meeting with Wilson had more or less convinced him that none would be forthcoming, and he explained to one journalist that speculation at this stage was pointless: 'The Liberal Party will wait for the Queen's Speech at the opening of the new parliamentary session on November 9th before declaring how far it will support or oppose the Government.'[3] It was hardly surprising that, by the time he flew north in mid August to spend the summer in Orkney, Grimond's growing weariness was becoming obvious to all. Although everyone assumed that he would carry on as leader through the next election, Jeremy Thorpe and his close cabal were beginning to manoeuvre in advance of the vacancy at the top that they expected to occur, sooner rather than later. At that time, the franchise in any leadership election was still confined to the party's MPs and, through his work in the target seats, Thorpe thought himself ideally placed to ensure that a healthy proportion of the likely electorate would owe him a debt of gratitude. He was rarely subtle in his campaigning, sometimes even promising jobs to his colleagues.

On Thursday, 2nd September 1965, Labour's precarious majority was again threatened, this time by the sudden death of the Speaker, Harry Hylton-Foster. There are traditionally three non-voting positions in the House of Commons: the Speaker and two deputies. Hylton-Foster was a Conservative and, at the time of his death, he had one Conservative deputy and one Labour. The Conservative leadership let it be known at once that they would not allow any of their number to accept a vacant, non-voting position. They wanted to force Labour to fill whatever vacancy arose, which would have reduced their voting roster in the House of Commons by one more, cutting their majority to one. James Margach of the *Sunday Times* predicted that Labour would now start to treat the Liberals with rather more respect, and it became a natural priority for them to avoid putting before the House of Commons measures that would antagonise them. He reflected that, quite suddenly, 'at the rate political events are moving the country will soon have a Wilson Government but a Grimond-controlled Parliament . . . Mr Grimond can no longer be taken for granted . . . history is about to make his leadership – and not in the narrow partisan sense – the most crucial influence of all in an incredibly confused and nationally dangerous situation.'[4]

Margach was partially right. Harold Wilson too had apprehended that the key to this precarious situation was to be found amongst the Liberals, but not with Grimond himself. Grimond was infuriated to learn that Wilson had gone behind his back by approaching Roderic Bowen, the longest-serving Liberal MP, to see if he might be willing to accept one of the non-voting deputy speakerships. On 8th September Grimond summoned a special meeting of the Liberal MPs to discuss the affair. Eight of the ten MPs attended – Thorpe and Hooson were on holiday – and most shared the strongly held view of Grimond and Eric Lubbock that it made no sense whatsoever for the Liberals to fill any non-voting vacancy. At this meeting Roderic Bowen conceded that, if he were to accept one of the deputy speakerships, the Liberals might be accused of helping to keep Labour in power. But still he kept his own counsel on how he might respond to any firm offer. Grimond responded irritably that it would be 'unfortunate' if Bowen were to allow his personal ambition to override his responsibilities to his colleagues. He was sufficiently angered by the whole situation to kick over the traces in public. If there was indeed a problem, it was for Harold Wilson and the Labour whips to find a solution to it:

> During the past week I have been asked several times by the Press if I will 'nominate someone for the Speakership'. In my view it is not for anyone to 'nominate' candidates simply for party advantage. A Speaker or his deputy should be acceptable to the majority of the House . . . This does not mean that their election cannot be contested. It has been in the past. But it should be remembered that occupants of the chair are the servants of the House and so, indirectly, of the electorate . . . This is a matter on which carefully thought out proposals must come from the Government.[5]

Grimond's temper was soon provoked further. Peter Bessell, the mercurial Liberal MP for Bodmin, somehow formed the impression during the meeting that Grimond was trying to discourage Bowen from putting his name forward because he himself wanted to become Speaker. Bessell told the Labour MP George Thomas that he thought Grimond would accept an invitation to become Speaker and even Grimond's legendary sangfroid boiled over the following Sunday when, in response to a highly speculative newspaper article that morning, Bessell suggested on television that he (Grimond) might be a generally acceptable compromise candidate for the Speakership. He also claimed to have good reason for believing that he would accept. As the story gained wide currency, calls began to flood in to Pratap Chitnis, who was now in charge of the party's press operations. He felt sure instinctively that there was no substance to what was being said, but recognised that only a direct quotation from Grimond would calm the waters. Grimond reluctantly agreed to issue a terse statement, to the effect that the reports were 'complete nonsense', since he was 'too busy to become Speaker of the House of Commons because he is expecting to be asked to become Prime Minister of Greece'.[6] Bessell soon issued a contrite statement of his own, explaining that he had misinterpreted tittle-tattle as truth, and that his support for Jo Grimond continuing as leader of the party was beyond question. Later that week Grimond summoned another meeting of all Liberal MPs. David Steel recalls that he had never before seen Grimond so furious. The official line agreed at that meeting was that the Liberals would support the claims on the Speakership of the Labour deputy speaker, Horace King, who already enjoyed Conservative support. In the unlikely event of Roderic Bowen receiving support from the Labour side, however, the party would not stand in his way. They were not keen, however, on his taking up a deputy speakership. Bowen again played his cards extremely close to his chest at the meeting, especially when asked whether he might consider one of the deputy positions, which would help Labour whilst conferring no obvious benefits on the Liberals themselves. Nor was it clear what Bowen himself stood to gain: he would lose his vote in the House of Commons but, unlike the Speaker himself, would still be opposed by the other parties at the forthcoming general election.

The autumn conference season was expected to be the last before a general election, and Grimond knew that the party's trumpet must sound a certain note. He decided to make one last play for an arrangement with Harold Wilson. In the run-up to the conference, Labour unveiled its so-called 'National Plan' for the economy. Some commentators immediately took the view that, since the Liberals set such store by planning, Wilson had now rather shot their fox. At a press conference, Grimond dismissed such unworthy sentiments with Asquithian calm, observing that the 'plan' was 'simply the basis for possible action, the nature of which in most respects we do not know'.[7] It was in fact an intelligence report, containing a great deal of information about the economy, but offering up only the scantest hints of possible future policies. Grimond was also displeased that Wilson had given the Liberals absolutely no insight into what the forthcoming Queen's Speech might contain. In view of Labour's decline in the opinion polls, Grimond expected 'overtures' from Wilson in advance of the speech, but they never came. He had spent the summer travelling up and down the country and talking to people from all walks of life, which had left him with a strong impression that the voters were by no means as 'fed up' with the government as they were generally said to be. Two polls in mid September confirmed this, as Labour moved back into the lead. The Liberals were down at 8½ per cent in the September Gallup poll, and Grimond too had lost ground. Although Liberal voters still had a good impression of him, the proportion across the country thinking that he was doing a good job as party leader had fallen to 57 per cent, down from 65 per cent in May. Nonetheless, as in 1964, on his travels Grimond had found Liberal Party workers to be unexpectedly buoyant. They were confident of gaining several of the party's target seats, and he was urged from all sides to remain robust. On that basis, he felt that his position was stronger than most people realised.

As the party assembly gathered in Scarborough, there came news that Grimond would not only be giving the usual end-of-assembly leader's speech. He had asked to speak at the beginning of the assembly too, immediately after the opening address by the president, Nancy Seear. He had foreshadowed the assembly with a piece in the *Guardian* a few days before, writing that, although Liberals should 'judge this Government with sympathy', it would be 'dishonest and unpatriotic to go on supporting a Government in which we had no faith, just to keep out the Tories . . . the throwing of life-belts at the last moment to a sinking Government is not a job I would welcome.'[8] His purpose in seizing the initiative at the beginning of the assembly was simple: he wanted to make the point that he should be allowed to keep his options open. When he stood up to speak, Grimond had been left in no doubt about the mood of the meeting: Miss Seear had won rapturous applause for her warning that, after all its years of subsisting in the wilderness, 'isolated but undefiled', this was hardly the time for the party 'to go, in a Biblical phrase, a-whoring after foreign women – and I am not referring to the Common Market!'[9]

Grimond had arrived in Scarborough only at 4 a.m. that morning, after his plane had been grounded, but his robust twenty-one-minute speech swept the gathered delegates before it. Although he spoke with his customary aplomb, Grimond in fact said nothing new. He affirmed that he regarded the Liberals as 'a radical and progressive party and not a conservative party'[10] and what was really important was always to fight, in Parliament and out in the country, for Liberal policies and Liberal solutions to the real problems of the people. They had to keep their nerve in the days ahead, he warned: 'our teeth are in the real meat and our muscles are exerted in the real struggle for political power.'[11] He made no apology for raising the question of how the parties should deal with the difficulties that would arise if Labour were to lose its majority:

> British politics have been bedevilled all my lifetime by the love-hate relationship of the Liberal and Labour parties . . . it would have been utterly wrong not to have raised the question at least of a working partnership . . . If the Government should lose its majority, we cannot escape our share of the decision as to whether an election should be held or not. It is no good trying to find some halfway house, half keeping the Government in, and half putting them out. If the occasions on which we vote with the Tories are important, out a minority government must inevitably go.[12]

The rest of the conference went surprisingly smoothly. Delegates evidently took the point that there was little to be gained by calling for the Liberals to 'side' with anybody, or in speculating on whether or not the party's MPs should support measures that had not yet been unveiled. Many speakers were highly critical of the government, but there were no calls to bring it down in Parliament. The only disturbance of note was a U-turn on how the Liberals might behave towards the government's proposals for land reform. The MPs, and Eric Lubbock in particular, had originally believed that the Liberals should oppose any Bill. Once the assembly had convened, however, there was no mistaking the party's mood. The thrust of the government's proposals, the details of which were still not known, was to make life far harder, and more expensive, for land speculators. By the end of the week, after at least one midnight meeting chaired by Grimond himself, Eric Lubbock let it be known that it was '99 per cent certain' that the Liberals would not, in fact, vote to reject an entire Bill. Perhaps of more interest to political aficionados was the question of Roderic Bowen's whereabouts. His name had by now been widely canvassed in the press as a possibility for Speaker, and his absence spoke volumes. The rumour mill worked overtime: there was talk of a trip to Sweden, which was then said to have been cancelled. One delegate commented wryly: 'I expect he's been too busy negotiating.'

Grimond himself helped to provide another bizarre interlude at the conference. Jimmy Saville, of *Jim'll Fix It* fame, was in town and very much wanted to meet Grimond, whom he greatly admired. Grimond was seized by an immediate and powerful aversion to such a meeting and spent several hours dashing around the assembly, desperately eluding his admirer. What he could not avoid, however, was an impending contest for the job of party treasurer. Not least as a consequence of its relocation into expensive new offices in Smith Square, the party had an accumulated deficit of £70,000 and Jeremy Thorpe decided to challenge the incumbent treasurer, Sir Andrew Murray, a former Lord Provost of Edinburgh. To avoid too much damaging publicity, the contest was deferred until after the conference, but Thorpe won and, by drawing upon his legendary fund-raising skills, got the party more or less back on to the financial straight and narrow. Thorpe once told Trevor ('Jones the Vote') Jones: 'Give me dirty money and I will clean it.'[13] The price the party paid is still open to speculation, but Grimond at least once forbade Thorpe from accepting contributions from organisations whose objectives he regarded as being inconsistent with what the Liberal Party wished to achieve, narrowly preventing the acceptance of a donation from the right-wing think-tank Aims of Industry. According to Christopher Layton, he also turned down the offer of very large donations from a Canadian businessman who wanted the Liberals to propose the abolition of income tax.

In Grimond's second and closing speech to the Scarborough assembly, gone were the tension and occasional defensiveness of his opening address. Grimond now felt able to go on to the attack. 'I do not want the left to fail and fail again,'[14] he told the assembly. It was time for the left to get its act together, to demonstrate that it could govern effectively for all the people: 'again and again we have to break out new hope from the chrysalis of the dead past.'[15] His closing words were crafted to inspire: 'if we have to go into an election before I see you again, we shall go in with confidence, knowing that the sun is shining on us.'[16] Grimond deservedly got an overwhelmingly positive press after the conference. Anthony Howard observed 'it is only necessary to hear Jo Grimond to realise how far he is head and shoulders above the other party leaders as a platform speaker.'[17] Howard also observed something else that must have been only too apparent to those in Grimond's immediate circle. His impatience with his party was becoming obvious. As Howard pointed out, Grimond increasingly prefaced his public statements with a weary, if residually good-humoured, phrase such as 'I shall have to be careful or I shall get another sixty protesting letters from Liberals tomorrow morning'. He would also talk of 'pushing the Liberals into the sea and making them swim'. In Grimond's view, too many Liberals thought of themselves as the unique receptacle of some timeless, oracular conscience, and the party still had too many supposed Arks of the Covenant and far too few willing foot soldiers.

Despite the disappointment of his meeting with Wilson in the early summer, Grimond did ask his old friend David Astor to go as an unofficial emissary to Cecil King, whom he knew to be close to Wilson, to make a last bid for an understanding. The two men met on the very day of Grimond's second address at Scarborough, and Astor openly sought King's advice on how best to promote a pact between Labour and the Liberals. King suspected at once that Grimond was behind the approach, and warned that the Liberals were hopelessly naïve about Harold Wilson's *modus operandi*. In King's view, 'Grimond was far too glamorous a character for Wilson to want him in the Government.'[18] King also counselled the Liberals against believing that Wilson might ever concede a change in the electoral system. This pessimism was well placed. For too long, Grimond had innocently assumed that all Labour's leaders were just like Roy Jenkins: urbane, subtle, liberal-minded *bons viveurs* with a penchant for political realignment. In practice, the best that Grimond could hope for was what came to be known as the 'parallel lines' approach: the Liberals would remain in opposition, but Labour would ensure its own survival for as long as its leaders wished by establishing, through contacts both formal and informal, which measures would win Liberal support or acquiescence. Harold Wilson made this only too clear in his speech to Labour's conference the following week, which was an example *par excellence* of his gift for tailoring his words to his audience. There would be no formal arrangement, he said, but he hoped that 'others will feel able to support these measures which we put forward because we believe them to be in the national interest . . . If they can, we shall welcome their support – if they cannot, we shall have to go on without them.'[19] Although at face value this all sounded very measured and reasonable, those close to Grimond at that time recall how crestfallen he was after Wilson's speech. Although his initial public response to Wilson's rebuff was ostensibly good-natured – 'we know Mr Wilson must pretend to scoff'[20] – Grimond in fact felt that he had lost a good deal of face, along with his last opportunity to participate in government.

After a few days' extra consideration, Grimond became even more belligerent. 'The Labour Party conference was remarkable not for the dogs which did bark,' he observed, giving a pretty clear indication of where his enthusiasm for detective novels began, 'but for the dogs which did not.'[21] Although Liberals were, by and large, rather pleased that the word 'socialism' had been virtually banned at Blackpool, Grimond thought that certain excisions were 'disgusting': there was no mention of Europe, for example, and no indication that a reappraisal of Britain's role in the Far East might be on the cards. Nor did Labour evince any intention of introducing pro-competitive or modernising measures for industry. 'In the new session,' warned Grimond, 'it looks as though the Liberals may find themselves more often in disagreement with things the Government leave undone, than with those they do.'[22] On Wednesday, 20th October, Grimond had lunch with Woodrow Wyatt and Desmond Donnelly. They discussed how best to ensure that Wilson would drop any residual thought of nationalising steel. With Grimond's help, the two Labour MPs drafted a letter to Wilson setting out their continuing objections to an 'old-style' nationalisation of steel. Grimond agreed to drop it off at the House of Commons for delivery to No. 10. He made the mistake of delegating the task to a Liberal Party messenger, who was recognised when he delivered it, which Wilson mentioned in his polite but dismissive reply to Wyatt and Donnelly.

When the House of Commons resumed at the end of October, it soon transpired that Roderic Bowen had accepted Labour's offer of the deputy chairmanship of committees, bringing with it the deputy speakership of the Commons. His parliamentary colleagues were not impressed, and Grimond issued a terse statement: 'Mr Bowen's decision . . . is an entirely personal one . . . We naturally regret any diminution of our strength in the House of Commons, and we have made it clear that it is no part of the Liberal Party's responsibility to help the Government maintain its majority intact . . . Since, however, both other parties are anxious that Mr Bowen should fill this post, we accept the position.'[23] On 9th November 1965 the Wilson government released its planned schedule of legislation for the new session of Parliament. Nationalisation of the steel industry was a notable absentee. Grimond was more than happy to take the credit for any putative realignment, saying on BBC Television that the Liberals could 'claim to have weaned the Labour Party away from the more ridiculous doctrines of old-fashioned socialism – nationalisation is dropped'. Writing some years later, however, Wilson claimed that the position of the Liberals had played no part in his attitudes: he had 'never considered accepting [Grimond's] proposal for one moment . . . a nine-inch tail trying to wag a three-hundred-inch dog'.[24]

Wilson's unquestioned skills as a party manager notwithstanding, the steel issue did now threaten to create a larger schism within Labour's own ranks. Throughout 1965 around fifty Labour MPs had been implacably hostile to the US intervention in Vietnam, which Wilson felt unable to oppose. When Americans resumed their bombing of North Vietnam in early 1966, the number of rebels came closer to 100. One Labour left-winger, William Warbey, who had already resigned the Labour whip two months earlier, complained that Wilson's concessions to pro-American forces marked a 'vital and decisive step' towards 'the formation of a non-Socialist centre grouping of parties to carry out a non-Socialist policy'.[25] Speaking to the Oxford University Liberals a few days later, Grimond asked rhetorically why the Labour left didn't demonstrate the courage of their convictions by forcing an election and putting their case to the electorate. He described them (and this was criticism indeed) as 'the National Liberals of modern politics – they have sacrificed their independence and beliefs for a comfortable ride in a well-oiled machine. They talk bravely and achieve nothing.'[26]

Despite these defiant words, Grimond must have been a worried man. A by-election in Westminster the previous week had seen the Liberal vote fall from 11 per cent to an execrable 6.3 per cent. This was directly followed by a fall in share from 14.4 per cent to a pitiful 7.1 per cent in Erith and Crayford. The latter result was a particular disappointment, as Grimond had drawn an enthusiastic crowd of 200 people to a public meeting a week before polling day. The dreaded two-party 'squeeze' seemed to be on again, with worse to come, and Iain Macleod taunted Grimond with the thought that the voters were trying to teach him a lesson: namely that 'votes cast in 1964 were not cast for socialism, and he is heading for suicide if he believes he can trade the Liberal Party to Mr Wilson.'[27] Although Grimond conceded that a 'lack of political drive in the Liberal camp'[28] had contributed to the poor by-election results, he continued to receive positive intelligence from areas where the Liberals were strong. Although the total Liberal vote looked likely to fall (not least because the party was finding it hard to enlist candidates so soon after the previous election), Jeremy Thorpe convinced Grimond that the party nonetheless stood to gain seats. Both men came to believe that the tide that had swept the Highlands would now carry into England.

Grimond's piecemeal approach to policy continued in the new session. The single issue on which he always instinctively and vehemently took Labour's side against the Conservative Party was on Rhodesia. The new Prime Minister of Southern Rhodesia, Ian Smith, was threatening to issue a Unilateral Declaration of Independence (UDI) in protest at attempts by the British government to steer his country towards majority rule. 'If you behave as rebels,' was Grimond's view, 'there is no conceivable possibility other than that any government in Britain should react by expelling you from the Commonwealth and imposing sanctions against your major industries.'[29] In contrast, many Conservatives were sympathetic towards Smith and his white supporters, and Heath had to take great care to prevent his party splitting publicly and rancorously on this emotive question, prevaricating on how Britain should respond if Smith acted on his threat. Grimond thought the Conservative position almost as disgraceful as that of Smith, whom he described as a man who 'has been offered every reasonable concession to his extreme position', adding that 'the widest measure of support should be rallied behind the attitude of *our* Prime Minister' (author's emphasis).[30]

At a Liberal rally in Westminster, Grimond maintained this attack. There was a serious risk that the rule of law might break down entirely, he warned, particularly if the Smith government was serious about UDI. The Archbishop of Canterbury, Dr Ramsey, had recently warned that the British government might have to reimpose the rule of law by force, and Grimond endorsed what he had said. His fear was that the British government had still not faced up to all the implications of Smith issuing a UDI, which would, after all, be an illegal act. 'It would be direct defiance of the Crown,' declared Grimond. 'For much less, constitutions have been suspended and Governments in British territories dismissed – if Mr Smith committed such an illegal act, the Crown could not go on treating him as Prime Minister . . . It is no reason for not supporting the law that the lawbreaker is your cousin – and, terrible as would be a struggle with the Rhodesians, the black Rhodesians have their cousins too.'[31] When, less than a fortnight later, Smith did issue a UDI, Grimond told an audience in Oxford that Rhodesia could easily turn into another Suez – with Britain again falling into the trap of enduring a massive setback on the international stage, then trying to shrug it off. 'We are now on trial,' Grimond wrote. 'We should take the lead in pressing for a worldwide embargo on trade with Rhodesia.'[32] As the crisis went on, Grimond continued to offer qualified support to Wilson, emphasising that, although force must never be more than an instrument of last resort, it could not responsibly be ruled out. This was a marvellous and natural *cause célèbre* for Liberals, and Grimond was in no mood to compromise: 'What is now required is steps which will be short, sharp and decisive enough to topple Mr Smith and replace him in Rhodesia by a government prepared to broaden the franchise and guarantee the rights of the black Rhodesians.'[33] As on all matters, however, Grimond retained and exercised his right to be critical of the government, on one occasion reflecting that: 'it seems highly probable that, had we at once deployed a few troops or even police . . . the Rhodesians would not in fact have fired on them and the illegal rebellion might well have collapsed.'[34]

Everyone now expected an election early in 1966. Labour's lead in the opinion polls had consolidated and, if he went to the country, Wilson could be confident of winning a decent working majority. Grimond and his team now had to face the fact that they must put aside any thoughts of an arrangement with Labour. The London Liberals had passed a motion calling on the party leadership to re-establish the Liberals 'as an independent fighting force' and to 'warn the country that the Government has not relinquished its Socialist dogmas, and the present moderation of their policies is designed by them firstly to safeguard their present small majority and secondly to delude the electorate into returning them to power in the next Parliament with a majority large enough to enable them to put into operation a full Socialist programme'.[35] These sentiments chimed perfectly with Grimond's new strategic thinking, and formed the basis of the calls that he would make during the forthcoming campaign for a sizeable Liberal vote as the best means of putting a brake on socialism. He also decided to talk up the achievements of the Liberals in Parliament since the general election of 1964, and warn the voters that this moderating influence must not be lost. As Christmas 1965 approached, Grimond gave further indications of a hardening line towards Labour, in another interview with Mark Arnold Forster. He was now highly critical of the government, and warned that it was unlikely to be improved by winning a larger majority. Despite pressure from the Liberals, Wilson had failed to address the underlying problems facing Britain. Grimond didn't feel that No. 10 was 'any sort of power house or centre of planning – far too much is played off the cuff, too little is followed through'.[36] He also warned that Labour would certainly wish to return to steel nationalisation if it managed to obtain a large enough majority to get it through the House of Commons.

Jo Grimond had already confided a year before to one or two of his closest confidants that he was growing very weary of leading the party. He had tried, and failed, to resurrect the position of a deputy leader after Donald Wade's defeat at Huddersfield, and he still desperately missed Mark Bonham Carter alongside him in the Commons. The demands on him were inevitably taking a toll on his health. He was also, although few other people had really noticed, becoming aware of the first signs of deafness. Grimond told his mother-in-law that:

> I want before I reach old age to do a different political job . . . Since the day after I was first elected to Parliament I have been whip or leader, tied to an endless succession of decisions, week-end tours, turning up day after day at questions and making speeches in and out of the Commons on all sorts of subjects, about many of which I know little or nothing . . . I mentioned my desire for change a year ago. I was and am anxious to do it as conveniently as possible for the Party – but no one took much notice and I must press the matter . . . Unfortunately I do not believe it will be any easier after an election than it is now. Personally I think Jeremy (or indeed Eric) would do admirably. But admirable or not they will be no better in a year's time. While I look forward with dread to more repeat performances given by myself at rallies up and down the country – and with particular dread to the election itself . . . Nor does there seem to be any halfway house. The Liberal Party is like a clock which has got to be constantly wound up . . . So long as the party has a leader it expects him to be constantly available. There are so few people available that he must constantly tour, follow up ideas, prod committees etc . . . if only Mark or Frank or both were in the House of Commons things would be different. But they are not.[37]

When Lady Violet discussed Jo's disillusionment for the first time with Laura, a week later, she discovered that the two of them had exactly the same reaction – a combination of 'complete understanding & regret'.[38] In the run-up to Christmas 1965, Grimond discussed the matter with a small circle of close confidents including Frank Byers, Mark Bonham Carter and Thorpe.

Between Christmas and New Year, rumours of Grimond's growing desire to call it a day suddenly burst into the public domain. Undeterred, he issued a trenchant New Year message, attacking Labour and the Conservatives in equal measure. 'Much was excused the Labour Party in 1965,' he warned, 'because of the situation which they inherited from the Tories – these excuses cannot be continued into 1966.'[39] The rumours about Grimond's own intentions persisted, however, forcing him to issue a statement about the future. It was highly equivocal about what he might do if his own prediction of a substantial Labour victory did, in fact, come to pass: 'There is no reason for speculation about my leadership of the party, since I am definitely not going to retire before the next General Election, nor, if there is a close result, will I retire before the election after that . . . If, however, the next election produced a decisive majority, the matter might then be considered. But whatever I do about the leadership, I will continue to sit as the Member for Orkney and Shetland.'[40] It turned out that the reports and rumours in the media had been stimulated by a throwaway remark that Grimond had made at a meeting of the Liberal Party Committee a few weeks earlier, to the effect that he would not, of course, be leader of the party *in perpetuo*. After evidence emerged that the press reports had probably emanated from Jeremy Thorpe in the West Country, Thorpe issued a suitably grovelling statement that Grimond was 'a far better leader than we deserve'.[41] Emlyn Hooson, always less of a Grimond fan than most of his colleagues, was less sycophantic. The suggestion that the party would die without Grimond as its leader was 'nonsense', he said: 'the Liberal Party is a far greater institution than something based on, and surrounding, one man.'[42]

Grimond's statement did not silence the speculation and, in an interview with Colin Cross shortly afterwards, he tried to clarify his thinking further. His reflections on how he might behave if the next general election produced a 'decisive majority' had been misunderstood, he explained. He was talking about possibilities, not firm intentions: 'I do not know whether I will be fighting just one more general election as leader, or two or three more – you cannot look that far ahead in politics.'[43] He added for good measure: 'I enjoy leading the Liberal Party . . . I hope one day to hold office.'[44] The New Year saw the departure of Harry Cowie, who had transformed the Liberals' research operations and had arguably done more than anyone, apart from Grimond himself, to transform and modernise the party's policy agenda. This left a gap that could not be filled, and the whiff of a Grimond *Götterdämmerung* was unmistakable. He now expected a spring election, and thought it to be desirable – in order to resolve the big issues faced by the country – and was now determined that, given the chance, the Liberals would vote against Labour on any motion of confidence, 'barring an alliance'.

Another serious challenge now loomed, in the shape of a by-election at Hull North. In 1964 Labour had won the seat by just over 1,000 votes. The third-placed Liberal had polled a scarcely respectable 15.9 per cent. Although Grimond knew that the Liberals faced being badly squeezed at the by-election, still he went up to Hull to campaign and put on a brave face. Again he had to brush off questions about his own future, all of which distracted from his essential message. 'I am going on,' he proclaimed at a public meeting, echoing Hooson, presumably intentionally, by adding, 'Everyone who is over the age of six knows that people do retire . . . It is flattering, but also untrue, that I am for all time indispensable.'[45] Labour increased its majority to 5,000 votes. The Liberal vote fell by more than half, but the Conservatives' failure to improve upon their 1964 share of the vote left them the most shell-shocked. This created an entirely different political situation and, quite suddenly, everyone now felt certain that the dissolution of Parliament could only be a matter of weeks away. Fortunately, Grimond did not allow the tensions of this time to undermine his sense of humour. When MPs were discussing the appointment of a new Parliamentary Commissioner, one of the Ulster Unionists asked Wilson whether the post would be open to a woman. Wilson confirmed that it would be, and Grimond intervened with the thought that 'this is indeed a most suitable post for a woman, who is far better able to create an effective row than most men, and that if [the Prime Minister] would get in touch with me in confidence, I should be delighted to give him a short-list of suitable women.'[46]

At the beginning of February the Liberal MPs held a private pre-election conference near Oxford. They were told by Jeremy Thorpe that the party stood a realistic chance of making gains in ten constituencies and, at the end of their meeting, they issued a robust statement that the party was confident of making gains 'whenever the election comes'. On Tuesday, 22nd February, senior Liberals put the finishing touches to their manifesto and, less than a week later, Grimond delivered a vigorous speech to the Liberal Party Council, in which he turned most of his fire upon Labour's economic and industrial policy. Perhaps Harold Wilson wanted to call an election, he joked, because 'he has run out of paper on which to print his White Papers'.[47] He also warned that 'Labour will revert to socialism not because it believes in it, but because it was brought up on it – because it is too conservative to change its ideas and because it has a mistaken sense of values . . . It puts equality before enterprise . . . It suspects success.'[48] The gloves were now off in advance of the election declaration that was expected any day. 'What 18 months of Labour government should have taught the country,' he went on, 'is that the present Labour Government does not have any overriding, long-term aim to which Liberals can subscribe . . . it will gradually emasculate the free-enterprise system.'[49]

Two days later, Harold Wilson called a general election for 31st March. In the course of the campaign, as in 1964, Grimond would travel some 6,000 miles. Frank Byers would once again hold the fort in London and take charge of press conferences. Although attempts were made to 'theme' these, as showcases for individual party policies, it was Byers's witticisms about the other parties that earned most of the Liberals' limited coverage during the campaign, as the press evinced little interest in either the Liberals or their policies. During the campaign, Byers would host Sunday lunches at which senior party figures, including Grimond, would have the opportunity to discuss tactics. When he was based in London during the campaign, as Michael Meadowcroft recalls with pleasure, Grimond liked to start his days at a leisurely hour – claiming that 'I must read the papers, y'know.' In fact, he was an excellent host at home in Kew, regaling those members of his entourage who accompanied him there with anecdotes and plying them with white wine well into the small hours. Although Grimond was always reluctant to have a personal assistant, even he conceded that he needed one during an election campaign, in addition to his trusty secretary, Cate Fisher. Tim Beaumont, head of the party organisation, was charged with finding someone suitable. He enlisted Keith Wedmore, a lawyer in his mid thirties, who had stood as a Liberal candidate in 1964. When Beaumont interviewed Wedmore, he asked how much he knew about Liberal policy. 'I don't actually have much knowledge of Liberal policy,' admitted Wedmore. 'I just say what I think and then I usually find that it is Liberal policy.' Beaumont concluded at once that this man would suit Jo Grimond 'right down to the ground'.[50] Wedmore had never actually met Grimond, so Beaumont arranged for the two men to have a private chat. Shortly before the campaign began, Wedmore was summoned to Grimond's room in the House of Commons. He didn't really know what to expect and does not now recall whether or not Grimond said 'hello' as such, but does remember being taken aback when Grimond asked him, before he had even settled into a chair, 'Should we do a hatchet job on our opponents?' There followed a period of silence. Seeing that Wedmore had no answer to offer, Grimond moved on, after a pause, to another topic and never raised that question again. In Wedmore's own phrase, Grimond had 'taken his breath away'.[51]

Grimond may not have done a 'hatchet job' on Labour, but it is striking just how quickly he began to attack the record of the Wilson government as soon as it was clear that his overtures had been rejected once and for all, and an election was imminent. Grimond felt genuinely deflated and disappointed at Wilson's refusal to offer any kind of arrangement. Cecil King had been absolutely right: Grimond had never understood what kind of Prime Minister he was dealing with. Wilson's intention all along had been to hang on until he was confident of a handsome victory, and then to go to the polls. The Liberals were useful, up to a point, and no more. Grimond's talk of realignment, with a collapse of the existing party and electoral systems, then as now, was anathema to most Labour politicians. Grimond was also disappointed with Labour's policies. They had been too defensive and insufficiently radical; in their way, every bit as conservative as the Conservatives themselves had been. They had done nothing to address the drift of Britain, which to Grimond now seemed to be 'full of those characters so familiar in nineteenth-century Russian plays, who sit around moaning that they are not in Moscow, yet never buying a ticket there'.[52]

Speaking in Shetland on 4th March, Grimond effectively conceded the election, but tried to pull a victory of sorts out of the jaws of Wilson's impending triumph

> It seems likely that Labour will be returned,' he said. 'If this should happen it will be vital to have strong Liberal representation in the House of Commons . . . we are speaking up for ordinary people . . . We don't want to see everyone lose control over their own lives . . . We want devolution for Scotland and Wales and we want a proper scheme of regionalism . . . Labour have moved a bit in the right direction under our pressure but not enough.[53]

The following day he was offering up some unfashionably plain speaking on the economy and industry, warning that 'the chart of our economic illness shows a steady decline under both Parties . . . unless we work our machines harder and our labour force more effectively we shall not maintain our foreign trade, nor shall we make the wealth to give us the higher wages, better houses, more schools, roads, hospitals or pensions or enable us to give aid to other countries.'[54] The answer, he said, was to attack monopolies and to decentralise pay bargaining. Co-ownership should be spread through the private sector, and the lessons of efficiency must be transferred across the border into the public sector, locally and nationally: 'Re-cast the grants system to local authorities so that they are rewarded not penalised for economy in both expenditure and manpower . . . Introduce pay-as-you-go on motorways'.[55] Even though there were a few new and radical elements to all of this, Grimond found it harder than ever to disguise his own sense of *ennui* at going through the same old motions, in the same old halls, all over again for the umpteenth time.

Even Jo Grimond could derive some interest, however, from being drawn into a three-way squabble with Heath and Wilson about whether or not the three of them should participate in at least one televised debate during the campaign. Although the initiative for a head-to-head debate originally came from Heath, he was unwilling to accept Wilson's condition that Grimond should also take part. Jo Grimond naturally echoed the Prime Minister, agreeing that a two-way debate would be pointless and unfair or, as he put it, a case of 'Pinky and Perky'. Such a debate never took place. It still has not. Grimond was on television soon enough, in his own right. He was the first of the party leaders to be featured on BBC TV's *Election Forum* and, although he generally acquitted himself well, as he had in 1964, he was judged to have tripped at one fence. The Liberals were once again fielding candidates in only a minority of seats (311 out of 630), and Grimond was asked how he might vote 'if there was no Liberal candidate standing in your constituency – and if the Tory was Mr Heath and the Labour man Mr Wilson'. Understandably, in the face of such an obvious trap, Grimond had recourse to humour. 'That would be a terrible fate, I must say,' he chuckled. 'I should move my domicile – faced with this, it would be too much to bear.'[56] A few days later, to a predictable and sententious chorus of disapproval from the other parties, Grimond would suggest that Liberals in constituencies without a Liberal candidate should, if neither the Conservative nor the Labour candidate seemed to them acceptable, spoil their papers by writing 'Liberal' across them. Frank Byers would subsequently claim that this argument had been fully thought out in advance – publicity was like gold dust for the Liberals, and even bad publicity was better than none.

In the rest of his big television interview, Grimond was anything but facetious. His answers were a model of clarity, terseness and concision that Wilson and Heath found impossible to match. One question put to him by Robin Day he turned around brilliantly. The questioner wanted to know whether Grimond really wanted the UK to play a full part in the development of the EEC, with all the attendant commitments and implications – and, emphasised Day, the questioner wanted no prevarication, just a straight, one-word answer. 'Yes,' replied Grimond with a smile, leaving his interlocutor floundering. In the middle of the campaign, some other plain speaking got Grimond into trouble, when he came under attack after touching upon the policy that, in those far-off days, dared not speak its name: putting forward the blindingly obvious proposition that, if prices continued to rise faster in the UK than elsewhere, then it might be best to have a 'controlled devaluation'. The other parties became splendidly self-righteous at this point, with Jim Callaghan going so far as to claim that the American markets had been panicked by what Grimond had said. Grimond was prompted to explain that he had not called for a devaluation: 'I said the strength of the pound depended upon action, not words.'[57]

Ludovic Kennedy was put in charge of the party's three television broadcasts. He himself was the star of the first, in which he made a direct appeal to the voters to entrust to the Liberals the responsibility for preventing the imposition of nationalisation. This broadcast received the highest viewing figures ever for a political broadcast, over 12 million (more than 80 per cent of the potential audience at that time). Kennedy then introduced David Steel and Jeremy Thorpe in the second, and the plan was to have Grimond himself as the star of the final broadcast. As in 1964, Grimond undertook a heavy speaking schedule, travelling in a private plane accompanied by Cate Fisher, Keith Wedmore and a small group of journalists. The plane was always strewn with papers and, early in the tour, Wedmore did not endear himself to his colleagues by exploding a can of fizzy drink over them all. But it was not until Grimond toured the West Country on Friday, 11th March that things really went horribly wrong. Grimond's schedule was for ten meetings in only nine hours, a schedule inevitably vulnerable to even the tiniest hitch. When the team's aeroplane was delayed by forty minutes at London Airport, losing more time as the day dragged on, disaster beckoned. The unpressurised plane often flew very low, sometimes hitting patches of violent turbulence. On this occasion, trying to make up time, the pilot flew even below the usual cruising altitude and the journey was interspersed with the regular, violent jolts of air pockets. As Keith Wedmore and Cate Fisher made their peace with their Maker, Grimond calmly read the day's newspapers – though he did send Wedmore off later on in search of precautionary travel sickness pills. Michael Meadowcroft instructed Jeremy Thorpe's legendary agent, Lilian Prowse, to cancel Grimond's first meeting, at Chivenor. She said she would. Then, when Grimond and his small entourage landed there, they discovered a crowd of 500 people still awaiting them, forcing Grimond to stop and speak after all. A frozen crowd of 150 at Bideford was less fortunate, waiting for an hour only to discover that Grimond really wasn't coming, and Tony Lacey, the candidate for Mark Bonham Carter's old seat of Torrington, ended up hauling Grimond out of the Hotel Rodeo at Hetherleigh, where he found him gulping down soup and coffee.

Both Grimond and the Liberals took a particular interest in ensuring that the party's new bridgehead in Scotland was nurtured and, if possible, extended. A separate, shortened manifesto for Scotland was produced, rather cheekily claiming, 'it is no coincidence that since Liberals were elected for [the Highlands] we have seen the Highlands and Islands Development Board, more development of Dounreay and real financial aid to counter depopulation.'[58] This slim document also quoted some of the nice things that newspaper commentators had written about Grimond and his Scottish colleagues. On the second day of a two-day tour of north-east Scotland, Grimond returned to Johnshaven, the tiny fishing port where, in 1935, he had made his first ever election speech. By 21st March, Grimond had notched up around 3,000 miles, and gave a half-time press conference in London. He reported that he had found morale amongst Liberals not only higher than anyone had expected – it was appreciably higher than it had been in 1964. He was confident of gaining seats, though the only such seat that he would name was Colne Valley.

On Tuesday, 22nd March, Jo and Laura Grimond returned to Orkney and Shetland, braving rough seas in a tiny boat to visit the small southerly island of Flotta, where Grimond was in his element, chatting with local fishermen about lobsters. The following day, the couple went their different ways, Jo making his way to Lerwick in Shetland, while Laura took the campaign to the northernmost islands of Orkney, North Ronaldsay and Papa Westray. That evening the manager of the Shetland hotel where Grimond was staying had to give him a piece of news which Grimond would describe as 'an unforgettable personal tragedy to Laura and myself'.[59] Jo and Laura's eldest child, Andrew, had been found dead at his flat in Edinburgh by a cleaner, three days before his twenty-seventh birthday. He had been feeling out of sorts for several days, and had cancelled a visit to Peterhead to help the Liberal candidate there. Less widely known is the fact that he had also fallen victim, through no fault of his own, to a purge of staff at the newspaper where he had been working. It is impossible to imagine how great a blow this must have been. Although Andrew Grimond's health had never been robust, nothing could have prepared his family for this shattering news. Orkney and Shetland were afflicted with appalling weather when the news came, so Jo and Laura were not able to use the light plane that Grimond had been employing during the campaign. As Laura made her way to Kirkwall by sea, a posse of journalists gathered to pester her. Edwin Eunson enjoined two female supporters to wait with him at the pier head at Kirkwall. The dockers provided a shed where they could wait with their car, and in which Laura was able to take a call from her husband. They then took her to the Old Manse and, from there, to the airport outside Kirkwall to fly south. One of the group that met Laura recalls that she seemed strangely calm, although she took violently against a journalist from the *Telegraph*, who pursued her even after she had said that she had no comment to make. She was particularly incensed, since he had been caught without food on the boat with her in the northern isles, and she had given him half of her lunch.

As soon as he heard the news, Harold Wilson telephoned Liberal headquarters and asked if there was anything he could do. At his instigation, an RAF plane was made available to fly Grimond to Edinburgh, where he had to perform the sombre task of identifying his son's body at the police mortuary. The news broke in an uncontrolled fashion. Many people close to Grimond, from his daughter Grizelda to Pratap Chitnis, first learned the news from journalists. Chitnis telephoned Mark Bonham Carter who confirmed the worst. Grizelda had been helping Robert Oakeshott, a family friend, in his campaign at Darlington and a cub reporter, Paul Routledge, who was staying in the same hotel, had to tell her what had happened. Johnny Grimond, then aged nineteen, was uncontactable on a camping holiday in Italy. Jo and Grizelda went from the Edinburgh police headquarters to the home of Lord Wemyss, where Laura joined them later. All Grimond's public engagements were cancelled for the next three days. Both Jo and Laura greatly impressed those around them with their fortitude in the face of tragedy. Jo's indispensable secretary, Cate Fisher, who was with him in Shetland, said that he had been 'terribly upset, but he is taking it remarkably well'.[60] A private funeral was held on Saturday, 26th March at St Andrews, which would

have been Andrew's birthday, where Andrew was buried in the family plot
alongside his Grimond grandparents. No police statement was ever made
about the cause of death. Two days later, Jo Grimond rejoined the general
election campaign for its closing days.

The *Express*, which broke the story, claimed that Andrew Grimond was
'believed to have died from natural causes'.[61] The press in those days was too
restrained ever to publish the fact, but Andrew had not died from natural
causes. Without warning and after another bout of illness and depression, he
had taken his own life. It says a lot for both Grimond himself, and for the press,
that they thought so highly of him that, once the funeral had been reported,
the matter was never referred to again in the papers. Perhaps there is little to
be gained from speculating about why Andrew Grimond committed suicide,
but it was a particularly grievous blow, coming just when, as his father wrote
in his *Memoirs*, 'he seemed to be settling down in Edinburgh'.[62] Grimond
himself had always been grateful for the fact that he had been able to enjoy
the company of mature parents and older siblings, and reflected that Andrew's
serious and introverted nature might have been attributable, in part at least,
to the fact that he had been born when his parents were so young, and so
soon after they married: 'I fear Andrew suffered from being the eldest, partly
because parents get mellower as they get older but also because being the
eldest is apt to wear the nerves.'[63] Andrew Grimond's early life had been
complicated by the war, which broke out when he was only five months old,
and used to have 'an occasional black fit'. Although, as a very small child, he
had enjoyed the company of his young uncle, Raymond Bonham Carter, who
had played war games with him and taught him about planes and warships,
he saw comparatively little of his father in those critical years and, by force of
circumstances, spent a lot of time with his grandmother, Jo's mother, when the
family relocated to St Andrews. On her death she had left him a lot of money,
which explained why, when Andrew's will was published, his net assets were
in excess of £56,000, an immense amount in those days for someone of his
age. He had then become the only one of Jo and Laura Grimond's children to
be sent to a boarding preparatory school. When he was there, he sent a series
of plaintive letters to his parents which, years later and with the benefit of
hindsight, they could interpret as youthful 'cries for help'. When they visited
him just before his tenth birthday, they found him 'apparently reconciled, if
not devoted' to his school, and 'calmer than he used to be'.[64] As a naturally
sensitive child, Andrew Grimond had grown rather too serious, 'old before his
time', a problem which was apparently compounded by his tuberculosis.

After being sent down from Oxford, Andrew successful completed his
history course at London University, but his working career then also had a
false start. For a time he worked in a merchant bank in London, living in
Sloane Street, but the City lifestyle did not suit him and he soon resolved

to switch to journalism. His parents warned him that he might not take to such a stressful and highly competitive world, but his mind was made up. Close associates of Grimond who met Andrew towards the end of his short life remember him as a shadowy and insubstantial figure – quiet, reserved and almost ethereal. In the months before his death he had evidently felt isolated, and he had been profoundly affected by the suicide of one of his closest friends. The timing of his death seems highly indicative – during an election campaign as well as a few days before his birthday – and it is hard not to feel that he in some sense lived in the shadow of his father. Andrew had for a number of years demonstrated clear signs of mental illness – manic depression certainly, and perhaps even mild schizophrenia. The Grimonds were the victims of their time and their class. If they failed to recognise the full extent of their son's symptoms, or went into denial about them, that was very much the norm at the time, when so little was known about mental illness. The thought of having Andrew hospitalised must have been anathema to them, though he did for a time endure a variety of treatments, many of them crude and quite possibly counter-productive. They always did the best they could for him, helping him to organise his finances and find an acceptable and stable job. Even though Andrew had apparently attempted suicide before, and some of those close to him had been expecting the worst, this was still a terrible blow for which nothing could have prepared his close family.

Accounts differ of how Jo Grimond had changed, if at all, when he returned to London on Monday, 28th March. Michael Meadowcroft recalls that he seemed older; that when he returned to the campaign somehow everyone at Liberal HQ instinctively knew that the end of the Grimond era could now not be far distant. Keith Wedmore, who again worked closely with Grimond for the final few days of the campaign, remembers things rather differently: 'What fascinated me was that the shock did not appear to – was not allowed to – affect him at all, in anything he did or said, to the smallest extent. It might not have happened. I have never seen anything like it. Impressed? I'll say.'[65] When Wedmore saw Grimond for the first time after his return, he expressed his sympathies, they were acknowledged, and the subject was dropped. Grimond threw himself into what remained of the campaign with no falling-off in the admirable determination and energy that he had brought to its earlier stages. Just before he received the terrible news about Andrew, he had set out an even more aggressive stance in an article he signed off for the *Daily Mirror*:

> What does Mr Wilson stand for? Nelson in Plymouth? Baldwin on the telly? President Johnson in America? President de Gaulle in Europe? Never before have we had a leader of a so-called progressive party whose convictions are less apparent. Never has this country been faced with two bureaucrats such as Messrs. Wilson and Heath anxiously trimming their image to catch the electoral wind.[66]

Frank Byers had substituted for his leader in the party's final television broadcast of the campaign, and Grimond now determined to make up for that with a late burst of activity. He started his press conference in London with thanks for the messages of condolence he had received, and moved straight on to a statement on foreign policy. With Labour poised to win with an increased majority and the Conservative campaign 'crumbling', he warned solemnly, only a sizeable Liberal vote could bring an 'effective check upon some of the excesses and follies' that the socialists might otherwise visit upon the nation. At this election, it was a Conservative vote that would be 'wasted', while 'an effective vote is going to be a Liberal vote'. This was why 'the Liberals are the one party of which Labour is frightened – we compete for the same sort of people, and offer an alternative way forward.'[67] Grimond also retook the reins for the party's final national radio broadcast, in which he reinforced the same message: 'Give us a massive response on Thursday, and you will get attention to your real needs and an insurance against Socialist folly'.[68] On his way back to Orkney and Shetland, Grimond dropped in on West Aberdeenshire, where the Liberal candidate, James Davidson, was hopeful of victory. There was a slightly light-headed quality to Grimond's final press conference of the campaign, understandably in the circumstances. Reviewing the campaign, he accused Labour of 'the most appalling complacency' and the Conservatives of 'still fumbling for a policy to put before the electorate'.[69] After a final tour of his own constituency on election day, Grimond flew back to London for the results via Biggin Hill, and Orpington. He had been forced to cancel his visit to this talismanic constituency after Andrew's death, and made a last-minute appeal to local commuters as they returned home from work. It was, recalls Eric Lubbock, a tense occasion, though Grimond was 'very Roman' about his bereavement. He then went to Liberal headquarters and waited.

The 1966 general election result was even more of a mixed bag for the Liberals than that of 1964. The total Liberal vote receded by almost 800,000 and the party's share of the total poll fell from 11.2 per cent only eighteen months earlier to 8.6 per cent, partly because the number of Liberal candidates had fallen by fifty-four. Had it not been for three days of furious telephoning by Frank Byers, that figure could have been far worse. Roderic Bowen's erstwhile colleagues shed few tears for him as he ceded the one-time Liberal fortress of Cardigan to Labour, but more bitter blows came as George Mackie lost Archibald Sinclair's old seat of Caithness by sixty-four votes to a youthful Labour candidate, Robert Maclennan, and Christopher Layton once again narrowly missed out at Chippenham. David Steel held on in Roxburgh, and four other gains, including one by James Davidson in Aberdeenshire, meant that the party matched its previous post-war high of twelve MPs. England also made up some ground on Scotland, as seat targeting south of the border paid its first real dividends. Richard Wainwright was finally rewarded for his tireless efforts with a win at Colne Valley and there was a surprise gain at Cheadle, where Dr Alan Winstanley won what was described as an 'Orpington of the North'. John Pardoe also gained the long-time Liberal target of North Cornwall. The Liberals' parliamentary 'gene pool' was significantly boosted. There was, however, a downside to the ruthless targeting strategy: whereas, in 1964, the Liberals had come second in fifty-five constituencies, in 1966 this figure fell to only twenty-nine constituencies. On the basis of comparable seats, the Liberals did better than they had in any of the elections of the 1950s – but worse than in 1964, 1945 or any other election before that, losing some three-quarters of the support gained between 1959 and 1964. In only eight constituencies throughout Britain were the Liberals within 5,000 votes of victory. Worst of all, Labour was back, with a parliamentary majority of just under 100 seats.

Grimond went on agonising about whether the Liberals might have achieved more in the Parliament of 1964–6. In his *Memoirs* he contradicts himself on this within the space of a few pages. He writes that: 'I do not see that much could have been done between 1964 and 1966 . . . Certainly we had to make a showing in the political fray . . . We had to pretend that we could influence events . . . But our influence on immediate events was very limited.'[70] Then, writing about the steel issue he adds: 'Looking back, I now feel on this as on other issues I did not press the Liberal luck hard enough.'[71] He echoed this in an interview a few years later, saying that he might have exploited the Liberals' position better 'for publicity purposes . . . I think that, if I had been a different character possibly . . . I would have boosted the whole idea that the Liberal Party were on the verge of this enormous breakthrough.'[72] Could Grimond have pressed his luck better? There is no definitive or final answer, but it must never be forgotten that Wilson did, throughout the lifetime of the Parliament elected in October 1964, have a Labour majority in the House of Commons and could have won a vote of confidence at any time. On the question of steel alone was his ability to command a parliamentary majority in the slightest doubt. Even on steel, the two potential Labour rebels would probably never have done more than to abstain and, in the event, they were bought off very cheaply by meaningless reassurances from George Brown. Furthermore, there was at least one Tory seat vacant for most of the Parliament. At one stage in the winter of 1964–5, there were five of them vacant.

All these factors greatly strengthened Harold Wilson's hand *vis-à-vis* Grimond and the Liberals. As it was, by electing to play his cards more subtly, Grimond extracted a number of minor compromises and concessions, particularly during the period in the summer of 1965 when the polls briefly suggested that a general election would result in a Labour defeat, Wilson had felt obliged to take some heed of the Liberals' position. For the rest of the Parliament, however, Wilson wanted an election more than the Tories did.

Perhaps a nastier and more ambitious man than Grimond might have gambled more recklessly. In the final analysis, however, the Liberals' position was never as strong as all that and, like the Ulster Unionists in 1992–7, the Liberals did at least allow the government to govern – insofar as it wanted, or had the necessary will, to govern. The 1966 result left Grimond's realignment strategy in ruins. As the Conservative Party's main publication for the campaign put it: 'Only on the basis of a crumbling Labour Party could the Grimond strategy hope to succeed. The period of Labour power has demonstrated the hollowness of Liberal pretensions.'[73] This was intentionally brutal, but Grimond himself would have recognised the element of truth in it. As the subdued leader left Liberal headquarters in the small hours of 1st April 1966, William Wallace, who had been in charge of the 'night team' throughout the campaign, watched this solitary figure depart and knew with a sinking feeling that the Grimond era must be drawing to a close.

13

THE GENERAL SENSE of anticlimax after the general election of 1966 left Liberals feeling deflated and disappointed. For Jo Grimond it was devastating. Asked on television the day after the election whether he had thought again about his future as leader, he answered with a snappy and monosyllabic 'No'. In fact, the electorate had delivered precisely the scenario in which he had said that he might consider quitting and, in the wake of personal tragedy as well as political peradventure, his only thought was of doing precisely that. Although he had told a journalist very firmly during the campaign that he still enjoyed his politics and was not at all unhappy 'operating . . . on the political fringes',[1] Grimond now told Frank Byers that he had decided to call it a day. In response, Byers asked Grimond whether he had enjoyed being leader, to which Grimond replied, 'Yes, of course.' 'In that case,' retorted Byers, 'you can disenjoy the job for a bit longer.' Perhaps unwisely, Grimond accepted that he owed it to the party to hang on for a time. The new front-bench team needed to bed down, and he could afford to relax more in the job, now the days of knife-edge parliamentary votes were over. Furthermore, the scale of Wilson's majority meant that this government was likely to last for at least four years. Even if Grimond decided to quit after a year or so, his successor would still have plenty of time to find his feet before the country next went to the polls. Always possessed of a certain streak of vanity, Grimond must also have enjoyed being told that he was indispensable. Rumours broke out in the north of Scotland that Grimond was considering standing down as MP for Orkney and Shetland, to be replaced by anyone from Laura to George Mackie or Basil Wishart. The rumours were soon dismissed, as Grimond began to demonstrate unexpected spirit in his parliamentary activities.

Progress in Parliament, if not spectacular, was steady. Within a month of the election, Richard Wainwright was establishing himself as the full-time economics spokesman and James Davidson was speaking for the party on foreign affairs. Although this lifted a tremendous burden from Grimond's shoulders, the months after the election would offer few genuine openings. Grimond immediately set about intensifying his criticisms of the Wilson government. After Wilson's rebuff to him the previous autumn, Grimond had curtailed all attempts at bridge-building and, with the Liberals well and truly in opposition in the new Parliament, this harder line would continue.

For a time at least, Grimond rather enjoyed the new situation. Although the government's standing was never particularly high once the election was out of the way, Edward Heath and his Conservatives were making no significant impact. Unfortunately the Liberals still had problems with making interventions in the House of Commons, and in getting their own motions debated. Grimond was their sole Privy Counsellor, and he was kept especially busy during the early months of the new Parliament by his political backyard. The re-election of the Labour government had been greeted by a seamen's strike, threatening dire consequences for Orkney and Shetland. Although Grimond tried to prevail upon the seamen's union to allow one of the regular supply vessels to run, his hopes that the union leadership would behave reasonably were misplaced. The tourist trade was virtually wiped out at a stroke; fishermen, crofters and small farmers were badly hit; and piles of eggs were soon going bad at the dockside. Within three weeks, oil and gas shortages were beginning to bite. An emergency committee in Shetland had to ask grocers and the islands' only coal merchant to introduce rationing. By the time the strike came to an end, after seven weeks, many in the islands were on the edge of bankruptcy.

The Liberals' Organising Committee was in robust form in the wake of the election, quickly resolving 'that a clarion call was required to be approved by Mr Grimond, and if possible sent out in time for the May local elections'.[2] All the language in the minutes of that meeting is aggressive and forward-looking. This 'call-to-arms' atmosphere left both Grimond and the voters cold. The 1966 local elections were disappointing as, yet again, the party recorded a net loss compared with three years earlier. Grimond's colleagues now realised that he desperately needed a break. For the first time in three years, he was told, he should go and enjoy a really good holiday. It was not exactly a holiday, but Grimond decided to arrange a trip to China under the aegis of the *Observer* newspaper, for whom he would write several articles about his experiences, travelling with two journalists from the paper, its foreign editor Robert Stephens and its China specialist, Ian Adie. While he was waiting for his visa, Grimond received a *cri de coeur* from Lord Reay, a good friend of Lady Violet, who informed him that London Zoo was having problems with its panda-mating programme. If he had the chance, Reay asked, might Grimond consider visiting the panda specialists at Peking Zoo, who never replied to letters from London, in order to ask them a series of important questions? Quite what Grimond made of some of these questions is a matter for conjecture. Examples include: 'Do pandas sleep together at night?'; 'Do they continue to fight throughout the period they are together, or do they settle down?'; and 'Do the giant pandas mind being watched while they are copulating?'[3] One can only admire Grimond's intrepid willingness to undertake such a mission. In the event, the regime evidently decided that a

Liberal would not be much to their taste, and refused him a visa. A visit would not, in the clipped phraseology of the Communists, 'be opportune'.

Grimond had long reconciled himself to the long journey between London and Orkney, but the poor state of the air connections was always a source of irritation. The old BEA was running flights directly from London, but always claimed that they were uneconomic. Grimond's complaint, however, was that there were simply too few flights. When he tried to book a flight at the end of June 1966, he was told that no seats were available until August. He therefore applied to the House of Commons Fees Office for permission to fly instead via Copenhagen, a longer journey, at a cost of £111 as against £37 for the more direct flights. The redoubtable Sir Barnet Cox, Clerk of the House, was having none of it: travel warrants were issued only for the most direct routes available. When Grimond accepted an invitation to speak at the inauguration on Tuesday, 15th August of a new air service to Orkney, he no doubt hoped for some improvement. Then, just the day before, the Board of Trade announced that the new plane bought by Loganair for the route – the Britten-Norman Islander – would not be allowed to fly the route. A board spokesman announced that the Islander must obey the same approach-and-landing rules as a Boeing 707 – even though the British plane was specially designed to land safely at only 50 mph, as against a landing speed of 150 mph for the 707. Grimond was incensed and insisted that the ceremony should take place anyway, using it to launch an attack on the bureaucrats of Whitehall, who again had failed to understand the needs of the islands. Grimond then fired off an angry letter to Peter Jay, the President of the Board of Trade, asking why plans for the new service had been allowed to proceed so far, given that the planes would not be allowed to fly, and protesting about increases of between 20 and 50 per cent that BEA had just imposed on its fares to Orkney.

Throughout the summer of 1966 Grimond found himself addressing a series of large and unusually tense Liberal meetings, as the party picked over the bones of its election campaign. Although the Liberals had gained seats at the general election and virtually held their own in the local elections, there were still recriminations about why they had not done better. On Monday, 18th July 1966 there was a huge meeting at the House of Commons, to which members of the executive, the parliamentary party, peers, the Scottish party and the Candidates' Association were all invited. Gruffydd Evans, the chairman of the executive, launched a direct attack on the MPs for what he saw as their poor communications with the party membership out in the country, and for their poor attendance record at meetings of the executive. Grimond was not impressed, and 'pointed out that as far as he was concerned . . . the Executive were at fault for not specifically inviting any member to attend their meetings.'[4] As the months went by, he became more and more robust in his dealings with the party. Two days later, on 20th July, the latest economic crisis came to a head and the government was forced to introduce an emergency package including some painful cuts in public expenditure. In a televised response to this announcement, Grimond poured scorn on how 'this government that believes in planning' also changed its mind every week. The government's senior economic adviser, Alec Cairncross, recorded in his diary that he found this particular attack 'quite devastating'.[5] The following Saturday, 23rd July, Grimond made a major speech to the London Liberal Party and, in line with the changed parliamentary situation, his talk was no longer of coalescence with Labour. He was scathing about Wilson's performance as Prime Minister, and even about his shortcomings as a party manager. Labour had now been in government for almost two years, he said, so it could hardly blame all the nation's woes on the old Tory government. The problem was that Labour still had not come forward with solutions for the problems it had inherited. He particularly attacked Labour's deflationary measures: 'Last Wednesday might well have been christened "Saint Selwyn's Day" [in honour of Selwyn Lloyd, another deflationary chancellor]. We had the same old incantations – "backs to the walls", "Britain always does her best under attack", "a fair day's work at a fair day's pay" – cliché upon cliché, only just stopping short of the actual mention of Dunkirk.'

A week later, in a speech to the party council, Grimond satirised the government's wage freeze, describing it as a return to mediaeval economics: 'it takes a Labour Government to set us back 200 years'.[6] Two days later, Grimond took the fight to Labour in the House of Commons by leading a move to block the government's Family Provision Bill, as a gesture against its handling of its Prices and Incomes Bill. Following normal convention, the principle of that latter Bill had been discussed, and passed, by the House of Commons at second reading. Many now felt, however, that the government's subsequent amendments had been so radical that the nature of the Bill had been fundamentally changed. Grimond was doubly angry: not only had Labour refused to allow a full debate in the House on those fundamental changes to the Bill, but the committee of twenty-five MPs to which the Bill had been referred included not a single Liberal. He tabled a motion condemning the government's high-handedness and deploring the refusal of the Leader of the House 'either to arrange for a second-reading debate as to the principle of the drastic amendments now put down . . . and wholly unforeseen by the Prime Minister as recently as 20th July, or to refer these amendments to a committee of the whole house'.[7] Although this motion was quickly rebuffed and forgotten, the days when Grimond had talked optimistically of coalescence on the centre left did now seem far distant. In the late summer, Grimond gave voice to some of his less liberal instincts. The newspapers had been filled with sensationalised accounts of violent crimes, and Grimond's response must have startled some of his own supporters. Where necessary, he said, the police should now be armed in order to put down such disorder. The argument that this would breach some kind of sporting code in a 'game' between criminals and police 'typified British complacency at its worst'.[8] The party soon did its best to rein him in, at least to some degree, by requiring him to spearhead a national party campaign. At the meeting of the Executive Committee on 3rd September, Pratap Chitnis explained that 'Mr Grimond would be launching the Autumn Campaign in his speech at the Assembly and also opening a factory in Scotland . . . It was felt that Mr Grimond could not be asked to work actively for the campaign due to the pressure of his other work although it was certain that Mr Grimond would mention the campaign in all engagements to which he was at present committed.'[9]

As Liberals gathered in Brighton for their autumn assembly, they hoped and expected that Grimond would give some indication of his intentions with regard to the party leadership. Throughout the assembly, Liberals followed their leader in attacking the government on a broad front, departing totally from the atmosphere of the previous year. Generally they did so from a radical or progressive angle, significantly to the left of Labour. Grimond himself marked the first day of the assembly with an unusual demonstration of vehemence during an argument with a traffic warden, Mr Albert Allen. After spending the morning listening to speeches in the hall, the Grimonds found that a refuse collection vehicle had blocked in their car. When Laura sounded her horn in protest, Mr Allen counselled 'patience, patience, patience'. This did not have the desired effect. Allowing his natural disinclination towards bureaucrats to get the better of him, Grimond got out of the car and caused a scene, demanding that the dustcart be removed forthwith. The remainder of the week was rather less electrifying, with Grimond beginning each day by going through his mail with Cate Fisher: 'when I'm in the news at a conference, everyone thinks it is time to write to me about their dog.'[10] This conference marked the first significant outing of the new, radicalised Young Liberals – the so-called 'Red Guards' – and, observing the convention of neither speaking nor voting on resolutions, Grimond was forced to sit and watch as delegates flocked back to the old days of self-indulgence. The party executive had failed to draft a coherent resolution on the future of NATO, and the compromise that it put forward at the assembly was ignominiously referred back, leaving the party without a policy. This disaster had been waiting to happen: in July, Emlyn Hooson, James Davidson and Lord Gladwyn had caused considerable waves at a press conference by calling for NATO to be 'reformed and overhauled considerably', a line that was agreed by the Foreign Affairs Committee but never properly endorsed as official party policy, leading to considerable confusion.

In retaliation, Grimond unexpectedly intervened in a private session mid way through the assembly, rebuking both executive and delegates for their attempts at self-immolation. He urged those responsible for organising the conference to ensure that delegates had the opportunity to discuss clear and straightforward resolutions that were likely to command their support. He also warned the Young Liberals and their supporters to show more care, reminding them that they were under constant scrutiny from the media and, by implication, the public. Frank Byers too made a robust attack on their conduct, warning that delegates had given the party 'a bad image'. It was not only Young Liberals who were causing problems. An aggressive motion on Rhodesia had been drafted in Grimond's absence, proposing a policy 'not necessarily excluding the ultimate sanction of force' and, on that same day, Friday, 23rd September, Jeremy Thorpe spoke about Rhodesia and clearly suggested that Liberals would support a targeted bombing campaign against railways there, as the most effective way of stopping the flow of oil to the Smith regime. Grimond would not repudiate what his spokesman on Commonwealth affairs had said, but he evidently could not explain it either: 'This is not a statement of Liberal policy or a phrase used in a Liberal resolution and I am speculating, of course, as to what Jeremy Thorpe may have meant by it.'[11] Meanwhile the party establishment lost another major vote, when a hard-hitting motion on sterling, moved by Christopher Layton, was passed, while a more cautious amendment from the leadership was roundly defeated. The party accordingly embraced a policy of allowing the pound to float and, by implication, to depreciate. In 1966, this smacked of wild and dangerous radicalism.

Despite all of this party mismanagement, Grimond's closing speech to the assembly was a *tour de force*. He even brushed aside the embarrassment of being interrupted at the outset by a tape-recorded message, broadcast across his sound system, from a dissident but technologically adept delegate who wished to object to the party's policy towards Rhodesia, attacking the divisions in industry and warning of the growing gulf 'between the government and the governed'. He also made a point of reaffirming his, and the party's, support for NATO. On the EEC, he claimed credit for the Liberals as the first party to advocate membership, but warned that: 'much as I would regret it, it seems to me not wholly impossible that we may have missed our chance.'[12] Entirely in accordance with the mood, Grimond blamed Labour fairly and squarely for the nation's economic predicament: 'the Labour government having inherited a problem in 1964 have turned it into a disaster . . . They have spread a fear and insecurity among weekly wage earners which has not been present since the war'; instead of turning No. 10 into a 'power house', Harold Wilson now inhabited a 'conjurer's parlour'. In short, 'a Labour Government with a majority of three may have been bad, but it was nothing like so bad as a Labour government with a majority of a hundred.'[13] By any token, this was a vigorous and impressive performance. The timing was as acute as ever; and the jokes, if anything, were rather better. The ovation was lengthy and heartfelt. It must have seemed to most of those present that Grimond had come through his trial by fire, and was again leading them towards the sound of the gunfire. In fact, despite Grimond's claim in a broadcast during the week that he would remain as leader 'indefinitely', this was to be his assembly swansong.

After all the ambiguities of the previous couple of years, this assembly effectively re-established the Liberals as an independent force, radical yet also moderate. Publicity literature was produced featuring both Wilson and Heath, with the slogan 'Which twin is the Tory?', and plans were unveiled for a concentrated campaign during the autumn in twenty-nine constituencies where the Liberals claimed to have hopes of victory. Under the coordinating hand of Richard Holme, MPs and 'commando units' of Young Liberals would visit these seats, making a particularly determined attempt to win Labour votes. Grimond was going to play a very limited part in this campaign. He was about to embark upon a lengthy autumn trip to central and Eastern Europe with the sponsorship of the *Guardian*. He would spend most of October on his tour, in the company of the paper's German expert, Norman Crossland. Not only did the duration of this trip indicate that Grimond was continuing to treat his responsibilities as leader more lightly post-election; some of his comments on the trip suggested that his thinking was starting to drift in directions that might seem less than agreeable to many of his colleagues, as he let his sense of disillusionment with the British political system get the better of him.

In a broadcast from Poland (his first port of call), Grimond went rather further than he had to when he praised Poland as 'a land of great equality', adding for good measure that 'as a Liberal, he was particularly enthusiastic about this'.[14] For some listeners back home, this must have sounded somewhat ingenuous, with faint undertones of George Bernard Shaw and his notorious praises in the 1930s for the system in Stalin's USSR. Before leaving the UK, Grimond had signed off a letter to the 'Red Guards', praising the 'vigorous performance' of Young Liberals at Brighton and claiming that the 'idealism and enthusiasm of your movement reinforced my belief that with your help we can radically change the face of British politics'.[15] To his astonishment, many of his hosts seemed to know all about the Young Liberals. They were full of questions about them – and enthusiasm for them. In Romania, Grimond was more provocative, sending a message to a Bucharest newspaper, *Lumea*, in which he explained how 'as a Liberal I look forward to the day when more Romanians can travel from Romania to counter-balance the large number of tourists whom you entertain from abroad, and when the restrictions upon liberty are still further loosened . . . I make no secret of the fact that I believe there is too little expression of opinion and too little freedom of choice within the Marxist philosophies.'[16] That section of his comments, unsurprisingly, had been excised when his piece was published the following January. This mood music did not impress all of Grimond's followers back home, nor was it enough to convince the Soviet Prime Minister, Mr Kosygin, that he was worth meeting while he was in Moscow. On his return, Grimond produced a series of articles, some surprisingly sentimental, for the *Guardian*. He was very diplomatic, and it was only in his *Memoirs* that he revealed how often he had been embarrassed or appalled by what he had seen behind the Iron Curtain.

Many aspects of what he saw behind the Iron Curtain left Grimond feeling decidedly touched or even moved. He greatly preferred the 'old-world' kitsch of the National Hotel in Moscow to the corporate anonymity of American hotels, commenting favourably upon 'the mirror supported by cupids improbably dressed in tricorn hat and bands like a professor, the clock round which a satyr chases a nymph . . . the ormolu, the rams' heads on the beds'.[17] He prayed, vainly as it has turned out, that the Communist countries could liberalise gradually in their own way, rather than succumbing to the tawdry and brash trappings of corporate America: 'surely to go through all the traumatic experiences of the last fifty years only to succumb at last to Coca-Cola and chewing gum would be an end not wholly to be desired.'[18] In a later article in the series, Grimond played *advocatus diaboli*, flimsily concealing some of his own darker thoughts by portraying them as arguments that Communists might use if they wished to compare their system favourably with that in the West. For example, democracy could very reasonably be attacked for its increasing propensity to degenerate into 'a squalid wrangle in which each interest attempts to get as much as it can at the expense of the common good'.[19] He would prefer to see things move in the direction of Tito's Yugoslavia, whose partial shift to direct (and strictly intra-party) democracy he described as possibly 'one of the most fruitful developments of the modern world'.[20] A year later any spell seems to have been broken, as he attacked the 'folly' of those who believed that 'by getting onto backslapping terms with fascists or communists you can sway them your way while not even grasping, far less making any concessions to, their interests and philosophy'.[21] Although Grimond generally proved admirably resistant to Communist propaganda, however, he did occasionally repeat one or two of its myths, such as the assertion that 'East Germany is already one of the most powerful industrial countries of the world.'[22]

Although Grimond, as a consequence of his disaffection with British institutions, was by his usual standards fairly emollient about the Communist bloc in most of his *Guardian* articles, he did sign off by reiterating his abhorrence of 'the brutal view that individuals don't matter, the spying on private life, the infliction of vindictive and apparently purposeless punishments . . . [that] have not even any economic justification'.[23] In fairness to him, what had impressed Grimond was not the state-socialist system *per se*: he had been cheered by the early signs of its ultimate disintegration, and by the robustness of the human spirit that he observed. The routine bugging of foreign embassies he derided as 'a tiny monument to the barbarism of Communist methods',[24] and he mocked the very thought that anyone could plan every aspect of a country's existence. Revisiting Budapest after an interval of thirty years he was appalled by the sepulchral atmosphere in the national Parliament: 'Communism is like the plague, it leaves silence behind it.'[25] Like many other Western visitors, he was impressed at least by the forceful and independent nature of Romania's appalling President Ceausescu, and resorted to a gigantic safe when he wanted a private chat with the British ambassador in Bucharest, Leslie Glass, who regaled him with tales of strange initiation ceremonies on a hunting trip in the Carpathians with Ceaucescu and his entourage. But the trip did not consist entirely of anecdotes and *grand guignol*. Grimond was conscious-stricken when, during his stay in Romania, he received a letter from an old member of the long-outlawed Romanian social democratic party. The man wanted to enlist Grimond's support in leaving the country. Grimond was warned that this man had once written in similar terms to a British delegation, which had agreed to see him. The secret police had punished him by smashing his ankles. Grimond was advised to ignore the letter, which he did.

In the final analysis, this long trip confirmed Grimond's belief that Communism – or state socialism – was irredeemably evil: 'to describe it as bestial is to malign animals . . . how repulsive is the admiration for Communist countries shown by cosy intellectuals in the West who thrive in free societies.'[26] One of the worst features of all was the evident emergence of a privileged class, encompassing party officials, wealthy foreigners and a few corporate businessmen, manifested in the 'dollar-only' bars and restaurants to be found in most hotels, and the prevalence of backhanders, usually also in dollars. 'Russia,' wrote Grimond, 'is a tragedy – a tragedy which strikes the heart, but it is also corrupt and grubby with depravity unequalled by the worst of capitalism.'[27] Yet he could still not convince himself that all was well in the free world. On his return, in contrast with the hard-pressed, bleak lives of the victims of Communism, he was struck by 'the triviality of the press, the aimless extravagance, most of all, the extravagance of the public authorities . . . I remember even in 1968 being struck by the advertising forever stimulating appetites.'[28]

Shortly after Grimond's return from his trip around the European Communist bloc, the Oxford University Liberals enlisted the assistance of Mrs Eleanor Bone, one of Britain's leading white witches, who called on the traditional elements of earth, air, fire and water in order to 'strengthen the Liberal Party'. Mrs Bone and her Liberal cohorts chanted an ancient incantation and concentrated upon a mental image of Jo Grimond walking up the steps of No. 10. She later commented that: 'I cannot guarantee Mr Grimond's chances, but I have had a large number of successes with my spells in the past.'[29] In fact all that happened was that Jo and Laura Grimond went off on a trip to Israel, where he made a plea for the 'Great Powers' – including the USSR – to negotiate a security pact to cover the Middle East. Two days before the Grimonds arrived, the Israelis had launched a vigorous reprisal raid on a Jordanian village. As he had on his trip to the Warsaw Pact countries, Grimond perhaps erred on the side of defending his hosts, saying that Israel had had 'no choice' in the matter, in the face of sustained provocation from Jordan. When Grimond returned to the UK, it was not his foreign policy that he found coming under attack. In an article in the influential Liberal journal *New Outlook*, a member of the party executive by the name of Richard Lamb had fired a tremendous broadside at his growing caution on economic policy. Christopher Layton, Lamb reminded readers, had convinced the recent Liberal assembly that sterling should be floated and strong new powers against monopolistic practices be introduced, with the force of the criminal law behind them. Lamb then argued (with some justification) that these were precisely the kind of radical, liberal policies that Grimond and his advisers used to favour. Why, then, had they not come out vigorously in support of the Layton line? Grimond, Lamb argued, was also being excessively cautious towards some of the radical thinking on the social services that was being propounded by his advisers, Professor Michael Fogarty and the new MP for North Cornwall, John Pardoe. Grimond made no comment about this attack, but as he prided himself upon his radicalism, it must have stung him.

In November 1966 the Wilson government announced that it wanted to commence accession negotiations with the EEC. This was a stunning U-turn. In a major speech at the National Liberal Club on 12th November 1966, whilst welcoming the government's belated conversion to EEC entry, Grimond echoed previous speeches by warning that Wilson and his ministers would have to change their attitudes radically: 'We must remember that we are negotiating with friends and not enemies.' Writing in the *Sun* a few days later, Grimond confessed that he was none too impressed with Harold Wilson's timing: 'This is not the best time to open negotiations. Our financial position is weak . . . were we already in the European Community, that Community would have been immeasurably stronger. It would have been a Community of eleven or twelve instead of six.'[30] He also, rather belatedly, appeared to endorse Jeremy Thorpe's hawkish stance on Rhodesia: 'To my mind, our main object in Rhodesia should be our obligations to the Africans – I am more concerned about them than about constitutional legality.'[31]

It was announced at the end of November 1966 that the Liberal Party's fourteen-member Organising Committee was to be wound up, to be replaced by a more streamlined directorate, to improve coordination between MPs, peers and the party beyond Westminster. Although the committee had been reasonably effective it had never really overcome the initial suspicions directed against it. Day-to-day organisation was left in the hands of Pratap Chitnis, who had taken over from Tim Beaumont as head of the party's professional staff in July, after Beaumont's reversion to 'amateur status' in the wake of the general election. Perhaps the last straw for Grimond – or at least *a* last straw – then came with the Executive Committee meeting of 26th November 1966, at which it was suggested that 'Mr Grimond should be released from *some of his responsibilities* in the House of Commons in order to spend more time in the constituencies' and that 'a record containing the engagements and activities of all Liberal MPs should be kept.'[32] Although Frank Byers strongly opposed such developments, on the grounds that they would mean extra work and pressure for headquarters staff, after discussion it was agreed that: 'at its January meeting the Executive should receive a diary of Mr Grimond's commitments for the first three months of next year.' Grimond's engagements diary reveals that he in fact resolved to spend the remainder of 1966 concentrating on social occasions – mainly lunches and dinners with friends, old colleagues and family – and on a small number of events held by younger members of the party, usually in the universities.

At least one of those social occasions also had a serious political purpose. Around this time, Grimond once listed to the *Guardian* journalist Edward Greenfield all the leading figures whom he wished to see together in the new progressive party that he envisaged. 'Ah, Jo,' responded Greenfield, 'you just want all the nice people inside it, and all the nasty people outside.'[33] Several of those 'nice' people were Conservatives. Grimond had a high regard for a number of senior Tories, notably Rab Butler whose liberal social instincts appealed to him. What he really wanted was a new party that could appeal to everyone who held moderate but radical, broadly liberal views. After the 1966 general election, Grimond hosted a dinner at Kew for a small cabal of those who, in his opinion, might be sympathetic. Butler was there, as was Roy Jenkins, and the pro-European journalist William Rees-Mogg was also invited (in a private and personal capacity). Grimond explained how he foresaw a new radical coalition coming into being, uniting initially around support for British accession to, and ultimately leadership of, a European Community that would in time unite politically. Grimond subsequently told Rees-Mogg that Rab Butler had put this argument to Ted Heath, who at least initially had shown some interest. Although nothing concrete ever came of this, talk of realignment did continue, and Jo Grimond was never far away from it. He was peripherally involved in a short-lived project called the Open Group, consisting largely of pro-European Labour and ex-Labour figures, and he had further discussions with parliamentary colleagues from the Labour and Conservative parties who shared his broad thinking about a grand alliance of the radical centre. The post-Grimond Liberal Party, however, would show little interest in such concepts.

Although Grimond had come unscathed through the 1966 party assembly, he was conscious that it had marked the tenth anniversary of his taking over the leadership from Clement Davies. He had reached his self-imposed deadline and, after many long talks with Laura, he resolved that it was indeed time to 'get out'. For a time he told no one else in the party of his intentions, but his reluctance to engage fully in discussions about future campaigns was all too apparent. The new LPO press officer, Mike Steele, protested that the leader's frustrating and lethargic behaviour was beginning to make his own position intolerable, and even had to be reprimanded by Pratap Chitnis in November 1966 for machinating against Grimond's leadership. Yet even such Grimond devotees as Chitnis and Tim Beaumont did now recognise that a very obvious 'leadership issue' was beginning to emerge. On Saturday, 10th December 1966 a new draft constitution for the party, prepared under Tim Beaumont's aegis, was put to the Liberal Party executive. It was received coolly, in particular because it appeared to threaten an emasculation of the party assembly. Debate on this draft was adjourned until January, giving members more time to ponder the merits or otherwise of change, and for learned documents to be circulated amongst them on the subject. This gathering storm must have added another unwelcome burden to the leader's life. Three days later, the new Political Directorate (successor to the Organising Committee) met for the first time, discussing a possible spring campaign centred on the qualities of the party leader. At the end of that meeting, Frank Byers warned Tim Beaumont privately not to devote too much of his time and energy to planning such a campaign: Grimond had now resolved to quit when Parliament rose for Christmas. Byers made one last attempt to dissuade Grimond from quitting, but succeeded only in getting him to defer his resignation slightly, pointing out that calling it a day at the beginning of a recess would inevitably open up wounds within the party, as possible leadership candidates took the opportunity to lobby for support. The new leader would be chosen only by the twelve MPs, after all, so there was no need for a long campaign. It should be as short as possible. Grimond reluctantly agreed to hang on until January – but no longer. Now a successor had to be found. Grimond's own choice was clear: he would support Jeremy Thorpe.

A number of senior Liberals (including Frank Byers, Tim Beaumont, Pratap Chitnis and Michael Meadowcroft) were less convinced than Grimond was about the merits of Jeremy Thorpe as a potential leader. They knew something of the allegations of homosexual activity that dogged him and, more importantly, they believed that he lacked both political substance and political judgement. The problem was, how to find a wholly plausible candidate to run against him. Eric Lubbock was steady and reliable, but lacked

Thorpe's charisma and showmanship; Emlyn Hooson was too right-wing for most people's tastes; and Richard Wainwright had come into the House of Commons only nine months before. Wainwright was their preferred choice, but he could not be talked into running. This left the anti-Thorpe caucus clutching at straws, lukewarmly supporting the claims of Eric Lubbock, now defending a wafer-thin majority in Orpington. As well as underestimating the extent of his support within the parliamentary party, Thorpe's opponents failed to appreciate how strongly the Grimond family would endorse his claims on the leadership. Although Grimond certainly recognised some of Thorpe's flaws, and had apparently been given indications by the security services that Thorpe might present problems as leader, he greatly admired his energy and flair, and felt too that the party had built up Thorpe as his heir-apparent. On that basis, it would, in his view, be patently unfair for the party to deprive him of the prize.

Richard Wainwright had once found himself confronted in the House of Commons by a young man who claimed to have had a sexual relationship with Thorpe. When Wainwright tried to warn Grimond that his chosen successor might have some serious skeletons in his closet, he was rebuffed. 'There are some people who think Jeremy is homosexual,' conceded Grimond tersely, 'but that's nothing to do with me.'[34] Thus ended the conversation. Some years later he explained that Thorpe had seemed to him to be the only possible candidate with the ability to do what any Liberal leader had to do: 'Keeping the Liberal ball in the air by different jets of water – otherwise the whole thing was apt to collapse'.[35] In the same interview he conceded that: 'of course, if I had known what was going to happen, I would no doubt have taken a different view.' Laura Grimond too was an admirer of Thorpe, and in particular of his more dangerous and risk-taking qualities. She had once joked to Harry Cowie that he would 'either end up as Prime Minister or in prison'. In mid December, Beaumont and Byers discussed the future with Laura over lunch, and attempted to lobby her on behalf of Wainwright. They soon realised that she could not be swayed. By Christmas 1966, Richard Holme too knew of Grimond's intention to resign, and joined Pratap Chitnis in making a doomed last-ditch attempt to dissuade him.

In his *Memoirs* Grimond wrote with obvious feeling about the sense of weariness and *ennui* from which he was now suffering:

> By 1967 I had been leader of the Liberal Party for ten years. The Tory and Labour parties go in and out of office . . . for the Liberal Leader there is no such relief. I found myself staring at the same grey boards in the same town halls. At General Elections when politicians must repeat the same speeches over and over again, by the end of the campaign I would listen to myself in a detached way, silently commenting that we were about to have this passage or that. I now caught myself indulging in the same trick even between elections. I found myself constantly 'striving' to obtain something or other. It was time to be gone.[36]

Grimond decided that he would renounce the leadership of the Liberal Party on Tuesday, 17th January 1967. More strictly, he would announce that he intended to hand over the reins of the parliamentary party. After the Christmas recess, Grimond told both Eric Lubbock and George Mackie of his intentions. Mackie called a meeting of the Scottish MPs to discuss how to proceed and, under the influence of Russell Johnston, who was a close friend and ally of Emlyn Hooson, Mackie advised his colleagues to support Hooson. Eric Lubbock said at first that, as chief whip, his responsibility now was to organise the election, not participate in it. Apparently Grimond, in his formal letter to him, had told Lubbock that he regarded Thorpe as having a 'certain claim' on the leadership. In the event this did not deter Lubbock from entering the race.

The weekend before the appointed date, David and Judy Steel and their infant son Graeme were staying with the Grimonds at the Old Manse. Before they set off to a dinner that Steel was due to address on his behalf, Grimond invited the younger man into his study for a private word. He told Steel that he must not indulge in any embarrassing eulogies about his leadership when he spoke, because he was going to quit as leader in a few days' time. Grimond had brought Steel into politics, and this was the younger man's first visit to Orkney and Shetland as an MP. It is easy to imagine how shocked, mortified even, he must have felt at that moment. Grimond recorded that Steel initially reacted with 'Asquithian calm', having realised at once that he was being informed, not consulted. Had the good people of Orkney known about this bombshell, they might have thought more kindly of Steel as he struggled through his speech to them. During the remainder of the weekend, Steel and Grimond discussed the future of the leadership. They agreed that Jeremy Thorpe was the obvious choice – he was radical, fluent and charismatic. 'It didn't seem that anyone else was a natural contender,' recalled Steel some years later, 'although we didn't know at that stage who would actually stand.'[37] Grimond left for London on the Monday, while Steel remained in Scotland, fulfilling a number of political engagements with a heavy heart.

In deference to fears that a protracted campaign for the leadership would split the party not only over who should be chosen, but also over the electoral process itself, a meeting of the parliamentary party on the day of Grimond's resignation agreed that it would elect a new leader the following day. Donald Wade, a suitable Caesar's wife for these purposes, was volunteered as the returning officer. In his resignation statement, Grimond assured his constituents that he hoped to represent them 'for many more years', and his many admirers and supporters across the country that he intended to remain as politically active as ever. He was no more interested in going to the Lords than he had been in becoming Speaker eighteen months earlier. At the impromptu press conference that he called to explain his intentions, Grimond conceded that it was 'certainly a sad occasion, but it is not a funeral – I have no intention of burying myself'.[38] He also explained that he had not left because of any disagreements with, or pressure from, his parliamentary colleagues, and expressed his confident belief that 'the party will well be able to supply a new leader'.[39] The general reaction was one of genuine surprise at Grimond's retirement. One newspaper speculated that Grimond had resigned from the leadership 'apparently for no other reason than that he was getting bored with the job'.[40] There was more than a hint of truth to this suggestion and, on television that evening, Grimond looked and sounded very disillusioned as he admitted that he was not pleased with his record as leader: he should, he said, have been more ruthless and less bogged down in internal party matters.[41] That evening the diplomat Nicholas Henderson had dinner with Grimond and Mark Bonham Carter, and asked him why he had quit. Grimond replied, 'You have no idea of the difficulties, not to say the exhaustion, that come with having to formulate a policy on everything from dog licences to atomic bombs at a minute's notice,' he opined. Thirty years later, Henderson still vividly recalled Grimond's sense of relief that evening.[42]

Jeremy Thorpe was well prepared. He was confident that he enjoyed crucial support from Jo Grimond and David Steel, plus the votes of his fellow MPs from the West Country, John Pardoe and Peter Bessell. Most of his colleagues knew only of rumours that there were allegations against him and most of those, like Grimond, were convinced by Thorpe's own account of events, that he had gone to the police after an attempt had been made to blackmail him. In his *Memoirs*, written after 'Rinkagate' but before the Thorpe trial, Grimond wrote: 'the Parliamentary Party elected Jeremy Thorpe to succeed me, with my whole-hearted encouragement.'[43] This was not quite true: Thorpe won six votes out of twelve (one of them Grimond's) against three each for Lubbock and Hooson. Peter Bessell went to see Grimond on the morning of the ballot to ask him whether he would reconsider his decision to quit. When Grimond said that his mind was made up, Bessell asked him to confirm that he would be voting for Thorpe, which he did. Although Bessell, in his peculiar way, was close to Thorpe, he later claimed that it was Grimond's firm, if lofty, endorsement that finally convinced him to vote for Thorpe. The other crucial vote was that of James Davidson, who had been prevailed upon to support Thorpe by Steel and Thorpe himself in the small hours of the morning before the vote. The die was cast. The fears of Beaumont and Chitnis had been justified: in the absence of any credible alternative, Thorpe was the victor. He moved into Grimond's shabby office and immediately arranged to have it completely redecorated. 'Oh,' said Grimond when he first saw the redecorated room, 'you have a new carpet.' 'Well yes,' replied Thorpe, 'there was a hole in the other one – people could trip over it.' 'Oh,' responded his predecessor, nonplussed and unimpressed.[44]

There was an almighty row in the party generally about the handling of this process. Members felt that they had not only lost their major asset overnight, but they had also been bounced into accepting a controversial successor without the slightest consultation. Two senior party figures, Gruffydd Evans and Roger Cuss, publicly condemned the process. In private Jo Grimond indicated that, although he rather sympathised with them, the matter had rapidly been taken out of his hands because those whom he had felt able to consult about the matter had all agreed that a swift hand-over would be in the best interests of the party. Just one day after he resigned, on 18th January 1967, Grimond attended a meeting of the party's Political Directorate. Whoever wrote the minutes did not attempt to disguise the tension of the occasion. The group did not attempt to conceal its collective displeasure at both the abrupt manner of Grimond's departure and the undemocratic method employed in choosing his successor. Frank Byers recorded his view that 'since the Parliamentary Party was not only expected to elect a Leader of themselves in Parliament, but for the whole Party, the Party had a right to some form of consultation'.[45] The meeting agreed with Byers, and requested that the Constitutional Review Committee look at reforming the procedure. Jeremy Thorpe arrived late, so his brittle ego was not forced to endure this onslaught. When he did arrive, he recorded his 'overwhelming sadness' at the retirement of his predecessor, and his view that no one could 'ever express adequately the gratitude the party owed to Mr Grimond or the affection in which he was held'.[46]

Grimond now set about rebuilding his life, first essaying his thoughts in a piece that he probably penned before the world knew of his intentions, or else within a few hours of stepping down:

> I shall miss it. 'Leader of the Liberal Party' is an honourable title and I shall also miss much that goes with it. There has been a constant thought at my elbow: Why not go on then? Another year will do no harm. No one is pressing you to go . . . but I am sure I am right to go now. At 53 I am still young enough to try something else in politics . . . I want to recharge my political batteries on some political issues . . . I have taken a gamble. I have given up a secure platform and position to find a new one. But to settle down to being perpetual leader of the smaller opposition party means ultimately that you sacrifice some freedom of thought, some opportunity of influence, for the trappings without the reality of power . . . I may have gone too early – but better that than too late'.[47]

Grimond's first action now was to curtail his parliamentary duties radically. Thorpe discussed with him what he might wish to do in future and it was agreed that Grimond would have 'general oversight' – which is to say, semi-official *carte blanche* – with regard to the areas of policy that most interested him, namely defence, foreign affairs and regionalism. The Liberals had at least one other spokesman on each topic, and Grimond certainly took advantage of the rather larger Liberal parliamentary party to step back from the more mundane and routine duties, trawling around for new opportunities outside the confines of politics. He continued to spend one or two weekends a month in the islands, while Cate Fisher too ensured that constituents were as well looked after as before. Grimond's sense of disaffection with British political institutions may have begun as a slightly bored affectation. Now, however, it began to harden into a way of life, as Grimond's extra-parliamentary commitments began to predominate in what continued to be a remarkably full diary. After Grimond stepped down as party leader, Cate Fisher was moved across the road from the Commons, to a building in Bridge Street. If he needed to dictate something in a hurry, he would call over to Miss Fisher and they would meet halfway, on the Embankment. Completely oblivious to the crowds milling around him – many of whom must have recognised him – Grimond would dictate letters or speeches, out in the street.

For several months afterwards, Grimond alternated between gloom about the country's prospects, and relief at the fact that, freed from the shackles of leadership, he could now spread his wings politically. Within two weeks of quitting, he was in fine and outspoken form at a Ditchley weekend conference on Europe, bemoaning the unwillingness of the major parties to discuss openly the political ramifications of accession to the EEC. At the party assembly at Blackpool, Grimond's entry to the hall was brilliantly timed. Coming at the end of a rancorous debate on defence, it dissipated all ill feeling at a stroke, as delegates stood to cheer their hero. Although Jo did not address the delegates, Laura did, making a splendid speech and earning a heartfelt standing ovation. Her husband commented wryly that he had never made one better. After that brief appearance, Grimond in a sense went full circle, by making a long trip to the United States, just as he had in 1956 upon his accession as leader. In November he visited Colombia and Mexico to spread the gospel of liberalism, under the aegis of Germany's Friedrich-Naumann Stiftung, also fitting in a brief stopover in Panama.

In Parliament, although there were fewer big set-piece contributions from Grimond, he still played a major role in the Scottish Committees of the House. Not only did this help keep his mind off his reduced status; it also gave him a fresh taste of, and for, the engine room of the legislative process. When the Labour government's Water Bill of 1966–7 first came before the Scottish Grand Committee, Grimond leaped to the defence of the water authorities in Orkney and Shetland, mocking the Labour government's plan to amalgamate services with those on the mainland, and demonstrating surprising technical mastery. 'Is it envisaged,' he asked, 'that engineers or supplies will be shifted from Wick to Shetland via Thurso, Kirkwall and Lerwick? If so, it will not only be costly but will make the donkey tracks in the Hebrides look like main roads.'[48] The proposal to locate the islands' water provision in an office in Wick seemed to Grimond 'a nonsense of bureaucracy and uniformity gone mad . . . Is a gentleman to be sent from Wick to visit Unst and Yell when anything goes wrong, carrying a washer in his waistcoat pocket? [*Laughter*].'[49] Less than two weeks after relinquishing his party's leadership, Grimond found that he still had battles to fight, not least against the march of insensitive bureaucracy.

Grimond, unusually for an elder statesman, continued the battle by leading for the Liberals on the Standing Committee scrutinising that Water Bill, which kept him occupied for two days a week during February and March 1967. His hearing difficulties resulted in one surreal exchange when the Minister of State, Dick Mabon, mentioned a former MP who had been born in Vancouver and, thanks to the naturally high levels of fluoride in the water there, still had perfect teeth at the age of sixty. For some reason, Grimond thought that Mabon was talking about him and denied vehemently that he had been born in Vancouver! On a more serious note, after these long sessions, Grimond reflected bitterly on how the government had refused to take account of his concerns: 'The Government find it inconvenient to make alterations in their original propositions in the Bill . . . All the discussions about what can be done are not centred round any benefit accruing to the community, but about Government convenience.'[50] It was not only with regard to water supplies that Grimond felt that the particular problems of the islands were given insufficient weight and understanding. He had been an early advocate of a Highlands and Islands Development Board, but now perceived the Labour Party gradually packing it not with business people – 'the type of young men, commercially minded, really knowledgeable and professional men whom I would like to see on the Board'[51] – but with retired civil servants and ambassadors, in Grimond's view admirable in their way, but completely out of place. Again he detected the tentacles of bureaucracy about its dastardly work.

There were even more bitter controversies in the world of Scottish politics that demanded Grimond's attentions. In March 1966, having gained it in 1964, Labour narrowly held the parliamentary constituency of Glasgow Pollok against the Conservatives in a straight fight, winning just over 52 per cent of the vote. At a by-election a year later, the Conservatives won the seat back, despite their share of the vote falling from 48 per cent to only 37 per cent, because the Labour vote had fallen by over 20 per cent. The cause was an intervention by the Scottish Nationalists, who won 28.2 per cent of the votes cast. Although their candidate had come third, with this result the Nationalists shook the Scottish political establishment to its core. On the same day Plaid Cymru ran a good second to Labour in Rhondda West. Despite a supporting visit from Grimond during the campaign (sound-relayed live to a Liberal meeting at the Albert Hall), the Liberal candidate at Pollok only narrowly beat the Communist into last place, with a miserable 1.9 per cent of the votes cast. In the wake of Pollok, Grimond penned an article in which he was highly critical of the Nationalists:

> The Scottish Nationalist Party expound nationalism in 19th-century nation-state terms. That will not run very far in an age when all sophisticated and industrial societies are seeking new forms of association . . . Too many Nationalists behave like grown men who, because they had unhappy school days, demand to be dressed up in shorts to have their youth over again . . . their frame of mind is sometimes bad-tempered, reactionary and unconstructive.[52]

Although between 1951 and 1964 Grimond had been the only Liberal representing a Scottish constituency, at the elections of 1964 and 1966 it was Scotland that had delivered the lion's share of the party's new seats. Grimond recognised that many of the Liberals' new votes since 1956 had come from 'anti-system' voters, people who were fed up with the established duopoly of Conservative and Labour. In England, the Liberals had become the natural beneficiaries of any hostility to the 'system'. In Scotland, however, which for a host of reasons felt far more disgruntled with the system, such voters had somewhere else to go: the SNP. Many Scottish Liberals, notably Ludovic Kennedy, took the view that it was folly for the Liberals to compete with the nationalists for what seemed to be the same voters. After moving to Scotland, Kennedy had quickly been invited to join the council of the Scottish Liberals, and had been dismayed by how little serious discussion about home rule there was amongst its members. In the months after renouncing the Liberal leadership, Grimond grew increasingly sympathetic to this argument. In private, however, Grimond was becoming convinced that the Scottish Liberals must, as a matter of considerable urgency, reach some kind of accommodation with the Nationalists. Before the 1964 general election the SNP had suggested an electoral pact to the Liberals and, although a deal had never been struck, in their choices of seats to fight the two parties had generally avoided cancelling each other out. Now the Liberals were on the wane and the SNP was gaining ground, and Grimond feared that the SNP might not prove merciful towards his party. His fundamental views had not changed – he was no advocate of independence – but he feared that pressure for radical change in the system of government might be dissipated if its advocates continued to fight amongst themselves. He believed that the Scottish Liberal Party (SLP) and the SNP could, in combination, establish the right of the Scots to take charge of their own destiny. As soon as the Scottish people were guaranteed a referendum, in which they could decide which form of home rule they preferred, the Nationalists and the Liberals would again be free to campaign against each other.

In 1966 Ludovic Kennedy had put forward to the Scottish Liberals' annual assembly a proposition that home rule should be the party's principal aim and object north of the border. As Kennedy wrote later, this motion had

been 'passed unanimously and thereafter . . . completely ignored'.[53] Before
their Perth assembly of May 1967, the Scottish Liberals put out feelers for
a strictly unofficial pact with the Nationalists and, at Perth, Kennedy put
down a motion calling for talks with the SNP. It was never called. Grimond
sidestepped the controversy in his speech to the assembly, concentrating
instead on his fear that Scotland might become a 'land exclusively run by
bureaucrats – life will be drained out of many parts'.[54] Many other Scottish
Liberals were appalled by any dalliance with the Nationalists, at that time
a very mixed bag politically with a strong streak of *poujadism,* and the
pact proposal was heavily defeated. In defiance of official policy, Kennedy
subsequently helped to arrange a meeting between Grimond, David Steel and
one of the SNP leadership, Billy Wolfe, prior to the Hamilton by-election in
the autumn of 1967. Russell Johnston and George Mackie got wind of this,
and continued to lead the way in opposing any deal. Both recall that this
ouverture came to nothing, as it unsurprisingly transpired at the Grimond-
Wolfe meeting that the Liberals and the SNP had virtually nothing in
common politically. Grimond always regretted this, believing that the Liberals
came off 'second-best' as a result. He wished in retrospect that the Liberal
leadership had felt able to appeal to the SNP membership over the heads of
their leaders. Kennedy subsequently quit the Liberals in protest and, although
he never actually joined the Nationalists, he did appear on a platform in
support of Winnie Ewing, the SNP candidate at Hamilton.

Many of those who stayed behind, including Grimond, continued to share
Kennedy's fear that the Liberals and the Scottish Nationalists could end up
dissipating precious energies and support by fighting each other to a standstill.
Yet when the Scottish Liberals decided in November 1967 that they should
in future make better use of Grimond, the task identified was not to do
any deal with the resurgent Nationalists. Although the door was left ajar
for deals at a local level, the SLP leadership wanted to find ways of beating
them off. In December 1967 Grimond initiated a counter-attack against this
strategy. At his instigation, he and three colleagues – David Steel, James
Davidson and Alasdair Mackenzie – wrote to George Mackie, apparently with
Jeremy Thorpe's express knowledge and approval, setting out the steps that
they would like to take towards a policy of cooperation with the Nationalists.
Since this ran counter to everything he had fought and argued for, Mackie
threatened to resign as chairman of the party's Scottish executive. When the
executive discussed the matter, however, it overwhelmingly backed Mackie.
When the party's Scottish council followed suit, it became clear to Mackie
that it would make no sense for him to resign, since he enjoyed such strong
support. The Scottish party was now dangerously divided over a substantive
issue of both tactics and strategy, however, and many people blamed Grimond
for the situation.

By the end of 1967, it was not only in Scotland that Jeremy Thorpe was having severe difficulties with his party. The autumn brought a series of by-elections in six disparate seats, and the party performed badly in all of them. At the end of November the party's Executive Committee virtually indicated a lack of confidence in the leadership, and some of the party's MPs began to murmur about bringing back Grimond. They had begun to realise just how much the Liberals' revival since 1956 had depended upon the personality of the leader. Before succeeding grimond in the post, Thorpe had a reputation as a raconteur rather than as a man of substance. In his early months, he over-compensated by becoming excessively earnest, delivering a number of highly turgid speeches, and soon he found himself being unfavourably compared, even by his own supporters, with his predecessor. He lacked Grimond's charisma, gravitas and sense of strategy, and rarely seemed to listen to people, which drove away many of the committed intellectuals whom Grimond had attracted to the party. 'Some of the mythology put out about Grimond was posthumous praise,' Thorpe later protested. 'Jo did have intellectually a fresh and good approach, but some of his ideas were totally incomprehensible. I think it was rather like modern music: people thought they ought to admire it.'[55] Grimond himself did little or nothing to help bolster the new leader whose election he had helped to secure, and he would later admit that he should have been less aloof.

Freed from the diary-filling routine engagements of the leader, Grimond was able to travel in a more leisurely fashion. He spent June 1967 in Yugoslavia, with a BBC film crew in tow, taking the opportunity to go off on another of his ideological flights of fancy. Although he had followed previous Liberal leaders in championing workers' rights and participation, Grimond had never really been able to give full expression to his more extravagant, not to say off-the-wall, ideas about direct democracy and anarcho-syndicalism. The trip to Yugoslavia positively inspired him in that direction. The resultant BBC film shows a tanned and vigorous Grimond reflecting upon the shortcomings of British government policy in the Gorbals and Orkney, and then taking genuine pleasure in the economic and social developments that the citizens of Tito's Yugoslavia were beginning to enjoy. He had one or two minor confrontations with officialdom, but nothing worse than the conflagration he had enjoyed a year earlier with a traffic warden in Brighton. In the light of what has happened since, one inevitably listens for some blinding insights into the ethnic tensions of the Balkans, but even the section of the film filmed in Bosnia has an almost idyllic quality to it.

Grimond did not attempt to disguise his respect not only for Tito's determination to remain independent of the USSR, but also for certain elements of the political reforms that he had introduced. On his return to the UK, he reflected that 'the British are one of the least enthusiastic peoples in the world – they don't believe in anything – in their party system . . . their religion . . . free enterprise . . . They are in grave danger therefore of being alienated, and being detached from everything . . . I don't think we need a rest from democracy . . . but I do believe that we should wipe the slate clean and start again – change isn't sacrilege.'[56] Although Grimond was understandably criticised at the time for praising what was by no stretch of the imagination a liberal system, in fairness to him it is well worth sieving out precisely those aspects of the system that he found agreeable. Above all, he admired the country's efforts to abolish class divisions not through concentration camps, but through a fundamental reorganisation of the industrial process not far removed from what he had been advocating. On his return to the UK, he praised the way in which Yugoslavia had already gone far beyond traditional notions of co-ownership: 'It is quite difficult to define who "owns" a factory or its machinery . . . they hope to achieve a situation in which management and workers are the same animal. It is not a question of "workers' representatives" but of all being workers.'[57]

Then there were Tito's experiments in democracy. Grimond was impressed to discover that, although a multi-party system was still entirely out of the question, the principles of direct democracy were being introduced in areas far beyond anything dreamed of in the UK. He met teachers who had to resubmit themselves for election every five years. For someone with Grimond's increasingly jaundiced view of British party politics, this kind of departure had an immediate appeal: 'Democracy is thereby introduced into activities from which in Western countries it is excluded. Diversity is encouraged . . . Next, in Yugoslavia it is considered natural that there should be regional autonomy.'[58] Most of all, however, Grimond admired the way in which Tito held his country together by rallying people against Soviet influence. For, despite this dalliance with Yugoslav collectivism, Grimond was as scornful as ever of pro-Soviet fellow travellers, particularly those on the left who only spoke out intermittently and in the wake of particularly eye-catching atrocities. When a Soviet clampdown on intellectuals in 1967 prompted just such a meretricious outburst from many of the West's fellow travellers, he was scathing: 'while it merely slaughtered the poor and those who were politically innocent many of the present protesters seemed very well pleased with the practice of communism.'[59]

Many of the 'Grimond Liberals' – the likes of William Wallace, Tim Beaumont, Richard Holme and Michael Steed – had never really tried to conceal their doubts about Jeremy Thorpe. They now took the opportunity to press for some kind of major ideological statement to be made before the party's drift became critical, followed by a period of intensive and serious policy development. They were desperate for the kind of intellectual stimulus that Grimond could give effortlessly, but to which Thorpe seemed unable to aspire. They soon pressed Grimond directly to consider a comeback. Although he still saw himself as the ideal leader for any new, broadly based progressive movement, Grimond never wanted his old job back. His specific interest in Scottish politics had also grown considerably. Rather than working either for or against Thorpe, he stuck to Scottish politics and his old crusade for a realignment of the left. When Roy Jenkins was appointed Chancellor of the Exchequer, Grimond's paean to the Labour man far exceeded anything that he had said about anyone within his own party. He described the appointment of Jenkins as 'one of the most hopeful political events since the war . . . the last chance for this Government . . . he inherits the Gaitskell-like belief in equality, he will for a change match words with action . . . he will bring intelligence and purpose to the office.'[60] Then Grimond launched an uncharacteristically personal attack on Harold Wilson, whose cabinet had just overturned his preferred policy towards South Africa. He rejected any thought of a national government led by Wilson: 'a Government under the leadership of the last few years, with a few Conservatives added . . . would make confusion worse confounded.'[61] Grimond evidently intended to keep the flame of realignment burning.

14

Jo grimond's first opportunity to develop his non-political activities after quitting as party leader came very quickly indeed. On the day of his resignation, 17th January 1967, an ambitious young independent television producer called Alasdair Milne was staying with Jo Grimond's old friends Ludovic Kennedy and Moira Shearer in their house in the Borders, celebrating Moira's birthday. Milne had decided to put together a consortium to bid against Lord Thomson's Scottish TV in the forthcoming round of franchising for independent television. He knew that they were vulnerable because of bad publicity they had received since being awarded their franchise – often referred to at the time as a 'licence to print money'. He had already discussed his plans with a number of distinguished figures and enlisted their support in a number of ways, including Esmond Wright, then a professor at Glasgow University and soon to become an MP, John Taylor of the Scottish TUC, Alistair Burnet of the *Economist* and Grimond's old friend David Astor. Three Scottish universities, including those of St Andrews and Edinburgh, were also on board. One major problem concerned Milne: he still hadn't found a suitably prestigious chairman.

When they heard on the news that Grimond had stepped down as leader of the Liberals, Milne knew at once that he had identified his man. Kennedy telephoned Grimond at once, and Grimond told Milne that he'd love to become chairman of the consortium. This seemed to be exactly the kind of new direction that he had wanted, and he threw himself into the three or four months of preparatory work with a gusto and enthusiasm that had been lacking in his political activities for some time. Although Grimond was a prodigious and skilled broadcaster, at the beginning of this process he knew next to nothing about the mechanics or financing of broadcasting. This did not inhibit him in the least. Milne recalls Grimond as 'a marvellous chairman – funny, urbane and amusing',[1] who merrily and devotedly got stuck into the nitty-gritty of drafting and redrafting, painstakingly mastering the complicated briefs given to him by Milne and Burnet. Grimond must surely have realised that, had the bid proved successful, he would in due course have become chairman of a major television company, a position which he could presumably not have combined with that of a member of Parliament. He must have been willing to quit politics altogether.

Having submitted their plans in written form, Grimond and his team from 'Central Scotland Television' were interviewed for ninety minutes by the Independent Television Authority (ITA). At the interview, according to Milne, the ITA chairman Charles Hill (a former Tory MP well known as the 'radio doctor') and his colleagues already had their minds made up: 'they made it perfectly clear that they thought we were interlopers really – STV had done a jolly good job.'[2] Milne got the message straight away that the group 'would have to run pretty fast to pull it off'[3] and, in retrospect, wondered whether he and his team had been too openly scornful of Scottish Television. Hill was particularly patronising towards Grimond during the cross-examination that followed the consortium's presentations, making it clear that, in his view, a recently retired Liberal leader could hardly be an authority on broadcasting – trying, again in Milne's words, 'to put him off severely'.[4] Despite this hostile atmosphere, Grimond and his colleagues came away afterwards feeling that they still had a reasonable chance of getting the franchise. The *Sunday Telegraph* 'Close-up' team later confirmed that their rivals had succeeded 'only by a whisker'.[5]

When they heard that he had lost, Grimond did not leave the stage quietly. He believed that the entire matter had been badly handled from the outset. Two members of the ITA were absent for the crucial interview, and he was certain that the authority must have had a private agenda that informed their aggressive attitude at the interview. Furthermore, in his view members of the authority 'were not particularly qualified' to judge the credentials of the consortium that he had chaired against those of its competitor, not least because only one of them came from Scotland.[6] Grimond felt that each region should have had its own committee, in order that the franchise decisions could be properly informed. He also objected to the arbitrary nature of the ITA's powers, and the fact that so much of the process was confidential, even though there was an obvious public interest in the applications and the outcome of the ITA deliberations: 'there are advantages in not giving reasons, but . . . it is indeed a strange position where the ITA can sit in private and make or break without appeal.'[7]

It was probably as well that nothing came of the television bid, for activities in and around the world of politics were still very much in Jo Grimond's blood, and he relished his new-found freedom. He had long argued that, in the quest to build a genuinely liberal society, a massive expansion of voluntary action, as well as the rebuilding of civic institutions, was an essential prerequisite. He was now able to get more 'hands-on' experience of helping with this crusade. He also turned his hand to producing a lot more journalism than hitherto. In March 1967 Laurence Scott invited Grimond to become the first outside director of the *Guardian* for many years (all the others were full-time officers of the company), and also appointed him as a trustee of the Scott Trust, which holds the ordinary share capital of the newspaper. These responsibilities took him to Manchester regularly, and Grimond played a leading part in the appointment process that led to Peter Preston becoming editor of the paper in 1975. Grimond's main concern was that the newspaper should increase its (already extensive) parliamentary coverage. Throughout his time on the board, Grimond took an active interest in the paper's affairs and brought an informed, and typically robust, view to parliamentary debates on the media. He remained on the board until he took over as 'caretaker' leader of the party in 1976, and continued to write for the paper.

In November 1967 it was announced that Grimond was to become a joint vice-chairman, with Selwyn Lloyd, of a new trust responsible for the administration and appointment of a unit of thirty young people, to be called the Young Volunteer Force, who would tour Britain establishing local voluntary service schemes. The first director of the unit was Anthony Steen, a young barrister and future Tory MP, who had already been active in the field of young volunteers. Steen always enjoyed his dealings with Grimond, who never patronised him and treated him as an equal. He regarded Grimond's involvement in this new undertaking as an extension of a well-established and genuine interest in helping young people who had fallen on hard times. He recalls that he would even use his house at Kew for putting up people who desperately needed accommodation. Grimond was less active than Selwyn Lloyd, but he did attend committee meetings, at which he would remain silent for long periods before interjecting the occasional pithy remark. Steen was consistently impressed by what he describes as Grimond's 'progressive optimism' and his genuine desire to encourage those who were more fortunate to reach out a helping hand to individuals who had been in some way 'hurt by society', whether they were young or elderly. Although Grimond probably committed no more than a couple of hours per week to this undertaking, he made a point of speaking to Steen at least once a week, and always seemed pleased to hear from him. His inspiration was essential to the whole enterprise, which had twenty-eight local units or 'task forces' up and running once it hit its stride. This lasted until the enforced austerity of the Heath government drove it out of business, by which time it had induced some 10,000 young volunteers to undertake useful activities – a substantial number, but only one-tenth of the original target from 1967. Most of them were digging gardens or decorating for elderly or disabled people, though some had taken a more positive and aggressive line, getting into trouble for their criticisms of local authority programmes.

In May 1968 Grimond agreed to become chairman of the Mental Health Trust, on whose behalf he launched a nationwide fund-raising appeal on 6th June that year, the target of which was to raise at least £250,000 to support urgently needed programmes of research and rehabilitation. He described mental health as the 'Cinderella' of the health service, which deserved to be given far greater priority. Students at Hornsey College of Art prepared a 'shock' exhibition on mental health as part of the campaign, which Grimond and Rab Butler opened that autumn at St Martin-in-the-Fields, Trafalgar Square. Grimond explained that the funds raised would be used to establish a national network of training and rehabilitation centres; to set up adolescent treatment centres; and to buy and convert houses into bed-sitters for discharged mental patients. Although they never spoke publicly about it, Jo and Laura Grimond were undoubtedly still feeling the loss of their eldest son very acutely, and they seemingly resolved to do whatever they could to help prevent other parents going through what they had endured. Laura involved herself in parallel activities in Orkney and Shetland.

As leader, Grimond had various dealings with the Joseph Rowntree Social Service Trust (JRSST). He admired not only the philanthropy of the Trust's founder, cocoa baron Joseph Rowntree, but also the fact that the Trust above all prized its freedom of action. Unusually for an organisation involved in good works, the Trust had not opted for charitable status. Since it was willing to pay the full burden of taxation, the JRSST enjoyed almost total freedom about how to disburse its considerable funds, using as much of its estimated annual income of £250,000 as it chose to on political projects. Thanks to the efforts of Richard Wainwright, it had also played a major part in keeping the Liberal Party afloat during its years of financial tribulation. Shortly after quitting as Liberal leader, Grimond was delighted to become a trustee, in which capacity he would take the opportunity to involve the Trust in several of his own 'pet' projects, one of which led to a generous donation in 1973–4 to the Orkney and Shetland Liberals. He also developed the habit of amiably shooting down one well-intentioned, but inadequately prepared, grant application after another. In 1969, thanks to Richard Wainwright's advocacy and what he himself describes as the 'nepotic system of the Liberal establishment', Grimond's protégé Pratap Chitnis went off to York to run the Trust full-time.

Grimond took immense pleasure in travelling up to York three times a year for trustees' meetings. He and Ted Goodman, another trustee, would usually travel up together from London and stay with Chitnis and his wife. By all accounts these were convivial occasions. On one occasion Chitnis himself travelled with Grimond and one of the gentlemen sharing their first-class carriage with them turned out to be an admirer of Grimond's. 'Let me buy you a drink,' insisted their prosperous-looking co-traveller. Once Grimond had established that Chitnis was included in the offer, he accepted it and the benefactor carried on buying them drinks all the way north. Suddenly they realised that the train was pulling into York station. Grimond pocketed their last, unopened miniatures and they dashed off the train just in time. At the hotel where the trustees assembled for their meetings, Grimond would usually be the first down to the bar. There was a strong non-conformist and teetotal angle to the Trust, and Grimond generally liked to make sure that he got a couple of strong cocktails down (preferably ones that looked like water from a distance) before his colleagues joined him. The Chitnis home in York had a second bathroom over the dining room and, during one of Grimond's visits, it started to leak one morning. Grimond sat eating his breakfast and reading the paper, quite oblivious both to the water pouring through the ceiling and the chaos around him as his hosts desperately struggled to deal with the impending flood. One evening, after the household had gone to bed in the wake of a particularly convivial dinner, Grimond got up during the night to go to the lavatory and, in the darkened house on his way back to his bedroom, took a wrong turning. He fell all the way down the stairs. He was by no means a small man, and lay on his back at the bottom of the stairs in an indignant state, waiting for lights to come on and the buzz of concerned onlookers to commence. There came nothing of the sort. The food and drink had also taken their toll on the rest of the household. He hauled himself back up the stairs and went back to bed.

It was not all fun and games, however: according to a later chairman of the Trust, Archy Kirkwood, it was Chitnis and Grimond who refashioned it into a modern and effective organisation. Grimond convinced his fellow trustees to support two projects of his own devising. The first was an urban project in Greenock, outside Glasgow, an area in which Grimond had identified particular problems of social and environmental decay. Although the project was comparatively short-lived, it at least taught Grimond and his fellow trustees some important lessons about social needs. On one occasion, Grimond and a number of colleagues from the Trust had flown up together to see Greenock for themselves. So foul was the weather by the end of the afternoon that flights back south were cancelled. The airlines commandeered as many places as they could on southbound trains, and Grimond pulled rank as an MP, obtaining the last available place in a first-class sleeper, while the rest of the Rowntree group had to spend the night in the Station Hotel in Glasgow. The second project was (at least for Grimond) closer to home, at Northmavine in Shetland, a far-flung habitation as far from the northern tip of Scotland as Darlington is from London. The community at Northmavine was typical of Shetland, unsettled by the discovery of oil and the threatened decline of fishing, and living in constant fear of depopulation. To no one's surprise, this project was more successful than its relative in Greenock, since the community was less alienated unto itself, less dependent upon the state and, perhaps, more naturally resilient.

Another important development encouraged by Grimond and Chitnis was the introduction of young parliamentary researchers who came to be known as the 'chocolate soldiers'. In 1971 the Trust decided to establish a total of six bursaries, split between the three main parties and worth £2,500 each per year. Although the Conservative Party turned down two such fellowships, the Labour chief whip Ted Short (later Lord Glenamara) at once recognised the potential of the scheme, as did the Liberals, and the chocolate soldiers would in due course be paid for out of public funds ('Short Money'). These bursaries enabled several senior frontbenchers, including Roy Jenkins, David Steel and John Pardoe, to employ researchers for the first time. When the Trust agreed to provide Grimond himself with a researcher to help with his own House of Commons activities, prior to interviewing each of the four or five young people on the shortlist, Grimond poured them a beakerful of whisky. Coping with this during the course of a twenty-minute interview in the middle of the day must have rivalled even the most fiendish test that the Civil Service Commission could devise.

Even as leader, Grimond had something of a reputation as a *bon viveur*. With more time on his hands, and fewer responsibilities, he could relax rather more. Although the family home in St Andrews was fairly abstemious – when his father died, the cellar was found to contain only a little port and a few bottles of champagne – Jo Grimond himself always enjoyed a drink. Though none of his colleagues recalls ever seeing him seriously the worse for wear as a consequence, they do remember quite a formidable capacity and a genuine enthusiasm for a good wine over dinner. One of his protégés attributes his constitution to his background and upbringing, likening it to that of a born-and-bred diplomat, required to match Eastern Europeans vodka for vodka, without showing the slightest ill-effect or losing face. Archy Kirkwood recalls how Grimond's voice could change when he drank a lot, becoming harder to understand, not because he was slurring his words, but because its Etonian qualities came more and more to the fore! He was a great connoisseur of his wine, as Hamish Gray recalls: 'He loved wine . . . He was a very, very shrewd judge of a bottle of wine . . . a very clubbable chap.'[8] His former parliamentary colleague Lord Geraint (Howells) reminisced with pleasure about attending a grand dinner in the City with Grimond. By each place setting stood six different glasses, in assorted sizes and shapes. Grimond grinned at Geraint and commented, 'it looks like it's going to be quite an evening!'[9] Visitors to the Old Manse would often be treated to unidentifiable wines from the cellar. Since most of the labels had come off because of the damp conditions, on occasions Laura just had to do her best for dinner parties to find bottles that looked the same. Grimond was as far-sighted in matters vinicultural as he was when it came to the economy or the constitution. He was among the first to sing the praises of Australian wine, taking his advocacy to the floor of the House of Commons: 'Some Australian wine which I have drunk is quite excellent . . . There is, in this House a drink called a carafe of wine . . . which,

I understand, is French . . . I do not say that it is bad; it is moderately good, but I am sure that we could find an Australian wine which is just as good.'[10]

Grimond had for some time been a member of the Other Club, founded in opposition to 'The Club' by Winston Churchill and F E Smith, but had only rarely been able to attend its meetings. He now became a regular. He also enjoyed the conviviality of the select Literary Society, of which he became president. This used to meet at the perennially fashionable Garrick Club in Covent Garden, devouring splendid dinners and fine wines. There are no speeches, and no demands are made of members, other than to provide engaging company. Grimond was amused and slightly nonplussed to find himself in the chair of such a society, and he certainly did no harm to membership numbers. If anyone asked about joining, he would ask if they had ever written anything. If the answer was 'No', he would usually deem them perfectly qualified for membership. Mark Bonham Carter was another member of the society whose literary credentials were open to question, earning his place not by writing tomes (although he did publish some) but by establishing a reputation as one of the most acerbic and entertaining neighbours to be had at the dinners. As president, Grimond risked controversy only once, when at his instigation, for the first time in its 200-year history, the society voted on whether to admit women. Grimond himself often brought lady guests to dinners, and he would have preferred the membership to be broader. Despite his advocacy, the result was a resounding 'No'.

Grimond's own literary efforts after he resigned as leader were scattered. As in 1964, Grimond again had the opportunity to gather his thoughts and put them into book form, but failed to do so. Between 1968 and 1971 a number of different publishers approached him with a wide variety of book proposals. In the space of three years Grimond could have had published, at the very least, two works on British politics, one on Scotland and a biography of Asquith. Grimond accepted two apparently firm commissions, the first to contribute a 40,000-word work that would be 'on a personal level, even slightly autobiographical'[11] to a series that Robert Maxwell's Pergamon Press hoped to publish under the heading 'What I Wanted to Say'. Nothing ever came either of the series or of the book, and the advance had to be repaid. The second commission, which Grimond accepted rather reluctantly, was improbably to provide a conclusion to a book about management development. No expert in management, Grimond was nervous that his bluff might be called if he got into specifics, and drafted something 'rather broad and probably hazy'.[12] This was at first accepted, and then summarily dropped, by the Gower Press. After struggling particularly hard on this piece, Grimond was for once genuinely furious, tersely observing that this was 'discourteous, to say the least of it' and asking for his fee and his draft to be returned forthwith. He also withdrew around £55,000 from the City of London after twelve years as an underwriting member of Lloyd's. 'I don't know whether I've made a profit or a loss since I joined,' he explained from the US in his most blasé fashion, 'but I'm perfectly satisfied.'[13]

Grimond had once turned down the possibility of writing a full biography of Asquith, but when in early 1973 he was invited to contribute a 5,000-word essay about his grandfather-in-law to a book about Prime Ministers, it seemed like a more credible proposition. He had contributed too many pieces in recent years to volumes that had never materialised, however, and sought reassurance from the book's editor Herbert van Thal, 'that this is a "hard" project'.[14] It was certainly 'hard', but it was by no means smooth. The publishers at first proposed excising a section towards the end of Grimond's essay about the way in which Asquith organised his private office and personal affairs. Grimond objected: 'I am all for having my articles edited. I wholly regret this particular excision, however. It seems to me one of the few interesting passages in the whole essay. I would much rather that you had deleted those rather boring strings of adjectives to which my prose runs.'[15] The editorial division reinserted the passage and, in the context of a new century, one or two sections make for interesting reading. Grimond always liked the fact that Asquith never had a government car, and watched the cab fare tick away like everyone else. 'Part of the yawning gap between politicians and the public,' mused Grimond, 'is due to the insulation of ministers from ordinary life . . . They do not notice rising prices or the breakdown of public services as they are wafted in their official cars from their official residences to their well-appointed offices . . . One cannot imagine Asquith tape-recording conversations or employing a personal bodyguard of public relations officers like a renaissance bravo.'[16]

Meanwhile Asquith's most celebrated grand-daughter, Grimond's wife Laura, was threatening to match his efforts at diversifying his activities. Laura was deservedly renowned for her energy and creativity and, in Orkney and Shetland, threw herself into countless local activities. She had long been a great campaigner for local heritage in the islands and, proudly reminding everyone that St Magnus' Cathedral in Kirkwall had been standing for nearly 500 years by the time Sir Christopher Wren began to design St Paul's in London, in the early 1970s she launched a campaign to draw attention to the importance of the buildings around the cathedral. Three houses on a short stretch known as the Strynd, some parts of which date back to 1380, ranking them amongst the very oldest in Kirkwall, were coming under threat. All three were very dilapidated and, using a legacy left to her by her mother, now Laura bought two of them for £1,600. She set about restoring the smaller one herself, gifting the other to Orkney Heritage Society. In 1973 Laura took the lead in a campaign to save the majestic island of Hoy from depopulation, helping to set up a charitable trust to take over the massive estate of the island's laird, Malcolm Stewart, which accounted for some two-thirds of Hoy. A once-thriving agricultural community had dwindled to around thirty people. 'What we need,' explained Laura, 'is not eccentrics and freaks, but tradesmen, craftsmen and builders.'[17] One notable figure to defy the tide of depopulation was the composer Peter Maxwell Davies (now Sir Peter), who rehabilitated a cottage high above the desolate Rackwick Bay. Laura couldn't praise him enough: 'he goes out in the worst weather and seems quite able to live without food.'[18] In due course, Peter Maxwell Davies inspired the annual St Magnus Festival in Orkney, which continues successfully to this day.

Jo Grimond played his own part in Orcadian tradition when, in 1968, he stood on a plinth outside St Magnus' Cathedral and launched the Ba' in the annual ball game in Kirkwall, doing his best to 'give the opposing scrummagers . . . a fair whack at it', while cries of 'have a go, Jo!' rose up from the throng below. Once the Ba' (a specially handmade ball) has been launched, two vast, opposing scrums of Orcadians – the uppies and the doonies – then try to bustle it, respectively, either up the hill or down it. It is a sport quite unlike any other, and Grimond wisely neither participated nor took sides! The affection between the Grimonds and the inhabitants of Orkney and Shetland was entirely mutual, and Grimond loved telling stories about the islands. One of his favourites was about his youngest son Magnus, who was once given a lift by some acquaintances of Jo and Laura who, by some chance, did not realise who he was. They tried to glean from the youngster what his father did and, after a series of evasions, he finally remarked that 'och well, he only gangs aboot'.

One development that helped to revitalise Grimond during this period was a greatly increased involvement in university life. He enjoyed few things more than the company of intelligent, articulate young people, once explaining that he simply enjoyed talking with young people about the things that interested them: 'no special virtue in this – it's a sign of old age, I like rambling discussions.'[19] Grimond's reaction to the famous student protests of the late 1960s was always slightly confused. At an intellectual level, he recognised that a liberal should not always condemn protest movements, particularly when they were at least in part reacting against an illiberal, or even corrupt, status quo. In one sense, the existence of rebellious students did demonstrate a healthy desire to question government and authority, which from a liberal perspective, was surely to be applauded. Grimond had always argued that universities should be 'places of re-birth', encouraging intelligent young people to engage positively with the ferment of new ideas. The student protests, although they were nominally directed against the universities themselves, could therefore paradoxically be cited as evidence that the universities were actually being rather successful. This all appealed to Grimond's anarchic streak, and he had an instinctive appreciation for what he would term 'the explosion of individualism . . . Carnaby Street and Rock & Roll and all that'.[20] At the 1968 Königswinter conference, he went so far as to tell fellow delegates that he positively 'welcomed the students' revolt and regarded it on the whole as a healthy sign . . . one could hardly expect young people to take part in a democracy which tells them that they are absolutely impotent to change anything except at elections.'[21]

On the other hand, there was a self-indulgent aspect to the student demonstrations that he found distasteful. He disliked the 'sit-ins' that were prevalent during this period, which he regarded as 'essentially disorderly'; the majority of the participants showed every sign of being 'obstinate and inarticulate'.[22] The unrest in Western universities must have seemed 'unbelievably frivolous' to people enduring genuine hardship and deprivation of civil liberties, he reflected: 'A great deal of the unrest is crude, muddled and intolerable . . . The need is for a liberal re-affirmation, the danger is that dissatisfaction will lead to reaction.'[23] He was even more trenchant in his regular newspaper slot

> My criticism is that they do not involve themselves enough in the politics of their own country . . . I welcome the Young Liberals because they do . . . If 'escapism' means anything, there is something profoundly escapist in caring passionately about Vietnam and yet doing nothing about either Vietnam or about the slums on your own doorstep. Students of a past generation actually *fought* in the Spanish Civil War.[24]

Grimond echoed these sentiments in a speech that he gave in support of Eric Lubbock just after a particularly virulent outbreak of unrest at the LSE:

> To ordinary people who pay for the students, the answer often seems to be: boot them out and fill their places with the hundreds of thousands of boys and girls in the world who are eager to learn and can't get places in further education – for students, some from the wealthiest country in the world, the United States, and all specially privileged and supported by the taxpayer to an extent which doesn't exist even in all Communist countries, to behave like this seems absurd.[25]

Towards the end of his time as party leader, Grimond had become president of the Scottish Union of Students. When he wrote to students in Scotland at the beginning of the 1967–8 academic year, he asked that protests should not be taken to extremes: 'what can be absurd is to remain creating trouble in a University when University places are eagerly sought by those who will make good use of them.'[26] Poignantly, some eighteen months after the death of his oldest son, he still described himself in that same letter as a '55-year-old father of four'.[27] Having so enjoyed his connection with Edinburgh University, after resigning as leader Grimond encouraged Liberal students to put his name forward for similar appointments, particularly in Scotland and the south-east of England. The first success came in 1969, with his election as rector of Aberdeen University, still enduring the after-shocks of student revolution. So strong were Grimond's credentials that one of the other candidates, the boxer Henry Cooper, dropped out in his favour. The appointment was controversial, as some students feared that Grimond might have too much on his plate already. At his installation, Grimond carefully played to the gallery, speaking up for freedom and diversity and mocking the popular perception of universities as 'well-upholstered nests for pampered but ungrateful layabouts'.[28] He also veered into controversial territory, referring to the confidential political files that were being held on students of the day, joking that he couldn't see why universities bothered, 'except to feed those ravenous computers'.[29] He must have been amused, indeed probably rather pleased, when an anonymous profile of him in the university newspaper described him as 'an adamant left-winger of the Liberal Party, a position well to the Left of the present Labour Government'.[30] One of Grimond's first tasks at Aberdeen was to appoint an assessor to the University Court, which he chaired. When it was suggested that he might appoint a student, Grimond tried to trump the radicals by finding a suitable woman, who might be free from the 'hierarchic ambitions' that devoured young men. Unfortunately, so free were the women from those ambitions that none of them would take on the post: 'they had the good sense not to waste the golden hours of their youth on University administration.'[31] He did, however, find a suitable young man, Kenneth Chew, who duly became the first student to find himself appointed as a full member of a British university governing body.

Geographically, Aberdeen was perfect for Grimond. He would take his usual sleeper up from London, breakfast in the main railway station and then go on to the university, usually staying in one of the halls of residence, opposite the old chapel. Then, if he was bound for the islands, he could fly on directly from Aberdeen airport. He acted, in his phrase, as a 'free floating' rector, not meddling too much in the affairs of either the university or the students, and generally avoiding social or political entanglements. As an influential but independent figure who had been elected by student supporters, he was always happy to help students with any difficulties they might be experiencing and always advertised his presence whenever he was in Aberdeen. He was always struck (and relieved) by how few cases of unhappiness or injustice were, in fact, brought to his attention. He concluded that his main interest should be in helping to foster non-academic interests – the 'hinterland' of university life. One of his main achievements was in getting together a group to raise money for a new arts centre at the university, to which he summoned one leading student light, the future broadcaster James Naughtie, with a letter headed 'Dear Naughtie' and signed off 'Yours, Jo'. In search of funds for this project, Grimond dined the then chairman of Harrods, Sir Hugh Fraser, telling Naughtie grandly that he had 'had dinner with that draper fellow'.

When Grimond went to the University Court to tell them of his progress, however, he would be disappointed. 'There is adequate display space for paintings,' he was portentously told, 'in the basement of the natural philosophy building.'[32] The project was stillborn. In alliance with Nigel Lindsay, the Young Liberal who had managed his campaign for the rectorship, Grimond helped to ignite a substantial Liberal resurgence in Aberdeen. Although the party never challenged seriously in any of the parliamentary constituencies in the city, Liberals did in due course establish a substantial bridgehead in local government.

Although Grimond certainly enjoyed his association with Aberdeen, it was another leading higher education institution that would provide him with the opportunity to prove his credentials with a really serious and engaging task – and, perhaps, to gainsay the charges of dilettantism that had always dogged him. In the second half of 1970 the vice-chancellor of Birmingham University, Sir Robert Hunter, who as a professor of medicine had attended Grimond's mother, asked him to chair a committee to look into that university's constitution and internal workings. This was by any token a major undertaking, and came to occupy much of Grimond's time between the beginning of 1971 and the autumn of 1972. Although Grimond was naturally sceptical of how much might be achieved by this, or indeed any, committee, he accepted without hesitation. He was reassured to be told that Sir Maurice Dean, a retired senior civil servant, would be in charge of the day-to-day running of the committee, and to be promised whatever secretariat he needed, to help with drafting and administration. Speaking to students and staff as he embarked on this task, Grimond explained that one of his main concerns was to explore ways of defending academic freedom: 'I do not believe that there is a severe threat to freedom yet – but if universities ever allowed themselves to be ruled by one dominant philosophy, or by the beliefs of the government in power, the threat would be very great indeed.'[33]

Like other British universities, Birmingham had endured its share of student sit-ins and the like during the late 1960s. At one point Robert Hunter's own office had been occupied. What prompted the establishment of this committee, however, was the widely held belief that, seventy years on from its foundation by Joseph Chamberlain, the university needed a fresh and objective analysis of the way in which its affairs were organised. One of the old 'civic' universities, Birmingham had seen its quota of students increase from 700 to 7,000. It also now depended predominantly upon the state, rather than private philanthropy, for its financial support. Yet its academic organisation, and its method of self-government, had hardly changed over all that time. The University Court, a worthy but rather archaic body comprised largely of the 'great and good' from outside the university, was still notionally the final authority on most non-academic matters. There was also some concern that the university was becoming specialised in a way unforeseen by its founding fathers: the Faculty of Science and Engineering, with twenty-two departments and over 3,000 students, already accounted for almost half of the students at the university, and planned to expand numbers by a further 1,000 within the decade.

The committee was given an open brief to consider how schools, departments or faculties might be merged or separated. To his intense frustration, Grimond's initial personal preference for a looser, federal type of structure between the departments found little favour. He later bemoaned: 'there appears to be a tendency to think that universities must either have the structure of schools or the structure of faculties and departments . . . yet it appears fairly obvious that they fulfil different purposes and both may be essential.'[34] From the outset, Grimond knew that many senior members of the university would expect this committee, like so many others he had encountered over the years, to be a palliative and nothing more. He wanted to err on the side of assertiveness as well as radicalism. He was slightly depressed to find that two students had taken great pleasure in joining the committee, an attitude that he had foreshadowed a few years earlier: 'I cannot see that preoccupation with administration . . . is the best way to use your time at a university . . . Administration can be a creeping blight . . . If you don't have to do it, keep clear.'[35] He could never understand the desire of students to devote themselves to office jobs. 'It is hard to see,' he wrote a few years later, 'why students long to sit on committees or take sabbatical years to play at politics, or worse, to become premature bureaucrats.'[36] He put it all down to a decline in the academic and social stimuli offered by modern universities – and ultimately felt powerless, even on a committee with a supposedly wide-ranging brief, to do anything about it.

Grimond rapidly perceived at Birmingham most of the very failings against which he had been railing more widely. Not only the students, but the academics too, seemed to have their priorities all wrong. He consulted with his old friend Sam Beer about how anyone could possibly make sense of a university where the academics were devoting so much energy and intrigue to the question of how the deans and heads of departments should be selected. Beer sympathised: in Harvard too it was almost impossible to get anyone to take on non-academic responsibilities, with the result that the most junior lecturers normally found themselves weighed down with them. Grimond burst out laughing: the problem at Birmingham was the precise opposite – everyone there absolutely loved empire-building, all too often at the cost of eating into the time available for teaching and research. The desire of almost everyone he met to be the head of this or that illustrated for him once again the endemic inflationary mentality that now applied as much to titles as to the currency. The home of much of this inflation seemed to be the university Senate, comprised of the vice-chancellor, the vice-principal, the deans, all the university's professorial staff and a panoply of advisers and observers – 190 members in all. Grimond was taken aback when representatives of the Senate, which had in 1969 set up its own Constitutional Committee to consider all the issues now before Grimond and his team, informed him that its membership, already almost 200, should probably be substantially expanded. Grimond himself favoured the view expressed by the Association of University Teachers, that forty or so 'senators' would be quite sufficient.

Grimond's commitment to his task was most impressive. During 1971 the committee met most weeks, including several 'working weekends' at a hotel in Oxfordshire. The plan was to spend its first year consulting interested parties and then drafting a consultation paper, after the manner of a government green paper. This would be followed, after a consultation period, by a definitive statement from the committee on the future of the university. The committee decided at its first meeting, in February 1971, that it should first invite written submissions from interested parties. Almost 200 such submissions were received, some running to dozens of pages. In addition, a series of discussions and interviews were held, often following up on the more important of these written submissions. Both the university Senate and the Guild of Students were allowed two hearings. Between March and December 1971, Grimond attended thirteen out of the fifteen 'discussion days' held at Birmingham, chairing twenty-seven individual sessions. Throughout, Grimond enjoyed the role of an informed outsider, disinterested but never uninterested. Reading the minutes of the meetings he held with manifold groups within the university, there is no mistaking the evidence either of Grimond's sense of humour or of his genuine and abiding interest in the subject at hand. He also used every opportunity to deepen not only his appreciation of the problems facing Birmingham, but of the world in general. Although his own background had left him in no doubt about the validity of academic excellence, Jo Grimond had always believed that universities should 'open their doors' – to industry, to other educational establishments and to students from as diverse a variety of backgrounds as possible – and that, as a general principle, they needed to take far more account of the longer-term needs of society. Given free reign as chairman of this committee, he was able to develop these thoughts.

Grimond first set out his own philosophical approach to educational matters in some prefatory remarks from the chair at the second meeting of the committee, on Friday, 26th February 1971. The minutes of the meeting record that:

> The Chairman felt that, in addition to producing engineers, lawyers etc., universities had a responsibility to society for studying and criticising the activities of governments. The importance of value judgment was not emphasised enough, nor the wider value of judgment and development of the

critical faculties . . . Universities provided the initial increment of knowledge
but there was a need for a further investment at later stages during a person's
life, both within and outside the university. People should be resilient to change
[sic] rather than predestined to particular careers. There was a tendency for
specialities to replace general studies but it should not be assumed that everyone
would follow the particular subject which he read . . . The Chairman asked
whether universities should be . . . for the clever only. He himself had always
thought that they should take others as well; this was generally agreed.[37]

In discussion with representatives of the Faculty of Arts, Grimond
ruminated that 'he felt that the quality of decision making in the country
was not as good as the expansion of education would lead one to expect.
Was there a lack in the courses of a requirement to assess material and
provide answers?'[38] Grimond also began to question whether a university
enjoying the benefits of Birmingham's geographical location might not be
better advised to devote more funds to academic priorities rather than to ever-
expanding student accommodation. Might not more 'day students', based in
the Midlands, be admitted? When cross-questioning representatives of the
Faculty of Science and Engineering, he 'referred to the fact that students away
from their homes cost a lot of money in the provision of residence. There was
a growing feeling that Polytechnics should get more money; in view of this
could large expenditure on residential accommodation really be justified?'[39]

A week later, Grimond pressed this point with representatives of the Guild
of Students, asking 'whether students should live at home as an economy . . .
whether it was the view of the representatives that the cost of moving students
from their home in one town to a University in another was justified.[40]
This provoked a dusty response from the students; only three years after the
events of 1968, they were hardly likely to welcome the language of priorities,
economy and hard choices. Jo Grimond proved also to be an early advocate
of coursework and continuous assessment. 'The Chairman asked whether the
prospect of assessment would not concentrate the mind and induce people to
get through the work. Might it not be that the less intelligent students were
the ones least likely to benefit from abolition of assessment?[41]

The committee finished its first wave of formal discussions with interested
parties in late June and, over the weekend of 1st–3rd July, went into conclave
at Whately Hall Hotel, near Banbury, to consider a series of eight draft papers
that had now been prepared by the secretariat. The process of drafting and
redrafting went into abeyance during the summer, but autumn brought a
flurry of committee meetings and interviews through which the arguments
of the review body were honed. A further long weekend at Whately Hall in
mid November broke the back of the drafting process. The first draft of the
consultation paper repeatedly stated that the review body was not qualified to
deal with certain internal matters, which should be left to the university itself.
Grimond countered:

on the whole I dissent from this attitude . . . The University, for better or for worse, has set up the Review Body to advise it. It must therefore be presumed that in the University's view we are qualified to do so . . . I believe we should be failing in discharging the task given to us if we did not make clear-cut proposals . . . I quite appreciate, however, that it is for the University to reject, accept or amend such proposals.[42]

By Christmas 1971 the Grimond Committee had approved the text of a seventy-six-page consultative document to be published and promulgated early in the New Year.

This document proposed a number of radical changes to the faculty structure at the university, including the breaking up of the Faculty of Science and Engineering into three faculties. The reaction was decidedly mixed. First of all the very status of the document seemed to be open to question. In places its tone was one of closing down arguments and making what read like firm suggestions for reforms, some of them quite sweeping. This did not suggest consultation. Secondly, despite Grimond's scepticism towards the committee process and his determination to avoid all the usual pitfalls, to some critical eyes the document in its final form demonstrated all the typical shortcomings of a committee outcome. Many of its milder suggestions were generally acceptable, but genuine indignation and uproar greeted the suggestions that the Court might be abolished, and the faculties radically redrawn. There was much criticism too of the rather general tone adopted, and the fact that too few recommendations seemed to be specifically targeted at Birmingham. Given that the preponderance of comment came from the academically inclined, both within and without the university, there was also a sense of disappointment at the fact that so eminent a committee had failed to go more deeply into the philosophy of education. The Guild of Students, in its elegant response, went so far as to quote Buddha, at some length, on the need for learning to take the form of sceptical questioning. Although Grimond had expected at least a degree of conservatism from academics, he was still shocked by this almost total resistance to change. Everyone claimed to be in favour of reform in principle, but nobody seemed able to agree on what it should be.

Ironically the Birmingham branch of the Council for Academic Freedom and Democracy was especially scathing about the report, lamenting its 'platitudinous conservatism' and 'failure to cite evidence . . . to argue a case at crucial points . . . [and] to make values and assumptions explicit'.[43] In fairness to Grimond, he never in fact lost sight of his firm belief that the university should if possible become more democratic. One suggestion put to the committee was that the existing structure, in particular the Court, should be abolished and everything be replaced with a mass meeting of staff and (some) students for two days every year. This horrified Grimond who commented privately that, 'many dictators have had their decisions justified by a show of hands at a mass meeting', and dismissed the suggestion out of hand. No doubt he was thinking too of the contemporary practices of many trades unions.

Grimond was always an interventionist chairman and, during the consultation period, he produced four written submissions of his own for his committee colleagues, two of which survive. The first was absolutely archetypal Grimond: a four-page discourse, dated 3rd May 1972, about the nature of a university, much of it waffly, but some of it very much ahead of its time. For instance, Grimond recognised that the committee had to look in a hard-headed way at questions of priorities: 'the need for good judgement will be of increasing importance . . . Do you want to build Concorde or save Venice?'[44] He also proclaimed the then controversial belief that education should be 'a process to which men and women return constantly through life'.[45] The second is a letter sent on 17th July 1972 – almost three weeks after the committee had signed off the final text – containing detailed suggestions for changes in the text, sent rather late in the day and including several complete paragraphs that he wanted to have inserted. Although many of his suggestions for smaller changes were accepted, none of his more substantive suggestions were taken on board. For his detractors, this was typical Grimond: dilatory and inconsiderate, ill focused and self-important. His committee colleagues must have felt that he was trying to 'bounce' them improperly with an intervention of this kind.

In the final report, formally presented and published on 21st September 1972, the review body stuck to its guns on most major issues, notably the question of the faculties. It also gave great emphasis to its collective desire to make university life more attractive to women. In his preface to the report, Grimond emphasised that the review body 'were conscious of the importance of not throwing out a vigorous baby because the bath water needed attention'.[46] When he presented the final report to the University Council, he demonstrated his usual judicious mixture of humour and earnestness. The official history of Birmingham University acknowledges that the comments of the review body on most of the 'big educational issues . . . still read judiciously and persuasively'.[47] At the time, however, it was still the constitutional proposals that caused some perturbation. The proposed realignment of the faculties was shelved in the face of opposition from the academics, and most of the more radically democratic proposals for student participation were also ignored. Indeed the only major internal recommendation to be accepted was the proposal that ultimate legal authority within the university should be transferred from the Court to the Council, which did no more than bring the constitution into line with the evident practical reality. The main thrust of the final report had been against entrenched, vested interests within the university and it can hardly have been surprising when those interests reacted by rejecting most of its proposals. As the authors of *The First Civic University* observe, the response to the Grimond Report was 'eclectic',[48] with some of its recommendations coming into force quietly and without ceremony in the years that followed. Although the neo-corporatism of the University Council survived, there was at least some symbolic consultation of students in the wake of the Grimond Report and, as some of the longer-established staff at Birmingham still maintain, the aftermath of Grimond marked a high-water mark for democracy at the university.

A longer lasting entanglement with the world of higher education came at the University of Kent at Canterbury, where Grimond was appointed chancellor in July 1970, in succession to the late Princess Marina, who had been the first holder of that office at this comparatively new university. This was a considerable honour, the equivalent of which had not been held by a Liberal leader since Gladstone had been Lord Rector of Edinburgh and Glasgow. The process by which Grimond came to be chosen was also of particular interest. The sudden death of Princess Marina had left the university ill prepared for embarking on the search for a successor and, in the spirit of the times, the authorities opted for a new and democratic method of selecting the chancellor. All the students and staff were given the opportunity to vote on a shortlist of candidates. Grimond won the ballot convincingly, and took particular pride in having won an unquestioned mandate. Grimond's main connection with the university was his firm friendship with Professor Bryan Keith-Lucas and his wife. Keith-Lucas had been one of the gifted academics attracted to the Liberal Party by Grimond, and nobody was more pleased than he was when he was able to repay that early inspiration with the offer of hospitality during Grimond's longer stays at Canterbury. Jo Grimond thoroughly enjoyed his time as Kent's chancellor, retaining the position for twenty years, and Kent was by all accounts proud of its chancellor. Although he had hardly any duties – the most time-consuming being the presentation of degrees – Grimond was nominally head of the university. He gave full rein to his sense of mischief, usually using his speeches to the degree congregation to get his political concerns of the moment off his chest. He did so with evident good humour and with the well-practised accompaniment of self-deprecation, so nobody ever objected.

On one occasion, he proved to be a poor recruiting sergeant for his own party. They should certainly think seriously about standing for Parliament, he told them, but 'only for a safe seat' which, he conceded, 'virtually rules out being a Liberal'.[49] Grimond made good use of his network of contacts on behalf of the university and took part himself, to good effect, in a number of political seminars. He was also given a modest expense account, whose funds he did not allow to fructify. He would periodically ask for the names of ten or twelve students, whom he would then invite for lunch, in the early days taking these little groups for bracing Sunday walks in the Kent countryside, followed by a pub lunch and discussions ranging from the abstruse and academic to the earthy and political. He also mixed well with the academic community and with the parents of the students and graduands and enjoyed the conviviality of university life to the full; in preparation for his visits, his hosts knew that they had to be well stocked with gin and tonics. Before the presentation of politics degrees, the Dean of Social Sciences would give the graduating students a tour-de-scène of politics and a brief pep talk on the ceremony itself. One graduand from the early 1980s recalls the dean's closing remark, which amused all those who had met their chancellor before: 'Oh by the way, the Chancellor has had a good lunch so in the likely event that he gives you a PhD, just smile, say thank you and move on.' Fellow travellers were regularly surprised to recognise him, travelling alone, on the last evening train back from Canterbury to Charing Cross after staying on at some event long beyond the call of duty. Occasionally he also invited little groups of academics to dinner in the House of Commons. These too were highly convivial, not to say bibulous, occasions. It is scarcely to be wondered at that Grimond is remembered at Kent with great affection.

Another agreeable academic appointment came in the shape of the presidency of the English Association for 1972. In his presidential address, Grimond did not so much praise the power of words, as warn against the danger of words being abused in public life. He was amongst the first to point out how television reporting had eroded the old distinction between 'news' and 'comment', often implicitly or even subliminally through the reporter's choice of words: 'When a particularly callous atrocity is carried out by the IRA, I have seen it referred to as an "execution" – now the word "execution" implies that it has some legality; the word "murder" implies that it is an illegal and immoral act. By using the word "execution" you make a comment on the act.'[50] In one sense, Grimond had identified an early strain of political correctness. In the second part of his address, Grimond returned to his views about democracy, and his belief that liberal democracy requires people to make rational and considered choices: 'literacy means . . . exploring areas available only to the literate . . . It means refining judgements in a way only possible through the application of argument and the acceptance of general ideas.'[51]

In the midst of all this there was cause for celebration. In January 1973 Jo and Laura became grandparents, when their daughter Grizelda had a child by the director and actor Tony Richardson. Then, on 11th May 1973, their son Johnny married Kate Fleming at St Bartholomew's Church, Nettlebed. The bride was the daughter of Peter Fleming, an old friend of the Grimond family, and his wife Celia Johnson, the celebrated actress.

One of Grimond's most notable speeches in the wake of Harold Wilson's narrow win in October 1974 came in a debate about the arts. While everyone else in the debate talked about levels of public subsidy, Grimond talked very impressively about the creative process, and about the destruction that had been visited upon so many of Britain's great cities by modern architects. This was a theme to which he had regularly returned since the 1950s. This genuine love for the attractive over the merely functional brought Grimond into conflict with the authorities at Edinburgh University when, in the late 1950s, they set about destroying the historic buildings of George Square in order to replace them with hideous concrete monoliths that they claimed would be more practical. Grimond's response to this act of architectural desecration was typical of him at his vitriolic best: 'Personally, I hope that an indestructible ferro-concrete monument will be put up on which will be carved the names, not only of the Secretary of State, but of the Principal of the University and the whole of the University Court commemorating the deed. Presumably, they are proud of pulling down George Square, and so they should be associated with its destruction.'[52] This was typical Grimond: his interest in architecture was profound, but his priority was never to see grander and grander temples to wealth. He was concerned that the homes of ordinary people should be improved, that city centres should be easy on the eye and practical. He resented the unending race to build yet higher office blocks, and bemoaned the fact that 'our town planning is largely in the hands of deplorable architects.'[53] Although Grimond counted several individual architects amongst his friends, he regarded that profession collectively as unusually pernicious, wrecking the country whilst collecting its 'routine hand-out of OMs, knighthoods and so on'.[54]

Although his tastes were never painfully highbrow and he was more or less tone-deaf, Grimond was certainly a cultivated man. He enjoyed reading (particular favourites included detective novels and the works of Proust), but his main enthusiasm was for the visual arts, notably Scottish paintings and fine architecture. He was one of the first people to recognise the qualities of Sir William MacTaggart, in whose paintings he enthusiastically invested. As a member of the committee assembled to advise on the selection and display of works of art in the Commons area of the Palace of Westminster, he gleefully took the opportunity of having as many works of art as he could disinterred and displayed, in order that people should actually be able to see them. He found deeply distasteful the very notion that there should be vast cellars full of works of art that were in theory in the possession of the British people, but which no one ever had the opportunity to see. 'Art is central,' he once wrote. 'It is not a diversion.'[55] When Grimond visited Madrid in mid November 1968, lodging there with the British minister, Sir Nicholas Henderson, he did little to press forward the interests of the Liberal Party during his stay, preferring to indulge his interests in architecture and paintings as his first visit to Spain in some thirty years reopened an entire culture to him. He gave his host a splendid book about the fountains of Rome and proved to be a wonderful companion, in Henderson's words, 'enthusiastic, unconceited, not too doctrinaire – a keen and assiduous sightseer'.[56] In May 1973 Grimond led a delegation to Mrs Thatcher, the Secretary of State for Education, to plead for a more flexible and informed governmental approach to art studies and to protest against the enforced merger of the arts colleges into the polytechnics. The delegation included the distinguished sculptor Henry Moore and the painters John Piper and Patrick Heron, as well as Patrick Gibson, chairman of the Arts Council. It did not win her over.

Another organisation that Grimond actively supported was the Minority Rights Group (MRG), which published during the 1970s a series of detailed and learned reports into the problems of minority groups not only in the United Kingdom, but also right across the world. No minority seems to have been ignored, from the Tartars of the Crimea to the Sahel Nomads and the Jehovah's Witnesses of Central Africa. Grimond regularly attended meetings of the group and, in 1976, delivered the fifth MRG annual lecture. He not only emphasised the benefits that immigrants can bring to nations (joking that 'as I have spent much of my life in England I can claim to have come from a family which has conferred inestimable benefits on two nations'), but also spoke up for the rights of minorities which were not bound together by racial characteristics or religious beliefs, but by 'refusal to accept the conformity which in this country is now a much more damaging restriction than even the class system'.[57] In a highly centralised, bureaucratic state, he argued, almost anyone who tried to go his or her own way or, even worse, desired to be 'eccentric', was likely to be treated as part of a seditious minority. This kind of state-sponsored pressure to conform had, in Grimond's view, greatly fuelled the movement for home rule: 'the chronic mismanagement of [Britain's] affairs and her lack of élan have led to centrifugal movements such as Scottish and Welsh nationalism.'

Always an advocate of cooperatives and co-ownership, in the 1970s Grimond decided to find out more at first hand about cooperatives that really worked. The most impressive and celebrated example was the Mondragon cooperative movement, which he visited in 1977. Mondragon was set up in 1955 in the Basque region of Spain with an initial workforce of two dozen men, with the active support and participation of the local Catholic priest, Father Arizemediaretta, who contributed to the strong element of Catholic-style social solidarity that underpins Mondragon. By the late 1970s it encompassed over seventy coops, with approximately 15,000 employees, working in a wide range of activities including banking, farming and retail distribution. Every employee has to make a down payment before joining a Mondragon cooperative, and everyone has an equal vote. Mondragon appealed to Grimond in a host of ways: he liked the dignity accruing to the worker-owners, and he was impressed with the transparency of the arrangements for social services, and the willingness of people to contribute what they could afford towards their cost. He also felt that areas like the Highlands and Islands could learn much from the way in which the Mondragon savings bank, the Caja Laboral Popular, made available for reinvestment money saved within a community for investment within that same community. In time what began as a tiny credit cooperative grew into one of the larger and more profitable banks in Western Europe. At a purely economic level, Grimond was also impressed by the manner in which Mondragon, though not entirely recession-proof, could survive more or less intact the ups and downs of the economic climate prevailing elsewhere in Spain. He did, however, express to Robert Oakeshott his fear that its values might be 'altogether too Cromwellian for our more easy-going fellow countrymen'.[58]

Grimond had long argued in favour of co-ownership in industry, not as a replacement for the free market system, but as a *modus operandi* that could easily thrive within it. In 1978 he became the first chairman of Job Ownership Limited (JOL), a non-profit organisation set up by Robert Oakeshott to encourage and assist in the establishment of cooperatives through a range of seminars and publications, inspired by the example of Mondragon. For its first two years, JOL was funded by the Rowntree Trust. Speaking at the launch of JOL, Grimond described the Mondragon model as 'socialism without the state' and called for a reassertion of old-style, community-based and decentralised 'guild socialism'. Oakeshott himself characterised the JOL paradigm as a combination of the socialist-style worker solidarity with the old Tory emphasis on individualism and self-reliance. Grimond remained chairman of JOL for eight years and, during the latter stages of his career in the House of Commons, he became an enthusiastic tabler of amendments relating to employee share-ownership. He also extracted an undertaking from the Thatcher government with regard to tax relief for employees who borrowed in order to invest in their employers.

In June 1979 it was announced that Grimond would be on the inaugural editorial board of the newly established Mainstream Book Club. Working with the Oxford-based publisher Basil Blackwell, this group set out to commission a series of short books (four per year) dealing with contemporary political themes. Others on the editorial board included two future Conservative cabinet ministers, John Patten and Leon Brittan, the Conservative historian Robert Blake and the free-market economist Alan Peacock. The group grew out of a series of dinners in Oxford organised by Patten, then a don at Hertford College and soon to become the Conservative MP for Oxford. The stated aim of Mainstream was to 'present a balanced and generally non-collectivist analysis of the country's problems . . . recognise the distinctive quality of British culture and society, and offer proposals for long-term change, adaptation and conservation'. Although Mainstream was not a Conservative organisation as such, there was no mistaking its right-radical tenor. What united this group was a sense that the post-war consensus must now be broken, and that a complete reassessment of the 'mixed economy' was essential. If necessary for the good economic health of the country, the public-private boundary should be shifted quite radically in favour of the private sector. The thesis was perhaps more 'supply-side' than monetarist, but there is no doubt that Mainstream played its part in shoring up the foundations of the intellectual revolution of the 1980s.

As an enthusiastic regular at dinners of the Literary Society, Grimond was a well-known and equally well-liked figure in publishing circles and, once his political career was acknowledged to have passed its zenith, there was a great deal of interest in extracting an autobiography from him. Grimond's own wish by the mid 1970s was to produce a definitive work on Scottish politics, but the traumas that engulfed the Liberals during and after the Thorpe crisis put paid to that. Although he did sketch out the synopsis of a book about the development of society and the need for political reform to re-establish the primacy of moral judgements over economic ones, that too fell by the wayside. At least six separate publishers were politely rebuffed between 1975 and 1977 when they asked Grimond to write for them about his life. He just had too many other distractions and, although his work with his 'ghost' Brian Neve had borne fruit not only effectively but amazingly quickly too, he would never have allowed anyone else to write even part of an autobiography for him. When Grimond did finally agree to contract for his autobiography, he was dealing with yet another publisher, Nigel Hollis of Heinemann, whose father Christopher had in 1963 published Grimond's second book. The contract was signed in May 1977, with the typescript due by the end of that year.

After all the false starts of the past decade or so, Grimond was able to recycle a certain amount of unused material, and to recast some of his ideas. Nonetheless, as he freely admitted, the process did rather drag out. He sketched out a synopsis almost at once (in which he proposed that his time at Oxford should be dealt with 'briefly, if at all'), but then appears to have done no more than sketch out a few pages of manuscript until the original deadline was past. A chasing letter from January 1979 suggests that Hollis Jr now lived in hope, not expectation. He was unduly pessimistic for, working away in railway stations, airport departure lounges and even on board ship, Grimond was indeed crafting his *Memoirs*. The editing of this work must have been an immense challenge – the structure is discursive, to put it mildly – but much of the material is affectionate and fascinating. The book was launched in October 1979, and Grimond was uncharacteristically enraged to discover that many of his proof corrections had been ignored, sometimes with embarrassing results.

The index in particular contains one or two howlers. Grimond's parliamentary colleague from the Highlands, Hamish Gray, inexplicably appears in the book as 'Hamish Troy' – and even more bizarrely in the index as 'Hamish Gray Troy'. For years afterwards, whenever he needed to discuss any matter of common interest with Grimond, Gray would announce himself, with Grimondish humour, with the words 'Hamish Troy here!'

The book was not a commercial success. Grimond had really left it too late and, although book signings were organised in the face of Grimond's initial reluctance, in many instances they were only sparsely attended. At a packed literary lunch in Yorkshire, attended by his old friends and colleagues Donald Wade and Richard Wainwright, Grimond was undaunted and in sparkling form, treating his audience to an amusing account of the manner in which production of the book had drifted, in which he allowed himself a deal of comic licence in the interests of effective humour. He had met Nigel Hollis after making a television appearance, he explained, the project had been agreed and then there was silence: 'Ten months later [in fact it was closer to twenty-five], after hearing nothing, I delivered the book and it took them all by surprise – they had forgotten they had asked me.'[59] He also revealed one literary clanger that he had dropped: 'I thought one family I had mentioned were dead and I am glad to say they are not bringing a libel action.'[60] He got his best laugh, however, when he recounted Laura's response at being told that he was at last going to embark on writing his autobiography. She had just asked him why he didn't wait until he was dead. Perhaps Grimond's tongue was only half in his cheek when he went on to share this thought with listeners: 'One of my hosts inferred there were too many Liberals and I agree with him. Donald Wade and I would have found it much easier to run the party had we not been pestered by its members. They are an infernal nuisance; their job is to pay up and shut up.'[61] Although its sales were disappointing, the book attracted a lot of publicity, and a wide range of reviewers. Most found plenty to enjoy in its pages, though there was little praise for the organisation of the text, and some reviewers identified a slightly disagreeable whiff of privilege and nepotism hanging over much of Grimond's early life – which sat uneasily with his own denunciations of the creeping abuse of privilege in Britain in the 1970s. Although Grimond's *Memoirs* are poorly organised, they are full of little gems, some of them reproduced in these pages. Few would attest to the accuracy of Grimond's anecdotes, however, some of which are impressionistic to put it kindly, and the book is probably best regarded as an enjoyable, discursive stream of consciousness – and not as an impeccably accurate source for a biographer!

15

By the end of 1967, though still by no means wholly comfortable in the peculiar role of 'ex-leader', Grimond was again deriving at least some enjoyment from his politics. He had been refreshed and recharged by his travels, and Labour's travails in government seemed to have confirmed his fears. Always a vain man, he also quietly enjoyed being compared favourably with Jeremy Thorpe, who was failing to provide the party with a cutting edge. A few years later, he would admit that: 'I think I should have done more for Jeremy when he was under attack – I didn't for a mixture of bad and good motives . . . Having given up being leader of the party, I didn't see why I should still have to enter into controversy. Also I was told that it wouldn't do him any good to have the father figure come swanning over the horizon.'[1]

It certainly didn't help Thorpe much when, in March 1968, a group of Grimond's closest supporters, including Chris Layton, Richard Holme and David Steel, launched the Radical Action Movement, supposedly as the seedbed of realignment, its objective to 'secure a dialogue between radicals in the Labour and Liberal Parties as well as those who sought solutions outside party politics in direct social action'.[2] Journalists and commentators immediately dubbed the movement 'Jo's Agents' and assumed that it was a conspiracy to oust Jeremy Thorpe and restore Grimond to the Liberal leadership. In May 1968 the Young Liberals called on Thorpe to quit and, in June, an abortive coup against him took place while he was on his honeymoon. In a speech during Thorpe's absence, Grimond endorsed his leadership: 'I reject criticism of Mr Thorpe – he is doing a splendid job.'[3] Yet, reading between the lines, Gordon Greig of the *Daily Mail* perceived support for Thorpe's persecutors, as Grimond conceded that the party should open itself up to the 'widest ranging discussion' about internal reform. The day he returned, Thorpe attended a critical meeting of the party's Executive Committee, at which his leadership was endorsed by 48 votes to 2. A few days later, he endured an interrogation on television during which he freely admitted that he would happily serve under Jo Grimond in a government of the realigned left.

By the summer of 1968, Grimond was beginning to admit, albeit in private, that he too was growing disillusioned with Thorpe's leadership. His successor, he felt, should have been far more opportunistic, latching on to protest movements such as the one against the proposed airport development at Stansted, and resurgent Scottish nationalism. He regretted too the tendency towards centralisation that Thorpe had brought to the party, and now claimed that he would like to see the party recast as a loose federation of semi-autonomous constituent parts. Above all, he deplored Thorpe's evident lack of interest in political ideas and questions of policy. Others who felt the same way – many of whom had opposed Thorpe from the outset – began by mid 1968 seriously to wonder whether Grimond might not be willing to stage a comeback, ousting his own successor after little more than a year. In early June 1968 Christopher Layton and John Pardoe went to see Grimond in order to try and persuade him to initiate a *putsch*. Grimond told them that he had no intention of becoming leader again – not out of any particular loyalty to, or enthusiasm for, Thorpe, but because he saw no immediate future for the party. His sense of detachment infuriated his supporters, but was not that hard to understand. He had done so much for the party, but was still young enough to explore new pastures. Why on earth would he wish to get embroiled in this mess? As soon as this message sank in, senior Liberals realised that, if they were to have any party left at all, they just had to make the best of the Thorpe leadership. There was no alternative leader waiting in the wings and the more radical elements in the party began to devote their energies to building up the party at the grassroots.

It was in the autumn of 1968 that Grimond found himself openly under attack from his fellow Liberals for the first time, charged with dividing his party and undermining its leadership. What motivated his behaviour before and during the assembly of that year may only be speculated at, but it nearly caused irreparable divisions. Although Grimond had felt obligated to support Thorpe in the leadership contest eighteen months earlier, he seemed by now to feel that any obligation had been discharged. As luck would have it, that autumn the Liberals held a joint assembly in Edinburgh for both the national party and the semi-autonomous Scottish Liberals. This threatened star billing for the running argument about relations with the Nationalists. But it was not that controversy in which Jo Grimond would become embroiled. In the run-up to the assembly, the Young Liberals published some remarks by Grimond in which he allegedly suggested that Britain would never get the reforms it needed through the democratic process, in which case would-be reformers would have to resort to non-parliamentary action:

> However unpalatable it may be, the truth is that again and again useful reforms have been achieved in Britain by force after argument has failed . . . the way to get to the public is to create a disturbance . . . Thus the temptation of action, not words, is increased . . . It is possible that many of the changes necessary would only be achieved by action which the organisers of the present bureaucracies would regard as illiberal and revolutionary.[4]

It transpired that some draft remarks penned by Grimond for a conference in Scandinavia that July had found their way into the possession of the Young Liberals, whose membership included everything from crypto-Marxists to fanatically devout libertarians. Only a couple of years earlier they had denounced Grimond as too old and out of touch. Now they revered him as a radical rebel and, with sublime timing, had leaked the contents of his note to the media just before the party assembly.

As soon as Grimond heard that his comments had been rush-released by the Young Liberals in time for the assembly, Grimond explained that he had not been endorsing 'direct action'; he was merely making a historical observation, with examples such as Ireland and India in mind. He was not suggesting for one moment that he wanted democratic processes to be bypassed; he was just observing that, throughout history, if political institutions failed to channel pressures for change, then those pressures had often led to violence. In any case, Britain was already increasingly beset by strikes – and didn't that represent a triumph of force against reason? 'Obviously it would be better if normal democratic methods could be equally effective,' he explained, 'but how can they be, when the party in power takes no notice of what people are feeling?'[5] On *The World at One* he explained that he wanted 'government by reason . . . I want more democracy, and this means making it effective.'[6] Grimond was echoing sentiments that he had expressed on many previous occasions: in the *Spectator* as early as 1956, in his famous 'Sound of Gunfire' speech in 1963 and, most recently, in a lecture less than a year earlier. At Königswinter, even more recently, Grimond's fellow delegates had apparently listened calmly as he set out his view that 'the basis of parties is being eroded and that a great number of people do not feel any deep attachment to any party . . . If they are not offered a place within a democratic process they may conceivably take to extremes.'[7] So the views attributed to Grimond were nothing very new. They were also, as the 1970s would brutally demonstrate, all too well founded. Russell Johnston, chairman of the joint conference committee, who had clashed with Grimond only a few months earlier about the party's relationship with the Scottish Nationalists, now performed the Liberal equivalent of swearing in church by denouncing him as a 'dilettante revolutionary'.[8] In contrast, John Pardoe and Tim Beaumont, who were putting themselves forward as 'anti-establishment' candidates for senior party offices, defended Grimond and tried to explain the frustrations that he was trying to express, Pardoe describing him as 'the leading politician in any party in the country – I still think he is the best Prime Minister this country has not had since the war.'[9]

Through the Rowntree Trust, Grimond was able to encourage many younger radicals to pursue their interests in the new political activism that emerged towards the end of the 1960s. In the autumn of 1964 the USA and the UK had both elected supposedly left-leaning figures: Lyndon Johnson and Harold Wilson. Both of them rapidly disappointed radical opinion, most violently through the prosecution of the war in Vietnam, which Johnson instigated and Wilson supported. Although Grimond retained some of the taboos that must have come with his upbringing, once he had resigned as Liberal leader he came to be regarded by many of these young radicals as both an inspiration and a kindred spirit. Like them, he somehow rejected both sides of the Cold War; like them, he always had a strong egalitarian streak; and also like them, he wanted to explore new forms of co-ownership and even anarcho-syndicalism. He quickly set out to encourage the younger radicals who crossed his path, using Rowntree money to send several of them out as 'scouts' to experience the new hotbeds of youthful radicalism for themselves. Grimond was fascinated to hear the first-hand accounts of his 'scouts' about the emergence of a new radicalism. He became more and more convinced that a massive 'dealignment' was taking place, socially and politically. His dalliance with the further shores of radical politics had now caught up with him.

In the wake of the furore, Grimond had a widely publicised forty-five-minute meeting with Jeremy Thorpe at his hotel, proclaimed his faith in his successor and appeared on the main platform, speaking on devolution and receiving a warm ovation. Then, to the irritation of the party leadership, he also honoured his agreement to appear at the Young Liberals' unofficial 'Free Assembly', to which members of other parties were also invited, sitting quietly at the back of the hall for twenty minutes with a group of supporters, and then failed to show up at a press conference which he was to share with Thorpe, claiming that he was 'too busy' to fit it in. While an embarrassed Thorpe sat waiting for him, Grimond was telephoning an article to a newspaper, fulfilling a television engagement and then having lunch only 100 yards away. In that article, Grimond first of all protests that: 'I am not in any circumstances – even if asked, which I have not been – trying to regain the leadership of the Liberal Party.'[10] He also claims, rather less plausibly, that his successor need have no fear of him. He had never criticised him and, furthermore, 'for what it is worth, I have said that Mr Thorpe has my confidence.'[11]

The following day, Russell Johnston earned a mixture of applause and booing when he followed up his earlier criticism of Grimond in a speech to delegates, commenting that: 'I don't think it is helpful for him to go round saying the whole basis of having a party is highly suspect – I want to know what he means and what he will put in its place.'[12] To attack Grimond once might have been regarded as a mistake, but to do so twice was wanton iconoclasm. Significantly, however, some 70 or 80 per cent of delegates accorded Johnston a standing ovation. So did a number of leading figures on the platform who shared his sense of infuriation about Grimond, including

George Mackie and Emlyn Hooson. Curiously, many of the same delegates applauded John Pardoe with the same fervour only minutes later when he praised Grimond in a speech of similar intensity, defending his right to express even his more wayward thoughts and to 'go off on intellectual safari'. Even though Russell Johnston had warned Grimond about what he was going to say, giving him the opportunity of slipping away from the platform in good time before the onslaught began, the older man apparently never forgave him. The following day Grimond and Johnston were again on opposing sides of the argument, when Grimond and John Bannerman spoke in favour of an amendment to the main policy on devolution. The executive's motion, in support of which Johnston spoke, called for a fully federal system of government with regional assemblies for England. The amendment endorsed by Grimond and Bannerman proposed instead the creation of a single English Parliament, to rank alongside those of Scotland, Wales and Northern Ireland, something in which Grimond believed passionately. It was defeated by the narrow margin of 365 votes to 335.

In the autumn and winter of 1968–9, Grimond certainly showed all the signs of wandering off on an 'intellectual safari', returning in rather wayward fashion to his favourite theme, the economic and political disintegration of Britain: 'I do not see that there is any reason why, in an affluent society, some people should not choose to live in idleness – it may not be very practical, but there is no reason why people should not try.'[13] In a more sober vein, he warned that the Soviet Union was looking to expand what it termed its 'legitimate sphere of influence', possibly with a view to intervening more directly in the affairs of the Middle East and Yugoslavia. During this period, Grimond was still often seen in the tearoom of the House of Commons, traditionally the haunt of plotters and would-be conspirators. Jeremy Thorpe subsequently laughed this off, commenting that he was 'a close Scot . . . Jo is seen getting off the Underground . . . he's seen around the tearoom for the simple reason that it's cheaper than the dining room.'[14]

Jeremy Thorpe was understandably eager to get Grimond 'back on board' and, during the Christmas recess of 1968–9, managed to talk him into taking on a formal front-bench role, as home affairs spokesman. In the wake of the recent party assembly, a story had appeared in the newspapers in which it was claimed that the Scottish Nationalists had approached Grimond and asked him to take the lead in a new movement campaigning for a self-governing Scotland. This was not quite correct, but Grimond was planning a short tour of Scotland in the New Year, during which he would call for a unified Scottish home rule movement. He seems to have felt that the SNP was vulnerable if the Scottish Liberals could make a concerted bid for its supporters. In advance of this, he re-entered the controversy about the Liberals and the SNP on Scottish Television, publicly calling upon everyone who favoured home rule to 'stand up and be counted and cooperate' by uniting in each constituency behind a single candidate.[15] Then, in a speech in Galashiels, he made sure that nobody had missed his point, by proclaiming his 'warm feelings towards the Scottish Nationalists'.[16] He blamed the fact that the parties were opposing each other on the 'narrow outlook' of some individuals within the SNP leadership. James Davidson was due to introduce a Bill for a Scottish referendum in the House of Commons in February, and Grimond argued that this would provide a perfect opportunity for putting party differences on one side, marking a total departure from the official line of the Scottish Liberals. Grimond's detractors were incensed by what they regarded as yet another irresponsible attempt to hijack the debate. The SNP leadership was no more enthusiastic. The party's chairman, Arthur Donaldson, rejected Grimond's proposals out of hand. Grimond later denounced him as a 'tiresome man'.[17]

The winter of 1968–9 brought no improvement in the political and economic situation. Grimond's dealings with ministers and their departments had confirmed his fears that the present generation of politicians and civil servants were simply not up to the job, and he began rather to revel in his doom-mongering. For example, after one lunch with him, the incorrigible diarist Cecil King recorded Grimond's belief that: 'the problems piling up – social, financial, constitutional – are so enormous as to be insoluble as far as he can see.'[18] He despaired totally of the Labour Party and, although he felt some sympathy for Ted Heath personally, he did not believe that the Tory leader would be able to succeed where others had failed, by eradicating the twin evils of bureaucratic centralism and endemic inflation. The failings of the economic and employment policies seemed to Grimond obvious: in Orkney and Shetland, a notional unemployment rate of almost 10 per cent coexisted with a chronic shortage of skilled and semi skilled workers. Meanwhile, much of the taxpayers' money that made its way to the islands was frittered away creating pointless jobs in the public sector.

In September 1969, for the second year running, Grimond caused controversy at the beginning of the Liberals' autumn assembly. In a television interview with Robin Day, he returned yet again the question of an alliance with the SNP, saying that the Liberals should 'march along with any other groups who are going our way'. When Day asked if he meant that the Liberals and the SNP should pool their efforts, Grimond replied, 'I do indeed.'[19] This provoked more tart remarks about him from Russell Johnston, who told the press: 'there are indeed some Liberals who would do well to study the nationalist parties they court, for they would find them far from liberal.'[20] Speaking to the press at the party's Edinburgh assembly the previous year, Jeremy Thorpe had enraged opponents of a pact by keeping this door very much ajar. If the Liberals and the SNP managed to win a majority of seats in Scotland, he thought that the prospects for a joint campaign for the 'limited immediate objective' of a Scottish Parliament were good: 'In my view it could be obtainable after three or four years.'[21] The assembly was a disaster. An anti-EEC undercurrent emerged, and attempts by Jeremy Thorpe and Chris Layton to ignite genuine enthusiasm for accession were less than compelling. Although the Liberals were enjoying considerable successes at local elections and, in June 1969, had gained the constituency of Birmingham Ladywood at a by-election, the general view was that they were ill prepared for a general election.

A week later, it was announced that the Scottish Liberal Party (SLP) was thinking of creating a new position of leader, which they would ask Grimond to take on. He indicated that he might be willing to accept and that, although he had for two years campaigned for some kind of pact with the Nationalists, he did now accept that 'the time for this has now passed, because the SNP have put up candidates against Liberals in all constituencies except my own'.[22] This position was entirely consistent with that of the SLP, whose executive had now decided to meet him half way by setting out its belief that 'all Scots who accept the right of Scotland to determine its own future should come together' and that they would, after all, have 'welcomed an electoral tactical agreement with the SNP despite our policy disagreements'. The idea of creating an SLP 'leader' died a quick death, however, amid fears that such a move might give the impression that the party's national leader had lost part of his bailiwick, and in due course it was announced that Grimond would instead be elevated to the established position of president of the Scottish Liberals, in succession to the late Lord Bannerman. On the day the announcement was made, 30th October 1969, the SNP had a disappointing result in a by-election in the constituency of Glasgow, Gorbals, and Grimond took the opportunity to gloat, saying that the result destroyed their pretensions to power. Below the surface, however, all was still not well between Jo Grimond and the Scottish Liberals.

The meeting that endorsed the proposal that the party should make better use of Grimond by making him president also rejected the idea of any 'common front' with the SNP as a matter of principle. Grimond thought that this went too far and, in November, he reopened the matter again by arguing forcefully that the Liberals should not contest the forthcoming South Ayrshire by-election; they should give the SNP a clear run, and they should issue a public statement to that effect. A parallel row between Grimond and the SLP was also brewing. Grimond had obtained a lump sum of up to £1,500 from the Rowntree Trust, to pay for the appointment of a full-time employee to take care of research and press relations at the SLP headquarters in Edinburgh. The person whom he had in mind was one of George Mackie's daughters, who was believed to be interested in taking on such a job. When she decided not to take the position, Mackie suggested paying half of the money to a former teacher called Donald Gorrie (latterly a Liberal Democrat MP) whom he wished to appoint as part-time head of research. Grimond was not keen; this was not at all what he had in mind, since Gorrie apparently had no experience of public relations. George Mackie dug his heels in, defending what he had done and calling Grimond's bluff, telling him that, if he wished to advise the Rowntree Trust to cancel the money, then he must of course do so.

Grimond had wanted to take an aggressive leading role over the winter of 1969–70 in promoting the party's policy on home rule. He received no support for this idea and sulked in his tent instead. Then he heard that his old friend Bryan Keith-Lucas, of Kent University, had been asked to draft the party's definitive policy on home rule. Much as he liked and admired Keith-Lucas, Grimond protested that such a delicate and controversial matter should surely be left to the political leadership of the party. He also heard that the new policy might include proposals for an 'English Grand Committee' of MPs, along the lines of the existing Scottish and Welsh Grand Committees. To have a committee that would consist of around 75 per cent of all MPs seemed to Grimond plain daft. In April 1969 Wilson had set up a commission under the chairmanship of Lord Crowther to look at all aspects of the constitution. Grimond was asked for his views on the party's draft submission to the commission, and duly submitted them. He was greatly piqued to discover that they had been largely ignored. He became even more dyspeptic when he was invited to join a small SLP group in giving oral evidence on a date that had already been fixed (by the commission itself). On top of that, he was invited to an SLP press conference, its date and time also fixed without consultation, to launch the printed version of the Crowther evidence, which he had still not seen in its final form. In March 1970 Grimond privately informed the SLP that he no longer wished to take on its presidency. He had never wanted the position, he claimed, and had always had misgivings about agreeing to take it on. He felt that the SLP had been thoroughly uncooperative and inconsiderate towards him, and the proposal was dead in the water. In any case, he had not the faintest idea of what would be expected of him in the position. He felt too old to be a stooge and too young to be a mere figurehead, and became convinced that he had been treated with less consideration than was his due; in effect, whether he realised it or not, he was hankering after his old status. Grimond had never been much of a 'team player'. After ten years as leader, he could be impossible.

Grimond claimed to be worried that the SLP was in danger of overstating its independence from the UK Liberals. Although the Scottish Liberals were in a sense 'independent', he felt that the SLP executive, under George Mackie, was pushing the point dangerously far by setting out to establish a full policy of its own on home rule independently of Liberals in the other constituent parts of the UK – a policy that might come into conflict with that of the party nationally. When he was party leader, Grimond explained to others in the SLP,

he had regarded himself both as leader of the British Liberal Party and of the
Scottish Liberal Party. It was therefore absurd for the SLP executive to take it
upon itself unilaterally to redraw its constitutional policy without reference to
the national leadership. George Mackie, Russell Johnston and Donald Gorrie
swiftly and robustly closed ranks against Grimond. They pointed out that he
had been the first Liberal outside the SLP headquarters to receive a copy of the
Crowther evidence, and that the date chosen for the press conference had been
the only possible day on which the main authors of the evidence, David Steel
and Russell Johnston, could have met the press without some unfortunate
clash. They also felt that, given Grimond's reputation for making capricious
and last-minute changes to his arrangements, it would have been absurd to
organise any major event around his supposed availability. The bad blood was
beginning to run deeply between Grimond and his senior Scottish colleagues,
who evidently felt that he was behaving like an over-indulged child, grown
paranoid in his desperate quest for recognition and appreciation.

When Grimond's fingerprints were detected on an abortive plan to replace
him as chairman of the SLP, George Mackie decided that enough was enough.
He warned Grimond that his behaviour was seriously jeopardising the Liberals'
prospects in Scotland and enjoined him to bury the hatchet, withdraw his
refusal to accept the presidency and row in the same boat as everyone else.
At Mackie's insistence, the two men attempted to clear the air at a stormy
meeting of the SLP executive on 4th April 1970. Grimond started off by
putting on the record the fact that others had put him under pressure to
become president of the SLP. He had, he said, assumed that this would
mean becoming the 'political leader of the Scottish Liberal Party'. Since he
had agreed to let his name go forward, however, he had not received due
support and cooperation from the SLP headquarters. 'He also,' according to
the minutes, 'contended that a large part of this lack of cooperation was due
to the fact that the Chairman, Mr George Y Mackie, liked to get his own
way.'[23] Mackie dissented, but offered an olive branch by suggesting that it
might be appropriate for the president to take the chair of the SLP office-
bearers' meetings. Grimond then set out his terms. Within the SLP, he said,
political leadership must come from the MPs. They and the elected office-
bearers should form a political directorate under the chairmanship of the
president and, after full discussion with the executive, the final say on policy
must rest with the 'leader' (i.e. the president). Grimond and Mackie then
left the room and, under the chairmanship of Russell Johnston, the executive
agreed to sue for peace – on Grimond's terms. A vote of confidence in George
Mackie's chairmanship was also passed. Grimond had won what he wanted –
a free rein to lead the party's battle in Scotland – and he announced that he
would, after all, allow his name go forward for the presidency. After three
years in the political wilderness, he had regained charge of a major part –

Grimond with Magnus, 1965

COCONUTS (1964)

Two Shy? Grimond takes a pot at his opponents (John Jensen/University of Kent)

Towards the Sound of Gunfire or just blunderbust? A fair summary of how realignment went off-track in 1964–6 (John Jensen/University of Kent)

The eyes have it: Grimond and his successor (Srdja Djukanovic)

Much Ado About Nothing: the famous, inconsequential, meeting at Orme Square, 3rd March 1974 (Srdja Djukanovic)

Basil Wishart, journalist, entrepreneur and some-time parliamentary candidate, was Grimond's most crucial supporter in Shetland

With Pratap Chitnis in Kirkwall (Dougie Shearer)

Jo, Laura and Magnus Grimond at the Old Manse with close neighbour and friend Jimmy Brown (Dougie Shearer)

With Edwin and Margaret Eunson in Kirkwall (Dougie Shearer)

Receiving a portrait from David Steel (*Liberal Democrat News*)

At the opening of an exhibition of cartoons by 'Vicky' (Victor Weisz) at the Cartoon Centre at the University of Kent

Introduction to the Lords, 1983: with Frank Byers and Pratap Chitnis (Srdja Djukanovic)

Jo and Laura receiving the
freedom of Orkney in 1987
(Dougie Shearer)

With long-standing friends and supporters from Shetland, Jim and Margaret Crossan in 1983
(Charles Tait)

A late portrait (Jane Bown)

his favourite part – of his old empire. This protracted and, at times, highly rancorous episode had at least resolved one issue: nobody in the upper echelons of the Scottish Liberal Party was left in any doubt that Grimond missed being party leader.

The cutting edge of nihilism that seemed to blight Grimond's relations with the SLP extended into his wider political philosophy at this time. Not only did he now feel that the party system was not up to the job: he feared that political thinking generally had become dangerously fatalistic, as a new doctrine took hold. In the previous century, Karl Marx had argued that capitalistic society would fall prey to inevitable economic forces. Marxism in practice had proved to be less than inspiring, but a new determinism was now taking a grip, in Grimond's view, as too many policy-makers were being seduced into believing that it was the development of science and management, rather than their own rational decisions, that would determine the future course of human history. He thought that Harold Wilson and Ted Heath in particular had been seduced by technology, allowing their political outlooks to be excessively influenced by this 'technological (or technical) determinism', rather than by social needs or philosophies. They were too concerned with prestige and the vainglorious, meretricious surface glamour of high-tech products, when far more basic human needs were still not being properly addressed, at home and abroad. He would also term this phenomenon 'Concordism', after the whitest elephant of all. Writing in a South African university magazine, he declared: 'The hand-maidens of technology are a series of bureaucratic organisations, the civil service, big business, the unions, the professions, operating in secret and invoking inevitability to justify their decisions . . . But there is a sizeable minority against this systemic fascism.'[24]

At the forthcoming election it would not only be Jo whose political activities were of general interest. There had long been talk of the party looking to harness Laura's abilities more effectively and attention suddenly focused on the selection of a Liberal successor to James Davidson, the MP for West Aberdeenshire, who felt obliged to stand down after only one term because of a family illness. Laura gave a wonderfully politically incorrect reply when she was first asked whether this possibility might appeal to her: 'It's like being asked whether you would marry a black man – how do you know until you are asked?'[25] In due course Laura was successfully wooed by the Liberals of West Aberdeenshire, saying that, if she won, 'I suppose I shall see a lot more of my husband.'[26] The couple's twenty-two-year old son Johnny was also selected to contest a Scottish seat, North Angus. Meanwhile, Laura went on a safari of her own, sampling Africa for the first time with a visit to Zambia and other southern African states. As an election in 1970 looked increasingly likely, the only ray of hope for Britain that Grimond could perceive came from across the Channel. In April 1969 Charles de Gaulle had resigned as President of the Republic after a comparatively technical referendum had gone against him, and his successor, Georges Pompidou, was far more emollient towards the British. On a visit to Brussels in December 1969, Grimond had a private meeting with Jean Rey, the President of the EEC Commission. In a follow-up letter, Rey struck an optimistic note: *'comme vous savez, les choses ont évolué depuis votre dernière visite et il y a maintenant des chances vraiment très sérieuses que les négociations commencent l'été prochain* [as you know, things have evolved since your last visit, and there is now a really serious chance that negotiations will commence next summer]'.[27] Wise words indeed.

In late 1969 Grimond introduced a Bill for home rule in the House of Commons, with support from his Liberal colleagues and Scottish Nationalists, and his last major contribution to the 1966–70 Parliament was his attempt to amend Labour's Race Relations Act, after a doctor in Eastbourne had found himself in hot water when he advertised for a 'Scottish daily able to do some plain cooking'. 'Racial harmony,' warned Grimond as he introduced his Bill at Second Reading, 'must be achieved by education and conciliation . . . Our whole approach to race relations depends upon carrying the public with us . . . If the public comes to think that the approach embodied in the Act is associated with what seems to it something quite contrary to common sense or natural justice, it will affect its whole attitude to the subject.'[28] Although the Government had initially indicated that it might help, in the event it opposed his Bill which was duly rejected by MPs.

Grimond's Bill for home rule was also killed off when Harold Wilson asked the Queen to dissolve Parliament in May 1970, with an election to be held on 18th June. In almost every conceivable way, the general election of 1970 was a disaster for the Liberals. Grimond nominally led the Liberals' campaign in Scotland, spending two days on a Scottish tour and the rest of his time in the islands, where he greatly missed the presence of Laura alongside him, at once energising and reassuring. Their daughter Grizelda filled the breach well enough, but Grimond's sense of foreboding never deserted him. Grimond knew that the Liberals' standing was not high and feared that even his northern stronghold might be afflicted. The Liberals always suffered when the Tories were on an upswing, and he sensed from the outset that this election would be no exception. On 18th June 1970 he received his lowest-ever majority, of below 3,000 votes. The party was almost wiped out: of its six surviving MPs, three (Steel, Thorpe and Pardoe) had majorities of below 1,000 votes. After a difficult campaign, Laura was comfortably defeated in West Aberdeenshire by the Tory candidate, Colonel Colin Mitchell ('Mad Mitch' of the Argyll and Sutherland Highlanders, famous for his bravery in Aden) and son Johnny lost heavily in Angus. In Scotland the Liberals retained three of their five seats (Steel, Johnston and Grimond himself), with the Conservative Hamish Gray surprising many people by gaining Ross & Cromarty. He was himself surprised when Grimond was among the first people to welcome him to Parliament:

> He stopped me in the lobby and congratulated me on winning my seat – while at the same time lamenting the fact that I had defeated his old friend Alasdair Mackenzie, for whom he had a great regard. He was extremely pleasant, and very informal, and said that, if anything ever cropped up that related to his constituency and also related to mine, not to hesitate to give him a ring and have a chat about it. I thought this was a very nice gesture, but I was to find later on that it was absolutely typical of Jo Grimond.[29]

Grimond also offered his congratulations to the incoming Prime Minister, Edward Heath, on a 'notable personal triumph, probably all the more so as being to many people unexpected'.[30]

Although Grimond would no doubt have liked his non-political activities to occupy more of his time after 1970, he was to be disappointed. Exactly a year before the election that brought Ted Heath to No. 10, he had predicted the result, not only of the election but also the consequences of Heath's managerial brand of Conservatism: '*I foresee a reasonable Tory majority at the next Election, a big Home Rule vote but few seats* . . . In Scotland there will be a big vote for Home Rule but unless there is some agreement between the Liberals and the SNP this will not be reflected in seats . . . *the next Government will be as entangled in financial management as is the present*'.[31] Few governments disappointed Grimond more than the Heath government did. He regarded its failure as both the personal failure of Heath, and a systemic failure of government itself. Before 1970, he had taken an unfashionably positive view of Heath, a fellow Balliol man, once describing him on television as 'a fair man whom people would trust'.[32] He had never doubted that the Conservative leader was well equipped for the highest office, and elements of the radicalism in those early days of 1970–1 appealed strongly to his liberal instincts. But the infamous U-turns that followed signified to Grimond a return to corporatism and a negation of freedom. They also appeared to confirm something else he had said in that broadcast: 'I don't think Ted has a very deep-seated political philosophy – when he comes up against a real political issue, you don't get the impression that he feels it in his stomach.'[33] As the 1970–4 Parliament progressed, Grimond spoke with increasing contempt and sadness of what he termed the 'rigid but constantly changing attitudes of Mr Heath'.[34] In particular he deplored the failure to tackle the inflationary culture that threatened to wreck not only the pound sterling, but also the social fabric of the country. This government, like its post-war predecessors, was failing to redefine the boundaries between collective and individual responsibility, notably in the sphere of industrial relations.

The nation's traumas of the early 1970s prompted a lot of soul-searching by Jo Grimond. In an apparently unpublished draft from 1971, he wrote that:

> More ubiquitous than the government are the pressures to conform to a world
> which seems to continually demand, hector, point to our inadequacies and
> threaten us with failure . . . always pointing at us from hoardings, admonishing
> us on television, shouting at us in newspapers. It is not our world. It menaces our
> freedom. Most people acquiesce. Indeed they might well be lost if released'.[35]

Grimond was by now much influenced by monetarist writings, and was
amongst the first politicians to warn publicly that the oil price shocks hitting
the economy would bring in their wake the long-term threat of ruinous
inflation. Heath's Chancellor, Tony Barber, allowed his fear of short-term
unemployment to dominate his thinking, and pressed on with expansionary
measures that would fan the inflationary flames. The irony is that Grimond's
fundamental faith in the *principles* of democracy at this time was, if anything,
stronger than ever. Even if he was convinced that metropolitan Britain had
gone quite mad, he continued to find solace and inspiration amongst the
people of Orkney and Shetland and never allowed his pessimism wholly
to burn out his idealism. He was increasingly convinced, however, that
the political and economic system prevailing in the United Kingdom was
incapable of delivering anything that could be in the 'general good'. One
interest group that found itself coming under withering attack from Grimond
was the BBC. In a lecture at Senate House, Grimond questioned whether
the normal viewer could be in the least stimulated by most of the BBC's
highly formulaic political programming. He argued that a major problem
lay amongst the corporation's 'hardy perennial' interviewers: 'They think the
same thoughts, they live in the same circles and it even seems that, if one dies,
his successor is better to have the same name – how many Dimblebys have
been employed by the BBC? Whether you are an artist, politician or journalist,
unless you are one of the dinner gongs to which the Pavlov's dogs of the media
respond, you have little chance.'[36] Two months later he attacked the 'declining
standards' of BBC news coverage.

Just before Christmas 1971, the royal family too were back in Grimond's
sights, when he and the Northern Irish MP Gerry Fitt were the only non-
Labour MPs to vote against a Bill to increase the royal finances. Next in line
for a colourful Grimond broadside were the Scots. Speaking in Linlithgow,
Grimond described his fellow Scots as 'the most politically incompetent people
in Western Europe, with the possible exception of the Poles'.[37] The problems
with Scots he enumerated as 'a certain venality'; 'a general softening of the
intellect in middle age'; 'toadyism'; and an ingrained love of bickering. The
first two characteristics were particularly pernicious, he said, because they
resulted in a 'plethora of successful and garrulous windbags without any moral
faith, an element fatal to political life'. This speech caused a mixture of hilarity,
bemusement and sententious criticism. The *Daily Telegraph* said in a leader: 'if
a Scottish Republican Army were established, Mr Grimond would certainly

be the man who blew up the pub with himself still inside it.'[38] Grimond's nerves were severely tested elsewhere on the Celtic fringe in January 1972 when, on a trip to Dublin, he found himself under physical attack from Republican students when he went to speak at the city's University College. This first-hand experience of intolerance in Ireland provoked one of the strongest speeches that he ever delivered. Addressing the Guild of Newspaper Editors, he said that the tactics of the IRA were worthy of the Nazis at their worst: 'There does not seem to me to have been adequate condemnation of this thuggery which, if it had been carried out by Fascists, would have raised a howl all over the world.'[39] Grimond's reaction to the Troubles in Northern Ireland generally demonstrated few illusions about a place that he had got to know fairly well during the war. He always recognised that, despite its best efforts, the British government could never effect a solution without the support of the people of Ireland: 'it is their quarrel, not ours.'[40] To send British soldiers to die in the province seemed to him the height of futility, and he despaired of the willingness of the 'moderate people of Ireland' to play some part in seeking out a settlement. 'The historical truth,' he once observed, 'is that the IRA has never achieved anything except murder and violence – and the indefinite postponement of the unity of Ireland.'[41]

By the end of 1972, with widespread strikes and intimidation, and the new development of violent picketing, Grimond feared that his apocalyptic prediction of 1968 was coming to pass. The hijackers, the IRA and the murderers of Munich seemed to him part of a single phenomenon: of violence and intimidation deliberately targeted at 'the wholly innocuous'. Even strikers were part of the same spectrum, since their actions generally harmed not the employers against whom they claimed to have grievances, but the ordinary public. More mundanely, Grimond took every opportunity to protest at the endless hankering after national prestige at the cost of lower living standards for the majority of the population. 'I long not to go to the moon,' he boasted during a debate on the future of Concorde.[42] On the economy, Grimond watched with a sense of growing despair as the Heath government dropped its earlier commitment to liberal economics, and warned that its attempts to deal with inflation through increasingly Byzantine incomes policies would result in 'a fairly agreeable totalitarian state, presided over by well-intentioned bureaucrats with an economy largely unresponsive to public demand'.[43] Now that the government had apparently abandoned free-market economics, Grimond felt that there was no advantage to be had by floating the pound, which was under constant pressure in the markets: 'It certainly relieves one of the traumatic experiences of devaluation . . . but if we are gradually floating down a river and sinking, it may be of some value to have an occasional weir at which we have to pull ourselves together.'[44] When in May 1973 he asked Heath to condemn Lonrho, Grimond unwittingly prompted his interlocutor

into the one utterance that has subsequently guaranteed him a place in most
dictionaries of quotations, as he denounced the 'unpleasant and unacceptable
face of capitalism'. A manuscript from December 1973 well characterises
Grimond's profound pessimism at the time:

> Inflation is an immediate and desperate danger to democracy. Unemployment
> is an evil but it can be handled by a free society. After a point inflation cannot.
> It not only weakens the economy, it undermines freedom. It debauches society.
> It breeds acquisitiveness, violence and fascism . . . the growing contrast between
> those who profit from inflation and those don't is the classic breeding ground
> of Nazism and communism.[45]

The two priorities in the fight against inflation were, he would argue, to
control the supply of money and credit and for those at the top to set a better
example by accepting less inflationary pay rises themselves.

Naturally Jo and Laura Grimond remained fully engaged with Orkney
and Shetland during this time. Their relationship with Jo's constituents was
still based upon a mixture of self-deprecating good humour and a crumpled
lairdishness. If a voter ever challenged him on a Liberal policy, he would tell
the elector not to worry: 'there is absolutely no chance of the Liberals putting
that into practice after the next election.' Grimond also entertained his local
troops by bringing big-name speakers to the islands. It didn't always work
out perfectly. David Steel, who had replaced the defeated Eric Lubbock as
chief whip, came to Orkney to speak and, as he walked along Kirkwall High
Street with Grimond beforehand, they met a group of supporters. Grimond
introduced his young protégé, saying, 'I'd like you to meet our chief whip
David Steel, who has come all this way to speak tonight. You will all, of
course, be coming?' 'Oh no, Mr Grimond,' one of the group responded,
'the branch have organised a whist drive.'[46] Steel accordingly spoke to an
audience of about twenty, after which they all went on to the whist drive,
where they found some 150 people. Laura too dabbled in elective politics
for the second time. Largely thanks to Grimond's interventions, the Heath
government's local government legislation had paved the way for new, single-
tier local authorities for Orkney and Shetland to be elected for the first time
in May 1974. Although Orkney had a population of only 17,000, the new
Orkney Islands Council would have almost full regional status, being all-
purpose (except for police and fire services), and all its meetings were to be
held in public. On 22nd January 1974 Laura deputised for her husband at a
big conference on the future of local government in Orkney, speaking about
the importance of voluntary activities. Then she decided to stand herself for
election as local councillor for the Grimonds' own home ward of Firth and
Harray (as an independent, since party politics are still kept out of the council
chambers in the islands). She was successful, and remained on the authority
until she resigned in 1980.

A less cheerful episode for Jo Grimond came in the shape of problems with a residential area at Hatston, on the Orkney mainland. At Grimond's instigation, in December 1973 the Secretary of State for Scotland, Gordon Campbell, had arranged for one of his officials to look around the place. Hatston had always been in the control of the public authorities, and consisted of hutted accommodation that had been part of a former Royal Naval Air Station, taken over in 1952 and converted into housing units by Kirkwall Council (sixty-six huts) and Orkney County Council (seventeen huts). Grimond himself had (in 1951) persuaded the government to hand them over, but only as a short-term, stopgap response to an acute and critical housing shortage. The huts had a timber construction, with felt-covered roofs. To add to the pleasure of living there, a food processing plant nearby was particularly squalid, pumping out untreated blood products directly into the sea nearby. The tenants were of all ages and backgrounds, but many of them were clearly adding to the environmental problems. Grimond had been drawing attention to the place's decline for fifteen years: 'a terrible example of the failure of planning . . . more and more money is spent on planning and consultants and yet simple matters which require immediate action appear to be neglected.'[47] Even if action was now forthcoming from the government, he warned, hundreds of children had already 'been brought up in slum conditions'. Greatly helped by Grimond's intervention, the area was eventually cleared and turned into an industrial estate.

Although the fortunes of the country were on the slide, those of the Liberal Party benefited considerably from the travails of the government. In 1972 the Labour seat Rochdale finally fell to the Liberals (in the shape of Cyril Smith) and, thereafter, no Tory seat seemed to be safe from their advance. In December of the same year, Sutton and Cheam tumbled. It was followed in July 1973 by the Isle of Ely and Ripon and then, in November, by Alan Beith's victory at Berwick upon Tweed. When one of the new MPs, Clement Freud, asked Grimond how he spent his days in the House of Commons, Grimond told him: 'I arrive at the Members' Entrance and hang up my coat, go to the post office for my mail . . . and then spend most of the day trying to remember where I put it.'[48] In early 1974 Grimond added the energy portfolio to his existing briefs on Scottish affairs and the arts. When Edward Heath called his 'back me or sack me' election for 28th February 1974, he telephoned Grimond at the Old Manse as a courtesy to inform him. He picked a bad moment. Grimond had recently decided that he wanted to introduce ducks to the Old Manse, and they had been delivered that day – in a box that had been left by the kitchen door, from which they promptly liberated themselves, preferring an exploration of the house to incarceration. As the No. 10 switchboard put through the Prime Minister, they waddled into Grimond's study and he had to make his apologies to Heath: 'Do you mind hanging on while I get the ducks back into their box?' Grimond later joked that Heath 'took this extremely hard, I may say – he thought it was a joke in very bad taste!'[49]

In the campaign of February 1974 Grimond shared one of the party's election broadcasts with David Steel. Viewers might have been forgiven for thinking that he had disinterred a script from 1966, as he asked of the government: 'What could they do after the election that they cannot do now? A bigger majority would not make them a better government . . . the election will only have been worth holding if it returns a large block of Liberals.'[50] The campaign in Orkney and Shetland was unusually rancorous. The Conservative candidate, John Firth, having first fought the seat in 1964, had fallen short by only 2,500 votes in 1970 – and now believed that he had a chance of winning. He therefore decided to fight a personal campaign, highlighting the record of the incumbent, and accusing him of treating his parliamentary duties too lightly and unduly favouring the Labour Party. Many of Grimond's supporters were more stung by these attacks then he was himself, and he contented himself with keeping above the fray, resolving to 'let those who brought the country to its knees, fight each other to death'.[51] His own majority more than doubled. The general election on 28th February 1974 marked a new post-war high-water mark for the Liberal Party. The party won almost 20 per cent of the vote and fourteen seats, playing a major part in reducing the Conservatives to their lowest share of the vote since the confused 'coupon' election of 1918. After the massive and almost terminal reverse of 1970, it is hard to overstate this achievement.

Although the election brought succour to Thorpe and the Liberals, however, it produced the worst possible result for the country, in the shape of a delicately balanced Parliament. Out of 635 MPs, Labour had 301, to the Conservatives' 297. The fourteen Liberals were not, therefore, in a position to give either party a majority in the House of Commons. With the balance made up of nine nationalists, two independents and twelve MPs from Northern Ireland, the chances of establishing a stable coalition looked limited. Although Labour had won the most seats, however, it was the Conservative Party that, despite losing over a million of its voters, had still won the most votes. Heath was therefore determined to try and stay at No. 10 and had his private office track down Jeremy Thorpe as soon as possible, to invite him in for talks. As soon as the indecisive outcome of the election was known, Liberals from all over the country began to send messages to Thorpe, imploring him not to do a deal with Heath. When he went to see Heath at Downing Street at teatime on Saturday, 2nd March, Thorpe was presented with three options: the Liberals might agree to support those aspects of a Conservative programme that they judged to be in the national interest; they might enter into systematic consultation with the Conservative government; or they might join a coalition. Thorpe stressed the importance of electoral reform to him and his party, and then went off to consult senior colleagues, including Grimond, before making any formal response. The message that he received was loud and clear: Heath had been discredited in an election held at a time of his own choosing and, even in the unlikely event of the Liberals reaching some accommodation with the Tories, they would do so only in support of a different Prime Minister.

The following day, Sunday, 3rd March, Thorpe publicly invited Jo Grimond, David Steel and Frank Byers to a working lunch at his home, to discuss Heath's offer. Although the party outside suspected that some kind of deal was being covertly concocted, in fact Thorpe and his colleagues all agreed more or less from the start that any coalition was a non-starter. The only word of warning came from Grimond: if the Liberals were serious about constitutional and electoral reform, they must at least be seen to have given Heath some kind of fair hearing. It must be made absolutely clear that they did not rule out working with others as a matter of principle. He also pointed out that, even if the Liberals did choose to support the Tories in the House of Commons, the two parties would not command a majority of votes: to command a majority over Labour, any administration would have to bring in the Ulster Unionists. This would mean dismantling the Sunningdale power-sharing agreement, a move that would have been unacceptable both to Heath and to the Liberals. That evening, Thorpe telephoned Heath at Downing Street and reported upon the results of his lunchtime meeting. He warned that the Liberals, with 6 million votes but only fourteen seats, were now determined that electoral reform should become a reality, and quickly. They were not interested in another Speaker's Conference or a Royal Commission. Both Thorpe and Heath knew that the Conservative Party would never acquiesce in the Liberal demand for electoral reform within a matter of months. Later the same evening, Thorpe returned to Downing Street in person, and told Heath that he now believed that it would be impossible to 'deliver' the Liberal Party into any kind of firm parliamentary arrangement, in the absence of a firm commitment to electoral reform.

The full parliamentary party met on the morning of Monday, 4th March and, although nobody actually endorsed a pact with Heath, several of those present, led by Grimond and including Cyril Smith and David Steel, reiterated the warning that the Liberals must not appear hostile to the concept of inter-party cooperation *per se*. During the meeting a letter from Heath was delivered, in which he confirmed that the best he could offer in return for Liberal support was a Speaker's Conference on electoral reform. The die was cast. With the support of his parliamentary colleagues, Thorpe issued a statement calling upon both the Tories and Labour to work for the creation of a government of national unity. He also wrote to Heath suggesting this, and emphasising that, although the Liberals had been willing to consider a limited parliamentary arrangement short of coalition, Heath had now rejected this.

Hurt and confused at his rejection by the electorate, Heath resigned. As the minority Labour government took charge, Grimond claimed that the Liberals were now 'the conscience of the nation, trying to influence Parliament for the good of everyone – don't forget, Labour won the backing of a third of the electorate, and lost more deposits than the Liberals!'[52] It was clear from the outset that a second election would probably come before the year was out, and Grimond was dismayed by the talk that quickly grew up about a government of national unity. These politics of the lowest common denominator were not, in his view, what the country needed. Its problems were too grave to be solved by anything less than a reforming government, truly radical and firm of purpose.

As inflation continued to blight any prospects of economic recovery, Grimond grew increasingly disgusted by the hypocrisy of a privileged establishment whose members constantly berated ordinary workers for demanding pay increases, whilst hanging on to every possible scrap of money and prestige for itself. At the very least, it should set some kind of example. In May 1974 he attacked Sir William Armstrong for agreeing to become chairman of the Midland Bank only three months after retiring as Head of the Civil Service. In July he once again called on the royal family to set an example in those difficult days by taking a voluntary pay cut, as a 'crude but important psychological way of drawing attention to the severe economic danger that we are in . . . it is something that should be done by businessmen and politicians as well'.[53] A spokesman for Buckingham Palace can hardly have done the monarchist cause many favours by responding tersely: 'everyone is suffering equally from inflation.'[54] Grimond emphasised at the time that he had no personal or political grudge against Her Majesty and her family and, a few years later, came apparent confirmation that there were no hard feelings. In the autumn of 1977 Grimond was buying some honey in a Shetland shop before heading south. The shopkeeper asked him if he would mind taking the Queen's personal consignment of the honey to London with him, as freight charges did seem to be rather a burden to impose on the Palace. Grimond consented, telephoning Buckingham Palace on his arrival and suggesting that they should 'come and collect the honey before the monarchy collapses', which they did.

The minority Labour government elected in February 1974 wasted little time in causing Grimond's heart to sink even further than it had in the Heath era. Even more than their predecessors, Wilson and his team seemed to believe that the state should play a major role in the economy. Their reluctance to deal with inflation seemed, to Grimond, to be a form of socialism by stealth: 'leave it to inflation and we shall not need a wealth tax – inflation will wipe out wealth far quicker than any government can do it.'[55] On Wednesday, 24th July 1974 Grimond and Richard Wainwright joined a group of maverick Tories, economic liberals all, who defied their party leadership by voting against the government's economic policy, instead of abstaining. At the Liberals' autumn assembly, Grimond won both a standing ovation and prodigious laughs when he promised that, when he was Secretary of State for Scotland under a Thorpe premiership, he would aim to bring together all shades of political opinion behind proposals for home rule. During the campaign for the general election of October 1974, Grimond accepted Jeremy Thorpe's invitation to share a party broadcast with David Steel. In this, he appeared to accept the Thorpe strategy, by enjoining voters to support the party in the middle – which alone could 'assert the national interest against the smash-and-grab tactics of some selfish people and some trade unions'.[56]

To prove that Grimond was not forgotten, he was featured in the closing titles of the last-ever edition of *Monty Python's Flying Circus* in December 1974, which gently ribbed him for his vanity – crediting him with 'make-up and hairdressing' for the show.[57]

The anti-Tory tide of the February election continued in October and Wilson was in – by a majority of three seats. The return of a Labour government did nothing to stem the tide of protest that had boosted the Scottish Nationalists, Grimond raised a lonely voice in favour of warmer relations between the Scottish Liberals and the SNP: 'the notion that they are the stuff from which Provisional IRA thugs are manufactured is a turnip-lantern of a scare which will not even frighten the children.'[58] He also pressed on with his calls for common sense in economic and industrial affairs. In one memorable phrase he pointed out that 'you can no more guarantee people against rampant inflation than you could guarantee the French aristocrats against the revolution.'[59] Two days later he made a marvellous intervention against ministerial hypocrisy in the light of government proposals for dramatic increases on petrol tax. The number of government cars had risen by fifty in recent years, and Grimond felt that ministers and senior civil servants were utterly incapable of comprehending the hardship that their policies would cause in Orkney and Shetland, where public transport was thin on the ground: 'when I regularly meet Ministers travelling on the tube lines in London, I shall believe that there is something in the argument about public transport.'[60]

The United Kingdom became a full member of the European Economic Community (EEC) on 1st January 1973. The Labour Party had been badly divided on this question ever since the days of Gaitskell and, in an attempt to resolve matters once and for all, the Wilson government called a referendum for June 1975, giving the people the opportunity to decide whether or not they wished to remain in the Community. Grimond had grown slightly equivocal about British membership, his long-held enthusiasm somewhat dampened by the evident bureaucracy of Brussels and the possible consequences for his constituents of European agricultural and fisheries policies. Although he generally took a fairly orthodox view of the need for representative government, on the very fundamental question of Britain's relationship with Europe he had been an early advocate of a referendum, voting for one in 1969 in the House of Commons and speaking out in favour of one after the 1970 election:

> I feel that there is a case on a constitutional issue like this for examining the possibility of a referendum . . . We are sent here to make up our minds and not to keep running back to our constituents for snap decisions, but over the Common Market there is much anxiety in the country, and there is the difficulty that no major party is opposed to our entry, so that the opposition is not argued on an effective scale.[61]

In Grimond's view, only the full endorsement of a referendum could draw a line under the controversial question of whether Britain belonged in Europe. What seems to have moved him most, however, was his firm belief that only a referendum campaign would force pro-European politicians to come together and put their case, including the case for political as well as economic integration, directly and explicitly to the people.

Shortly before the referendum, Grimond nominally co-authored a book with a young academic, Brian Neve, about the political and constitutional background to the referendum (in reality the text was almost entirely produced by Neve). When polling day turned out to be rather earlier than expected, the book had to be rushed out and its print run was dramatically curtailed. Consequently, although it provides a perfectly readable and cogent beginner's guide to the referendum process, this slim volume has made virtually no impact. Perhaps it may be taken up again in 2002 or 2003. During the campaign, virtually every moderate, mainstream British politician supported British membership of the EEC, and many subsequently perceived in the 'Yes' campaign the first glimmerings of a realignment of the parties. Overcoming his initial doubts, Grimond was convinced by Roy Jenkins at Königswinter to become the leading Liberal in the 'Yes' campaign, speaking at meetings in Birmingham and Portsmouth and taking part in press conferences, enjoining his fellow citizens to vote to stay within the EEC. He never underplayed the importance of the nation's verdict, warning in his most significant speech of the campaign that, since the Prime Minister and most members of the government wanted the country to vote 'Yes', if it voted 'No', the government would be dead in the water: 'they would have surrendered their judgement and their honesty – they would have broken every canon of political morality.'[62] In one message, he described the Community as 'the grouping which embraces the cradle of our civilisation' and warned that 'a "No" vote would be a disaster'.[63]

Although the country as a whole voted by a massive majority of two to one in favour of remaining within the Common Market, for Grimond personally the result was a little embarrassing. Although Orkney followed the national trend, Shetland became one of only two areas (the other was the Western Isles) to follow the citizens of Norway in voting against the EEC. The reason was clear: strong anti-EEC feelings amongst the fishermen had won out, thanks to the general apathy (the Shetland turnout was only 47.1 per cent, the lowest in the country). Grimond had held a meeting in Shetland during the campaign, to which only eleven people had come, and the *Shetland Times* had received only one letter about the EEC during the entire referendum campaign. The growing influence of the oil industry was feeding the sense of independence that is never far below the surface in Shetland, adding financial security to geographical isolation. Grimond joked that, although his constituents were lovely people and he was devoted to them, 'I have always suspected that they did not know what I stood for'. In the wake of the referendum, Grimond suggested that perhaps the country did after all need a government based upon the broad coalition that had recently been united on the single issue of Europe – a coalition that should be established before serious decline turned into real crisis. When Roy Jenkins hosted a celebratory dinner at Brooks's after the referendum result, the guest list looked suspiciously like the seedbed of just such a coalition, bringing together the likes of Ted Heath and Willie Whitelaw, Shirley Williams and David Steel, Jenkins and Grimond.

Although his activities in the political frontline were by now fairly intermittent, Grimond remained greatly in demand as a speaker for both social and political occasions. Having been something of a cricketer himself in his youth, he was no doubt particularly delighted when he was invited to propose the toast to Sir Garfield Sobers, the great West Indian cricketer, at a dinner at London's Café Royal in June 1975. He gave his listeners a marvellous insight into the domestic life of the Grimonds:

> It is my wife who is the real cricket expert of the Grimond family. At the age of ten . . . she wrote a sharp letter to the *News Chronicle* denouncing the dropping of APF Chapman as captain of England in favour of RES Wyatt. As a result, she was asked to report the Oval Test Match for that great paper . . . she has remained devoted to cricket ever since. Frequently she reads herself to sleep on *Wisden*. Occasionally in the middle of the night I am aware of something digging sharply into my back, to find that Tait's *Fight for the Ashes* has slipped down between the bedclothes!'[64]

In autumn 1975 Grimond was one of only three Liberal MPs to opt out of a gruelling speaking campaign during which nine of his colleagues, between them, would address over 150 meetings. He was nonetheless still a busy man, delivering a number of speeches in places of his own choosing. In one such speech, to a group of London solicitors, he likened the contemporary political situation to that faced by Britain in medieval times and the sixteenth or seventeenth centuries, when powerful interests, feudal barons, 'Renaissance bravos etc.' had threatened both the individual and the state: 'in that situation

Magna Cartas, Bills of Rights and so forth were necessary, and so they may be today.'[65] As politics settled down, Grimond returned to his favourite theme of bureaucracy. In a series of articles for *The Times,* later edited together for a pamphlet entitled *The Bureaucratic Blight,* he distilled his fears and hopes for Britain. His thesis was that the traditional division between the classes had broken down. The problem now was that society as a whole was in danger of following suit. Politicians seemed increasingly powerless as they tried to hold the ring in the public interest, while countless organisations hammered at their door threatening every kind of sanction, unless they got whatever they were demanding. In this situation, Grimond argued, only the bureaucrats would benefit, calmly building up their closed, unaccountable empires of index-linked patronage, chauffeur-driven cars, supersonic aircraft and expense accounts. Through the economic difficulties of the past ten years, the civil service had grown from a complement of 662,000 to some 747,000 people. More than half of that increase had taken place between April 1975 and April 1976. By bureaucrats, however, Grimond meant not only civil servants, but also 'corporate man' more generally. Quite what Grimond might have expected a 'grand coalition' of the centre to do about reversing this tide is an open question. Little did he expect that, within only a few short months, he might have to push his drafts and pamphlets to one side as, once again, the call came to lead his troops towards the sound of gunfire.

As in 1964–6, the Liberals were having a fairly miserable time in a House of Commons with a slender Labour majority. Although the 1974 results marked a tremendous personal achievement for Jeremy Thorpe – as Grimond was always the first to acknowledge – the edge again seemed to have gone off him, as he was increasingly beset by rumours and speculation. Between mid 1973 and late 1974 Liberal support in the polls had been around 20 per cent. By early 1976 that level had halved. It is hard to see precisely where Jeremy Thorpe had gone wrong, but as he had between 1967 and 1969, so between 1974 and 1975 he somehow lost the initiative. The downfall of Jeremy Thorpe began in May 1971, when a young man called Norman Scott came to the House of Commons to visit David Steel, and made a series of allegations about Thorpe, which were subsequently investigated by an internal enquiry headed by Frank Byers. Although the allegations of homosexual activity were dismissed as unproven, the rumours continued to recur in subsequent years, and neither Steel nor Jo Grimond was wholly privy to the increasingly desperate attempts by some senior Liberals to contain them. Grimond first learned of the allegations against Jeremy Thorpe at one of the *Private Eye* lunches that he so much enjoyed attending, when a convivial Auberon Waugh let valour be the better part of discretion. Only a few months later, in early 1976, the allegations began to emerge into the public domain, after an outburst against Thorpe from Scott when appearing at an unrelated hearing at Barnstaple magistrates' court. Former MP Peter Bessell, now living in the USA, also intervened, with tales of how he had covered up for Thorpe.

After the Liberals performed particularly badly at a by-election at Coventry North-West in March 1976, their vote falling by a third, Grimond did not exactly rush to the aid of his successor. He was informed of the result when he arrived, jetlagged, at Heathrow after a trip to New York. 'Oh dear,' he responded, 'that's very bad.' When asked whether he thought that recent controversies relating to Thorpe had contributed to the party's decline, Grimond replied, 'Well, it certainly begins to look like it.' He also suggested that Thorpe 'must think of stepping down . . . after all, he has been there for nine years and you can't go on for ever.'[66] The combination of private rumours and public humiliation was too much even for some of Thorpe's strongest supporters. In the wake of that by-election, David Steel, always a loyal supporter of Thorpe, told him privately that he should quit the leadership. Shortly afterwards, Steel and John Pardoe, Thorpe's likeliest successors, had a private meeting about the future and, after a sombre discussion, agreed that the party could be grievously damaged by a divisive leadership election at such a difficult time. It needed someone behind whom everyone could rally, who could heal the wounds of recent months. There was only one possible candidate: Jo Grimond. In a radio interview on Sunday, 14th March 1976, Grimond appeared to indicate that he was indeed considering a full-scale comeback as leader. He was not interested in being a stopgap, he said and, 'if by some extraordinary fluke or peculiar situation anyone wanted me back as leader, they would have to face up to it that I would be there for five to ten years.'[67] Almost at once, he had to issue a statement in which he claimed that he was 'not a candidate for the leadership, temporary, permanent or in any other way'.[68] It was too late: John Pardoe had already gone on the record saying how delighted he would be to have Grimond back as leader, adding that it would be 'the most exciting thing that could happen in British politics'.[69] The press were on the case.

The Thorpe leadership limped on for two more months, coming to an ignominious end on Monday, 10th May, after the publication in the weekend press of embarrassing letters from Thorpe to Scott. Steel and Pardoe immediately approached Grimond again, asking him to return as leader. Grimond went on television that night, defending Thorpe and saying: 'I don't blame him for resigning . . . he was hounded and there was no way out for him.'[70] The following day, the Liberal MPs met, with representatives of the peers and the party president, Margaret Wingfield, also in attendance. They asked Jo Grimond formally to take over as leader. This move was particularly supported by the chief whip, Alan Beith, and the three probable candidates in any leadership election: Emlyn Hooson, John Pardoe and David Steel. Grimond made it plain that this was something that he really did not want to do, pointing out that there was no shortage of perfectly suitable, younger candidates for the job and protesting to the party president, Margaret Wingfield that: 'I'm too blind, I'm too deaf, I'm too old.'[71] She told him that he was wasting his time with this argument – she was two years older than he was! In response he asked for twenty-four hours in which to consider the proposition.

Though he had for a time missed his old status very much after relinquishing it, Jo Grimond's reluctance to return as leader was genuine, and he repeatedly told David Steel that he was past it ('I cannot read a teleprompter, which is what gives my broadcasts that air of unmistakable sincerity'[72]). Quite independently of his infirmities, Grimond was uncomfortably aware that he and the Liberal Party had grown further apart over the years. For his taste, Liberals had become insufficiently aggressive in addressing the nation's economic problems, and far too tolerant of Labour's bumbling 'democratic socialism'. Most Liberals seemed content to leave the public-private demarcation in the economy where it was, whereas Grimond was increasingly influenced by the arguments for privatisation. He also felt that Liberals were too tolerant of the shortcomings of the social services which, in his view, were unresponsive, ineffective and administratively top-heavy. Grimond even admitted in a television interview on the day of Thorpe's resignation that he didn't 'know that the Liberal Party has really been very keen on the sort of things I've been suggesting'.[73] Nonetheless, the pressure on Grimond to return was immense: the party was in a state of total confusion, from which no one else could possibly rescue it. The situation was exacerbated by the fact that, after the controversy in 1967, the party still hadn't come up with a new system of electing its leader. Although it had eventually been agreed that the old method would not be acceptable again, the party had been planning to agree upon a new method of electing its leader at the 1976 autumn conference. It was now left both without a leader, and without a satisfactory method of electing a successor. Not for the first time, there was only one man who could come to the salvation of the Liberal Party.

16

J O GRIMOND ANNOUNCED on Wednesday, 12th June 1976 that he was indeed coming back as leader of the Liberal Party. He would, however, do so only for a period of approximately two months, until a new, long-term replacement could be elected under a new system, still to be determined. The first task was to initiate a special conference, at which the party could resolve once and for all how the leader should be chosen. When asked if he might be a candidate, Grimond laughed and replied, 'you never know . . . a couple of months or so might stimulate the appetite.' He then explained carefully that he was jesting: 'I am too old – I have done it before – I am not Mr Gladstone.'[1] At a press conference the same day, Grimond joked that 'whatever the party may feel now, I strongly suspect that in a matter of months they will be driven round the bend by my old mug on the telly all the time.'[2] Waiting outside a television studio the same day, Grimond bumped into David Steel and joked, 'Hello, I've won my election, you've still got yours to win!'[3] Steel told him, 'Ssssh, I'm not a candidate.'[4] As he settled into his temporary position, Grimond did not even bother to occupy the party leader's suite, telling his secretary Cate Fisher that it wasn't worth moving for only two months. He at once dictated an article for the day's London *Evening News,* in which he claimed that, far from despairing, he saw a 'break in the political clouds . . . The Labour Party is now unashamedly the party of the ruling classes, of the leaders of the big trades unions and the big-time bureaucrats.'[5] What the Liberals could bring to politics was 'No gimmicks . . . Example from the top: power to the people, protection from exploiters and more of their own wealth left in their own pockets.'[6] The following day in the *Guardian,* he developed his themes, warning against the new predominance of 'bureaucratic interest groups'[7] and promoting the Liberals as the only party that could exploit the gap on the centre-left of politics, with a radical programme of decentralisation and a reduction in the functions of government. He also restated his view that, with the battle of Britain in Europe now over, the 'so-called social democrats . . . have come to the end of the road',[8] their actions in government failing to measure up to their rhetoric.

Since Grimond had resolved from the outset that the interregnum would be as brief as possible, he did not try to put an undue imprint upon the party.

He did, however, break new ground by denouncing what he regarded as the government's hypocritical decision to ban the Rhodesian cricket team from playing in the UK: 'they would no doubt have received a Russian cricket team with acclamation if the Russians were foolish enough to play cricket.'[9] He also sent out a series of messages to prospective candidates, in the first of which he proclaimed that 'the Labour Party have abandoned the Left Centre; we must occupy it.' There followed several restatements of Liberal principles, and Grimond's repeated calls for a political debate between 'Liberalism and bureaucratic socialism'. He also launched a formidable attack on the Leader of the House of Commons, Michael Foot, accusing him of manipulating the workings of Parliament for party advantage. Within days of Grimond resuming as leader, John Pardoe invited him and David Steel for dinner at his home in Hampstead, to discuss the special conference to resolve the electoral system to be used in electing the new leader. Pardoe told Grimond that, after an extensive search for a suitable venue, only one place of an appropriate size had been identified, but he was not at all sure that it was suitable: Belle Vue Zoo in Manchester. 'On the contrary,' responded Grimond, 'in the circumstances, there could hardly be anywhere more appropriate!'[10] The conference was scheduled for Saturday, 12th June. Three days before, in the House of Commons, the Conservative Party moved a vote of censure against the government. Neither the Ulster Unionists nor the Liberals supported it, and the government survived. As he had been in similar circumstances in 1964–5, Grimond was scathing about the Conservatives' parliamentary tactics. The debate, he said, had demonstrated that Mrs Thatcher and her party had no alternative policy to offer. If the motion had been passed, and a general election had ensued, she would have lost the pound, the pay policy and the election itself. She was, he said, 'a very lucky woman to be saved from the folly of her own party'.[11] The opposition parties should be constructive, rather than playing 'party games' by attacking the government whenever it took steps necessary to 'try and get the country out of this terrible and perpetual slide'.[12]

Grimond's speech to the special conference at Manchester was the only keynote speech that he made during his brief tenure to a gathering of the entire party. His style had not changed. He opened in a light-hearted and nostalgic vein, moved on to the substance and then closed with more telling humour. He also made a long and earnest tribute to Jeremy Thorpe. 'Now, chairperson,' he began, to ripples of laughter that such a remark would scarcely be likely to prompt at a Liberal Democrat conference nowadays, 'I really don't think I need disguise from you that I'm really rather fond of being leader – and it really would save a lot of trouble if I went on.'[13] This was greeted with an uproar of laughter, applause and cheers. The only thing that deterred him from doing so, he explained, was that he would not deprive his audience of 'this top-hole day in Manchester . . . there is nothing that Liberals love more than a long day of constitutional wrangling.' In fact, he now well understood 'the appeal of those advertisements in the London Underground for temps, and I intend to put in for a good many more – if anyone needs a Bishop for a week or two, here I am!'[14] Delegates should also be grateful, he counselled, because the prospective candidates for the leadership would not be allowed to speak during the proceedings, and his own idea of making them parade along a catwalk had been rejected. Grimond also gave what appeared to many people to be a thinly veiled endorsement of David Steel, something that he later denied.

Grimond's tribute to the achievements of Jeremy Thorpe was well received, not least his praise for the way in which his successor had 'built up the party from the general shambles in which I left it'.[15] Then there followed a section of political philosophy and advice for his next successor. Grimond warned that it was no longer possible to take it for granted that the people of Britain either appreciated or understood liberal values or principles – in a whole host of ways, through the closed shop, patronage, rampant inflation and the gradual breakdown of civil society, this was 'ceasing to be a liberal country'.[16] Without making any explicit criticism of the ideological direction that the party had taken since 1967, Grimond set out his own credo, that the private sector should be encouraged to flourish, and that any good Liberal should be thinking not in terms of more government action, but in terms of which laws and regulations should be repealed: 'we need smaller – and stronger – government.'[17] He also warned that the special assembly must reach a conclusion, by the required majority of two-thirds, or else they would all look like 'utter Charleys': 'have a happy day, have a happy day, but the coach comes at 5.20 and, after that, you're all pumpkins.'[18] Delegates had to bear in mind that, if they were deadlocked, then the parliamentary party would choose the leader; and, if the parliamentary party were deadlocked, then he and Jeremy Thorpe would choose the leader. For once, the message hit home. An electoral college was approved, weighted in favour of seats where the Liberals had more members and support.

A week later, Grimond addressed the Scottish Liberals in Perth and, once again, he was in top form, playing to the gallery and showing every possible sign of enjoying himself thoroughly. He was there, he said, as a 'sort of lay John the Baptist – who hopes to retain his head' or, alternatively, as a 'housemaid who is left dusting the house while the new tenants gad round the country in a cloud of oratory'.[19] Neither David Steel and John Pardoe had wasted any time in getting on the campaign trail once the voting system had been chosen and, in the space of only a few days, their comments about one another had degenerated into personal rancour. 'It looks as though it may become a competition,' said Grimond to nervous laughs, 'as to who is the bigger bastard . . . now, I should be hard put to give a ruling . . . for many years, I have made it a rule to keep my guard up, and to transfer my notecase to my trouser pocket, when dealing with either of them.'[4] The campaign between Steel and Pardoe reached its nadir when Steel unwisely hinted to a group of journalists that Pardoe wore a toupee, which provoked a bitter and virulent response from Pardoe and his supporters. Steel's greater popularity amongst the activists, and in the country at large, was reflected in a decisive victory by 12,541 'national' votes to 7,032. The press had strongly favoured Steel throughout, and Grimond conceded after the result was declared that Pardoe had been 'badly done by'.

After handing over the reins for a second time, Grimond once again found it rather difficult to adjust to being an ex-leader. He felt very downhearted after the party assembly in autumn 1976, drafting a commentary for the *Sunday Times,* in which he wrote that the Liberals might as well come to terms with the fact that they were never going to form a government. Michael Jones, the political journalist responsible for commissioning and sub-editing the article, asked Grimond whether he really wanted to say that. Grimond took his point, and the finished piece contains the qualified observation that the Liberal Party 'is not going to form a government in the immediate future'.[21] The rest of the article was less helpful to Steel, Grimond calling once again for a restatement of liberalism from his party, rather than more watered-down, middle-of-the-road social democracy. The Liberals should be banging home, he opined, the fact that all the things about which people supposedly cared – healthcare, schools and housing – 'depend on the creation of wealth . . . surely that is the message which should be shouted by Liberals again and again'.[22] Nor, he rumbled, had anyone at the assembly shown any sign of caring about the hegemony of bureaucratic centralism: 'a rather moth-eaten version of Mussolini's state'; 'on the contrary, the majority earnestly debated policies which presume that 1984 must be embraced'.[23]

After the second general election of 1974, under both Thorpe and Grimond, so long as Labour still had a majority in the Commons, the Liberals had judged individual pieces of legislation on their merits, much as they had done after the almost identical result in 1964. They also had to contend with a lot of knife-edge votes. The Liberal whip at that time was Cyril Smith, who recalls that, each week, he would inform Grimond of the following week's business, drawing particular attention to any three-line whips. 'Well yes, Cyril,' Grimond would respond, 'but you realise I ignore such things and am not promising to be there.'[24] Nonetheless, Smith cannot a recall a single occasion when Grimond let the side down: 'he was loyal, faithful, kind, considerate and a "gentleman" in every sense of the word.'[25] After Labour lost its parliamentary majority at by-elections in November 1976, however, they had to take some tough decisions. David Steel's view was that the Liberals should consider negotiating a pact with Labour, in return for a number of concessions, in particular with regard to economic policy. The issue was then forced in March 1977 when Margaret Thatcher and the Conservatives put down a confidence motion against the minority government. Steel negotiated a draft agreement with the government, including provision for a consultative committee between government representatives and the Liberals, a renewed bid for devolution and a commitment to draw a line under nationalisation. When Steel put these proposals to his parliamentary colleagues, he was shocked and disappointed when, of all people, it was Jo Grimond who was least keen on entering into such an arrangement.

Grimond's objections to the proposed pact were manifold. First of all, the government had already done a lot of highly illiberal things, and the perception would inevitably be that the Liberals were now proposing to offer a retrospective endorsement of its record. He also felt that it was wrong to blur the line between government and opposition. Grimond perfectly understood that the Liberals, whether as part of a more general realignment or not, might sooner or later find themselves in coalition with another party; but Callaghan was not offering the Liberals a coalition. On the contrary, they would play no part whatsoever in the closeted decision-making processes of government. They would just be allowed to say their piece at a series of private meetings with ministers, a few of their objections or suggestions might (or might not) be taken into account and they would then be honour-bound to support the entire package that the government brought forward. Grimond was substantially adhering to his principles of a decade earlier: 'What I think might be damaging to the party would be if it went into the Government for the sake of doing so, and without any common agreement. A lot of people would then ask, "What has become of Liberal beliefs?"'[26]

In Grimond's opinion, the pact as envisaged by Callaghan and Steel would completely undermine and contravene the role of an MP. He did not wish to be silenced for the convenience of Jim Callaghan, David Steel or anyone else. He also, as it happened, believed that the Liberals had far less to fear from an election than most of them thought. The polls suggested that the Liberals had a reasonable chance of retaining most of their seats, while the Tories gained seats from Labour across the country. At one point the Tories had a twenty-point lead. An election then might have precipitated the fissure in Labour for which Grimond had so long prayed. When the Liberal MPs gathered for a late-night meeting at which they had to decide how they should vote on the confidence motion, however, all but two of them agreed to a short-term pact, which would be re-evaluated by the parliamentary party in the spring. The two dissentients were Jo Grimond and David Penhaligon, both of whom believed that Steel could and should drive a harder bargain. In particular they felt that the Liberals should have extracted a firm commitment that the first direct elections to the European Parliament, due in 1979, should be conducted under a system of proportional representation. Although Grimond opposed the pact from the start, his personal loyalty to Steel and his acceptance of collective responsibility within the Liberal parliamentary party bound him to it. He nonetheless continued to act as a source of 'cautionary advice' for David Steel. In acknowledgement of his special interest in the subject, Grimond was now energy spokesman. He therefore found himself 'shadowing' Tony Benn, the Secretary of State for Energy, who opposed the pact just as resolutely as he did himself. It would be quite a pairing.

At the end of June the Liberals MPs held a weekend meeting in London to consider whether the pact should be continued. Both Grimond and Penhaligon were still opposed to it in principle, but agreed that it might be 'least-worst' option, so long as Steel took a robust line in his dealings with the government. By late July 1977 Grimond was running out of patience with the pact. He had been 'consulted' about the government's proposals to reorganise the electricity industry, but felt that the entire exercise had been pointless. His colleagues from that time vividly recall him giving a hilarious account of that meeting to the Liberal parliamentary party, as an illustration of how fatuous the pact was. Tony Benn was another opponent of the pact who recognised in Grimond a kindred spirit who was not 'enough of a technocrat' to enjoy taking part in its machinery. Grimond's account ran as follows: 'Tony and I are the most accommodating people in politics – we eventually decided, for the good of the party . . . that possibly we ought to see each other, so I went off to the Ministry and we had a short conversation, and then we had tea, and we had some buns, and we had an agreeable conversation and agreed that the pact was hopeless – and we parted on extremely good terms.'[28]

A few days later, Grimond accidentally turned up in his battered Fiat at Blenheim Palace during a Tory rally hosted by the Duke of Marlborough. As soon as he paid over his 50p, he realised what was going on and excused himself, saying, 'Oh dear, I think I am in the wrong place at the wrong time.'[29] Although defection to the Tories was never on Grimond's mind, he was profoundly unhappy about being forced to support Labour at all times, and on all issues. When David Steel summoned a meeting of the MPs for Tuesday, 26th July to discuss tactics, Grimond was unable to attend. He did, however, write a letter to Steel saying that he no longer felt able to support the pact, which he copied to all other Liberal MPs. In his letter, Grimond set out his principled argument against renewing the pact, warning of a long-term danger that 'the more Liberals collaborate with Labour, the more difficult it will be to break out.'[30] He did not argue that the Liberals should necessarily oppose the government on everything. On the contrary, he just thought that they should be free to treat proposals on their merits, rather than continuing to 'bolster up a government which is losing the confidence of the country'.[31] The letter was leaked on the eve of the meeting. Amidst the ensuing furore, Grimond was interviewed on television by Noel Lewis of the BBC. If a majority of his colleagues decided to renew the arrangement, he said, he would probably go along with them, but he could not in good conscience countenance a deal that committed the Liberals to 'supporting the government in all circumstances for a whole session . . . as we are an opposition party, we reserve the right to vote when we think that the government are wrong and I therefore don't think one can give up that right for a whole session.'[32] On the morning of that crucial meeting, a modified version of the letter to colleagues appeared as an article in the *Daily Mail.* Grimond dealt with the issues very frankly, including the question of why he, 'the original advocate of realignment on the left', so objected to the pact. The answer was 'precisely because I do not think it will lead to realignment'. In fact, explained Grimond, he thought that David Steel was doing a splendid job as leader of the Liberals – and even that Jim Callaghan had 'turned out to be a good Prime Minister', who had 'operated the pact with scrupulous fairness'. The problem was that the country continued to face huge problems, notably the level of inflation, and, in his view, only a massive change in the system of government itself could provide the necessary solutions. 'So,' he concluded, 'while I don't necessarily want to bring down the Government, I want to return to freedom.'[33]

Grimond's immediate fear for the Liberals was that, when the election came, they now increasingly stood to lose both ways. If the tide turned back to Labour, it would be returned with an absolute majority in the House of Commons, and there would be a return to socialism; if the country turned against Labour, the Liberals would likely suffer from guilt by association. With the summer recess only days away, however, the Liberal MPs again backed the pact, and both Grimond and Smith, who had now turned strongly against the pact, decided to keep their own counsel until the autumn. At the party assembly in September 1977 David Steel won the support of delegates for his stance by a vote of almost two to one. Grimond and Smith absented themselves from the hall as the vote was taken. Smith resigned at once as employment spokesman, and Grimond followed suit a few days later, quitting his post as energy spokesman, something he had been minded to do for some time. Another motion less to the taste of the leadership was also passed, demanding that, as a precondition for the pact being maintained, Labour MPs should support PR for the European elections by 'a substantial majority'. Two months later, Grimond warned that the Liberals were now caught in a trap of their own making: 'once the Liberal oysters started on their stroll along the sands with carpenter Jim, to run away was difficult and has become more difficult.'[34]

Jo Grimond's fundamental objections to the Lib-Lab pact, and the government that it was sustaining in office, hardened with the passing months. This was not a government that did conspicuously liberal things, and it showed no signs, in the era of the pact, of becoming more susceptible to liberal

influences. Meanwhile the recurrent crises of conscience and wranglings over
the pact were distracting Liberals from the real job at hand. 'We must,' wrote
Grimond, 'shake off our obsession with the pact and with our troubles . . .
we should be the party of relevant new ideas . . . we are a party of protest –
a most honourable role . . . there are great numbers of Liberals in Britain
[who] need leadership . . . It is not for us to shore up the rickety planks of a
rickety system of government.'[35] What Liberals urgently needed to address, he
warned, was the question of why anyone might wish to vote for them. The
Lib-Lab pact certainly did the Liberals no electoral favours while it was in
operation. In two by-elections in the spring of 1977, Liberal candidates lost
their deposits. Shortly after becoming leader, David Steel had been to stay
with the Grimonds in Orkney, and Grimond must fervently have wished that
the younger man had heeded the heartfelt 'cautionary advice' about dealing
with Labour that he had given him on that visit.

Then in December 1977, unbelievably, it was Grimond who rescued the
pact when most of his colleagues looked like disowning it once and for all.
He did so primarily out of loyalty to David Steel, whose position as leader
might have been jeopardised, but there was also calculation in his caprice. The
House of Commons had finally voted on the question of PR for the European
elections and, after Callaghan allowed Labour backbenchers a free vote on the
measure, had rejected electoral reform by a majority of almost 100. Although
some ministers had supported the motion, PR now seemed to be dead in
the water, and many Liberal MPs were furious. Steel summoned them to a
meeting the following morning, by which time several had still not calmed
down. Although Grimond could not get to the meeting, he saw Steel later in
the day and surprised him by explaining that, in his view, this reverse would
be a singularly bad reason for breaking the pact. After all, the vote had been
on the List system (latterly introduced) and, although the Liberals preferred
this to 'first past the post' on grounds of its proportionality, it was by no
means their preferred option. Furthermore, Callaghan had behaved entirely
honourably and, most importantly, this was hardly an issue likely to win
sympathy for the Liberals in the country. Grimond argued that the Liberals
should settle down and take some pleasure in hailing the unprecedentedly
high vote in the Commons for electoral reform, then get on with the real job
in hand: promoting liberal values and Liberal policies. At an evening meeting
of the parliamentary party, Grimond repeated these arguments, to general
astonishment. It was a critical intervention and, once again, the pact was saved
as Grimond joined the pro-pact faction, which won by six votes to four, with
two abstentions (Jeremy Thorpe and John Pardoe).

The defeat of PR in the House of Commons triggered a special Liberal
assembly in January 1978, at which the wider party could again make its voice
heard on the pact. Although he still disliked the arrangement in principle,

Grimond resolved to help David Steel weather what looked like becoming a very difficult time, writing in advance of that assembly that, although he personally had always been against the pact, even he had to concede that, 'since it was struck, things have undoubtedly got better as far as the country is concerned . . . [Steel] has attracted more attention and put the party nearer the centre of power than did his immediate predecessors . . . So it would be crazy, having entered into the pact, to tear it up at this moment.'[36] Although David Steel had been perfectly justified in educating his party on the need to work with others, Grimond believed he should have done far more to reassert the values of liberalism; and he should also have borne in mind that politics is not only about gaining even the tiniest influence over government, at whatever price. Parliament also has an important role in standing for the governed against the government, and the Liberals had an honourable part to play in that process. On one occasion when the Liberals were needed to help steer the government through some close late-night votes, Grimond told his colleagues that he couldn't stay on any longer, because he wanted to catch the last tube home. David Penhaligon organised a whip-round to pay for a taxi for him, and each of his parliamentary colleagues put 50 pence on to the table. Grimond agreed to stay and, with a characteristically mischievous smile, pocketed the proceeds. The Lib-Lab pact survived the special assembly, but died a natural death in he summer of 1978.

Jo Grimond always believed that the Liberals should have demanded electoral reform, with Labour whips on to get it, and later claimed to have been told 'on the highest authority' that, had David Steel pressed this demand, the cabinet would probably have agreed to it. All the Liberals got was the debate and lost vote on the possibility of adopting a proportional voting system for the forthcoming elections to the European Assembly. Christopher Mayhew, a former Labour minister who had defected to the Liberals, had assured him that Labour MPs were so terrified of an election that even they would probably have fallen into line. In fact, David Steel did not even see the point of raising this possibility with Jim Callaghan: he was always utterly convinced that the Labour leader simply could not deliver. What Grimond would eventually concede was that David Steel had at least succeeded in forcing the Liberals to come to terms with the need to work with another party.

Supported by an alliance of Liberals and Scottish Nationalists, Grimond had in November 1973 introduced a Bill to establish Parliaments in Scotland and Wales, which was killed off after its first reading when Ted Heath went to the country in February 1974. The issue of devolution predominated throughout the 1974–9 Parliament – before, during and after the Lib-Lab Pact – more or less independently of other considerations. In September 1974 the short-lived minority Wilson administration published a White Paper on devolution; and after the second general election of that year, a second White

Paper was issued, in November 1975. Although Jo Grimond had always been in favour of home rule for Scotland, he believed that devolution must, at the very least, be accompanied by a profound reassessment of local government functions in Scotland, with a view to abolishing one of its tiers. He was uncomfortably aware that the Labour Party had it in mind to add to the burdens of government, rather than reducing them – when the last thing the country needed was 'a fifth wheel to the overburdened and creaking coach of government'[37] – and engaged in a protracted correspondence with Harold Wilson on this question. Wilson disappointed him, confirming that he 'would not expect any savings to occur in Whitehall as a result of our devolution proposals to Scotland'.[38]

Grimond knew for a fact that his own constituents had a highly equivocal view of an Edinburgh Parliament, and he would often quote an unnamed constituent who had grumbled to him that he could imagine 'nothing more awful than being in a country run by Glasgow trade unionists and Edinburgh lawyers'. Grimond warned that the Wilson government's first proposals might cause the UK to break up, in which case nobody should assume that Orkney or Shetland would inevitably wish to be part of an independent Scotland whose politics would be dominated by the big cities: 'we might return to Scandinavia, or we might retain some links with England, Wales and Scotland'.[39] The Scottish Nationalists had suggested that Orkney and Shetland should acquire a status similar to that enjoyed by the Faroe Islands, which are virtually independent attachments to Denmark. He picked up this idea with enthusiasm: 'If Scotland is willing to pay the subsidy, similar to that which is received by Faroe, we should be likely to accept that position.'[40] When he had been restored to the Liberal leadership, Grimond again denounced the Labour proposals, in the House of Commons, as 'pretty awful'.[41]

Labour's Scotland and Wales Bill was finally introduced in late 1976. The minority parties supporting devolution – the Liberals and nationalists from Scotland and Wales – were not consulted, but they still gave it a fair wind in the House of Commons and it was passed at second reading. Grimond's initial view was that the Liberals should support the Bill only if the government promised to bring in proportional representation for elections to the Scottish and Welsh assemblies. Labour was reluctant to provide the necessary time for debate on the Bill, and matters came to a head in February 1977 when Labour introduced a motion in the House of Commons to impose a 'guillotine' on it. Grimond told David Steel from the outset that the Liberals must oppose the government's proposed guillotine. If it was voted through, he argued, whole chunks of the Bill would go through without the chance of even briefly debating important Liberal amendments, still less of voting on them. The government had to realise that it could not take for granted the Liberals' continuing support for the Bill. Ministers should be told, in no uncertain terms, that Liberal support would henceforth be contingent upon proper consultation. The guillotine was voted down by MPs, effectively killing off the Bill. The successor Bills sprang directly from the negotiations establishing the Lib-Lab pact. Although, once again, the government was either unwilling or unable to deliver a more proportional voting system, with support from the Liberals it did get the Scotland and Wales Bills on to the statute book. Fully supported by the Shetland Islands Council, which feared that one of the first priorities for a Scottish Parliament would be to grab hold of the islands' oil assets, Grimond was also less than enthused with the new measures, describing the Scotland Bill as 'a thoroughly bad Bill'.[42] Nonetheless, on 17th November 1977, the Liberals (including Grimond) supported a government guillotine motion for the Bill, helping it to make it on to the statute book.

Grimond was surprised by some of the opposition to devolution that emerged in Shetland while these Bills were being considered. Some reputable voices on the Shetland Islands Council were raised in favour of UDI and, in January 1977, Grimond had to tell them that, in his view, although their special needs had to be protected, 'going it alone just is not on'.[43] He even brought representatives of the Isle of Man and the Faroes to explain how complicated were their systems of semi-autonomous government. As Labour continued with its protracted attempts to introduce devolution, Grimond would find himself more and more tied up with the parliamentary battle to ensure that the islands were not done down and, on 25th January 1978, he moved an amendment to the Scotland Bill at committee stage in the House of Commons to allow Orkney and Shetland to opt out of devolution if they voted against it at the referendum. The government did not welcome Grimond's amendment and, with the assistance of a couple of SNP MPs, its deputy chief whip, Walter Harrison, tried to prevent the House voting on it, which Grimond subsequently described as 'obstruction not seen since the days of the Irish members'.[44] The guillotined debate was due to end at 11 p.m. that day and, together with his co-conspirators, Harrison tried to block the voting lobbies of the House of Commons as the 'Grimond Amendment' approached. When David Steel discovered them there at 10.40 p.m., he remonstrated with them and asked what they were playing at. Harrison confirmed that they wanted to prevent Grimond speaking – 'he'll call a division and we'll lose'[45] – and the deputy speaker, Sir Myer Galpern, had to send in the Serjeant-at-Arms to clear the lobbies. The rebellious malcontents were moved on just in time and Grimond had only a few seconds left in which to move his amendment. His only words were 'a damned close thing, if I may say so'.[46] The House was not impressed with the behaviour of Harrison and his allies: Grimond's amendment was passed by 204 votes to 118. On the following day, the Speaker formally reproved Harrison and his co-conspirators.

The relentless campaign by Labour anti-devolutionists that had put paid to the Scotland and Wales Bill of 1976–7 was maintained against the new Bills, with the result that devolution itself was virtually discredited by the time referenda on home rule were at long last held in Scotland and Wales on 1st March 1979. Grimond voted 'Yes' with a public show of reluctance, because the form of devolution on offer was to his mind so inadequate. He could not see how the proposed Scottish Assembly would be able to deal with any of the major problems facing Scotland, nor could he understand how adding 'another thousand or so civil servants to be carried by productive industry' could bring relief to a land already groaning under the deadweight of bureaucracy.[47] He rued the fact that Labour had not been forced to concede that at least one tier of local government should have been abolished as part of the new settlement, with some powers being delegated down not only to the assembly, but also to local councils, and blamed his own party for not making a better case for full-blooded federalism. Although Grimond's own amendment had been amended in turn by the government, he had at least ensured that, if the assembly was set up, it would be bound by statute to take particular account of the special interests of his constituency. In the general election campaign that followed shortly thereafter, Grimond felt able to set out an uninhibited demand that 'the Scotland Act should be consigned to oblivion and government reform designed to give us less and better government nearer home, and allow greater freedom for Orkney and Shetland to run their own affairs . . . This should be reconsidered in the new Parliament.'[48]

One of the main sensitivities in the islands by this time was the degree to which local people would benefit from North Sea oil. As the MP for Orkney and Shetland, Grimond was well placed to play a major part in the debate about North Sea oil, before and subsequent to the commencement of extraction. It was arguably in Orkney and Shetland that the existing, quite delicate, balance between man and nature stood to be changed. As the 1970s progressed, particularly after a major strike 100 miles east of Shetland by Shell-Esso in 1972, oil became the dominant feature of economic life in the islands. At the time of writing, North Sea oil has been with us for thirty years and, even for those who remember the earliest days of the industry, it will probably require a special effort of memory to conjure up the almost neurotically close attention paid in those far-off days to political affairs in the Middle East, and their possible implications for the availability of oil in the West. The folk memory of the Suez crisis still lingered. Quite rightly, therefore, Parliament gave itself time to debate the discovery of oil in the North Sea in a thorough and reasoned way. With confirmation that considerable reserves of oil and gas had been located, the Scottish Grand Committee met on 5th December 1972 to discuss 'the matter of North Sea oil and the Scottish economy'. From the outset, the question of oil could never be separated from the debate about home rule and the cry soon went up that this was 'Scotland's oil'. Grimond was highly sympathetic to that point of view, heralding the advent of the oil industry as 'one of the greatest events that has taken place for Scotland for many years', but regretting the fact that 'we are not having this important debate in a Scottish Parliament or Scottish Assembly'.[49] Yet Grimond could not conceal his pessimism about Scotland's ability to respond to the challenge of oil being discovered off its shores.

His main parochial concern was that the oil industry must not be allowed to 'crowd out' other better established and more sustainable economic activities, and that the short-term burst of income that it would generate should be, at least in part, reinvested in the islands: 'we must not repeat the mistake of the nineteenth century . . . [leaving] in Scotland derelict areas with natural resources exhausted and the communities totally disrupted'.[50] He wrote privately to Ted Heath's Secretary of State for Scotland, Gordon Campbell, warning 'generations to come will not forgive us if we make a mess of our opportunities . . . It is for the people themselves to express a view as to what they want . . . They want to know what is being considered.'[51] The last thing Grimond wanted was to blight, or disparage, a development that would clearly bring jobs and prosperity to his constituents, but from the outset he enjoined them to bear in mind that the oil bonanza would not last forever, that they must think to the longer term. He feared that traditional activities, far more sustainable than oil in the long run, would be displaced by oil, and that skills could be lost forever. He likened oil to a huge cuckoo that would inevitably disturb the native birds. Yet he would have been the last person to begrudge the people of the islands their time in the sun, and he deplored anyone else who did: 'For the first time many work people and crofters who have lived in semi-poverty for generations see the prospect of a decent wage and an increase in the value of their land. *It is not for the Home Counties tourists nor the well-heeled middle class to reprove them.*'[52]

Grimond waged a continuous campaign for more generous treatment of the islands as the oil bonanza came on-stream. He argued that the islands councils should receive money directly from the oil companies and reflected 'in the past we've always had to go on hands and knees to London for small subsidies – now we're going to be the Texas of Britain . . . It'll be us who'll have to subsidise Concorde!'[53] On 23rd February 1973 in a speech to a dinner held by engineering contractors in Glasgow, he posed the rhetorical question: 'Can Scotland again seize the chance? I detect a strange lack of confidence . . . it seems to be accepted as inevitable that America will call the tune through London . . . It is assumed that all the technology associated with oil must come from across the Atlantic. Why? . . . We could be having a second industrial revolution at this moment in Scotland.' Two weeks later, through the LPO press office he issued a statement about oil. He criticised the generous terms awarded to the oil companies by successive governments.

He also warned that, whatever he and his constituents might say or do, nobody should pretend that the exploitation of the oil, and its effects on Orkney and Shetland, could be stopped. They just had to do everything in their power to ensure that their environment, their social life and their culture were protected, and that they received a fair deal financially. He praised the Shetland County Council for its initiative in producing a county plan anticipating the needs of the industry, and supported the council as it sought powers over compulsory purchase of land equivalent to those of a harbour authority, which would enable it both to protect the environment of the islands, and to ensure that local people got a fair deal from the oil companies. In 1973 Grimond piloted the Zetland County Council Bill through Parliament, temporarily granting the new Shetland Islands Council most of the powers that it wanted. From an early stage, he also advocated that financial provision be made for reinstatement of the environment once the oil reserves had been exhausted.

In October 1973 hostilities between Egypt and Israel erupted again, and petrol supplies within the United Kingdom were restricted almost at once. With this in mind, speaking to the Commons Public Accounts Committee in December of that year, Grimond urged the government to take steps to speed up the provision of the housing, road and other services that would be needed by the oil industry. He continued to speak on this subject during 1974 and 1975: he was still particularly concerned about planning procedures, believing that failure to define and enforce them clearly would have damaging consequences for the local population, and about fishing, which, despite its indigenous nature, was in danger of becoming a 'poor relation'. During the election campaign of February 1974, Grimond denounced the deals signed between the government and the oil companies. It had been estimated that the six major companies had made almost £250 million in Britain in 1972, he said, and yet they had paid virtually no tax at all. Annual profits were expected to reach £400 million by 1980, yet 'four-fifths of the exploration could end up being paid for by the taxpayer'.[54] There was no mistaking the sense in the islands that an unduly high proportion of the benefits had been appropriated by others. In his election address for Shetland in October 1974, Grimond made a point of declaring: 'it is not only a question of obtaining a bigger share of the oil revenues for Scotland – but for Shetland.'[55]

In December 1976 the first oil came ashore at Flotta, Orkney, from the Piper field, which had been discovered in 1973. Shetland, with its huge terminal at Sullom Voe, was some two years behind. As Grimond feared, all too little of the wealth generated found its way into local investment and, once the construction boom in Shetland came to an end, the islands were left with a lost generation of 'young Shetlanders used to high wages but with no particular skills and with no jobs which will yield the return to which they are accustomed'.[56] This fuelled Grimond's fear that local traditions were less likely to be honoured and practised by the new breed of hard-working commuter. In March 1979 a series of oil spillages, one accidental and the rest intentional, near Sullom Voe, destroyed a large number of birds and a number of sheep, the latter of a rare local breed. The environmental lobby called for the terminal to be closed forthwith, but Grimond took a cooler view, writing to the Prime Minister pointing out that closure would constitute a 'serious economic setback' and should not even be contemplated. His view prevailed. Nonetheless, in his election addresses in 1979 Grimond would acknowledge the local sentiment that the benefits of oil had been less dramatic than might have been expected: 'as I forecast, oil is bringing as many problems as benefits . . . It is Britain, not Shetland [Orkney], that is the main beneficiary from oil.'[57] By 1986, when oil production had been running for just over a decade, Grimond would feel able to attempt a considered assessment of its effects, concluding that the most obvious impact had been not in Orkney or Shetland, but in Aberdeen, with the arrival of large international companies and a fleet of supply vessels. Although workers in the islands enjoyed a bonanza for a time, and the old airstrip at Sumburgh had been transformed into an impressive airport, Grimond concluded that the long-term effect of oil was 'unlikely to be as great as was once supposed . . . certainly the general public have not benefited',[58] adding in a final note of irony that, despite North Sea oil, 'petrol is one of the commodities which is more expensive in the North.'[59]

Although he was willing to offer it qualified support in individual votes, in Grimond's view the Callaghan government, wittingly or otherwise, was threatening to usher in an age of what he described as 'corporate fascism': the negation of democracy and freedom. In a speech to the Insurance Debating Society at Lloyds he used his strongest language yet to describe the threat: 'Lust for power is rife, but the checks and balances are eroded . . . Christianity is weakened . . . The very heart of our affairs is eaten by a canker, the lack of any morality – that is to say, any attention to the general interest . . . Each organisation, unchecked, goes all out for its own aggrandisement.'[60] The new bureaucratic elite was unlikely to do anything to improve matters, and Grimond would cite with grim humour an example in Shetland of bureaucratic nonsense in practice. At the end of a ten-mile mud track, he had been astonished to find four new houses built in a row, with a pavement outside. The pavement was there purely and simply because regulations stipulated that no house could be built without a pavement outside: 'It was totally useless, of course, although the sheep loved lying on it in the sun.'[61]

At the London end of their lives, the Grimonds were engaged in what is now known as 'down-sizing', selling their grand family house on Kew Green in 1976 and taking up residence in a smaller dwelling in Bedford Park, Hammersmith, retaining a direct link to Westminster thanks to Grimond's favoured District Line. On the Underground, Grimond would pick up some of his more outré ideas, as fellow commuters recognised him and unburdened themselves to him. The talk, once again, was of Grimond giving up politics altogether and taking on one last, high-profile job. For a time it was rumoured that he would become chairman of the Highlands and Islands Development Board. In fact, after his attempt to break into Scottish Television in 1967, Grimond seems never again to have seriously considered opting out of party politics. Grimond's disenchantment with the Beveridge settlement, and his growing belief that the social services needed to be completely reinvented, hardened dramatically in the mid 1970s. In October 1976 he warned in a speech in Edinburgh that centralised social services had 'sapped the will to follow our own consciences'.[62] He was delighted to be attacked for proclaiming these views only ten days later in *Social Work Today*, the journal of the Association of Social Workers. His work with organisations outside the party political mainstream convinced him that social services provided centrally by the state were never going to put civic society back on to the rails. Indeed they were now in many instances doing more harm than good.

As early as 1972, Grimond had observed that 'to treat as piecemeal housing, transport and employment, health and education, is doomed to failure',[63] and he gradually came to the view that the original welfare state, founded by the Liberal government of 1905–12, got off on the wrong foot: 'the foot of Bismarckian state socialism instead of radicalism'.[64] This he attributed to the closeness of several leading Liberals, including the party's future leader Herbert Samuel to the Webbs and other leading socialists of the period. What was needed was a more preventative and coordinated approach. In 1976 he ruefully pointed out that 'unlike medicine, the better the social worker in some respects discharges his or her work, the more dependent does the patient become'[65] and, by 1978 he felt certain that, 'with six million on national assistance of one sort or another, the Welfare State has patently come to the end of the road'.[66] Social work seemed to Jo Grimond to be largely the preserve of well-intentioned but misguided people who offered palliatives, but no long-term answers to the vicious circle of hopelessness, poverty and unemployment. In an unpublished draft article from this time, Grimond reflected that: 'in ancient Greece, I believe, when the accretion of committees, taxation, public expenditure and bureaucrats grew intolerable, there was a "seisacthia" – a cutting off of burdens . . . that is what is needed here.'[67] In Grimond's view, this applied to the private sector just as much as to the public sector. On a trip to the old-style *Daily Mirror*, Grimond was once told that: 'if all the people on the Mirror payroll turned up, their printing works would be so crowded that they could not function . . . certain employees . . . were reading books while bundles of newspapers passed before them.'[68]

During the 1970s Grimond became increasingly attracted by the radical, free-market ideas of some of Mrs Thatcher's closest advisers, notably Sir Keith Joseph and his own distant relative by marriage Nicholas Ridley. At the end of his interregnum as leader, shortly before leading his troops into the lobbies against a Conservative motion of censure, Grimond echoed, and then praised, Joseph: 'A great deal of government expenditure today is not helping the poor or anyone – it is positively harmful . . . There is much to be said for [Keith Joseph's] public statements about the market economy in a free society.'[69] Socially and politically, Grimond continued to gravitate towards the economic Liberals of the Conservative Party. In July 1978 he addressed the Adam Smith Institute and praised the stand taken by George Ward against the closed shop at Grunwick; he also allied himself with the National Association For Freedom (NAFF), a right-leaning umbrella organisation with few friends within Liberal ranks, and associated with the free-market Institute of Economic Affairs (IEA), which provided much of the intellectual backbone of the 'Thatcher Revolution'. As a participant in IEA seminars and a contributor to some of its publications, Grimond found an excellent platform from which to proclaim his belief in the liberal market economy – and a welcoming and interested audience for his argument that the unions were now guilty of abusing their power and wrecking the prospects of ordinary people. Writing for the IEA in 1978, he likened the leaders of the trade unions to 'mediaeval barons, ganging up against the common people . . . and against any government which tries effectively to control them',[70] and he regularly lambasted the Tories for their unwillingness to commit themselves to dismantling the closed shop, which he described as 'a direct infringement of freedom'.[71]

In a longer essay for the IEA entitled 'The Point of No Return?' Grimond warned that the free market, which provided the essential foundations not only for prosperity, but also for political freedom, might not indefinitely withstand the unrelenting demands, taxes and regulations of the corporate state. What was required now was nothing less than a reassertion of the 'primacy of the individual as a moral creature capable of developing his talents and making his choices within a community'.[72] Grimond had lost none of his enthusiasm for cooperatives, and argued in this piece that there should be a greatly increased role for them, and for other forms of co-ownership, both within existing private sector concerns and within units that should be privatised. The state also had to play a more positive and active role in guaranteeing the interests of the consumer, with trust-busting, pro-competitive measures. In the economic sphere at least, what we now recognise as the natural territory of the Conservative Party had by that stage been ploughed and cultivated by a lonely Grimond for some three decades. These were therefore all policies for which Grimond had long argued, and there was no great 'shift to the right' implicit

in his advocacy of them now. Nonetheless, on 28th March 1979, Grimond
did irritate many fellow Liberals by speaking at the second Ross McWhirter
memorial dinner, at which the controversial industrialist George Ward was
awarded an honour for his 'leadership at Grunwick in his fellow workers'
struggle to preserve the rule of law'. An even more controversial attachment
came with Grimond's short-lived patronage of CUT, an organisation set up to
inspire a rates revolt in the hugely mismanaged London Borough of Southwark.
He had not realised that CUT was closely associated with two right-wing
campaigning outfits, the Freedom Association and Aims of Industry.

Later in the decade, Grimond had to concern himself with an entirely
different species, grey seals. The grey seal population of Orkney was estimated
at 14,500, a population that was supposedly depriving fishermen of their
livelihoods by consuming some 2,000–3,000 tonnes of salmon each year. In
response, the Labour government of the day decided that the seals should
be culled. It was decided that a 'disappointing' cull in 1977 necessitated a
really big one in 1978, possibly involving the demise of 5,000 seals, all to
take place on what was supposed to be a seal sanctuary. Grimond was not
impressed with this. For one thing, on a global scale, the grey seal was a
comparatively rare mammal. There was also a lot of anger in the islands.
On 12th May 1978 Grimond wrote to the Secretary of State for Scotland,
Bruce Millan, expressing his doubts about the scientific basis for what was
being proposed. He was referred to the 'Seals Advisory Committee', chaired
by Lord Cranbrook. By 23rd May, Grimond had received over 110 letters,
far more than he had ever received about subjects such as Europe or home
rule. In response to the public outcry, Cranbrook plus some Scottish Office
officials came to Orkney in August 1978. One of the officials began with an
opening remark that could hardly have been calculated to endear him to an
audience of Orcadian nature-lovers – 'I don't know how many of you have
ever seen a seal' – and Grimond formally complained to Millan in a letter a
few weeks later that the official had 'seemed to think that the whole matter
was something of a joke'.[73] Grimond was incensed to learn that it was now
proposed that a Norwegian commercial interest would be brought in, at an
estimated cost of £20,000. It would also be allowed to sell the seal pelts for
£30 each. The protests were ignored, a decision that Grimond described as
'a scandal'.

Although the Lib-Lab pact had come to an end in mid 1978, the Callaghan
government survived as a minority administration until the spring of 1979.
Despite his well-established loathing of general elections, Grimond went into
the 1979 general election with higher hopes than usual. The Conservative
leadership seemed to have some genuinely liberal intentions, at least in the
economic sphere, and Grimond hoped that the 'bureaucratic blight' might
now be curbed. The election reduced the Liberal parliamentary party from

fourteen to eleven, and Grimond rejoined the front bench as spokesman on foreign and Commonwealth affairs. Undaunted, he carried on writing, and speaking, on whatever subjects took his fancy. Jo Grimond's attitude towards the government elected in 1979 was endlessly fascinating. In opposition, Mrs Thatcher had radicalised the Conservative Party, sweeping away the vestiges of Heathite corporatism and giving rein to a new breed of free-marketer. The policy proposals that emerged did not tally precisely with what Grimond had been advocating over the years – there was hardly a trace of his beloved cooperatives and wider share ownership scarcely earned a mention – but this intellectual revolution did seem to him to be pointing in the right direction.

Grimond had therefore at first hoped that a restatement of liberalism might come from that unlikeliest of sources, a Conservative government. He would defend Keith Joseph as someone who was merely 'putting stress upon the market economy because the British had gone too far the other way'.[74] Within a couple of years, however, he concluded that Margaret Thatcher and her advisers had lacked the courage of their convictions. Within only a few months of Mrs Thatcher coming to power, Grimond had warned that 'the danger is not that the Tories will do too much towards reducing the size and powers of government, but that they will do too little.'[75] In his opinion, by 1981 Mrs Thatcher was 'in danger of being hanged for virtues her Government does not possess'.[76] He believed that the press had completely misread the balance of power within the Conservative Party ('as usual'), for it seemed to him perfectly obvious that the 'conservatives', not the radicals, had been in the ascendant. There had been no serious attempt at making structural changes, government spending had risen and, now, the level of taxation had risen too. Efforts to reduce the public sector had been 'feeble' and there had been no sign whatsoever of the supply-side measures that were desperately needed to inject some dynamism into a dropsical economy. The government had set up quangos all over the place ('Mr Heseltine in particular has proved a disaster') and Grimond doubted whether 'British Leyland would have got as much out of Mr Eric Varley as it did out of Sir Keith Joseph'.[77] It was now not at all clear to Grimond that the Thatcher government stood for anything very much, despite all the brave rhetoric; its economic policy had consisted of nothing more refined or radical than punitively high interest rates and a crude attempt at tightening the money supply. He wrote sadly of his disappointment in the *Spectator*:

> I fear that I must abandon my hopes that the Tories might become the radical anti-establishment party . . . their animosity to private enterprise is amazing . . . there have been no structural changes . . . there has been no serious assault on the water boards, quangos, or, indeed, on excessive government . . . I tried one or two mildly Thatcherite amendments to a recent Bill only to be treated by Ministers as a not too well-intentioned half-wit.[78a]

Grimond was particularly incensed that the process of reforming industrial relations had been even more timid than under the Heath government. Along with David Steel and Cyril Smith, Grimond himself had voted for an amendment to the 1980 Employment Bill calling for the abolition of the 'closed shop'. The majority of Conservatives and Liberals disagreed with them, and the amendment fell. What Grimond described as a form of 'barbarism' was allowed to carry on for two more years, with, as Grimond observed, the support of so-called social democrats. Labour, wrote Grimond, 'once the party which stood up for the poor and the oppressed . . . is now associated with the powerful and the bully . . . and like all representatives of the top class it resists all change'.[79] Grimond believed too that the Conservatives should have appealed to people's patriotic instincts, as well as their immediate self-interest, re-igniting their self-esteem and independence of spirit, in order to lead them out of the dark vale of bureaucratic corporatism. He desperately wanted the first Thatcher government to succeed, as a necessary first step towards establishing a credible and sustainable alternative to state socialism. No Conservative produced a more coherent or more telling radical-liberal critique of the policies of 1979–81, and the failure fully to re-establish the necessary social and political foundations for a market economy.

The other interesting question in the longer term was whether the disintegration of the Callaghan government, followed by Labour's defeat at the polls, might now precipitate a political realignment on the left. In the event, more than anything else (along with the conflict in the Falklands) what kept Mrs Thatcher and the Conservatives in power throughout the 1980s was the pitiful state of the Labour Party. From the mid 1970s on, Grimond had been far from impressed by the conduct of many leading social democrats, too many of whom had 'retired hurt'. When Roy Jenkins abjured domestic politics to become President of the European Commission, Grimond felt that he had abrogated his responsibilities towards his country. 'Socialism,' he commented, 'has become the path to office, big salaries and perks . . . In fact, the highest paid British today, after tax, are socialists working in Brussels.'[80] Ironically, the opening gambit in the battle for realignment soon came from Jenkins himself in the autumn of 1979 when, towards the end of his term in Brussels, he called for a strengthening of what he termed the 'radical centre' of politics. Grimond decided that this was not at all what he had in mind. He did not attack Jenkins by name, but he did warn that, in his opinion, 'the social democrats have been discredited – most of them have put up a poor fight inside the Labour Party and too many have left it for lucrative jobs outside . . . They ought in many instances to call themselves pluto-democrats.'[81] Furthermore, 'they have not spelled out what they now stand for . . . It can hardly any longer be equality: is it now some watered-down version of state socialism, or a mixed economy in which the mix is a muddle?'[82] Writing in the *Listener*, Grimond reiterated his point that too many of the social democrats had opted out of public life, carping from the sidelines and pulling in good salaries while David Steel and the Liberals put their shoulders to the wheel. If the social democrats wished to influence politics, he suggested, they should get back into the real fray, rather than issuing portentous proclamations from the sidelines. Everyone knew what the Liberals' priorities were: 'if Mr Jenkins agrees, let him come down into the battle.'[83] Coming from someone as respected as Jo Grimond, these uncharacteristically dyspeptic comments hardly marked an auspicious start to Roy Jenkins's latest campaign. Jenkins recalls feeling a sense of 'disappointment – though not an obsessive disappointment'.[84]

Although Grimond was personally disenchanted with many of the leading social democrats and self-proclaimed centrists within Labour ranks, he did nonetheless call for them to make the break and join in the foundation of a new 'Liberal/Social Democratic Party . . . if the social democrats are going to get anywhere, they have virtually got to join the Liberal Party.'[85] Events during the remainder of 1980 made that far more likely. At the end of May David Owen was jeered when he spoke on defence policy during a special Labour conference at Wembley, and there were moves to remove Bill Rodgers as official defence spokesman. In June a party commission recommended the mandatory re-selection of sitting MPs and, in August, David Owen, William Rodgers and Shirley Williams (the so-called 'Gang of Three') published an open letter, expressing their growing disquiet at developments within the party. They did so to no avail: by the autumn of 1980 Labour had adopted positions on defence and the EEC inimical to the fundamental beliefs of most social democrats, accepted the principle of mandatory re-selection and deprived the party's MPs of the power to elect the party leader (without, as yet, agreeing on the make-up of the new electoral college). Despite all this, however, Grimond doubted that the social democrats would ever find the necessary vision and courage either to desert their party or to embrace the kind of liberal radicalism that he espoused. He also grew critical of some of David Steel's centrist (and centralist) tendencies, gently mocking the vagueness of it all. When Steel proclaimed his belief in a 'balanced, sustainable economy', Grimond countered: 'Um, ah. Does this mean that control of the money supply will be slackened whenever some powerful interest threatens? Does it mean a certain amount of government interference, a certain amount of government investment? If so, what amount? According to what principles? Decided by whom?'[86]

In the wake of Labour's rancorous 1980 autumn conference, Grimond delivered his most notable speech for years, the inaugural 'Eighty Club' Lecture to the Association of Liberal Lawyers. In this he did much to re-ignite the cause not only of Liberalism, but also of a realignment that could not be founded upon the politics of the lowest common denominator: 'At this moment there is a temptation to win votes by a rather woolly moderation or by emphasising that latter-day conservatism which would preserve the accepted tenets of the past thirty-five years – what has been called the doctrine of a better yesterday.'[87] What was now needed, asserted Grimond, was a restatement of liberal values, and, unless that came soon, there was a serious risk that liberalism would be forgotten entirely as different forms of nationalism and corporatism vied for supremacy. Even in Britain, historically the home of so many great Liberals, there was now a genuine threat that liberalism might die out altogether. Though he confessed that he was still 'not impressed by what we hear from most of the social democrats', Grimond acknowledged too that the Liberals were in no position to rebuff the overtures of anyone who sincerely wished to become an ally: 'I am deeply impressed by the need to welcome allies and to cooperate with them'. The Liberals could not, he warned, afford to 'remain painted into a corner of the political room, hugging their illusions of coming power and clutching at all sorts of illiberal fashions to prove that they are courageous iconoclasts of the left'.

Not for the first time, there are also unmistakable echoes of contemporary Conservative thought in this speech. He strikes a robust line on defence, mocking the would-be unilateral disarmers ('let no one expect the Russians to leave pacifists in peace any more than nuns were left inviolate by the Goths, Turks and Vandals') and pays heartfelt tribute to the importance of continuing institutions, and the notion of personal responsibility. He also perceives in the Conservative Party others who share his desire to see a resurgence of liberal values as a rejoinder to state socialism and its bureaucratic allies: 'Much of what Mrs Thatcher and Sir Keith Joseph say and do is in the mainstream of liberal philosophy.' Grimond chimes perfectly with the intellectual revolution that was just then beginning, by restating views that he had maintained throughout his political life: 'the market for economic purposes is by far the best means . . . Liberals must stress at all times the virtues of the market, not only for efficiency, but to enable the widest possible choice.' There is also a curious and unexpected tribute to the positive aspects of nationalism: 'Nationalism has often shared some of the generous features of liberalism. It can be a rival for allegiance to much more soul-destroying sirens . . . it can be an extension of the community . . . it gives men and women that feeling that they have something to belong to, and work for, and rejoice in, it gives them some security from the knowledge that their fellow patriots are on their side.'

Less than six months before the 'Gang of Four' led the breakaway from Labour to the new Social Democratic Party (SDP), it is fascinating that Grimond should still have taken such a jaundiced view of them and their supporters. He looked in vain for some echo from them of his own belief in the free market, in personal responsibility and in cooperative and communitarian liberalism. They can hardly have felt very encouraged.

At another special Labour conference in January 1981, again held at Wembley, the party decided upon the new method of electing its leader and David Owen's call for 'one member, one vote' was heavily defeated. An electoral college was instituted, giving the trade unions a 40 per cent stake, to only 30 per cent for the parliamentary party and 30 per cent for constituency parties, who would be free not to ballot their members. This was unacceptable to the social democrats: Jenkins, Owen, Rodgers and Williams issued the 'Limehouse Declaration' that weekend, which effectively committed them to the creation of a new party. When the 'Gang of Four' did finally indicate their willingness to break with the Labour Party in early 1981, Grimond felt obliged to make a kindlier assessment of the social democrats, recognising for instance that David Owen's 1981 book *Face the Future* would play a major part in cementing them to the Liberal Party. At one meeting of the Liberal parliamentary party, he grew exasperated with his colleagues as they descended into discussions of the Liberal catechism. 'I really don't know what all the fuss is about,' he proclaimed. 'Have any of you read any of these books? They set out exactly the same case that we have been arguing for the past twenty years.'[88] Nonetheless, he would later confess that the leaders of the SDP had not emerged in answer to 'of any prayers of mine'.[89]

The SDP came into being on 26th March 1981, with a flurry of media attention. The first parliamentary election fought by the new party was the by-election at Warrington on 16th July. Although the Liberals and the SDP had no formal electoral arrangement, the Liberals were happy enough to stand down in a seat where they had won only 9 per cent of the vote two years earlier. Roy Jenkins was selected as the SDP candidate. Grimond was at his most characteristically detached when, in Jenkins's phrase, he 'just blew in'[90] to Warrington on the Saturday before polling day to cast a sceptical eye over what Jenkins and his by-election campaign team were up to. He was astonished to observe the enthusiasm for campaigning evinced by Jenkins and his team, soon dispensed with his scepticism and ended up helping out actively for most of the day. Laura was out delivering 'good morning' leaflets at 5 a.m. on polling day, helping Jenkins to cut the Labour majority from over 10,000 votes to under 2,000. This was all very well, but Grimond still felt that there was too much emphasis amongst both social democrats and Liberals on the need to find 'that old political nirvana, the middle ground'.[91] The only radicalism that he found to cheer him came in a seminal article by one of the founding MPs of the SDP, John Horam, who shared (and shares) his radicalism and his active mistrust of the corporate, bureaucratic state.

Grimond was unsettled not only by the emergence of policies that he disliked. He was also disturbed by a parallel with the 1960s, when under his own leadership the Liberals had attracted so much support from people who agreed with very little of what the party actually stood for. This could mean that image could triumph over substance, as the Liberals and their new allies lazily adhered to illiberal, indeed conservative, attitudes (notably an incomes policy) as a safety measure, under the malign influence of traditional right-wing Labour: 'the conservative state socialist wing responsible for the present set-up in the nationalised industries'.[92] At their 1981 autumn assembly at Llandudno, the Liberals had to decide whether or not to endorse an alliance with the SDP and, despite Grimond's appearance at Warrington, many of his colleagues perceived a lack of enthusiasm on the part of their revered former leader for this new enterprise. In fact, he always recognised that a formal electoral alliance would be necessary, to prevent the two parties neutralising one another. He also believed that it could be made to work, once wryly commenting that it was bound to succeed 'because Roy Jenkins is such a good liberal and David Steel is such a good social democrat'.[93]

Although most Liberals perfectly understood the practical case for an electoral pact, there was still a considerable emotional barrier to overcome, and David Steel arranged for a fringe meeting to be held at Llandudno that would be more or less as large as the assembly itself, at which Shirley Williams and Roy Jenkins would speak. The hope, spectacularly realised in the event, was that this meeting would generate such fervour that the assembly would be swept along into endorsing the alliance the following day – something of a 'con-trick', as David Steel would later admit. Symbolically, however, it was Grimond who would be the star of the show. Alan Watson, the party president, took his car to pick up Grimond from the railway station. He watched the train arrive and waited until the last person disembarked. Characteristically, Grimond was that last person, clambering down to the platform wearing a heavy coat and a balaclava. Sitting in the car on the way to what promised to be a historic fringe meeting, Grimond asked, 'Ah, Alan, what is it I must do?' Watson explained to Grimond that he must tell everyone that the true Liberal thing to do was to back the proposed alliance with the SDP. 'Ah,' responded his passenger, non-committally. Grimond followed the advice and, at lunch with Watson the day after, evidently knew that he had played his part in history.

The meeting was attended by a majority of those at the conference, and Grimond spoke with genuine passion, skilfully leavened with his characteristic humour. His talismanic role was underlined by the fact that, alone among those on the platform, he received a standing ovation before uttering a word. He had never dreamed, he told the audience, that all his hopes of a great political breakthrough could be realised as they were being at that moment:

> Now I beg of you to seize this chance – do not get bogged down in the niceties of innumerable policies. I spent my life fighting against too much policy in the Liberal Party! I do not believe that we have to have a policy on dog licences and the details of world government. But also make quite sure that your major

policies are right and that you are going to defend them – because you may have to put them into practice!'[94]

He even praised the social democrats for putting the public interest ahead of their own interests, having foregone 'prestigious and lucrative jobs' in order to go back out on to the stump as they attempted to create a new political movement from scratch. The following day, only 112 dissenting votes were recorded from amongst 1,600 delegates as the alliance was endorsed after a highly charged debate. Steel's tactic had paid off: he had played his trump card, Grimond, the night before and won before the sun rose over his day of destiny. Roy Jenkins would subsequently christen Jo Grimond as the 'father of the Alliance'.

Grimond had never believed that realignment would come about quickly; indeed, for a time he had thought that it would never happen. Now, thanks to the 'courage of Roy Jenkins' and his followers, it seemed that what he had always dreamed of was now coming to pass. Grimond rewarded Jenkins for that courage by joining him at the launch of his by-election campaign in Glasgow, Hillhead, and then returning to help with the campaign. In Grimond's view the hunger for, and experience of, high political office amongst the social democrats was a perfect complement for the Liberals, who still in many instances prized ideals above power. When Roy Jenkins, duly returned to the House of Commons after his hard fight at Hillhead, was elected as the SDP's first leader, Grimond publicly accepted that he and many others had misjudged him: 'This is no fat cat sipping claret instead of cream but a taker of risks and a formidable vote-getter.'[95] Although Grimond had lost none of his charisma or talismanic qualities, his regular appearances at the series of by-elections that sustained the Alliance sometimes proved to be a mixed blessing. Grimond appears never to have had a great deal of respect for Shirley Williams, particularly disapproving of her decision to go on the picket lines during the Grunwick dispute, though he did once praise her for the fact that 'she can't get her tights on the right way round . . . it shows a desire not to get out in front'.[96] The press had an easy time driving a wedge between the two of them during a press conference in Crosby. She had long believed that everything possible should be done to drive independent schools out of existence and, although Grimond was willing to concede 'I suppose I do find it rather hard to believe, as an OE, that Eton was a charity,' he could not disguise his opposition to her policy. 'Well, we agree on the aims of education,' he protested half-heartedly. It all confirmed his fears that liberalism, as he had always understood it, was going to have a difficult time of it under this new arrangement. He foreclosed the debate in an abrupt, if surreal, fashion by moving on to the subject of the sexual frustrations of public schoolboys.

Then came the Falklands War, which dramatically revived the sense of purpose, and the political fortunes, of Margaret Thatcher and the Conservative

Party. Although Grimond described the conflict as 'the culmination of blunders', he joined most of the political establishment in paying tribute to the armed forces which, he commented, had demonstrated an ability to get things done that was rare in 1980s Britain. Indeed, he suggested that, in the aftermath of the Falklands expedition, could not a study of the armed services be undertaken, to learn from them 'both for what purposes the public service is suitable and by what motives and methods it should be conducted'.[97] As in the case of Suez, he feared that the difficult questions would be evaded once the islands had been retaken and, along with many Conservatives, deplored the performance of the media throughout. Grimond had some years before warned of the growing propensity of the media to focus on 'the fashionable and often the trivial in both news and comment' and 'the pursuit of selfish interests or gladiatorial displays to titillate our taste for violence'.[98] Now he denounced both the 'horror-comic treatment' of the conflict in the *Sun,* and the propensity of the BBC to echo the 'orthodox opinions of its own London, vaguely left, middle-class staff'.[99] Hearing that some relics of the age were to be buried at Castle Howard, Grimond suggested adding to the collection one of the most appropriately gruesome icons that he could envisage: 'the mummy of a newsreader, tastefully embalmed, as the idol of 20th-century television'.[100] At the Falklands service at St Paul's some months later, solemn thanks were offered up to the Almighty for providing mankind with the BBC. As Grimond commented wryly, 'in mediaeval times the BBC might well have acquired a patron saint'.[101]

As expectations of an early election gained currency in the autumn of 1982, Grimond knew that he had to decide whether or not he should defend Orkney and Shetland one more time. He decided not to. He was almost seventy years old, and evidently felt increasingly self-conscious and out of place in the Commons after thirty-two years there. His best friends in his House of Commons career had probably been Reggie Paget, a Labour MP, and the Tory Dick Law, son of Bonar Law, both of whom had long since left the House. For years now his failing hearing and unreliable eyesight had made life increasingly difficult and embarrassing for him. His constituents always preferred to raise their problems with him in person, and he often found that he simply could not hear what they were saying. He therefore regretfully came to the view that seventy was a 'very suitable age' for calling it a day, sending handwritten letters to a number of his closest supporters and confidants in October 1982 to inform them that: 'I don't think that I should fight the next general election – 70 & deaf' and to solicit their views on possible replacement candidates. On the day the news became public, Grimond was interviewed on Radio Orkney by Howie Firth, a one-time SNP candidate for the islands who had become a good friend. It was not all bad, he told Firth, at least now 'we can have long, uninhibited conversations about the awfulness of it all!'[102]

Grimond's final months in the House of Commons were marked by a series of pleas to the SDP-Liberal Alliance to become more radical. 'Most of the Liberal agenda,' he warned, 'sets out a diet of nursery fare, unlikely to upset the children or cause their nurses anxiety . . . More money is to be spent, more cosseting arranged, a few old nursery favourites are served up.'[103] He particularly deplored the parties' reliance upon an incomes policy 'minted in the thinking of 1945'[104] and representing 'an easy way out . . . It would be an attempt to disguise the faults of our public relations instead of getting to the root of the problem.'[105] He also begged the joint Alliance leadership to mix in a bit of populism along with all the reheated middle-of-the-road fare. He could not disguise his relief at avoiding a campaign of his own at the general election for the first time since 1945. 'Like a cold bath,' he remarked, 'the only pleasure in a general election is getting out of it successfully.'[106]

17

EVEN THOUGH GRIMOND was standing down from the House of Commons, in the run-up to the 1983 general election his party still made good use of him, employing him as a keynote speaker at the major lunch and evening rally when the Alliance was 're-launched' in January of that year. At the rally Grimond went for broke, describing the Alliance as a 'great adventure, something I thought beyond my wildest dreams'.[1] He then agreed to undertake a heavy programme of constituency visits during the campaign. The last major trial that Grimond had to endure as a member of Parliament was an appearance with Eamonn Andrews on *This is Your Life*, recorded in February 1983. Although he retained his composure and good humour throughout the show, Grimond looked out of place, greeting the opening ambush from Andrews with the words 'Oh God, how very alarming' and a characteristic dry chuckle – and appearing increasingly nervous about who might next emerge from behind the set. There were, however, several touching tributes on the show, not least that from veteran broadcaster David Frost, who described Grimond as someone who had 'always put the national interest above party interest and never confused the two'. Ester and Barry Slater, the Grimonds' neighbours who looked after the Old Manse when they were away, came down to London to appear on the show and, as Grimond greets Mrs Slater, he can be heard saying, 'I've rung you up today – no wonder I couldn't find you, what!' When the 1979 Parliament was dissolved, the *Daily Telegraph*, by no means known for its admiration of Grimond, mourned the departure of 'arguably the last Independent to sit in Parliament'.[2] In the *Guardian*, Edward Pearce wrote that he left the House of Commons with 'the affection of almost everybody . . . An agnostic among zealots, indifferent to the sound of his own voice, on the side of the angels in most questions but never immoderately so, he was a lesson in good manners, a classy guy.'[3] Grimond's successor as Liberal candidate for Orkney and Shetland was Jim Wallace, a twenty-eight-year old advocate from Edinburgh who before being selected had only been to the islands on three occasions, and had never even met Grimond. The Grimonds took to him at once, and Laura acted as his agent.

As the Alliance almost overtook Labour during the campaign, Grimond relished the opportunity to fire a shot or two across socialist bows: 'It is amazing to me that Labour have not fielded Eric Varley and Peter Shore more,' he observed. 'To swing from Michael Foot, whom I regard as a hypocrite of the first order, to the arch-bully Denis Healey is crazy.'[4] He also appeared alongside Jim Wallace at election meetings in the islands. Nationally the 1983 general election brought another highly equivocal result for the Liberal Party. Despite winning over 25 per cent of the vote, the Liberals and their SDP allies won a combined total of only 23 seats. Jim Wallace won in Orkney and Shetland, making him the first Liberal candidate since the war to have successfully inherited a candidacy from an incumbent MP at a general election. In the years that followed, Jo Grimond always remained in the background unless and until his help was required, allowing Wallace breathing space to establish himself. Laura, however, determinedly took Jim Wallace's wife Rosie under her wing, teaching her how to cajole local people into supporting various Liberal and other causes, on one occasion virtually dragging her round a series of shops in search of prizes for the Liberal raffle, at every stop reminding the intimidated shopkeepers what they had given the year before.

When he decided to call it a day as an MP, Grimond was clear in his own mind that he was only retiring from frontline politics, not from life. Although he looked forward to looking at pictures and 'pottering around', he also intended to do a certain amount of exercise for as long as he was able, telling Keith Kyle that he thought it was 'frankly immoral'[5] not to make at least some effort to keep reasonably fit. He would also 'entertain and be entertained'.[6] Grimond knew that a seat in the Lords was his for the asking – if he wanted it. He had always been rather opposed to the House of Lords, once affirming that he 'would not take a seat in any House of Lords reformed in any way which is possible at the moment'.[7] As he contemplated the impending end of his career as an MP, however, he confessed that he was inclined to change his mind. He was 'coming round – as many people do – to think there's more in it than meets the eye'.[8] Very wisely, he dealt with this looming inconsistency with his usual good humour and robustness, explaining that, although he intended to go on living at the Old Manse of Firth, he also wished to carry on coming to London and, as a member of the House of Lords, he would be able to go on claiming his travel costs. He would joke too that the Liberals would never get rid of him. Shortly after the 1983 general election, Margaret Thatcher conferred a viscountcy – a hereditary peerage – on William Whitelaw, who had no male heir. The journalist Alexander Chancellor asked Grimond whether he expected the same. 'Certainly not,' was his response, 'I have heirs!'[9]

Before Jo Grimond could take his seat in the House of Lords, however, there were other important matters to which he had to attend. First of all, in the summer of 1983, he was wheeled out in defence of David Steel's determination to retain his right of veto, as leader, over the party manifesto.

In the end it was arguably Laura who won the day, with a marvellous speech at the party's 1983 autumn assembly, in which she said how absurd it would be for Steel to be in a position where he could be forced to admit on television that there were aspects of his party manifesto with which he disagreed. Shortly afterwards, and back at Westminster, the Grimonds and many friends and colleagues together commemorated the end of an era. Although she would go on deciphering his manuscript notes for some years yet on an *ad hoc* basis, Cate Fisher, Jo Grimond's private secretary for the past thirty years, was retiring from the Palace of Westminster. The retirement party that the Grimonds hosted in October 1983, in the Cholmondely Room in the Lords, was a classic Liberal gathering, and Jo graced it with a vintage speech, recalling one occasion on which he had returned from a lengthy trip around the world and, upon his return, had telephoned Cate to ask, 'Has anything happened?' 'No.' 'Do I need to come to the Commons tomorrow?' 'No.' 'Do I need to sign any letters?' 'No.' This had been one of the great Westminster partnerships.

In November 1983 Grimond did take his seat in the House of Lords, as Baron Grimond of Firth, in the County of Orkney. He was formally introduced into the chamber by Pratap Chitnis and Frank Byers. When Roy Jenkins and Mark Bonham Carter hosted a dinner party to celebrate Grimond's peerage, it was obvious that he had achieved a perfect transition to his new status. 'People ask me, having been a member of the House of Commons, what's it like now, being in the House of Lords,' he reported in his speech of thanks. 'Well, when I go home to Orkney for the weekend and go shopping on Saturday morning, if anyone says "Hello, Jo", I can now just scowl at them!'[10] Grimond carried on in a similar vein for his entire time in the House of Lords, where he commanded respect and affection, if anything, to an even greater degree than he had in the Commons. Although Grimond had always argued that the House of Lords should be elected, he believed too that it had to be different from the House of Commons in a number of ways, and never doubted that even an unreformed upper chamber could make a positive and distinctive contribution: 'I am in favour of the House of Lords doing nothing in particular but doing it very well,' he once wrote.[11] Although Grimond's own manners were always impeccable, he very much missed the cut and thrust of the Commons, comparing the atmosphere in the Lords to that in a 'well-run old folk's home'[12] and never quite settling into its more gentle atmosphere or mastering its topography. He once bumped into Richard Holme and told him vaguely: 'I think there's someone looking for you – in that room where the stone women are', by which he meant the celebrated Prince's Chamber, adorned with vast sculptures by John Gibson of Queen Victoria flanked by allegorical statues of Justice and Clemency.

Grimond also contributed to the ongoing debate about the future of the SDP/Liberal Alliance. Although many senior figures in both parties continued to emphasise their 'radical' credentials, Grimond believed the Alliance had paid a price in 1983 for looking like precisely the kind of centre party he had repeatedly denounced, writing that, even if it did replace the Labour Party, that would only mean that 'the Tories will continue to assert the conservative side, the Alliance the progressive side, of state socialism'.[13] Grimond's great hope now was that the new SDP leader, David Owen, might give the Alliance a radical cutting edge: 'He favours the market, smaller Government and social services whose aims are to be achieved in some cases by new methods . . . But has the Alliance accepted Owenism?'[14] To his great disappointment, Grimond gradually became convinced that this kind of radicalism was not to the taste of most Liberals and Social Democrats. They appeared to be happier in the political centre ground, preferring to espouse a form of Gaitskellite social democracy. 'I detect in the Liberal Party,' he mused sadly, 'a slackening of interest in new ideas.'[15]

It never crossed the Grimonds' minds to break their connection with Orkney merely because Jo was no longer the local member of Parliament. Visitors to the islands often commented on how he was regarded, with good-humoured respect, as a kind of benign squire, just as much as a servant of the people, and as an integral part of the local ecosystem. It therefore surprised nobody that Grimond decided to carry on living amongst the Orcadians, that 'notably peaceful race, unassertive, unabrasive and anxious to live in harmony with one another'.[16] He also acted as a kind of MP emeritus, quietly offering moral and practical support to his successor Jim Wallace as he fought for the rights of the Orcadians, notably when Orkney was caught up in a controversy allegedly involving child abuse. The great contribution that the Grimonds had made to Orkney was formally recognised on 22nd April 1987, when they became the first people ever to receive not only the freedom of the Borough of Kirkwall, but also the freedom of Orkney itself. This was given at a ceremony presided over on the steps of St Magnus' Cathedral in Kirkwall by Jo Grimond's long-time supporter Edwin Eunson, in his capacity as the convenor of the Orkney Islands Council. Grimond as usual raised a good few laughs when he spoke, contemplating his new freedoms and grumbling, 'I haven't heard anything about free drink.' He closed with a moving tribute to the Orcadians, to their enduring qualities and to their ability to adapt when necessary to new methods of existence. Quoting Housman's *A Shropshire Lad*, he closed with the couplet, 'Get you the sons your fathers got, And God will save the Queen' (it will not have been lost on Grimond that the reference, and the tribute, in the original poem was to the qualities of the 'Lads of the Fifty-third'). In his post-Commons life, Grimond also blossomed as a journalist. He was already well established as an engaging, if occasional, contributor to the *Spectator* and the broadsheets, but he now became a regular columnist in both the *Field* magazine and the *Daily Telegraph*. It is impossible to do full justice to the combination of gentle humour and wisdom that pervades this late opus, but his outpourings provide insight not only into the older Grimond, but also into his earlier life. His contributions in the House of Lords mirrored his journalism: they were scattered and unpredictable, almost always gentle and genial but sometimes serious and more often than not witty. He combined detailed and well-informed interventions about higher education with his continuing and highly articulate devotion to more recherché subjects, such as the habits of the Highland midge, on which he was surely rather less of an expert than he liked to imply.

During his ten years in the Lords, Grimond stuck mainly to familiar territory, making a series of sustained attacks on bureaucracy and quangos, in particular those dealing with 'heritage' and 'conservancy'. In his maiden speech he denounced contemporary legislation: 'legislating and regulating have become a national disease throughout the country . . . Yet the strange thing is that a great deal of it is clearly trivial and much of it harmful, while very important matters go untouched.'[17] The burgeoning volume of mediocre, complicated and ill-prepared legislation that threatened to swamp the parliamentary system seemed to be symptomatic of the general dysfunction of the public sector: 'a lack of skill is shown in the mending of London Transport escalators and in the drafting of Bills.'[18] Grimond pressed the Thatcher government on why it had not done more, particularly when privatising large industrial concerns, to spread ownership of shares or to make industry more competitive, and continued to make the case for the cooperative movement. He also made telling contributions on questions of national heritage (a phrase he detested), conservation and, most significantly, human rights. He spoke up for the Kurds and the people of Tibet, and for forgotten and oppressed minorities, such as the Hungarians in Romania. He was appalled that any democratically elected government should pull its punches on the international stage on questions of human rights, for fear of jeopardising trade relations (all too often involving the large-scale sales of arms, military hardware or munitions) with another state. He also became increasingly outspoken in his denunciations of the Provisional IRA, criticising the hypocrisy of the US administration in allowing fund-raising activities to take place on its behalf in the USA: 'Americans,' he observed, 'would be outraged if large sums of money were collected in Britain to equip the Red Indians with bombs and rifles.'[19]

On two areas of policy Grimond's interventions in the mid 1980s were especially detailed and significant. The first was the community charge (poll tax), which was introduced between 1987 and 1988. Like most people, Grimond objected to this measure in principle: 'The Government themselves do not know how it will work, and there will be widespread evasion. In the end it will not result in people paying for the things they use. It will be a random poll tax.'[20] He was particularly concerned for the impecunious crofters in his old constituency of Orkney and Shetland, who potentially faced ruinous increases in local taxation. Like most Scots, Grimond was also particularly angry that a government with so few MPs from Scottish constituencies should have gone out of its way to add insult to injury by introducing such a controversial measure in Scotland first:

> the Government are treating Scotland as a test-bed . . . this is a dangerous situation to ignore . . . I am not suggesting for a moment that there would be anything like an uprising in Scotland, but . . . if after the next election Scotland is still governed by a party that has a small minority in Scotland, and if that party introduces major legislation of this sort, the mood may turn sour, possibly with bad results for the parliamentary system in general.[21]

The poll tax, in summary, threatened to 'bring the administration of local government into total disrepute'.[22] The other major piece of legislation to attract Grimond's attention was the Thatcher government's Education Reform Bill of 1987–8 (the 'GERBIL').

During the GERBIL debates, Grimond treated the House to several brilliant expositions of what he meant by a liberal education. First of all, he emphasised that he believed in high standards: 'there is a danger that we may encourage universities not to go for excellence, which has its dangers, but for the safe second-rate – I do not believe that that would be at all desirable in the case of British universities.'[23] His conception of a university was 'a free and independent community of scholars in a wide range of subjects . . . at the core of the idea is freedom, including the freedom to be eccentric and unorthodox.'[24] Always Grimond rejected the 'sausage machine' conception of education, within which a publicly funded system would aim to churn out young people trained purely according to economic and industrial criteria, and he was suspicious of some of the centralising tendencies apparent in this Bill. He was no more impressed by the same government's proposals to introduce the student loans scheme:

> The purpose of higher education is not only to produce an excellent chemist or doctor; it is to produce an excellent person . . . higher education is not simply specialised technical education, important though that is . . . It is equally essential to introduce as many students as possible to a wider education and to a real knowledge of history, of the habits of their country and Europe, and of European civilisation.[25]

One other role that Grimond fulfilled late in life remains shrouded in mystery, and with good reason. Along with Conservative former chief whip Francis Pym and Labour's Lord Shackleton, in 1986 he became part of the political honours scrutiny committee, set up during the First World War after Lloyd George had been criticised for selling peerages. The committee is traditionally comprised of three distinguished peers, one from each of the main parties. Grimond took over from Lord Franks. Perhaps the most striking feature of this committee is the fact that virtually nobody knows anything at all about it. Its job is to ensure that only 'the most suitable' candidates for major honours are seriously considered. During Grimond's time on the committee, it is understood that the vetoing of a peerage for Jeffrey Archer became something of a regular ritual, and it was reported from time to time that talk of an honour for the media tycoon Rupert Murdoch had been raised and then quelled, allegedly at the say-so of the committee. Grimond was as discreet as every other member of this committee has been, the extent of his whistle-blowing on the subject being that he once admitted that the committee existed, and met a few times a year. For all his protestations, no other position could have so unquestionably underlined Grimond's ascension to the uppermost tier of the political establishment. Nonetheless, as his hearing faded and his eyesight fell victim to an unpredictable thyroid condition, Grimond did in some ways become a rather isolated figure. At one party, he joked with a journalist from the *Sunday Times*: 'I am a little deaf, so I'll talk anyway and let's hope I answer the question I think you asked me.'[26] Although he did eventually acquire a deaf aid, he didn't much like it, likening the rush of sound that it created to the 'Brixton riots' and grumbling that it never enabled him to pick out the words that he wanted to catch, amidst the crackling of newspapers and the 'clatter of cocktail parties'. He regularly made good use of the hearing aid, however, discreetly turning it off when he was collared by anyone particularly boring. One of his colleagues well remembers him being cornered by someone who had an axe to grind. Grimond's face at first betrayed considerable discomfort as he endured the verbal torrents. Then his hand slipped almost imperceptibly into his jacket, and to the inside pocket, where a switch was imperceptibly thrown, whereupon his face was transformed into the very picture of beatific bliss. Grimond's deafness certainly never affected his ability to amuse, and invitations to speak continued to come in, as did honorary degrees and doctorates, from universities such as Stirling and Buckingham. In February 1984 Grimond became an honorary fellow of Balliol College.

Jo Grimond was again brought out of political semi-retirement for the so-called 'relaunch' rally held by the Alliance parties on Saturday, 31st January 1987 at the Barbican Centre in London, as a curtain raiser for their general election campaign. 'No other party could persuade two and a half thousand people to pay £7 to hear eighteen speeches,' he proclaimed. 'It must strike terror into the hearts of our opponents!' The Alliance had attracted unwelcome attention only a few days before when its MPs had split three ways on a crucial division, with David Steel, Charles Kennedy and Roy Jenkins supporting a Labour motion attacking the City of London, while David Owen and Paddy Ashdown, *inter alia,* opposed it. 'At least when we have a cock-up,' joked

Grimond, 'it's not on party lines'. His only concern, he told his enthusiastic audience, was that the Alliance might have lost the votes of animal lovers, 'now that they know that the dogs of Battersea may have to eat Eric Lubbock' (who had recently announced that he intended to leave his body to Battersea Dogs' Home). He warned his colleagues to beware their tendency to have too much in the way of policy and counselled them to streamline their campaigning by concentrating on the economy and the health service, adding, with stylish and canny understatement, that 'Scotland will have to be attended to.' The Alliance had endured some difficult times since 1983. The personality clash between David Steel and David Owen had been underpinned and, at times, even overshadowed by policy disagreements, notably about nuclear weapons. The Barbican rally helped to recreate a sense of unity and purpose, but Labour's modest recovery in 1987 damaged the Alliance at the polls. The Alliance did extremely well to win twenty-two seats, only one fewer than in 1983. There were five casualties, the most notable of whom was the former SDP leader Roy Jenkins, defeated at Hillhead by 3,000 votes.

In the wake of the 1987 general election David Steel wasted no time in launching his campaign for a merger between the Liberals, who had won seventeen seats, and the SDP, now down to only five seats. Grimond was more interested in Alliance policies than in its organisation, merely expressing relief that a divided party – or parties – had been spared the very mixed blessing of holding the balance of power (which he now termed the 'balance of impotence') in the new House of Commons. In an article written just days after the 1987 poll, he coined an interesting phrase, one that would, in time, achieve a wide currency indeed: 'for me, the Alliance is not a middle way, but a *third way* [emphasis added] . . . the problem is not to achieve socialism, but to make capitalism work for all.'[27] He still believed that the long-term tide was flowing towards a realignment of centre-left politics, but wished that its leaders would send clearer signals about what kind of country they wanted to help create. In Grimond's view it had not been the dual leadership of Owen and Steel that had caused difficulties in the election campaign; it had been the 'lack of a clearly defined political stance'.[28] He also wished that David Steel in particular had taken a far firmer line against the unilateral nuclear disarmers who had so riven the Alliance from its inception, with their policy that would 'either increase the chances of war or leave Britain in a most dishonourable position'.[29]

More or less from the outset, Grimond had believed that the SDP and the Liberals were wasting their time and dissipating their energies by attempting to coexist as separate parties. They either agreed on the basics of policy, he felt, in which case they might as well merge, or they did not, in which case they should go their separate ways. As early as 1970 Grimond had written that: 'I have never thought all local pacts immoral. But when it comes to a general pact with another party, the point which strikes me is that there must be some identity of view and, if there is, why not some permanent alliance or amalgamation?'[30] In the wake of the 1987 general election, Grimond was one of the first supporters of a merger, though he showed more consideration for the sensitivities of SDP members than did many of his Liberal colleagues, and believed that David Steel had been badly mistaken in forcing the issue in the immediate wake of the election, and, 'having forced it, his failure to take a grip on the aftermath was a greater mistake . . . Having suffered the fiasco of the policy document which had to be withdrawn, he took no steps to clarify the future of the leadership, nor to make the broad political stance of the party clear.'[31] When some of his colleagues attempted to play the sentiment card in opposition to a merger, however, Grimond was very robust about the need to condemn the old Liberal Party, in name at least, to death: 'I would willingly forgo the name for the substance of liberalism.'[32] Once David Owen had resigned as SDP leader at the beginning of August 1987, the way to merger seemed to be clear and, in January 1988, a special Liberal assembly met in Blackpool to resolve the issue once and for all on the Liberal side. Many party campaigners had their doubts about the proposed merger, and the result was far from certain. In a deliberate and conscious rerun of the famous eve-of-vote rally at Llandudno in 1981, David Steel asked Grimond and Roy Jenkins to star in a similar event at Blackpool. The assembly voted for merger by the unexpectedly decisive margin of 2,009 votes to only 385. Grimond responded by ignoring David Steel's request for a 'close season' on the leadership of the merged party, calling for Steel to put himself forward as the new party's first leader.

Despite his continuing involvement with the Liberals, there is no doubt that Grimond in later years, on economic policy at least, continued to identify himself with some of the more radical thinking more normally associated with Margaret Thatcher and the Tories, whom he continued to regard as being in some respects excessively cautious and conservative. In 1988 Grimond became one of the prime movers in the new Radical Society, an anti-collectivist group bringing together politicians from all parties who had been inspired by the 'raised individualist ethic' that had sprung up in the 1980s. Its leading figure was Norman Tebbit, once again free from the constraints of office, for whose demotic strain of radicalism Grimond had considerable sympathy. 'Had it not been for such as Tebbit,' he once wrote, 'the Tory party under its nabobs might well have continued as before . . . His strength lay in being a populist with an understanding of technology and the world of technologists who intended to be upwardly mobile.'[33] The 1987 Budget had brought massive tax cuts for high earners, who had responded not by trimming back their gross pay, but by increasing their largesse towards each other – high salaries now being so much more worth having. In July 1988 Grimond used a lecture under the aegis of the Radical Society to warn that British companies might soon pay a price for their profligacy towards their directors and senior staff. The lean times that he predicted were not too long in coming and, ultimately, he was disappointed in the Thatcher government.

By the mid 1980s he had already feared that she had forsaken her self-proclaimed mission to 'speak for the comparatively silent majority against the paternalists and the socialist mandarins', having been taken in by the cult of monetarism: 'her Government seems to worship the public sector borrowing requirement as the Israelites bowed before the Golden Calf.'[34] As the Thatcher years came to a fairly ignominious end, he reflected wistfully: 'this belief that the Government can do everything is now the hallmark of the Tory Party.'[35] One very serious measure that Grimond opposed vigorously in the Lords was the Thatcher government's War Crimes Bill, which he described as 'a disgrace, only to be surpassed by our treatment of Hong Kong and with no parallel excuse'.[36] Even some of Grimond's admirers were a little hard put to defend one comparison that he made in this connection, when he drew the parallel that dare not speak its name: 'If the Nazi torturers are to be hounded down, why not others? Why not the Stern gang?'[37] Though Grimond might have chosen his words more diplomatically, it can hardly be disputed that this particular Act has proved to be far from successful.

As ever for the Grimonds, it was not all politics. In May 1988 Jo and Laura's daughter Grizelda organised a party to celebrate the couple's fiftieth wedding anniversary, going to great lengths to ensure that as many surviving members of the original congregation as possible were present. According to Woodrow Wyatt, Laura commented at this event that it was remarkable that two such 'cantankerous' people had lived together for so long: 'perhaps it's because he is deaf and I won't listen!'[38] In February 1989 Grimond took the chair at a Foyle's lunch celebrating the publication of the autobiography of his old friend and comrade-in-arms Ludovic Kennedy, enthusing in his speech about the 'many passages of lamentable taste' in the book. Grimond carried on as chancellor of the University of Kent until 1990, cementing his reputation as a raconteur and *bon viveur*. When Grimond finally came to the end of his chancellorship after twenty years, he noted that he would be leaving behind a gold and green robe that had been designed for his predecessor, Princess Marina, by no less a luminary than Christian Dior. 'It once had a train,' he mentioned gleefully in one of his last speeches to the university congregation, 'with a small boy at the end of it – but we used to jack-knife, so I did away with it!'[39]

Towards the end of the 1980s Grimond's political journalism began to peter out, and his contributions in the House of Lords became less regular. In one of the last overtly political pieces he penned, he fleshed out what he meant by what he still termed the 'third way' that, in his view, his party ought to be following. The Labour Party had now gradually dropped the four totems of the left that had scared off the voters – on defence, nationalisation, Europe and the trade unions – and the gap between the two main parties was therefore narrowing. Grimond warned against a strategy that would leave the Social and Liberal Democrats (SLD), as they then were, squeezed in that ever-diminishing gap. His 'third way' was emphatically not that of the 'New' Labour Party. It was a return to the kind of social liberalism that had first brought Grimond into politics – a combination of Conservative-style social obligations with a concern for equality – a third way enshrining 'great devolution of power and influence as well as wealth'.[40] The SLD must promise to do something that neither Labour nor the Conservatives had ever done, although Mrs Thatcher had made encouraging noises in the early days, namely to curb the power of the bureaucratic, centralised state.

In his senescent journalism, Grimond continued to register benign personal protests against the intrusions of the modern era. In one article he reveals that his mother-in-law, Violet Bonham Carter, who was hard put to be half-hearted about anything, had a particular penchant for the telephone, and convinced herself that all calls cost the same. This, believed Grimond, was a peculiarly Liberal trait. He recalled Eric Lubbock, when chief whip, sitting in the House of Commons, 'the telephone clasped to his ear as are comforters to the lips of children'.[41] One can only try to imagine what he would have made of today's streets, filled as they are with people clasping mobile telephones to their ears even as they go about their business. He also revealed that he had endured an intestinal operation, in which two polyps had been removed. 'What particularly gratifies me,' he wrote, 'is that they were said to be "benign" . . . perhaps it is a pity that I have lost them.'[42] When Grimond insisted on returning to the House of Lords shortly afterwards, before it was advisable for him to do so, staff there noticed that Laura was following devotedly around behind him, at a discreet distance, lest he suffer a medical emergency or a fall.

Throughout his life Grimond enjoyed shopping, a characteristic that he believed to be hereditary, having inherited it from his father and passed it on to his children. Once he even used his expertise to advise readers of a broadsheet newspaper on how to go about selecting presents. It is one of his most hilarious pieces, full of deadpan advice such as: 'beware of buying presents on holiday . . . Avoid pottery and fabrics, particularly from the East.'[43] He also harked back to his own earliest triumph in the art of present buying, when he had improbably talked his parents into buying a parrot for someone: 'but the wisdom of the world and the wishes of parents,' he warned, 'are on the whole against birds and animals'.[44] Closer to home, Grimond struggled with his gardening, to which his approach seemed very similar to that he had adopted towards cultivating the Liberal Party in earlier years: he continued to sow and to dig with all the outward appurtenances of the optimist, though in fact he was doing so in conscious defiance both of the odds and of his own more realistic expectations. By his own admission, as a gardener he was relentless, rather than inspired. Although he had problems with his legs, he managed to mow the lawn quite comfortably, and weeded away well into his late seventies without the slightest concession to decrepitude. Year after year, he bemoaned, he was caught out by the capricious Orcadian seasons, as he notched up more white Easters than white Christmases. He also found himself constantly ambushed by plants that he had forgotten, plants that he had not expected – and plants that he not even planted, including an importunate blackcurrant bush that made an incursion into what was supposed to be a herbaceous border.

By the late 1980s the years had begun to weigh more heavily, and more visibly, on Jo Grimond. He accepted all the exigencies of old age with his customary good humour. Indeed he constantly used the infirmities and indignities that he experienced to enliven his journalism – usually in what he described as his 'self-appointed capacity as the geriatric correspondent of the Daily Telegraph'.[45] Endeavouring to establish for himself the sense of routine that his public life no longer provided for him, he would grumble about the poltergeists and sprites that hid things from him, or pestered him into going upstairs, invariably making him forget why he had clambered up by the time he arrived. He came to regret his own habit of leaving jobs half-done and grumbled that, although he constantly mislaid things he needed, if he tried to throw away anything that he didn't want, it would 'bounce back like a mischievous boomerang'.[46] Seeking out space for Christmas presents, he tried the bottom drawer of a chest of drawers, believing it to be empty. In it he found 'one old pullover [full of holes], an assortment of leather straps and a metal contraption which might have been part of a coffee percolator or a device for keeping flowers upright in a vase'.[47] It is easy to see what marvellously amusing company Grimond was in his 'anecdotage'.

He also minted 'Grimond's Law': that inanimate objects increase to fill any available space. 'I am almost converted to animism,' he once wrote, after surveying the inexplicably jam-packed attic at the Old Manse, which had once been a huge, empty space. 'Inanimate objects seem to be by no means inert.'[48] One of the few innovations that he welcomed was the Screwpull, invented by someone whose professed calling, that of the 'professional inventor', inspired both fascination and jealousy in Grimond. After years of frustration with conventional corkscrews, Grimond had at first tried a contraption that was supposed to blow corks out of bottles. After one or two spectacular accidents, he gave up on that and discovered the Screwpull. So impressed was he by this particular breakthrough that he enjoined its inventor to turn his hand to ameliorating other aspects of geriatric purgatory. He also suggested that elderly people would make excellent spies: they would have no need of debriefing, since most of them 'have an excellent and automatic debriefing machine which constantly drains their memories'.[49] Another trick of the unseen tormentors of the old would come when Grimond was crunching up an old newspaper to light a fire, and his eye would catch a fascinating paragraph, which he had missed when the newspaper was current. 'Back I go on my haunches,' he opined, 'and much of the morning is taken up reading pieces of stale, but gripping, news.'[50]

Some of Grimond's problems could not be attributed to the supernatural activities of unseen imps. He was a terrible hoarder, and admitted that his meanness sometimes got the better of him. For instance, he collected pre-paid envelopes, just in case they might ever come in handy. When he had his desk repaired, he was appalled by the volume of accumulated clutter that he had to extract from its drawers, including several articles whose progeny and practical uses, if any, were shrouded in the mists of time, such as a 'small conical object made of bone and decorated with a round pad of chamois leather'.[51] Grimond also regretted that telephone numbers and addresses were becoming longer and more complicated, deprecating the fact that, whereas in earlier years he carried round a handy selection of useful numbers in his head, this was now quite impossible. With regard to addresses, Grimond again detected that the British search for meretricious status was at work: 'some firms and indeed individuals seem to think that their importance is enhanced by the length of their addresses – Moron & Co, PO Box 73, Nutcase House, 250 Twit's Lane, Madman's Way, Bedlam, Lunaticester, Barmyshire LC5 9TP.'[52] The main lunacy that irritated Grimond, however, emanated not from the private sector but from government. The highly intrusive form that he had to fill in for his poll tax seemed to imply, to his mind, that 'it was I who was begging to pay this new impost and causing the local authority a great deal of bother'.[53] He was also less than impressed to learn that, when the government was reported to be paying out £19 million of taxpayers' money in response to the 1988 panic about salmonella in eggs, 'like many other people I assumed it was to help the old and frail poisoned by salmonella, only to find it was to help the purveyors of this disease'.[54] The final indignity was on public transport, although Grimond noticed that young women were increasingly disposed to give up their seat for the elderly and infirm, 'you do have to be fast on your feet, however, to forestall the young men who try to bag them'.[55]

Grimond continued to cast a sceptical and questioning – though never jaundiced – eye over the ever-lengthening tentacles of government. Everywhere the bureaucratic attitude seemed to prevail, with more forms to be filled in, more irritating and pointless intrusions, more futile yearning for prestige and grandeur. Towards the end of his life, Grimond was appalled to receive a letter from the Students' Association at Edinburgh University, proudly informing him that the association now employed 280 people and 'enjoyed' ('I bet it does,' commented

Grimond wryly) an annual turnover of over £6 million. Driving innocently along in Grimond's car one day, one of his sons saw a dog run over. The police were soon in touch with Grimond, demanding details of his insurance policy. 'It is a wonder to me that the police catch any burglars,' reflected Grimond, 'if they are forced to spend their time checking on the insurance of the owners of cars from which witnesses have seen sad but minor accidents.'[56] Driving on the M2 through Kent he found himself, along with thousands of others, herded by bollards into one or two lanes while 'outside the bollards the forbidden stretches of asphalt slept peacefully in the July sun untroubled by any repair work'.[57] It was high time that the British public stopped being so supine about all of this, opined Grimond: 'we could . . . strike against filling up irrelevant forms . . . we could insist upon a more intelligible tax system . . . some protest should be mounted against the rising tide of nonsense . . . If you treat people as morons, you will end up by making them morons.'[58]

Another of Grimond's bugbears in later years was the apparently ever-expanding tourist industry which, he feared, was set to destroy most of the 'heritage' that it so vigorously and ruthlessly promoted. He suggested that, since 'we all expect now to be bribed to behave decently',[59] the government should consider paying £25 to anyone who could produce a certificate proving that they had visited London without crossing the over-used threshold of Westminster Abbey: 'no more ridiculous than paying farmers not to farm or landlords not to dig up sites of scientific interest.'[60] When he discovered that the steps up to St Paul's were believed to act as a deterrent to a significant proportion of would-be visitors, he reflected that it might make sense to erect obstacle courses outside ancient monuments, requiring visitors to swing across a moat on ropes, or, at the very least, to follow the example of one of Orkney's historical sites, Maes Howe, by introducing the widespread use of low tunnel-like entrances. Grimond himself continued travelling well into the 1980s, particularly to Italy, where he usually stayed with Mark Bonham Carter and his family. Another invasion that Grimond dreaded was that of an American-style love of litigation: 'Coupled to our Legal Aid system it could be disastrous . . . In America litigation has become a way of life . . . People sue for palimony, bad advice, mental stress: every mishap real or imagined. If the habit spreads it could well hamper all sorts of activities including medicine.'[61]

Physically, Grimond suffered a great deal in his later years. His recurrent back problems continued to plague him and, after a bad fall, one of his legs played him up constantly. In the morning, he once wrote, he would 'totter from [his] bed as though enduring a hangover plus the after-effects of riding a horse for the first time in years'.[62] By his own admission, he was at his brightest until lunchtime, all right for 'light work' until teatime and then needed to be amused – usually by reading a detective novel or making a speech in the House of Lords. On the question of television, Grimond was no addict but, as in most matters, a man of taste and moderation. He was a particular admirer of the early situation comedies, notably *Dad's Army* (whose stylish and laid-back Sergeant Wilson could almost have been modelled upon him), and never looked down upon those who admired television's ability to entertain. He once likened a nonplussed Alec Douglas Home to Alf Garnett, when Sir Alec had defended Britain's role in the Middle East. During his early election campaigns, he would use the Crossan family home in Shetland as a local base, often having tea there before going on to a round of election meetings. On one occasion, he came to the Crossans' to discuss politics, but Margaret Crossan recalls that he preferred to sit with her children, watching children's television programmes with them. As in all things, he made the connection between competition and the rewards of the free market and the stimulation of creativity, still recognising at once that the introduction of competition, in the shape of commercial television, was no straightforward matter. In the early days of TV advertising he was amongst many who feared that advertisers would generally steer clear of 'good talks and music and the like',[63] but he did nonetheless support the introduction of some competition into television, admitting that he did so not because he thought that the sum of human knowledge would be greatly enhanced by the introduction of commercial television: 'I do not think that the Aeropagitica are answered by allowing Lever Brothers on the air'.[64]

Grimond found increasing solace in familiar and time-honoured activities: cooking eggs, making speeches or pottering about in the garden. He also continued to derive great pleasure from observing the flora and fauna of Orkney, and would give hilarious accounts of his dealings with his favourite animals, notably ducks and other birds, seals and rabbits. Once he found a wren in possession of his tool-shed and was unsure about how to react. The wren 'seduced' him into trying to photograph it with his less than sophisticated camera. It then refused to perch still for an instant, so Grimond decided to shoo it out. This it took to be the opening gambit of a game of hide-and-seek, now popping behind deckchairs, then scuttling like a mouse behind a watering can. The septuagenarian former hope of the Liberal Party had to capitulate, conceding defeat, abandoning the tool-shed and leaving the door open for the convenience of the tiny avian intruder. The following day, his feathered tormentor was still waiting for him, eager for the second round of this fine game. Grimond recounted too how he tried to drive rabbits from his Orkney garden, without recourse to violence of any kind. Although he had hunted as a youngster, Grimond in his dotage could hardly bring himself to kill, or even to harm, an animal. Fearful of a mass invasion by the rabbits of Orkney, however, he did scatter noisome rags, soaked in preparations said to be repulsive to rabbits, across the lawn. Alas, the creatures had never been informed that these smells were supposed to appal them, and carried on contentedly munching away at the Grimonds' lawn. 'What with looking for things, trying to remember things and endless diversions from such as wrens and rabbits, I sometimes long for the well-regulated peace of an office,' he bemoaned. 'At any rate, by six in the evening I am ready for a glass or three of wine, or even something stronger.'[65]

Throughout his parliamentary career, Jo Grimond was an avowed advocate of avian interests. For many of his first encounters with birds, he was probably trying to shoot them, but in later life he wholeheartedly turned his attentions to preserving them. As early as 1953, during the passage of the Protection of Birds Bill, he came to the defence of a whole series of unfashionable species, defending the right to life of the humble tomtit, which had suddenly incurred the wrath of humanity by mastering the art of getting into unguarded milk bottles. A few months later he demonstrated his affection for the lapwing – when told that it was under threat because it could only lay up to five clutches, he commented: 'Poor bird . . . I feel more and more for the lapwing' – and for the moorhen, whose rights had been threatened by an amendment in the House of Lords: 'We all have a great many moorhens among our constituents, and . . . our human constituents very much enjoy watching them. The moorhen has everything to commend it. It is of unquestionable British parentage . . . It is mildly eccentric and very democratic . . . Also, it will not bite anyone.'[66] The same could not be said of all birds: 'The experience of trying to help an ostensibly injured owl in Orkney which malingered for weeks, feasting on prime liver and biting everyone who fed it, makes me think that no owls are ever tame . . . They are savage though sagacious birds who exploit any human that they can seduce into looking after them'.[67] He regarded owls as 'the kind of scroungers on the Welfare State that Mrs Thatcher is trying to stamp out'.[68]

Another bird much admired by Grimond was the cormorant, which he regarded as the victim of either a cruel twist of fate or a celestial joke. Although it feeds on fish, the feathers of the cormorant are not waterproof. Grimond likened its dives into the sea to 'continually diving into cold water in a rather thick tweed suit and then having to stand with outstretched arms resembling a scarecrow while it dries – the cormorant should either have moved inland or become extinct through pneumonia.'[69] He also rather admired the bumblebee, aerodynamically incapable of flight but flying around regardless ('luckily no one has told it, nor can it see itself in the mirror . . . When it looks at other bumblebees it no doubt suffers from that very human failing of believing it has a better figure than they have'[70]). On balance, Grimond felt that smaller birds were probably to be preferred, in defiance of naturalists, who tended to echo Grimond's political opponents, in believing that bigger was better. 'When I say smallish birds are better,' Grimond explained, 'I do not only mean more friendly, which they are, but of superior character.'[71] Grimond also believed that birds had more in common with humanity than most people realised, observing that thousands of Orcadian kittiwakes were in the habit of flying daily from Westray to a loch on an adjacent island. 'I suspect that their expedition,' he chortled, 'is the equivalent of bingo or the WRO outing for humans – boredom looks to me to be rampant in some areas of nature.'[72] His favourites were ducks. When he had to name the three things that he most desired on a BBC programme, Grimond included a duck pond, for a species that he found 'very soothing . . . their restful quack and refusal to be diverted from the direction in which they are proceeding is an antidote to the stridency and restlessness of the human race'.[73]

In the *Field* and *Country Life,* Grimond was able to write constantly about his beloved flora and fauna. He alternated in the *Field* with Phil Drabble, but didn't meet him, once memorably meeting the magazine's editor at a party and observing that 'Phil Drabble writes a good column . . . Who is she? Sister of Margaret?'[74] Grimond quietly admired fish too, not least for the effortless fashion in which they routinely evaded his hapless attempts to catch them. He was astounded that so few people ever raised any objection to fishing since, in his view, fish showed every outward sign of feeling pain. 'As someone who has long taken part in blood sports,' he once wrote, 'the sight which has most poignantly brought home to me the cruelty of death is the heaving aboard of a seine net with crushed struggling fish which are then gutted alive.'[75] He was always critical of 'the hypocrisy of those who condemn foxhunting and shooting but condone fishing . . . because there are so many fishermen and they include so many weekly wage-earners.'[76] Another marine life form that occupied Grimond was the seal; a creature that every so often became the object of culling in the islands. Grimond's postbag on this question was immense, but he was cautious about taking sides too avowedly. His advice to his successor as member of Parliament for Orkney and Shetland, Jim Wallace, if the issue was ever raised with him on any significant scale, was to 'go on holiday'.

For the record, Grimond robustly opposed any proposals to outlaw hunting, something that he had experienced in both childhood and adulthood, and he did so on the basis of a sound liberal analysis. In earlier life, shooting had been one of Grimond's greatest pleasures and, even in his seventies, he would still have recourse to his gun *in extremis* when rabbits invaded the inner sanctum of his walled garden in Orkney. When the Liberal assembly passed a resolution calling for a ban on foxhunting, he described it as 'one straw of many blown by the wind which carries the nanny state from one meddlesome folly to the next'.[77] He regarded the furore against hunting as an unacceptable extension of the class war, observing 'of course the most potent motive for the anti-hunting lobby is that hunting gives pleasure, and pleasure to a comparatively small number of people.'[78] Grimond's line on hunting was part of his wider liberal view regarding the relationship between state and citizen: 'The state encroaches on what is rightfully the province of morality and free choice. In doing so it destroys morality. For there is no virtue in doing what I am compelled to do, whether it is loving my black neighbour or remaining sober . . . By constantly extending the criminal law . . . we destroy personal responsibility.'[79] The sapping of personal responsibility was a theme to which Grimond constantly returned, in writings and in speeches. With a robustness that eludes many liberals, he had long rejected any notion that criminality could be in any way excused by economic or social circumstances:

> For some, unemployment or even the suppression of crime seems an adequate excuse for violence . . . But communities cannot expect bounty from a State which they are not prepared to uphold. It is a funny sort of patriotism, a queer form of social conscience, which constantly claims rights but rejects responsibility . . . Liberals are under no obligation to succour those who would destroy a liberal country.[80]

Although he never became morbid, Grimond did from time to time contemplate eternity, writing once: 'it is no good holding out promises of Heaven – the prospect of death is always unpleasant and does not grow any more pleasant as it gets nearer.'[81] Jo Grimond was not a religious man, yet he seems to have nurtured throughout his life a strong spiritual sense. He would attribute this in large part to his Christian upbringing, and it seems also to have derived from his liberal humanism. The relationships of human beings with each other seem to have had a semi-divine quality in his eyes. Witness this unexpected flight of fancy from *The Liberal Challenge*, a work that for many long stretches is, to put it kindly, workmanlike or even prosaic:

> Human beings, huddling together in terror of being left alone, baffled by the prison of their own sensations, long for some support, for some assurance that they are of importance, that life has meaning. Before they face the ultimate loneliness of death they look for some assurance that their endeavours on earth have some immortality. Society and the state its servant must help to meet this yearning.[82]

This is a most heartfelt utterance – and one that certainly suggests that, with Jo Grimond as Prime Minister, the state might have had rather more on its hands than Adam Smith ever envisaged. At the very end of his life, Grimond did on occasion reflect upon questions of faith, sometimes describing himself as a 'lukewarm Presbyterian' (exactly how he had described himself to the military authorities in 1939). In a short contribution to a fascinating and eclectic collection of essays published after his death, Grimond admitted that, although he had 'had no personal experience of the Divine . . . I resemble a large proportion of mankind in calling myself a Christian but acknowledging that I am a wavering candle . . . but totally to reject the Divine seems contrary to our nature.'[83] Although, with his incurable habit of mislaying things, Grimond recognised that, were he to make a habit of seeking the help of Saint Anthony, he would end up persecuting him, he would sometimes light a candle to a saint, on one occasion doing so unprompted on behalf of a sick, non-believing friend. The said friend began to recover at once, to his own intense irritation. 'The more his blood pressure grew, the better he grew,' joked Grimond.[84]

As Grimond approached the grand age of eighty, those around him were increasingly aware of his age. His features lost the incisive and striking quality that had made him so eye-catching in earlier years. His posture deteriorated, and the rather affected academic stoop of the younger Grimond became an integral part of a distinctive shuffle. Despite his evident physical decline, however, Grimond's intellect remained virtually as sharp as ever and, to general alarm, he continued to drive himself around. By the beginning of the 1990s, he no longer involved himself in the details of legislation in the House of Lords, but he did continue to make regular appearances, and his commitment to Liberal principles remained as firm as ever. When he rose to his feet, his fellow peers would still totter in more than they would totter out. Although his journalism gradually ground to a halt, his last book, an affectionate and heartfelt tribute to St Andrews, was published in 1992 to a deservedly warm critical reception. By a cruel irony it was not Jo, but Laura, who would be the first to succumb to a condition that was seriously debilitating and, ultimately, mortal. After she suffered a serious stroke in December 1992, life could never be the same again for either of the Grimonds. Laura was on her way to meet Jo from Grimsetter airport in the family car when she blacked out, careering into one of the outbuildings at the Old Manse. She was attended at once by a friend and, though she seemed confused, the extent of her illness was not at first apparent. Laura never fully recovered and, although Jo continued to commute between Orkney and the Lords, he willingly devoted much of his remaining time to nursing her. Tragically, Laura, who had always been so energetic and articulate, always the first to offer an opinion, found that her ability to speak had been badly affected. Although she benefited greatly from intense physiotherapy and regained much of her movement, she continued to have problems with words. She could neither understand words properly, nor could she articulate her own thoughts clearly. For her many friends and admirers, seeing someone so energetic and vital reduced to this state was a heart-rending experience.

In contrast Jo Grimond, in defiance of declining health and a series of operations and accidents, remained remarkably active right until the end of his life. Only a few weeks before he died, he appeared on the doorstep of Ruth Williams, one of his closest friends and supporters in Orkney, on the day of her son's marriage. 'I thought the mother of the groom might need a dram,' he said with a smile, proffering a bottle of excellent malt whisky. On Thursday, 21st October 1993, he made a fine speech in the House of Lords, appropriately about one of his favourite causes, co-ownership, in which he reiterated his lifelong belief in a more even spread of wealth. 'If we are to have a decent and satisfactory country, whatever our party, it is essential that the gap between rich and poor should not grow . . . unless we are careful, and the capitalist system gives some better reward to the majority of people in this country, among whom, most prominently, are the unemployed . . . to my mind we shall see a return to state socialism, which I would much regret.'[85] The following day Jo Grimond made his way home to Orkney where, sitting in his study at the Old Manse making notes for a speech, he suffered a massive stroke. Laura, by now so frail herself, remained at his bedside at the Balfour hospital in Kirkwall, as he managed to hang on to life until the rest of the close family was able to join them there. Three days after suffering his stroke, at the age of eighty, Jo Grimond was dead.

His funeral, held in Orkney, was like a royal occasion. Flags flew at half-mast throughout Kirkwall, as many colleagues joined Grimond's family in paying homage to a man whom the Liberal Democrats' leader, Paddy Ashdown, had described as a 'lion of the Liberal cause'.[86] Grimond's old agent, Jackie Robertson, gave the address: 'He could walk with Kings but still remained Jo to all who knew him and so he will remain to us . . . I was proud and privileged to have known Jo, a gentleman in the truest sense, and to have played a small part in his elections. We shall miss him greatly – we may not see his like again.' Just a few short months later, on St Valentine's Day 1994, Laura died at the age of seventy-five, bringing to mind Sir Henry Wotton's celebrated lines of 1651: 'He first deceased; she for a little tried/To live without him: liked it not, and died'. A memorial service for the couple was held in London later that year, attended by their extended family, along with their many friends and admirers from countless walks of life. Roy Jenkins delivered the tribute to Laura, while Mark Bonham Carter spoke movingly of his sorely missed brother-in-law Jo, praising one who 'was not a construct put together by some public relations firm – he was himself – intelligent, irreverent, brave, eloquent, speaking for all of us far better than we could speak for ourselves'.

Although he never allowed it to corrode his character, Grimond did ultimately feel that his political career had ended in failure. What saddened him above all was the fact that his tea and buns with Tony Benn were the closest that he ever got to becoming a minister. For a man with his gifts, this must have been profoundly frustrating. He was never anxious to achieve office for its own sake, but would have liked to test himself against the major political yardstick of running a department. In fact, as he told Keith Kyle, 'what one would like to be is Prime Minister – an excellent job – and I really think that I would have been better at that than at anything else . . . I think I'm in the Callaghan class – I regard him as a hopeless Minister, but rather a good Prime Minister . . . But also Foreign Secretary, Chancellor of the

Exchequer . . . all that, of course one would like to be that.'[87] Jo Grimond was no saint. He could be stubborn and inconsiderate as well as inconsistent, self-centred and insensitive. Though he was generally easy-going, he could still have a sharp tongue, which, at times, could become decidedly bitchy and even unkind. In his idiosyncratic way he was a driven man, and not an easy husband. As Laura admitted after almost forty years of marriage: 'There have been times, as in all marriages, when it's been tough going, when one gritted one's teeth but never gave up. The easy acceptance of your generation to say "well, that's that", and dissolve a marriage, was not how we saw things. One expected to stay married so one tried harder.'[88] Though he was, by his own admission, 'moderately rich', and was more often than not a hospitable and generous host, he could also be famously mean – especially where small sums were concerned. Nonetheless, as a private as well as public figure, Grimond was deservedly far more loved than not.

Perhaps the great question, then, is why Jo Grimond, even in the long, dark days between 1935 and 1956, stuck to his guns and remained true to the Liberal Party. After all, most people agree that a man of his charm, views and talent could have flourished in either of the major parties. It is best to let Grimond himself explain:

> I am sometimes asked why I became a Liberal. With my upbringing and temperament, it would have been difficult not to be a Liberal. But I might I suppose have joined the Labour Party. I should find it easier to do so today than in the thirties. Which strikes me as odd. It must be due to changes in myself . . . No doubt had events taken a different turn I might have found myself in a different party. But it would not, as far as I can see, have made much sense . . . Apart from the fact that I am not by temperament attracted to certain elements in the Tory Party, I hope that had I ever joined it I should have left it over Munich, Suez, its resistance to political reform to mention two or three concrete examples of issues where I think it went totally wrong. I also hope that I should have been driven out of it by its general attitude to community and social services . . . As to the Labour Party, I do not believe in state socialism. Many people in the Labour movement I have admired, many of their hopes I share, but I do not think that the areas of agreement, the common sympathy, was enough to get over my disagreements with the party.

These excerpts from Grimond's first draft for his *Memoirs* are all the more intriguing for the fact that nothing quite so candid and reflective made it into the published version.

It is perfectly possible to argue that Jo Grimond was indeed the 'best Prime Minister we never had'. He certainly propounded many interesting and challenging ideas, some of which have latterly become accepted wisdom. Quite rightly he criticised that post-war British attitude that always proclaimed that *'they* ought to do something about it', which amounts to a negation of initiative and personal responsibility, and called for a welfare society, in place of the burgeoning welfare state. Yet he too could often be found calling for planning, for subsidies or for new government bodies to be established. It is also difficult to reconcile his calls for international integration with his lifelong belief in devolution and decentralisation, and his oft-stated hostility to the growing power of unaccountable bureaucracies. But then the job of Liberal leader is virtually impossible, requiring the occupant to hold together a coalition of outspoken individuals, ranging from unreconstructed advocates of free trade to middle-of-the-road social democrats and anarcho-syndicalist Young Liberals. Jo Grimond in fact proved to be remarkable dextrous in riding so many unpredictable horses at once, but it was only after he finally renounced the leadership of the party that he was able to give voice to a coherent and courageous liberal response to the problems of the nation. He recognised that liberalism depends, above all, upon individual responsibility and shared values, not upon constitutional rights and extended use of the state and judicial apparatus. Many people still judge that vision to be just as valid, and as inspiring, as it ever was. Did Grimond therefore fritter away his talents by joining the Liberals? Taken at face value, he would have been a perfect Tory. He had the right background and qualifications, a private income and the natural manner of the ruling class. Yet, as he once told John Strachey: 'apart from ideological differences I knew that if I became a Tory I should always be tacking up against a wind from the right'.[89] A counter-case can be made just as convincingly, to the effect that Grimond was a lightweight political dilettante well suited to the semi-detached politics and way of life in Britain's furthest-flung constituency. Certainly his political philosophy, 'like the aurora borealis' as one of his former colleagues puts it, could be unpredictable and insubstantial as well as eye-catching. Furthermore, some commentators have argued that his positive influence on the fortunes of the Liberal Party is easily exaggerated, that his talent was confined to riding a wave that others had created for him. There are also those who never warmed to his lackadaisical, not to say intermittently lethargic, style.

The truth, predictably perhaps but not unreasonably, probably lies somewhere in between the two viewpoints. It is certainly true that the party had begun a modest recovery as early as 1954, under the leadership of Clement Davies, largely thanks to the declining reputation of the Conservative Party, and to the increasingly rancorous disputes within the Labour Party. It is also true that, by the time Davies stepped down in 1956, there was only one possible successor. Donald Wade and Arthur Holt were wholly dependent upon their pacts with the Conservatives in Huddersfield and Bolton; Roderic Bowen was at least as devoted to his legal practice as to his party; and Rhys Hopkin Morris was enjoying his splendid isolation as deputy speaker. Had there been no Jo Grimond to take over the reins, the party would surely have perished there and then. Furthermore, Grimond undoubtedly did bring a fresh style and intellectual stimulus to a tired party, making a major personal contribution to its long-term recovery. Even if, as in the case of Dr Johnson's woman preacher and the dog that walked on two legs, what mattered most is not that he did it well, but that he did it at all, the fact does remain that he did do it rather well. Perhaps the author's favourite reflections on Grimond the leader come from the anonymous 'Report on a Liberal leader' carried in *The Times* on 18th January 1967, the day after Grimond resigned as leader of the Liberals: 'Watching him from the press gallery, he had always seemed to be one of *us*, rather than one of *them*. He has been everyman gifted with the powers of lucidity, spotting the flaws in entrenched attitudes which seem so obvious to those outside.'

Appendix 1
CONSTITUTIONAL AND EUROPEAN AFFAIRS

E VER SINCE THE Liberal Party lost power in the 1930s, its most consistent and distinctive policies have related to the constitution and Britain's relationship with continental Europe. In opposition, both the Conservative and Labour parties have at times evinced radicalism in this area; in government, both have become more conservative. In some respects, on these matters Grimond stood in the Liberal mainstream. Yet with his questioning nature, his close relationship with Orkney and Shetland and his instinct to play devil's advocate, he never inclined to embrace any nostrum wholly unquestioningly. Grimond was perhaps never a 'European' after the style of Edward Heath or Roy Jenkins, Christopher Soames or Chris Patten. Although he did generally advocate British participation whenever European treaties were being discussed, particularly in the 1950s, the case he made had been arrived at more rationally than emotionally. As leader he was surrounded by devout supporters of European integration, most notably Mark Bonham Carter and Arthur Holt, both of whom played a major role in establishing the primacy of the party's pro-European policy. In many ways, Mark Bonham Carter was more of a natural politician than Grimond himself. Grimond paid tribute to his incisiveness, writing of him that he 'delves down to the bones of problems, marshals arguments and proposes right and often original solutions . . . His speeches had a cutting edge and his advice fertilized the thinking of the parliamentary Liberal party.'[1] He had more drive and aggression and, at times, did not bother to disguise his frustration when other people, including Grimond himself, appeared to be insufficiently resolute. He was altogether more categorical, ruthless and outspoken than his more prominent brother-in-law, and many people still cite examples of what they regard as his rudeness and abrasiveness. Much of this drive came from his mother. Although, had he held Torrington in 1959 and through into the 1960s, he would surely eventually have been a contender for leadership, Bonham Carter's brief stint as an MP was not altogether successful. So burdened was he with responsibilities to the national party that he built up a huge backlog of constituency mail. Lady Violet paid out of her own pocket for secretarial assistance to clear it up.

Less celebrated, but perhaps even more significant, was the influence on Grimond of Arthur Holt, between 1951 and 1964 the Liberal member of

Parliament for Bolton West. Holt was a Liberal of the old school, a strong advocate of free trade and a devoted anti-imperialist, who advocated free and fair trade between nations but rejected the extreme *laissez-faire* position that was still a force in the Liberal Party as late as the 1950s. Holt was an invaluable supporter for Grimond in countless ways, but his greatest influence was surely as the leading pro-European force in his inner counsels. He was a quietly heroic man, who had been captured by the Japanese at the fall of Singapore in February 1942, as a captain in the Reconnaissance Corps. He and his men were sent to work on the Burma Railway. His bravery in the terrible conditions earned him two mentions in despatches, once when he was beaten almost to death by a Japanese commandant for refusing to move sick British prisoners to another camp. Arthur Holt was an easy man to underestimate. Emlyn Hooson never did so after a particular trip to the north of England with a legal brief. The lawyer who met him off the train knew that he was a Liberal MP. He was not a Liberal himself, he told Hooson, but there was one Liberal for whom he would do absolutely anything: he had been a POW under Holt: 'and none of us would have survived if it hadn't been for him'.[2] Holt's wartime experiences gave him a lasting interest in foreign policy, and an absolute conviction of the need for ever closer European cooperation. He was a parliamentary delegate to the Council of Europe in the fifties and an early and consistent advocate of joining the European Economic Community for both economic and political reasons.

Grimond was convinced by the likes of Bonham Carter and Holt that, if Britain was to embrace membership of the European Community, then it should embrace wholeheartedly the aspirations for political integration that lay at the heart of the Treaty of Rome, as well as its promises of freer trade and economic convergence. Typically, as soon as he had arrived at a view, and by whatever process, Grimond became a tireless and inspiring advocate. Once he had been convinced that the post-war nation-state must wither away, Grimond turned all his rhetorical skills to convincing others. In the edition of *Liberal Orkney* published for the 1951 general election, Grimond enthusiastically welcomed the founding of the new Council of Europe, which marked the first step towards 'a great new design for human government'. It is still important, however, to work out exactly what he meant by that.

While negotiations were under way between the 'Six' (West Germany, France, Italy, Belgium, Holland and Luxembourg) during the mid 1950s to establish an European Economic Community (EEC) under the Treaty of Rome, the UK was playing the leading role in setting up a far looser organisation, the European Free Trade Area (EFTA), which would explicitly abjure the objective of political integration favoured by the Six. At first the Liberals supported only the EFTA negotiations and, just as the Six were on the verge of signing their deal, an article appeared in *Liberal News* with Jo

Grimond's endorsement, explicitly stating that 'Liberals support the proposals that the United Kingdom should join the free trade area – not the customs union'.[3] Within a few months, however, the Liberals in Parliament were openly and repeatedly advocating British accession to the EEC. Inspired by Arthur Holt, the small band of Liberal MPs repeatedly divided the House of Commons after debates on Europe, most notably in December 1959 and July 1960, to draw attention to what they regarded as the government's dithering over the question.

To his immense credit, unlike many others who shared his belief in international political integration, particularly within the Tory party, Grimond never minced his words. For example, speaking to the tenth anniversary congress of Liberal International, in Oxford on 29th August 1957, he said plainly that: 'We are faced with the need of this country, and all countries, to accept some abatement of sovereignty . . . it is absolute criminal folly for the western world to remain disunited in foreign policy and to attempt to maintain a nineteenth-century conception of sovereignty.'[4] Later that year he asked:

> Are we to remain bumbling on in the old way, edging a little towards interdependence perhaps, paying lip-service to the United Nations, dipping a shivering toe into the Free Trade Area? Or are we, as Liberals claim, faced with an inevitable decision in an unavoidable situation? Must we not abandon many of our ideas about sovereignty, pool much of our resources, our arms and indeed our foreign policy? And take a lead in doing so – not merely trail along behind the Americans.[5]

When the Conservatives' negotiations to set up a new European free trade area started to founder in 1958, Grimond urged Macmillan to make a fresh start by dropping the whole idea, and applying to join the Common Market.

In a debate on the first set of measures laid before the House of Commons by the re-elected Macmillan government in 1959, Grimond again called upon the Conservatives to embrace the EEC, but only if they were genuinely willing to face up to the implications of doing so: 'It does mean giving up the power to take unilateral decisions on some subjects . . . I believe that we have misunderstood a good deal of what the European movement is about, because it is not primarily an economic movement but a political movement. To be left out of a major political movement in the West would be very serious for this country.'[6] Less than six months later, as the first straws began to appear in the wind about a Conservative change of heart on Europe, Grimond was again on the attack. This was sorrow, not anger. He knew that Britain's great chance had already been missed: accession from now on would take place only on terms dictated by the Six, above all the French. Whatever happened now would be, at best, second best. Nonetheless, he pressed the Macmillan government to show the courage of its emerging convictions and indicate, in principle at least, that it now intended to apply for EEC membership:

We should let it be known that at the right moment we are now ready to join the Common Market . . . when mutually agreeable terms have been negotiated . . . I suggest that instead of trying to pretend that the Common Market will eventually come to an agreement on our terms, we must make an effort to establish better relations with it . . . The sad feature is that, fifteen years ago, Britain was at the peak of her power and influence, and the leadership of Europe was hers for the asking. We have thrown it away on grounds which have largely proved wrong . . . I believe that we may see Germany take our position as the leading power of Europe.[7]

It is impossible to separate Germany from the seismic events of European history, and Grimond took a particular interest in German affairs. The creation of the European Coal and Steel Community (ECSC) and, subsequently, its transformation into the European Economic Community (EEC) in the 1950s was inspired by a perceived need to tie the Germans into supranational institutions as a method of preventing a resurgence of German nationalism and expansionism. As Grimond put it: 'those who fear a violently chauvinistic Germany should remember that the one way to avoid this is to build her into European Unity . . . People in the position of the Germans are apt to show their worst side if treated as pariahs or sent to Coventry'.[8] Grimond was also very interested in the 'social market economy' of West Germany, created as a means of maintaining the balancing act between the market economy and social cohesion. Perhaps this was the 'halfway house' that Liberals should be advocating between state domination and collectivisation on the one hand, and the extremes of *laissez-faire* on the other. Grimond became a regular at the Königswinter conferences established in the late 1940s by the German-English Society under the leadership of a redoubtable German lady called Lilo Milchsack. Grimond's mother-in-law Lady Violet Bonham Carter was another enthusiastic participant in these conferences; and their 'godfather' on the British side was none other than Sir Robert Birley, the enthusiastic Germanophile who had so influenced Jo Grimond when he was a pupil at Eton and who had subsequently become headmaster of the school. Birley had written a celebrated letter to *The Times* on 5th May 1945, while Grimond was taking possession of the Hotel Atlantic in Hamburg, warning that 'the "re-education" of Germany by the allies will not be a pious aspiration, but an unavoidable duty.' The occupying powers needed to learn the lessons of history. The Germans had for a century 'been fatally ready to accept any government which would save them from having to make decisions for themselves', so the first task now was to 'teach the Germans to face responsibility'. A land that had produced Beethoven and Goethe ought to have the appropriate foundations for a civil society. An enlightened policy on the part of the allies could help them to rediscover those foundations.

Birley had a house in Bad Rothenfelde, near Bielefeld, and in the immediate post-war time he gave parties there for Germans who were known to share a liberal outlook and whose activities he was encouraged to stimulate (he was well briefed by MI5). He established a crucial conduit between a community of politically active and liberally inclined Germans and a number of people involved in British public life who recognised the imperative of building bridges with the new, democratic Germany. For a time Grimond joined the Königswinter steering committee and he was a guest of honour at the twenty-fifth anniversary conference in 1975, staying at the ambassador's residence in Bonn along with Ted Heath, Shirley Williams and Roy Jenkins. The overall guest list included over twenty MPs and several senior journalists. When Roy Jenkins referred disparagingly to the building in which the conference was held, the Adam-Stegerwald Haus, Grimond was amused. 'It's a bit thick, Roy complaining about the discomfort of the Adam-Stegerwald Haus,' he commented to Nicholas Henderson later. 'He has scarcely spent five minutes in it – he is always with you in the Embassy guzzling caviar.'

In July 1960 the first of the *New Directions* pamphlets, *Britain Must Join*, was published, very explicitly with Grimond's personal imprimatur, and its authors did not mince their words. The pamphlet emphasised that British accession to the EEC, as soon as possible, would not only be in Britain's interest – it would be in the best interests of the existing members, since the UK alone could counter-balance the influence of France and Germany. Indeed *Britain Must Join*, unlike so many other texts of the period, brims over with enthusiasm for the political aspects of European integration: 'the objective is a growing political unity, and it is this which Britain cannot afford to ignore or remain outside . . . this new political strength in Western Europe provides a much more effective bulwark against communism than any military forces can.' Nor were the authors impressed by the Conservative government's recent feint at joining the two older parts of the European Community: Euratom and the Coal and Steel Community, neither of which had the far-reaching political implications inherent in the Treaty of Rome. 'If Britain is to solve its European problem it must join the European Community as a whole,' stated the final sentence of *Britain Must Join*, 'and that means joining the Economic Community as well.' On the day of publication, Grimond was amongst the forty-two signatories of a statement urging Britain to initiate accession negotiations with the Common Market. Roy Jenkins and Grimond's old boss from UNRRA, Sir Frederick Leith-Ross, also signed up.

In his own pamphlet, *Let's Get On With It!*, published later that year, Grimond wrote that: 'we have to build that Europe des Patries of which De Gaulle has spoken and which is a new edifice, but soundly founded on the different national pillars of European civilization.'[9] At the Liberal assembly that autumn, the party signed up once and for all to the leadership's pro-EEC policy, as Mark Bonham Carter successfully urged delegates to embrace EEC membership. The BBC film of Bonham Carter's speech shows Grimond sitting at his brother-in-law's left hand, nodding and murmuring 'Hear, hear' at every stage of the argument that he was setting out so cogently, especially during his attacks on what he regarded as the duplicity and cowardice of the other parties on the question of sovereignty. Grimond returned to the same theme in his pamphlet *Growth not Grandeur*, co-written with Harry Cowie in 1961:

> We have to accept the political as well as the economic implications of joining Europe. Time and time again the Government have, in fact, made concessions when it is too late. Mr Heath's recent speech [on the tariff negotiations in which he was involved] is a good example. He is apparently willing now to accept a harmonised tariff which in effect involves some political integration. Eighteen months ago the Government was saying this was impossible. Then, it might have been the basis for negotiation, now it is not enough.[10]

When the Liberal Party carried a resolution at its 1960 assembly calling for negotiations with the EEC, to take place in conjunction with other interested parties including 'other members of the Commonwealth', its pro-European credentials were affirmed. When accession negotiations with the EEC began in earnest in 1961, for domestic consumption the government always laid great emphasis on the terms. This seemed to Grimond no more than a smokescreen, a 'get-out' clause if the political situation at home became too difficult and backbench opinion had to be appeased. He likened the accession negotiations to buying a house. First, he said, you had to decide whether or not you liked the house; then you could worry about the price. Although Grimond never favoured unconditional entry, he did consistently argue that the government needed to demonstrate, openly and freely, that in principle at least it wanted the UK to play its full part in the European venture: 'it is no good going into Europe holding one's nose, so to speak.'[11] This is why the government had a responsibility both to be honest about the implications of entry, and to show some enthusiasm for it. When Hugh Gaitskell made a broadcast in which he argued that the pros and cons of entry should be weighed up as if on a balance sheet, Grimond was scornful: 'There must be some emotion and desire about this decision on Europe . . . This decision will affect people's lives for generations . . . You cannot reach that decision simply by weighing up temporary and doubtful "facts" on a computer.'[12] He echoed this sentiment in his book *The Liberal Challenge*, where he wrote that 'no great enterprise has been managed in such a niggardly, shivery spirit as our gradual approach to Europe . . . But a sense of purpose cannot be imposed; it must be evoked.'[13] At their autumn assembly in 1962 the Liberals adopted a strengthened pro-EEC policy – one that made no mention of the terms, EFTA or the Commonwealth, prompting a number of resignations from the party.

Grimond's vision of Europe was not that of the bureaucrats. In European matters, as elsewhere, Grimond never lost his love of diversity and of openness.

Conrad Russell recalls Laura describing to him the former headquarters of the Commission in Brussels as 'the symbol of everything we, as Liberals, should be against'. Where Grimond differed from the demagogues of European integration was in his historian's analysis of the role of the nation-state. He never subscribed to the simplistic view that, since most modern wars have been initiated by nation-states, all that is required to prevent further wars is to abolish those nation-states. He would even, on occasions, praise the positive aspects of nationalism. In a book review written when he was at the very height of his powers, Grimond set out this case: 'The thing which makes me pause about the Common Market – to which I believe nevertheless we are right to be negotiating our entry – is that up to now nationalism, with all its faults, has been the main bulwark against Communism and other totalitarian movements. If nationalism is doomed it is imperative that we find something instead.'[14] In 1963 Grimond echoed these sentiments in *The Liberal Challenge*, indicating that, although he favoured a gradual movement towards world government, he never believed that the 'sentiment of nationality' should, or could, be abolished or eradicated. Indeed, 'it ought in all its cultural aspects to be encouraged.'[15] What he sought, above all, was an international rule of law, something really effective that could prevent disputes turning into conflicts or all-out wars.

Another important strand in Grimond's approach to the entire European question was his fervent and consistent belief that, if pro-European politicians shared their vision openly and honestly with the people, there was every chance that the country would embrace internationalism with genuine enthusiasm. He deplored the way in which Conservative pro-Europeans would pussyfoot around the issue, always understating the political implications of the Treaty of Rome:

> The Bonn Declaration [by the Six] was a declaration that the Six would pursue the political unity of Europe, and we know from what has appeared in Hansard that the Lord Privy Seal [Edward Heath] has said that we are in favour of that . . . But when the Prime Minister was asked what this meant, he referred vaguely to *l'Europe des patries* . . . I think that the confederal idea as envisaged by de Gaulle will lead to a greater abrogation of sovereignty and to more problems than some of the ideas of those who are called the European federalists . . . I do not think that the European Movement was ever intended to be a defence arrangement. It was never intended to be an anti-Communist alliance, and I should hate it to become that . . . All these matters require firm decisions by the Government now, but, above all, they also require that the Government should take the people of this country rather more boldly into their confidence.[16]

Jo Grimond also flagged up well before most others the need for some element of direct accountability in a system that would otherwise be liable to corruption or elitism of the worst kind. Although the Commission needed extensive powers, these should be countervailed by a strengthened European Assembly that 'will not have sufficient strength until it is directly elected'.[17] He noted the need to ensure that the new and powerful hybrid officials – 'a new animal, half civil servant and half politician' – of the Commission were properly scrutinised, and he was the first to admit that: 'unless some political changes are brought about in Europe, even those of us who support Britain's entry may feel that it may not bring about a very satisfactory situation.'[18] These were important questions, yet the government had 'deliberately played down the political implications of the Common Market'.[19]

In January 1963, after over a year of accession negotiations, French President Charles de Gaulle vetoed the United Kingdom's application to join the EEC. Grimond believed that much of the blame should be attached to Harold Macmillan, who had taken the insensitive decision to negotiate a bilateral defence treaty with the Americans (at Nassau) behind de Gaulle's back, just when the Common Market negotiations were at their most delicate. Grimond's response to the veto was subtly different from those of many others, which his close adviser from that time, Christopher Layton, attributes to the fact that Grimond was in the USA visiting President Kennedy at the time of the veto. The Conservatives were dealt a shattering blow by the failure of the negotiations, and many of Grimond's supporters felt that he missed a great opportunity upon his return to seize the political initiative – by coming forward with radical new proposals for political union. President Kennedy had apparently told Grimond that the British should disregard de Gaulle. Their moment would come: they just had to be patient and wait for things to settle down. On reflection, Grimond wasn't so sure. He felt that the Macmillan government had been guilty of yet another error of judgement:

> Many British people have convinced themselves, with their invincible complacency, that it is mainly due to General de Gaulle's malevolence that their generous offer to join the Common Market was turned down. They forget our long refusal to take the Common Market seriously . . . one of the major objections to the Nassau Agreement was that its timing was such that it was all too likely to wreck what was at the time the major foreign affairs objective of the government.[20]

The Wilson government of 1964–6 was no more honest than its predecessor about political union in Europe. In 1965 Grimond pressed Harold Wilson to be more rigorous and honest about the long-term implications of membership: 'If the movement towards political unity in Europe progresses, is it not inevitable that there must in time be a pooling of sovereignty and a coming together on foreign and defence policy?'[21] On the campaign trail in the 1966 general election campaign he pursued a similar line. Although Britain was certainly pursuing its economic interests by joining the Common Market, he told an audience in Yorkshire, that was not the whole story: 'The European

Community is a new sort of economic organisation, and it should be followed by a political community – and in that Britain should play a leading part – we have contributed again and again to the political development of the world . . . Now we have a chance again, to take our full share in the exciting new adventure in Europe.'[22] In Grimond's view this approach by both major parties was not only dishonest; in the longer term, it was certain to be highly counter-productive, because the British people would discover in time that they had been misled. If ministers really believed that Britain's best interests lay inside the EEC, why could they not share their enthusiasm with the people? In 1971 he challenged Foreign Secretary Alec Home on this point: 'I appreciate the Right Hon. Gentleman's argument that we shall have a veto on political developments. The implication of that is that we do not want political development. Many people think that possible political developments are the most important thing about the Community. Are the Government saying that they would resist and oppose political developments in Europe?'[23]

Although Alec Home certainly played down the political aspects of integration in favour of economic arguments, he was not a man to prevaricate in response to a direct question and his reply to Grimond, beginning with the words 'not at all', is illuminating thirty years on. Although Emlyn Hooson was the only Liberal to vote against British accession to the EEC in the historic 'free' vote of 28th October 1971, Grimond did express his own reservations about the terms that were now on offer. Accession at this late stage was, for him, hardly even a 'second-best' outcome; it was a rather disagreeable necessity. After Ted Heath had become leader of the Conservative Party and, within a couple of months, begun to proclaim the need for immediate UK accession to the EEC, Grimond's response had been very telling. 'The Tory proposals,' he remarked acerbically, 'illustrate the genius of the Tory party for being twenty years too late – the time to be enthusiastic about Europe was in the 1950s.'[24] He would echo this during the 1966 general election campaign: 'Almost everyone now realises that we shall have to join the Common Market . . . but the time this needed saying most was in the 1950s, when the Liberals alone said it, for then the problems of adjustment would have been so much smaller.'[25] Grimond never forgave the Conservative Party for its failure to give a lead in the early days of European integration. He believed that a strong British input from the outset might have helped create a political movement that was less centralised and less *dirigiste* than that which emerged.

Towards the end of the 1960s, although Grimond never turned against European unity in principle, he began to express some serious reservations of his own about the form that it seemed likely to take. 'We do not want a European megalopolis stretching from Rotterdam to the Ruhr,' he warned.[26] Yet the trend towards bureaucratic centralisation in the Commission threatened precisely that, and seemed to have particularly worrying implications for constituencies such as his own: 'if you inquire in Brussels about transport and freight policies which are at the heart of development, the answers are alarming . . . They presuppose both an impossible centralisation and a policy on freight charges which could only lead to further depopulation of the rural areas.'[27] Before the UK agreed to join the Community, he argued, it must therefore seek to extract 'some assurances on regionalism as against centralisation . . . we must not end up under a chaotic blanket of authorities, whose relationship has not been considered, nor under too many layers of bureaucratic government.'[28] When Grimond found himself attacked, in particular by John Pardoe, for his apparent born-again scepticism, he defended himself unapologetically. His perfectly reasonable view was that, as a long-standing and loyal supporter of European integration, he was perfectly entitled to make such points. He felt that his position could be contrasted very favourably with that of the Tory establishment, which had failed to take the European initiative in good time, but now pretended that the EEC was beyond reproach or criticism.

Grimond never doubted that Britain's long-term future lay with Europe, but he thought that it was the responsibility of Europe's true friends to explain a few home truths first. He also thought that it was intellectually dishonest of the pro-Europeans to argue that failure in the negotiations must not be considered, because it was simply unthinkable for Britain to remain outside the EEC. Grimond himself played devil's advocate, arguing that there would be plenty on the credit side if the country did not sign up. He pointed out that the UK carried out 80 per cent of its trade outside the EEC and, despite being outside the Common Market, also satisfactorily carried out plenty of trade with its members. Furthermore, by remaining outside the EEC, 'we shall be free of the common agricultural policy . . . we should be free of the threats which some aspects of EEC policies pose to regional development, e.g. the fisheries policy.'[29] These were negatives to be avoided, but there were also positives that might be embraced: outside the EEC, Britain might in fact be better placed to take a lead on the truly global issues that were outside the domain of Brussels: pollution, free trade, the exploitation of natural resources. He also admitted that he was repelled by the 'power bloc' argument for European integration increasingly advanced, in private at least, by the likes of Edward Heath: 'We are told that only in an expanded EEC can Western Europe become like Russia, Japan or America . . . The answer to this is that no sane or humane man wants Western Europe to be like Russia and one must hope that we will not copy in all respects the recent history of Japan and America.'[30]

This approach to European integration was a perfect example of the belief in bureaucratic power, prestige and the 'bigger is better' philosophy – the creed of the power worshippers, not the democrats. If the negotiations failed, Grimond concluded, it would not be the end of the world. British politicians should not allow a breakdown to result in 'recriminations and disintegration'.

They should just put their own house in order, and devise new economic and industrial policies to play to the strengths of what was still 'a humane country which retains some human values in an environment that has not been entirely destroyed'.[31] Grimond had long foreseen that the fishing industry, which was treated with indifference by both Tories and Labour, stood to be sacrificed during accession negotiations. Witness his thoughts during the 1966 general election campaign: 'Look out from Shetland and you will see lights like a town. They are the lights of the Russian or Polish fishing fleets; scooping up our fish; with a catching power unknown to Labour, who in the National Plan have written off what they are pleased to call inshore fishing!'[32] When the Heath government indicated that it intended to press forward with accession negotiations, Grimond declared 'the present terms for British entry into the Common Market are unacceptable even to people such as myself who were keen to go into Europe in the days when it was extremely unpopular.'[33] His main objection was that the interests of Scotland's inshore fishermen were threatened, and he even went so far as to suggest that, since the applicant nations – England, Scotland, Ireland, Norway, Denmark and Wales – all had an interest in fisheries, they should present a united front on fisheries policy. He described the UK's approach to the negotiation as a 'fiasco' and a 'total failure',[34] and Grimond took a dim view of the manner in which the Six ensured that the foundations for an agricultural and fishing regime unfavourable to the British were quickly put into place before UK accession was ratified. This did not, he wrote, 'seem a very good way to show goodwill'.[35]

Throughout the negotiation period of 1970–2, Grimond persistently heckled the government about the need to do more to protect the interests of Britain's in-shore fishermen. He was not in the least convinced by repeated assurances from ministers that they were taking the problem of protecting the fishermen seriously: 'we are constantly assured about concern, but in the meantime the common fisheries policy is drawn up without our being represented, with potentially disastrous effects for our fishing industry.'[36] At the beginning of June 1971 the Heath government backtracked on its hitherto stated intention of holding out for exclusive fishing rights up to twelve miles from the coast, reducing its proposed limit to only six miles. This was political dynamite. On 9th June 1971 Grimond wrote one of a series of letters to Geoffrey Rippon, the minister in charge of the negotiations, in which he reiterated: 'I cannot understand how a Government which, when it was in opposition, assured the fishermen that a 12-mile limit was essential, now say that they are willing to abandon it.'[37] In due course, after two peaks in the 'cod war' with Iceland, Grimond would argue that what was needed was a treaty going far beyond anything likely to come out of the EEC, to limit how far away from their own national coastlines boats should be allowed to fish: 'the ultimate solution to these difficulties is an international agreement for . . . ideally an extension up to 200 miles, as well as some agreement on conservation.'[38] Later in the year, Grimond warned Rippon to 'make it abundantly clear to our European friends that, if they insist upon free fishing up to a six-mile limit, they are going to destroy the fishing industries for all countries on the North Sea to no advantage whatever, and that all who consider themselves good Europeans will stick on this point'.[39]

Grimond was annoyed by the government's apparent view (one rather confirmed in Con O'Neill's official account of the negotiations, now published) that fishing was a small and declining industry of marginal importance. In fact, he argued again and again, in Shetland it was not only a staple industry, it was one that in recent years had seen considerable investment and development – development that had come about 'since the introduction of the 12-mile limit – it is between the six and 12-mile limits that most of the fish going to the processing factories have been caught'.[40] Any uncertainty about the government's resolve in this matter would deter fishermen from investing for the future. He took a dim view of the government's insistence that British fisheries could be protected by means of the 'Luxembourg compromise', a convention that any EEC nation should have a *de facto* veto over any community policy that threatens to harm its 'vital national interests'. As Grimond pointed out in the House of Commons, this did not appear to have been very effective in the past: 'I am not clear what happened over the common agricultural policy, which no one seems to like except the French . . . Our influence can be most effectively deployed inside the Six – but the Government have to carry rather more confidence on this issue in the country than they do at present.'[41] This attitude brought Grimond into conflict with his old friend Con O'Neill, the senior British official in the negotiations. Although O'Neill recognised that Grimond's growing doubts about the EEC could not be dismissed out of hand, he regarded him as being 'rather typical of a number of European enthusiasts in public life who had always imagined that entering the Community would be an easy, pleasant and comfortable process – they had never bothered to discover how intensely technical and difficult the process was bound to be, and had relied too much on mere idealism and good fellowship to do the trick.'

In spite of his doubts, Grimond did ultimately join four of his Liberal colleagues in voting with the Heath government in the crucial division on 17th February 1972 that secured the second reading of the Accession Bill. The government's majority was only eight votes, so this Liberal support was crucial. The Liberals were surrounded afterwards in the chamber of the House of Commons by furious Labour MPs, one of whom physically assaulted Jeremy Thorpe before being pulled away by his own chief whip, Bob Mellish. The UK had, through its elected representatives, chosen to join the Six, but without particular enthusiasm or interest. 'Having missed the dawn when it appeared a prospect with glory,' Jo Grimond told an American audience in 1973, 'now belatedly we have slouched in, rather dusty and without great public acclaim – it is always a sign that things are pretty dreary when the British decide on a festival!'[43] Once the UK was actually in the European Community, Grimond recognised that he would have to live with the consequences of EEC fisheries policies, and his criticism became more muted. In May 1972 he welcomed the chief representative of the EEC, in the UK, M Georges Berthoin, on a week-long visit to Orkney and Shetland. Berthoin assured the Shetlanders in particular that their needs were recognised in Brussels, adding for good measure that one of Grimond's speeches in the House of Commons had decisively influenced EEC decisions on fisheries. When the minority Labour government of 1974 arrived, Grimond hoped that its more equivocal stance towards Europe, and its pledge to look again at the accession terms, might result in a harder line on agriculture and fisheries: 'I'd look for alterations in the EEC's common agricultural policy – at the moment it's expensive, inefficient and may become against the interests of Britain in general, and many of my constituents . . . Many of them have grave fears, too, about the Common Market policies on fisheries.'[44] At the very end of his career in the House of Commons, Grimond rather came full circle, upsetting fishermen in the islands by defending the fisheries policy to which Peter Walker had signed up on behalf of the Thatcher government.

In the final analysis, although he never lost sight of the pro-European 'bigger picture', Grimond seems to have remained uncomfortably aware that the burgeoning bureaucracy of Brussels was not what he had had in mind when he first campaigned for closer cooperation in Europe. It was more bureaucratic blight than golden age – with all the accoutrements that he so abhorred in any bureaucracy: index-linking (at least) of salaries, tax-free perks and generous allowances, all operating under conditions of minimal democratic scrutiny and accountability. Nor was he much impressed by the supposed *largesse* of the Community, whose apologists constantly pointed to large grants 'for this purpose or that . . . some of these grants seem to me extremely ill-judged . . . money is being wasted on a large scale'.[45] Why, he asked, did the EEC bureaucracy never turn its attention to the need to reduce expenditure, and why could they not curb their 'propensity to make irritating or positively objectionable regulations'.[46] In his election address in 1979, Grimond admitted, 'as a supporter [of the EEC] I am gravely disappointed in the way things have gone'.[47] Later, looking back upon Hugh Gaitskell's reluctance to engage in Europe, he commented, 'his disbelief has proved fairly well founded.'[48] Yet always he retained that sense of the wider perspective, recognising that the main objective of European integration – the prevention of another war between the old nation states of Western Europe – had been achieved, which was 'worth any petty tribulations that the EEC may inflict'.[49]

From the moment he arrived in the House of Commons, Grimond had felt that something was wrong – neither with democracy in principle, nor with his fellow MPs as such, nor even with the goodwill of most of the people involved. He identified a number of fundamental problems preventing Parliament from undertaking what he believed to be its main task: 'not to govern, but to prevent the government doing too much'.[50] Never renowned as one of the greatest speakers in the House, Grimond was for a long time one of its most notable questioners and it was in that function that he acknowledged perhaps the most important historical function of the member of Parliament: 'In no other assembly that I know of do those who wield the power come to it and answer questions in person, questions sometimes wounding, often petty, but which are collectively one of the great foundations of our liberties.'[51] Jo Grimond's most detailed analysis of the workings of Parliament is contained in the 1957 volume, *The Unservile State,* edited by the academic George Watson. In this essay, Grimond lamented the way in which 'individual Members of Parliament habitually urge the Executive to do more', rather than putting a check on its activities, a development that he described as 'a threat to individual liberty'.[52] He was highly critical of the practice of outside organisations 'sponsoring' MPs, and argued that MPs should be paid enough to guarantee their financial comfort and independence. He conceded that the whips may, in fact, work to the benefit of the country at large in at least some instances, by applying to MPs a pressure to countervail those of particular constituencies or interest groups. 'Nevertheless,' he concluded, 'the power of the Whip has grown very much and ought to be curtailed . . . Discussion by party meetings is the Communist method. We are rightly scornful of Reichstags and should beware of sowing the seeds within our own system.'[53] He argued for a reformed upper house, with a democratic mandate, which could deal with more routine legislation and reduce the burden on MPs, and for greatly improved parliamentary scrutiny of public expenditure. Electoral reform was presented very much as a second-tier priority, and attached to the endorsement of devolution is the warning that 'the strictest watch must be kept to see that such devolution genuinely spreads the work of government more widely and does not merely create new jobs, new functions and new committees making work for themselves.'[54]

First of all, in his view, although the state in general was doing far more than ever before – notably as a consequence of nationalisation – Parliament had not adapted to the consequent new demands upon it. As he explained in the 1967 Herbert Samuel Lecture, once the British people are 'faced with an executive they elect a Parliament to examine, criticise and control it . . . This presupposes a small sphere for government and a Parliament with leverage and sources of power outside the control of government.'[55] This historic relationship between Parliament and the government had been gradually corrupted, and the arrangements of the House were being increasingly abused to suit the larger parties, making it harder all the time for MPs to do their job, of scrutinising the executive. In practice, too many MPs thought of little except furthering their chances of preferment: 'A Government want MPs who are patient oxen, strong in health, weak in ideas and, above all, silent, who can put their programme through the Commons. Members who know their place and, like children, are to be seen but not heard and, above all, ask no awkward questions'.[56] Furthermore, in contrast with their opposite numbers in other modern democracies, MPs were appallingly equipped for doing their jobs. This thought lay behind Grimond's early advocacy of specialist committees of the House of Commons – what became the select committees.

After the 1966 general election, Grimond discerned a rapid worsening of the situation: 'Most of the new MPs are young . . . They have come with their sleeves rolled up to do a job. There is plenty of work to be done, yet the Palace of Westminster is a palace of time-wasting. You can gossip and drink tea or beer, and sleep and debauch yourself on innumerable papers, daily and weekly. But it is a difficult place in which to work.'[57] There were too many professional politicians, tied to the House of Commons not because they had constructive activity to undertake there, but because the whips wanted to keep an eye on them: 'Now . . . most MPs depend on the party, not on interests outside it . . . Power flows from office . . . More and more members want office, or at least the shadow of it . . . Ministers in theory can be chucked out by MPs if they make too much of a mess . . . If the potential chuckers-out are going to join their potential victims, who is going to keep a hostile eye on Government?'[58] This undermined democracy: 'Party machines must stop behaving like grandmothers who try to enforce their habits on their grandchildren.'[59]

As party leader, he had described what he regarded as the three tasks of MPs. They should 'provide the bulk both of the Cabinet and the potential Cabinet'; 'subject the activities of the Government to scrutiny, some friendly, some hostile'; and 'must be able to get grievances not only aired, but righted'.[60] Historically, of course, Grimond was quite right. Even today the levying of taxation is notionally a matter for members of Parliament; the government's job is to put forward its proposals, which MPs debate and vote upon. Getting a Budget through Parliament is by any token a matter of confidence, and the party system is such that most significant negotiations within the governing party take place well before proposals reach the floor of the House. This is what so frustrated Grimond:

> Under our present Parliamentary system, an MP's job is, in theory, primarily to keep an eye on the Government, to see it doesn't encroach too much on our liberty or our pockets, and to raise our grievances . . . Even Government supporters find themselves eventually criticising the Government. As for the

Opposition, its role at present is inevitable. It must oppose . . . The situation, then, in theory ought to be this: a House of Commons divided into a Government side with a majority, and an Opposition side on which sits everyone who is not of the Government party – everyone who is not prepared to keep the Government in office at almost all costs. But a fair voting system would mean that frequently the Government would not have a majority. It would depend on support from other parties, which on some issues disagree with it. The parties are no longer rigidly divided by different political beliefs. Therefore it is no longer sufficient for MPs in general and the Opposition in particular simply to oppose. The public expect the House of Commons to be constructive in many fields of government. Particularly at this moment they want things done. We have had too long a bout of conservatism.[61]

Grimond always greatly admired the United States, not least because of the framing of its constitution in such matters. The US constitution was designed not to facilitate strong, one-party government, but to foil any attempts at state high-handedness. The checks and balances are manifold, with a genuine and clear separation of powers between the two Houses of Congress on the one hand, and the President and his administration on the other. So long as ministers were overwhelmingly drawn from the membership of the House of Commons, giving MPs the incentive to seek preferment rather than to follow their congressional equivalents by giving the executive branch problems at every turn, Grimond despaired of MPs from the major parties ever acquiring any real independence. He also found the standing orders of the House of Commons maddening. The archaic expectation that MPs should be happy to stay up all night debating – whilst also taking unusually long holidays – seemed to him both bizarre and impractical. Rather controversially, he was an early advocate of the routine guillotining of bills, based on a consensus in the House about how much debating time is actually necessary. He also wished that MPs could vary their activities more, occasionally leaving the confines of the Palace of Westminster and making greater efforts to solicit the views of outsiders. 'I have gone there [the House of Commons] on a sunny morning,' he once wrote, 'and been quite unaware until midnight that it had been snowing heavily all day.'[62] It was this sense of the remoteness and isolation of Parliament that informed his advocacy of genuine devolution.

Many Liberals have long argued that the shortcomings of the House of Commons are a direct consequence of the system employed for electing its members. Moving to a system of proportional representation has long been a sacred tenet of Liberal policy, yet Grimond was always conscious of its negative effects, and was never doctrinaire on this question. When his old school friend William Douglas Home stood for the Liberals at a by-election in South Edinburgh in 1957, he asked Grimond which policy he should emphasise. 'Proportional representation,' he replied, adding with feeling, 'wouldn't it be awful if we ever got it?'[63] Douglas Home attributed this remark to Grimond's irreverent sense of humour, but a couple of years later Grimond voiced his doubts publicly. Asked during the 1959 general election campaign whether the Liberals would attempt to insist upon the introduction of PR if they held the balance of power in Parliament, Grimond had replied that he would not: 'The tail of the dog has certain rights, but does not have the right to wag the whole dog. We might try to get the other parties to have a conference about it.'[64] On this question, Grimond was of course greatly influenced by his personal experiences as MP for the furthest-flung electorate in the United Kingdom. Although he accepted the moral case for a voting system that more accurately reflected votes cast, he became increasingly sceptical about any system that would jeopardise the kind of close bond that he enjoyed with his constituents. He never forgot the importance of playing his part, as MP for Orkney and Shetland, in an important process of direct and straightforward accountability. He summarised his position thus: 'the total dependence on the single-member, single constituency system must go. The Single Transferable Vote in multi-member constituencies seems, *for most places*, [emphasis added] to be the answer.'[65]

In the delicately balanced parliamentary situation of 1964–6, Grimond quickly recognised that Harold Wilson was in no position to deliver a radical change in the voting system and in public, therefore, he did not demand that he should do so. A week before polling day he had said that, in the event of a hung Parliament, 'it would not be our object to make political capital . . . we would not expect a Government to bring in proportional representation . . . we would try to press policies which certainly we want enacted, but which we also think would be particularly relevant to the situation and command wide support in the country.'[66] The day after the election, with some seats still hanging in the balance, Grimond again preferred caution to threats: 'Some time we shall have to change the electoral system . . . not immediately . . . the most important thing to face is the economic situation.'[67] Once he had given up the party leadership, Grimond finally made public the extent of his doubts about PR for the House of Commons: 'I believe we still need a chamber such as the House of Commons elected by the generality of the nation . . . it would be concerned with the traditional political issues. I see no reason why it should not be elected much as now. I then favour a second chamber . . . elected indissolubly for say seven years by proportional representation from very large constituencies.'[68] When the Young Liberals began a campaign for PR in 1974, Grimond was amongst a minority of Liberal MPs who let it be known that, with the country in a state of near-crisis, the public would probably regard such a campaign as frivolous and insensitive. Although he felt that the Liberals should have demanded some kind of electoral reform as the price for their participation in the Lib-Lab pact, Grimond also felt that PR would be a bad issue on which to fracture the pact in late 1977. In 1978 he went further, writing in *The Common Welfare,* that 'though proportional representation must be introduced somewhere in the system there is still a strong case for preserving the first past the post method because it gives a direct link between the constituency and one member.'[69] He had decided that he would settle for a more powerful upper house, elected by PR.

Grimond feared that all systems of government were prone to political entropy and bureaucratic dropsy, a view that underpinned his approach to the twin questions of 'community politics' and devolution. He always had a general predisposition against too much government, writing in one unpublished manuscript that: 'it is no good transferring from Westminster to Edinburgh the diseases which are bringing Britain and British democracy to its knees.'[70] He was bitterly disappointed when Harold Wilson confirmed that Labour's proposals to create Scottish and Welsh Parliaments in the 1970s would not entail any reduction in bureaucracy elsewhere, and even considered withdrawing his support for devolution at that time. Home rule must bring real responsibility, openness and accountability closer to the people, and 'not to go far enough may be worse than going too far'.[71] In the edition of *Liberal Orkney* produced for the October 1974 general election, Grimond voiced his fear that home rule might provide cover for narrow-minded nationalism or isolationism, demanding that: 'we must keep our links with Europe, especially Scandinavia . . . we have suffered as much from St Andrews House as from Whitehall.'[72] In a typescript dated 20th December 1974 he revealed the inevitable difficulties that a pro-European devolutionist faced if he also happened to believe in pushing back the boundaries of the state: 'I and my party believe in a Scotland within the UK, but I am beginning to wonder . . . Is humanity to be smothered by over-government from above, from Brussels, London, Edinburgh, the regions, the districts? Should we not take a break – strike off the burdens, start again?'[73] Grimond's attitude was entirely consistent: as early as the 1950 general election campaign he had remarked: 'it is not strong government that we need – but less government, better government and government nearer home.'[74]

What Grimond never embraced was the old SNP vision of an independent Scotland, which he parodied mercilessly:

> My quarrel with many Scottish nationalists is that they still think in terms of out-of-date sovereign states . . . They want Scotland to be created in the middle of the twentieth century as a model nineteenth-century state. They feel that she was deprived. But if someone has led a deprived childhood you don't, when they are in middle age, dress them in rompers and try to give them all the delights of the school holidays.[75]

It is quite true that Grimond's natural scepticism, combined with his distaste for the inward-looking form of Scottish nationalism, did sometimes lead him to equivocate slightly about Scottish home rule. In 1958, for instance, he wrote that 'the Scotch [sic] are by nature long-winded . . . they have always been bad at running their own affairs and rather good at interfering in other peoples.'[76] Some of his supporters were also critical of the very limited vision for home rule to which he seemed to confine himself in his 1959 book *The Liberal Future,* in which he called for 'a Parliament in Edinburgh . . . dealing, among other subjects, with subjects like Town and Country Planning and the Arts'.[77] There was also the special perspective of Orkney and Shetland, Grimond once observing that 'we have very little truck with Scotland . . . No one wears a kilt or speaks Gaelic . . . I am an old Danish colonial.'[78]

After ten years of Grimond's leadership, a brash federal approach informed the Liberal Party's approach both to domestic government and to European government. In a party political broadcast on 29th November 1966, George Mackie said that the new Scottish and Welsh Parliaments proposed by the Liberals would not mark the end of the United Kingdom: 'I think we need overall planning in the United Kingdom, and to do this we must have this federal framework.' The Liberals did not, however, propose giving England its own Parliament; originally this meant that Scotland and Wales would have an extra tier of government compared with their larger neighbour. The Scottish Liberals also proposed the establishment of regional councils within Scotland, an idea picked up by the party in England. By the mid to late 1960s, the Liberals were proposing that central government should also hand over many of its responsibilities to English regional assemblies. Whether these would have been more like the Parliaments in Scotland and Wales, or the regional authorities in those territories, is hard to ascertain.

Some of Grimond's detractors now claim that he preferred advocating 'devolution' rather than a Scottish Parliament. Although he did once slip up rather badly by appearing to suggest that he foresaw a Scottish Parliament with only the most basic powers and responsibilities, the evidence overwhelmingly tells a rather different story. In 1976, for instance, he wrote that the Callaghan government's proposals for devolution were doomed, because they proposed a Scottish Parliament that would be 'a further tier of government joining the bureaucratic clamour for more subsidies and more haphazard interference'.[79] What was required was a fundamental rethinking, and streamlining, of government: 'Home Rule, not devolution'.[80] Grimond's favoured phrase all along, in fact, seems to have been 'home rule' and, if anything, he rather disliked the very concept of 'devolution', with its implication that the Scots were humble petitioners, desperately hoping that Westminster might graciously hand down some of its God-given powers. Grimond's core principle was that sovereignty should come upwards from the people. 'The regional and social policies of Britain have failed,' he told an audience of American students in 1973, 'because they are handed down from above . . . democracy will only flourish where political power is seen to reside in the people at large – the power of each authority is delegated upwards, so to speak . . . local or state government is not that part of its power which London or Washington so graciously delegate, still less is it a present from Brussels – the centre must be seen as given powers from below.'[81]

This philosophical foundation also underpins Grimond's long-held view that devolution should not begin and end with the creation of Parliaments in Edinburgh and Cardiff. He disagreed with his party in believing that England deserved similar and equal treatment, not through the creation of costly regional authorities that would command little or no loyalty, but through the creation of an English Parliament to stand alongside those of Scotland, Wales and Northern Ireland. In 1975 he wrote of his fear that 'pressure for self-government for the regions of England will not be based on any genuine wish for better government, nor from a desire for . . . expression of regional differences, but simply from a demand to keep up with the Scots and the Welsh'.[82] Grimond was never much impressed by the calibre of the MPs sent to Westminster by Scottish constituencies. As the years went by, being an MP at Westminster became more and more a full-time job, which meant that fewer talented people in Scotland were willing to become parliamentarians, whereas 'you would get a wider section of Scottish ability in Edinburgh than you do in London'.[83] He did, however, reject any thought that he himself might seek election to a devolved Parliament: 'I am 60 years old. I don't see the point of being a Scottish MP in my 70s.'[84]

Grimond's most considered outpouring on this subject was his pamphlet of 1976, *A Roar for the Lion*, in which he argued that the United Kingdom needed an entirely new, and coherent, constitutional settlement, based upon a clear statement of principles. In the case of Scotland, this required politicians to 'start with the Scottish people and ask what sort of government they should create – we must not start with Westminster and ask what powers it should delegate'.[85] He pointed out that even Scotland was not homogeneous. Therefore, unless the new settlement had checks and balances built into it to prevent all groups and areas from predominating at the expense of others, then it could hardly be a success. When Grimond drafted his own home rule bill in the late 1960s, he soon discovered how difficult it is to unscramble the many lines of taxation and expenditure coming in and out of government. He was always convinced, however, that government and civic society depended upon a balance between power and responsibility, meaning that home rule would necessitate extensive tax-raising powers: 'one can imagine how irresponsible a Scottish Parliament or Government might become if it were free to demand expenditure in the safe knowledge that it would not have to find the money.'[86] By the 1970s he could argue that this might easily be sustained if around one-third of oil revenues were to go directly to the Scottish administration. The principle of decentralisation should not be confined to the elected parts of government; this was also an ideal opportunity to look again at a whole range of social policies, too many of which had become centralised and unresponsive.

A less centralised state, argued Grimond, could change the fundamental nature of the social services, making them less remedial and more preventative. The structure of local authorities should be streamlined as part of the package, and a higher proportion of their budgets should be raised locally. Grimond feared that Labour's proposals for devolution were a recipe for over-government and for bad government. For him, 'the main argument for democracy is that properly handled it can be the most efficient form of government . . . If it is not, then the burden laid on people will be too great. They will reject it.'[87] During his brief interregnum as Liberal leader in 1976, Grimond took the opportunity to rebel against the conventional wisdom on devolution by asserting his belief that 'the demand for Home Rule is not a demand for more government . . . It is a protest against too much government . . . It is also an assertion that Scotland is a nation.'[88] Grimond's point was not lost on his own constituents: given the chance to vote on Labour's devolution proposals in 1979, they did indeed reject them. He explained: 'Scotland is a foreign country, from their point of view.'[89] Although he obviously saw a role for himself at Westminster post-devolution, Grimond also advocated something that few home rulers, even today, have ever even discussed: that, if Scotland, Wales and Northern Ireland get Parliaments, then Westminster should be left with 'a much smaller Parliament' and 'the English must be left to make their decisions as to how to run their affairs.'[90] The so-called 'West Lothian' question has not always been the exclusive preserve of anti-devolutionists.

It was from such conceptions of what might be termed subsidiarity that Grimond developed his philosophy of what he termed 'community politics'. This was not merely about cracked pavements, but also about an entirely new, preventative, approach to social and community services, requiring a new attitude towards politics itself. In recent years, the Liberals and their successor party, the Liberal Democrats, have made considerable strides thanks to what has become known as 'grassroots' or 'community' campaigning, which has provided the foundations upon which the present-day Liberal Democrats have built their success. The approach may have delivered votes and seats, but it is nonetheless easily and widely criticised. In many people's eyes, it debauches and cheapens politics. With its reliance upon negative and oppositional campaigning, 'grumble sheets' and the exploitation of local grievances, it tends to weaken any conception of the 'general good' and reduces politics to a series of unilateral appeals to separate interest groups. The rapid development of professional lobbyists, within both the commercial sector and the charitable sector, has mirrored this change in politicians' behaviour. It is surely not excessively partisan to record that the first Blair government played this game with unusual skill, increasing taxes where the least attention would be generated, then issuing a seemingly never-ending and increasingly incomprehensible series of hand-outs to particular groups.

This was not what Grimond meant by 'community politics'. Indeed he would often express his admiration for John Stuart Mill's view that MPs should not take up constituency matters at all, and one of his major fears in the early 1970s was that government and society were being pulled hither and thither by a number of divergent and sometimes rather powerful interest groups. If government were to appease them all, in proportion to the amount of trouble they could cause, Grimond argued, that was something very different from the lofty concept of the 'general good' nobly set out by the great liberal political thinkers. Politicians had to bear in mind that 'democracy . . . implies that by argument you may change people's views . . . the reconciliation of different demands within the community is essentially a job for politicians . . . It is to my mind essentially a job which requires both, on the one hand, some firmly stated principles and, on the other hand, constant negotiations on particular matters over the application of these principles.'[91] Grimond was always determined that his brand of politics 'based on the community' should not be confused with what he disparagingly termed 'politics as the taking up of grievances', something that he found strongly distasteful. What Grimond meant by 'community politics' was that social and community services should be fundamentally reorganised, with far greater involvement for local people. They should not merely try to patch up the ills of society; they should prevent problems by 'improving the whole environment, including employment . . . and in the process participation is vital'.[92] 'It is important to distinguish between schemes designed to encourage communities to help themselves and schemes which simply prod people to clamour for more public funds and more bureaucracy,' he once observed.[93]

As the Liberal Party began to expand its activities under his leadership, and under the influence of Pratap Chitnis, however, Grimond had danced to a rather different tune. For a start, he realised how successes in local government, where for decades the Liberals had been virtually moribund, lifted morale and created the first strands of a network that could sustain the party in leaner years as well as better ones. In his closing speech to the party assembly in 1960, for example, Grimond said that 'every time a Liberal councillor gets a bus stop moved to a better place he strikes a blow for his party.' A few days later he wrote proudly of how the Liberals were 'getting Labour workers and Labour votes coming over at constituency level . . . That's where the movement to Liberalism is growing . . . Of course it will take time to reach the top but it is much healthier that it should begin at the roots.'[94] By that time, the foundations of Liberal parliamentary success were already being built up in long-time Conservative strongholds up and down the country. Grimond's views about society and politics changed with the years as he grew more disillusioned about the party system, and more than ever convinced that it could not deliver what the country needed. In particular he felt that there were individual groups whose needs were being neglected, either deliberately or unwittingly.

After the Liberals' debacle in June 1970, Grimond consciously switched away from his old strategy of realignment of the left and towards a new political model. The Liberals, he argued, should give up trying to compete on old party lines and become more of a community party, to 'stand for the people and against growing bureaucracy'.[95] He hoped that the growing proliferation of left-leaning pressure groups that had sprung up in recent years would 'soon come together to try to find some common outlook in political philosophy . . . This would once more give content to politics and justification for the pursuit of office.'[96] To succeed politically, Grimond would argue, this new radical movement should coalesce into a grouping 'based on genuine agreement among the rank and file of the movement about common aims and a common view of society . . . it cannot simply be a new party on the old model'.[97] 'Community politics,' Grimond explained a few weeks later:

> should mean more than taking up grievances or showing a deep interest in local matters – admirable though both of these activities are . . . It should mean the way to a more satisfactory, equal and democratic society . . . this entails improvement of the surroundings, housing, transport, education, welfare, health and employment in the less well off communities and a determined communal effort in all communities to exploit their potential to the full.[98]

This would be developed most impressively in Grimond's book *The Common Welfare*, published in 1978. There is no denying, however, the dramatic effectiveness of Liberal community campaigning over the years: the election of over fifty Liberal Democrat members of Parliament in 2001 is by any token a remarkable and eloquent tribute to the patient and tireless endeavours of generations of loyal party workers over the last forty-five years.

Appendix 2
THE DEVELOPMENT OF JO GRIMOND'S
POLITICAL PHILOSOPHY

Throughout most of his life, Jo Grimond was a prolific speechmaker and writer. His journalism runs almost unbroken from the mid 1930s to the late 1980s, and he produced a plethora of pamphlets in addition to his six full-length books. He always believed in the importance of both policy and political philosophy, and his intellectual pretensions never dimmed. His thoughtful and original contributions to the political debate from the 1950s on proved increasingly attractive to an impressive collection of academics and intellectuals who would, even five years before, hardly have considered wasting their efforts on the Liberal Party. Jo Grimond's journalistic utterances run like a golden thread through this book, as do excerpts from a wide range of his most important speeches in Parliament and beyond, but his weightier expositions deserve a section devoted exclusively to them, so that the development of his political philosophy between the 1950s and the 1980s can be more easily followed. The influence of his ideas belies the comparative weakness of the party that he led. Perhaps the first serious exposition of Grimond's philosophy came when he addressed the twenty-sixth Liberal Summer School, held in Southampton during the summer of 1952, taking the opportunity to draw a clear distinction between socialism and the brand of liberalism that he favoured. Partly under the influence of Lady Violet and Clement Davies, and partly because of the behaviour of the Bevanites, during the early part of his parliamentary career, Grimond became increasingly concerned about the threat of full-blooded socialism.

In a speech that resonated with echoes of the slightly pompous PPE student who dominated *Isis* magazine in the 1930s, Grimond praised the tradition of the empiricists, whose philosophies and policies are derived not from inspirations but from experimentation and observation. He wanted to see people taking far greater responsibility for their own development, and he believed that the onus of proof should be on those who wanted to expand the activities of the state, not on those who wanted to see greater responsibility given to individual citizens. Socialism had created a monster, and the Conservatives were performing their usual dismal function, he argued, of defending without question whatever they inherited. Liberals understood that the job of government was not to impose grand plans on the people, but to help them to improve their condition steadily and incrementally, by enhancing the opportunities available to them and by ensuring that the state was both well regulated and impartial. This meant that the government and its officials should not set out to arbitrate between different groups in society according to a master plan. The state should act impartially and fairly, on the basis of 'the general good', not favouring certain sectional interests according to political preference: 'The Socialists do not believe this . . . All the phrases which bespatter their writings boil down to the assertion that the State knows what is right and will pursue it and the individual will not . . . I believe in social equality . . . but I do not believe in a doctrine of equal pay for unequal work . . . If we must have high-sounding phrases I prefer liberty and fraternity to equality.'[1]

In 1953 Grimond had another good opportunity to commit his thoughts to paper, as part of a special section on the Liberals featured in the learned *Political Quarterly*. While such figures as Philip Fothergill and Arthur Holt dealt elsewhere with more practical matters, Grimond contributed a lengthy treatise on how advocates of liberalism, and the Liberal Party in particular, might find a way out of their predicament. It all went wrong for liberals with the industrial revolution, he reasons, because just when society was threatened with disintegration as a consequence of massive economic change, liberal thinkers went into a blind alley of their own making. They did not react to the utopian dogmas of Marx and Engels by restating their own rational and empirical philosophy, rooted in the thinking of Locke and Hume and 'in opposition to all abstractions'.[2] Instead, the Liberal Party retreated into a form of hardline individualism far beyond anything that Adam Smith or John Stuart Mill would have advocated, and 'forgot that man is a social animal who has always lived in communities and who has never been moved by purely economic considerations'. When they should have been making the case for some kind of sensible halfway house between state direction and absolute *laissez-faire*, Liberals had instead fallen for what Karl Popper termed the 'poverty of historicism', abandoning the politics of gradual amelioration and deceiving themselves into thinking that liberalism, like Marxism, must offer some ultimate end to mankind, some Utopia or perfect state that could mark humanity's historical destination. They had succumbed to a kind of fatalism, a belief in technical or technological determinism, which was in fact the very antithesis of liberalism.

This desiccated and degraded form of liberalism was anathema to Grimond, whose beliefs sprang from an abiding faith in the power of rational political choices and a piecemeal approach to improve the human condition. Liberalism was never likely to possess the pseudo-religious power that was exploited by the false messiahs of state socialism or nationalism, but Grimond argued here that the very relativism of liberalism was ultimately its strength not its weakness: 'the moralists have created far more misery than the cynics.'[3] If only Liberals could rediscover their belief in themselves, and in their fellow human beings, they could enjoy a renaissance by virtue of their ability to withstand the very process of sceptical questioning that they advocated. They also had to face the fact that their belief in equality of opportunity naturally entailed an acceptance of unequal outcomes. They could then design policies to ameliorate inequality, without resorting to excessive compulsion or falling into the trap of believing that 'the gentlemen in Whitehall know best not only in technical but in moral matters.'[4] He derides state socialism as 'the promise of sherbet and dancing girls in the future coupled to controls in the present'[5] and set out in clear contrast his own principles for a liberal society: 'To begin with, the starts in life must be reasonably fair: secondly, the fabric of society must be maintained: thirdly, a reasonable life must be guaranteed to even the slowest in the race. But in the infinite changes of human life politicians should not be too rigid in their views, nor attempt to fix the ends of human existence.'[6]

This exposition makes for a fascinating comparison with the basis for a 'just society' expounded just a few years later by the leading American liberal John Rawls. His 'difference principle', the foundation of so much subsequent liberal thought, is in fact extremely similar. In his masterpiece *A Theory of Justice*, Rawls stepped beyond the utilitarianism of J S Mill – 'the greatest happiness for the greatest number' – by tackling head-on the questions of distribution and inequality that had unsettled liberals for generations. He set out two principles as the ideal foundations for society: 'The first requires equality in the assignment of basic rights and duties, while the second holds that social and economic inequalities . . . are just only if they result in compensating benefits for everyone, and in particular for the least advantaged members of society.'[7] Rawls shared with Grimond a clear emphasis on equality of opportunity, and on duties alongside responsibilities. He also made no bones about the need for a stable society, which should be based upon generally agreed and rational principles. This is not necessarily to claim that Grimond was ahead of his time, or even that he might have directly influenced Rawls. But the two men, one an academic and the other an elected parliamentarian on the other side of the Atlantic, had clearly identified the same gaping hole in liberal thinking. It is hardly surprising that a Harvard philosopher should have been better able to find the requisite time and tranquillity to flesh out these ideas than someone who spent much of his life commuting between London and Kirkwall, but it is immensely to Grimond's credit that he always believed in the force and importance of ideas in politics, and always enjoyed making people think. He never lost his faith that, even in the era of 'Butskellism', when politics seemed to have been reduced to squabbles about the price of butter or the marginal benefits accruing to different, non-existent missile defence systems, ideas did matter. He believed in liberalism as a broad, generous and practical philosophy – and one with a future. In contrast, conservatism wasn't a philosophy at all, and socialism had manifestly failed. The question now was whether he would ever be in a position to bring about the liberal renaissance of which he dreamed.

In a foreword at the beginning of 1957 to a radical and cogent pamphlet written by two young Cambridge-educated Liberals, Timothy Joyce and Frank Ware, about 'Opportunity', Grimond made plain his desire to see more such pamphlets, and more Liberals rising to the challenge of 'the prickly questions'. He wanted Liberals everywhere to toss up new ideas, which could then be melded into an election platform for the party. 'So many of the old arguments are dead,' he wrote, 'and the old socialist answers have a strong whiff of the grave.'[8] This was an open invitation to absolutely anyone who had a contribution to make, however groundbreaking or offbeat, to throw their hat into the ring with the Liberals. He set up a Political Research Unit to keep him up to date with the shifting sands of public opinion. In time it concluded that the Liberals needed to present a modern and positive face to the voters. Grimond set about doing precisely that.

In July 1957 Grimond produced the first pamphlet of his own, *The New Liberalism*. This was clearly intended to be accessible rather than profound. The text was spare and in large print; various phrases or sections are emphasised through the use of italics or capital letters. As the *News Chronicle* put it: 'his testament is staccato in tone, brash in presentation, but this is of the age.'[9] In this he attacked the way in which both the Conservative and Labour parties had to be dragged kicking and screaming into facing the new challenges of the nuclear age. 'We want to see a British Government,' proclaimed Grimond, 'behaving as if they were MAD KEEN on spreading healthy opportunity in all directions: MAD KEEN on European integration.'[10] He also advocated a thorough reassessment of the social services. There must be greater targeting of welfare services, which should neither be provided 'with groans and misgivings as a necessary bribe' nor 'accepted by the receivers as part of their inalienable perks'.[11] There was a great emphasis on the need to dissipate responsibility back into society and to reduce reliance on the state: 'Responsibility rests with the people – Government is residual.'[12] In the section on individual freedom, Grimond set out the objective of protecting the individual worker, in particular, *against the tyranny of* employers, Trades Unions *or* other Associations'.[13] Internationally, the Liberal objective set out here is for the United Kingdom to play its full part in every international organisation going, especially in Europe. The Liberals would *go wholeheartedly into the creation of wider groupings such as the Free Trade Area, Euratom and the Schuman plan – going not reluctantly but as leaders*'.[14] Defence was considered in a similar context: 'Britain's place today in the world is not that of Rome but that of Greece . . . *We don't mean ever to go it alone, and so we can reduce arms to a minimum consonant with putting our share into the Western pool.*[15] The tenor of *The New Liberalism* was that of a clear, concise and bold recruitment statement for those who were already sympathetic to the Liberals. It was an effective opening salvo for Grimond's leadership. He did not pretend that his party expected to form a government after the next election – indeed he dismissed the very thought – but he did set out a new direction in politics.

In the wake of Torrington, something rather more substantial was required. This came in the shape of a second pamphlet, *The New Liberal Democracy*, published on 5th June 1958. This was an altogether more polished piece of work than its predecessor, which kicked off with an extended account of the Liberals' deep sense of grievance towards the voting system. Opinion polls and by-elections since Grimond had taken over the Liberal reins in 1956 all suggested that the party could plausibly look to win 15 per cent or so at the forthcoming election. Under the first-past-the-post voting system, however, that could deliver no more than a handful of additional seats, the injustice of which Grimond bemoaned at length in his opening exposition. More interesting is Grimond's hypothesising about how the Liberals might behave in certain post-election scenarios. He effectively rules out Liberal participation in a coalition government, unless their parliamentary party was comparable in size to those of the other parties. In the event of a smallish Liberal group holding the balance of power, he argued, they should stick to treating each piece of legislation on its merits. The formula ran thus: 'we should think it our duty to enable the majority party [the largest party, presumably] to carry on the government of the country for the time being so long as it did not attempt drastic or reactionary measures which clearly no Liberal could support . . . We should not join the Government.'[16] The clear drift was that the Liberals were out to bust the existing system – 'We believe that the place of the Socialist Party on the left should be taken by a non-Socialist progressive party'[17] – not to participate in it on anyone else's terms. This section was also strongly centrist in tone: the emphasis was not on radicalism, but on the way in which Liberals might moderate the policies of other parties. On certain issues – for example the proposed renationalisation of steel – they might find it impossible to support Labour. On others – notably any further expeditions *à la* Suez – they might find themselves unable to support a Tory government. On less fundamental issues, the party might have a free vote, or abstain.

So how would this new progressive party be constituted, and by what process would it be arrived at? The most interesting section of all is that on 'A New Alignment in Politics', the strategy that would characterise Grimond's tenure as Liberal leader. Grimond argued that the party system, based upon increasingly redundant class cleavages and political questions, had outlived its time. He had predicted the previous year that, in due course, the working class would disappear and the Liberals would come to be recognised as 'the party of the new middle class . . . soon an all-embracing class'.[18] Now, he argued, the important disputes were not between homogeneous class-based blocs, but between liberals and authoritarians – or between nationalists and internationalists. Both of the 'old' parties contained people on each side of the argument. Therefore, wrote Grimond, 'we might see a new Liberal Party attracting Liberal, Tory and Labour sympathizers and opposing a new conservative party which included non-Liberal Tories and Socialists.'[19] More likely, however, was a slightly less dramatic shift in the political landscape, with 'a Tory Party on the right and Liberal and Labour Parties on the left'.[20] Alternatively, if Labour were to move in a liberal direction, the two parties might not merely cooperate but could actually merge, 'leading to a new party of the Left'.[21] At this stage it is not clear whether Grimond was thinking in terms of an electoral arrangement with Labour, occasional post-election coalitions with it, or a sustained competitive-cooperative relationship sustained by proportional representation. All this bridge-building with Labour would, however, require it to renounce its attachment to state socialism. There was nothing remotely socialistic in Grimond's substantive policy proposals, and his fiercest criticism of the Tories was that they have 'in fact been conserving Socialism for the last eight years'.[22] A few days after the publication of this pamphlet, speaking at Taunton, Grimond would echo that even more harshly, describing the post-war consensus as 'a socialist way of life embalmed under a Tory government'.[23] In Grimond's view, socialism had left a terrible legacy: 'the growth of the State, protectionism, a weak currency, high taxation, high Government expenditure and its mistaken economic and financial policies which have led to restriction in industry and indirectly to recurrent financial crises'.[24] It is hard to see much common ground with Labour in such an indictment. It was little wonder that the *Daily Telegraph* should see fit to comment in a leading article that Grimond had here provided the voters 'with a set of arguments which are all pro-Conservative, and a set of conclusions which are mainly pro-Socialist'.[25]

In March 1958 Charles Monteith of Faber & Faber wrote to Grimond, proposing that he should write a book about politics, not a heavy treatise nor a manifesto manqué but 'a short, forceful book, designed for the general public, putting forward the Liberal political case'.[26] Grimond invited Monteith to the House of Commons and, within the month, they had agreed that he would write the book. He received the grand sum of £100 as an advance, with more royalties to follow. Grimond had no illusions that he was writing a bestseller, accepting in a letter to his publisher that he quite accepted that 'this is not a book of which the film rights are likely to be very valuable'.[27] He was right about that: two years later Fabers offered 1,000 remaindered copies of the book to the party's Organising Committee for only 2s 6d per copy – against the original price of 12s 6d. Nonetheless, the work that Grimond produced, *The Liberal Future*, published on 10th April 1959, remains a classic of its kind. It must be one of the most persuasive and cogent statements ever made – or ever likely to be made – of social liberalism since the heyday of H H Asquith. In its 190 pages, Grimond successfully killed off most of the old canards about liberalism and sets out a radical, humane vision of the future of democracy.

This work arguably represents the most important contribution that Jo Grimond made to political debate. 'All who profess and call themselves politically adult should read his book,' proclaimed an anonymous reviewer in the *Times Literary Supplement*. 'It may not give his party a future; but it may in that case assure a better future for some other party, and certainly for the nation.'[28] What is perhaps most striking about *The Liberal Future* is that, in contrast with many more recent statements of what purports to be liberalism, it laid most of its emphasis not upon the rights of citizens, but upon their responsibilities. The kind of civil society that Grimond posited can exist only if people are actively committed to the well-being of their fellows, if they understand the importance of public service and give freely of their time and endeavours for the community and the country, if they are courteous and considerate, and do not abuse their freedoms. This is a direct and deliberate throwback to the groundbreaking liberalism of John Stuart Mill, who equally preached that liberty can only be sustained when inextricably bound up with an ingrained sense of what constitutes responsible and acceptable social behaviour: 'The liberty of the individual must be thus far limited; he must not make himself a nuisance to other people.'[29] This statement by Mill is sometimes used to define the difference between 'freedom' and 'licence'.

Grimond's liberalism was highly 'communitarian' throughout. Perhaps the most potent criticism of classical liberalism is that it is too abstract, too abstruse and altogether too prone to treat the individual human being as a blank slate, as some kind of absolute Platonic construct floating in an imaginary no-man's-land removed from time and space, where there are no traditions, no communities and no shared experiences and values. Grimond rejected that intellectual foundation outright, calling for a reassertion of the individual *and* community spirit that had been eroded and usurped by post-war collectivism, of the shared values and aspirations that underpin a true society. 'We hear a good deal about Opportunity,' wrote Grimond in the Appendix to the book, 'but not so much about Responsibility, which is the other side of the coin . . . Personal, political and economic responsibility are all weak today . . . Too many people hug committees because they offer release from individual responsibility . . . too many people hope to throw their troubles on to someone else . . . Responsibility is not popular.'[30] It seems so obvious today, but in 1959 this was a magnificently bold restatement of an almost forgotten truth. The one slight slip of the pen, which Scottish

Nationalists long quoted with glee, came when Grimond suggested that he foresaw a Scottish Parliament 'dealing, among other subjects, with subjects like town and country planning and the arts'.[31] He would have been well advised to expand rather more on those 'other subjects'.

Grimond was also careful to emphasise that liberalism was no foreign, academic construct. It had roots in Britain's long history of maintaining a tolerant and decent civil society. It should still be sustainable here; it had been sustained, and it had sustained, in the past. He would develop the theme of participation more deeply four years later in a subsequent work, but it has its place here too. In an unyielding denunciation of socialism, he condemned not only the hypocrisy of Labour's attacks on capitalism, but also accused socialists of whittling away true democracy by stealth through the creation of a 'proletariat', which treated people like 'marbles in a bag' and crushed the individual spirit, but all-importantly delivers the vote for Labour at election time. They were 'the ruled'; left to slump indifferently in front of the television between elections, constantly assured that their class interests were being protected. As Grimond wrote, the existence of a proletariat is not solely the result of economic factors: however prosperous the country may be in financial terms, a proletariat is the opposite of a society. It is the negation of individual responsibility and activism in its best sense: 'a proletariat may be copiously supplied with cars, houses, television sets, and still be a proletariat, while a society may be primitive, but still be a society . . . America today has some symptoms of a proletarian state.'[32] In other words, Labour, through advances in technology, was contriving new opiates for the masses.

In economic matters, Grimond blazed a trail for better incentives, and lower direct taxation. He was an unabashed advocate of the free market, but rejected the extreme view that a totally free market should be either encouraged, or revered as some kind of natural order, a superior 'state of nature'. There is a strong Christian Democratic influence here; although Grimond did not use the phrase, he was effectively advocating the principles of the 'social market economy', as pioneered by Ludwig Erhard in post-war West Germany, where a strong social state is founded upon the wealth that can be generated only by a successful market economy. Spread ownership, set the people free, unleash democracy and creativity in the economic sphere as well as the social sphere – all this has a social market ring to it. 'One asset of the free enterprise system,' wrote Grimond, 'is that decisions are taken by a great number of people . . . That alone is a safeguard against one overriding disastrous error.'[33] A free economy is a corollary of any genuinely liberal democracy. When the state gets too involved, not only does creativity run dry, but also the bureaucrat's love of prestige over utility, for the 'grand project', comes to the fore. 'If the State makes too much use of the system to serve its own ends of national prestige or "social" justice it promotes those very vices which Socialists most decry . . . I believe that the concentration of economic power in the hands of the State is a threat to Freedom and Liberalism.'[34] These are ideas that influenced the likes of Arthur Seldon, Ralph Harris and Keith Joseph – and, in her turn, Margaret Thatcher, when she was at the height of her powers.

With regard to the social services, Grimond was again ahead of his time. He advocated an expanded assisted places scheme to open up the independent schools and a new commitment to preventive medicine, and even toyed with introducing vouchers into the education system. He foresaw the need for 'encouraging voluntary pensions, always allowing for a basic State pension in cases of need . . . This must, however, depend upon . . . making it easier to transfer [voluntary pensions] when the man or woman concerned changes employment',[35] and argued that the principle of targeting benefits had to be reintroduced more widely. This would mean finding ways of getting away from the stigma that used to be attached to means testing: 'the means test of the thirties was objectionable because of the methods used, rather than because of any inherent indignity in the process itself.'[36] Though he accepted that the social services, allowed to grow unchecked, might 'encourage fecklessness, waste, the idler, the sponger',[37] Grimond's main concern was that they might contribute to the creation of 'pressure groups and vested interests'.[38] This led him to propound the notion of a 'national minimum income', above subsistence level, guaranteed to all, shorn of the disincentive effects of most state benefits and any residual stigma of targeting. Today's 'Citizen's Income' proposals from the Liberal Democrats owe everything to Grimond. There were one or two conservative flourishes too. Grimond recognised that, if the influence of the state was to be reduced, then other, smaller social units would have to provide greater support to individuals as they had in the past. In this connection he wrote that: 'I hope we shall restore family life.'[39] There was also his continuing war against the horrors of modern architecture and his advocacy of the traditional 'representative' role of MPs, as critics of the executive rather than its creatures.

On Europe there was a burst of the radicalism to which Grimond was gradually being converted under the influence of Arthur Holt and Mark Bonham Carter. It had always been the political aspects of European integration that most appealed to Grimond, and he made the case forcefully here. Indeed, he went one better, setting out an ultimate aspiration of establishing some system of world governance. Nowhere is his thinking more clearly set out. Grimond's fear was that, in the absence of effective intervention on behalf of the consumer, business has a tendency towards oligopoly or monopoly, not only domestically but also trans-nationally. Unchecked, economic and industrial power tend to become concentrated in too few hands, not only denying to citizens as consumers the benefits of price competition, but also raising fundamental questions about accountability. Grimond foresaw the arguments that we are now having about what today is termed 'globalisation'. The only way he could see of reasserting the interests of the consumer-citizen in the face of these agglomerations of power was if government, in its benign and liberal form, also grew and crossed national boundaries with the same sangfroid as big business. This would mean that national sovereignty would have to be pooled – as it already had been 'with America and their Western allies'.[40] Furthermore, 'a Liberal foreign policy towards Europe would be based on the firm belief that Britain is a part – a leading part – of Europe, and that international bodies should be executive and not merely advisory.'[41]

On Europe in particular Grimond made a remarkable contrast with the rather shifty and apologetic approach demonstrated by most advocates of EEC accession in the other political parties. He proclaimed that 'every Liberal must rejoice that developments in politics and science point to unity not division among the people of the world . . . If we are to have peace it is essential to break up the bellicose robber baron states who have torn the world apart in the last fifty years.'[42] That is as clear a statement as can be found in the English language of the thinking that actuated the Treaty of Rome, the desire to transpose feelings of attachment and loyalty away from the old nation-states to a new European model. Liberals need not excoriate feelings of national pride or even nationalistic sentiments, ran the argument, but these need to be separated from a fetishistic attachment to that artificial and outmoded historical conception, the wholly independent and self-reliant nation-state. It is possible to disagree with this thesis – to argue for instance that the nation-state has at times been a necessary and admirably liberal bulwark against tyranny, or that democracy cannot effectively be applied in too large a unit (as Grimond himself sometimes did) – whilst still admiring its clarity and honesty.

So what exactly is the liberal society that Grimond set out here, and how would it have differed from the prevailing conditions in Britain in the late 1950s? One thing that emerges in *The Liberal Future*, really for the first time, is Grimond's loathing for the British class system. He perceived a nation bedevilled by too much self-destructive confrontation: bosses against workers, government against governed, even region against region. His prescription was a harder-edged version of the kind of things that Liberals had long advocated: wider share ownership or even co-ownership, unions denuded of their privileges and bound by the normal rule of law, profit sharing and so forth. He advocated that ownership and responsibility should be far more widely diffused, within a new industrial system possessing many of the features normally associated with anarcho-syndicalism. This was a new streak in Grimond's thinking, and one that would develop further over the years, not always to the acclaim of his colleagues. Full-blown syndicalism would have meant the abolition of shareholders, in particular outside shareholders, but what Grimond put forward in *The Liberal Future* is less dramatic than that. The main thrust of his argument was that it was unreasonable to expect real commitment from workers unless and until they were properly consulted by management, and had a direct interest in the success of the enterprise.

One or two of the policies floated in *The Liberal Future* got an airing in the House of Commons in early 1959. In particular, Grimond wanted to draw attention to the new Liberal policy on defence, which he used to emphasise divisions in the other parties:

> We of the Liberal Party say that Britain should not make its own nuclear deterrent. We believe the nuclear deterrent should be held by the West on behalf of the West as a whole and not by individual countries in the West. We recognise that at present America is so much the most powerful nuclear power that the development of the Western deterrent must rest largely with her, but we are perfectly willing that this country should make a contribution to her nuclear programme if it is wanted . . . If we could limit the possession of the bomb to Russia and America, that would be excellent. But even if we could not, I think that, on balance, we should not make our own bomb.[43]

Grimond also pressed home some of his more radical economic ideas in the House of Commons. Leading for the Liberals in the 1959 Budget debate, he was scornful of the government's own proposals which, in his opinion, did nothing to stimulate the long-term investment that Britain needed. He followed Enoch Powell in the debate, echoing his concerns about the fact that government expenditure was now rising under a Conservative government. He adhered very much to his themes of recent years, calling for reductions in direct taxation to improve incentives, and for measures to encourage private savings to go into industrial investment instead of into government securities. One of the few taxes to have been cut was the duty on beer, and Grimond was especially scornful of this, accusing the Chancellor of producing a bottle of beer in the debate 'with the air of extreme respectability usually seen only in old family retainers, absolutely above suspicion . . . It seems like Marie Antoinette to reduce the cost of living by taking 2d. off the pint.'[44] He would have preferred to see a cut in fuel duty, which would at least have helped industry.

The second of the *New Directions* pamphlets, *Better Buys*, published in 1960, resonates with the influence of Jo Grimond. It argued the case against too much *laissez-faire*, and for firmer action by government against private-sector monopolies. This pamphlet argued that only some comparatively modest legislation would be required to bring consumer protection up to speed. Presaging a notable parliamentary battle to come, there was a short section on the subject of Resale Price Maintenance (RPM), which used to limit price competition between retailers. The pamphlet fell short of demanding that RPM should be abolished, but even the careful drafting did not conceal that this was the direction in which Liberals would like things to go: 'undoubtedly many enterprising businessmen, manufacturers and retailers are keen to see individual RPM abolished . . . Being enterprising they welcome competition.' In this pamphlet Grimond and his colleagues also dipped their toes, with due qualification, into the chilly waters of deregulated shopping hours: 'it is right, of course, that shop workers should be protected from exploitation . . . But it is not in the shopper's best interest that the opening hours of shops should be restricted by Act of Parliament.'

It is also possible to detect Grimond's hand in the repeated denunciations of the malign effects of advertising. Grimond's response to the growing slickness of advertising was impeccably Asquithian, just like his views on press freedom. As a liberal, he found the idea of restricting freedom of expression repugnant. On the other hand, he desperately wished that people would restrain themselves from infringing reasonable standards of honesty and decency. 'It is very doubtful whether . . . restraint of advertising would help consumers,' conceded the text. On the other hand, 'this does not mean that all is well with advertising.' The problem was that advertisements, through hyperbole or through the bogus association of ideas or events, can so easily mislead people – consciously or unconsciously – without actually containing a lie: 'Many advertisements, to the sophisticated, appear to make misleading statements. These are not merely harmless untruths, as practitioners on the defence are prone to claim. Any untruth, particularly when it is widely publicised, must serve to erode moral standards.' This may sound slightly pious or censorious, but it reverberates with Grimond's deeper fears about the effects of advertising.

On the eve of the party's 1960 autumn assembly, Grimond produced a substantial pamphlet entitled *Let's Get On With It!* As its impatient title implies, although this pamphlet was perfectly cogent, it was perhaps rather less elegant than most of Grimond's work, and rather more aggressive. It consisted of a demolition job on state socialism followed by a lengthy section in which the author 'argues the need for a new leap forward by the Left'.[45] Grimond criticised the Labour Party, as epitomised by Richard Crossman, for its belief that the British should 'tighten our belts and get behind our moat'[46] and for its continuing adherence to nationalisation. Crossman had recently produced a pamphlet in which he argued that the West could compete with the Communist bloc economically only if it expanded the public sector, and politically in the eyes of the developing world if it dropped its obsession with consumer goods in favour of something more like 'the solid respectability of the Communist way of life'.[47] That a senior figure from the 'legitimate' Labour left should peddle Soviet propaganda in this fashion seems surprising today. For Grimond, it was proof of the bankruptcy and intellectual dishonesty of Labour. His rejoinder was that 'if respectability means a society which is stupefyingly orthodox and dull while all human values of humanity and decency stand at a discount, this seems to be having the worst of both worlds . . . You have the appalling tyranny of Russia plus aesthetic stagnation.'[48] As for the nationalised industries, they were hopelessly and irredeemably inefficient: furthermore, 'the appointment of Labour establishment figures to run them is holding up their image as part of our heritage, like half-timbered houses and the Church of England . . . It is not that way that dynamism lies . . . nationalisation on our model has made the problem worse . . . The most unmanageable part of the economy is now the nationalised part.'[49]

Grimond's own thesis was not that a *laissez-faire* economy would be the answer. Whilst rejecting the proposed solutions of the state socialists, he did accept that 'there is . . . the feeling that we have got our priorities wrong.'[50] He took forward, this time under his own name, much of the thinking initially set out in *Better Buys*. As much on grounds of good taste as economic efficiency, he takes to task many of the practices of the private sector. At the heart of *Let's Get On With It!* was a treatise against the trend towards ostentatiousness, and the growing problem of 'private indulgence amid public squalor'. His distaste for modern advertising techniques again came to the fore – 'we are led by the nose in directions which we don't really want'[51] – and he argued that politicians must take a heavy share of the blame for the modern obsession with 'ostentatious expenditure'.[52] He feared that 'the competitive, free enterprise system has degenerated into private monopoly – and the politician has gloried in the shoddy workmanship purveyed by many of these monopolies.'[53] The obsession with prestige and profit has debased civil society. Those who undertook voluntary work, for example, or were responsible for other forms of 'valuable, uncommercialised services' are accorded little or no prestige. Grimond also quoted – approvingly – Alan Peacock's statement that 'the true object of the welfare state is to teach people how to do without it!'[54] Having identified problems that were as much spiritual as they are economic or social, Grimond suggested some disappointingly pedestrian solutions.

He also highlighted the importance of education, advocating opening up the public (independent) schools on the basis of ability, rather than wealth. He argued for a redefinition of the mixed economy, founded upon a re-evaluation of services which really must be provided by the public sector, as against those (such as the railways) that should be approached pragmatically, on the basis that 'there is no moral virtue in government management'.[55] Grimond was not against public ownership, as such, but warned: 'we must ensure that we are getting value for money.'[56] The underrated role for government, he argued, was in assisting certain important industries to find the funds necessary for capital investment. The government's role in this should be geared more to the long term, and there should be far more transfers of personnel between the public and private sectors. He reiterated the Liberal view that the position of trade unions needed to be rationalised – 'the use of the strike weapon against the public or other unions, under the privileged legal position of trades unionists, must give way to the general interest'[57] – and argued that, through schemes of profit sharing and co-ownership, the remuneration of workers should be far more closely linked to changes in their productivity, rather than to their ability to cause trouble for the employers. Grimond also took the opportunity to pour scorn on the advocates of unilateral nuclear disarmament.

The closing section of the pamphlet contained a naked appeal to liberal-minded social democrats to play their part in a realignment of politics. As part of what Grimond termed the 'Darwinian revolution in politics',[58] the state socialists should get out of the way and allow the new, liberal radicals to the fore. This required the break-up of the Labour Party, he argued, because it was utterly impotent as a vehicle for change. Despite the vast efforts of its more liberal members, its credibility was continually destroyed by the deadweight of state socialists, who revelled in industrial confrontation, preached the virtues of nationalisation in the face of all the evidence and refused to countenance the pooling of national sovereignty: 'the elements which are strangling it should form their own socialist national party . . . They would then leave the only possible road of advance clear.'[59] Then Grimond came back to what seems to have been, for him at least, the main liberal dilemma. He believed in freedom, and rejected a homogeneous, orthodox way of life; he had the true liberal's love of diversity and free expression; but, as a man of good taste and moderate views, he was always discomfited by the way in which society was prone to degeneration if people abused their freedoms. For example, in the case of one of his own favourite bugbears, Grimond accepted that there are attractive arguments for legislating against the kind of advertising that promoted 'the indefinite production of consumption goods on the margin of luxury and deliberately designed for obsolescence'.[60]

Jo Grimond was the first to acknowledge that liberalism can be a knotty and tricky philosophy. By definition it does not set out to provide any definitive, absolute answers to the problems of the human condition. At most, it can be used to justify the gentle steering of individuals or groups in certain directions. Almost the only principle of liberal government is a general assumption against state interventions, with the onus of proof always on the advocates of expanding the role of the state. Furthermore, despite its many vulgar and disagreeable aspects, Western society was by any token preferable to the horrors of the Soviet bloc. The same freedoms that sometimes indulge anti-social behaviour and the grotesque self-indulgence of the wealthy also allow positive free expression at all levels, stimulating the creativity of everyone from artists to entrepreneurs. As Grimond put it here, even if one accepts the case for some state intervention in the workings of a free society, 'it would be an extremely delicate operation to cut out the bad and leave the good . . . I pin my faith on education and on improved public example.'[61] Grimond's parting shot on advertising supplied an example of what he meant. To ban it would entail an obvious curtailing of freedom. Yet the state actively encouraged advertising by allowing it to be offset against tax which, after all, implied a value judgement. Grimond never objected to consumption *per se*; indeed he mocked the Stalinist machismo of economic planners who vaunt investment as an end in itself, contrasted with the self-indulgent evils of consumption. 'All investment in a free society is for the purpose of ultimate consumption,' reflected Grimond. 'A country in which power stations are built to make more power stations to make more power stations would indeed be a sort of puritan cloud-cuckoo-land.'[62] Forty years on, this might sound a bit feeble, but it is always essential to bear in mind that proclamations of absolutes and ultimate objectives are the antithesis of liberal democracy.

Two more policy pamphlets emanated from the 'New Directions' groups. The first, drafted by Harry Cowie but going out under Grimond's name, was entitled *Growth not Grandeur*. At its 1960 assembly, the Liberal Party had adopted two five-year plans – itself an unexpectedly Stalinist-sounding gambit. The first was to raise industrial production, the second to 'make Britain a better place to live in'. The second, 'quality of life', agenda was developed quite dramatically here. For example, education was very pointedly dealt with not in a cold-blooded 'investment in people' fashion, but in the context of passing on the values of civilisation, its stated purpose 'to civilise our affluent society'.[63] On the question of economic growth, Grimond and Cowie's pamphlet was an odd mixture of the old-fashioned and the groundbreaking. For example they suggested that, if the government were to adopt a firm growth target, that would of itself give industry greater confidence, inducing it to invest more. This seems a little naïve, to put it kindly. More plausibly, there was also a restatement of the Liberal belief in greater competition and a suggestion that the government should establish tax-free savings accounts very much akin to the Personal Equity Plans (PEPs) or Independent Savings Accounts (ISAs) that prevail today. They also proclaimed the virtues of hypothecated taxation, in order that the electorate should be able 'to judge any particular proposal with regard to the cost, who would have to pay for it and how much they themselves would have to pay'.[64] Nothing less, in the view of the authors, would put an end to the prevailing 'auction between political parties who advocate reforms which no one really wants to pay for'.[65]

Another *New Directions* pamphlet followed hot on the heels of *Growth not Grandeur*. In *Opportunity Knocks*, published at the end of July 1961, Professor Michael Fogarty of Cardiff University set out to put the 'social' back into the social market economy. More generous terms for redundancy, combined with retraining schemes, were proposed and the concept of 'co-responsibility' is introduced here for the first time, as a development of previous Liberal policy.

Various forms of co-responsibility were dealt with, including German-style co-determination, consumer representation at board level and the creation of representative works councils. This led on to what must at that time have seemed like rather novel reflections on the social responsibilities of industrial concerns, and on the ways in which the government might intervene more actively in industrial disputes, in the interests of the general good, particularly as a means of curbing inflation. Most interesting of all, perhaps, was the call for a form of 'inflation tax' – still the policy of the SDP/Liberal Alliance over a quarter of a century later – to deter private-sector employers from granting unsustainable pay increases. 'If persuasion fails,' warned the text, 'the State should be prepared to ensure, by adjustment of taxation, that the offenders pay back through taxation what they have gained by their selfishness.'[66] Decentralised pay bargaining and intensified government action to reduce prices for consumers would intensify the war against inflation. In the 1964–6 Parliament, though he had a larger parliamentary team to help shoulder the burden, Grimond continued to lead across a broad front. Although few voters raised the question of inflation with him, he remained convinced that few, if any, greater problems faced Britain in the long term. He also doubted whether a government so mindful of its own popularity, or lack of it, would ever take the necessary decisions to curb price rises: 'One of our troubles in the past . . . is that constantly one body, whether it be a union, or the farmers, or a profession, or, indeed, politicians themselves, says that it must have an increase because someone else has had one already. It is these across-the-board increases which have bedevilled the economy in the last 10 or 15 years.'[67]

As Grimond tried to steady Liberal nerves in 1962–3 after post-Orpington euphoria had subsided into a general gloom, his thoughts again turned to the writing of a book, in advance of the forthcoming general election. This time Bodley Head were the publishers, paying an advance of £100 against royalties. The handwritten manuscript was produced on several hundred sheets of House of Commons notepaper, and Grimond claimed to have written this tome 'on planes and trains' (Laura confirming that 'I've never seen him write a word – he certainly doesn't do any of it at home'). In places, it shows. Though Grimond did take forward his thinking on some of the specific social services, *The Liberal Challenge*, published in October 1963, lacked the focus and force of its notable predecessor, *The Liberal Future*. He carried on very much along the lines put forward during the early 1960s by the semi-official policy groups that he had set up. As one would expect with Grimond, many of these passages were packed with interesting and radical ideas far ahead of their time. The book also showed itself to be an odd hybrid: interwoven with some dry sections about the possible mechanics of policy were seriously philosophical passages about aesthetics and the nature of civilisation. Grimond loved setting out complex and thoughtful ideas, but he was sensitive too to the charge that the Liberals were too idealistic, and lacked both common sense and practical policies. The marriage of ideals and policies attempted here didn't quite work, but it certainly kept the reader guessing about what was coming next.

Even more than in *The Liberal Future,* Grimond set out here to establish the rational and ethical basis of his political outlook: 'for me the content of politics is all important'.[68] He set out to be radical in the etymological sense of the word, by going to the very roots of political problems, and of human society itself. If there was one theme that recurs throughout the text, was is his fear that the democratic political process was being subverted by the emergence of certain interest groups strong enough to bring sustained pressure to bear on the political class. Members of Parliament, he feared, were losing sight of their real responsibility, namely keeping a critical eye on the executive branch of government. Meanwhile, pressure groups were attempting to influence ministers, MPs and government officials with their special pleading, resulting in an ever more complex web of subsidies and grants, all based on the supposition that anyone who can organise and bring pressure to bear must be a 'special case'. Consequently 'it is almost impossible now to argue against the claims of any group for more state aid, because they can always show either that some other comparable group gets aid, or that the state has intervened to deprive them of their own natural advantages.'[69] In this world of competing interests, argued Grimond, it was not the natural justice of the case that counted: it was how loudly its advocates could shout, and how much trouble they were capable of causing. Meanwhile, the role of the state in arbitrating according to the 'general good' went out of the window, and public expenditure was likely to go on rising indefinitely unless politicians had the courage to say 'No!' As Grimond put it: 'economy may be approved of in general, but it is the sum of the particulars which counts and each particular interest wants more expenditure.'[70]

There is an obvious flaw here and, if more of Grimond's opponents had possessed the necessary patience they might have exploited it more effectively. For Grimond himself had only recently enjoined Liberals to take full advantage of the politics of protest – the single-issue, oppositional style of politics that fanned the flames of the cynicism that he was deploring here. In his closing speech to the party assembly in 1960, for instance, he had proclaimed that 'every time a Liberal councillor gets a bus stop moved to a better place he strikes a blow for his party'. A few days after that he wrote proudly of how the Liberals were 'getting Labour workers and Labour votes coming over at constituency level . . . That's where the movement to Liberalism is growing . . . Of course it will take time to reach the top but it is much healthier that it should begin at the roots'.[71] Under his leadership, the Liberals were deliberately contributing to the culture of complaint, exploiting grudges rather than synthesising aspirations. Grimond's basic argument here about government expenditure of taxpayers' money – that there was too much of it – is also hard to take totally seriously. The book was full of assertions that more money should be spent on this or that. There was his proposed Highland Development Board, which would be 'manned with experts' and have 'money to spend'.[71] Then, Grimond asserted, 'Liberals would increase total expenditure on education.'[72] He conceded too that 'the total taken by the social services may rise for a considerable time.'[73] Meanwhile pension rates too must rise substantially[74] and spending on 'communal services . . . should be extended'.[75] Then, in the one burst of real, out-and-out eccentricity, there was Grimond's apparent endorsement of a proposal from J K Galbraith that 'unemployment pay should be at much the same rate as basic wage rates, so that there was an incentive for more people to choose leisure rather than work.'[76] Grimond was always scornful of the sort of unworkable ideas that the liberal intelligentsia were prone to propounding over their claret, yet here he was surely leading the charge. He and his colleagues knew that they were vulnerable to the charge of trying to be all things to all voters yet in this book, perhaps as a consequence of writing it in too many different times and places, Grimond was as woolly as anyone.

This is a shame, because much of the more orthodox liberal material in the book was so very good. Grimond came closer here than he did anywhere else to explaining what he meant by 'planning'. What he meant by it was not state intervention on a vast scale, or the enforced reallocation of resources. First of all, he believed that many of the country's troubles stemmed directly from insecurity about the future and uncertainty about future economic policy. He felt too that the tax system encouraged consumption rather than saving and investment, which reduced potential growth in the medium term and stability in the longer term. By economic 'planning' Grimond really meant what today might be termed 'coordination' of economic and fiscal policy. He certainly did not mean nationalisation or further encroachments on the operations of the free market: 'Liberals believe that private enterprise is an important freedom and a protection for private liberties which will wither if the state takes too much power into its own hands.'[77] This was not to be taken as advocacy of a *laissez-faire* economy, however. Once again this was very much the 'social market' (though Grimond never used the phrase), where private enterprise was expected to 'justify the support the community gives it'.[78] This means operating on a fair, even-handed and non-monopolistic basis, with legislation used primarily to advance the interests of consumers and workers.

In the section on international affairs, Grimond detailed his latest thoughts on internationalism, setting an ultimate objective of 'world government'. World government, for Grimond, was a preferable alternative to a development that he observed in the early 1960s, the emergence of regional groupings, united and defined in most cases by little more than their opposition to each other. Grimond feared that this limited form of 'internationalism' would in time do more harm than good, merely replacing 'the old selfish nation states with their belligerency and their protectionism by more powerful bodies behaving in the same way'.[79] So what did Grimond actually mean by 'world government'? He does not seem to have been thinking literally, in terms of a body possessing a directly elected assembly or a head of state. What it appears to boil down to is a beefed-up United Nations, less hamstrung by vetoes from an out-of-date Security Council and better able to police trouble spots. He foresaw the potential development of 'rogue states' in the nuclear age, and wanted civilisation to set up a force capable of dealing with them. In effect, what Grimond meant by 'world government' was 'world rule of law'.

This book ultimately struck an optimistic note. Although Grimond was deeply disturbed about the prevailing political situation at home, he was evidently (and rightly) proud of the role that he had played in establishing a reasonably credible alternative to the Tory-Labour duopoly. He regarded Labour and the Tories as the terrible twins of politics, operating in much the same way, through a corrupted form of tripartism between government, the trade unions and industry, and systematically failing to address the structural needs of the UK economy. The only appreciable difference between them was that Labour favoured the unions and the Tories favoured the bosses. There is no mistaking in the *Liberal Challenge* Grimond's feeling that the carapace of the party system really may have cracked, that the essential foundations of a political realignment could be in place. With regard to international affairs, Grimond was always warning, in a measured and thorough fashion, of the continuing threat from Communism. He also foresaw the emergence of China as a force on the world stage, but nowhere was his essential faith more apparent. He believed in civilisation and civilised values, as distinct from the barbarism of fascism or Communism, and he believed too in the ability of liberal democracy not only to endure where it was already well established, but also to prosper and to expand its sphere of influence.

It was fifteen years before Grimond produced his next major book, a work about the social services entitled *The Common Welfare*. Its thesis would not have surprised anyone familiar with his speeches: the welfare services were too centralised, at best ameliorating and, at worst, exacerbating social problems. Furthermore, the mistake was constantly being made of trying to separate people from institutions that were supposed to serve them. A distinctly 'conservative' aspect to Grimond's thinking emerged here, as he emphasised not so much the individual as the sustainable nature of shared values. He conceded that 'Conservatives are right to stress the importance of institutions and of loyalty to them, for institutions are the instruments of the community and their multiplicity a guarantee of choice and freedom'[80] and that 'just as freedom depends on order, personal choice and expression . . .

can only flourish in a community which has a common loyalty among its members.'[81] This was worlds away from the individualism of the classical liberals, and from the centralised collectivism of social democrats of Grimond's generation. Welfare should be taken in the round, he argued, embracing all aspects of governmental or communal activity, which should generally be as decentralised as possible. He also restated his belief in the 'social market': a society built upon the foundations of the market economy, rejecting the bureaucratic outlook but giving the utmost priority to the creation and maintenance of social cohesion. This belief did nothing to blunt the radical edge that Grimond was again demonstrating: he advocated more charges in the healthcare system, student loans and education vouchers. He also reasserted the 'Golden Rule' (to do unto others . . .) and picked up on the writings of the US political thinker John Rawls, who had recently produced a modern, liberal definition of the 'general good', in the form of his 'difference principle'.

It is possible to discern the confluence of several diverse influences in this book. Grimond's almost neo-conservative emphasis on the acceptance and continuity of institutions sat alongside a restatement of his belief in co-ownership and a voluntary form of guild socialism: 'socialism without the state'. He also made a strong claim for the importance of home ownership: 'I find it difficult to believe that a community largely composed of weekly or monthly tenants will be a satisfactory society.'[82] There was an informed reassessment too of the thinking of Grimond's fellow Scot, Adam Smith, and a clear exposition of the indissoluble link between political freedom and economic freedom. More fundamental is the distinction that Grimond draws between the centralised welfare state, with the citizen as the powerless client, and a 'welfare society', in which the citizen was expected to be an interested participant, rather than the supine recipient of handouts. Finally there was Grimond's touchstone of decentralisation in all its forms, with responsibility and accountability at the lowest practicable level.

There is no disguising the main thrust of this book. Grimond was still a 'social liberal', but he was convinced that the pendulum had swung too far in the direction of the state. Radical action was therefore needed before freedom was lost, perhaps forever. He was challenging the nostrums of a society so economically degenerate and politically dropsical that it seemed doomed. In that spirit of no-holds-barred radicalism, he challenged all the assumptions that had poisoned political discourse since the late 1940s: that the free enterprise system was morally dubious, that despite being undermined and attacked at every turn, it would go on producing the wealth to sustain all the non-productive people and sectors, and that it was better to spend other people's money than one's own. Ludicrously, such thoughts, rooted in the best liberal traditions and in basic common sense, were often seen as the preserve

of the 'radical right'. They were nothing of the sort. Perhaps the choicest
Grimondism in this book came when he wrote of an unnamed woman who
had given up a job in Marks & Spencer for what she described as a more
'worthwhile' job in the social services. This was too much for Grimond:

> Apart from the fact that a job in social services carries complete security and
> a pension linked to prices and beyond the dreams of most producers, I would
> suspect that Marks & Spencers have done more to improve the living standards
> of the worse-off than do most social workers. But the climate of the time
> deludes people into thinking that civil service jobs are more meritorious than
> production or distribution.[85]

Forty years before, Grimond had been one of the many Liberals who had
taken up the Beveridge Plan as a panacea for all the land's troubles. He had
now broken free. Only three years later he would go even further, claiming
that the welfare state had become 'positively' malevolent in the eyes of those it
should be helping.[84]

In 1983 Grimond produced another remarkable book, arguably both his
most radical and readable of all. Originally contracted under the title
Policies for the Alliance, Grimond's *A Personal Manifesto* distilled much of
his later radicalism quite beautifully. Written in less than two months, the
book revolted against what Grimond regarded as the centripetal, nascent
'Butskellism', of the SDP-Liberal Alliance as it went into the election. He was
horrified that the leadership of the Alliance, far from being genuinely radical,
was returning to many of the nostrums of old consensual politics, presenting
itself not as a fresh alternative but as a grouping of the 'safe centre'. These
were the politics of the lowest common denominator and Grimond felt that
someone had to speak out. As he wrote to the publisher: 'Liberal views are
sometimes much nearer to the SDP than they are to "Grimond".'[85] The final
version of his book made that point only too clearly, in a text so accessible and
congenial that the *Economist* likened its style to 'that of a man thinking aloud
in the company of friends'.[86]

Grimond's target had not changed, but much of his thinking comes into
sharper focus than it had for a long time. The journalistic mosaic of recent
years was replaced by a single, coherent political thesis in which Grimond
attacked not only the bureaucratic accretions of the pre-Thatcher era, but
also the apparent failure of Conservative ministers post–1979, despite their
very clear mandate, to 'roll back the frontiers of the state'. Although some
critics professed themselves unimpressed, or even offended, by Grimond's
occasionally dismissive attitude towards other parties, the book was certainly
intellectually impressive. Its air of patrician loftiness would never be to
everyone's taste, but Grimond was certainly right in predicting that the
policies of the Alliance would soon be stranded by the strong political tides
that were beginning to appear. The vein of decentralisation runs like gold

through the text, as Grimond restated the all-important parallels, so often neglected by Liberals and Social Democrats alike, between the social and economic spheres: in both of which freedom, responsibility, accountability and democracy were under threat from bureaucratic corporatism. In the preface, Grimond warned that the Alliance 'sometimes appears a little bland, even conservative',[87] and it was this fear that informed most of what followed, as Grimond floated a number of familiar ideas that had found no place in official SDP-Liberal thinking.

It was perhaps in the realm of economics that Grimond went furthest out on a limb. It seems odd now, but at that time a belief in a statutory incomes policy was almost a *sine qua non* for Liberals and Social Democrats, few of whom foresaw that the largely unfettered free market might overcome inflation by natural economic forces alone. Although Grimond did not wish to appear disloyal or tackle alone a particularly favoured sacred cow, he could not bring himself to endorse anything more than a very short-term incomes policy, and that only as an emergency measure, to be kept 'as simple as possible'.[88] He was clearly shocked that Liberals, out of habit or laziness, should have fallen into the habit of relying on an incomes policy as a routine instrument: 'it shows that common feelings, the bonds of a liberal society, have collapsed . . . It renounces the market and one important liberty, the liberty of everyone to sell his labour.'[89] Unlike most of his colleagues, Grimond did believe that a programme of structural reform could obviate the need for any intervention of this kind in the long term, which would kill off once and for all serious discussion of a policy that he likened here to 'an attempt to drive the economy with one foot on the accelerator and the other on the brake'.[90] Other chapters of the book covered more time-honoured ground. Grimond's dalliance with anarcho-syndicalism was revisited, as he cited Mondragon again in advocating a system of 'socialism without the state' in which the 'genuine entrepreneur, not the financial gambler' will be both respected and rewarded.[91] He also rehearsed once again the arguments for a radical rethink of the welfare state, expressing his hope that the welfare services, like the centralised state itself, will in time wither on the vine, to be replaced by a liberal society. He also called for less distortion in the housing market, with a transition from subsidised housing to targeted income support for those in need. His parting shot to the unilateralists was agreeably robust: 'The rabbit sets a splendid example of non-belligerence. The stoat eats it just the same.'[92]

Grimond signed off his last political book by explicitly emphasising his common ground with the 'One Nation' tradition within the Conservative Party. Consciously or not, Grimond echoed a piece that he himself had written almost thirty years earlier: 'I find myself in agreement with much Conservative policy, but I cannot say that I think it has always been put into practice. Progress towards a "property-owning democracy" has been slow.

How can it be hastened unless Conservative governments take steps to spread ownership in industry and land?'[93] He desperately regretted the way in which the bureaucratic state had helped to accentuate the differences between groups in the country. 'Politics,' he wrote in the conclusion to *A Personal Manifesto*, 'has become not so much a means of achieving some common good as a means by which various interest groups can pursue their own advantage.'[94] He might have added that any political system is likely to go the same way unless its leaders are constantly alert to the dangers. He continued:

> a free, individualist, liberal society can exist only when there are strong bonds to hold it together. Some of these bonds – such as common tradition, respect for generally accepted values, reverence for institutions, restraint upon greed – have weakened. All are essential to liberalism . . . The order imposed by dictatorships takes over when natural order breaks down. The machinery of the state must then enforce some sort of order based on fear, not consent.[95]

Can there have been a clearer or more compelling exposition since 1979 of a society based upon shared values of tolerance and personal responsibility, economic freedom and social cohesion? Could there ever be a better statement of 'One Nation'?

REFERENCES

Chapter One

1. *W E Gladstone* (2 vols, 1880).
2. Jo Grimond, *Memoirs* (Heinemann, 1979), p. 2.
3. Sun, 5th September 1968.
4. Grimond, *Memoirs*, p. 34.
5. Kyle I.
6. Daily Telegraph, 31st January 1983.
7. Grimond, *Memoirs*, pp. 40–41.
8. Ibid., p.30.
9. Sun, 16th March 1967.
10. Jo Grimond, *The St Andrews of Jo Grimond* (Alan Sutton, 1992), p. 32.
11. Grimond, *Memoirs*, p. 31.
12. Spectator, 16th January 1982.
13. Grimond, *Memoirs*, p.35.
14. Kyle I.
15. Bernard Fergusson, *Eton Portrait* (John Miles, 1937), p. 1.
16. Ibid., p. 185.
17. Grimond, *Memoirs*, pp. 45–6.
18. Ibid., p. 45.
19. Ibld.
20. Grimond, *Memoirs*, pp. 54–5.
21. Ibid., p. 44.
22. Astor interview with the author.
23. Handwritten essay by Jo Grimond, Eton College Archive.
24. Change (one-off Eton journal,1935).
25. Grimond, *Memoirs*, p. 43.
26. F. Bolkestein (ed.), *Modern Liberalism* (Elsevier Science Publishers, 1982), p. 82
27. Handwritten essay by Jo Grimond, Eton College Archive.
28. Change.
29. William Douglas Home, *Mr Home Pronounced Hume* (William Collins, 1979), p. 46.
30. Spectator, 16th January 1982.
31. Isis, 9th May 1934.

Chapter Two

1. Ann Thwaite (ed.), *My Oxford* (Robson Books, 1977), p. 111.
2. Isis, 2nd May 1934.
3. House of Lords Official Report, 19th May 1988, col. 451.
4. Thwaite, *My Oxford*, p. 114.
5. Isis, 9th May 1934.

6. Philip Toynbee, *Friends Apart* (MacGibbon & Kee, 1954), p. 48.
7. Isis, 25th October 1933.
8. Ibid., 29th November 1933.
9. Ibid., 17th January 1934.
10. Ibid., 9th May 1934.
11. Ibid., 25th April 1934.
12. Ibid.
13. Ibid., 30th May 1934.
14. Ibid., 24th May 1934.
15. Ibid., 24th January 1934.
16. Thwaite, *My Oxford*, p. 116.
17. Letter, VBC Collection, n.d.
18. Sunday Telegraph, 19th June 1994.
19. Submission on future of Birmingham University, RB 148, 3rd May 1972.
20. Hansard, 13th May 1953, col. 2525.
21. The Times, 25th March 1993.
22. Grimond, *Memoirs*, p. 66.
23. Grimond, *St Andrews*, p.46.
24. Sun, 21st April 1966.
25. Mearns Leader and Kincardineshire Mail, 21st November 1935.
26. Grimond, *Memoirs*, p. 66.
27. Oxford Guardian, 26th October 1937.
28. Grimond, *Memoirs*, p. 67.
29. Ibid.
30. Ibid.
31. Jo Grimond, *The Liberal Challenge* (Hollis & Carter, 1963), p.220.
32. Observer, 16th May 1976.
33. Ibid.
34. Grimond, *Memoirs*, p. 79.
35. Lionel Brett, *Our Selves Unknown* (Gollancz, 1985), p. 62.
36. Letter dated 16th September 1937, VBC Collection.
37. Letter dated 26th September 1937, VBC Collection.
38. This Is Your Life, 1983.
39. Letter dated 29th September 1937, VBC Collection.
40. Letter, VBC Collection, n.d.
41. Letter dated 27th November 1937, VBC Collection.
42. Ibid.
43. Grimond, *Memoirs*, p. 71.
44. Postcards dated 28–31 December 1937, VBC Collection.
45. Letter dated 8th February 1938, VBC Collection.
46. Colin Coote, *The Other Club* (Sidgwick & Jackson, 1971), p. 128.
47. Letter dated 7th August 1938, VBC Collection.

Chapter Three

1. Spectator, 16th March 1985.
2. Letter to the author.
3. Sun, 26th February 1967.
4. Annette Penhaligon, *Penhaligon* (Bloomsbury, 1989), p. 70.
5. Letter, VBC Collection, n.d.
6. Ibid.
7. Letter postmarked 28th December 1940, VBC Collection.

8. Letter dated 28th December 1940, VBC Collection.
9. R. J. B. Sellar, *The Fife and Forfar Yeomanry, 1919–1956* (Blackwood, 1960), p. 141.
10. Letter to the author.
11. Letter dated 4–5 May 1941, VBC Collection.
12. Daily Telegraph, 11th October 1990.
13. Grimond, *Memoirs*, p.91.
14. Mark Pottle (ed.), *Champion Redoubtable* (Weidenfeld & Nicolson, 1998), p.268.
15. Grimond, *Memoirs*, p.98.
16. Ibid., p. 99.
17. Letter dated 19th February 1945, VBC Collection.
18. Ibid.
19. Brett, *Our Selves Unknown*, p. 91.
20. This Is Your Life, 1983.
21. P. Delaforce, *Red Crown and Dragon* (Tom Donovan, 1996), p. 216.
22. Kurt Grobecker, *Das Atlantic Hotel zu Hamburg* (Maria Faber Verlag, 1999), p. 148.
23. Grimond, *Memoirs*, p.128.
24. Letter dated 13th April 1945, VBC Collection.
25. Letter dated 21st October 1944, quoted in Duncan Brack and Robert Ingham, *Dictionary of Liberal Quotations* (Politicos, 1999).
26. Letter dated 31st May 1945, VBC Collection.
27. Ruth McInry interview with the author.
28. Ibid.
29. George Woodbridge, *UNRRA* (Columbia University Press, New York, 1950) vol. I, p. 251.
30. Cable dated 29th August 1945, UN Archive, New York.
31. Daily Telegraph, 4th May 1987.
32. Minute Ref S 213, 23rd January 1946.
33. Grimond, *Memoirs*, p.135.
34. McNeil to Gale, 29th January 1947, UN Archive, New York.
35. UN Archive, New York.

Chapter Four

1. Orkney Liberals Minute Book.
2. Field, 1st November 1986.
3. NTS Executive Minutes, 27th November 1946.
4. Minutes of meeting of NTS Council, 5th February 1948, NTS Archive, Edinburgh.
5. NTS Archives, Edinburgh.
6. NTS Executive Minutes, 29th September 1948.
7. Houses of Outstanding Historic or Architectural Interest: Report of a Committee Appointed by the Chancellor of the Exchequer (HMSO, 1950), para. 74.
8. Ibid., para. 75.
9. Hansard, 3rd July 1953, col. 783.
10. Dalyell conversation with the author.
11. Ibid.
12. Interview with the author.
13. Orkney Liberals Minute Book, 19th November 1948.
14. Letter dated 4th December 1948, VBC Collection.

15. Ibid.
16. Ibid.
17. Letter dated 14th December 1948, VBC Collection.
18. Letter dated 14th February 1949, VBC Collection.
19. Cited in Mark Pottle (ed.), *Daring to Hope* (Weidenfeld & Nicolson, 2000), pp. 62–3.
20. Letter dated 6th March 1949, VBC Collection.
21. Pottle, *Daring to Hope*, p.65.
22. Shetland Times, 16th June 1972.
23. Orkney Liberals Minute Book.
24. Minutes of NTS Council meeting, 13th April 1949, NTS Archive, Edinburgh.
25. NTS Executive Minutes, 22nd June 1949, NTS Archive, Edinburgh.
26. Letter dated 30th July 1979, GP/NLS.
27. Orkney Herald, 2nd August 1949.
28. Ibid.
29. Ibid.
30. Ibid., 1st November 1949.
31. Ibid., 22nd November 1949.
32. Ibid.
33. Ibid.
34. Letter dated 14th December 1948, VBC Collection.
35. Grimond Collection, Kirkwall Library.
36. Orkney Herald, 14th February 1950.
37. Rosie Wallace (ed.), *Jo and Laura Grimond* (Orkney and Shetland Liberal Democrats, 2000), p. 84.
38. Meadowcroft interview with the author.
39. Private source.
40. Orkney Herald, 21st February 1950.
41. Wallace, *Jo and Laura Grimond*, p. 14.
42. Grimond, *Memoirs*, p. 145.
43. Ibid., p.142.

Chapter Five

1. Grimond, *Memoirs*, pp. 147–50.
2. Ibid., p. 148.
3. Hansard, 10th March 1950, col. 626.
4. Ibid., cols. 628–9.
5. House of Commons, 27th June 1950.
6. Daily Telegraph, 15th May 1950.
7. The Times, 11th November 1950.
8. Ibid.
9. Letter dated 16th September 1950, VBC Collection.
10. Letter dated 18th September 1950, VBC Collection.
11. Letter dated 20th September 1950, VBC Collection.
12. Kirkwood interview with the author.
13. Official Report, Standing Committee C, 27th February 1951, col. 1121.
14. Grimond Collection, Kirkwall Library.
15. Liberal Orkney, 1951.
16. Pottle, *Daring to Hope*, p.117
17. Hansard, 1st May 1953, cols. 2539–42.
18. Grimond, *Memoirs*, p. 176.

19. The Times, 13th May 1953.
20. Hansard, 11th March 1954, col. 2535.
21. Ibid., col. 2539.
22. Ibid., 29th July 1954, col. 785.
23. Ibid., 23rd March 1955, col. 2140.
24. Ibid., 25th March 1955, col. 2468.
25. Conversation with Alan Beith.
26. Official Report, 1st July 1953, cols. 2716–19.
27. *Scottish Committee Official Report*, 24th April 1956, col. 602.
28. Scottish Committee Report, 13th July 1954, col. 1781.
29. Manchester Guardian, 18th April 1955.
30. Ibid.
31. Ibid.

Chapter Six

1. Reproduced in *Liberal Orkney*, 1955, Grimond Archive, Kirkwall Library.
2. Daily Mail, 13th May 1955.
3. Ibid.
4. Observer, 22nd May 1955.
5. Manchester Guardian, 25th July 1955.
6. Daily Telegraph, 3rd August 1955.
7. Manchester Guardian, 14th October 1955.
8. Hansard, 20th June 1956, cols. 1487–8.
9. Manchester Guardian, 25th July 1955.
10. Ibid.
11. Minute dated 14th May 1954, LSE Collection.
12. Sunday Express, 23rd September 1956.
13. Grimond, *Memoirs*, p. 188.
14. Manchester Guardian, 29th September 1956.
15. Daily Telegraph, 29th September 1956.
16. Kyle II.
17. The Times, 1st October 1956.
18. Conversation with John Cole.
19. Coventry Evening Telegraph, 29th September 1956.
20. The Times, 1st October 1956.
21. Kyle II.
22. BBC Television, 29th September 1956.
23. New Statesman and Nation, 6th October 1956.
24. Manchester Guardian, 20th August 1956.
25. The Times, 3rd November 1956.
26. Northern Daily Echo, 5th March 1955.
27. News Chronicle, 12th November 1956.
28. Hansard, 8th November 1956, col. 293.
29. The Times, 29th December 1956.
30. News Chronicle, 18th December 1956.
31. Liberal Collection, LSE.
32. The Times, 12th January 1957.
33. Liberal Collection, LSE.
34. Daily Mail, 26th March 1957.
35. Manchester Guardian, 16th February 1957.
36. Grimond, *Memoirs*, p.157.

37. Manchester Guardian, 4th March 1957.
38. Ibid.
39. Bolton Evening News, 9th March 1957.
40. The Times, 1st April 1957.
41. Grimond, *Memoirs*, p.192.
42. Manchester Guardian, 22nd April 1957.
43. Oxford, 20th July 1957.
44. Ibid.
45. Oxford, 2nd August 1957.
46. Hansard, 25th July 1957, col. 616.
47. Manchester Guardian, 22nd July 1957.
48. The Times, 20th September 1957.
49. Southport, 21st September 1957.
50. Ibid.
51. News Chronicle, 2nd October 1957.
52. Bolton Evening News, 7th February 1958.
53. Daily Telegraph, 7th February 1958.
54. Minutes dated 15th February 1958, Liberal Collection, LSE.
55. Daily Telegraph, 20th February 1958.
56. Manchester Guardian, 12th March 1958.
57. Liberal Collection, LSE.

Chapter Seven

1. Pottle, *Daring to Hope*, p.194.
2. The Times, 21st March 1958.
3. Daily Telegraph, 26th March 1958.
4. Cited in Ian Gilmour and Mark Garnett, *Whatever Happened to the Tories?* (Fourth Estate, 1997), p.146.
5. Daily Telegraph, 19th February 1958.
6. Ibid, 14th April 1958.
7. Liberal Collection, LSE.
8. Ibid.
9. Margaret Wingfield interview with the author.
10. Evening News, 12th August 1958.
11. Speech at Burray, 15th October 1957.
12. Hansard, 11th February 1958, col. 272.
13. The Times, 22nd September 1958.
14. Liberal News, 25th September 1958.
15. Daily Telegraph, 11th November 1958.
16. Ibid.
17. Official Report, 10th July 1958, col. 224.
18. Official Report, 12th May 1959, col. 67.
19. Ibid.
20. Daily Telegraph, 11th July 1959.
21. Observer, 5th July 1959.
22. Bolton Evening News, 21st February 1959.
23. Ibid., 14th April 1959.
24. Daily Telegraph, 15th April 1959.
25. Ibid., 3rd August 1959.
26. Ibid.
27. Unst, 27th September 1955.

28. Grimond, *Memoirs*, p. 35.
29. Daily Telegraph, 4th September 1959.
30. Liberal News, 5th February 1959.
31. The Times, 16th September 1959.
32. Daily Telegraph, 17th September 1959.
33. People Count (1959), p.4.
34. Pottle, *Daring to Hope*, p.212.
35. Daily Mirror, 26th September 1959.
36. Basil Wishart, *Memoirs* (Beatrice Nesbit, 1998) p.140.
37. Ibid, pp. 136–7.
38. Daily Telegraph, 20th October 1959.
39. Wishart, *Memoirs*, p. 137.
40. Hunter Davies in the *Sunday Graphic*, 8th November 1959.
41. Ibid.
42. Robin Day, *Grand Inquisitor* (Weidenfeld & Nicolson, 1989), p. 137.
43. Ibid., p. 140.
44. Grimond, *Memoirs*, p. 202.
45. Guardian, 10th October 1959.
46. Observer, 11th October 1959.
47. The Times, 12th October 1959.
48. Kyle II.
49. Daily Telegraph, 17th October 1959.
50. Political Quarterly, vol. 31 (1960), p. 299.
51. Mark Abrams and Richard Rose, *Must Labour Lose?* (Penguin, 1960), p.119.
52. Ibid., p. 121.
53. Daily Telegraph, 30th November 1959.
54. Southport, 18th September 1957.

Chapter Eight

1. Liberal News, 19th November 1959.
2. Ibid., 17th December 1959.
3. The Times, 1st March 1960.
4. Ibid.
5. Liberal Collection, LSE.
6. Interview, *Journal of Liberal Democrat History*, Summer 2000, p. 3.
7. Minute dated 28th March 1960, Liberal Collection, LSE.
8. Daily Telegraph, 11th April 1960.
9. Ibid.
10. Southport, 19th March 1960.
11. Hansard, 8th April 1960, cols. 787–93.
12. Official Report, 10th December 1959, col. 26.
13. Official Report, 16th February 1960, col. 137.
14. Official Report, 12th July 1960, col. 36.
15. Official Report, 9th February 1961, col. 34.
16. Liberal Collection, LSE.
17. Ibid.
18. Bolton Evening News, 20th July 1960.
19. Observer, 29th May 1960.
20. Ibid.
21. Ibid.
22. The Times, 8th July 1960.

23. Ibid.
24. Daily Telegraph, 14th September 1960.
25. This is YOUR PARTY, p. 6.
26. Ibid.
27. Ibid., p. 7.
28. The Times, 3rd October 1960.
29. Ibid.
30. Daily Mail, 5th October 1960.
31. News Chronicle, 6th October 1960.
32. Minutes of Standing Committee Meeting, 29th November 1960, Liberal Collection, LSE.
33. Minutes of Standing Committee Meeting, 8th February 1961, Liberal Collection, LSE.
34. Daily Mail, 18th October 1960.
35. Guardian, 18th November 1960.
36. Evening News, 18th November 1960.
37. Hansard, 2nd November 1961, col. 370.
38. Ibid, 1st March 1961, col.1575.
39. Daily Telegraph, 16th March 1961.
40. Hansard, 22nd March 1961, cols. 487–90.
41. Peter Bartram, *David Steel: His Life and Politics* (W. H. Allen, 1981), p. 34.
42. Sun, 9th February 1967.
43. Transcript from the Edinburgh University Archive.
44. Pottle, *Daring to Hope*, p. 235.
45. Ibid.
46. Student, 12th January 1961.
47. Ibid.

Chapter Nine

1. Alistair Horne, *Macmillan* (Macdonald, 1988–9), p. 255.
2. Guardian, 26th April 1961.
3. The Times, 18th November 1961.
4. Guardian, 8th December 1961.
5. Hansard, 2nd November 1961, col. 368.
6. Philip Williams, *Hugh Gaitskell* (Jonathan Cape, 1979), p. 696.
7. Sunday Times, 19th November 1961.
8. Sunday Telegraph, 28th January 1962.
9. Daily Telegraph, 29th January 1962.
10. Daily Mail, 14th December 1961.
11. The Times, 15th March 1962.
12. Ibid.
13. Chitnis interview with the author.
14. Daily Telegraph, 22nd March 1962.
15. Harold Macmillan, *At the End of the Day* (Macmillan, 1973), p. 60.
16. Guardian, 30th March 1962.
17. Ibid.
18. The Times, 10th April 1962.
19. Sunday Telegraph, 15th April 1962.
20. Political Quarterly, vol. 33 (1962), p. 254.
21. Daily Sketch, 11th May 1962.
22. The Times, 19th May 1962.

23. Ibid.
24. Sunday Times, 20th May 1962.
25. Ibid.
26. Ibid.
27. Sunday Telegraph, 20th May 1962.
28. Ibid., 27th May 1962.
29. The Times, 26th May 1962.
30. Aberdeen, 25th May 1962.
31. Daily Telegraph, 2nd June 1962.
32. Ibid.
33. Sunday Telegraph, 24th June 1962.
34. Daily Mail, 15th June 1962.
35. Pottle, *Daring to Hope*, p. 259.
36. Ibid.
37. Daily Telegraph, 14th July 1962.
38. Melrose, 22nd July 1962.
39. Hansard, 26th July 1962, cols. 1786–90.
40. Daily Telegraph, 26th March 1962.
41. Melrose, 22nd July 1962.
42. Hansard, 11th December 1962, col. 24.
43. Beaumont interview with the author.
44. Sunday Telegraph, 23rd September 1962.
45. Sunday Times, 23rd September 1962.
46. Ibid.
47. BBC Radio, 24th September 1962.
48. The Times, 25th October 1962.
49. Daily Telegraph, 9th October 1962.

Chapter Ten

1. Hansard, 17th December 1962, col. 962.
2. Minutes of Executive Committee meeting, 26th January 1963, Liberal Collection, LSE.
3. Hansard, 22nd January 1963, col. 48.
4. The Times, 6th February 1963.
5. Cate Fisher interview with the author.
6. Kenneth Rose, *Sunday Times*, 31st October 1993.
7. Kirkwall, 26th January 1963.
8. Strasbourg, 7th February 1963.
9. Hansard, 10th April 1962, col. 1191.
10. Ibid., col. 1193.
11. Sunday Telegraph, 2nd June 1963.
12. Ibid., 9th June 1963.
13. Scotsman, 15th June 1963.
14. Ibid.
15. The Times, 15th June 1963.
16. Hansard, 17th June 1963, cols. 77–8.
17. Sunday Times, 23rd June 1963.
18. Liberal Collection, LSE.
19. Hansard, 16th July 1963, col. 336.
20. Aberdeen Press and Journal, 19th July 1963.
21. Sunday Telegraph, 2nd June 1963.

22. Guardian, 14th August 1963.
23. Kyle II.
24. Daily Telegraph, 12th September 1963.
25. Brighton, 14th September 1963.
26. Ibid.
27. Daily Telegraph, 11th October 1963.
28. The Times, 19th October 1963.
29. Hansard, 24th October 1963, col. 921.
30. Ibid., col. 924.
31. Bristol, 22nd November 1963.
32. Guardian, 9th December 1963.
33. Ibid.
34. Daily Telegraph, 31st December 1963.
35. Ibid, 6th February 1964.
36. Guardian, 13th February 1964.
37. Ibid., 8th April 1964.
38. Kirkwall, 24th April 1964.
39. This Is Your Life, 1983.
40. Liberal Collection, LSE.
41. Sunday Express, 21st June 1964.
42. Sunday Telegraph, 28th June 1964.
43. The Times, 30th June 1964.
44. Orkney, 29th August 1964.
45. David Steel, *Against Goliath* (Weidenfeld & Nicolson, 1989), p. 31.
46. Steel interview with the author.
47. Sutton Coldfield, 8th September 1964.
48. Sunday Times, 6th September 1964.
49. Ibid.
50. The Times, 7th September 1964.

Chapter Eleven

1. Daily Telegraph, 23rd September 1964.
2. The Times, 15th September 1964.
3. Daily Telegraph, 23rd September 1964.
4. Ibid.
5. The Times, 2nd October 1964.
6. Daily Telegraph, 22nd September 1964.
7. Ibid.
8. Evening Standard, 30th September 1964.
9. Quoted in D. E. Butler and A. King, *The British General Election of 1964* (Macmillan, 1965), p. 125.
10. Sunday Telegraph, 11th October 1964.
11. Kirkwall, 14th October 1964.
12. Jay Blumler and Denis McQuail, *Television in Politics* (Faber & Faber, 1968) p. 187.
13. Independent, 14th November 1992.
14. Guardian, 8th October 1964.
15. Basil Wishart, *Memoirs*, (Beatrice Nesbit, 1998) p. 142.
16. Daily Telegraph, 15th October 1964.
17. Broadcast interview, 13th October 1964.
18. The Times, 17th October 1964.

19. Guardian, 17th October 1964.
20. Ibid.
21. Evening Standard, 16th October 1964.
22. The Times, 19th October 1964.
23. Hansard, 18th February 1960, col. 1495.
24. Minute dated 31st October 1964, Liberal Collection, LSE.
25. London, 31st October 1964.
26. Minute dated 31st October 1964, Liberal Collection, LSE.
27. London, 31st October 1964.
28. Hansard, 4th November 1964, col. 250.
29. Ibid., col. 253.
30. Ibid., 9th November 1964, cols. 718, 723–4.
31. Ibid, 10th November 1964, col. 829.
32. Liberal Collection, LSE.
33. Ibid.
34. Daily Telegraph, 16th October 1964.
35. Letter dated 16th November 1964, GP/NLS.
36. Ibid.
37. Liberal Collection, LSE.
38. Ibid.
39. Nicholas Henderson interview with the author.
40. Hansard, 28th July 1964, cols. 1243–4.
41. Daily Telegraph, 25th January 1965.
42. Sun, 28th January 1965.
43. Liberal Collection, LSE.
44. Ibid.
45. Ibid.
46. Hansard, 2nd February 1965, col. 942.
47. ITV interview, 2nd February 1965.
48. Sun, 4th February 1965.
49. Sunday Telegraph, 7th February 1965.
50. Sun, 18th February 1965.
51. Hansard, 4th November 1964, col. 251.
52. Glasgow, 19th March 1965.
53. Hansard, 18th March 1965, col. 1478.
54. The Times, 8th March 1965.
55. Ibid.
56. Mackie interview with the author.
57. The Times, 25th March 1965.
58. Eastbourne 1st April 1965.
59. Hansard, 7th April 1965, col.546.
60. Ibid., col. 551.
61. Television interview, 30th April 1965.
62. Hansard, 10th May 1965, col.101.
63. The Times, 12th May 1965.
64. Inverness, 28th May 1965.
65. Wadebridge, 15th May 1965.
66. Sun, 1st April 1965.
67. Ibid., 3rd June 1965.
68. The Times, 12th June 1965.
69. Transcript from Liberal Collection, LSE.
70. Ibid.

71. Guardian, 24th June 1965.
72. Ibid.
73. Ibid.
74. Transcript from Liberal Collection, LSE.
75. Ibid.
76. Financial Times, 25th June 1965.
77. Guardian, 25th June 1965.
78. Ibid., 26th June 1965.
79. Sunday Telegraph, 27th June 1965.
80. Daily Mail, 5th July 1965.
81. Ibid.
82. Sunday Telegraph, 11th July 1965.
83. Daily Express, 12th June 1962.
84. Alastair Hetherington, *The Guardian Years* (Chatto & Windus, 1981), p. 324.
85. Richard Crossman, *The Diaries of a Cabinet Minister* (Hamish Hamilton/ Jonathan Cape, 1975–7), 12th September 1965.

Chapter Twelve

1. Tony Benn, *Collected Diaries* (Hutchinson, 1995), 6th August 1965.
2. Hansard, 2nd August 1965, col. 1117.
3. Birmingham Post, 14th August 1965.
4. Sunday Times, 5th September 1965.
5. Sun, 9th September 1965.
6. Chitnis interview with the author.
7. The Times, 18th September 1965.
8. Guardian, 20th September 1965.
9. Ibid., 23rd September 1965.
10. The Times, 23rd September 1965.
11. Ibid.
12. Ibid.
13. Simon Freeman and Barry Penrose, *Rinkagate* (Bloomsbury, 1996), p. 110.
14. Sunday Telegraph, 26th September 1965.
15. Ibid.
16. Sunday Times, 26th September 1965.
17. Ibid.
18. Cecil King, *The Cecil King Diary 1965–1970* (Jonathan Cape, 1972), 25th September 1965.
19. Blackpool, 28th September 1965.
20. The Times, 29th September 1965.
21. Sunday Times, 3rd October 1965.
22. Statement, 2nd October 1965.
23. Daily Telegraph, 26th October 1965.
24. Harold Wilson, *The Labour Government 1964–70* (Weidenfeld & Nicolson, 1971) p. 139
25. The Times, 10th November 1965.
26. Oxford University, 13th November 1965.
27. Nigel Fisher, *Iain Macleod* (André Deutsch, 1973), p.273.
28. Guardian, 16th December 1965.
29. Sunday Times, 10th October 1965.
30. Orkney, 16th October 1965.
31. Central Hall, 1st November 1965.

32. Sun, 25th November 1965.
33. London, 27th November 1965.
34. Chippenham, 11th December 1965.
35. Liberal Collection, LSE.
36. Guardian, 16th December 1965.
37. Letter dated 9th December 1965, VBC Collection.
38. Pottle, *Daring to Hope*, p. 306.
39. Daily Telegraph, 31st December 1965.
40. Ibid., 3rd January 1966.
41. Ibid., 6th January 1966.
42. Sunday Telegraph, 16th January 1966.
43. Observer, 16th January 1966.
44. Ibid.
45. Hull, 18th January 1966.
46. Hansard, 17th February 1966, col.1546.
47. London, 26th February 1966.
48. Ibid.
49. Ibid.
50. Beaumont interview with the author.
51. Wedmore interview with the author.
52. Observer, 20th February 1966.
53. Guardian, 5th March 1966.
54. Gerrards Cross, 5th March 1966.
55. Ibid.
56. BBC TV, 8th March 1966.
57. Leeds, 18th March 1966.
58. We Need a Liberal Scotland.
59. Grimond, *Memoirs*, p. 220.
60. Daily Telegraph, 25th March 1966.
61. Daily Express, 24th March 1966.
62. Grimond, *Memoirs*, p. 220.
63. Ibid., p. 16.
64. Letter dated 14th February 1949, VBC Collection.
65. Wedmore interview with the author.
66. Daily Mirror, 25th March 1966.
67. Daily Telegraph, 29th March 1966.
68. BBC Home Service, 28th March 1966.
69. Aberdeen, 29th March 1966.
70. Grimond, *Memoirs*, p. 217.
71. Ibid.
72. Kyle II.
73. Conservative Campaign Guide, 1966, p. 327.

Chapter Thirteen

1. Observer, 6th March 1966.
2. Minutes of the Organising Committee meeting, 18th April 1966, Liberal Collection, LSE.
3. Correspondence from 1966, GP/NLS.
4. Minutes dated 18th July 1966, Liberal Collection, LSE.
5. Alec Cairncross, *The Wilson Years: A Treasury Diary 1964–69* (Historians' Press, 1997), p. 154.

6. The Times, 1st August 1966.
7. House of Commons, 1st August 1966.
8. Kirkwall, 28th August 1966.
9. Liberal Collection, LSE.
10. Evening Standard, 23rd September 1966.
11. Daily Telegraph, 24th September 1966.
12. Sunday Telegraph, 25th September 1966.
13. Guardian, 26th September 1966.
14. Ibid., 7th October 1966.
15. The Times, 11th October 1966.
16. MS in GP/NLS.
17. Guardian, 31st October 1966.
18. Ibid.
19. Ibid., 8th November 1966.
20. Ibid., 2nd November 1966.
21. Spectator, 8th September 1967.
22. Ibid.
23. Guardian, 12th November 1966.
24. Grimond, Memoirs, p. 220.
25. Ibid., p. 221.
26. Ibid., p. 223.
27. Ibid., p.225.
28. Ibid., p.226
29. The Times, 1st November 1966.
30. Sun, 17th November 1966.
31. Ibid., 8th December 1966.
32. Liberal Collection, LSE.
33. Conversation with the author.
34. Wainwright interview with the author.
35. Kyle III.
36. Grimond, Memoirs, p. 228.
37. Steel interview with the author.
38. Daily Express, 18th January 1967.
39. Ibid.
40. Ibid.
41. 24 Hours, BBC TV, 17th January 1967.
42. Henderson interview with the author.
43. Grimond, Memoirs, p. 228.
44. Cate Fisher interview with the author.
45. Liberal Collection, LSE.
46. Ibid.
47. Sun, 19th January 1967.
48. Official Report, 31st January 1967, col. 25.
49. Ibid., col. 27.
50. Sun, 27th April 1967.
51. Official Report, 13th July 1967, col. 272.
52. Sun, 16th March 1967.
53. Ludovic Kennedy, On My Way to the Club (Collins, 1989), pp. 306–7.
54. Perth, 18th May 1967.
55. Sunday Times, 3rd March 1974.
56. BBC TV, 21st October 1967.
57. GP/NLS.

58. Ibid.
59. Unpublished draft article dated 7th December 1967, GP/NLS.
60. Kirkwall, 2nd December 1967.
61. Shetland, 16th December 1967.

Chapter Fourteen

1. Milne interview with the author.
2. Ibid.
3. Ibid.
4. Ibid.
5. Sunday Telegraph, 18th June 1967.
6. Sun, 22nd June 1967.
7. Ibid.
8. Gray interview with the author.
9. Conversation with the author.
10. Hansard, 13th July 1956, col. 811.
11. Letter dated 20th March 1971, GP/NLS.
12. Correspondence held in GP/NLS.
13. Daily Express, 4th October 1967.
14. Letter, GP/NLS.
15. Letter dated 10th April 1974, GP/NLS.
16. Herbert van Thal (ed.), *The Prime Ministers* (George Allen & Unwin, 1975), p. 208.
17. The Times, 20th December 1973.
18. Ibid.
19. Sunday Times, 3rd March 1974.
20. Kyle III.
21. Official Record of the 1968 Königswinter Conference (Deutsch Englische Gesellschaft, 1968), p. 87.
22. London, 8th December 1968.
23. MS for *Wits Student*, GP/NLS, dated April 1970.
24. Sun, 9th February 1967.
25. Orpington, 18th March 1967.
26. Letter, 1967, to Scottish Union of Students, GP/NLS.
27. Ibid.
28. Gaudie, 11th March 1970.
29. Ibid.
30. Ibid.
31. Grimond, *Memoirs*, p. 180.
32. Naughtie interview with the author.
33. Birmingham, 20th January 1971.
34. English Association Presidential Address, 1972.
35. Sun, 9th February 1967.
36. Grimond, *Memoirs*, p. 181.
37. University of Birmingham Archive RB (M) 2.
38. UBA RB (E) 48, 30th April 1971.
39. UBA RB (E) 61, 14th May 1971.
40. UBA RB (E) 67, 21st May 1971.
41. UBA RB (E) 132, 21st October 1971.
42. Comments by Jo Grimond on first draft of consultation paper, University of Birmingham Library.

43. UBA RB (C) 45.
44. University of Birmingham Special Collection.
45. Ibid.
46. University of Birmingham, 1972.
47. Eric Ives, *The First Civic University: Birmingham 1880–1980* (University of Birmingham, 2000), p 397.
48. Ibid., p. 397.
49. Canterbury, 2nd July 1977.
50. English Association, 1976.
51. Ibid.
52. Official Report of Scottish Grand Committee, 4th June 1959, col. II.
53. Birmingham, 9th May 1968.
54. Ibid.
55. MS dated 28th February 1973, GP/NLS.
56. Henderson interview with the author.
57. London, 17th November 1976.
58. Oakeshott, Robert, *Jobs and Fairness* (Michael Russell, 2000), p. 15.
59. Yorkshire Post, 16th November 1979.
60. Ibid.
61. Ibid.

Chapter Fifteen

1. Sunday Times, 3rd March 1974.
2. Daily Telegraph, 26th March 1968.
3. Birmingham, 18th June 1968.
4. Sun, 11th September 1968.
5. Evening Standard, 11th September 1968.
6. BBC Radio, 12th September 1968.
7. Königswinter, March 1968.
8. Daily Telegraph, 12th September 1968.
9. Guardian, 12th September 1968.
10. Sun, 19th September 1968.
11. Ibid.
12. Daily Telegraph, 20th September 1968.
13. Manchester, 31st October 1968.
14. Sunday Times, 3rd March 1974.
15. Scottish Television, 6th January 1969.
16. Guardian, 22nd January 1969.
17. Kyle III.
18. King, *Cecil King Diary*, 13th March 1969.
19. BBC, 17th September 1969.
20. Brighton, 18th September 1969.
21. Daily Telegraph, 19th September 1968.
22. Scotsman, 13th October 1969.
23. Minute dated 4th April 1970, Scottish Liberal Party.
24. MS for *Wits Student*, GP/NLS, dated April 1970.
25. Evening Standard, September 1968.
26. The Times, 31st May 1969.
27. Letter to Grimond, 12th December 1969.
28. Hansard, 6th February 1970, col. 769.
29. Gray interview with the author.

30. Hansard, 2nd July 1970, col. 96.
31. MS for *Scotland* magazine, dated June 1969, GP/NLS; italicised sections excised before publication.
32. Thames TV, 20th March 1969.
33. Ibid.
34. Unpublished MS, GP/NLS.
35. GP/NLS.
36. London, 4th November 1971.
37. Linlithgow, 2nd February 1972.
38. Daily Telegraph, 3rd February 1972.
39. Bournemouth, 21st April 1972.
40. Hansard, 14th July 1972, col. 2030.
41. Ibid., 24th July 1972, col. 1339.
42. Ibid., 15th February 1973, col. 1520.
43. Ibid., 8th March 1973, col. 647.
44. Ibid., 11th July 1973, col. 1572.
45. GP/NLS.
46. Kirkwood interview with the author.
47. Grimond to Campbell, 11th January 1974.
48. The Times, 30th October 1993.
49. This Is Your Life, 1983.
50. Election broadcast, 13th February 1974.
51. The Times, 27th February 1974.
52. Sunday Post, 10th March 1974.
53. The Times, 15th July 1974.
54. Ibid.
55. Hansard, 16th May 1974, col. 1567.
56. Party political broadcast, 25th September 1974.
57. BBC TV, 5th December 1974.
58. Unpublished MS from 1975, GP/NLS.
59. Virginia Water, 1st March 1975.
60. Hansard, 3rd March 1975, col. 1185.
61. Ibid., 2nd July 1970, col. 101.
62. Birmingham, 21st May 1975.
63. Press cutting, Britain in Europe Archive.
64. Speech notes, GP/NLS.
65. London, 28th October 1975.
66. The Times and *Daily Telegraph*, 6th March 1976; also Peter Bessell, *Cover-up!* (Simons Books, 1980), pp. 313–14.
67. Daily Express, 15th March 1976.
68. Daily Telegraph, 16th March 1976.
69. Guardian, 15th March 1976.
70. BBC, 10th May 1976.
71. Wingfield conversation with the author.
72. Steel, *Against Goliath*, p. 111.
73. Daily Mail, 11th May 1976.

Chapter Sixteen

1. The Times, 13th May 1976.
2. Daily Express, 13th May 1976.
3. Guardian, 13th May 1976.

4. Ibid.
5. London *Evening News*, 12th May 1976.
6. Ibid.
7. Guardian, 13th May 1976.
8. Ibid.
9. Hansard, 20th May 1976, col. 1714.
10. Steel interview with the author.
11. BBC, 10th June 1976.
12. Ibid.
13. Manchester, 12th June 1976.
14. Ibid.
15. Ibid.
16. Ibid.
17. Ibid.
18. Ibid.
19. Perth, 19th June 1976.
20. Ibid.
21. Sunday Times, 19th September 1976.
22. Ibid.
23. Ibid.
24. Letter to the author from Sir Cyril Smith, dated 19th September 2000.
25. Ibid.
26. Birmingham Post, 8th October 1964.
27. Daily Telegraph, 2nd May 1977.
28. Kyle III.
29. Sunday Express, 24th July 1977.
30. The Times, 26th July 1977.
31. Ibid.
32. BBC News, 26th July 1977.
33. Daily Mail, 26th July 1977.
34. Ibid., 27th November 1977.
35. Ibid.
36. Spectator, 21st January 1978.
37. The Times, 17th December 1975.
38. Ibid., 23rd December 1975.
39. Sunday Telegraph, 9th November 1975.
40. Hansard, 4th November 1974, col. 741.
41. Ibid., 9th June 1976, col. 1473.
42. Spectator, 10th June 1978.
43. Lerwick, 7th January 1977.
44. Daily Telegraph, 6th April 1987.
45. David Steel, *A House Divided* (Weidenfeld & Nicolson, 1980). p. 96.
46. Hansard, 25th January 1978, col. 1548.
47. Spectator, 10th February 1979.
48. Election address 1979, Grimond Collection, Kirkwall Library.
49. Official Report, 5th December 1972, col. 31.
50. Ibid., col. 35.
51. Quoted in *Shetland Times*, special interest feature on North Sea oil, 2001.
52. MS from GP/NLS; italicised section had been deleted.
53. Sunday Telegraph, 13th August 1972.
54. Orkney, 19th February 1974.
55. Grimond Papers, Kirkwall Library.

56. Jo Grimond, *The Common Welfare* (Temple Smith, 1978), p. 179.
57. Grimond Collection, Kirkwall Library.
58. Julian Critchley (ed.), *Britain: A View from Westminster* (Blandford Press, 1986), p. 25.
59. Ibid.
60. London, 20th October 1976.
61. The Times, 4th September 1978.
62. Guardian, 1st November 1976.
63. Scottish Grand Committee, 10th July 1973, col. 228.
64. Daily Telegraph, 13th January 1992.
65. Edinburgh, 19th October 1976.
66. Spectator, 16th September 1978.
67. GP/NLS.
68. MS among GP/NLS.
69. Hansard, 9th June 1976, cols. 1475–6.
70. Jo Grimond, 'Trade Unions Harm the Poor', in *Trade Unions: Public Goods or Public 'Bads'* (IEA, 1978).
71. Ibid.
72. Jo Grimond, 'The Point of No Return', in *Confrontation: Will the Open Society Survive to 1989?* (IEA, 1978) p. 171.
73. Letter dated 19th September 1978, Grimond Collection, Kirkwall Library.
74. F. Bolkestein (ed), *Modern Liberalism* (Elsevier Science Publishers, 1982), p. 93.
75. Spectator, 22nd September 1979.
76. Jo Grimond, 'Two Wasted Years or Too Little, Too Late?', in *Could Do Better* (IEA, 1981). p. 25.
77. Ibid., p. 23.
78. Spectator, 14th March 1981.
79. Daily Mail, 3rd May 1980.
80. London, 1977.
81. Statement, 27th November 1979.
82. Ibid.
83. Listener, 13th December 1979.
84. Jenkins interview with the author.
85. The Hague, 8th March 1980.
86. The Times, 23rd June 1980.
87. London, 28th October 1980.
88. Jeremy Josephs, *Inside the Alliance* (John Martin, 1983), p. 91.
89. Spectator, 20th March 1982.
90. Jenkins interview with the author.
91. Spectator, 31st January 1981.
92. Ibid. 11th April 1981.
93. Steel interview with the author.
94. Llandudno, 15th September 1981.
95. The Times, 3rd July 1982.
96. Sunday Telegraph, 11th July 1982.
97. Daily Telegraph, 14th June 1982.
98. 1980 Romanes Lecture.
99. Spectator, 22nd May 1982.
100. Ibid.
101. Ibid., 21st August 1982.
102. Radio Orkney, 16th November 1982.
103. Spectator, 25th September 1982.

104. Ibid.
105. Mail on Sunday, 21st November 1982.
106. Spectator, 18th December 1982.

Chapter Seventeen

1. Josephs, *Inside the Alliance*, p. 245.
2. Daily Telegraph, 13th May 1983.
3. Guardian, 15th May 1983.
4. The Times, 9th June 1983.
5. Kyle III.
6. Ibid.
7. London, 17th January 1967.
8. Kyle III.
9. Sunday Telegraph, 24th July 1983.
10. Charles Kennedy interview with the author.
11. Spectator, 1st June 1985.
12. Holme interview with the author.
13. Spectator, 18th June 1985.
14. Daily Telegraph, 7th February 1984.
15. Ibid., 17th September 1985.
16. Ibid., 7th March 1991.
17. Official Report, 29th November 1983, col. 570.
18. Official Report, 31st January 1990.
19. Daily Telegraph, 11th November 1985.
20. Official Report, 30th March 1987, col. 381.
21. Ibid., col. 400.
22. Official Report, 31st March 1987, col. 509.
23. Official Report, 19th May 1988, col. 450.
24. Ibid., cols. 450–51.
25. Official Report, 27th February 1990, cols. 647–9.
26. Sunday Times, 11th November 1984.
27. Daily Telegraph, 22nd June 1987.
28. Ibid., 7th August 1987.
29. Ibid.
30. MS dated 18th September 1970, GP/NLS.
31. Daily Telegraph, 13th May 1988.
32. Sunday Telegraph, 6th September 1987.
33. Daily Telegraph, 15th October 1988.
34. Ibid., 7th January 1985.
35. Official Report, 31st January 1990, col. 390.
36. Spectator, 9th June 1990.
37. Ibid.
38. Woodrow Wyatt, *Journals* (Macmillan, 1998), vol. 1, p. 576.
39. Sunday Telegraph, 23rd July 1989.
40. Daily Telegraph, 13th May 1989.
41. Spectator, 16th June 1990.
42. Ibid.
43. Daily Telegraph, 16th November 1987.
44. Ibid.
45. Daily Telegraph, 13th December 1990.
46. Ibid., 4th February 1985.

47. Ibid.
48. Ibid.
49. Ibid., 4th May 1987.
50. Ibid., 19th October 1987.
51. Ibid., 21st April 1990.
52. Ibid.
53. Ibid.
54. Ibid.
55. Ibid.
56. Ibid., 27th January 1990.
57. Ibid., 15th July 1989.
58. Ibid.
59. Ibid., 22nd May 1990.
60. Ibid.
61. Ibid., 18th July 1983.
62. Ibid., 17th October 1989.
63. Hansard, 14th December 1953, col. 149.
64. Ibid., col. 150.
65. Daily Telegraph, 19th October 1987.
66. Hansard, 21st May 1954, col. 2507.
67. Grimond, *St Andrews*, p. 102.
68. Daily Telegraph, 12th April 1980.
69. Ibid., 6th February 1984.
70. Ibid.
71. Spectator, 14th February 1981.
72. Ibid.
73. Field, 22nd February 1986.
74. Daily Telegraph, 26th October 1993.
75. Spectator, 15th May 1982.
76. Country Life, 27th September 1990.
77. Field, 14th June 1986.
78. Ibid.
79. Ibid.
80. Daily Telegraph, 27th April 1981.
81. Ibid, 11th October 1990.
82. Grimond, *Liberal Challenge*, p. 205.
83. Dan Cohn-Sherbok, *Glimpses of God* (Duckworth, 1994), p. 105.
84. Daily Telegraph, 6th February 1984.
85. House of Lords, 21st October 1993, cols. 678–9.
86. The Times, 26th October 1993.
87. Kyle III.
88. Evening News, 5th June 1976.
89. Grimond, *Memoirs*, p. 151.

Appendix One

1. Grimond, *Memoirs*, p. 202.
2. Hooson interview with the author.
3. Liberal News, 1st February 1957.
4. The Times, 30th August 1957.
5. Liverpool Daily Post, 25th November 1957.
6. Hansard, 29th October 1959, cols. 471–7.

7. Ibid., 14th April 1960, cols. 1522–9.
8. Daily Telegraph, 10th March 1960.
9. Jo Grimond, *Let's Get On With It!* (LPD, 1960).
10. New Directions Group, *Growth not Grandeur* (New Directions Paper No. 3, 1961), p. 10.
11. Hansard, 6th June 1962, col. 561.
12. Daily Sketch, 11th May 1962.
13. Grimond, *Liberal Challenge*, p. 138.
14. Sunday Telegraph, 6th August 1961.
15. Grimond, *Liberal Challenge*, p. 123.
16. Hansard, 2nd November 1961, cols. 373–5.
17. Guardian, 4th June 1962.
18. Hansard, 6th December 1962, col. 1493.
19. Ibid., 26th July 1962, col. 1790.
20. Ibid., 23rd November 1964, col. 981.
21. Ibid., 17th June 1965, col. 884.
22. Denby Dale, 19th March 1966.
23. Hansard, 21st October 1971, col. 921.
24. Hillswick, 7th October 1965.
25. Daily Sketch, 23rd March 1966.
26. Guardian, 29th December 1969.
27. Ibid.
28. Ibid.
29. Sunday Telegraph, 9th May 1971.
30. Ibid.
31. Ibid.
32. Daily Mirror, 25th March 1966.
33. Aberdeen, 9th February 1971.
34. Sunday Telegraph, 14th January 2001.
35. The Times, 5th April 1971.
36. Hansard, 2nd December 1970, col. 1263.
37. Con O'Neill, *Britain's Entry into the European Community* (Frank Cass, 2000) p. 263.
38. Hansard, 20th January 1979, col. 1141.
39. Ibid.,1st December 1971, col. 449.
40. Ibid., 20th January 1972, col. 709.
41. Ibid., col. 713.
42. O'Neill, *Britain's Entry*, p. 247.
43. Indiana, 23rd October 1973.
44. Sunday Post, 10th March 1974.
45. Jo Grimond, *A Personal Manifesto* (Martin Robertson, 1983), p. 152.
46. Ibid.
47. Grimond Collection, Kirkwall Library.
48. Spectator, 17th September 1983.
49. Ibid.
50. Grimond, *Memoirs*, p. 167.
51. Hansard, 28th July 1964, col. 1244.
52. George Watson (ed.), *The Unservile State* (George Allen & Unwin, 1957), p. 27.
53. Ibid., p. 34.
54. Ibid., p. 52.
55. Senate House, 13th November 1967.

56. Sun, 28th April 1966.
57. Ibid., 21st April 1966.
58. Ibid., 9th March 1967.
59. Ibid., 26th January 1968.
60. Sunday Telegraph, 12th January 1958.
61. Sun, 19th November 1964.
62. Ibid., 6th July 1967.
63. William Douglas Home, *Old Men Remember* (Collins & Brown, 1991), p. 103.
64. Daily Telegraph, 17th September 1959.
65. Jo Grimond, *The Liberal Future* (Faber, 1959), p. 40.
66. Birmingham Post, 8th October 1964.
67. Evening Standard, 16th October 1964.
68. Manchester, 13th March 1969.
69. Grimond, *Common Welfare*, p. 36.
70. GP/NLS.
71. Ibid.
72. Orcadian, 3rd October 1974.
73. GP/NLS.
74. Orcadian, 2nd March 1950.
75. Scotsman, 8th April 1963.
76. Spectator, 30th May 1958.
77. Grimond, *Liberal Future*, p. 51.
78. London, 16th November 1967.
79. Daily Telegraph, 11th June 1976.
80. Ibid.
81. Indiana, 23rd October 1973.
82. Unpublished MS, GP/NLS.
83. Where Do We Go From Here?, BBC TV, 5th April 1968.
84. Radio Times, 11–17th May 1974.
85. Jo Grimond, *A Roar for the Lion* (LPD, 1976), p. 1.
86. Ibid., p. 6
87. Ibid., p. 16
88. Guardian, 13th May 1976.
89. BBC Database of Quotations.
90. Daily Telegraph, 3rd December 1988.
91. Presidential Address to the English Association, 1972.
92. Indiana, 23rd October 1973.
93. Daily Telegraph, 17th September 1985.
94. Daily Mail, 5th October 1960.
95. Sunday Telegraph, 27th September 1970.
96. The Times, 4th July 1970.
97. Ibid., 3rd October 1972.
98. Ibid., 9th December 1972.

Appendix Two

1. News Chronicle, 2nd August 1952.
2. Political Quarterly, vol. XXIV (1953), p. 236.
3. Ibid., p. 238.
4. Ibid.
5. Ibid., p. 239.
6. Ibid.

7. John Rawls, *A Theory of Justice* (Clarendon Press, 1972), pp. 14–15.
8. Introduction to Timothy Joyce and Frank Ware, *What Liberals Mean by Opportunity* (LPD, 1957), p. 5.
9. News Chronicle, 11th July 1957.
10. Ibid., p. 4.
11. Ibid., p. 6.
12. Ibid., p. 8.
13. Ibid., p. 11.
14. Ibid., p. 12.
15. Ibid., p. 17.
16. Jo Grimond, *The New Liberal Democracy* (LPD, 1958), p. 7.
17. Ibid., p. 6.
18. Liberal News, 26th June 1958.
19. Grimond, *New Liberal Democracy*, pp. 8–9.
20. Ibid., p. 9.
21. Ibid., p. 16.
22. Ibid., p. 17.
23. 10th June 1958; cited in Brack and Ingham, *Liberal Quotations*, p. 73.
24. Grimond, *New Liberal Democracy*, p. 17.
25. Daily Telegraph, 12th June 1958.
26. Letter dated 6th March 1958, GP/NLS.
27. Letter dated 28th April 1958, GP/NLS.
28. Times Literary Supplement, 10th April 1959.
29. John Stuart Mill, quoted in Brack and Ingham, *Liberal Quotations*, p128.
30. Grimond, *Liberal Future*, p. 184.
31. Ibid., p. 51.
32. Ibid., p. 17.
33. Ibid., p. 32.
34. Ibid., pp. 59–60.
35. Ibid., pp. 105–7.
36. Ibid., p. 106.
37. Ibid., p. 111.
38. Ibid., p. 112.
39. Ibid., p. 113.
40. Ibid., p. 47.
41. Ibid., p. 164.
42. Ibid., p. 158.
43. Hansard, 25th February 1959, cols. 1190, 1223.
44. Ibid., 8th April 1959, cols. 257–8.
45. Let's Get On With It! (LPD, 1960), Foreword.
46. Ibid., p. 6.
47. Ibid., p. 7.
48. Ibid.
49. Ibid., p. 9.
50. Ibid., p. 15.
51. Ibid.
52. Ibid., p. 16.
53. Ibid., p. 17
54. Ibid., p. 21.
55. Ibid., p. 22.
56. Ibid.

57. Ibid., pp. 25–6.
58. Ibid., p. 34.
59. Ibid., p. 35.
60. Ibid., p. 37.
61. Ibid.
62. Ibid., p. 38.
63. New Directions Group, *Growth not Grandeur* (New Directions Paper No. 3, 1961), p. 6.
64. Ibid., p. 15.
65. Ibid., p. 16.
66. Professor Michael Fogarty, *Opportunity Knocks* (LPD, 1961), p. 32.
67. Hansard, 7th April 1965, col. 544.
68. Grimond, *Liberal Challenge*, p. 7.
69. Ibid., p. 30.
70. Ibid., p. 93.
71. Grimond, *Liberal Challenge*, pp. 64–5.
72. Ibid., p. 180.
73. Ibid., p. 201.
74. Ibid., p. 203.
75. Ibid.. p. 204.
76. Ibid., p. 279.
77. Ibid., p. 142.
78. Ibid., p. 143.
79. Ibid., p. 268.
80. Grimond, *Common Welfare*, p. 213.
81. Ibid., p. 241.
82. Ibid., p. 233.
83. Ibid., p. 105.
84. Jo Grimond, *New Outlook,* September 1981.
85. Letter dated 2nd March 1983, GP/NLS.
86. Economist, 11th June 1983.
87. Grimond, *Personal Manifesto*, p. viii.
88. Ibid., p. 75.
89. Ibid.
90. Ibid.
91. Ibid., p. 101.
92. Ibid., p. 158.
93. Spectator, 13th May 1955.
94. Grimond, *Personal Manifesto*, p. 166.
95. Ibid.

Bibliography

Abbreviations

GP/NLS   Grimond Papers, National Library of Scotland
Kyle (I, II, III)   three BBC TV interviews with Grimond by Keith Kyle,
                broadcast in 1983 as part of the *Twentieth Century
                Remembered* series
LPD   Liberal Publication Department
VBC Collection Violet Bonham Carter Collection, Bodleian Library,
                University of Oxford

Abrams, Mark, and Rose, Richard, *Must Labour Lose?* (Penguin, 1960)
Allen, A J, *The English Voter* (English Universities Press, 1964)
Amery, Julian, *Approach March* (Hutchinson, 1973)
Arlott, John, *Basingstoke Boy* (Willow Books, 1990)
Ashdown, Paddy, *Citizen's Britain* (Fourth Estate, 1989)
Ashdown, Paddy, *Beyond Westminster* (Simon & Schuster, 1994)
Ayerst, David, *Biography of a Newspaper* (Collins, 1971)
Ball, Alan R, *British Political Parties* (Macmillan, 2nd edn, 1987)
Bartram, Peter, *David Steel: His Life and Politics* (W. H. Allen, 1981)
Beer, Samuel H, *Modern British Politics* (Faber & Faber, 2nd edn, 1982)
Beith, Alan, *The Case for the Liberal Party and the Alliance* (Longman, 1983)
Benckendorff, Count Constantine, *Half a Life* (Richards Press, 1954)
Benn, Tony, *Collected Diaries* (Hutchinson, 1995)
Bessell, Peter, *Cover-up!* (Simons Books, 1980)
Blumler, Jay and McQuail, Denis, *Television in Politics* (Faber & Faber, 1968)
Bogdanor Vernon (ed.), *Liberal Party Politics* (OUP, 1983)
Bolkestein, F (ed.) *Modern Liberalism* (Elsevier Science Publishers, 1982)
Brack, Duncan and Ingham, Robert, *Dictionary of Liberal Biography*
    (Politicos, 1998)
Brack, Duncan and Ingham, Robert, *Dictionary of Liberal Quotations*
    (Politicos, 1999)
Bradley, Ian, *The Strange Rebirth of Liberal Britain* (Chatto & Windus, 1985)
Brett, Lionel, *Our Selves Unknown* (Gollancz, 1985)
Brivati, Brian, *Hugh Gaitskell* (Richard Cohen, 1996)

Brivati, Brian, *Lord Goodman* (Richard Cohen, 1999)

Bullock, Alan, and Shock, Maurice (eds.) *The Liberal Tradition from Fox to Keynes* (A & C Black,1956)

Butler, David, *British General Elections since 1945* (Blackwell, 2nd edn, 1995)

Butler, D E, *The British General Election of 1951* (Macmillan, 1952)

Butler, D E, *The British General Election of 1955* (Macmillan, 1955)

Butler, D E, and Rose, Richard, *The British General Election of 1959* (Macmillan, 1960)

Butler, D E and King, A, *The British General Election of 1964* (Macmillan, 1965)

Butler D E, *The British General Election of 1966* (Macmillan, 1966)

Butler, David, and Kitzinger, Uwe, *The 1975 Referendum* (Macmillan, 2nd edn, 1996)

Butler, David, and Stokes, Donald, *Political Change in Britain* (Macmillan, 2nd edn, 1974)

Cairncross, Alec, *The Wilson Years: A Treasury Diary 1964–69* (Historians' Press, 1997)

Checkland, S G, *The Gladstones: A Family Biography* (Cambridge University Press, 1971)

Chester, Lewis, Linklater, Magnus, and May, David, *Jeremy Thorpe: A Secret Life* (André Deutsch, 1979)

Clark, Alan, *The Tories* (Weidenfeld & Nicolson, 1998)

Cobbett, William, *Cobbett's Tour in Scotland* (ed. Green), Aberdeen University Press, 1984

Cockett, Richard, *Thinking the Unthinkable* (HarperCollins, 1994)

Cohn-Sherbok, Dan, *Glimpses of God* (Duckworth, 1994)

Cole, John, *The Thatcher Years* (BBC, 1987)

Collingwood, R G, *An Autobiography* (Clarendon Press, 1978 edn)

Conservative Campaign Guide 1959

Conservative Campaign Guide Supplement 1959

Conservative Campaign Guide 1964

Conservative Campaign Guide 1966

Conservative Campaign Guide 1970

Cook, Chris, *A Short History of the Liberal Party 1900–97* (Macmillan, 1998)

Cook, Chris, and Ramsden, John, *By-elections in British Politics* (UCL Press, 1997)

Coote, Colin, *The Other Club* (Sidgwick & Jackson, 1971)

Cowie, Harry, *Why Liberal?* (Penguin, 1964)

F W S Craig, *Chronology of British Parliamentary By-elections 1833–1987* (PRS, 1987)

Crewe, Ivor, and King, Anthony, *The Birth, Life and Death of the SDP* (OUP, 1995)

Crick, Michael, *Michael Heseltine: A Biography* (Hamish Hamilton, 1997)

Critchley, Julian (ed.), *Britain: A View from Westminster* (Blandford Press, 1986)

Critchley, Julian, *A Bag of Boiled Sweets* (Faber & Faber, 1994)

Crossman, Richard, *The Diaries of a Cabinet Minister* (Hamish Hamilton/ Jonathan Cape, 1975–7)

Crossman, Richard, *Backbench Diaries* (Hamish Hamilton/Jonathan Cape, 1981)

Cursiter, Stanley, *Peploe* (Thomas Nelson, 1947)

Cyr, Arthur, *Liberal Party Politics in Britain* (Calder, 1977 (or 1988 2nd edn))

Dangerfield, George, *The Strange Death of Liberal England* (Stanford University Press, 1997)

Day, Robin, *Grand Inquisitor* (Weidenfeld & Nicolson, 1989)

De Groot, Gerard, *Liberal Crusader* (Hurst, 1993)

Delaforce, P, *Red Crown and Dragon* (Tom Donovan, 1996)

Donnelly, Desmond, *Gadarene '68* (William Kimber, 1968)

Douglas, Roy, *History of the Liberal Party 1895–1970* (Anchor Press, 1971)

Douglas Home, William, *Half Term Report* (Longmans, Green, 1954)

Douglas Home, William, *Mr Home Pronounced Hume* (William Collins, 1979)

Douglas Home, William, *Old Men Remember* (Collins & Brown, 1991)

Drucker, Henry (ed.), *Multi-Party Britain* (University of Edinburgh, 1979)

Eccleshall, Robert, *British Liberalism* (Longman, 1986)

Economics of Politics, The (IEA, 1978)

Evans, Harold, *Good Times, Bad Times* (Weidenfeld & Nicolson, 1983)

Fergusson, Bernard, *Eton Portrait* (John Miles, 1937)

Finer, Sam, *The Changing British Party System* (AEI, 1980)

Fisher, Nigel, *Iain Macleod* (André Deutsch, 1973)

Fisher, Nigel, *Harold Macmillan* (Weidenfeld & Nicolson, 1982)

Fogarty, Michael, *Opportunity Knocks* (LPD, 1961)

Freeman, Simon, and Penrose, Barry, *Rinkagate* (Bloomsbury, 1996)

Fulford, Roger, *The Liberal Case* (Penguin, 1959)

Furnell, Patrick, and Ware, Frank, *Planning with a Purpose* (LPD, 1962)

Gilmour, Ian, and Garnett, Mark, *Whatever Happened to the Tories?* (Fourth Estate, 1997)

Goodhart, Philip, *Referendum* (Tom Stacey, 1971)

Gordon Walker, Patrick, *Political Diaries 1932–1971* (Historians' Press, 1991)

Grimond, Jo, *The New Liberalism* (LPD, 1957)

Grimond, Jo, *The New Liberal Democracy* (LPD,1958)

Grimond, Jo, *The Liberal Future* (Faber, 1959)

Grimond, Jo, *Let's Get On With It!* (LPD, 1960)

Grimond, Jo, *Industry, Profits and People* (Industrial Co-Partnership Association, 1960)

Grimond, Jo, *Take Britain Ahead* (LPD, 1961)

Grimond, Jo, *The Liberal Challenge* (Hollis & Carter, 1963)

Grimond, Jo, *Eastern Europe Today* (*Guardian*, 1966)

Grimond, Jo, *Has Democracy a Future?* (Young Liberals, 1974)

Grimond, Jo, *The Bureaucratic Blight* (Unservile State Group, 1976)

Grimond, Jo, *A Roar for the Lion* (LPD, 1976)

Grimond, Jo, *The Common Welfare* (Temple Smith, 1978)

Grimond, Jo, 'Trade Unions Harm the Poor', in *Trade Unions: Public Goods or Public 'Bads'* (IEA, 1978)

Grimond, Jo, 'The Point of No Return', in *Confrontation: Will the Open Society Survive to 1989?* (IEA, 1978)

Grimond, Jo, *Memoirs* (Heinemann, 1979)

Grimond, Jo, 'Two Wasted Years or Too Little, Too Late?', in *Could Do Better* (IEA, 1981)

Grimond, Jo, *A Personal Manifesto* (Martin Robertson, 1983)

Grimond, Jo, *The St Andrews of Jo Grimond* (Alan Sutton, 1992)

Grimond, Jo, and Neve, Brian, *The Referendum* (Rex Collings, 1975)

Grobecker, Kurt, *Das Atlantic Hotel zu Hamburg* (Maria Faber Verlag, 1999)

Hailsham, Viscount, *A Sparrow's Flight* (Collins, 1990)

Harvie, C, *Scotland and Nationalism* (George Allen & Unwin, 1977)

Haseler, Stephen, *Death of British Democracy* (Elek, 1976)

Henderson, Nicholas, *Mandarin: The Diaries of an Ambassador* (Weidenfeld & Nicolson, 1994)

Hetherington, Alastair, *The Guardian Years* (Chatto & Windus, 1981)

Horne, Alistair, *Macmillan* (Macdonald, 1988–9)

Howard, Michael, *War and the Liberal Conscience* (Maurice Temple Smith, 1978)

Hunt, Norman (ed.), *Whitehall and Beyond* (BBC Books, 1964)

Hutchinson, George, *Edward Heath* (Hutchinson, 1970)

Ives, Eric, *The First Civic University: Birmingham 1880–1980* (University of Birmingham, 2000)

Jenkins, Roy, *Partnership of Principle* (Secker & Warburg, 1985)

Jenkins, Roy, *A Life at the Centre* (Macmillan, 1991)

Jenkins, Roy, *Gladstone* (Macmillan, 1995)

Johnston, Brian, *It's Been a Lot of Fun* (W. H. Allen, 1974)

Johnston, Brian, *Someone Who Was* (Methuen, 1992)

Jones, Mervyn, *A Radical Life: The Biography of Megan Lloyd George* (Hutchinson, 1991)

Josephs, Jeremy, *Inside the Alliance* (John Martin, 1983)

Joyce, Peter, *Giving Politics a Good Name* (Liberal Democrat Publications, 1995)

Joyce, Timothy, and Ware, Frank, *What Liberals Mean by Opportunity* (LPD, 1957)

Kennedy, Ludovic, *On My Way to the Club* (Collins, 1989)

King, Anthony, *Britain Says Yes* (AEI Studies, 1977)

King, Cecil, *The Cecil King Diary 1965–1970* (Jonathan Cape, 1972)

King, Cecil, *The Cecil King Diary 1970–74* (Jonathan Cape, 1975)

Kinnear, Michael, *The British Voter* (Batsford, 2nd edn, 1981)

La Guardia, Fiorello, *Making of an Insurgent* (J. B. Lippincott, 1948)

Lamb, Richard, *The Failure of the Eden Government* (Sidgwick & Jackson, 1987)

Leonard, R L, *Elections in Britain* (Van Nostrand, 1st edn, 1968)

Liberal Party, *This is YOUR PARTY* (LPD, 1960)

Livingston, William S. (ed.), *A Prospect of Liberal Democracy* (University of Texas Press, 1979)

Mackintosh, John, *The Devolution of Power* (Penguin, 1968)

Macmillan, Harold, *Riding the Storm* (Macmillan, 1971)

Macmillan, Harold, *Pointing the Way* (Macmillan, 1972)

Macmillan, Harold, *At the End of the Day* (Macmillan, 1973)

Magee, Bryan, *The New Radicalism* (Martin Secker & Warburg, 1962)

Mandela, Nelson, *Long Walk to Freedom* (Macdonald Purnell, 1994)

Martin, Graham, *From Vision to Reality* (University of Kent, 1990)

Mayhew, Christopher, *Time to Explain* (Hutchinson, 1987)

Michie, Alistair, and Hoggart, Simon, *The Pact* (Quartet, 1978)

Mole, Stuart (ed.), *The Decade of Realignment* (Hebden Royd, 1986)

Morgan, Kenneth, *The Age of Lloyd George* (George Allen & Unwin, 1971)

Mortimer, John, *Murderers and Other Friends* (Viking, 1994)

Nabarro, Gerald, *Exploits of a Politician* (Arthur Barker, 1973)

New Directions Group, *Britain Must Join* (New Directions Paper No. 1, 1960)

New Directions Group, *Better Buys* (New Directions Paper No. 2, 1960)

New Directions Group, *Growth not Grandeur* (New Directions Paper No. 3, 1961)

New Directions Group, *Opportunity Knocks* (New Directions Paper No. 4, 1961)

Nicolson, Nigel, *Long Life* (Weidenfeld & Nicolson, 1997)

Oakeshott, Robert, *The Case for Workers' Co-ops* (Routledge, 1978)

Oakeshott, Robert, *Jobs and Fairness* (Michael Russell, 2000)

O'Neill, Con, *Britain's Entry into the European Community: Report by Sir Con O'Neill on the Negotiations of 1970–1972* (Frank Cass, 2000)

Owen, David, *Time to Declare* (Michael Joseph, 1991)

Pearce, Edward, *The Senate of Lilliput* (Faber, 1983)

Penhaligon, Annette, *Penhaligon* (Bloomsbury, 1989)

Pimlott, Ben, *Harold Wilson* (Harper Collins, 1992)

Pottle, Mark (ed.), *Lantern Slides* (Weidenfeld & Nicolson, 1996)

Pottle, Mark (ed.), *Champion Redoubtable* (Weidenfeld & Nicolson, 1998)

Pottle, Mark (ed.), *Daring to Hope* (Weidenfeld & Nicolson, 2000)

Pulzer, Peter, *Political Representation and Elections in Britain* (George Allen & Unwin, 1967)

Rasmussen, Jorgen Scott, *The Liberal Party* (Constable, 1965)

Rawls, John, *A Theory of Justice* (Clarendon Press, 1972)

Rhodes James, Robert, *Bob Boothby: A Portrait* (Hodder & Stoughton, 1991)

Richardson, Tony, *Long Distance Runner: A Memoir* (Faber & Faber, 1993)

Roberts, Geoffrey, *Political Parties and Pressure Groups in Britain* (Weidenfeld & Nicolson, 1970)

Sampson, Anthony, *Macmillan* (Allen Lane, 1967)

Sampson, Anthony, *The Changing Anatomy of Britain* (Hodder & Stoughton, 1982)

Samuel, Viscount, *Memoirs* (Cresset Press, 1945)

Sellar, R J B, *The Fife and Forfar Yeomanry, 1919–1956* (Blackwood, 1960)

Shepherd, Robert, *Iain Macleod* (Hutchinson, 1994)

Shepherd, Robert, *Enoch Powell: A Biography* (Hutchinson, 1996)

Shonfield, Andrew, *British Economic Policy since the War* (Penguin Special, 1958)

Shrapnel, Norman, *The Performers: Politics as Theatre* (Constable, 1978)

Sked, Alan, and Cook, Chris, *Post-War Britain* (Penguin, 2nd edn, 1990)

Slesser, Sir Henry, *A History of the Liberal Party* (Hutchinson, 1944)

Smith, Cyril, *Big Cyril* (W. H. Allen, 1977)

Smith, Cyril, *Reflections from Rochdale* (Liberal Democrat Publications, 1997)

Smith, David, *The Rise and Fall of Monetarism* (Penguin, 1987)

Steel, David, *A House Divided* (Weidenfeld & Nicolson, 1980)

Steel, David, *Against Goliath* (Weidenfeld & Nicolson, 1989)

Stevenson, John, *Third Party Politics since 1945* (Blackwell, 1993)

Strong, Roy, *The Roy Strong Diaries 1969–1987* (Weidenfeld & Nicolson, 1997)

Thorpe, Jeremy, *In My Own Time* (Politicos, 1999)

Thwaite, Ann (ed.), *My Oxford* (Robson Books, 1977)

Tonypandy, George Thomas, *Mr Speaker* (Century, 1985)

Toynbee, Philip, *Friends Apart* (MacGibbon & Kee, 1954)

Tregidga, Garry, *Liberal Party in South-West Britain since 1918* (University of Exeter Press, 2000)

Tulloch, Bobby, *Bobby Tulloch's Shetland* (Macmillan, 1988)

Van Thal, Herbert (ed.), *The Prime Ministers* (George Allen & Unwin, 1975)

Wade, Donald, *Our Aim and Purpose* (Liberal Movement, 1989)

Wade, Donald, *Behind the Speaker's Chair* (Austicks, 1978)

Wallace, Rosie (ed.), *Jo and Laura Grimond* (Orkney and Shetland Liberal Democrats, 2000)

Wasserstein, Bernard, *Samuel: A Political Life* (OUP, 1992)

Watkins, Alan, *The Liberal Dilemma* (MacGibbon & Kee, 1966)

Watson, George (ed.), *The Unservile State* (George Allen & Unwin, 1957)

Watson, George (ed.), *Radical Alternative* (Eyre & Spottiswoode, 1962)

Waugh, Auberon, *The Last Word* (Michael Joseph, 1980)

Williams, Philip, *Hugh Gaitskell* (Jonathan Cape, 1979)

Wilson, Des, *Battle for Power* (Sphere, 1987)

Wilson, Harold, *The Labour Government 1964–70* (Weidenfeld & Nicolson, 1971)

Wishart, Basil, *Memoirs* (Beatrice Nesbit, 1998)

Woodbridge, George, *UNRRA* (Columbia University Press, New York, 1950)

Wyatt, Woodrow, *Turn Again, Westminster* (André Deutsch, 1973)

Wyatt, Woodrow, *What's Left of the Labour Party?* (Sidgwick & Jackson, 1977)

Wyatt, Woodrow, *Confessions of an Optimist* (William Collins, 1985)

Wyatt, Woodrow, *Journals*, Vol.1 (Macmillan, 1998)

Young, Hugo, *This Blessed Plot* (Macmillan, 1998)

Index